SHAKESPEARE *into* FILM

1. R+J
2. Vision
3. Jumps
   Kurosawa
4. World Shakespeare bibliography – internet
5. The concept of reinterpreting
   - many movies

SHAKESPEARE *into* FILM

JAMES M. WELSH

RICHARD VELA

JOHN C. TIBBETTS, et al.

Preface by
Kenneth S. Rothwell

Checkmark Books®
An imprint of Facts On File, Inc.

Shakespeare into Film

Copyright © 2002 by James M. Welsh, Richard Vela, John C. Tibbetts

All rights reserved. No part of this book may be reproduced or utilized in any form or by any means, electronic or mechanical, including photocopying, recording, or by any information storage or retrieval systems, without permission in writing from the publisher. For information contact:

Checkmark Books
An imprint of Facts On File, Inc.
132 West 31st Street
New York NY 10001

Library of Congress Cataloging-in-Publication Data

Welsh, James Michael.
Shakespeare into film / James M. Welsh, John Tibbetts, Richard Vela, et. al.
p. cm.
Includes bibliographical references and index.
ISBN 0-8160-4944-0 (pb. : alk. paper)
1. Shakespeare, William 1564-1616—Film and video adaptations.
2. English drama—Film and video adaptations. 3. Film adaptations.
I. Vela, Richard. II. Tibbetts, John C. III. Title.
PR3093 . W46 2002
791.43'6—dc21   2001052984

Checkmark Books are available at special discounts when purchased in bulk quantities for businesses, associations, institutions, or sales promotions. Please call our Special Sales Department in New York at
(212) 967-8800 or (800) 322-8755.

You can find Facts On File on the World Wide Web at
http://www.factsonfile.com

Text design by Cathy Rincon
Cover design by Semadar Megged
Illustrations by John C. Tibbetts

Printed in the United States of America

VB FOF 10 9 8 7 6 5 4 3 2 1

This book is printed on acid-free paper.

The following essays originally appeared in *Literature/Film Quarterly*, © Salisbury State University, Salisbury, Maryland, and are reprinted here by permission of the editors, James M. Welsh and Thomas L. Erskine:

Christopher Andrews, "*Richard III* on Film: The Subversions of the Viewer," *Literature/Film Quarterly* 28, no. 2 (2000): 82–94.

Normand Berlin, "*Macbeth*: Polanski and Shakespeare," *Literature/Film Quarterly* 1, no.4 (1973): 291–298.

Mark Thornton Burnett, "The 'Very Cunning of the Scene': Kenneth Branagh's *Hamlet*," *Literature/Film Quarterly* 25 no. 2 (1997): 78–82.

Mariacristiana Cavecchi, "Peter Greenaway's *Prospero's Books*: A Tempest between Word and Image," *Literature/Film Quarterly* 25, no. 2 (1997): 83–89.

Lucy Hamilton, "Baz *vs.* the Bardolaters, Or, Why *William Shakespeare's Romeo + Juliet* Deserves Another Look," *Literature/Film Quarterly* 28, no. 2 (2000): 118–124.

Diana Harris and MacDonald Jackson, "Stormy Weather: Derek Jarman's *The Tempest*," *Literature/Film Quarterly* 25, no. 2 (1997): 90–98.

Jane E. Kingsley-Smith, "Shakespearean Authorship in Popular British Cinema," *Literature/Film Quarterly* 30, no. 3 (2002).

Arthur Lindley, "Scotland Saved from History: The Welles *Macbeth* and the Ahistoricism of Medieval Film," *Literature/Film Quarterly* 29, no. 2 (2001): 96–100.

Michael Pursell, "Playing the Game: Branagh's *Henry V*," *Literature/Film Quarterly* 20, no. 4 (1992): 268–275.

Kenneth S. Rothwell, "How the Twentieth Century Saw the Shakespeare Film: 'Is It Shakespeare?'" *Literature/Film Quarterly* 29, no. 2 (2001): 82–95.

James W. Stone, "Black and White as Technique in Orson Welles's *Othello*," *Literature/Film Quarterly* 30, no. 3 (2002).

James M. Welsh, "'To See It Feelingly': *King Lear* through Russian Eyes," *Literature/Film Quarterly* 4, no. 2 (1976): 153–158.

Ramona Wray, "Nostalgia for Navarre: The Melancholic Metacinema of Kenneth Branagh's *Love's Labour's Lost*," *Literature/Film Quarterly* 30, no. 3 (2002).

Yong Li Lan, "Returning to Naples: Seeing the End in Shakespeare Film Adaptation," *Literature/Film Quarterly* 28, no. 2 (2001): 128–134.

This book is dedicated to Charlton Hinman and Paul Murray Kendall, both of whom taught me to appreciate Shakespeare and how to write productively while also teaching full time. Their commitment to and love of Shakespeare was an inspiration, and I dedicate this book to their memory with heartfelt gratitude. And also to a third mentor at the University of Kansas, Ken Rothwell, whose bibliographical survey, originally published in Literature/Film Quarterly *(29:2) serves as our preface.*

—*J. M. W.*

Contents

PREFACE
How the 20th Century Saw the Shakespeare Film:
   "Is It Shakespeare?"
   KENNETH S. ROTHWELL   IX

INTRODUCTION
Seduced by Shakespeare, Transfixed by Spectacle
   JAMES M. WELSH   XXIII

ENTRIES A TO Z   1

ESSAYS

The "Very Cunning of the Scene": Kenneth Branagh's *Hamlet*
   MARK THORNTON BURNETT   113

Playing the Game: Branagh's *Henry V*
   MICHAEL PURSELL   117

"Every Project Has Its Season": Mel Gibson and Franco Zeffirelli
   on the Challenges of *Hamlet*
   JOHN C. TIBBETTS   125

To "See It Feelingly": *King Lear* Through Russian Eyes
   JAMES M. WELSH   129

Macbeth: Polanski and Shakespeare
   NORMAND BERLIN   135

Scotland Saved from History: Welles's *Macbeth* and
   the Ahistoricism of Medieval Film
   ARTHUR LINDLEY   141

Richard III on Film: The Subversion of the Viewer
CHRISTOPHER ANDREWS
147

Baz versus the Bardolaters, or Why *William Shakespeare's Romeo + Juliet* Deserves Another Look
LUCY HAMILTON
159

Peter Greenaway's *Prospero's Books*: A Tempest between Word and Image
MARIACRISTINA CAVECCHI
167

Stormy Weather: Derek Jarman's *The Tempest*
DIANA HARRIS AND MACDONALD JACKSON
175

Returning to Naples: Seeing the End in Shakespeare Film Adaptation
YONG LI LAN
183

Black and White as Technique in Orson Welles's *Othello*
JAMES W. STONE
189

Nostalgia for Navarre: The Melancholic Metacinema of Kenneth Branagh's *Love's Labour's Lost*
RAMONA WRAY
193

Shakespearean Authorship in Popular British Cinema
JANE E. KINGSLEY-SMITH
201

APPENDIX
Backstage with the Bard: Or, Building a Better Mousetrap
JOHN C. TIBBETTS
207

CONTRIBUTORS 227

BIBLIOGRAPHY 229

INDEX 231

Preface

How the 20th Century Saw the Shakespeare Film: "Is it Shakespeare?"

In the beginning, when the fledgling cinema evolved out of the helter skelter of magic lantern shows, peep shows, Kinetoscopes, Mutoscopes, Zoöpraxiscopes, Steele Mackaye's Spectatorium (1893), and Scenitorium (1894), with accompanying stage wonders such as the "luxauleator," "illumiscope," "nebulator," and "proscenium adjuster," and even picture postcards,[1] criticism of the Shakespeare film was pretty much limited to asking the single question: "Is it Shakespeare?" This nagging interrogation concealed a deeper insecurity, what might be called "the anxiety of inauthenticity," the fear that any derivative of Shakespeare, "mechanical reproduction" as Walter Benjamin would put it, must necessarily lose the "aura" of the original. By "aura," Benjamin apparently meant the ineffable identity surrounding the work of art, like holding the 1594 quarto of *Titus Andronicus* in your own trembling little hands at the Folger. The reproduction of Shakespeare by the new medium, however, represented but one segment of a larger revolution in taste and aesthetics that has alienated the consumer-crazed, Kmarted, Walgreened, Costco-ized masses even from the aura of their own souls, as it were. Now a century later, with film on the edge of digitalization, things haven't changed very much. Shakespeare films still trigger the cry: "Is it Shakespeare?"

Literature-and-film criticism always operates at cross purposes as the writer attempts to serve two masters at once. Roughly speaking, then, Shakespeare-on-film criticism has flip-flopped through three stages, evolving from a kind of positivism to hermeneutics, as William Uricchio has described film criticism in general ("Film History" 113). First, commentators rose to the bait of the impossible question: "Is it Shakespeare?"; next, they avoided it or manipulated it; and, lastly, ignored it altogether. It has been a movement from Victorian conservatism to modernist expansiveness to postmodernist permissiveness. That is to say, a text-focused preoccupation with literal translation of Shakespeare's language into film language has gradually and sometimes imperceptibly given way to a more open and adventurous foray by both auteurs and critics into discovering that which is special and unique about each movie.

Initially, however, all film critics, including Shakespeareans, expended most of their energies on defending movies against charges of immorality, licentiousness, and indecency. The darkened movie theaters were thought to be veritable cesspools of vice, a branch of Sodom and Gomorrah, where no young woman could ever be safe from the base, importunate concupiscence of lurking louts. As a result, the defenders of Shakespeare in the movies toiled under a double load of baggage—it was bad enough to ravish Shakespeare but even worse to perpetrate the vile and unspeakable act in a movie theater. They felt the full wrath, contempt, scorn, and contumely of the Shakespeare "purists," a phantom group who tolerated Shakespeare on stage, but certainly not in low music halls. Actors successfully conspired with moralizing clergy to have the New York nickelodeons branded firetraps and shut down on Christmas Eve, 1908.

Enter, in 1908, Mr. W. Stephen Bush of Philadelphia, the patron saint of Shakespeare-on-film critics, and defender of the silent Vitagraph Shakespeare films against the animadversions of choleric purists. His bully pulpit was the indispensable journal *The Moving Picture World and View Photographer*, volume one having appeared in March 1907 at the cost to readers of five cents a copy. There he railed against the assumption that a sacralized Shakespeare belonged to the classes rather than to the masses and saw the Shakespeare movie as a wedge for enticing "the best class of people" into the dingy storefront movie houses. A paradigm for the sacralization of Shakespeare emerges in the prologue of Edwin Thanhouser's 1916 *King Lear* which shows Frederick B. Warde, the actor playing Lear, seated stiffly in a wingback chair reading from the Globe edition. Warde was the epitome of the well-bred Victorian gentleman who could savor Shakespeare's exquisite language, while hoi polloi kept their places in the rowdy music halls.

Putting Shakespeare in silent movies, or "the wordless drama," as it was often called, was a curiously inept way to give Shakespeare mass appeal. Ironically, it was the bombastic wordiness, the sound and fury (a bravura "to be or not to be"), not the sense, of stage actors that had appealed to the powerful oral impulses in an earlier, semiliterate American culture. When movies and radio eventually usurped the place of the orators and actors, the result was further to exacerbate the split between low and high culture.[2] It was also somewhat naively thought by some cohorts that Shakespeare in the nickelodeons would give a good dose of Anglo-American culture to the mostly eastern European immigrants, the tired masses who huddled in the darkness yearning for a morsel of joy. Although Bush filled a threefold technical, cultural, and political need, he did have a hidden agenda. In a conflict of interest, he frequently advertised his services in trade journals as a lecturer who supplemented high-quality films such as *Othello* and *Romeo and Juliet*, as well as Dante's *Inferno*, with epilogues or even a complete lecture during and between the running of the reels.[3]

In Europe, France's influential Film d'Art put the great Jean Mounet-Sully in a *Hamlet* graveyard scene, thus making the Comédie Française available to the meaner sorts of persons. Great literature like Shakespeare's dramas, and great actors like Mounet-Sully and Sarah Bernhardt made movies great. No one had yet thought that movies in themselves could be art. Bush was pleased to see J. Stuart Blackton's Vitagraph company, inspired by Film d'Art, include one-reel Shakespeare movies in its "Quality" products. The Vitagraph 12-to-14 minute, 1,000-foot, one-reel Shakespeare movies (though at a production cost of 10¢ a foot sneered at as the "cheap for the cheap") did adumbrate lengthier and better quality story films, especially those of independents like Adolph Zukor.[4] The audience didn't need to know a lot of Shakespeare to follow an easily apprehensible series of sketches or tableaux: the assassination of Caesar, the balcony scene in *Romeo and Juliet*, a mad King Lear on a heath, and so on. These vignettes did advance slightly ahead of the *actualités* that were already the staple of the storefront electric theaters and their boxing matches, belly dancers, and marching soldiers.

In a very few years, however, critics ceased being defensive and began coming up with fairly sophisticated interpretations. Critic Brian Hooker's 1916 *Century* essay, "Shakespere [sic] and the Movies," compared the similarity in form between Shakespeare and "the modern photodrama," and illustrated its argument with rare stills from the 1916 *Macbeth* starring Sir Herbert Beerbohm Tree. Others also saw aesthetic possibilities for cinema beyond the passive role of merely recording stage action. By 1917 an anonymous critic in *Bioscope* (Nov. 22, 1917, 47) precociously theorized about different ways to put Shakespeare on screen. Which, he asked, of three means of adaptation should be chosen? ". . . the first being to treat the play as a condensation . . . ; the second to . . . present a human story; the third, . . . to materialize the philosophy of the Bard in a series of symbols." The first method presumably describes the stage codes of *tableaux vivants* and statue-like acting that characterized the Vitagraph *Julius Caesar*. The second fits Edwin Thanhouser's 1916 reinvention of the old king and his daughters in the sentimental pathos of a D.W. Griffith film. The third method, calling for capturing the Bard in "symbols," anticipated postmodernist films such as Jean-Luc Godard's *King Lear*, which makes no attempt to represent Shakespeare's tragedy except though a montage of unique images and a medley of voices and sounds.

In the years between World War I and World War II, commentary on Shakespeare films continued to be limited to the journalists, the Shakespeare movie being déclassé in academic circles. The *New York Times* praised the 1920 Gade *Hamlet*, which was elevated into one of the 10 best pictures of the year, and in 1922 poked fun at the unintended comedy in a revived Cines *Julius Caesar* (1914) that even after only eight years seemed old-fashioned. In 1929, British audiences underwent severe culture shock when, for the first time, they heard American voices speaking Shakespeare's words in Mary Pickford and Douglas Fairbanks's *The Taming of the Shrew*. There were rumblings about "indignation meetings" in London as if Hollywood had committed lèse majesté. The notorious credit line "With additional dialogue by Sam Taylor," which, as James M. Welsh quoting R.H. Ball has argued, may never have existed, induced a feeding frenzy of hostility. The movie's reception, which in the rapidly evolving distributorship protocols of the film industry would have gone not into a dingy nickelodeon, but to a first-run downtown theater with tickets priced at 50¢ or more, was sufficiently ornery to send poor

PREFACE

Sir Herbert Beerbohm Tree as King John (1899) (MILESTONE FILM & VIDEO)

Mary Pickford, the star who virtually owned the movie industry, into a deep depression from which she apparently never fully recovered. Even critic Mordaunt Hall's belief that "Miss Pickford is delightful in her fits of fury"[5] was insufficient to console her. At the London Bijou gala premiere, critic James Agate knowledgeably argued that the movie, rather than being a travesty of Shakespeare's play, was essentially a reworking of David Garrick's famous stage adaptation, *Katherine and Petruchio*. Ironically, the ambitious movie, designed by William Cameron Menzies of *The Thief of Bagdad* and *Gone With the Wind* fame, eventually found many defenders, especially after its 1968 rerelease and subsequent recording on laser disk.

The specter of the dreaded purist haunted the producers of the 1930s Hollywood Shakespeare extravaganzas, Warner Bros.'s *A Midsummer Night's Dream* and Metro-Goldwyn-Mayer's (MGM's) *Romeo and Juliet*. Maybe to exorcise the demons, they made much of the special effects in *A Midsummer Night's Dream*—Reinhardt's cobweb machine, Cagney's donkey's head with "eyes which roll . . . ears which wag, and mouth which opens and closes with the spoken lines," and the weird masks for the elfin orchestra.[6] Stained with a sleazy reputation for spawning gangster movies, Warner Bros. sought exculpation with a highbrow Shakespeare movie directed by the celebrated Max Reinhardt, the guru of *A Midsummer Night's Dream* stage productions. Hence, a snarling gangster like James Cagney was "translated" into Bottom. Despite these perturbations, some critics, among them the *New York Times* reviewer P.W. Wilson, stopped asking the question, "Is it Shakespeare?" and boldly asserted that "if the screen can rescue Shakespeare from the trammels of the stage . . . , the Elizabethan urge within us all—boisterous and brave and sentimental and sad—may again encircle the globe."

MGM producer Irving Thalberg and his director George Cukor launched a preemptive strike against

Mary Pickford and Douglas Fairbanks's Kate and Petruchio

British rage over American voices in Shakespeare movies by casting only authentic Pukka Sahib types like Basil Rathbone, Leslie Howard, Dame May Oliver, and C. Aubrey Smith, prominent names in Hollywood's British expatriate colony. As a sop to American elitists, they also hired the Shakespearean expertise of Cornell University's Professor William B. Strunk, coauthor with *The New Yorker*'s E.B. White of the ultimate freshman composition handbook, *The Elements of Style*. Perhaps mesmerized by the movies pretentiousness, most American critics raved about it, even though its pompous sets were the acme of inauthenticity and turned Verona into a cemetery. The aging Norma Shearer and Leslie Howard were technically impeccable but ultimately wooden and incapable of capturing the passion of Romeo and Juliet. Sinclair Lewis's Carol Kennicott of Gopher Prairie would have loved it for all the wrong reasons.

While these Hollywood-sound Shakespeare movies never entirely caught fire with either classes or masses, they were sufficient to stir the interest of the academy. In the 1950s and 1960s, Alice Griffin's intelligent essays, "Through the Camera's Eye," appeared in *Shakespeare Quarterly*. There were distinguished essays by Orson Welles in *Sight and Sound*, by Ian Johnson in *Films and Filming*, by Meredith Lillich in *Films in Review*, and Constance Brown in *Film Quarterly*. I still remember reading Constance Brown's 1967 essay on the Olivier Richard III and being bowled over by the deft way that she used the shadow imagery to show how the cross-fertilization of verbal and visual elements could reify Shakespeare into moving graphics.

A *History of Kinetograph*, and Kinetoscope had been published as early as 1895 by the pioneering W.K.L. Dickson, and brief allusions to Shakespeare flickered across the pages of Benjamin Hampton's engrossing 1931 *A History of the Movies*, but the first book-length study devoted only to Shakespeare on film emerged in 1968: Professor Robert Hamilton Ball's *Shakespeare on Silent Film*. To build this monumental work of scholarship, Ball dug through hundreds of pages of trade journals, tracked down blurry prints in remote archives, examined paper film prints, screened ancient 35mm silents in the dingy old National Film Archive in Soho, wrote dozens of letters of inquiry about lost films, interviewed surviving cast members from the earliest days of cinema, and completed an indexed manuscript of notable accuracy, especially considering the absence then of word-processing software. His essays on the films oscillate between charming commentary and tedious scene-by-scene plot outlines, and his rambling style sometimes obscures the exact fact one may be searching for, such as the name of a film's director, yet no book on this subject is ever likely to surpass it. Thought slightly eccentric in its time (Shakespeare on silent film was an oxymoron), Ball's fascination with the silents has been recently revived by the release of Milestone's video of the British Film Institute (BFI) films and by a flurry of interest from such archivists and critics as Buchanan, Freedman, Guntner, McKernan, Pearson, Terris, and Uricchio. Uricchio and Pearson in *Reframing Culture* (1993) employ the rigorous language of sociocultural theory (movie theaters become "sites of cultural contestation") for their probing analysis of the Vitagraph company's "Quality" films, which bridged the tawdriness of the storefront theaters and the opulence of the emerging palaces.

Ball had planned a sequel covering the sound films of Shakespeare, which never materialized, though his copious notes and clippings for the project remain housed in the Folger Library archives. Instead, the first full-length treatise on the talking Shakespeare movie, *Shakespeare and the Films*, came a few years later, in 1971, from film historian Roger Manvell, a former director of the British Film Academy, and at the time of his demise, a beloved visiting professor at Boston University. As a film person, Manvell stressed the practical problems of filmmaking and included revealing interviews with Lord Michael Birkett, who produced Peter Hall's 1969 *A Midsummer Night's Dream* and Peter Brook's 1971 *King Lear*. In his subsequent book, *Theater and Film* (1979), Manvell worked out the first full-scale taxonomy for Shakespeare films (36).

In the meantime, the scorekeepers, even well before the final gun had sounded, could hardly wait to begin. Shakespeare filmographies surfaced everywhere, not just in Anglophone countries. They include, chronologically, work by F. Silva Nobre of Brazil (1964), Tue Ritzav of Denmark (1964), Max Lippman of Germany (1964), Nachman Ingber of Israel (1967), Peter Morris of Canada (1972), Sergei Yutkevich of Russia (1973), Alexander Lipkov of Russia (1975), Ralph Condee of the United States (1976), Andrew McLean of the United States (1980), Graham Holderness and Christopher McCullough of Great Britain (1987), Kathy Grant of Great Britain (1992), Luke McKernan and Olwen Terris of Great Britain (1994), Jo McMurtry of the United States (1994), Yoshio Arai of Japan (1996), José Ramon Díaz-Fernández of Spain (1997), and Vanni Borghi of Italy (1999). Are there others? Yes, of course—a latecomer arrived only yesterday, out of the blue, to coin a cliché: Eddie Sammons's, *Shakespeare: A Hundred Years on Film* (London: Shepheard Walwyn, 2000).

What should have set the gold standard was Barry M. Parker's *The Folger Shakespeare Filmography* (1979), which stemmed from the admirable O.B. Hardison's dream of making the Folger preeminent in Shakespearean cinema, a project that lost impetus after his untimely death. The filmography was sabotaged by a dyslexic proofreader who confused Helen Haye with Helen Hayes, turned Alan Webb into Alab Webb, Roger Manvell into Roger Manuell, and so forth, though the book still shows expertise on offshoot and derivative Shakespeare films.

I should mention parenthetically the 1990 *Shakespeare on Screen: An International Filmography and Videography*, compiled by one Kenneth S. Rothwell with some help from Annabelle Melzer, which despite flaws and obsolescence remains the most complete inventory. In danger of upstaging everyone is the Internet's International Movie Database, which spews out thousands of names and dates, though rarely gives its sources, which can be unsettling. Errors, howlers, and mistakes can spread alarmingly, like some pestilent computer virus. For example, recently I read in the pages of the *International Film Index* (495) the amazing information that Sir Johnston Forbes-Robertson starred in an 1898 *Macbeth*, one year prior to Tree's *King John*, which I thought had been safely enshrined as the first Shakespeare movie. A polite query in January 2001 to the London editor remains unanswered.

Not surprisingly, the tempestuous zeitgeist of the 1970s, which displaced traditional continuities with postmodernist discontinuities, also triggered miniupheavals in Shakespeare studies. Jack J. Jorgens intrepidly announced in his outstanding *Shakespeare on Film* (1977) that the Shakespeare movie was "less a maimed rite than a source of fruitful confusion." To Jorgens, Shakespeare on film offered advantages and opportunities, not just impediments and barricades. At the same time, the *Shakespeare on Film Newsletter* squeaked onto the scene at the 1976 Modern Language Association convention in New York City, the editors, Rothwell and Kliman, fully expecting to be hissed out of the Hotel Statler book displays by irate purists. Now absorbed by *Shakespeare Bulletin*, the newsletter in its 16-year career encouraged many emerging scholars, stimulated established scholars to write about the Shakespeare movie, and evolved into a useful research tool. By good fortune, it was at just this time that the epic, perhaps even megalomaniacal, BBC/Time-Life television series was inaugurated and shared its generous advertising budget with the impoverished newsletter. I hasten to add, however, that there was nothing about this largesse that kept the editors from being ingrates. In a stinging indictment, reviewer O.B. Hardison accused the BBC producers of not so much "doing Shakespeare" as "doing Shakespeare in."[7] The editors begged, cajoled, and wheedled to get first-rate reviewers like James Bulman, Ann Cook, Irene Dash, Barbara Hodgdon, Michael Manheim, and Lois Potter. Embarrassingly, everyone fell all over themselves to agree with Roger Manvell's 1987 prediction that inexpensive television productions heralded the demise of the multimillion-dollar Shakespeare movie (Fox 278), never imagining the powerful renaissance that would begin only two years later with Kenneth Branagh's *Henry V*.

This decade was indeed the best of times, for the first of some 100 essays on filmed Shakespeare by 67 authors began appearing in special Shakespeare issues of *Literature/Film Quarterly* (*LFQ*). In general, authors leaned more toward the literary than the filmic, though as the years went by and English department commentators became more comfortable with film, this duality began to wither away. The essays clustered around five categories: "pedagogical," "normative," "aesthetic," "positivist," or "heuristic," with as many overlaps and crossovers as the dialogue in a Robert Altman movie. For example, pedagogically, Michael A. Anderegg in 1976 writes about using Shakespeare movies in the classroom at a time when it was still a no-no. Normatively, Normand Berlin fulminates over the wreckage of

King Lear perpetrated by Peter Brook, who is guilty of a "self-indulgence" that "obliterates Shakespeare for the sake of a limiting, preconceived idea" (303). In a similar vein, William P. Shaw deplores the violence in the Brook *Lear* and Polanski *Macbeth* that "creates an exaggerated, darker, and less complex vision of humanity than we find in Shakespeare's plays" (213). As for the aesthetic, it must impinge on almost every discussion, though some, such as Michael Pursell's "Art and Artifice in Franco Zeffirelli's *Romeo and Juliet*" (*LFQ* 14.4), which calibrates the interplay between the authentic and artificial, can more plausibly claim that label. More positivist and neutral is Ace G. Pilkington's sober assessment of the BBC "Henriad," in which he liberates it from invidious comparison with Olivier's *Henry V* (*LFQ* 21.1). In a revisionist mode, Walter R. Coppedge's essay on the widely denounced Paul Mazursky *Tempest* (1982) made a case for viewing the film in a gentler, kinder way (*LFQ* 21.1).

As to the fifth category, the heuristic, or essay of discovery, I find relatively few along the lines of what Peter Donaldson describes as his own "heuristic auteurism, a skeptical bardolatry" (xiv). Nevertheless, Barbara Hodgdon's "Two King Lears: Uncovering the Filmtext" went far in the theoretical direction of sorting out the nexus between film and play text.

Most recently, the tendency has been to move toward trendy sociological analysis of pop culture, as, for example, in Elsie Walker's "Pop Goes the Shakespeare: Baz Luhrmann's *Romeo + Juliet*" (*LFQ* 28.2), or in a kind of quasi-Marxist political vein, Anthony Miller's "*Julius Caesar* in the Cold: The Houseman-Mankiewicz Film" (*LFQ* 28.2). Of course, editor James M. Welsh has himself significantly contributed at least eight Shakespeare-centered articles and reviews.

Among these 100 essays, *Hamlet* was the most frequently written about, with at least 22 essays on Branagh's version, though other strong contenders were Olivier, Gade, Kozintsev, and Zeffirelli. *King Lear* ran second with 15 articles, many of them on the Brook version. *Macbeth* and *Romeo and Juliet* came in third and fourth, respectively, with *Othello* running a poor fifth.

Leslie Banks as the Chorus in Olivier's Henry V (UNITED ARTISTS)

Among the other genres, the Olivier and Branagh *Henry V*'s did very well with 11 essays, and not surprisingly, since so few films have been made of them, the comedies and romances were poor also-rans, except for *A Midsummer Night's Dream*.

In the late 1980s there was another spurt of book-length commentaries. Anthony Davies's *Filming Shakespeare's Plays* (1988) showed how in *Chimes at Midnight* the vertical planes of light in the castle reinforce the power of monarchy, while the horizontal planes of light at the Boar's Head tavern situate Falstaff in the midst of frivolity, squatness, and subversion. Davies's originality made awareness of cinematic space a key element in the quest for visual and verbal equivalents. In a different approach altogether, John Collick, in *Shakespeare, Cinema and Society* (1989), followed the cultural materialists in his proto-Marxist commentary on such films as the Olivier *Henry V*. He interrogated the widespread assumption that *Henry V* functioned as a morale-builder for the armed forces in World War II, for that would require "the mythical idea of a wholly integrated British culture" (47). Indeed common sense suggests that for Tommies and Joes, Vera Lynn and Betty Grable carried more clout than William Shakespeare. In yet another approach, Bernice W. Kliman in *Hamlet: Film Television and Audio Performance* (1988) exhaustively studied the history of *Hamlet* films beginning with silents like Mario Caserini's 1910 version, and working through the midcentury sound versions such as Kozintsev's. She also showcases Ragnar Lyth's sensational televised Swedish *Hamlet* (1984), starring a wonderfully sullen Stellan Skarsgård, which in its gothic style mocks the received wisdom that television cannot match film. Without the indefatigable Kliman, Americans would have little knowledge of this jarring *Hamlet*, with, for example, its terrifying graveyard scene in which Ophelia in a postmodernist memento mori sprawls horribly out of her cheap coffin. Taking another tack, Bridget Lyons combines a continuity script taken from the soundtrack of *Chimes at Midnight* with a discussion by such significant critics as C.L. Barber and Dudley Andrew of the Wellesian textual alterations and commentaries.

Speaking of Lyons's work reminds me of an important subspecies of Shakespeare on film commentary—film scripts and costume/design sketches. They appear as early as the Strunk edition of the 1936 Thalberg/Cukor *Romeo and Juliet*. More than 40 years ago, CBS issued a handsomely engraved script for the Old Vic *Hamlet* (1959), and in 1971 there was the unadorned but useful Garrett and Hardison script of Olivier's

The French Court in Laurence Olivier's Henry V
(UNITED ARTISTS)

Henry V. Since then, scripts have appeared in sumptuously illustrated volumes for Branagh's *Henry V*, *Much Ado About Nothing*, and *Hamlet*, Trevor Nunn's *Twelfth Night*, the Loncraine/McKellen *Richard III*, and Baz Luhrmann's *Romeo & Juliet* [*sic*]. They make life infinitely easier for critics who can't recollect the particular details of a film, though in some instances they may perplex more than clarify, as when the fabulously ornamental script for Michael Hoffman's *A Midsummer Night's Dream* has Bottom doused in donkey manure (16) instead of the red wine actually seen in the film. Peter Greenaway's beautifully made script for *Prospero's Books* (1991) further validates his credentials as a graphic designer, nor should anyone overlook the 1986 screenplay of *Ran*, personally illustrated by the versatile Akira Kurosawa, who was both accomplished artist and cineaste.

Something also must be said about Shakespeare on television, which was once condemned as hopelessly inferior to film by so respected a critic as Jack Jorgens. Again one gets into a morass. The most trenchant single study is Susan Willis's 1991 *The BBC Shakespeare Plays*, based on the author's presence on the set during the shooting of the plays. In a *Shakespeare on Film Newsletter* (*SFNL*) review, O.B. Hardison skewered Edward Quinn's *The Shakespeare Hour: A Companion to the PBS-TV Series* (1985) for peddling "banalities," and parenthetically shrugged off its bibliography, which I compiled, as a mere "cursory list" (*SFNL* 12.1). Herbert Coursen and James Bulman stitched together the most complete anthology on televised Shakespeare in their 1988 *Shakespeare on Television*. (Herbert Coursen himself deserves a presidential medal with oak leaf clusters as the world's most prolific writer on Shakespeare in moving images, with contributions to the *Shakespeare on Film Newsletter*, *Shakespeare Bulletin*, his own periodical *Shakespeare and the Classroom*, and his more recent *Watching Shakespeare on Television* [1993], though so far as I know he has never contributed to *LFQ*.) There is one other indispensable resource for televised Shakespeare, however, in the Mayflower and BBC complete Peter Alexander texts with literary consultant John Wilders's cogent prefaces, Henry Fenwick's notes on design and costuming, and David Snodin's, or Alan Shallcross's, textual notes on the BBC's alterations.

It's time now to squeeze in a few remarks about the 130 essays in ten anthologies of criticism that further embellish the critical landscape. These books (listed chronologically) are edited by Charles Eckert (1972), Stanley Wells (1987), Anthony Davies and Stanley Wells (1994), Michael Skovmand (1994), Lawrence Guntner and Peter Drexler (1995), Lisa Starks (1997), Lynda Boose and Richard Burt (1997), Robert Shaughnessy (1998), Neil E. Béchervaise (1999), Mark Burnett and Romana Wray (2000), and soon forthcoming is Russell Jackson's *Cambridge Companion to Shakespeare On Film*, 4 (2000). There is also the year 2000 issue of *Early Modern Literary Studies* entirely devoted to Shakespeare on screen. This landslide suggests that the question "Is it Shakespeare?" no longer really concerns anyone. The Shakespeare film has struck out on a path of its own. Stanley Wells deserves credit for bridging the gap between bardophile and cinephile with his 1987 *Shakespeare Survey* (39) devoted to Shakespeare on film. It included scholar/critic Robert Hapgood's estimable essay on Orson Welles's *Chimes at Midnight* in which he untangled Welles's five ways for textual rearrangement of the Henriad. In Davies's *Shakespeare and the Moving Image*, he situated Kurosawa in Japanese culture and ferreted out subtle parallels between the costume drama *Ran* and the modernized *Hamlet*, *The Bad Sleep Well*. In the Boose and Burt collection, Hapgood does not fret over the question "Is it Shakespeare?" but embraces Zeffirelli as a "popularizer" of such talent, so that the term becomes honorific rather than pejorative.

Burnett and Wray's thematically unified *Shakespeare, Film, Fin de Siècle*, self-referentially seizes on the end of the millennium, as Judith Buchanan says, "to read these Shakespeare films, made on the cusp of the new millennium, in the light of anxieties attendant upon a moment of historical transition" (197). Its contributions demonstrate the liminality, or transitional phases, of the Shakespeare film. Andrew Murphy fearlessly goes to the crossroads at midnight to drive a stake into the heart of the demonic creature who under the full moon endlessly howls "Is it Shakespeare?" Noting the disjunction between the received Shakespeare text and its filmed versions, he advocates ditching the "tired old critical paradigms that have governed the study of filmed Shakespeare for the past several decades" (21).

As if the 238 essays and some 24 books are insufficient data for a history of Shakespeare on film criticism, I must now triumphantly but wearily report the existence of a flood of commentary scattered hither and thither in such locations as the eminent University of Manchester "Shakespeare in Performance" series. The authors include familiar performance and Shakespeare-on-screen scholars like Jay Halio, Bernice W. Kliman, and Graham Holderness. Holderness directly addresses the key theoretical questions. To the real film critic, he says, a Shakespeare film ". . . is not truly a film at all, but a hybrid amalgamation of two hostile cultural discourses, tainted by the noxious traces of the stage, of high art, of cultural elitism and of British cultural imperialism" (51). Here one feels the terror of being squeezed between the pitiless inquisitions of the film purists and the Shakespeare purists. The question is no longer "Is it Shakespeare?" but "Is it film?" Holderness reassuringly goes on to say that he will not allow a theoretical impasse between stage and film to dissuade him from evaluating Zeffirelli's *Taming of the Shrew* " . . . in its own specifically *filmic* terms rather than in comparison with some ideal model of an authoritatively Shakespearean realisation" (53).

There still remains an avalanche of commentaries in journals and newspapers, though my waning energies have prevented me from compiling an exact count. As an example of the researcher's potential nightmare, simply look at the website of the electronic *World Shakespeare Bibliography*. The entry for the Ragnar Lyth *Hamlet* lists 27 reviews in Swedish publications (everything from the *Kvällsposten* to the *Svenska Dagbladet*) and one in English by the tireless Bernice W. Kliman. But as the great Al Jolson said, "You ain't seen nothing yet." The Ragnar commentary pales into insignificance next to the Branagh *Hamlet* entry, which includes more than 250 journal and newspaper articles in languages ranging from Hebrew to French to German to English. If the reviews for all films of *Othello*, *Macbeth*, *Hamlet*, and *Midsummer Night's Dream* alone were laid end to end, they would doubtless encircle the Globe—well, anyway, Sam Wanamaker's Bankside Globe. Such journalists as Jonathan Rosenbaum, Vincent Canby, and the late Pauline Kael, with no time for the luxury of the second thoughts that we cloistered academics enjoy, often shoot from the hip. That slashing style gives their work a certain flair, a *je ne sais quoi*, so that in a model of conciseness Pauline Kael could simply say of the Peter Brook *King Lear* "I hated it." Essays also pop up in unexpected places so that a piece so brilliant as Albert R. Cirillo's 1969 exegesis of the circle imagery in Zeffirelli's *Romeo and Juliet* might have sunk without a trace in the journal *Tri-Quarterly* except for its having been later anthologized.[8]

Now I can finally speak of the dozen new books from the last decade. An early entry was Lorne Buchman's *Still in Movement* (1991), which examined how the multiple perspectives of film help to reinterpret the Shakespeare text. A hostile reviewer charged him with "conceptual vagueness" but his analysis of the opening scene of Polanski's *Macbeth* is about as thoroughly specific as any I've ever seen. A decade ago, Ace G. Pilkington in *Screening Shakespeare* (1991) was enchanted by the user friendliness of videotape, which granted the Shakespeare film "the kind of scholarly attention that has traditionally been given to printed texts" (155). No longer would the screening of old films involve onerous forays to remote archives. Pilkington uses the new technology to explore the ambiguous link in Olivier's *Henry V* between Renée Asherson's Katherine and the Globe playhouse Player Queen.

Peter Donaldson's 1990 book *Shakespearean Films/Shakespearean Directors* employs a heuristic criticism that would have been totally unimaginable to Mr. W. Stephen Bush. His psychoanalytical readings of the Olivier *Hamlet*, and his approach to the Welles *Othello* from the standpoint of film theorist Jean-Louis Baudry's conception of the "cinematographic apparatus," move a long way from cautious empiricism. Donaldson joins the consensus that sees the Shakespeare film as an independent object. He recuperates the much maligned Jean-Luc Godard *King Lear* by revealing how the film filters the power of Shakespeare's unsettling tragedy through a montage of startling images and the iterative voice of Burgess Meredith.

Samuel Crowl's *Shakespeare Observed* (1992) ventures that the period from 1957 to 1970 was "the richest in the history of sound-filmed Shakespeare," which was certainly true at the time he finished his book in 1991, though by the end of the book he has managed to include Branagh's 1989 *Henry V*. He brings special strength to the issue of the intertextuality of stage and film, citing such former stage directors as Welles, Reinhardt/Dieterle, and Hall. He believes that "film gave us our liberty in thinking and writing about Shakespeare, and that led us and our students back to the theater" (4). To Crowl, Welles's self-referential *Chimes at Midnight* represents a "long-good-bye" for Falstaff (that is, Welles). In one telling example, he points out how Jeanne Moreau as Doll Tearsheet addresses Jack as a "whoreson tidy Bartholomew boar-pig"; "whoreson" miraculously comes out sounding like "Orson."

It's possible that since he dedicated it to me I need to make a disclaimer before evaluating Herbert Coursen's 1996 *Shakespeare in Production. Whose History?*, though the book's innate virtues make any such declaration redundant. Nicely complementing Crowl's work, Coursen attacks his duties as a critic like the fighter pilot he once was, with guns blazing. Influenced by Robert Weimann, he builds this latest of his many books around the concept of the locus (or "the thing represented"), and the *platea* ("the specifics of production"), the latter having an inherent ability to radicalize, problematize, or even subvert, the former. Thus, for example, the locus of Papp's *Much Ado About Nothing* could be wit play between Beatrice and Benedick, but the *platea* destabilizes the performance by reinventing Messina as Teddy Roosevelt's America. Coursen examines Christine Edzard's film society *As You Like It* (1992) in which *platea* turns the Forest of Arden into an urban wasteland, plus a cornucopia of stage productions on both sides of the Atlantic. For his reception study of the Branagh *Much Ado About Nothing*, he catalogs dozens of reviews, as well as examining the debate swirling around Branagh: saint or hero? Brilliant popularizer or running dog of cultural imperialism?

There is yet more. My survey would be incomplete without citing three of the most recent entries: Michael A. Anderegg's *Orson Welles: Shakespeare and Popular Culture*; Robert Willson's *Shakespeare in Hollywood 1929–1956*; and Kathy Howlett's *Framing Shakespeare on Film*. There is yet a fourth, Douglas Brode's *Shakespeare in the Movies: From the Silent Era to Shakespeare in Love* (2000), that I prefer not to comment on but rather refer you to James M. Welsh's and Tom Pendleton's penetrating reviews in *LFQ* (28.2) and *Shakespeare Newsletter* (Spring 2000). Anderegg's wonderful book does more than provide an absorbing account of Welles's career—we already have many of those—but goes beyond that to rebut the miasma of hostility enveloping him. Welles, Anderegg says in his defense, "acted out of a very American conviction that art . . . ought to have an educational function and serve a social purpose" (167). Robert Willson focuses on the material conditions in Hollywood during the era of the pre–World War II studio system. He embeds the Thalberg/Cukor *Romeo and Juliet* (1936) in the studio politics at MGM, when Thalberg, a "doomed prince" (top executive at MGM by 20 years of age and dead at 36), seized the double opportunity to imprint his signature on a major classic and to star his talented wife, Norma Shearer. In dealing with "selected offshoots" like Ernst Lubitsch's *To Be or Not to Be* (1942) and *A Double Life* with Ronald Colman (1947), Willson convincingly shows how derivatives can sometimes draw attention to Shakespeare's text and subtext even while apparently meandering away.

Kathy Howlett's *Framing Shakespeare* returns directly to the original question "Is it Shakespeare?" For her there is no "anxiety of inauthenticity." She resists the idea of "getting back to the original Shakespeare" as "an impossible one," even inconsistent "with Renaissance theatrical practice" (7). Shakespeare remains "centrally in" a variety of mainstream films such as the Zeffirelli/Mel Gibson *Hamlet* 1990) and Gus Van Sant's *My Own Private Idaho* (1991), an argument graphically supported with appropriate frame shots, stills, and Carpaccio paintings, the last showing the source for the tiny dog in Welles's *Chimes*. Howlett revels in the company of theoreticians like Inez Hedges, Linda Woodbridge, and Linda Charnes, whose abstruse discourses reinforce Howlett's baroque vision of the Shakespeare movie as a cultural phenomenon of extraordinary flexibility.

Lastly, I cite two highly unorthodox studies by Richard Burt and Lloyd Kaufman that are so postmodernist as to shock even post-postmodernists. Richard Burt's indefatigable zest for collecting recondite shards from Shakespeare references sedimented in popular culture lies behind his amazing *Unspeakable ShaXXXspeares: Queer Theory and American Kiddie Culture* (1998). Burt is not, however, just slumming (his word) in writing about unspeakable Shakespeare—dumbed-down youth culture, porn films, gay treatments—so much as charting the interaction between existing sites of cultural authority and these quasi-subversive products of youth culture. I say "quasi" subversive because it's not clear how uncomprehending youth, itself lobotomized by commodity-driven mass communications, can in any authentic way be considered subversive. Ironically, it seems to be the academic attempting to understand the new dumbed-down culture who turns out to be the "loser." Having rejected the Faustian bargain of complicity in pop culture, the professor is left only with his melancholy, so to speak. Burt is a brilliant allegorizer, using, for example, the 1994 film *Quiz Show*, about the fall of Charles Van Doren, as a talisman of how mass culture has co-opted elitist values. Come to think of it, Van Doren's gloomy fate works a variation on Professor Rath in Von Sternberg's film *The Blue Angel* (1930)— the professor as entertainer who at the very moment he becomes an entertainer ceases to be a professor, though Burt has himself written a whole book about entertainment in which he warns against the folly of the middle-aged attempting to hip hop with kiddie culture. It's exasperatingly convoluted and double-edged, and even sublime in the Burkean sense that anything entirely clear cannot be powerfully moving. One of Burt's chief admirers, Lloyd Kaufman of Troma Studios, cogently defends his own X-rated movie *Tromeo and Juliet*, in the hilarious *All I Need to Know about Filmmaking I Learned from The Toxic Avenger: The True Shocking Story of Troma Studios* (1998). For Kaufman the best movie is one of "no redeeming social value" (193), a tongue-in-cheek sideswipe at the banality of vapid Hollywood mainstream cinema.

In conclusion, after having dragged you through the entire catalog of Shakespeare-on-film commentary comprised of some 100 articles in *LFQ*, another 138 in anthologies, about 30 essays scattered everywhere else, hundreds of newspaper reviews, 17 filmographies, nearly two dozen books, and so forth, I end by quoting Peter Holland's pessimistic view: "The study of Shakespeare on film has often seemed intensely and agonizingly preoccupied with searching for answers to the self-imposed question of the films' relation to Shakespeare, and has usually triumphantly managed to come up with no better solution than that film is and is not Shakespeare."[9] I think, however, that the situation is not quite so bleak, at least in the way that these books and articles have evolved toward new ground. Gradually, subtly, we have ceased to ask "Is it Shakespeare?" but instead "Is Shakespeare in it?" Has the anxiety of inauthenticity evolved into the inauthenticity of anxiety? The ultimately unanswerable question "Is it Shakespeare?" belongs with similar mischievous speech acts such as "Have you stopped beating your wife?" In film, the aura of Shakespeare may be gone, but in the lingering afterglow, the Shakespeare-on-film critic finds a niche.

—Kenneth S. Rothwell
University of Vermont

NOTES

1. A. Nicholas Vardac, *Stage to Screen: Theatrical Method from Garrick to Griffith* (Rpt. 1949; New York: Benjamin Blom, 1968) passim. See also Ben Brewster and Lea Jacobs, *Theatre to Cinema: Stage Pictorialism and the Early Feature Film* (Oxford University Press, 1997) passim.
2. For full discussion, see Lawrence Levine, *Highbrow/Lowbrow* (Cambridge, Mass.: Harvard University Press, 1988), and Michael Bristol, *Shakespeare's America, America's Shakespeare* (New York and London: Routledge, 1990).
3. See *Moving Picture World*, July 4, 1908, and July 29, 1911.
4. For an excellent account of Zukor's career from the viewpoint of a contemporary film worker, see Benjamin B. Hampton, *A History of the Movies* (New York: Covici-Friede Publishers, 1931. Reprint, Arno Press, 1970) 252–80, and passim.
5. See Hall's review, *New York Times*, Nov. 30, 1929; cf. Pickford, 312.
6. Public Relations blurb, Warner Brothers 1929, in British Film Institute library.
7. See *Shakespeare on Film Newsletter* 12.1 (Dec. 1987): 8.
8. "The Art of Franco Zeffirelli and Shakespeare's *Romeo and Juliet*," *Tri-Quarterly* 16 (1969): 69–92. Reprinted in Fred Marcus, ed. *Film and Literature: Contrasts in Media* (Scranton: Chandler, 1971) 205–27.
9. Foreword, *Shakespeare, Film, Fin de Siècle*. Eds. Mark Thornton and Romana Wray (New York: St. Martin's Press, 2000) xii.

WORKS CITED

Anderegg, Michael. "Shakespeare on Film in the Classroom." *Literature/Film Quarterly* 4.2 (Spring 1976): 165–75.

———. *Orson Welles: Shakespeare and Popular Culture*. New York: Columbia University Press, 1999.

Ball, Robert Hamilton. *Shakespeare on Silent Film: A Strange Eventful History*. London: George Allen & Unwin, Ltd., 1968.

Béchervaise, Neil E. *Shakespeare on Celluloid*. Rozelle, Australia: St. Clair Press Pty Ltd., 1999.

Benjamin, Walter. "The Work of Art in the Age of Mechanical Reproduction," in *Illuminations*. Ed. Hannah Arendt. New York: Schocken Books, 1979. 217–51.

Berlin, Normand. "Peter Brook's Interpretation of *King Lear*." *Literature/Film Quarterly* 5.4 (Fall 1977): 299–303.

Boose, Lynda E., and Richard Burt, eds. *Shakespeare, The Movie: Popularizing the Plays on Film, TV, and Video*. New York and London: Routledge, 1997.

Brewster, Ben, and Lea Jacobs. *Theatre to Cinema: Stage Pictorialism and the Early Feature Film*. New York: Oxford University Press, 1997.

Bristol, Michael. *Shakespeare's America, America's Shakespeare*. New York and London: Routledge, 1990.

Brode, Douglas. *Shakespeare in the Movies: From the Silent Era to Shakespeare in Love*. New York: Oxford University Press, 2000.

Brown, Constance. "Olivier's *Richard III*—A Re-evaluation." *Film Quarterly* 20 (1967): 23–32.

Buchman, Lorne. *Still in Movement: Shakespeare on Screen*. New York: Oxford University Press, 1991.

Bulman, J.C., and H.R. Coursen, eds. *Shakespeare on Television: An Anthology of Essays and Reviews*. Hanover, N.H.: University Press of New England, 1988.

Burnett, Mark Thornton, and Romana Wray, eds. *Shakespeare, Film, Fin de Siècle*. Foreword by Peter Holland. Interview with Kenneth Branagh. New York: St. Martin's Press, 2000.

Burt, Richard. *Unspeakable ShaXXXspeares: Queer Theory and American Kiddie Culture*. New York: St. Martin's Press, 1998.

Cirillo, Albert R. "The Art of Franco Zeffirelli and Shakespeare's *Romeo and Juliet*," in *Film and Literature: Contrasts in Media*. Ed. Fred Marcus. Scranton, Pa.: Chandler, 1971. 205–27.

Collick, John. *Shakespeare, Cinema and Society*. Manchester, England: Manchester University Press, 1989.

Coppedge, Walter R. "Mazursky's *Tempest*: Something Rich, Something Strange." *Literature/Film Quarterly* 21.1 (1993): 18–24.

Coursen, H.R. *Shakespeare in Production. Whose History?* Athens: Ohio University Press, 1996.

———. *Shakespearean Performance as Interpretation*. Newark: University of Delaware Press, 1992.

Crowl, Samuel. *Shakespeare Observed: Studies in Performance on Stage and Screen*. Athens: Ohio University Press, 1992.

Davies, Anthony, and Stanley Wells, eds. *Shakespeare and the Moving Image: The Plays on Film and Television*. Cambridge, England: Cambridge University Press, 1994.

Davies, Anthony. *Filming Shakespeare's Plays: The Adaptations of Laurence Olivier, Orson Welles, Peter Brook and Akira Kurosawa*. Cambridge, England: Cambridge University Press, 1988.

Díaz-Fernández, José Ramon. "Shakespeare on Screen: A Bibliography of Critical Studies." *Post Script: Essays in Film and the Humanities* 17.1 (Fall 1997): 91–146.

Donaldson, Peter S. *Shakespearean Films/Shakespearean Directors*. Boston: Unwin Hyman, 1990.

Drexler, Peter, and Lawrence Guntner, eds. *Negotiations with Hal: Multi-Media Perceptions of [Shakespeare's] Henry the Fifth*. Technische Universität Braunschweig: Braunschweiger Anglistische Arbeiten, 1995.

Eckert, Charles W., ed. *Focus on Shakespearean Films*. Englewood Cliffs, N.J.: Prentice Hall, 1972.

Fox, Levi. *The Shakespeare Handbook*. Boston: G.K. Hall & Co., 1987.

Garrett, George P. et al., eds. *Film Scripts One— [Henry V]*. New York: Appleton Century Crofts, 1971.

Geduld, Harry M. *Filmguide to Henry V*. Bloomington: Indiana University Press, 1973.

Grant, Cathy, ed. *As You Like It: Audio Visual Shakespeare*. London: British Universities Film & Video Council, 1992.

Greenaway, Peter. *Prospero's Books: A Film of Shakespeare's The Tempest*. New York: Four Walls Eight Windows, 1991.

Halio, Jay L. "A Midsummer Night's Dream": *Shakespeare in Performance*. Manchester, England: Manchester University Press, 1989.

Hampton, Benjamin B. *A History of the Movies*, 1931. Reprint, New York: Arno Press and the New York Times, 1970.

Hardison, O.B. "The Shakespeare Hour," *Shakespeare on Film Newsletter* 12.1 (Dec. 1987): 6+.

Hodgdon, Barbara. "Two King Lears: Uncovering the Filmtext." *Literature/Film Quarterly* 11.3 (1983): 143–51.

Holderness, G. *Shakespeare in Performance:* The Taming of the Shrew. Manchester, England: Manchester University Press, 1989.

Hooker, Brian. "Shakspere [sic] and the Movies." *Century* 93 (Nov. 1916): 298–304.

Howlett, Kathy M. *Framing Shakespeare on Film*. Athens: Ohio University Press, 2000.

Jorgens, Jack J. *Shakespeare on Film*. Bloomington: Indiana University Press, 1977.

Kaufman, Lloyd, and James Gunn. *All I Need to Know about Filmmaking I Learned from* The Toxic Avenger: *The True Shocking Story of Troma Studios*. New York: Berkley Boulevard Books, 1998.

Kliman, Bernice W. Hamlet: *Film, Television, and Audio Performance*. London and Toronto: Associated University Presses, 1988.

———. Macbeth: *Shakespeare in Performance*. Manchester, England: Manchester University Press, 1992. 173–78.

Kozintsev, Grigori. King Lear: *The Space of Tragedy: The Diary of a Film Director*. Trans. Mary Mackintosh. Berkeley: University of California Press, 1977.

———. *Shakespeare: Time and Conscience*. Trans. Joyce Vining, New York: Hill & Wang, 1966.

Kurosawa, Akira. *Ran*. Illustrated by Akira Kurosawa, screenplay by Akira Kurosawa, Hideo Oguni, Ide Masato, trans. Tadashi Shishido. Boston and London: Shambhala, 1986.

Levine, Lawrence. *Highbrow/Lowbrow: The Emergence of Cultural Hierarchy in America*. Cambridge: Harvard University Press, 1988.

Lyons, Bridget Gellert, ed. Chimes at Midnight: *Orson Welles, Director*. New Brunswick, N.J.: Rutgers University Press, 1988.

Manvell, Roger. *Shakespeare and the Film*. 2nd printing. Cranbury, N.J.: A.S. Barnes, 1979.

———. *Theater and Film: A Comparative Study of the Two Forms of Dramatic Art, and of the Problems of Adaptation of Stage Plays into Films*. Cranbury, N.J.: Associated University Presses, 1979.

McKellen, Ian. *William Shakespeare's* Richard III: *A Screenplay*. New York: The Overlook Press, 1996.

McKernan, Luke, and Olwen Terris. *Walking Shadows: Shakespeare in the National Film and Television Archive*. London: British Film Institute, 1994.

McLean, Andrew M. *Shakespeare: Annotated Bibliographies and Media Guide for Teachers*. Urbana: National Council of Teachers of English, 1980.

Miller, Anthony. "*Julius Caesar* in the Cold War: The Houseman-Mankiewicz Film." *Literature/Film Quarterly* 28.2 (2000): 95–100.

Morris, Peter, ed. *Shakespeare on Film*. Ottawa, Ontario: Canadian Film Institute, 1972.

Nelson, Ralph, ed. Hamlet. *A Television Script*. New York: CBS, 1976.

Nunn, Trevor, ed. Twelfth Night *by William Shakespeare. A Screenplay*. London: Methuen Drama, 1996.

Parker, Barry M., ed. *The Folger Shakespeare Filmography*. Washington, D.C.: The Folger Library, 1979.

Pearce, Craig, and Baz Luhrmann. William Shakespeare's Romeo + Juliet: *The Contemporary Film, The Classic Play*. New York: Bantam Doubleday Books, 1996.

Pickford, Mary. *Sunshine and Shadow*. New York: Doubleday, 1955.

Pilkington, Ace G. "The BBC's Henriad." *Literature/Film Quarterly* 21.1 (1993): 25-32.

———. Screening Shakespeare from Richard III *to* Henry V. Newark: University of Delaware Press, 1991.

Pursell, Michael. "Art and Artifice in Franco Zeffirelli's *Romeo and Juliet*." *Literature/Film Quarterly* 14.4 (1986): 173–78.

Quinn, Edward, ed. *The Shakespeare Hour: A Companion to the PBS-TV Series*. New York: Signet Classics, 1985.

Rothwell, Kenneth S. *A History of Shakespeare on Screen: A Century of Film and Television*. Cambridge, England: Cambridge University Press, 1999.

Rothwell, Kenneth S., and Annabelle Henkin Melzer. *Shakespeare on Screen: An International Filmography and Videography*. New York and London: Neal-Schuman, 1990.

Sammons, Eddie. *Shakespeare: A Hundred Years on Film*. London: Shepheard-Walwyn Co., 2000.

Shakespeare, William. Romeo and Juliet. *A Motion Picture Edition*. New York: Random House, 1936.

Shaw, William P. "Violence and Vision in the Brook *Lear* and Polanski *Macbeth*." *Literature/Film Quarterly* 14.4 (1986): 211–13.

Skovmand, Michael, ed. *Screen Shakespeare*. Aarhus, Denmark: Aarhus University Press, 1994.

Starks, Lisa, ed. *Post Script: Essays in Film and the Humanities* 17.1 (Fall 1997); 17.2 (Winter/Spring 1998).

Taranow, Gerda. *Sarah Bernhardt: The Art within the Legend*. Princeton, N.J.: Princeton University Press, 1972.

Taylor, Geoffrey, ed. *Paul Mazursky's* Tempest. New York: Zoetrope, 1982.

Uricchio, William. "Film History at the *Fin de Siècle*," *Iichiko: A Journal for Transdisciplinary Studies of Pratiques* 64 (Autumn 1999): 112–23.

Uricchio, William, and Roberta E. Pearson. *Reframing Culture: The Case of the Vitagraph Quality Films*. Princeton, N.J.: Princeton University Press, 1993.

Vardac, A. Nicholas. *Stage to Screen: Theatrical Method from Garrick to Griffith*. 1949. Reprint, New York: Benjamin Blom, 1968.

Walker, Elsie. "Pop Goes the Shakespeare: Baz Luhrmann's *Romeo + Juliet*." *Literature/Film Quarterly* 28.2 (2000): 132–39.

Warde, Frederick B. *Fifty Years of Make-Believe*. New York: International Press Syndicate, 1920.

Wells, Stanley, ed. *Shakespeare Survey 39*. Cambridge, England: Cambridge University Press, 1987.

Welsh, J.M. "Shakespeare, With- and-Without Words," *Literature/Film Quarterly* 1.1 (1973): 84-88.

Welsh, J.M. and J.C. Tibbetts. *His Majesty the American: The Films of Douglas Fairbanks, Sr.* Cranbury, N.J.: A.S. Barnes, 1977.

Wilders, John, et al., eds. *The Shakespeare Plays*. Shakespeare texts by Peto Alexander. New York: Mayflower Books, 1979.

Willis, Susan. *The BBC Shakespeare Plays: Making the Televised Canon*. Chapel Hill: University of North Carolina Press, 1991.

Willson, Robert F., Jr. *Shakespeare in Hollywood 1929–1956*. Madison, N.J.: Fairleigh-Dickinson University Press, 2000.

Wilson, P.W., Rev. *MND*. *New York Times Magazine* (Oct. 13, 1935): 9, 19.

Introduction

Seduced by Shakespeare, Transfixed by Spectacle

Let's begin with some warm, fuzzy assumptions. Shakespeare (1564–1616) was a universal poet and playwright; film is a universal "language." Therefore, had he lived in the 20th century, Shakespeare would surely have written for the cinema, not for the stage. Instead of poetry, he would have written screenplays. He would have won multiple Oscars and basked in the glory of sunny Hollywood, because, after all, Hollywood *loves*, admires, and respects writers. After having written and produced 36 or 37 memorable scripts, he would have retired not to Stratford-upon-Avon but to Palm Springs, where he might have composed sonnets and played golf. Seven years after his death, the First Folio of his screenplays would have been published (in Pasadena, perhaps), and these would be read and studied and analyzed by anxious students for centuries to come. His reputation would eclipse that of Preston Sturges and Mitchell Leisen for comedy and Robert Towne, Herman J. Mankiewicz, and even Ingmar Bergman for melodrama, if not tragedy. And the world, no doubt, would be a far better place because movies would be better than ever.

Now, there is a fantasy beyond belief. It supposes that the semiliterate 20th century is congenial to poetry (as it is not) and exquisitely sensitive to language and wordplay, like, you know, like it most certainly ain't. It supposes that blank verse would easily be adapted to the screen. And the most egregiously wrong assumption of all, it supposes that theater and film are one and the same, whereas in fact they are, at best, distant cousins who do not really speak the same language. The soliloquy is the highest manifestation of Shakespeare's dramatic art and the most challenging of his dramatic devices to capture on screen. No, Shakespeare did not write for the screen. The best a film director can do is to trick the audience into thinking he might have done so.

And yet, Hollywood has been seduced by Shakespeare and has done its damnedest—if not its best—to exploit him. It has used his plays for star vehicles, first casting America's Sweetheart and the original Zorro,

William Shakespeare

Mary Pickford and Douglas Fairbanks, Sr., as Kate and Petruchio in *The Taming of the Shrew*, and much later, Elizabeth Taylor and Richard Burton—the play being a natural vehicle for celebrity couples who are not quite getting along. Hamlet has been played by Sir Laurence Olivier, by Richard Chamberlain, by Nicol Williamson, by Kenneth Branagh, by Mel Gibson, and even by Arnold Schwarzenegger (spoofing Olivier's Hamlet in *Last Action Hero*). Moreover, who better to handle the language of *Romeo and Juliet* than Claire Danes and that splendid, Italianate *Titanic* boy, Leonardo DiCaprio?

Those who suppose Shakespeare would have written for the screen should consider that cinema is not the same as theater, that the shot is the basic unit for constructing a film, whereas the scene is the basic unit for dramatic construction, that on stage the actor is the creator, whereas on film the actor is the created, that theater is an artificial medium but that film is by its very nature a realistic one, that theater audiences are conditioned to accept the theatrical artifice and attend carefully to the language, whereas moviegoers are increasingly rude, vulgar, and inattentive. Film is laconic: The language is minimal and simplistic and merely supports the action. Theater is verbal: The action is fabricated to give the actors opportunities to speak and declaim. There is ample reason for anyone who loves Shakespeare to *hate* movies. In significant ways Shakespeare is simply *too good* for the movies. Why, after all, should the very paradigm of elitist art be forced into a mechanical form of mass entertainment?

Let's consider the plays as performance texts. One could regard a screenplay as a performance text, but no one would consider the experience of reading a screenplay the equivalent of seeing a film. A screenplay is a mere sketch, an incomplete verbal framework that is extremely malleable and likely to be changed while the film is in production. In other words, "the script serves the representation," whereas in theater "the representation serves the play" (Gerdes 14). On stage "the play's the thing," whereas on film the thing's the play, or supposed to be. Because of the poetry and the language, Shakespeare's plays can be read for pleasure. As Peter Gerdes has noted, "The drama text is an independent art work to be read *or* performed" (Gerdes 11). A film script, by contrast, is merely "a preparatory element for a future art work." Notions of Hamlet or Lear or Macbeth or Othello will have been set in the minds of educated readers—ideals hardly to be realized by any given actor or production. For some, Olivier reaches or surpasses the ideal in his film of *Richard III*, stagebound though it may be. For others, Ian McKellen will hit the mark better in his flamboyant cinematic version of 1996, an ahistorical incursion that shoves the play into the Nazi nightmare of the mid-20th century.

In fact, every one of Olivier's "great" movie renderings of Shakespeare had been eclipsed by the end of the century: His loose-lipped, posturing Othello in blackface now seems a mere embarrassment in comparison to Laurence Fishburne's more natural rendering for Oliver Parker. Olivier's wheyfaced, patriotic Henry V reshaped Shakespeare's play into anti-Nazi propaganda and simply excised the antiwar elements in order to do some service to the state, but a disservice to Shakespeare. Nearly 40 years later Kenneth Branagh would show what the play was really about, a calculating and potentially cruel modern ruler rising out of a medieval morass of chivalric pageantry, manipulative and tough when he needed to be, Machiavellian and

Laurence Olivier

cynical, a king with a sense of public relations and something more than a windy rhetorician. Olivier's best innovation in his *Henry V* is the way he begins the film in a model of Shakespeare's Globe Theater, then gradually opens the action out of this stagebound theatrical framework until, by the time the "mirror of all Christian kings" gets to Agincourt, the film has finally moved the action out of the theater and into "the vasty fields of France" (though the battle of Agincourt was actually filmed in Ireland, since France was occupied by the Germans when the film was shot).

Olivier's greatest achievement is the way he mounts the play as a meditation on the differences between theater and film and a demonstration at the climax of how a well-funded cinema spectacle might be used to enhance the play's potential. Shakespeare's history play invites the sort of spectacular treatment Olivier provided, even though it may be framed as a patriotic, medieval fairy tale. Kenneth Branagh offered, by contrast, a far more realistic battle scene and a far more cynical king, who better resembles the sort of modern politician Shakespeare surely had in mind. Branagh's "muse of fire" was able "to write history with lightning" better than Olivier, or D.W. Griffith, for that matter.

Times change, icons fall. Orson Welles's *Macbeth* now seems about as authentic as Jeanette Nolan's zipper (awkwardly in evidence in the film), a mere shadow of the murderous monster so well portrayed by Jon Finch in Roman Polanski's wickedly evil treatment. But Polanski had seen the world differently, growing up in Poland during World War II, and had been touched by Evil personally. The thugs who murder Lady Macduff and her children and servants in his film behaved like Nazi Storm Troopers he had seen in his youth. His Macbeth was shaped by 20th-century notions of Satanic cults, a Charles Manson with a political agenda who gave a high definition to the witches' imperative: "be bloody, bold, and resolute."

Distractions of Spectacle and the Shock of the New

We just suggested that in cinema "the screenplay serves the representation." What this has come to mean in filmed Shakespeare is that the screenplay serves the spectacle—in Polanski's *Macbeth*, for example, in Baz Luhrmann's *Romeo + Juliet*, in Richard Loncairne's *Richard III*, and, egregiously, in Peter Greenaway's *Prospero's Books*, which cannibalizes the words of *The Tempest* without adapting it, exactly. The tendency of cinema is toward the spectacular, and spectacle can strip poetry of its sense. Baz Luhrmann's

Orson Welles

characters in *Romeo + Juliet* speak in anachronisms, conversing in language that is Shakespearean but disjunctive, language that is muted by explosive action and all but erased by the visual spectacle.

Shakespeare's contemporary Ben Jonson, who loved language that was "pure and neat . . . yet plain and customary" understood the proper harmony, balance, and proportion between poetry and spectacle and fought to preserve the integrity of his own poetry in his work with the architect Inigo Jones, as they worked together to design court masques that were intended to be spectacular in their visual display, because he knew the spectacle could quite overwhelm the poetry. This is also the case with the filmed Shakespeare. Viewers can be seduced by the visuals rather than being seduced by the poetry of Shakespeare. Add to this the tendency to reinvent the plays, moving the action out of the Renaissance and out of antiquity and nudging it toward modern times to make it seem "relevant."

As Ben Jonson wrote in his commonplace book *Timber, or Discoveries*, "Expectation of the vulgar is more drawn and held with newness than goodness;... so it be new, though never so naught and depraved, they run to it, and are taken." *Vide* Baz Luhrmann and Peter Greenaway and Julie Taymor—or even Kenneth Branagh, whose "complete" *Hamlet* was wrenched out of time if not teased out of thought. "I look upon a monstrous giant, as Titus," Jonson wrote, "and mine eye sticks upon every part; the whole that consists of those parts will never be taken in at one entire view." Jonson was not writing about *Titus Andronicus*, but he might have been, had he been able to see Julie Taymor's *Titus* (2000).

BIG SCREEN, SMALL SCREEN?

"Too vast oppresseth the eyes and exceeds the memory," Jonson wrote; "too little scarce admits either." We've had Big Hamlets and Little Hamlets, comprehensive Hamlets and incoherent Hamlets (such as Franco Zeffirelli's). Kenneth Branagh's *Hamlet* is coherent—he certainly respects the language—but it is overlong and overwrought. Conflating the Folio and Quarto texts stretches the play to well over three hours (arguably, too much of a good thing); but Branagh also adds at least a half-hour of visuals and special effects, as Rufus Sewell's Fortinbras draws near to Blenheim's Elsinore to build a smashing and even bloodier conclusion than Shakespeare wrote. The language is not lost, in other words, but the text has to compete with the shattering, "too vast" visuals that may "oppresseth the eyes."

Arguably, Tony Richardson took the better approach back in 1969, even though he trimmed the text to half its length and totally ignored young Fortinbras at the end. Richardson's *Hamlet* was not distracted by the visual splendor of Blenheim Palace. His film works within the more limited framework of filmed theater, highlighting the verbal skills of his actors, most notably Anthony Hopkins as Claudius and Nicol Williamson as Hamlet. This "performance text," an actual record of the production mounted at the Round House Theater in London, works perfectly well on the video screen. The actors are framed in medium-shots or close-ups, and the emphasis is placed squarely upon the language, as the spectacle is scaled down. And that, perhaps, is the paradigm of what the filmed Shakespeare should be—barebones cinema, with text and actors front and center.

Of course Richardson's *Hamlet* does not provide absolute textual fidelity, but the text is so cunningly cut that the whole play *seems* to be intact, although it demonstrably is not. Branagh's film is probably closer to what Shakespeare might have intended—lines added or discarded, they're all there in sometimes awkward profusion (the lengthy exposition of Act One, Scene One, for example); the language is for the most part wonderfully conveyed by Branagh's international cast (though one might suppose that Jack Lemmon, an otherwise splendid actor, was not born to play Shakespeare's spear-carrier). No, the problem here is not textual but in the flamboyant nature of the imagined action—the larger-than-life ghost played by Brian Blessed, in particular, and the fantastically staged duel at the end, which recalls the stage spectacle of *The Phantom of the Opera*.

The 1990s experienced a "Bard Boom," as it was called in the popular press, culminating in the tremendous box-office success of no single Shakespeare adaptation (though many were produced, some good, some not) but of a biofantasy fabricated from the imagined early career of *Shakespeare in Love*, patched together by director John Madden and his two scenarists, Marc Norman and Tom Stoppard. They managed to put an appealingly human face on the Droeshout engraving of the balding Bard, indulging in a biographical fantasy that turned Shakespeare into a sexy and energetic young lover who knew how to thrill with his quill. It's an understandable, made-up Shakespeare make-over that presents a young stud (Joseph Fiennes) rather than a balding Bard struck by the blind bow-boy's butt shaft. It's a backstage drama offering the best bits of *Romeo and Juliet* squeezed into a *faux*-biographical framework that turns the boy Bard into slick Willy, a lovesick puppy pining androgynously for blonde bombshell Viola DeLesseps (Gwyneth Paltrow), a poetry groupie who earns her hour on the stage before being sent to Virginia Beach and an arranged marriage in the Brave New World, but only after Queen Elizabeth (Judi Dench) grants her a night of love. The payoff for this slick confection? Thirteen Academy Award nominations and seven Oscars.

Hollywood loved *Shakespeare in Love* because Hollywood loves success. There is no particular respect here for the real Shakespeare and no real interest at all in his early, obscure London years. Just as his plays can be distorted and bent out of shape in the interest of making money, so can his life be falsified. It's Shakespeare made cute and commodified. No doubt the film is entertaining, even though it is biographically challenged, but it is not really very instructive. This is spectacular exploitation. "Though a man be hungry," Ben

INTRODUCTION

Jonson wrote, "he should not play the parasite. That hour wherein I would repent me to be honest," Jonson continued, "there were ways enow open for me to be rich." Screenwriters and directors should take note.

FROM ACTUALITY TO ADVERTISEMENT: REDUCED SHAKESPEARE WITHOUT WORDS

The first Shakespeare film ever made was not much to look at and involved only a scrap of one of Shakespeare's lesser known plays, *King John*, about three minutes of British actor Sir Herbert Beerbohm Tree as the king, poisoned and squirming on his throne in the play's death scene. W.K.L. Dickson filmed this scene from *King John* on September 20, 1899, on the same day that Tree's stage production of the play opened at Her Majesty's Theater in London. Intended to promote the stage production, the film was shown in variety theaters and also released as a Mutoscope "peepshow."

This and five other early Shakespeare films can be seen on the British Film Institute compilation video *Silent Shakespeare*, digitally mastered from original 35 mm nitrate materials made between 1899 and 1911, but none of these are true adaptations. The Percy Stow *Tempest* (1908), for example, offers vignettes showing Prospero's arrival at the island where he will be exiled, Miranda in arms and books in hand, his release of the spirit Ariel from a tree (not exactly a "cloven pine," as in the play), the discovery of Caliban, and other benchmark moments from the play. J. Stuart Blackton and Charles Kent's *Midsummer Night's Dream* (1909) reduces that comedy to a series of skits. The Italian Gerolamo Lo Savio production of *King Lear* (1910) also reproduces and dramatizes some of the play's big moments, but the play is simplified and compressed. The Edgar/Edmund subplot is not included, for example, nor is the storm scene where Lear goes mad.

In 1996, in Oregon, a nitrate print of a "lost" 1912 film was discovered; it is, historically important because it is the first extant "feature" film of the American cinema. Significantly, it is a Shakespeare film, *Richard III*, a silent five-reeler directed by James Keane and starring the British actor Frederick B. Warde (1851–1935) as Shakespeare's villainous Richard, the Duke of Gloucester, who would be king regardless of the odds against his succession. Warde discovered that he could profitably tour America with the film, interpreting the lines and providing commentary during the reel changes, as Kenneth S. Rothwell notes in his *History of Shakespeare on Screen*. Seen under these circumstances, this film was not exactly an example of Shakespeare without words, but Shakespeare without dialogue—not exactly a substitute for a dramatic production of the play, but a means of showing and telling what the play was about. The film ran to 55 minutes.

Such films are of obvious historical importance, but they cannot qualify as true adaptations. The best research on this arcane period of Shakespeare films was done by Robert Hamilton Ball's groundbreaking book *Shakespeare on Silent Film* (1968), which was the definitive work for over 30 years. Ball's work was later updated by Kenneth Rothwell's *History of Shakespeare on Screen* (1999). Anyone interested in such primitive novelties will find them listed and discussed in these two books. But the point is clear that almost from the beginning, from the turn of the cinema century, filmmakers saw the plays of Shakespeare as marketable and exploitable commodities, although such early attempts could do little more than illustrate and mime the texts of the plays. The language and poetry of Shakespeare could not be approached until after the coming of sound in 1929.

SHAKESPEARE SPEAKS! DIALOGUE TRADITIONS IN HOLLYWOOD

After talking pictures had arrived, theater people themselves wondered about the impact these films would have on real theater. In 1929 playwright Luigi Pirandello responded in the following way to the question "Will Talkies Abolish the Theater?" Pirandello claimed that both the classical theater and the music hall could "rest easy in the certainty that they will not be abolished for one reason: Theater is not trying to become cinema; cinema is trying to become theater. The greatest success to which film can aspire, one moving it even farther along the road toward theater, will be to become theater's photographic and mechanical copy, and a bad one at that. Like all copies, it must arouse a desire for the original."

With the coming of sound, Hollywood was deluged with an influx of theatrical talent and voice coaches to help the silent stars make the transition to sound. To make Garbo speak would be a triumph for MGM; to make John Gilbert speak in a manner befitting his image was more of a challenge. Early dialogue conventions make speech patterns in early talking pictures extremely awkward. When Fairbanks and Pickford entered the talking arena with *The Taming of the Shrew* in 1929, the text was cut back as much as possible to make way for knockabout farce. In 1936 Elisabeth Bergner's German accent in Paul Czinner's *As You Like*

It gave the character of Rosalind a certain charm but was decidedly odd and awkward.

In *Hamlet* the Prince informs the court "we'll *hear* a play." Four hundred years later people think in terms of *seeing* a play, either on stage or at the movies. If a movie presumes to adapt Shakespeare, however, his lines deserve to he *heard* as well as "seen." In Shakespeare's time educated people were more enamored of language than they are today. Shakespeare's plays are verbally intensive, and even if Shakespeare spoke of "the two-hours traffic of our stage," full dramatic productions today would run to three or four hours. That's rather more talk than a movie can bear, even if the language is expertly handled by an authority as gifted as Kenneth Branagh, whose extended *Hamlet* fully seems as long as it is—four hours, plus an intermission.

Linguists have speculated that, because the Renaissance was so language sensitive, English was spoken much more rapidly in Shakespeare's time than it is today, and that audiences were better conditioned to listen closely in order to follow the dialogue. The coming of sound in Hollywood coincided with the burgeoning popularity of radio in America, which surely had a conditioning listening effect. After the movies learned to talk in the 1930s, the dialogue expectations and the tolerance for dialogue of the 1940s differed from what was to follow during the age of television. Consider, for example, Clarence Day's *Life with Father* (1947), first converted to a play and then adapted to a film by Michael Curtiz, very popular in its day, but now hopelessly dated in terms of gender sensitivity and political correctness. The film seems much longer than it is (117 minutes) because it is all talk and little action. That might not have been a problem when the film was originally released, to be seen *and heard* by a radio-conditioned, radio-intensive audience. Viewers conditioned by radio drama would have listening skills far superior to audiences later in the century.

By the end of the century, moreover, stage dialogue had become simpler—brief, snappy, and profane—so that it might register more effectively for audiences unaccustomed to listening carefully. Movie dialogue now works to echo contemporary speech, to be conversational and "natural." In their everyday affairs, people do not speak in complete, fully-formed sentences, as playwright Harold Pinter realized early in his career. Pinter people express themselves in uneven, fragmented cadences, as if they are thinking while they are speaking and have to pause in order to collect their thoughts and complete their utterances. In America David Mamet would later imitate Pinter, translating Pinter patterns into a distinctively profane American idiom. People in general are not "poetic." They tend to resort to clichés as a means of short-circuiting the thinking process. Increasingly such clichés have involved a great deal of profanity in American films, on television (as in *The Sopranos*, where cursing and clichéd swearing are the building blocks of dialogue) and on stage, especially in the drama of David Mamet—a profane, American Pinter. Such realistic conventions of language and dialogue are far removed from the poetry of Shakespeare, whose language may seem more dated and complex than ever.

"Something Rotten": Postmodern Approaches to the Plays of Shakespeare

"Suit the action to the word, the word to the action," Hamlet advises the players in Act Three, Scene Two. Michael Almereyda, director of the Ethan Hawke *Hamlet*, took this advice as his mantra, "so smart and simple it's almost stupefying," he told the *New York Times*. But Hamlet also cautions his players not to "O'erstep . . . the modesty of nature," lest it be "overdone," distorting the mirror held up to nature. Defining and visualizing the action is another challenge, however, and the problem with the postmodern spectacle is that it can distort the action. The language of Shakespeare is preserved in the Baz Luhrmann *Romeo + Juliet*, for example, but the late-20th-century urban setting refigures and recontextualizes the action, twisting and teasing it out of thought. The anachronistic language of Shakespeare floats above the rubble of a contemporary urban setting and the vulgar Capulet mansion with its fishtanks and swimming pool, even above the helicopters that pursue desperate young Romeo into the candlelit cathedral where Juliet lies in state.

When Michael Almereyda described his own contemporary *Hamlet*, he could also have been describing the Luhrmann *Romeo + Juliet:* "Entire scenes were dropped, Shakespeare's text was further trimmed and torn, and the result is, inevitably, an *attempt* at *Hamlet*—not so much a sketch, but a collage, a patchwork of intuitions, images, and ideas." Almereyda claims that *Hamlet* has been filmed at least 43 times, so what can he presume to offer that is new, besides shifting the action to a contemporary urban setting? Despite evidence in the play to the contrary, he opts for a younger prince in his 20s, even though Kenneth Branagh at 35 was just about the right age for the role, on the evidence of what the Gravedigger says about how long poor Yorick has been interred. The mantra in *Entertainment Weekly* is

"Shakespeare *has* to be about what we want now," so forget art: The goal is to serve the imagined wishes of consumers. And following the advice from Jan Kott's *Shakespeare Our Contemporary*, Almereyda believed an "ideal *Hamlet* would be one most true to Shakespeare and most modern at the same time," as if Branagh's *Hamlet*, set sometime before the turn of the 20th century, was not "modern" enough.

Almereyda sets the action of his modern-dress *Hamlet* in Times Square, where a power struggle is going on at the "Denmark Corporation." Elsinore is transformed into a luxury hotel. A skeptical David Denby noted that by abbreviating the text, Almereyda "has lost the players, a great deal of wit, and some extraordinary metaphysical speculation," but these losses are compensated by some fresh dimensions. The film, in his opinion, is "not a travesty," but "a ripely melancholy version of the play," and a "gripping" postmodern translation. Almereyda wanted viewers of his *Hamlet* "to recognize the frailty of spiritual values in a material world, and to get a whiff of something rotten in Denmark on the threshold of our self-congratulatory new century." Such an approach deserves to be taken seriously.

No doubt the contemporary setting of the postmodern approaches can be distracting, as is the case in *Romeo + Juliet*, further hyped by its spectacular excesses. The same could be said of the Richard Loncraine *Richard III* (1995), which refigures Shakespeare's history play as a neo-Nazi nightmare that shows Jan Kott's "Grand Mechanism" of history in all its frightening and wicked manifestations; but that postmodern production is sustained through its wartorn wasteland spectacle by its bravura performances, which make the World War II setting seem almost secondary. Similar claims could be made for the Branagh *Hamlet* and possibly for the Julie Taymor *Titus* (1999), though her disgusting and flamboyant spectacle is distracting, as are the shifts in chronology, when the performance is wrenched into the modern-day Roman Coliseum at the end. Taymor effectively makes a point about primitive violence in the modern world, however, and the film is ultimately coherent, though at times it threatens to be otherwise. The plays of Shakespeare are constantly being reimagined and reinvented, as they should be, to demonstrate the universal implications of dramas that have not become dated over the past 400 years.

Derivative Approaches and "Shakespeare-Influenced" Films

The approach of this book is intended to be "encyclopedic," but it cannot be utterly comprehensive. If 43

Akira Kurosawa

versions of *Hamlet* have been filmed, we simply lack the space and resources to cover *all* of them, though we will attempt to round up the usual suspects. Out of obligation we should include the films of Akira Kurosawa "inspired" by Shakespeare, such as *Throne of Blood* (1957), an international classic that some have considered the best adaptation of *Macbeth* ever filmed, even though the action is set in medieval Japan, the characters reconfigured (one spooky witch instead of three), the message and ending changed, and the original poetry lost. Kurosawa's later film *Ran* (1985) is even looser in its transformation of *King Lear*.

Therefore, a major problem is posed by what Robert F. Willson, Jr., has called "Shakespeare-influenced" movies, some of which are treated in Chapter 4 of his book *Shakespeare in Hollywood, 1929–1956*. Other authorities have long since recognized *Forbidden Planet* (1956) as an "off-shoot" of *The Tempest*, with Walter Pidgeon playing Dr. Morbius, the Prospero figure, who is lost in space. A better candidate might be Paul Mazursky's *Tempest* (1982), which is a less radical transformation and follows the structure if not the dialogue of Shakespeare's play. But if these "derivatives" dispense with Shakespeare's poetry, should they be treated seriously as adaptations? Even more problematic is Peter Greenaway's postmodern transformation entitled *Prospero's Books* (1991), which shows Prospero (John Gielgud) in the process of writing *The Tempest* as the action unfolds around him. The film begins as he scratches out the opening words of the play, and Greenaway reconfigures much of the action, but the film is more a product of Greenaway's imagination than Shakespeare's.

Willson pays particular attention to *Joe MacBeth* (1955), an updated gangster version of the Scottish play directed by Ken Hughes and set in Chicago, where no one speaks in the cadences of Shakespeare. He also discusses Delmer Daves; *Jubal* (1956) as a "Western *Othello*" and Edward Dmytryk's *Broken Lance* (1954) as a "*King Lear* on Horseback." Another shoot-'em-up "off-shoot" is John Ford's classic *My Darling Clementine* (1946). Well, Victor Mature's Doc Holliday may recite the "to be or not to be" soliloquy with some feeling, but Jack Benny does it better in *To Be or Not to Be* (1942), Shakespeare "touched" by Lubitsch, who uses tragedy for comic purposes in his film and then comedy for tragic purposes, when he has a Jewish actor in Nazi-occupied Poland recite Shylock's "Hath not a Jew eyes?" defense.

Just as *Hamlet* is embedded (so to speak) in the Ernst Lubitsch film, so *Othello* is embedded in George Cukor's *A Double Life* (1947), another "Shakespeare-influenced" film. Of course, "influence" is not adaptation per se, but Willson's chapter indirectly poses a larger question: What exactly constitutes an adaptation? Is *Last Action Hero* (1993) "Shakespeare-influenced" because of its three-minute spoof of the Olivier *Hamlet*? ("So, you killed my fodder," Arnold Schwarzenegger says as he turns Hamlet into an action hero ready to "take out the trash.") Should *A Thousand Acres* (1997) be considered an "adaptation" of *King Lear* because Jane Smiley used *Lear* as a model for the Iowa farmer who goes round the bend in her novel? Smiley exploits *King Lear*, taking Shakespeare's concept for high drama and reducing it to a cornfed soap opera about a drunken and abusive, cantankerous father who turns two of his daughters against him. The film has some emotive power, but the language belongs to Iowa, not Shakespeare.

In his *History of Shakespeare on Screen*, Kenneth Rothwell offers a taxonomy for seven kinds of Shakespeare derivatives: "Those of the first kind (recontextualizations) will keep the plot but move Shakespeare's play into a wholly new era and jettison the Elizabethan language (*Joe MacBeth*); the second kind (mirror movies) will meta-cinematically make the movie's backstage plot about the troubled lives of actors run parallel to the plot of the Shakespearean play that the actors are appearing in (*A Double Life*); the third kind (music/dance) will turn the plays into musicals (*West Side Story*) or ballets and operas such as Zeffirelli's *Otello* (1986) . . . the fourth kind (revues) will use the excuse of a biography (*Prince of Players*), or of a documentary (*Looking for Richard*), or even a horror show (*Theater of Blood*) to showcase Shakespeare for embellishment, and/or graft brief visual or verbal quotations onto an otherwise unrelated scenario . . . the sixth kind (animations) . . . will put Shakespeare into cartoon images (*The Lion King*); and finally the seventh kind (documentaries and educational films) will make a variety of pedagogical films that in turn may overlap with any of the permutations and combinations in the previous categories."

Rothwell therefore defines a wide variety of the so-called Shakespeare derivatives. To find many such films discussed in detail, the reader will have to look elsewhere. Some of the "derivatives"—Pacino's *Looking for Richard*, Merchant-Ivory's *Shakespeare Wallah!* Cukor's *A Double Life*, Madden's *Shakespeare in Love*, for example—are examined in our Appendix. We have attempted to include most of the titles that readers and playgoers are likely to think of. That was also our guiding principle in selecting the major Shakespeare films covered here. For a more comprehensive listing, readers will want to consult *Shakespeare on Screen: An International Filmography and Videography*, compiled by Kenneth S. Rothwell and Annabelle Henkin Melzer in 1990.

—James M. Welsh

Postscript: On a personal note, the present book fulfills a lifetime ambition, since I first undertook the study of Shakespeare as a research assistant in analytical bibliography and textual criticism at the University of Kansas, working as research assistant for Charlton Hinman and Paul Murray Kendall as they were editing a student edition of Shakespeare's plays and as Hinman was working on *The Norton Facsimile of the First Folio of Shakespeare* (1968). But life and career demands brought about a change of course, and I eventually found myself teaching film (and Shakespeare) while editing the academic journal *Literature/Film Quarterly* for more than 30 years. I collaborated with Heyward Brock on *Ben Jonson: A Quadricentennial Bibliography* (1974), but that was the nearest I came to Renaissance drama, aside from the "Shakespeare on Film" special issues of *LFQ*. For many years I had hoped to anthologize some of the better essays published in *LFQ*, but keeping an academic journal on track while also teaching was more than a full-time commitment. After the publication of *The Encyclopedia of Stage Plays into Film* in 2001, however, the opportunity arose when Facts On File commissioned me to edit this book, *Shakespeare into Film*. Part One expands the A-to-Z entries from the earlier encyclopedia; Part Two is a "reader," offering an interview with Mel Gibson and his *Hamlet* director, Franco Zeffirelli, as well as a dozen essays written by a global assortment of Shakespeareans, originally published in *Literature/Film Quarterly* between 1973 (volume 1) to 2002 (volume 30), some of them long out of print. All of these essays are published here with the permission of the copyright holder, *Literature/Film Quarterly*, since they deserve, I believe, a wider audience than was heretofore possible.

—J.M.W.

WORKS CONSULTED

Almereyda, Michael, "A Live Wire to the Brain: Hooking Up 'Hamlet,'" *New York Times* (May 7, 2000), sec. 2, 19–22.

Ball, Robert Hamilton. *Shakespeare on Silent Film: A Strange, Eventful History*. London: George Allen and Unwin, 1968.

Denby, David, "Flesh and Blood," *The New Yorker* (May 15, 2000): 105–107.

Fierman, Daniel, "The Dane Event," *Entertainment Weekly*, 543 (June 2, 2000): 40–42.

Gerdes, Peter R, "Film and/or Theater: Some Introductory Comments," *The Australian Journal of Screen Theory*, 7 (1980): 1–17.

Jonson, Ben. *Timber, or Discoveries, Being Observations on Men and Manners*. London: J.M. Dent, 1951.

Kott, Jan. *Shakespeare Our Contemporary*, tr. Boleslaw Taborski. Garden City, N.Y.: Doubleday Anchor Books, 1966.

Norman, Marc, and Tom Stoppard. *Shakespeare in Love: A Screenplay*. New York: Hyperion/Miramax, 1998.

Pirandello, Luigi, "Will Talkies Abolish the Theater?" in *Pirandello & Film*, ed. Nina DaVinci Nichols and Jana O'Keefe Bazzoni. Lincoln: University of Nebraska Press, 1995.

Rothwell, Kenneth S. *A History of Shakespeare on Screen: A Century of Film and Television*. Cambridge, U.K.: Cambridge University Press, 1999.

Rothwell, Kenneth S., and Annabelle Henkin Melzer. *Shakespeare on Screen: An International Filmography and Videography*. New York: Neal-Schuman, 1990.

Silent Shakespeare: Such Stuff As Dreams Are Made on . . ., 1899–1911. British Film Institute National Film and Television Archive, 1999. 88 minutes.

Willson, Robert F., Jr. *Shakespeare in Hollywood, 1929–1956*. Madison, N.J.: Fairleigh Dickinson University Press, 2000.

Entries
A to Z

A DOUBLE LIFE

See OTHELLO

ANTONY AND CLEOPATRA (1606–07)

Antony and Cleopatra (1972), U.K./Spain, directed by Charlton Heston, adapted by Pamela Davis; Folio Films.
Antony and Cleopatra (1974), U.K., directed by Jon Scoffield and Trevor Nunn, ATV Network.

The Play

Antony and Cleopatra is regarded by many critics as Shakespeare's most romantic tragedy, even more moving than *Romeo and Juliet*. Its mature hero and heroine qualify as fascinating figures, marked by many contradictions. In addition, they express their mutual passion in compelling and highly erotic poetry. Shakespeare locates their complex affair on a historical stage that features a struggle between Roman destiny and Egyptian luxury and decadence. This drama of a monumental love brought down by lovers blind to their self-destructive natures has fascinated audiences for centuries.

As the play opens, Antony has spent long days and nights in the arms of the Egyptian queen Cleopatra. Yet with news of his wife Fulvia's death, he suddenly feels the urge to return to Rome; that urge is intensified by reports from Octavius Caesar and Lepidus, who with Antony form the ruling triumvirate, that their power has been challenged by young Pompey. (A peace settlement is reached with Pompey aboard his yacht, but during the celebration it becomes clear that Octavius plans to destroy the upstart.) Upon his departure from Egypt, Antony confronts an angry, frightened Cleopatra, who worries that Rome and Octavius will keep her lover from returning. While in Rome, Antony agrees to an arranged marriage to Octavia, Caesar's sister, but his longing for Cleopatra prompts him to leave his new bride behind and return to Egypt. Before he arrives, however, Cleopatra learns of the marriage from a messenger whom she soundly whips in her rage. This behavior reveals the queen's petulance and lack of reason, prompting this wise remark from the messenger: "Gracious madam, I that do bring the news made not the match."

Antony's desertion of his new wife outrages Octavius, who now plans to move against Egypt and Antony without delay. But an aroused Antony, reunited with Cleopatra and relying on her navy, vows to fight with the fury that marked his earlier career. However, his greatness was achieved in land battles and not at sea; Antony's blindness to this and other military realities prompts scornful criticism from his chorus-like follower Enobarbus. When, after the first encounter with Caesar's forces, Cleopatra and her sailors desert the battle, Antony rebukes his mistress and harshly attacks himself for falling prey to her wiles. Desperate and stung by guilt, Cleopatra apologizes and wins back an uxorious Antony's love. But when Antony later sees her showing favor to one of Caesar's ambassadors, Antony loses control, orders the beating of the messenger, and accuses Cleopatra of being a whore. Again, the two are somehow reconciled; in that day's battle, Antony manages to drive back Caesar's land forces. Despite the victory, his loyal follower Enobarbus decides to leave him, convinced that a weakened Antony has lost his ability to lead. When Antony sends his belongings after him, displaying not anger but love, Enobarbus is so moved by this magnanimous act that he dies of a broken heart.

In the final battle, Cleopatra's navy again flees the scene, leaving a shamed, defeated Antony in a suicidal mood. He turns once more on Cleopatra and tells her to rush to the "boy" Caesar, believing that she has betrayed him to save herself. Now despondent and frantic, Cleopatra sends word to Antony that she has killed herself. When Antony receives the dreadful news, he begs his fittingly named servant Eros to dispatch him; after Eros refuses and kills himself instead, Antony falls on his own sword. With Caesar closing in on them, the two lovers find refuge in Cleopatra's monument. Here the wounded Antony expires, describing himself ironically as "a Roman by a Roman/Valiantly vanquished." Left alone, Cleopatra devises a plan to avoid falling into Caesar's hands, to be paraded through the streets of Rome and scorned by gleeful citizens. When a clown brings her a basket of poisonous asps, she takes one and presses it to her breast, dying after her servants have dressed her in royal robes. Caesar enters too late to win his Egyptian prize but seizes the moment to praise Antony and comment on the great "solemnity" of these tragic events.

The Films

Charlton Heston's version of *Antony and Cleopatra* was rehearsed for weeks in London before being shot in Spain; Heston was following the advice of his mentors, Olivier and Welles, in his approach. When it was finished, the film was not widely distributed, perhaps because the actor-director did not feel his product met the demanding standards of his predecessors. One of the reasons for regarding it as a disappointment is the production's derivative quality. It looks much like earlier Hollywood attempts at Roman epics, films like *Quo Vadis?* (1951) and *Ben-Hur* (1959). Indeed, sea-battle scenes from *Ben-Hur* were intercut to represent the Actium encounter—and to save money. Action scenes involving ships ramming other ships and Roman cavalry charging Antony's foot troops likewise dominate the screen. When Antony negotiates his marriage to Octavius's sister, the scene occurs against the backdrop of gladiators struggling on the Colosseum floor below. As one combatant throws down the other, Antony and Octavius conclude their compact, and the crowd heralds Caesar's power with a thumbs-up gesture. The musical score by John Scott and Augusto Algero relies heavily on strings to create a Hollywood-style romanticism and to accentuate the film and Cleopatra's many mood changes. The sybaritic atmosphere in Cleopatra's Court, with billowing curtains, seductive servants, and reclining bodies recalls the settings from biblical epics like *David and Bathsheba* (1951) and *The Robe* (1953).

Heston's Antony and Hildegard Neil's Cleopatra lack the fire that we might expect from such passionate characters. Neil in particular fails to achieve the stature of a queen; she seems more the spoiled bad girl striving to seduce the handsome quarterback. Shots of her speaking while being made up or massaged dominate the Egyptian court sequences. Perhaps Heston couldn't escape the god-like identity he had established as Moses in *The Ten Commandments*. Both appear to be acting on a stage, rather than in the naturalistic context of film. Their relationship relies heavily on props as well: To keep her Antony from leaving, Cleopatra loops a long string of pearls over his neck, pulling him slowly toward her. The death scenes likewise appear wooden and staged, with neither actor achieving the mix of pathos and sensuality that Shakespeare's lines call for.

Some notable performances are delivered by John Castle as Octavius and Eric Porter as Enobarbus. Castle manages to catch the equivocal nature of Octavius, a man destined for imperial rule who can also be petty and vengeful. Porter's Enobarbus is forced to deliver his description of Cleopatra's barge to an Athenian servant and to speak the lines of deleted characters, but he looks and sounds like Antony's only true admirer. Jane Lapotaire, who would play Cleopatra in the 1981 BBC-TV production, performs convincingly as Charmian and Roger Delgado enacts his roles as soothsayer and clown with considerable skill. On the whole, however,

Heston's attempt at epic Shakespeare in the manner of Olivier and Welles leaves much in the way of verbal and visual power to be desired.

Trevor Nunn's 1972 Royal Shakespeare Company production of *Antony and Cleopatra* was the basis for the version directed for television by Jon Scoffield and broadcast in 1974. Widely acclaimed at the time as "a standard for what televised Shakespeare should be" and "a model for all that followed," it nonetheless "hit an all-time prime-time low rating," and many who did watch it complained of the commercial interruptions. Among its virtues is the thoughtful use of the medium of television. Nunn and Scoffield made no attempt to reproduce battle scenes and other physical details of the Roman and Egyptian worlds, choosing instead to contrast the hazy-edged and indistinct Egypt of Antony (Richard Johnson) and Cleopatra (Janet Suzman), suffused with a golden glow, with the antiseptically white world of Rome, where clusters of senators and soldiers orbit around Octavius (Corin Redgrave). Interiors are suggested with curtains, pillows, and, for the last third of the play, from the monument scene to the ending, Egyptian scenes are shot against a black background. The film's opening montage dramatizes Philo's description of Antony by contrasting black-and-white shots of disapproving Romans with color shots of Antony luxuriating in the decadent pleasures of Cleopatra's company. Throughout the film, close-ups turn the attention from the absence of spectacle to the images of the actors wrestling with the more interior conflicts of the divided world of the play. A rich use of sound—armies, winds and waves, gulls, barking dogs and buzzing flies—effectively supplements the impressionistic visual imagery of this production and establishes an unseen dimension that helps to suggest the wide world reflected in this play. Even at almost three hours, this version moves rapidly.

Janet Suzman has received ample praise for her ability to convey the range of the dark-complected Cleopatra as a queen of contradictions; she is both temptress and shrew, and both faithless lover and dying bride to Antony's noble wreck. Though Cleopatra says she is "with Phoebus's amorous pinches black / And wrinkled deep in time," she is also playful, taunting, and entrancing, pausing only briefly to stare into a mirror of polished metal in a moment of doubt, rising to a royal fury but then giving way to generosity as she interrogates the messenger who tells her of Antony's marriage to Octavia. Suzman skillfully shows how Cleopatra grows from the opening image of her wearing Antony's helmet and brandishing her sword as she rides on his back to the final image of her rigid in a bejeweled dress, wearing a golden wig, a figure of Isis, shot in profile as though she had herself become a monument. Richard Johnson, as Antony, seems alternately more earnest and puzzled than actually divided between his Roman obligations and his Egyptian temptations, but he is also a weathered soldier and, at the core, a mature man trying to make the best of newly stirred emotions that soften and confuse him.

Many other roles are ably played. Corin Redgrave's Octavius is a cool politician who projects a discipline and sense of purpose that will doom Antony. Taller than those around him, he appears in several close-ups that allow him to convey his contempt of those around him through narrowing eyes. Patrick Stewart makes a noteworthy Enobarbus, an adaptable and experienced soldier who laughs at Antony's concern over Fulvia's death but delivers his description of the first meeting of Antony and Cleopatra with a genuine sense of awe. A very young Ben Kingsley is excellent in the role of Thidias, the man whom Octavius sends to negotiate a surrender with Cleopatra and whom Antony has beaten and sent home. Finally, Mary Rutherford gives a touching performance as Octavia, who appears here as a victim of Antony's indifference and Octavius's rage.

REFERENCES

Bulman, J. C., and H. R. Courson, *Shakespeare on Television*; (Hanover and London: University Press of New England, 1988); Crowl, Samuel, "A World Elsewhere: The Roman Plays on Film and Television," in *Shakespeare and the Moving Image: The Plays on Film and Television*, ed. Anthony Davies and Stanley Welles (Cambridge: Cambridge University Press, 1994), 146-162; McKernan, Luke, and Olwen Terris, *Walking Shadows* (London: British Film Institute, 1994); Rothwell, *A Brief History of Shakespeare on Screen* (Cambridge: Cambridge University Press, 1999), 110; Rothwell, Kenneth S., and Annabelle Henkin Melzer, *Shakespeare on Screen: An International Filmography and Videography* (New York; Neal-Schuman, 1990); Rosenthal, Daniel, *Shakespeare on Screen* (London: Hamlyn, 2000): 191.

—*R.F.W. AND R.V.*

AS YOU LIKE IT (1599)

As You Like It (1912), U.S.A., directed by Charles Kent, adapted by Margaret Birch; Vitagraph.

As You Like It (1936), U.K., directed by Paul Czinner, adapted by R.J. Culen and J.M. Barrie; Twentieth Century British Fox.

As You Like It (1978), U.K., directed by Basil Coleman, adapted by Alan Shallcross; British Broadcasting Company/Time-Life Television.

As You Like It (1985), Canada, directed by Herb Roland, adapted by John Hirsch; Canadian Broadcasting Corporation.

As You Like It (1992), U.K., directed and adapted by Christine Edzard; Sands Films.

The Play

When Orlando, youngest son of Sir Rowland de Boys, complains to his brother, Oliver, that he is tired of being confined to menial farm work rather than receiving the training appropriate to a gentleman, he is told by Oliver to leave and take with him Oliver's servant, old Adam. Oliver then tries to get the wrestler Charles to injure Orlando in the next day's competition. Best friends Celia, daughter to Duke Frederick, who rules the court, and Rosalind, daughter of the banished duke Senior, who lives in the forest of Arden, "like the old Robin Hood of England," go to the match. Rosalind falls in love with Orlando and tries to persuade him not to fight. When he wins, she gives him a necklace, leaving him tongue-tied but equally smitten. Duke Frederick congratulates Orlando on the victory, but becomes angry when he learns Orlando is the son of Sir Rowland, so angry that he shortly tells Rosalind, whose banished father was a friend of Sir Rowland, that she must leave his court. Not wanting to be separated, the two women decide to disguise themselves and go into the woods. Rosalind will become the young man, Ganymede, and Celia will be Ganymede's sister, Aliena, a name that reflects her state in life. When Duke Frederick finds out that Rosalind, Celia, and Orlando have all left at the same time, he speculates they went together and tells Oliver to bring Orlando back or forfeit his lands.

Meanwhile, the woods are a paradise to Duke Senior and his followers, except for Jaques, a melancholic who moralizes that the duke's men are all "usurpers" and "tyrants" for hunting. Orlando, having arrived in the forest with old Adam, who is exhausted and unable to go on, breaks into the duke's camp, sword drawn and expecting the men to be "savage," and demands food. While Orlando goes to bring Adam, Jaques delivers his "seven ages of man" speech, concluding, ironically, with the image of dismal old age just as Orlando returns carrying Adam into the camp where they are welcomed and fed. At the same time and elsewhere, Rosalind, Celia, and their fool, Touchstone, appear, buy a cottage, and meet Silvius, a shepherd hopelessly in love with Phebe, who barely tolerates him. Rosalind, Celia, and Touchstone all find poems nailed to the trees, poems praising Rosalind. While Touchstone parodies them, Celia realizes that Orlando must be their author, and shortly they encounter him in the forest. Rosalind complains that someone, clearly sick from love, is defacing the trees. When Orlando confesses he is the one, she offers to cure him by taking Rosalind's part and being fickle and demanding. Rosalind also tries to tell the shepherdess, Phebe, to be kinder to poor Silvius, but her scolding only makes Phebe fall in love with the person she knows as Ganymede. When Orlando shows up an hour late, Rosalind scolds him and then has Celia act as priest for a mock wedding. Later, when he is again late, not Orlando but his brother Oliver arrives, saying he has a message from Orlando, who has been injured saving Oliver's life from a lion. Seeing a handkerchief with Orlando's blood, Rosalind faints. Oliver and Celia fall instantly in love.

Reunited with Orlando, Rosalind says she has magical powers and will solve the various love problems. She will satisfy Orlando, Silvius, and Phebe in their separate desires. Meanwhile Touchstone has met, won, and wedded a simple country-woman named Audrey. Rosalind enters dressed now as a woman. Unable to pursue Ganymede, Phebe agrees to marry Silvius; Oliver will marry Celia, and Rosalind will marry Orlando. Duke Senior recognizes Rosalind as his daughter. The group receives word that Duke Frederick, on his way to find and kill Duke Senior, has met a holy man, converted, and renounced the world. Duke Senior is the new ruler. The melancholy Jaques says he will go to find Duke Frederick. The rest of the company dance, and then Rosalind steps forward and delivers an epilogue.

The Films

One of America's first film companies, the Vitagraph Company of America, located in the Flatbush section of Brooklyn, New York, devoted only a small portion of its filmmaking to Shakespeare, but the effort was significant in developing the tradition of filmed Shakespeare. The director of the Vitagraph *As You Like It*, Charles Kent, had earlier filmed outdoor Shakespeare in *A Midsummer Night's Dream* (1909) and *Twelfth Night* (1910), and he made good use of locations for the pastoral elements of this play. *As You Like It* was somewhat longer than earlier Vitagraph Shakespeare films, three reels rather than two, and it was unusual in relying on the celebrity appeal of stage actress Rose Coghlan, who had played the role of Rosalind in the 1880s. Robert Hamilton Ball quotes from a contemporary review that calls her "one of America's most celebrated actresses," but in spite of her energetic performance it is impossible to overlook the fact that she was 60. The Robin Hood motif is apparent in all the woods scenes, and, unlike some versions of the play, this one shows Rosalind making a serious effort at creating a woodsmanly appearance. Coghlan clearly indicates in broad gestures when her actions are intended to show how Orlando's beloved might act. She is playing at being a man imitating a woman rather than being a woman trying to act like a man. At one point, when Rosalind accidentally leans against Orlando's chest, Oliver and Celia laugh at the accidental contact, and Rosalind quickly straightens up.

The film creates an odd tension between its written and visual elements. Ball makes the point that the film uses extensive titles, "472 feet, a total of almost half a reel." The complications of the play, of course, need a certain amount of explaining, but scenarist Margaret Birch's script sometimes invents scenes that Shakespeare only implies through dialogue. For example, the opening of the film shows Duke Frederick banishing Duke Senior but making his daughter, Rosalind, stay in court as companion to Celia. The following scene shows Sir Rowland De Boys, on his death bed, asking his oldest son, Oliver, to take care of the two younger brothers. Only after these scenes does the film reach the point at which Shakespeare opened the play—with Orlando's complaint about his forced rusticity. Another example occurs when the film illustrates Jaques's "seven ages of man" speech by cutting away to shots of characters in each of the seven stages. Rothwell and Melzer say that "The cinematic peak occurs with the use of cross-cutting to illustrate Jaques' Seven Ages speech," and they may be right, but the device seems confusing at first partly because it is not immediately apparent that these shots are intended to illustrate the speech. Finally, it seems as though the sequence could easily stand separate from the rest of the film. A similarly awkward moment occurs when Orlando must rescue the sleeping Oliver from the lion. Shakespeare has Oliver tell the story briefly in about 20 lines to Celia and Rosalind. The film dramatizes the situation. Orlando first sees Oliver sleeping, then sees a truly ridiculous lion's head sticking out of the bushes, then starts to walk away, realizes he cannot, takes off his jacket, pulls out his sword, and goes into the bushes, presumably to fight the lion. Oliver is apparently awakened by the movement in the bushes, which are shaking violently, and then Orlando comes out injured and bleeding. Ball points out that Vitagraph did not own a lion and did what it could with what it had, but the real problem again seems to be adding scenes that distract from the narrative flow and slow it down.

In discussing Paul Czinner's 1936 *As You Like It*, probably the first thing to get out of the way is the issue of Elisabeth Bergner's Rosalind. Bergner, the wife of director Czinner, had some reputation on the German stage, and it was Bergner who suggested getting Laurence Olivier to play the part of Orlando after she saw him in *Romeo and Juliet*. Olivier himself in an interview before he made the film said "No one can play with Bergner without learning something from her." Some years later, however, in his book, *On Acting*, Olivier said she "crucified the verse with her German accent." Critics who like Bergner's Rosalind find her charming, sprightly, and kittenish, but those who do not like her find her performance irritating, "disastrous," and "anxiously inappropriate." Her accent certainly does affect her reading of the lines. When she gets excited, for example, when she tries to find out who has been nailing poems about Rosalind on the trees in Arden forest, she is extremely difficult to understand.

The core problem with her performance, however, has to do with an issue that would probably not have occurred on Shakespeare's stage. Bergner seems to make absolutely no attempt to develop a pattern of action that could be taken as masculine behavior. Instead she is feminine in a coy, mincing, and effervescent manner. At the end of the mock marriage ceremony, for example, she calls after Orlando, hangs on the long vowel sounds in "Adieu" and "two," as in "two o'clock," hugs and kisses a tree, and then does a somersault to demonstrate her enthusiasm. Not a few critics have complained specifically about the somersault. On the Elizabethan stage, Rosalind would, of course, have been played by a man who was playing a woman playing a man. Perhaps that particular arrangement of societal construction versus stage construction would solve the problem, but Anthony Holden, in his biography of Olivier, says that when Olivier saw that no audience could possibly imagine that this Orlando could mistake this Rosalind for a man, he "tried to make up for it by adding an edge of madness to Orlando's high spirits."

As this dilemma might suggest, in some respects the film often seems unsure of its direction and fluctuates between the real and the artificial. Quite a few of the ribald or more cynical lines have been cut, and the intent seems to have been to make this a pretty play, with real clouds floating in the sky, and real sheep wandering through a somewhat stylized forest—itself a combination of actual and painted elements. The interiors of Duke Frederick's castle have an ornate but very physical quality to them. Celia's room, in particular, is in a very large, late-medieval castle, but it is a mixture of elaborate, almost confectionery effects and solid stone. Likewise, the opening scenes of Olivier in the peasant environment seem to be modeled on earthy characters and compositions from Bruegel, but the first view of Rosalind and Celia, in their pointed hats and wimples, seems to come from French illuminated manuscripts. Rothwell points out that designer Lazare Meerson's "sudden release of genuine sheep, rabbits, and squirrels into the mise-en-scène shattered the fragile world of his imaginary barnyards and woods." These ambiguities of style, along with the gender ambiguity, perhaps explain the ending of the film. Bergner steps outside the gates, which have enclosed the other members of the wedding party, and, in some of the most heavily accented and unintelligible delivery in the film, speaks the epilogue to the play. When she speaks to the women, she appears in men's clothing and waves a stick that she has carried for the last several scenes of the film, but when she speaks to the men, she reappears in her wedding dress and curtsies, as the line requires, when she finishes the speech. Rather than pursue Shakespeare's original emphasis on the ambiguity of roles, the film instead tries to have it both ways, and both images, male and female, appear in a somewhat stylized pair of characterizations.

Christine Edzard's 1992 modern-dress version of *As You Like It* is interesting, at least in part because of its particular emphasis on contrasting the opposing situations and attitudes in the play and underscoring them by clearly paralleling some of its characters. The major difference between Edzard's version and Shakespeare's play, the issue at any rate that most critics seemed to react to, was that while Shakespeare emphasizes the difference between court and country by drawing on the conventions of the romance, and especially on the idealized conventions of the pastoral world, Edzard draws on a very different set of conventions. In her production the opposition seems to be between bankers and homeless people, the haves and the have nots, or, as Kenneth S. Rothwell puts it, "the wretched of the earth . . . implicitly condemn the callous Thatcherites."

When this film's scruffy-looking Orlando is cast out by his pinstriped and overcoated banker brother (both parts played by Andrew Tiernan), he ends up not in Arden forest but in an urban wasteland where a man stands warming his hands over something that is burning in a 50-gallon metal drum. The economic context gives a new shade of meaning to, for example, wrestler Charles' lines when he tells Oliver "I wrestle for my credit," or when he boasts of how he will defeat Orlando and "give him his payment." Adhering effectively to the logic of the economic context Edzard imposes on the play, this Orlando articulates his love for Rosalind by spray-painting graffiti on walls and fences rather than by hanging poems on trees. Another benefit from this approach may be that the contemporary ambiguity in dress and gender roles makes this Rosalind more easily able to function as a young man. In jeans, pea jacket, and watch cap, she is certainly more believable, if that is a valid criterion, than many of the Robin Hood-attired actresses who usually try this role. In addition, Emma Croft emphasizes physical activity in a way that other Rosalinds do not, or, recalling Elizabeth Bergner's somersaulting performance, certainly Croft is more effectively physical than any other Rosalind. She very simply works at being a tomboy. She tends toward under-expressing emotion rather than being coy. In the mock wedding scene, she seizes Tiernan's hand as though she were about to arm wrestle. When he has to leave, she runs after him and they shout their lines as they run together.

Several writers have objected to Edzard's modernization, but while it is true that much of the film simply does not succeed, the concept behind the Rosalind-Orlando characterization seems promising even if it does not quite achieve that promise. An odd logic sometimes seems to control the handling of other parts of the play. The two incidents that might be dangerous to Orlando, for example, are inexplicably muted. The wrestling match at the beginning of the play seems well enough prepared for, but when the time arrives for the bout, the crowd that gathers completely blocks out any view of even the slightest action. This evading of one of the set-pieces of the play mostly calls attention to the scene's absence. Later, when Oliver tells Celia and Rosalind that Orlando was injured while rescuing him, the film cuts to a very dark flashback scene in which Orlando apparently stops a tramp from robbing the sleeping Oliver and is injured in the process. A similar muting seems to occur in some of the other characterizations. The vaguely pained expression on James Fox's face throughout the film suggests, for example, that his Jaques may be more dyspeptic than melancholic, a characterization that is probably not intended as an allusion to the Jaques/jakes pun embedded in the implied pronunciation of this character's name. Finally the visual pairing of characters at the end seems a little forced, so Oliver and Orlando, Duke Frederick and Duke Senior, Corin and LeBeau, among others, all seem to gaze oddly at each other, as though they had just now understood Edzard's true intentions.

The two made-for-television productions of *As You Like It* are in many ways better than most television versions tend to be. Helen Mirren as Rosalind and Richard Pasco as Jaques bring an exceptionally high level of acting to the BBC production, although both tend to play their roles more seriously than one might expect in this play, which is one of Shakespeare's greenest pastorals. The BBC version perhaps should not really be called a taped stage production since it was all shot at Glamis Castle and in the Scottish countryside. In fact, critics who were used to stage presentations and more stylized versions of the play seemed to be struck by the sheer leafiness of the BBC production of the play—real trees in a real forest. Maurice Charney, for example, says this version "evoked all the wish-fulfillment images of pastoral," while Jack Jorgens says "seldom have natural settings been used to less effect." J.C. Bulman probably frames the issue best when he says that "The more realistic the setting, the more we are inclined to apply the criteria of naturalistic drama to the action. Thus, inevitably, we begin to question the logic of the play." The visual impact of the forest is impressive, but there is no question that it sometimes overwhelms the actors by pointing up somehow the artificiality of the entire enterprise. Hence, for example, when Celia (Angharad Rees) comes on carrying one of Orlando's poems, it is apparent that the parchment, which might have worked well on a stage, in this setting looks as though Orlando (Brian Stirner) has been writing his poems on a giant corn chip. An artificial stage setting would have allowed everything to be taken as convention, but the sheer reality of vibrantly green trees blowing against a very blue sky accentuates the contrast. Jorgens says that there is "warfare" between the realistic setting and "a play which is essentially a fairy tale in verse," but Bulman finds several examples where director Basil Coleman manages to use the real setting as a way to "put quotation marks around the pastoral artifice."

The question of how reality intrudes on the artifice of the play perhaps extends to the characterizations as well. Helen Mirren is an exceptionally attractive and buxom Rosalind in this play and could not easily be taken for a young man. The film's Orlando, on the other hand, is slender, seems somewhat younger, and is not, according to most reviewers, someone who might inspire Rosalind's interest. How then is an audience to believe that Orlando does not notice that the character before him is clearly not a young man? Approaching the issue from another way, Bulman says that the actors must play their love scenes as "a game that neither mistakes for reality," but the fact is that the very reality of the setting diminishes the ability to suspend as many levels of disbelief as one must to enjoy all the things that this play tries to do.

Like other films from the Stratford (Ontario) Shakespeare Festival, Herb Roland's film of the John Hirsh production of *As You Like It* records an excellent performance of the play, apparently before a live audience. The staging is imaginative, the characterization very well thought out, and the several levels of comedy operating in this play all seem to work unusually well. Jaques (Nicholas Pennell) is here perhaps more thoughtful than he is sometimes presented. He is certainly not just vituperative, not just a scold who is occasionally funny. Instead he is presented as a clever man whose humor digs at both the pastoral and romantic conventions of the play. Touchstone (Lewis Gordon) is vigorous, with plenty of stage business to flesh out his long speeches. His bantering about the philosophies of court and country, for example, include magic tricks with an egg and some miming of a golf swing and lining up a pool shot. Silvius and Phebe (Mary Haney and John Jarvis) are appropriately daffy in their respective bouts of love sickness. More than these, Rosalind (Roberta Maxwell) and Celia (Rosemary Dunsmore) manage to fill their roles with humor; both seem to operate from a basic sense of decorum that immediately seizes on the peculiarity of many of the situations in the play. Rosalind is especially good at suddenly adopting a hale-and-hearty masculine manner as soon as she realizes that her bubbling affections threaten to create an embarrassing situation with her buddy (and secret love) Orlando. For his part, Orlando (Andrew Gillies) does a good job of demonstrating the silly side of sincerity, a quality that the literary criticism of his sonnets clearly implies, but a quality that is not often explored by actors who take this role.

Visually this production is most striking in its opening scenes where the icy world of the cruel duke Frederick is presented as a real winter, with heavily dressed characters going back and forth in a very palpable representation of cold weather. More metaphorically, Duke Frederick's entourage consists of men and women dressed entirely in black and silver, with some of the men even wearing dark glasses. They are, of course, additions to the play, but they add considerably to the characterization of this world to which the pastoral world of Duke Senior stands in clear contrast. Contrary to some productions, the handling of the scenes in the woods tends here to be somewhat restrained, and, indeed, the effect seems to accumulate. When Orlando first goes into the woods, his poems are stuck on what seem to be branches stuck in stumps. By the end of the play, at the wedding scene, the pillars supporting the upper playing area are trees green with leaves, and the "country copulatives" gather at both levels as a half-dozen women in white dresses dance in a circle holding lighted candelabras. The effect of the green and white and the glowing candles is the visual counter to the darkness of the opening scenes. Rosalind's delivery of the closing lines is, like the production itself, clear, simple, and straightforward.

REFERENCES

Ball, Robert Hamilton, *Shakespeare on Silent Film* (London: George Allen and Unwin, 1968); Bulman, J.C., "'As You Like It' and the Perils of Pastoral," *Shakespeare on Television*, eds. J.C. Bulman and H.R. Coursen (Hanover, N.H.: University Press of New England, 1988), 174–179; Holden, Anthony, *Laurence Olivier* (New York: Atheneum, 1998); Jackson, Russell, "Shakespeare's Comedies on Film," *Shakespeare and the Moving Image*, eds. Anthony Davies and Stanley Wells (Cambridge: Cambridge University Press, 1994), 99–120; Manville, Roger, *Shakespeare and the Film* (New York: Praeger, 1971); Olivier, Laurence, *On Acting* (New York: Simon and Schuster, 1986); Rothwell, Kenneth S., *A History of Shakespeare on Screen* (Cambridge: Cambridge University Press, 1999); Rothwell, Kenneth S., and Annabelle Melzer, *Shakespeare on Screen* (New York: Neal Schuman, 1900); Willis, Susan, *The BBC Shakespeare Plays: Making the Televised Canon* (Chapel Hill: University of North Carolina Press, 1991).

—*R.V.*

CHIMES AT MIDNIGHT/CAPANADAS A MEDIANOCHE/FALSTAFF

See HENRY IV, PART I (1596–97); HENRY IV, PART II (1598)

CHINA GIRL

See ROMEO AND JULIET

CYMBELINE (1609–10)

Cymbeline (1913), U.S.A., directed by Frederick Sullivan; Edwin Thanhouser Films.
Cymbeline (1982), U.K., directed by Elijah Moshinsky, adapted by David Snodin; British Broadcasting Company/Time-Life Films.

The Play

Cymbeline, king of Britain, beguiled by his duplicitous new queen's beauty and angered by his daughter Imogen's refusal to marry the queen's foolish son, Cloten, banishes Posthumus, the "poor but worthy" man Imogen has married. In Rome, Posthumus almost immediately falls into a wager with the crafty Iachimo, who bets that he can easily seduce Imogen, in spite of Posthumus's description of her goodness. In Britain, Iachimo tells Imogen that Posthumus has been untrue and she should sleep with Iachimo to revenge herself. Rebuffed by the virtuous Imogen, Iachimo says it was only a test of her honor and asks to store a treasure for the emperor in her bedroom. Later that night, Iachimo himself leaps out of the trunk, takes note of the room and of Imogen's marks, steals the bracelet Posthumus gave her, and hides back in the trunk. That morning, when Cloten again attempts to convince her to love him, Imogen tells him she loves Posthumus's "meanest garment" more than she could ever love Cloten. Back in Rome, Iachimo describes the room, shows the bracelet, and, when Posthumus concedes that his wife is unfaithful, Iachimo goes on to describe the mole on Imogen's breast. Having won the bet, Iachimo leaves a disillusioned Posthumus ranting against all women.

When King Cymbeline, urged by the queen and Cloten, rejects Rome's request for tribute, General Caius Lucius threatens war. Meanwhile, Posthumus's servant, Pisanio, has received one letter from Posthumus telling him to kill Imogen and another asking Imogen to meet him at Milford-Haven. Excited by the letter Pisanio shows her, Imogen makes plans to leave disguised. When they reach their destination, Pisanio tells her Posthumus's real plan, promises to lie to Posthumus, and urges her to disguise herself as a boy and serve "the noble" Caius Lucius, who will keep her safe. In Wales, Belarius, the old courtier exiled 20 years before by Cymbeline, has raised the king's sons, Guiderius and Arviragus, as his own and taught them to recognize simple virtue and disdain the devious courtly life. Cloten, in the meantime, has found out about Imogen's flight to Milford-Haven and gets Pisanio to take him there, secretly planning to be dressed in Posthumus's clothing and rape Imogen when he finds her. But Imogen has been found by Belarius and the princes, her brothers, who feel an instant attraction to Fidele, as Imogen is calling herself. Cloten encounters Guiderius, who kills and beheads Cloten. Belarius recognizes Cloten and realizes they now are in danger of discovery. Just then, Arviragus discovers the body of the apparently dead Fidele. Imogen, exhausted and feeling ill, had taken the restorative potion that Pisanio got from the queen. Luckily, rather than the poison the queen thought she had given him, the medicine is only a drug substituted by Cornelius, the court physician, who suspected the queen's intentions. Nonetheless, Fidele seems dead, so the boys sing over the dead bodies of Fidele and Cloten. When she later awakes, Fidele sees the headless body, dressed in her husband's clothing, and believes it is Posthumus. Caius Lucius arrives and takes the mourning Fidele into his service.

While Cymbeline prepares to battle the Romans, a repentant Posthumus, dressed as a Roman, vows to take off "these Italian weeds" and fight dressed as "a Briton peasant," thinking to expiate his crime through battle. So dressed, Posthumus defeats Iachimo, who does not recognize him but takes his defeat as a sign of his own crimes. Belarius, Guiderius, and Arviragus rescue Cymbeline from the Romans, and the ragged Posthumus helps them defend their position. After the battle, Posthumus changes back into Roman clothing and allows himself to be taken by the victorious British. The jailed Posthumus has a dream in which his dead parents and brothers pray for Jupiter to help him, and Jupiter, descending on an eagle and casting lightning bolts, leaves a prophecy to be interpreted later. Posthumus awakens and is brought before Cymbeline.

Gathered before King Cymbeline, the various characters now sort out their stories. Cornelius, the physician, says the queen has died and confessed to her treachery. Lucius asks for mercy for his servant Fidele, and while Fidele and Cymbeline talk, Belarius and the king's sons recognize the visitor they thought dead. Imogen, as Fidele, asks Iachimo where he got the ring he wears. Iachimo confesses his deception and his offense against the king's daughter. Posthumus steps forward, identifies himself, and threatens Iachimo. When Imogen tries to calm him, Posthumus knocks her down. Pisanio then recognizes Imogen and tells Posthumus that he has just struck his wife, who is still alive. Cornelius adds the information about the drug, which explains how Imogen apparently died, and Pisanio tells how he took Cloten to Milford-Haven. At this point, Guiderius confesses to killing Cloten, and is ready to be punished, but Belarius says Guiderius killed someone who was of lesser rank, since he and Aviragus are the king's lost sons, which he proves by showing their birthmarks. King Cymbeline pardons everyone. The Roman soothsayer explicates Jupiter's message to mean that the king's sons are restored and Rome and Britain can live in peace. Cymbeline agrees to pay a tribute and declares peace.

The Films

Although this play has its enthusiasts and has been produced more often in the last decade than in most of the rest of the century, many people have agreed with Samuel Johnson on "the folly of the fiction, the absurdity of the conduct, the confusion of the names and manners of different times and the impossibility of the events in any system of life." Perhaps not surprisingly then, no modern commercial film of *Cymbeline* has been attempted. Edwin Thanhouser made a silent version in 1913, and the BBC filmed the play in 1982, as part of its series.

Edwin Thanhouser and his wife, Gertrude, brought the benefits of an extensive theatrical background to their filmmaking. Establishing his Thanhouser Film Corporation in New Rochelle, New York, in 1909, Thanhouser used literary sources for several films that he made between 1909 and 1912, when he sold the company. Kenneth S. Rothwell and Annabelle Melzer call him "the supreme *auteur* of the silent Shakespeare film in America" and note particularly his "effective *mise en scène*," "cinematically based exterior action shots," and "sharp even lighting." Recently arrived from England, Frank Sullivan, who directed *Cymbeline*, directed more than a dozen films and toward the end of his career had several uncredited acting parts in Marx Brothers films. James Cruze, later to become famous for directing *The Covered Wagon* (1923), played Posthumus, and Florence LaBadie, the best-known and most popular actress of Thanhouser's group, played Imogen.

They had acted together in other Thanhouser films, such as the previous year's *Dr. Jekyll and Mr. Hyde*.

This silent *Cymbeline* has several qualities to recommend it. Among these is the clear emphasis on Imogen as the virtuous heroine who undergoes a series of catastrophic events. This theme of the virtuous heroine beset by multiple misfortunes was a popular melodramatic device of the time, and the Thanhouser script casts the play in that mold. Shakespeare's play is not at all as straightforward in its emphasis, but, although the silent film loses some in accuracy, it gains from the focusing and cutting that was necessary to get it down to about 40 minutes. This film also does a good job of keeping the various groups in the film clearly separated by easily identifiable means. The members of the British Court wear Germanic-looking costumes, with horned helmets and metal breastplates, while Belarius, Guiderius, and Arviragus wear furs and have a more rustic appearance. The Romans wear the traditional togas, but the soldiers invading Britain wear the short tunic under a breastplate. British men have long hair, while the Romans all have short hair.

The film frames the action somewhat differently from Shakespeare's method and opens with a forest scene of Belarius and the king's sons, so the emphasis immediately is on a divided family. The titles indicate that the king's sons are being raised by a courtier who stole them. From here, the scene shifts back to King Cymbeline's Court and follows the sequence of the play with several omissions. In a series of brief scenes, alternating between the Court and a garden area, the film makes clear that Imogen is being coerced to marry Cloten, but loves Posthumus, whom King Cymbeline then exiles. The queen's role as evil stepmother seems perfectly clear, although details of her story, such as her attempt to poison Imogen, are left out of the film. Cloten is introduced as a suitor of Imogen, but the script does not make clear that he is the queen's son, and, later, his pursuit of Imogen, his death in the fight with Guiderius, and the discovery of his body by Imogen are all left out. With the connecting device of the funeral services missing, Imogen is here instead simply captured by Caius's troops. The elaborate dream scene, the prophecy, and the whole connection of Posthumus with his ancestry and with the future of Britain is omitted. Instead the ending of the film consists of a series of confessions and forgivings. Belarius immediately confesses his guilt in having taken the boys, and Cymbeline immediately forgives him. Next Iachimo confesses his crime and gives the ring back to Posthumus. Imogen embraces him, and the brothers embrace their father, King Cymbeline. In this film, the family is reunited, even if all the cosmic and historical forces Shakespeare outlined are largely subordinated or ignored.

The BBC, in its dedication to mount relatively uncut television productions of all the plays, forces its *Cymbeline* into another set of problems and solutions. The changes are less in the lines of the play than in its visual impact. For example, the lines spoken by one of the Gentlemen, a minor character Shakespeare uses to develop background information in the opening and to comment on Cloten's (Paul Jesson) cloddishness later in the play, in this production are given to the physician, Cornelius (Hugh Thomas), another character with, in his case, an important few lines. The effect is to make Cornelius a recognizable character who seems to be commentator and mover behind the scenes throughout the entire play. In Shakespeare's play, he substitutes a nonlethal drug for the poison the queen (Claire Bloom) requests, apparently giving her something like the drug Juliet must have taken in *Romeo and Juliet*. He appears again at the end to tell Cymbeline (Richard Johnson) that the queen died confessing her crimes. In the BBC production he appears in the opening scene and then intermittently to comment and reflect or simply to stand in the background. By the end of the play, when he appears with the news about the queen, the impression is that he is probably the only person in the play who had a clear idea of what was happening underneath all the appearances.

Another visual simplification occurs with the handling of Shakespeare's four separate loci in this play, places that represent values as much or more than actual physical location. Shakespeare was, of course, working on a bare stage, but clearly the world of Cymbeline's Court is contrasted with the woodland world of Belarius and the princes who have retreated to a place where they can find simpler values that have been lost in the more sophisticated but corrupt Court. Rome is also two places; it is both the world of ancient Rome, inhabited by the noble Caius Lucius, and the corrupt world of Renaissance Rome, represented by the treacherous Iachimo. The BBC *Cymbeline* tends to simplify these distinctions into a case of Rome versus Britain. Caius Lucius (Graham Crowden) is dressed in the general soldier costume worn by other Romans. The anachronistic costuming of Thanhouser's silent version is lost. Instead the BBC *Cymbeline* tries to present Renaissance Rome as the evil city that Imogen imagines will ruin Posthumus. In this Rome, for example, the chess players are being served by bare-chested waiters and a dwarf, left over from *A Midsummer Night's Dream*. The impression is meant to convey a dangerous sensuality, and Iachimo's scenes with Imogen (Helen Mirren) carry out the suggestion. In this production, she seems genuinely tempted by Iachimo's offer to betray her husband. Later, in the bedroom scene, Iachimo is, for some unknown reason, bare-chested, and the camera visually links him with the sleeping Imogen, resulting in a scene that Susan Willis calls "lurid."

The suppression of certain physical effects may be part of this same effort at unity. For example, Shakespeare's final act in this play contains some spectacular scenes as well as actions that strain both credulity and convention. J.M. Nosworthy, in the Arden Edition, calls *Cymbeline* "transitional and experimental in style, as in other matters." One of the riskiest of these efforts perhaps is the event the stage directions describe this way: "Jupiter descends in thunder and lightning, sitting upon an eagle: he throws a thunderbolt. The Ghosts fall on their knees." In the BBC version, Jupiter (Michael Hordern) appears, does his business, and disappears. Roger Warren calls the scene "oddly unspectacular," and it may be that Shakespeare's scene would seem silly presented through the more realistic medium of television, but the shift seems to be part of the way the play is being read for this production. Again, Shakespeare merely uses stage directions to describe the fights, but these battles are significant, almost symbolic, shifts of power. First Posthumus (Michael Pennington), disguised as a "poor soldier," defeats Iachimo (Robert Lindsay), who, as a result, reflects that he "belied a lady,/The princess of this country" and thinks this defeat is a judgment on him and a sign of what is to come. Immediately after this, Cymbeline is captured by the Romans and then rescued by Belarius (Michael Gough) and the two princes, with Posthumus joining them to fight off the Roman army. Several characters later comment on the importance of the fight. In the BBC version, Posthumus stands in the foreground with the fires of battle behind him and simply describes what happened. The action is here discussed rather than presented.

When Katherine Duncan-Jones, reviewing the production, notes that the characters often sit, she may be commenting on this approach that makes the play seem more unified but also talkier than the play seems to be when read. Characters in this production sit when they might easily be doing something. Cymbeline sits at the beginning of the play, as though overhearing what the Gentlemen are saying about the condition of the kingdom. When Posthumus visits Rome, the Romans sit and play chess. When Pisanio introduces Iachimo to the British court, Imogen is sitting and then sits while Iachimo sits next to her. Pisanio is sitting when he reads Posthumus's letter asking him to kill Imogen. At the end of the play, the Soothsayer sits to decipher the message from Jupiter. In addition, lines that Shakespeare has characters speak, here are sometimes delivered as voice-overs, with the camera moving in as if to enter the mind of the speaker, but also filling the screen with a static image of a face that is saying nothing. As a result, the play, in spite of excellent performances from an unusually fine cast, seems more meditative, and, without its battles and its descending Jupiter, somewhat less dynamic than it might have been.

REFERENCES

Ball, Robert Hamilton, *Shakespeare on Silent Film* (London: George Allen and Unwin, 1968); Bowers, Q. David, *Thanhouser Films: An Encyclopedia and History*, Thanhouser Company Film Preservation, Inc., CD-ROM (Lanham, Md.: Scarecrow Press, 1998); Duncan-Jones, Katherine, "Sitting Pretty," *Times Literary Supplement* (July 22, 1983), 773; Nosworthy, J.M., ed. *Cymbeline* (London: Methuen, 1969); Rothwell, Kenneth S., and Annabelle Henkin Melzer, *Shakespeare on Screen: An International Filmography and Videography* (New York: Neal Schuman, 1990); Willis, Susan, *The BBC Shakespeare Plays* (Chapel Hill: University of North Carolina Press, 1991).

—*R.V.*

FIRE WITH FIRE

See ROMEO AND JULIET

FORBIDDEN PLANET

See THE TEMPEST

GIULIETTE E ROMEO/ROMEO AND JULIET

See ROMEO AND JULIET

HAMLET (1602)

Hamlet (1948), U.K., directed by Laurence Olivier, adapted by Laurence Olivier and Alan Dent; J. Arthur Rank/Two Cities.

Hamlet (1953), U.S.A., directed by George Schaefer and Albert McCleery, adapted by Mildred Freed Alberg and Tom Sand; NBC Hallmark Hall of Fame.

Hamlet (1960), Germany, directed and adapted by Franz Peter Wirth; Bavaria Atelier.

Hamlet (1964), USSR, directed and adapted by Grigori Kozintsev from Boris Pasternak's Russian translation of the play; Lenfilm/Sovexport.

Hamlet (1964), U.S.A., directed by John Gielgud (originally for the stage) and Bill Colleran, adapted by John Gielgud; Electronovision.

Hamlet (1969), U.K., directed and adapted by Tony Richardson; Woodfall.

Hamlet (1970), U.K./U.S.A., directed by Peter Wood and adapted for television by John Barton; NBC Hallmark Hall of Fame.

Hamlet (1980), U.K., directed by Rodney Bennett, adapted by Alan Shallcross, British Broadcasting Company/Time-Life Television: The Shakespeare Plays.

Hamlet (1990), U.S.A., directed by Franco Zeffirelli, adapted by Franco Zeffirelli and Christopher DeVore; Warner Bros.

Hamlet (1990), U.S.A., directed and adapted by Kevin Kline and Kirk Browning; WNET "Great Performances"/Corporation for Public Broadcasting.

Hamlet (1996), U.K., directed and adapted by Kenneth Branagh; Castle Rock Entertainment/Columbia Pictures.

Hamlet (2000), U.S.A., directed and adapted by Michael Almereyda; Miramax Films.

The Play

Arguably Shakespeare's most famous play, *Hamlet* first appeared in a corrupt, pirated edition, the so-called Bad Quarto of 1603, published by Nicholas Ling and John Trundell, which was later augmented by the corrected Second Quarto of 1604, "Newly imprinted and enlarged to almost as much again as it was, according to the true and perfect copy," as described on the title page. The First Folio edition of the play in 1623, published after Shakespeare's death by John Heminges and Henry Condell, contains approximately 90 lines not published in the Second Quarto, even though the Second Quarto is otherwise the most complete and substantive text. It is a very long play as a consequence.

The action begins with sentries on the castle walls at Elsinore, discussing with Horatio, the friend of Prince Hamlet, visitations by a mute ghost who seems to resemble the dead king. They decide to tell the prince what they have witnessed. In the next scene, set at court, the new king, Claudius, who has married Gertrude, his sister-in-law and Hamlet's mother, seems regal in his rhetoric and attentive to matters of state, particularly the potential foreign policy threat posed to Denmark by young Fortinbras, prince of Norway, who has raised an army and apparently intends to invade Denmark. After sending ambassadors to old Fortinbras, king of Norway, with instructions to keep the young prince in check, Claudius turns to domestic affairs and grants permission to Laertes, son of his councillor, Polonius, to travel to France. Finally, Claudius turns to domestic affairs and addresses Hamlet, who is still dressed in mourning clothes, grieving the death of his father. Claudius seems especially interested in establishing that Hamlet will stay in Denmark and not return to his studies in Wittenberg, presumably because this was an elected monarchy and Hamlet also had a valid claim to the throne. Hamlet's answer is laced with insolence, but, in deference to his mother, he promises to stay.

In the first soliloquy that follows ("O that this too too sullied flesh would melt,/Thaw, and resolve itself into a dew," I.ii.129–159), Hamlet is defined by his melancholy attitude and is extremely resentful of his mother's decision to marry Claudius, especially so soon after his father's death. Horatio and the guards visit him in this melancholy and suicidal state and tell him about the ghost that Hamlet will soon seek out. The ghost tells Hamlet of foul play, claiming that he was murdered while sleeping in his orchard by Claudius, who poured poison into his ear. Hamlet wants to believe what the ghost has told him but questions whether this "disturbed spirit" is truly the ghost of his dead father or a spirit sent from hell to tempt him into murdering his uncle. Hamlet makes Horatio and the guards swear not to divulge what they have seen and tells them of his plans to "put an antic disposition on" in order to give him license to make inappropriate comments under the guise of craziness.

Later, when a troupe of itinerant players arrives at Elsinore, Hamlet devises a way to test the veracity of what the ghost has told him, requesting that they perform a play called "The Murder of Gonzago," the plot of which resembles the scenario of his father's murder. Hamlet inserts a dozen additional lines to make this play more closely resemble what the ghost had told him. Hamlet and Horatio watch Claudius closely to see if he will register guilt when he sees the play. Claudius takes the bait in what Hamlet calls the "mousetrap," and Hamlet then knows that he must kill Claudius to avenge his father's murder.

Meanwhile, Claudius is spying on Hamlet, whom he rightly considers a threat to his Crown. His adviser Polonius offers to "loose his daughter," Ophelia, on Hamlet and to eavesdrop so as to learn more about Hamlet's intentions. By following her father's wishes, Ophelia must betray Hamlet, whom she loves, and Hamlet soon becomes aware of her intentions. Feeling betrayed by her, he turns on her and treats her roughly and indecently. Later still, Polonius hides behind an arras (a tapestry) while Hamlet meets privately with his mother in her bedchamber. Hamlet is so abusive of Gertrude that she calls out, evoking a response from hidden Polonius, whom Hamlet runs through with his sword, thinking it may be Claudius. Outraged by Hamlet's rash action, Claudius sends him to England with Hamlet's false friends, Rosencrantz and Guildenstern, who carry instructions to the English king to have Hamlet put to death upon his arrival there. Hamlet anticipates this villainy, however, and arranges to be rescued at sea by pirates, who will return him to Denmark.

In Hamlet's absence, Ophelia, emotionally disturbed by Hamlet's rejection of her and by the fact that the man she loves has murdered her father, goes quite mad and eventually drowns herself. Her enraged brother Laertes then returns from France, having heard about the death of his father, and finds his sister pathetically insane. Laertes holds Hamlet responsible for the death of his father and his sister. Hamlet arrives back in Denmark and is confronted by Laertes at her gravesite burial. Claudius plots the death of Hamlet with Laertes, arranging a duel between them. Laertes conspires to anoint the tip of his sword with poison so that Hamlet will be killed if scratched by his opponent's sword. Claudius arranges a drugged and poisoned cup of wine for Hamlet at the duel, but his plot backfires when Gertrude drinks the wine intended for Hamlet and dies. Hamlet is a better swordsman than Claudius imagined him to be, however, and after he is scratched by Laertes's sword, he manages to exchange weapons and wound Laertes, whose dying words alert Hamlet to Claudius's villainy. Hamlet kills Claudius, then dies, just before the arrival of the English ambassador and Fortinbras, who has crossed Denmark with his army and who claims the throne.

The Films

Since *Hamlet* has been filmed something like 43 times, this essay cannot be comprehensive and will cover only the best-known adaptations. Oddly enough, two of the earliest silent film treatments presented Hamlet as a cross-gendered Dane. The first film, released in France in 1900, featured Sarah Bernhardt as Hamlet, but only in the duel scene, lasting a mere five minutes. In a 78-minute film released in Germany in 1920, shaped by Edward P. Vining's book *The Mystery of Hamlet* (1881), the prince (Asta Nielsen) is actually a princess, whom Gertrude had raised in disguise as a man. In 1913 Cecil Hepworth produced a 22-minute version of the play, especially notable because it featured the celebrated Victorian Shakespearean actor Sir Johnston Forbes-Robertson, who was, of course, far too old for the role. We shall pass over such oddities and move on to the sound features.

Laurence Olivier's *Hamlet* (1948) set the standard at mid-century because it was Olivier's interpretation, following upon the critical success of *Henry V*, which established the actor-director as the leading interpreter of the filmed Shakespeare. Olivier's *Hamlet* was honored by two Academy Awards, for Best Actor and for Best Picture. In approaching *Hamlet*, Olivier followed the Freudian interpretation of the play popular among critics in the late 1940s. Hamlet kisses his mother full on the mouth several times, for example, and the Freudian link is also emphasized both at the beginning and at the end, when the camera roams through the castle to the royal bedchamber, then zooms in on the "incestuous sheets." After the murder of Polonius (Felix Aylmer), Hamlet throws Gertrude (Eileen Herlie) down on the incestuous bed, and the sexual appeal of the queen is conveyed by the way she looks at her son. That glance seems to be a come-hither stare, but it also conveys a sense of anguish and concern.

The film now seems mannered and stylistically overdone, far too conscious of its attempt to be "cinematic." One effective touch is the way scene changes are signified by the camera's roving through the castle corridors. Hamlet's means of returning to Denmark after Claudius (Basil Sydney) sends him to England is doubly emphasized, by his words and by the visual enactment of his encounter with the pirates. Hamlet is made out to be the only survivor after having boarded the pirate ship: We see the other ship sinking. There is a general tendency here to sacrifice poetry for spectacle. The camera work is too often self-conscious and draws attention to itself through moving camera shots, zooms, and dissolves. Ophelia's floating on her back, singing, comes near to being ludicrous, while at the same time being eerie and pathetic. Contemporary critic James Agee generally praised Jean Simmons's portrayal of Ophelia, however. Michael Kustow described the ghost as "an out-of-focus vaporous apparition."

Olivier portrays Hamlet as a sensitive, superior, magnificent young man, overly made up to emphasize his Danishness. There are too many shots of Hamlet lolling about on the throne trying "to make up his mind." The rendering also makes Hamlet appear to be distant and aloof, and there is little cause to be much in sympathy with him for that reason. All in all he is too much the delicate Dane. Hamlet is perhaps at his best when he is bantering with Polonius. The way he poses, leaning against a pillar with his elbow and his hand covering his eyes gets an intentional laugh from the audience and helps to set up the "Fishmonger" scene (II.ii.: by calling Polonius a "fishmonger," Hamlet suggests that the "good old man" is a pimp, willing to prostitute his daughter for his own ends).

In general, Hamlet's lines have been cut back. One listens in vain, for example, for the "O what rogue and peasant slave am I" soliloquy (II.ii). With regard to textual fidelity, Charlton Hinman once remarked that Olivier's treatment was not so much one of modernization as of vulgarization. Hinman, a textual scholar and a "purist," would have objected, of course, to the way Olivier cut the play by nearly 1,900 lines, shortening and simplifying the drama and even sacrificing the "What a piece of work is a man" meditation (II.ii). In his defense, just reproducing the text was not his main agenda. Certainly Shakespeare's organization is disrupted, however, and scenes are rearranged or abridged to make the play conform to the conventions of film pacing and film narrative.

The film is simplified by the way the text has been cut to achieve a running time of two and one-half hours and by Olivier's voice-over at the beginning that proclaims "This is the tragedy of a man who could not make up his mind," which puts rather too much emphasis on the issue of Hamlet's alleged procrastination, as if that were a tragic flaw. Fortinbras and the issue of Norway are missing in Olivier's film, which ends with Hamlet's body being carried up the castle wall to the parapet where Hamlet had earlier delivered his "To be

Maximilian Schell's adaptation of Hamlet *was directed by Edward Dmytryk.* (COURTESY NATIONAL FILM SOCIETY ARCHIVES)

or not to be" soliloquy. Also gone are Rosencrantz and Guildenstern, which diminishes the theme of friendship so carefully worked out by Shakespeare. There is no second gravedigger. Reynaldo is not sent to France by Polonius to spy on Laertes.

There are many other omissions and changes. The "mousetrap" is reduced merely to the "dumb show" Hamlet had requested the actors to avoid, which in this production causes Claudius's discomfort and departure from the great hall. The film's "cinematic" flourishes are flamboyantly overdone, as in the "To be or not to be" soliloquy, spoken as an interior voice-over while the camera zooms in on the back of Hamlet's head to a tight close-up, then dissolves to the waves breaking below the castle wall, supposedly taking the viewer into the turmoil of his mind. The film was regarded as a benchmark production but now seems a bit musty and dated.

The next major *Hamlet* was a Hallmark Hall of Fame production for NBC television, directed by George Schaefer and starring Maurice Evans, broadcast on the anniversary of Shakespeare's christening in 1953. It was called a two-hour production, considered at the time "the longest drama ever done on American television," but the running time was only 90 minutes, according to Alice Griffin. Evans, who had played Hamlet on the Broadway stage, wanted to portray "the inner conflict" of a man "caught up in a web of circumstances which sets him to questioning the values and standards by which he has lived." Barry Jones provided good support as Polonius, but Sarah Churchill as Ophelia and Ruth Chatterton as Gertrude were judged "inadequate." Joseph Schildkraut was "adequate" as Claudius, however, as was Wesley Addy as Horatio.

The Maximilian Schell *Hamlet*, directed by Franz Peter Wirth for West German television in 1960, was respected in its day because of Schell's intelligent rendering of the prince. The film begins with an establishing shot of two empty thrones, one of which will be filled by Schell's dying Hamlet at the end, interpreted as a possible political reference to a divided Germany and evoking Jan Kott's Grand Mechanism of history. Schell's prince is notable for his emotional stability, well acted and "most royal," Lillian Wilds contended, in comparison to Hans Caninenberg's one-dimensional Claudius and Wanda Rotha's over-acted Gertrude. The film was shot on a low budget, the sets stylized and claustrophobic, the action filmed predominantly in medium and close-up shots. The film might have retained its critical favor had the language been subtitled rather than dubbed into English from the German.

The Russian *Hamlet* directed by Grigori Kozintsev in 1964 is far more successfully cinematic, though it works many substantive changes on the text. The first scene is missing from the beginning, for example, and lines concerning Fortinbras at the end, as well as Horatio's declaration that he will tell Hamlet's story. Kozintsev adds magnificent visual sequences, however, such as Hamlet's passing through a war-torn village on his way back to Elsinore. Writing for *Sight and Sound* (1964), Michael Kustow was transfixed by Kozintsev's ghost, "a giant figure in glinting armour, his black cloak flaming and fluttering like a turbulent storm-cloud, his face shadowed by a vizor." To demonstrate that "Denmark's a prison" (as Hamlet tells Rosencrantz and Guildenstern), Kozintsev packs his mise-en-scène with telling details: "a massive portcullis, a vast drawbridge, guards with muskets, and a harsh iron corset into which Ophelia is strapped as she dresses to mourn Polonius." Add to this the music of

Dmitri Shostakovich, and the style that results was, for Kustow, "realistic-operatic."

Kozintsev dramatizes scenes that are merely narrated in the play, such as Hamlet's changing the death warrants on ship before his "rescue" and Ophelia's body floating in a pool. In the Kozintsev version, a bundle of dried kindlewood is substituted for the wildflowers Ophelia brings to the king and queen to demonstrate the queen's sad comment, "Alas, she's mad." But that point is also made visually by the way Ophelia dances to the tinkling music of Shostakovich, delicately played on a cembalo.

Jack Jorgens described "an incomplete list of omissions and alterations" in his essay on the film in *Literature/Film Quarterly* (1973), including "all mentions of suicide in the first soliloquy" and the last part of the "O what a rogue and peasant slave am I" soliloquy, references questioning the authenticity of the ghost, "nearly all of Hamlet's instructions to the players, Hamlet's praise of Horatio, the dumb show," Polonius informing Claudius that he will "loose" his daughter on Hamlet, the king's prayer scene, "Hamlet's description of the pirate adventure," and "all of the lines between the killing of Claudius and 'the rest is silence.'"

Absolute fidelity is not the only measure of a successful adaptation, however, and Jorgens praises Kozintsev's rendering and interpretation for its focus throughout "on Hamlet's integrity, his refusal to act without understanding his own motives and the meaning of his action, the moment when he takes arms against the sea of troubles represents a narrowing, a reduction in stature, a compromise," creating the impression that "Hamlet is finer than the world he lives in, greater than language or actions could express, and this feeling is confirmed in his death." In comparison to Olivier's film, which captured what Jorgens called "the inner *Hamlet*," Kozintsev's epic treatment emphasized "the outer *Hamlet*." In the Olivier film "the complexity of the central character grows primarily out of [Olivier's] performance," whereas in Kozintsev's film "the fragmented and conflict-ridden personality grows from within" the character as represented by Innokenti Smoktunovski. In this film Hamlet's first soliloquy ("O that this too too solid flesh would melt . . .") is voiced-over as Hamlet walks through a crowd of smiling courtiers. Jorgens rightly praised the film's mise-en-scène, which captures more of the play's "complexity and mystery" because Kozintsev's "visual texture is denser" and "the images and connections more consistently meaningful."

The other filmed *Hamlet* of 1964, directed by John Gielgud in America, was not intended to be "cinematic" at all, but a filmed theater record of Gielgud's stage production that first opened at Toronto's O'-Keefe Center before moving to the Lunt-Fontanne Theatre in New York. It starred Richard Burton as Hamlet, Alfred Drake as Claudius, Hume Cronyn as Polonius, Eileen Herlie as Gertrude, Linda Marsh as Ophelia, and Robert Milli as Horatio, with Gielgud himself providing the voice of the ghost. Although the theater reviews were mixed, the stage production was immensely popular and ran for 138 performances on Broadway. Gielgud trimmed "only about 500 lines, or approximately 12% of the text," according to Jay Halio, including "Horatio's description of Fortinbras's threatened invasion (I.i.70–112) and Claudius's first admission of guilt" (III.i.46–54), but retained almost all of "The Murder of Gonzago," written "in a purposely archaic dramatic style" more likely to be understood by theater audiences. The only wholesale unit cut Gielgud made was in Act Four, Scene Four, the scene in which Horatio reads Hamlet's letter concerning his adventures with pirates at sea and his "most strange return." This was a barebones approach, "stripped of all extraneous trappings" and filmed with the actors in rehearsal clothes. Burton told Gielgud that he was "anxious not to have to wear a period costume with tights." As a consequence, this led Gielgud "to conceive a production of *Hamlet* in modern dress on a stage with bare walls and only a few platforms and essential furniture." Gielgud recalls the production that was filmed as "bleak and unattractive," despite its enormous success on stage. Burton's performance was judged to be "powerful," but "uneven." The action was recorded by a mysterious technological innovation called "Electronovision."

A far more lively production was directed by Tony Richardson in 1969 at the Round House Theatre in London, starring Nicol Williamson as Hamlet and Anthony Hopkins as Claudius. The film captures a defining performance of Williamson, revising and rethinking the character of the prince for a whole generation of viewers. Richardson's filmed-theater approach, like Gielgud's, was far different from "cinematic" ones of Olivier and Kozintsev. The ghost is heard but not seen, for example. A bright spotlight is used merely to suggest the presence of the ghost, illuminating the faces of those privileged to see it; the voice of the ghost is in fact the voice of Nicol Williamson, electronically enhanced. This low-budget film is innocent of special effects.

The film was spun off from Richardson's stage production and financed by Woodfall Productions, the company Richardson had formed with playwright John Osborne to film *Look Back in Anger* (1959) and *The Entertainer* (1960). Richardson shot the film by day while the play was still being performed nightly. Williamson's Hamlet was as innovative as Olivier's was traditional, angry, and impudent, and was far more relaxed under the camera's scrutiny. The text was reduced by half, but the trimming of the text was done so seamlessly that the play appears to be intact. All of the major characters are in place except for Fortinbras, and when Hamlet dies, "the rest is silence."

Richardson pushes the theme of incest beyond the limits of the play to include Ophelia (pop star and decidedly unvirginal Rolling Stones groupie Marianne Faithfull) and her brother Laertes (Michael Pennington), who seem to kiss on his departure for France in a way a brother and sister never should. The actress does not convey much of a sense of Ophelia's innocence and virginity and seems to be contaminated, since the atmosphere of this film suggests moral rottenness. Since she seems to be an experienced tart rather than a frail innocent, the rationale for Ophelia's madness and suicide is a bit flawed. Gordon Jackson's Horatio, though a little old for the role, is fully in place as Hamlet's friend and confidant, and his loyalty is effectively paired against Rosencrantz (Ben Aris) and Guildenstern (Clive Graham). Judy Parfitt's Gertrude seems to dote upon both Hamlet and her oily and devious husband.

The strength of Richardson's *Hamlet* is what some might have considered its weakness. It was done essentially as filmed theater and shot in such a way that it would work for the television screen. Most of the set-ups are two-shots or close-ups, so that the emphasis is always upon the actors and their lines. There are almost no distractions of the mise-en-scène and the focus is always upon language and inflection, expertly rendered by Nicol Williamson, Anthony Hopkins, and their subordinates. Mark Dignam's Polonius is a memorable comic performance, as is that of Roger Livesey as the gravedigger. If, as Hamlet says, the point is to *hear* a play, this production is well worth listening to.

Less successful, perhaps, in cutting and emending the text seamlessly was Peter Wood's 1970 *Hamlet*, starring Richard Chamberlain as the prince, Martin Shaw as Horatio, Richard Johnson as Claudius, Margaret Leighton as Gertrude, Ciaran Madden as Ophelia, and Alan Bennett as Osric, all of them in Regency period costumes. This production cut large blocs of text—something like 2,100 lines—all but the last five lines of Act Four, Scene Two, e.g., and all of the dialogue of the play-within, retaining only the Dumb Show to spring Hamlet's "mousetrap." The Chamberlain version also removes Act Two, Scene One, and, more significantly, Act Four, Scene Four, and therefore Hamlet's last soliloquy: "How all occasions do inform against me." In this film Chamberlain's prince was well supported by Michael Redgrave's Polonius and John Gielgud as the ghost. When Claudius comes to Laertes (IV.vii) to plot Hamlet's death, he interrupts Laertes at his prayers, so that Gertrude's entrance with the news of Ophelia's death seems, as Jay Halio noted, "a retribution against Laertes" for his complicity in Claudius's diabolical scheme. Ophelia was earlier seen at her prayers in the background as Hamlet recites his "To be or not to be" soliloquy before the nunnery scene, as this adaptation emphasizes the Christian morality violated by Claudius and Laertes. Like Olivier's version, the Chamberlain *Hamlet* is agreeable enough, Halio asserts, "taken on its own premises as a romantic version of a passionate, sensitive young prince."

Derek Jacobi's performance in the 1980 BBC *Hamlet* received generally better notices than did the production itself, although this version of the play is not without its virtues. At 210 minutes, it was the most complete film version of the play until Branagh's 242-minute *Hamlet*. With a wealth of television experience but none with Shakespeare, director Rodney Bennett rejected his medium's naturalistic tendency and decided on a minimalist set that suggests locations through a few stage properties, sound effects—cannon, trumpets, shouts—and effective use of lighting. From some points of view, the virtue of this nonrepresentational arrangement is that it emphasizes actors and props in a manner similar to the flexible and unlocalized conditions of Shakespeare's stage. Kenneth Rothwell, however, believes that the result "looked in its bareness more like a budgetary than an artistic decision," although, he says, "it did move away from realism toward expressionism." The only use of a realistic background occurs in the play-within-the-play where Bennett places a Renaissance perspective background behind the actors of "The Mousetrap." Generally, however, he keeps perspectives fluid and indeterminate, making scenes flow from one to the next with minimal transitions.

Bennett develops several significant contrasts between Hamlet and the other characters in the play and seems to make him occupy a somewhat different level of reality. Jacobi's Hamlet is ironic, questioning, even mocking, aware of the audience on the other side of the camera, and, to a degree, inconsistent, perhaps even manic-depressive. By contrast, as Neil Taylor points out, Claudius (Patrick Stewart), Gertrude (Claire Bloom), and Polonius (Eric Porter) become "essentially warm, sensitive, reasonable people." Patrick Stewart's Claudius, in particular, never seems to approach the villainous hypocrisy of other performances. In the prayer scene, for example, he genuinely seems to struggle with his conscience in a way that justifies Hamlet's decision to wait and kill him in another, more damnable, moment. Indulging in what Rothwell calls a "metatheatrical" turn, Hamlet, after the "dumb-show," intrudes on the acting space being used by the players, interpreting, directing the action, and actually standing over the actors when the "player-king" is killed. H.R. Coursen says that "Jacobi's finest moments occurred within the climactic play-within-the-play scene," where Jacobi wears a death's head mask, simultaneously becoming a jester and an emblem of death, thus anticipating the graveyard scene's recollections of Yorick. The soliloquies in the play present another point of contrast. Claudius is never aware of the presence of the camera, but Hamlet seems to play to it. His soliloquies tend to be long, single takes of isolated moments in which he turns to the camera as though trying to work through issues he must keep from sharing with anyone else in the play but somehow feels free to share with an audience that only he seems to know exists.

The Mel Gibson *Hamlet*, directed by Franco Zeffirelli and superbly photographed by David Watkin in 1990, is not only lively but cinematic as well. The problem is that the screenplay by Zeffirelli and Christopher DeVore makes hash of the text, transposing lines capriciously and removing whole scenes that are necessary for properly contextualizing the action. The opening of the film springs back in time, for example, to the funeral of the old king Hamlet, stealing lines from the court scene in Act One, Scene Two, which is severely and stupidly abridged. "Let the world take note, that you are most immediate to our throne," Alan Bates's Claudius remarks to Mel Gibson's Hamlet as the prince sifts a handful of soil onto his father's bier. Zeffirelli cuts the first scene entirely, and seriously diminishes the role of Horatio. The screenplay also completely ignores Hamlet's fourth soliloquy, in which he states his resolution, finally, to take action against his uncle.

Franco Zeffirelli's Hamlet *starred Mel Gibson as Hamlet, Glenn Close as Gertrude, and Alan Bates as Claudius.* (COURTESY ICON PICTURES)

The faults of this adaptation concern the director's strategy. The medieval atmosphere is most pleasing and the acting, in general, is difficult to fault. Mel Gibson encompasses much the same attitude and impudence as Nicol Williamson had 20 years earlier. His Hamlet is energetic and animated, though at times his lunacy seems more real than imagined. Glenn Close is a fawning, sentimental Gertrude, supposedly innocent of the conspiracy that took her first husband's life. Helena Bonham-Carter's Ophelia, obedient to her father's wishes but resentful nonetheless, is among the best Ophelias ever captured on screen. Ian Holm's Polonius is self-consciously aware of his foolishness, more a snoopy busybody than a sinister figure and

Claudius's henchman. There is nothing terribly wrong with Stephan Dillane's Horatio other than the fact that he is not given sufficient screen time. Paul Scofield makes a stately ghost. John McEnery, who had played Mercutio brilliantly in Zeffirelli's *Romeo and Juliet*, is truly sinister as Osric, a far cry from Peter Gale's homosexual fop in Richardson's film. Only Alan Bates might be faulted for his rendering of Claudius, something of a meddlesome buffoon rather than a truly dangerous and sinister politician, and certainly not Hamlet's equal intellectually.

Zeffirelli has a flair for staging operatic spectacles, and this talent is put to excellent use in the duel scene, which is well choreographed, though arguably longer than it needs to be. Gibson's acting deserves to be taken seriously and is more than merely a Danish confection. So much of the play has gone missing, however, that the film might be incoherent to those who have not read and studied Shakespeare. Zeffirelli would have done better to study John Dover Wilson's book *What Happens in Hamlet?* (1967) so as to better understand the complexity of the play and the way in which the pieces should fit together. Unfortunately, he restructured the play without regard to the consequences.

Working with veteran television director Kirk Browning, Kevin Kline codirected a more ephemeral adaptation for American public television, broadcast on November 2, 1990, in which he played the lead opposite Diane Venora's Ophelia. Derived from the New York Shakespeare production for the "Great Performances" series, this presentation was more complete than the Zeffirelli film because Kline, a classically trained actor as well as a movie star, took Shakespeare seriously and argued to keep as much of the text as possible. "In *Hamlet*," he told observer Mary Maher, "every cut bleeds." Cutting only about 15 percent of the text, the production ran to two hours and 50 minutes in comparison to the stage production, which ran three hours and 20 minutes. This was Kline's directorial debut, and he was well supported by the stage players who would not be recognized, by and large, by filmgoers. Although long and relatively "academic" in its filmed-theater approach, the performance was praised as "elegant and riveting," and provided an interesting alternative to the mass-audience Zeffirelli version.

Likewise, actor-director Kenneth Branagh had a far superior understanding of the play, which he intended to film in all its complexity and wholeness. Running to just over four hours, Branagh's *Hamlet* is a monument of scholarship, taste, and judgment, and the longest Shakespeare film ever made. Branagh conflated the text of the First Folio of 1623 with that of the Second Quarto, the one version containing lines that the other lacked. The length might be a problem for some viewers, but not for those enthralled by Shakespeare's language. In this case, the usual complaints about textual fidelity simply do not apply. In his published screenplay, Branagh explained the "principles" that guided his adaptation: "a commitment to international casting; a speaking style that is as realistic as a proper adherence to the structure will allow; a period setting that attempts to set the story in a historical context that is resonant for a modern audience but allows a heightened language to sit comfortably," and, above all, "a full emotional commitment to the characters, springing from [a] belief that they can be understood in direct, accessible relation to modern life."

Branagh achieves these goals brilliantly. He clearly wants to help his viewers understand lines that may be difficult, such as those of the player king (Charlton Heston), whose words are illustrated as he speaks them by John Gielgud as Priam and Judi Dench as Hecuba

Kenneth Branagh directed the first full-text Hamlet.
(COURTESY CASTLE ROCK ENTERTAINMENT)

in cameo roles. He has assembled an unbelievably strong cast in keeping with his notions about international casting. Although Jack Lemmon fails to impress viewers at the outset as a spear-carrier, later on Billy Crystal is perfect as the comic first gravedigger. Other pleasant surprises include Robin Williams as Osric. Gerard Depardieu plays Reynaldo, sent by Polonius to France to spy on Laertes (Michael Maloney). Julie Christie came out of retirement to play Gertrude. Kate Winslet was on board as Ophelia before her maiden voyage on the *Titanic*. Richard Briers is a sleazy and potentially dangerous Polonius, Nicholas Farrell a dignified and loyal Horatio. And in Derek Jacobi, Branagh landed one of the most distinguished actors in the English-speaking world to play Claudius, and his Claudius is second to none in his villainy and deviousness, a truly worthy opponent for Hamlet.

The action is moved forward in time to the 19th century and filmed at Blenheim Palace rather than in the Middle Ages, for Branagh intends to demonstrate the play's timeliness. The film begins with a statue of the dead king Hamlet (Brian Blessed) coming to life and ends, after the shift of power to Fortinbras, with that statue being pulled down, as heroic statues of Lenin were in Iron Curtain countries after the fall of communism in 1989. Every detail in the film is meant to point up and clarify the text. When Hamlet confronts the ghost, for example, there are strange eruptions in the realm and Hamlet has good reason to be terrified. The final spectacle of the duel scene is arguably overdone in the way Claudius is killed, perhaps, but the arrival of Fortinbras and his army is a crashing success. Students of Shakespeare will be delighted by Branagh's absolutely clear delivery of the soliloquies. His disappointment in Ophelia is complicated by flashbacks that suggest they have been lovers, a visual departure, to be sure, but this detail also helps to explain her suicide and Hamlet's bizarre behavior at her graveside. It is entirely appropriate that *Hamlet* of all plays should have been given such a thorough treatment.

Michael Almereyda directed the first *Hamlet* of the new century in 2000, starring Ethan Hawke as the prince in a version that runs to a mere 112 minutes, nearly two hours shorter than Branagh's full-text adaptation and updated to New York City in the present day. This postmodern adaptation sets the power struggle in the confines of "The Denmark Corporation," where Claudius (Kyle MacLachlan) is now CEO. Elsinore becomes a luxury hotel, and the Hawke-Hamlet in modern dress recites his "To be or not to be" ironically, in the "action" department of a Blockbuster video store. The ghost (Sam Shepard) appears to Hamlet in a laundry room, wearing a leather jacket. One reviewer described Bill Murray's Polonius as "a slick spin doctor who uses wiretaps" on Ophelia (Julia Stiles). Diane Venora plays Gertrude as a social-climbing Manhattan socialite, not too tenderly. Almereyda rose to the challenge of low-budget filmmaking, shooting the picture on Super 16. Although the director discards huge blocs of text, he retains Shakespeare's language.

Reviews were mixed. Elvis Mitchell of the *New York Times* praised the "boldness and veracity" of Almereyda's trimming of the text and the "bemused hollowness" that Bill Murray "first discovered in sketch comedy" and here spun into "a worn, saddened undercurrent." The more theatrically experienced Stanley Kauffmann was more difficult to please, though he thought that Ethan Hawke was "the perfect choice for this Hamlet because his slithering, mumbling approach fits the essentially off-handed feeling of the film." Kauffmann considered the classically trained Liev Schreiber "out of place" as Laertes because Almereyda otherwise avoided "any touch of the theater or of classical tradition in the performances." Besides Schreiber, the only actor in the cast capable of giving "some sense of the size of the work that is here being battered is Sam Shepard." The play has survived "because of and through its language," and "to rip out great chunks [of the text] because they do not fit a director's design is like altering a giant's robe for a pygmy." Kauffmann concluded, brutally, that "to mash the language as an obstacle that must be cleared away for the modern audience is to cheat that audience." If Kauffmann finds an adaptation only "mildly entertaining," that does not bode well for the film's critical reception, once the novelty has gone stale.

REFERENCES

Branagh, Kenneth, *Hamlet, by William Shakespeare: Screenplay and Introduction* (New York: W.W. Norton, 1996); Burnett, Mark Thornton, "The 'Very Cunning of the Scene': Kenneth Branagh's *Hamlet*," *Literature/Film Quarterly*, 25:2 (1997), 78–82; Coursen, H.R., "Three Televised Hamlets: in *Shakespeare on Television*, ed. J.C. Bulman and H.R. Courson (Hanover, N.H.: University Press of New England, 1988), 101–110; Fierman, Daniel, "The Dane Event," *Entertainment Weekly*, 543 (June 2, 2000), 40–42; Gielgud, John with John Miller, *Shakespeare—Hit or Miss?* (London: Sidgwick and Jackson, 1991); Griffin, Alice, "Shakespeare Through the Camera's Eye," *Shakespeare Quarterly*, 4:3 (1953), 33–34; Halio, Jay, "Three Filmed *Hamlets*," *Literature/Film Quarterly*, 1:4 (1973), 316–320; Jorgens, Jack J., "Image and Meaning in the Kozintsev *Hamlet*," *Literature/Film*

Quarterly, 1:4 (1973), 299–315; Jorgens, Jack J., *Shakespeare on Film* (Bloomington: Indiana University Press, 1977); Kliman, Bernice W., *Hamlet: Film, Television, and Audio Performances* (Rutherford, N.J.: Fairleigh Dickinson University Press, 1988); Kustow, Michael, "Hamlet," *Sight and Sound*, 33:3 (1964), 144–145; Maher, Mary Z., "An American Hamlet for Television," *Literature/Film Quarterly*, 20:4 (1992): 301–307; ———, "Hamlet's BBC Soliloquies," *Shakespeare Quarterly* (1985), 417–426; Mullin, Michael, "Tony Richardson's *Hamlet*: Script and Screen," *Literature/Film Quarterly*, 4:2 (1976), 123–133; Taylor, Neil, "The Films of *Hamlet*" in *Shakespeare and the Moving Image*, ed. Anthony Davies and Stanley Welles (Cambridge, England: Cambridge University Press, 1994), 180–195; Welsh, James M. and John C. Tibbetts, *The Cinema of Tony Richardson: Essays and Interviews* (Albany, N.Y.: SUNY Press, 1999); Wilds, Lillian, "Maximilian Schell's Most Royal *Hamlet*," *Literature/Film Quarterly*, 4:2 (1976), 134–140; Willis, Susan, *The BBC Shakespeare Plays* (Chapel Hill: University of North Carolina Press, 1991).

—*J.M.W. AND R.V.*

HENRY IV, PART I (1596–97)
HENRY IV, PART II (1598)

Chimes at Midnight/Campanadas a Medianoche/Falstaff (1967), Spain/Switzerland, directed and adapted by Orson Welles; Internacional Films Espagnol (Madrid)/Alpine Films (Basel).

My Own Private Idaho (1991), U.S.A., directed and adapted by Gus Van Sant; New Line Cinema/Fine Line Features.

The Plays

In these two plays, the core of Shakespeare's second tetralogy of history plays that begins with *Richard II* and ends with *Henry V*, Shakespeare dramatizes the education and development of the politician destined to become King Henry V, "the mirror of all Christian kings." But here he is known mainly as Prince Hal, whose father, Henry Bolingbroke, now King Henry IV (r. 1399–1413), assumed the throne after a civil war that usurped the poetic but ineffectual Richard II. The action of *1 Henry IV* begins in the summer of 1402 and concludes a year later during the summer of 1403, after the battle of Shrewsbury, when the royal army defeated a rebellion led by the fierce Welshman, "that great magician" Owen Glendower and the Percy family—Thomas, earl of Worcester, Henry, earl of Northumberland, and Henry's son, called Hotspur.

Although troubled mainly by civil rebellion, the king is also concerned about the dubious behavior of his son, Prince Hal, an apparent playboy who spends much of his time at the Boar's Head tavern in Eastcheap in the company of a fat old rogue, Sir John Falstaff, and his associates Poins, Bardolph, Peto, and Gadshill, indulging in drinking, gambling, wenching, and practical jokes (such as a botched robbery prank, in which Hal and Poins in disguise scare off the boastful Falstaff and Bardolph, averting the planned robbery). Prince Hal's "loose behavior" is not what it seems, however. Rather, it is a calculated ploy at image-making that foreshadows Hal's later "redemption" as King Henry V. Hal clearly states his intentions when he says (I.ii.239–40): "I'll so offend, to make offence a skill/Redeeming time when men least think I will." Hal proves his mettle at the battle of Shrewsbury when he defeats and kills Harry Hotspur in single combat. Later, Falstaff attempts to take credit for the death of the hotheaded Hotspur.

Civil discord continues into *2 Henry IV*. The earl of Northumberland discovers that his son Hotspur is dead and that the royal army under the command of Prince John of Lancaster and the earl of Westmoreland is moving against him. Northumberland takes his wife and daughter-in-law and retreats into Scotland. The earl of Westmoreland urges the remaining rebels, Mowbray and Hastings, to make peace with Prince John, who promises that their grievances shall be redressed, then has them arrested for treason. This news reaches the king after he has learned of the death of Owen Glendower (Act Three) and the defeat of Northumberland in the north (Act Four). In Act Five the king advises his son "to busy giddy minds/With foreign quarrels," as Hal will later do as King Henry V.

In *2 Henry IV* Prince Hal gradually withdraws from Falstaff, who is seen as even more disreputable and conniving and has taken on another boon companion, a "swaggering rascal" named Pistol, whom Shakespeare stereotypes as a braggart soldier, a drunken whore named Doll Tearsheet, and a corrupt country justice, Master Shallow. Owing money to Master Shallow, Falstaff approaches the new king (Henry V) in Act Five expecting favoritism, but is soundly rejected: "I know thee not old man: fall to thy prayers;/How ill white hairs become a fool and jester!" Hal then adds, "Presume not that I am the thing I was" and banishes Falstaff from his presence.

The Films

One could argue that Orson Welles was born to play the role of Falstaff, or that he grew into it as his own career fell onto hard times after the initial brilliance of

Citizen Kane. For years Welles was obsessed with his Falstaff project. Early on he had combined and compressed the texts of *Henry IV* Parts I and II and *The Merry Wives of Windsor* on the stage, but he later had difficulty funding the film project. Shakespeare's so-called Henriad introduces Prince Hal as a calculating playboy who proves his valor in *1 Henry IV,* assumes the throne at the end of *2 Henry IV,* and conquers France in *Henry V.* In these three plays Shakespeare dramatizes the growth and development of a Christian prince destined to become England's first modern king and a hugely popular politician.

In *1 Henry IV* Hal's relationship with Sir John Falstaff is playful and affectionate, regarding Falstaff as a sort of surrogate father who teaches the prince to relate to the common man. At the time *Chimes at Midnight* was made, Falstaff had been seen only fleetingly on screen, at the beginning of Laurence Olivier's *Henry V,* as Mistress Quickly tells Pistol, Nym, and Bardolph of how Falstaff died of a broken heart in Act One. Welles considered Falstaff "the most completely good old man in all drama" when he presumed to rewrite Shakespeare's plays as "a dark comedy [and] the story of the betrayal of a friendship." Understandably, then, Welles pulled Falstaff out of the background and thrust him into the foreground as he presented for the first time in cinema Shakespeare's greatest comic creation. The film is a true adaptation that reworks and restructures Shakespeare's dramatic materials into a cinematic narrative that arches over the two plays.

The film begins with Falstaff (Welles) and Justice Shallow (Alan Dent) remembering their younger days (*2 Henry IV,* III.ii), with Falstaff speaking the lines that gave the film its title: "We have heard the chimes at midnight, Master Shallow." The film then cuts to "the Royal Castle" as Ralph Richardson's voice-over narration from Holinshed's *Chronicles* (Shakespeare's major source for the play) provides exposition summarizing the action of *Richard II* and the political circumstances of *1 Henry IV.* The ransom of Edmund Mortimer, held hostage by Owen Glendower, is demanded. However, King Henry IV (John Gielgud) is unwilling to empty his coffers "to redeem the traitor home," to the chagrin of Northumberland (Jose Nieto), his son Hotspur (Norman Rodway), and Worcester (Fernando Rey), setting up the conflict for the play.

Welles divides the narrative into two parts, paralleling the two parts of Shakespeare's original plays, separated by Richardson's voice-overs, which are also used to conclude the film. Welles presents an amalgam intended to showcase Falstaff, and to present the character more sympathetically than he finally appears in Shakespeare, who makes it clear that Prince Hal is finally forced by politics to reject Falstaff, since Falstaff would surely have exploited his friendship with the king had he been granted a position at Court. The joviality of the character in Part One gives way to a distasteful cynicism in Part Two, but Welles shows that the prince's decision, though arguably necessary, was not an easy one to make.

There is an intuitive stroke of editorial genius in this film in the way that Welles handles the rejection and, finally, the demise of Falstaff. First of all, Welles stages the rejection scene in such a way as to emphasize the utter presumption of Falstaff's approaching the king. Falstaff breaks through the guards to interrupt the royal procession, as no one else there would dare to do. Hal speaks his opening line ("I know thee not, old man") with his back turned; he pauses ever so slightly, but there is no question that he recognizes the voice. After banishing Falstaff "on pain of death . . . Not to come near our person by ten mile," Welles leaves the impression that Falstaff has been imprisoned for his presumption.

Welles then takes us into the beginning of *Henry V* as the new king, about to embark for France, speaks the lines: "Enlarge the man committed yesterday/That railed against our person. We consider/It was excess of wine that set him on,/And on his more advice, we pardon him." Dramatic time and space are here compressed, but it suits Welles's purpose to suggest that the king's mercy is here being granted to Falstaff, which serves to put Hal in a new and perhaps more human and compassionate light. This compaction and shift works very well for the director, and the description of Falstaff's death from *Henry V* (II.iii) follows immediately, with Pistol, Nym, Bardolph, the boy, and Mistress Quickly being grouped around a huge and portly casket.

After the rejection, as Roger Manvell has noted, Falstaff attempts to rally his self-respect: "I shall be sent for in private to him. Look you, he must seem thus to the world." But thereafter the camera isolates Falstaff, walking "the empty streets at night, alone." Mistress Quickly (Margaret Rutherford) gives her account of Falstaff's death from *Henry V,* getting a final tug of sympathy ("the King hath killed his heart") as the coffin is carried off. Pauline Kael considered the film "a near masterpiece" but criticized the "maddening" cutting and the way the actor's voices fail to match the images, producing a "crazy mix" of long shots and Shakespearean dialogue. Given the director's budget constraints, the film is far better than one might have expected and, arguably, his best Shakespeare film.

My Own Private Idaho (1991), Gus Van Sant's updated and loosely adapted remake of *Chimes at Midnight*, was intended as an homage to Orson Welles but is set in the homosexual netherworld of modern Portland, Oregon. The language, of course, is not Shakespeare's, and many liberties have been taken. Prince Hal becomes Scott Favor (Keanu Reeves), the son of Portland's mayor (Tom Troupe plays the King Henry IV figure), who is currently alienated from his father because of his associations with gay street hustlers and drug addicts. The older Bob Pigeon (William Richert), Scott's former lover, mentor, and "true father" (or so Scott proclaims), steps into the role of Falstaff. Budd (a musician named Flea from a band called "The Red Hot Chili Peppers") and company represent Shallow and company. Jane Lightwork (Sally Curtice), who owns the old hotel where the characters spend their time (the film's equivalent of the Boar's Head tavern), assumes the role played by Mistress Quickly, although her name also alludes to Jane Nightwork, an old friend whom Shallow mentions to Falstaff in *2 Henry IV* (III.ii.204) and also at the beginning of *Chimes at Midnight*, as Falstaff and Shallow recall how old they have become.

The central role of Mike Waters (River Phoenix), a narcoleptic hustler who becomes Scott's companion and lover, is more complicated. A literal reading of the film would consider Mike as Ned Poins, Hal's friend and fellow prankster, if Van Sant had created a literal transfer of the story, but the Poins role could also be ascribed to fellow hustler Gary (Rodney Harvey). Mike is also a younger Falstaff figure who cavorted with Hal as a brother in earlier days. Both Mike and Bob have lived in Idaho. The trans-gendering effect replaces Falstaff's connections with Doll Tearsheet. Ultimately Scott rejects both Mike and Bob.

Scott is heterosexual—his attachments to Mike and Bob are mainly a rebellion against his Establishment father—as evidenced when he comes into his inheritance and marries Carmella (Chiara Caselli), breaking with Mike and his former friends. Mike and Bob encounter Scott and Carmella outside a posh Portland restaurant. When Mike and Bob approach Scott, he rejects them, saying "Now that I've changed, and until I change back, don't come near me." Bob dies of a broken heart that night. The next day the hustlers gather for Bob's burial at the same cemetery where Scott's father is also being buried. The film begins and ends with Mike, collapsed in a narcoleptic seizure on an Idaho highway. *My Own Private Idaho* is an adaptation twice removed from Shakespeare and more of a tribute to Orson Welles than to the Bard, whose lines are parodied but seem only marginally appropriate, given Van Sant's harsh urban environment.

REFERENCES

Anderegg, Michael, *Orson Welles, Shakespeare and Popular Culture* (New York: Columbia University Press, 1999); Kael, Pauline, *For Keeps* (New York: Dutton, 1994); Kline, Jim, "My Own Private Idaho," *Magill's Cinema Annual 1992*, ed. Frank N. Magill (Pasadena: Salem Press, 1992); Manvell, Roger, *Shakespeare and the Film* (New York: Praeger, 1971).

—*J.M.W. AND H.H.D.*

HENRY V (1599)

Henry V (1944), U.K., directed by Laurence Olivier, adapted by Olivier, Reginald Beck, Alan Dent, and Dallas Bower; Two Cities/Eagle-Lion.

Henry V (1989), U.K., directed and adapted by Kenneth Branagh; Renaissance Films.

The Play

The Life of Henry the Fifth represents a culmination of the tetralogy of history plays that began with *Richard II* and continued on through the two parts of *Henry IV*, which traced the development of the modern English monarchy from the medieval rule of Richard II, whose arrogance and belief in the divine right of kings led to his downfall and deposition, to his successor, Henry Bolingbroke. Having assumed the title of King Henry IV, Bolingbroke had to put his realm in order and deal with a decidedly disunited kingdom, as well as his rakish and apparently dissolute son, Prince Hal. It is Hal who will become King Henry V, "the mirror of all Christian kings," as Shakespeare's Chorus describes him.

The play begins with the king's seeking advice from his churchmen, the bishop of Ely and the archbishop of Canterbury, concerning his right to wage war on France to reclaim French territory once ruled by Edward, the Black Prince, the mention of whose name strikes fear in the heart of the French king, Charles VI. Canterbury goes into a long-winded exposition about the French succession and "the Salic Law they have in France," until the king finds the bottom line: "May I with right and conscience make this claim?" (I.ii.96) and is then given the archbishop's "blessing," so to speak. The

French ambassador then brings Henry an insulting gift of tennis balls from the French dauphin, to which the king responds in dignified rhetorical anger: "We shall in France, by God's grace, play a set/Shall strike his father's crown into the hazard," then sets about his plans to invade France from Southampton.

A parallel subplot is also set in motion at the Boar's Head tavern, where Prince Hal in his youth had disported himself with his low-life friends, Pistol, Nym, Bardolph, and their ringleader, Sir John Falstaff, who is now on his deathbed, presumably dying of a broken heart because Hal had rejected him upon assuming the Crown. "The king hath killed his heart," Mistress Quickly remarks, after describing the death of Sir John to the others, who then prepare themselves to go to war. They are not honorable soldiers, however. Bardolph is executed in France, by order of the king, for stealing from a church. Nym, a cutpurse also interested in pillage, is killed in the battle. Pistol, having been reprimanded by his nemesis, the fierce Welshman, Captain Fluellen, will return home to become a cutpurse: "To England will I steal, and there I'll steal."

The first skirmish of the main plot is fought outside the gates of Harfleur, and the city is captured. King Henry then advances with his army, which is weakened by sickness en route, to meet, in the battle of Agincourt (October 25, 1415), a vastly superior army representing the very flower of French chivalry. The technological superiority of the English longbow, which could propel arrows capable of piercing French armor, results in a great victory against superior odds.

The denouement deals with the aftermath of the victory at the French Court, with King Henry claiming the French princess Katherine as his bride-to-be. The play would seem to be a patriotic celebration of England's greatest victory, but the Epilogue delivered by the Chorus (who comments on the action throughout) calls into question the ultimate significance of this triumph, since Henry's successor, "Henry the Sixth, in infant bands crowned king," so mismanaged his rule that England "lost France, and made his England bleed."

The Films

There are two remarkable adaptations of *Henry V*, the first of which, directed by Laurence Olivier, set the standard for Shakespeare adaptations to come, though it was not entirely faithful to the play nor to the character of the king, who seems to have been far more benevolent and far less calculating than the character Shakespeare created. This is considered Shakespeare's most patriotic play, and for that reason, Olivier was approached by Jack Beddington of the Ministry of Information and given a budget that would allow him to make a spectacular film in Technicolor. Olivier's film was therefore financed as part of the war effort to bolster morale and the spirit of the English people, then under siege by air and sea by Germany during World War II.

As a propaganda film, *Henry V* parallels the intent of *Alexander Nevsky*, directed in the Soviet Union by the great Sergei Eisenstein in 1938, portraying a mythic, unifying Russian hero, whose army drove the invading Teutonic Knights out of Russia. This was clearly intended as a prophetic warning to Nazi Germany, which was later to suffer horrendous losses on the Eastern Front. Like Nevsky, King Henry also had to unify his country before facing the enemy, and he cleverly uses the French campaign to consolidate his power. Olivier's film, with its parallel warning, is oddly critical of the French, whose nobles, as represented in *Henry V*, are indolent, vainglorious fops, and whose king is represented as a senile old man. Perhaps Olivier is unduly critical of the French, who allowed their country to be captured; arguably, his film would seem to insult the French Resistance effort. The weakness of the French nation in Olivier's rendering would seem to undercut the English victory, and this might be considered mistaken strategy in terms of propaganda value.

The film is much more than simply an exercise in propaganda, however. Olivier won a Special Academy Award for his "Outstanding Achievement as an Actor," but his achievement as director is equally noteworthy. What makes the Olivier adaptation still interesting and relevant is the way that Olivier framed the action, as a sort of meditation on the nature of theater as opposed to film. If any Shakespeare play was designed for a filmed treatment, *Henry V* is the one, built upon a battle spectacle that could not possibly be appropriately mounted on the stage. Although Olivier could not take his camera to "the vasty fields of France" then under German occupation, the film opens up the play gloriously by shooting out of doors in the Irish countryside. Olivier rises to the challenge of the Chorus's injunction at the play's opening—the memorable "Muse of fire" prologue—when he apologizes for the stage's limitations and entreats the audience, "On your imaginary forces work." He then implores the audience to "Suppose within the girdle of these walls/Are now confined two mighty monarchies;" and to "Piece out our imperfections with your thoughts."

Olivier begins his film as if it were a performance of the play in Shakespeare's time at the Globe Theatre.

The camera circles in a 360-degree pan of the audience taking their seats. The camera then takes us backstage, where the bishop of Ely (Robert Helpmann) is quaffing a tankard of ale with the king of France (Harcourt Williams). An actor wearing a crown emerges. He clears his throat as he makes himself ready for the stage. He is King Henry V (Olivier). Thus, the film begins as pure filmed theater, providing a textbook example of what a production at the Globe might have been like.

Some of the potentially boring bits of the text for a mass audience are judiciously pruned, such as the pedantic ecclesiastical "justification" for the war the king wants to wage, given by the archbishop of Canterbury (Felix Aylmer) and turned into a comic routine by Olivier's comedian churchman. Olivier later cuts all of the scene where the king uncovers a plot against his life and orders the execution of the conspirators, Cambridge, Grey, and Scroop, at Southampton (II.ii).

In the first scenes, up to Southampton, the acting is purposely "theatrical" and overstated. At the Boar's Head (II.i), for example, the low comedy is broadly played for the groundlings by Pistol (Robert Newton), Nym (Frederick Cooper), and Bardolph (Roy Emmerton), but the second Boar's Head scene is handled quite differently, for by that time Olivier has begun his gradual transition from the theatricality of the Globe to a more realistic treatment. Certainly, in the second Boar's Head scene the dialogue is delivered in a more natural and "cinematic" style. Gone are the broad gestures and the buffoonery, and the characters seem far more believable when Mistress Quickly (Freda Jackson) gives her account of the death of Falstaff (George Robey), earlier seen on his deathbed, with an offstage voice off repeating Hal's rejection speech from *2 Henry IV*—"Think not I am the man I was." The flamboyant theatricality of Act Two, Scene One, is recalled later in the scenes involving Pistol's dispute with Captain Fluellen (Esmond Knight), another potentially comic figure.

The Chorus (Leslie Banks) no longer takes the stage after Southampton, for the "stage" is gone thereafter until the final moments of the film, when Olivier swings the action back into the Globe Theatre, breaking the dramatic illusion so wonderfully created by the film. As the English fleet moves across the Channel, the Chorus floats, as if hovering over the mise-en-scène. Thereafter, only Chorus' disembodied voice is heard, but by that time its voice is recognizable.

The early scenes in France are wrenched out of the theatrical frame and seem oddly dislocated in an impressionistic medieval mise-en-scène, imitating the design of such illuminated texts as *Les très riches heures du Duc de Berry* and the *Book of Hours of Anne of Cleves*. The French Court is framed in such a flat, one-dimensional setting as Olivier gradually makes his visual transition between filmed theater and the realism of the final battle. Even so, the battle spectacle has the appearance of a tastefully decorated illustration. In the actual battle setting, rain would have soaked the field; in Olivier's film there is only a token mud puddle in evidence. For a truly "realistic" rendering of the battle of Agincourt, audiences had to wait for the Branagh adaptation of 1989.

For 45 years no one dared to readapt or upstage Olivier's "classic" treatment, but Kenneth Branagh fully understood the limitations and distortions of Olivier's wartime approach and intended to restore the play and the character of the king to Shakespeare's original design, without the burden of Olivier's political agenda. He also intended to make the play as entertaining and accessible as possible. He achieved both of these goals brilliantly in his 1989 adaptation of *Henry V*, which is far different from Olivier's earlier approach in both interpretation and design.

Branagh begins his film with Derek Jacobi's Chorus standing on a soundstage (or possibly in a television studio), surrounded by props that would later be seen in the film. From the beginning, then, there is no question about Branagh's filmed approach. Jacobi, an accomplished Shakespearean actor, was at the time playing the lead in alternating productions of *Richard II* and *Richard III* at the Phoenix Theatre on Charing Cross Road, taking the train from London to Brighton during the day to film the Chorus for Branagh. Jacobi's Chorus is not so well integrated into the action as Olivier's had been, and keeps appearing as a "You-Are-There" sort of interpreter at awkward moments that disrupt the cinematic flow of the narrative. On the other hand, he does help the audience to understand the flow of events, as when he identifies the conspirators, Cambridge, Scroop, and Grey, seen in the background before King Henry (Branagh) accuses them of treason. Branagh restores that scene, as well as the king's fearsome warning to the citizens of Harfleur of what fate may await them if they refuse to surrender their city.

Branagh's king is a far more tough-minded politician and warrior than Olivier's had been and therefore closer to Shakespeare's design. His response to the ambassadors in Act One, Scene Two, is cold and calculating, and far more menacing than Olivier's had been. As Michael Pursell noted in *Literature/Film Quarterly*, his first appearance in silhouette as he enters the Court visually recalls Darth Vader and Batman, and these popular culture allusions clearly suggest that the king has a dark side. Pursell also demonstrates how visual allusions to soccer and rugby in the way the battle of Agincourt is filmed would resonate meaningfully for younger British and European viewers.

Like Olivier, Branagh adds lines from both parts of *Henry IV* that recall Hal's rejection of Falstaff, and later in the film sets up Bardolph (Richard Briers) as another Falstaff figure. Branagh dramatizes the hanging of Bardolph (merely reported action in the play), as further evidence that the king has rejected his earlier raffish ways. Before the noose is tightened, their eyes lock and both of them seem to remember better times at the Boar's Head before Hal became king. Branagh dramatizes this memory by adding lines from *1 Henry IV* in a far more extensive excavation of that earlier play than Olivier had attempted.

The battle scenes are extended and "realistic" (though the death of the constable of France as he is pulled off the battlefield by his troops is recorded in slow-motion, as is the death of the duke of York). Branagh intends to demonstrate the human cost of the victory, further emphasized by a long tracking shot after the battle, in which the king carries a wounded squire (Christian Bale) the length of the battlefield, accompanied by Patrick Doyle's musical rendering of the *Te Deum* and *Non Nobis*, transformed into a victory anthem.

In this film, the French are worthy opponents, with the exception of the dauphin. The French king (Paul Scofield) seems old and weary, but certainly not senile. Nor is Ian Holm's Captain Fluellen the ethnic caricature he appeared to be in the Olivier adaptation. Brian Blessed's Exeter is contemptuously defiant when he appears as ambassador to the French king, and later, on the battlefield, he is a veritable killing machine, who, in full armor, seems to recall Robocop. Such allusions may weaken the film for some purists, but would no doubt help to maintain the interest of younger viewers. Above all, Branagh wants his film to be understood by a mass audience.

The challenge for Branagh was to adapt the play in such a way that it would not seem a mere imitation of Olivier's achievement. The only scene in Branagh's film that clearly seems to recall Olivier is the king's rousing, patriotic speech to his troops on St. Crispin's Day (IV.ii) before the battle of Agincourt: "We few, we happy few, we band of brothers;/For he today that sheds his blood with me/Shall be my brother; be he ne'er so vile,/This day shall gentle his condition." The speech makes a virtue out of what ought to be a military disadvantage (the fact that the English are seriously outnumbered), and Branagh's delivery, as well as his camera movement,

Kenneth Branagh's Henry V *was the first adaptation of Shakespeare's battle epic since Olivier's version more than 40 years before.* (COURTESY BRITISH FILM INSTITUTE)

starting in tight on the king, then pulling back as the speech builds resonance, would seem a sort of tribute to Olivier. Otherwise, the film stands entirely on its own merits, and launched Branagh's career as a latter-day Olivier among adaptors of Shakespeare.

REFERENCES

Branagh, Kenneth, *Henry V, by William Shakespeare: A Screen Adaptation* (London: Chatto and Windus, 1989); Geduld, Harry M., *Filmguide to Henry V* (Bloomington: Indiana University Press, 1973); Jorgens, Jack J., *Shakespeare on Film* (Bloomington: Indiana University Press, 1977); Manvell, Roger, *Shakespeare and the Film* (London: J.M. Dent, 1971); Olivier, Laurence, *Confessions of an Actor* (London: Weidenfeld and Nicholson, 1982); Pursell, Michael, "Playing the Game: Branagh's *Henry V*," *Literature/Film Quarterly*, 20:4 (1992), 268–275.

—*J.M.W.*

JOE MACBETH

See MACBETH

JULIUS CAESAR (1599)

Julius Caesar (1953), U.S.A., directed and adapted by Joseph L. Mankiewicz; MGM.
Julius Caesar (1969), U.K., directed by Stuart Burge, adapted by Robert Furnival, Commonwealth United Production.

The Play

Julius Caesar was one of four Roman plays (the others being *Antony and Cleopatra, Coriolanus,* and *Titus Andronicus*) in which Shakespeare explored systems of government and themes of despotism and decadence. In this play, Julius Caesar has just returned to Rome after defeating Pompey in a civil war and is on the point of proclaiming himself absolute dictator. However, a soothsayer has warned him to "beware the ides of March"; and there is indeed a conspiracy afoot, fostered by Cassius, Casca, and others, to depose him. Their cause is strengthened when they win over the noble Brutus to their side. Caesar is assassinated in the Capitol, with Brutus striking the final blow. However, Brutus' attempt to justify the act to the populace by arguing that it was for their political good is negated by the speech of Caesar's friend, Mark Antony, whose impassioned rhetoric rouses the mob into a mood of fury against the assassins. In the subsequent political turmoil, Antony and Caesar's successor, Octavius, unite against the forces of Brutus and Cassius and defeat them at the battle of Philippi. Brutus and Cassius both die a Roman death; and over the body of the former, Antony proclaims that "this was the noblest Roman of them all."

The Films

Julius Caesar was made on a modest budget by MGM, utilizing some of the costumes and sets left over from its 1951 blockbuster, *Quo Vadis?* Producer John Houseman had been closely involved with Orson Welles's legendary 1937 modern-dress production, which had stressed the play's contemporary relevance. A film version, declared Houseman, should translate "Shakespeare's bloody and turbulent melodrama into a medium where both mass emotion and personal conflict can be more closely observed and more fully revealed." Thus, although the film was not set in modern dress, it nonetheless invoked the demagogues and political rallies of the recent past. Accordingly, Houseman, in defiance of MGM's preference for color, reasoned that black-and-white photography was essential to convey the impression of contemporary newsreels. Much to the chagrin of his former colleague, Orson Welles, Houseman chose Joseph Mankiewicz to direct. His direction of such films as *A Letter to Three Wives* (1949) and *All About Eve* (1950) had established him as the best director of civilized dialogue in Hollywood. Together, Houseman and Mankiewicz agreed on an unusual shooting strategy—as far as possible, they eliminated reaction shots in order not to disrupt the rhythm of Shakespeare's lines.

As was characteristic of MGM's Roman epics of the 1950s, such as *Quo Vadis?* and *Ben-Hur* (1959), the cast combined the accents and styles of British and American actors. English players such as James Mason as a thoughtful Brutus and John Gielgud as a volatile Cassius were balanced by Americans Louis Calhern as an imposing Caesar and Edmond O'Brien as a crafty, cynical Casca. The most contentious choice was Marlon Brando as Antony. Associated with the Method style of naturalistic mumbling, Brando nonetheless gave a performance that attracted an enormous amount of comment and astonished many with its authority and clarity. Brando's charisma shifted the balance of the play away from Brutus' tragedy, in accordance with Mankiewicz' conception of Brutus as an "Adlai Stevenson-type figure," cultured, intelligent, but a bit at sea amid the hurly-burly of opportunistic politics. Oddly, the film made little attempt to exploit the opportunities presented by the play for spectacle and action, and the battle at Philippi emerges as a pretty tepid affair. More impressive were the small individual touches—the use of chiaroscuro lighting to suggest Brutus's uncertainty and inner torment; the deployment of statues as adornment of, and ironic commentary on, the action; and an electrifying moment when Brutus's speech to the mob is upstaged by Antony's suddenly producing Caesar's body as a bloodcurdlingly effective theatrical prop.

At the end of the 1960s, Peter Snell, a Canadian producer with only two previous film credits, began assembling a cast of British and American actors for a new version of *Julius Caesar*. Charlton Heston, who had played Mark Antony in a filmed college production, was so eager to take the role again that he agreed to a $100,000 fee and a percentage of the film. Robert Vaughn, from television's *Man from U.N.C.L.E.*, would play Casca, while Richard Chamberlain, who had stared as television's *Dr. Kildare*, would be Octavius, and Jason Robards, who had made his reputation playing in works by Eugene O'Neill, agreed to take the role of Brutus. British actors included John Gielgud as Caesar, Richard Johnson as Cassius, and Diana Rigg, who had played Emma Peel in *The Avengers*, as well as Helena in Peter Hall's *A Midsummer Night's Dream*, would have the role of Portia. The director, Stuart Burge, had done the Olivier version of *Othello* and a televised version of *Julius Caesar* in 1959. The failure of the resulting film, according to Kenneth Rothwell, "remains one of the great mysteries in the history of filmed Shakespeare." Roger Manvell says that the Mankiewicz film "haunted them like some unlaid ghost," and made them "determined to achieve something quite different." Samuel Crowl argues that "The film's look and tone and feel reflect its times," namely "the end of the decade dominated by the assassination of John Kennedy, the war in Vietnam, and the student revolt in Europe and America." Rothwell suggests that "it is time to acknowledge that far from being one of Shakespeare's most accessible plays, *Julius Caesar* remains as remote and aloof as the statue of Pompey before which great Caesar fell." Whatever the causes, the results are undeniable.

The opening of this somewhat garish Technicolor film sets the tone for its visual and moral context. As a voice-over gives the background of Caesar's war with Pompey, a soaring eagle dissolves into a vulture sitting on the debris of a battlefield. When the voice says the people named Caesar "perpetual dictator," the camera zooms in to a helmeted skull, from which a dry, rasping voice seems to call Caesar and then to become the voice of the crowd in the first scene of the play shouting Caesar's name. The film offers no moral baseline, with Cicero's lines omitted, the roles of Portia (Diana Rigg) and Calpurnia (Jill Bennett) abbreviated, and Calpurnia's dream presented as a disconnected montage. Gielgud's Caesar is at once superior and eager to please. In the death scene, after receiving many wounds, Caesar walks over to Brutus, who stands with his back turned to him. Brutus turns and stabs Caesar, but here Casca, rather than Brutus, gives the final blow. Even ambiguity is compromised, when Mark Antony, after delivering his speech over Caesar's body, pauses, then goes to a nearby room where he drinks a cup of wine and says "Now let it work." The image robs his speech of all emotion and reduces it to the calculated work of an opportunist. Heston is an aggressive, physical Mark Antony, larger than life and more at home in the battle scenes than in negotiations. Against this portrayal, Jason Robards, as Brutus, almost seems to be a character from a different play. According to Manvell,

Robards was "determined to give the part a new, untraditional and modern slant—a man troubled by the morality of the political assassination," and he tried "to capture Brutus's dilemmas before the camera, not in the rehearsal room." The effect is that he often seems to be doing a cold reading, not so much conflicted as emotionless. Heston, in his autobiography, comments, "I have never seen a good actor so bad in a good part."

REFERENCES

Crowl, Samuel, "A World Elsewhere: The Roman Plays on Film and Television," in *Shakespeare and the Moving Image: The Plays on Film and Television*, ed. Anthony Davies and Stanley Welles (Cambridge, England: Cambridge University Press, 1994), 146–162; Geist, Kenneth L., *People Will Talk: The Life and Films of Joseph L. Mankiewicz* (New York: Charles Scribner's Sons, 1978); Heston, Charlton, *In the Arena: An Autobiography* (New York: Simon and Schuster, 1995); Houseman, John, *Unfinished Business* (London: Chatto and Windus, 1986); Jorgens, Jack J., *Shakespeare on Film* (Bloomington: Indiana University Press, 1977); Manvell, Roger, *Shakespeare and the Film* (London: Vents, 1971), 91–95; Rosenthal, Daniel, *Shakespeare on Screen* (London: Hamlyn, 2000), 58–59; Sinyard, Neil, *Filming Literature: The Art of Screen Adaptation* (London: Croom Helm, 1985).

—*N.S. AND R.V.*

KAROL LIR

See KING LEAR

KING LEAR (1606)

King Lear (1909), U.S.A., directed by J. Stuart Blackton and William V. Ranous; Vitagraph.

King Lear (1916), U.S.A., directed by Ernest C. Warde; Thanhouser Film Corporation.

The Yiddish King Lear (1934), U.S.A., directed by Harry Thomashefsky; Lear Pictures, Inc.

King Lear (1948), U.K., directed and adapted by Royston Morley; British Broadcasting Corporation.

King Lear (1953), U.S.A., directed and adapted by Andrew McCullough and Peter Brook; CBS Films/Omnibus Productions.

Karol Lir (1970), USSR, directed and adapted by Grigori Kozintsev; Lenfilm Studio.

King Lear (1971), U.K., directed and adapted by Peter Brook; Athena-Laterna Films.

King Lear (1975), U.K., directed and adapted by Jonathan Miller; British Broadcasting Corporation.

King Lear (1977), U.S.A., directed and adapted by Edwin Sherin for Joseph Papp; Theatre in America.

King Lear (1982), U.K./U.S.A., directed by Jonathan Miller; adapted by David Shodin and Patricia Preece; BBC/Time-LifeTelevision Productions, Inc.

King Lear (1983), U.K., directed and adapted by Michael Elliott; Granada Television.

Ran (1985), Japan, directed by Akira Kurosawa, adapted by Kurosawa, Hideo Oguni, and Masato Ide; Nippon Herald Films.

King Lear (1987), France, directed and adapted by Jean-Luc Godard; Cannon Films.

King Lear (1997), U.K., directed and adapted by Richard Eyre; BBC/Chesterfield Ltd./WGBH-Boston.

The Play

With the exception of Shakespeare's other major tragedies (*Hamlet*, *Othello*, *Macbeth*), few plays approach *King Lear* in portraying and evoking the wretchedness of human existence, and even those plays are hard-pressed to equal the devastating spectacle of brutality and misery visited upon Lear and the earl of Gloucester, the play's two protagonists. The play's complex double plot provides a rich orchestration like no other Shakespeare play. King Lear misjudges his children; he disinherits his loving daughter Cordelia in favor of the duplicitous Goneril and Regan; Gloucester falls prey to Edmund's deceptions, disinherits his loyal son Edgar. Both are exiled: Lear is turned out into the storm by his false daughters and, in his madness, realizes his fault against Cordelia; Gloucester, branded a traitor by Edmund, is deprived of his eyesight but at last "sees" the truth about Edgar. Both fathers are finally cared for by their loving children and belatedly reconciled to them, but die bereft and brokenhearted. Cordelia's death, in particular, implies a wanton universe and exemplifies despair. In no other Shakespeare play does injustice triumph so ferociously for so long. It is not surprising, then, that *King Lear* has eclipsed *Hamlet* for many critics as Shakespeare's greatest tragedy.

Gloucester and Lear symbolize the plight of the elderly—whether guilt-ridden and dethroned monarchs or powerless, lonely outcasts haunted by memories and facing poverty and imminent death. The story of these two old men distills the experience of growing old—its despair and panic, its desperation for dignity and affection, and its sense of ingratitude and neglect—as the world goes on without them. Add to that plight the devastating pessimism regarding justice in an indifferent universe, and Shakespeare paints a malignancy at the core of the human heart. Enlightenment comes only through suffering; this enlightenment for Lear comes at the expense of his kingdom and the life of his faithful daughter Cordelia; for Gloucester spiritual wisdom arrives at the cost of his own vision. Just as Lear achieves spiritual wisdom when he goes mad, Gloucester achieves it when he is physically blinded.

Yet, to say merely that Lear and Gloucester learn something precious and significant is not to deny that they are broken and devastated by their brutal humiliation. Misery teaches Lear what he never could know as king about other poor wretches who have been pelted by the storm of existence: "O, I have ta'en/Too little care of this! Take physic, pomp;/Expose thyself to feel what wretches feel,/That thou mayest shake the superflux to them/And show the heavens more just" (III.iv.28–36). Both Gloucester and Lear drive virtuous children into exile (Cordelia and Edgar) and place themselves at the mercy of the wicked (Goneril, Regan, and Edmund). By the play's catastrophe, the appearance and the reality of justice have changed places along with folly and wisdom and blindness and seeing. *King Lear* repeatedly questions the existence of heaven only to provide ambiguous answers: "If you do love old men/If your sweet sway/Allow obedience, if you yourselves are old,/Make it your cause" (II.iv.191–193), Lear implores the gods, his exhortations mounting into frenzy before finally the heavens send down an answer—a storm on Lear himself.

Yet good does exist in this malignant universe: Servants obey their better instincts and turn against Cornwall to minister to Gloucester, doomed Cordelia forgives and cherishes her father, and Edgar ministers to Gloucester. These displays go directly against Edmund's amoral view of humanity and his naturalistic view of the universe in which morality, religion, and conscience are empty myths. The play suggests that villainy will indeed destroy itself, not simply because the gods are just but because insatiable ambition leads to violent death. Edmund, Goneril, and Regan all are consumed by their own lust and thus doom themselves. Yet despite this reassurance that villainy eventually undoes itself, *King Lear*, in its appalling devastation, refuses to answer its central questions about justice. Poetic justice and cause and effect do not account for political order or the enormity of personal disaster. Love's power is at last discovered in its very defeat, though it is learned far too late.

Shakespeare wrote *King Lear* no earlier that 1603 or 1604 and probably in 1605, between *Othello* (ca. 1603–04) and *Macbeth* (ca. 1606–07), while at the height of his literary powers. It was performed at Court in December 1606. However, throughout its earlier history, the ancient Lear story always ended happily. The earliest known version of the story appears in Geoffrey of Monmouth's *Historia Regum Britanniae* (ca. 1136) and records that Lear is overthrown by his sons-in-law—more than by his daughters—and restored to the throne by the intervention of the French king. Shakespeare was familiar with 16th-century Tudor versions that retained the happy ending: John Higgin's account in *The First Part of the Mirror for Magistrates* (1574), Raphael Holinshed's *Chronicles* (1587), Edmund Spenser's *The Faerie Queen*, and a play called *The True Chronicle History of King Leir* (1594, though not published until 1605). But Shakespeare's probable source for the tragic pattern and the Gloucester-Edgar-Edmund plot is Sir Philip Sydney's *Arcadia*, in which the Paphylagonian king falls victim to filial deceit and ingratitude. Yet Shakespeare's authority was not enough to overcome the public's craving for a happy resolution. In 1681, Nahum Tate's adaptation—which banished the fool, united Edgar and Cordelia in marriage, and restored Lear to the throne—held the English stage for nearly 150 years. David Garrick restored a portion of Shakespeare's lines, and Edmund Kean restored the tragic ending, but it was not until 1838 that *King Lear* was again performed more or less as Shakespeare had intended.

The Films

Shakespeare's tragedy first appeared on the screen in a handful of forgettable efforts in the Silent period and in the 1930s. In 1909, J. Stuart Blackton and William V. Ranous directed the first film adaptation of *King Lear*, followed in 1916 by Ernest C. Warde's version. In 1934, Harry Thomashefsky brought *The Yiddish King Lear* to American moviehouses, but film adaptations of the play did not appear again until the advent of television. The first television adaptation was produced by the BBC and directed by Royston Morley with William Devlin in the title role and Patrick Troughton as Edmund. In 1953, CBS and Omnibus featured director Andrew McCullough and producer Peter Brook's adaptation starring Orson Welles in the first American television version.

In 1970, Russian filmmaker Grigori Kozintsev released the first major foreign film version of Shakespeare's play with *Karol Lir*, adapted from Boris Pasternak's Russian translation of *King Lear*; it took few liberties with the structure, except, as Nigel Andrews noted, for one "startling omission," Gloucester's "illusory suicide attempt at Dover." Kozintsev's *Lear* is a Christian-Marxist tale of redemption and social renewal that presents the story of an individual's journey from insensitive ignorance to self-knowledge and pity. It follows the New Testament adage: To find oneself, one must first lose oneself. It is a meditation on the nature of reality and stoic endurance after civilization is stripped away. Though there is tremendous suffering and cruelty, there is also a discernable progression from materialistic tyranny to basic questioning and a deepening understanding. For Kozintsev, *King Lear* is a play localized both in cruelty and in mercy. His is a more romantic film. Yuri Jarvet's Lear is a weaker, more pathetic figure than is usually presented. This frailty heightens the sense of injustice in the suffering he endures. This Lear's violent responses become more interior. The end is not meaningless; rather, it is the beginning. Cruelty will still go on, but there are signs of renewal everywhere. For Kozintsev, *Lear* is not merely "a drama of a particular group of people who are linked by plot, but also a stream of history. Whole structures of life and social situations are carried along and tumbled together. Not only single voices are heard in the din of tragedy but combined and mighty ensembles, whole choruses." From Kozintsev's perspective on Russian and Soviet history, absolute dictatorship is both a cultural legacy and a living historical memory.

Kozintsev's film is a superimposition of the Middle Ages and the Renaissance. Visually, it is elaborate. Musically, Shostakovich's orchestral score moves the film toward a Russian romantic epic style, structurally significant by adding a more ornate, denser texture. Though it romantically builds toward large dramatic moments, Kozintsev's treatment is brutal and animalistic. Technically, the Russian uses associative montage more consistently to generate meaning between shots and uses camera movement to sweep upward at emotional peaks, or restless tracking shots as characters both pursue and are pursued. Kozintsev's central scene is the capture of Lear and Cordelia in which good triumphs over evil, even as evil prepares to destroy it. Here, in the depiction of the love between father and daughter, and in Edmund's uncomprehending hatred of it, lies the film's most powerful confirmation of love's power and it overrides the suffering at the end. Kozintsev's film represents the life of a willful ruler through its reflection in the lives of his subjects. The tragic destiny of Lear expresses at the same time the destiny of a people.

Having once said that Shakespeare was impossible to film, director Peter Brook in 1971 released his major adaptation of *King Lear*. Shot during the winter of 1968–69, on location in North Jutland, Denmark, Brook set the tragedy in a pagan, pre-Christian society that would still be sophisticated enough in its commentary on social relationships as to be viable for both the Elizabethan and the modern audience. Brook's version is a bleak, existential tale of meaningless violence in a cold, empty universe, beginning in silence and ending with civilization left in ruins. He shows the apocalyptic decline and fall of an archetypal kingdom and its rulers. His is a story of lust for power that consumes the bonds of love between parents and children, a story of jealousy, blindness, and vanity. It is a highly violent film, which assaults its audience with mental cruelty. Nature, though amoral and nihilistic, is infused with aggression and brutality. The absence of justice leaves evil destroying both itself and the good with devastation, emptiness, and scarred individuals too stunned to continue. Lear's generalized pain reflects the shattering of Christian humanist values like forgiveness, compassion, and humility.

Brook's interpretive vision duplicates in cinematic terms Shakespeare's blend of stage artifice and imaginative reality. He also avoids sentimentality to heighten the bleakness of the tale and the power of the scenes

Opposite Paul Scofield's King Lear was Jack MacGowan as the Fool. (COURTESY NATIONAL FILM SOCIETY ARCHIVES)

between Lear (Paul Scofield) and Cordelia (Annelise Gabold) and between Lear and Gloucester (Alan Webb); one effect is the total elimination of Edmund's reformation and attempt to save Lear and Cordelia's lives. (Edmund is played by Ian Hogg, Edgar by Robert Lloyd; Goneril is played by Irene Worth, Regan by Susan Engel; Jack MacGowran plays Lear's Fool.)

The central scene in Brook's version is Lear's beach conversation with Gloucester; here, the simplicity of a blind subject meeting his insane king is heightened by the ferocity and expressionism of the rest of the film. This scene's emotional power lies in its adherence to Shakespeare's mixture of the general and the specific. Brook concludes his perspective on *Lear* in the film's final shot. Contrasting with the film's opening darkness, this version ends on a gravel beach bathed in glaring white light with Lear, kneeling over Cordelia's body; surrounded by nothingness, he falls backward in slow motion, disappearing from the screen. This image leaves a sense of unrelieved hopelessness and emptiness.

Brook's interpretation of *King Lear* is raw, primitive, ascetic, and stripped to nothingness. He uses disjointed images, superimpositions, surreal appearances, crude surfaces, washed-out and grainy black-and-white images, close-ups, and shallow depth of field to increase a sense of solipsism. The actors understate their lines in slow, gruff whispers, which are essentially devoid of music. Much of Shakespeare's exposition is stripped away and the subplot pared to the leanest elements. Though criticized as self-conscious and flashy, Brook's character-centered version is also a minimalist response to the decorative spectacle of previous Shakespeare adaptations.

Adaptations of Shakespeare's tragedy during the remainder of the 1970s and early 1980s were television productions. In 1975, Jonathan Miller directed a BBC adaptation with Michael Hordern as Lear; then, in 1982, Miller directed a joint American-British venture between BBC and Time-Life that also featured Hordern as Lear. In 1977 the Joseph Papp "Theatre in America" series featured the leading African-American actor James Earl Jones as Lear in a New York Shakespeare Festival production that also featured Paul Sorvino (Gloucester), Raul Julia (Edmund), and Rene

Auberjonois (Edgar); the production was not successful with the critics. In 1983, Michael Elliott mounted a Granada Television production starring Sir Laurence Olivier as Lear, Dorothy Tutin (Goneril), Diana Rigg (Regan), Leo McKern (Gloucester), Colin Blakely (Kent), and John Hurt as Lear's Fool. Thanks to such an outstanding cast, this production was much praised, though some liberties were taken with the text and perhaps too much emphasis was placed on Lear's enemies rather than on his suffering. (One possible Shakespeare derivative should arguably be mentioned in passing, Paul Mazursky's *Harry and Tonto* [1974], for which Art Carney won an Academy Award; but to consider this otherwise touching story of a 72-year-old English teacher evicted from his New York apartment with his cat, Tonto, as an updating of *King Lear* is perhaps too much of a stretch.)

In 1985, Japanese director Akira Kurosawa relocated *King Lear* to medieval Japan, rendering Lear an aging feudal warlord. In doing so, he offers a variation on legend and history that contradicts orthodox, institutionalized culture. *Ran* (translated as "chaos") ironically represents the historical conditions of samurai power. Though the first inspiration for the movie came through his idea to invert the legend of Motonari Mori (1497–1571), Kurosawa, in scripting *Ran*'s story of a feared but aging ruler deposed by his disloyal sons, noticed the similarities with Shakespeare's tragedy. However, in considering *King Lear* Kurosawa was puzzled that the English dramatist had not given his characters a past: How did Lear acquire the power that, as an old man, he abuses with such disastrous effects and what accounted for his daughters' ferocious response to their father's attempts to step down? Kurosawa answered such questions by creating a past political career for the ruler and setting events in a specific era. Since the setting is medieval Japan, the fictional Great Lord Hidetora Ichimonji's line of descent had to be male—to divide a kingdom among daughters would have contradicted history. Though Kurosawa drew plot elements, significant incidents, and central metaphors from Shakespeare's tragedy, his treatment is controlled by his original intention of inverting Japanese ideals of family and political loyalty.

In Kurosawa's perspective on the era of Japanese history in which he sets the events of *Ran*, absolute power is based on a legacy of ruthlessness. Amidst the suffering and chaos that results from Hidetora's ill-conceived plans for peace through shared power with his three sons, he encounters the survivors of his own savage conquest of the kingdom years earlier. This dramatic movement through the ruins of past ambition and war is distinctly different in structure from the immediacy of the tragedy that follows from King Lear's demand for professions of love and from his rash temper, which theater audiences directly witness. This aside, *Ran* has a stronger intertextual connection to Shakespeare in terms of the play's figurative language rather than in terms of incident, characterization, or description. The narrower dramatic action eliminates the Gloucester subplot while transposing other elements from it. Kurosawa condenses and intensifies events and character traits. Through its remarkable costumes, sets, scenes, and cinematography, Kurosawa considers his film more hopeful, less pessimistic, and less tragic than Shakespeare's play. While King Lear has no regrets, does not contemplate his past, and needlessly falls, Hidetora reflects on his past and regrets it. *Ran* lacks the archetypal pattern of Western tragedy's sacrifice of the hero and its promise of redemption for his society. However, in creating a detailed past of misdeeds by the main character, Kurosawa renders Hidetora not only less tragic but also less heroic than Lear. In the film's final shot of the blind Tsurumaru (Kurosawa's parallel for Gloucester and Edgar), unattended and moving toward the edge of a castle rampart, a blind and unprotected humanity stands near the edge of a precipice. This is a summation of Kurosawa's vision of what humanity is, in having brought itself to the brink of extinction. This situation is a final indication that human suffering has entirely human origins; thus, the tragedy is historical, existential, and unheroic.

The most recent film versions of *King Lear* are Jean-Luc Godard's ludicrous version, which updates Shakespeare's play to a bizarre, contemporary punk-apocalyptic setting, featuring Burgess Meredith as "Don Learo," Molly Ringwald (Cordelia), Woody Allen as a film editor, Peter Sellers as "Will Shakespeare," Godard himself as a "Professor," and Norman Mailer (for whatever reason) playing himself. This oddity was followed by Richard Eyre's 1997 television adaptation for American Public Television starring Ian Holm as a cranky, imperious Lear and Victoria Hamilton as a high-strung, quivery Cordelia.

REFERENCES

Andrews, Nigel, "King Lear," *Sight and Sound*, 41:3 (1972), 171–172; Bevington, David, ed., *The Complete Works of Shakespeare* (New York: HarperCollins, 1992); Goodwin, James, *Akira Kurosawa and Intertextual Cinema* (Baltimore: Johns Hopkins University Press, 1994); Jorgens, Jack J., *Shakespeare on Film* (Bloomington:

Indiana University Press, 1977); Kozintsev, Grigori, *King Lear: The Space of Tragedy* (Berkeley: University of California Press, 1977); Manville, Roger, *Shakespeare and the Film* (New York: Praeger, 1971); Rothwell, Kenneth S., and Annabelle Henkin Melzer, *Shakespeare on Screen: An International Filmography and Videography* (New York: Neal-Schuman, 1990); Welsh, J.M., "'To See It Feelingly': *King Lear* through Russian Eyes," *Literature/Film Quarterly*, 4:2 (1976), 153–158.

—*J.N.Y.*

KISS ME KATE

See THE TAMING OF THE SHREW

LOOKING FOR RICHARD

See RICHARD III

LOVE'S LABOUR'S LOST (1594–95)

Love's Labour's Lost (2000), U.K., directed and adapted by Kenneth Branagh; Pathe Pictures/Miramax.

The Play

Perhaps written as early as 1593 or 1594, *A Pleasant Conceited Comedie Called Love's Labour's Lost* was first published under that full title in the First Quarto edition of 1598 and was the first time that Shakespeare's name appeared on a title page. It was advertised as having been "presented before her Highness [Queen Elizabeth I] this last Christmas." The play is an academic satire about young King Ferdinand of Navarre, who has decided to take his books rather too seriously, removing himself and three courtly gentlemen—Dumain, Longaville, and Berowne—from his Court and from the company of women for a three-year period. His dedication to celibacy and scholarship is challenged, however, by the presence of four attractive noblewomen, embedded in the plot to shake the men's resolve. There is much pedantry and wordplay in evidence here. The king's "little Academe" in the play pokes fun at the pretensions of French and Italian philosophical debating societies, which had become popular among the educated in Shakespeare's time.

Balanced against the high-minded courtly characters are low-comedy types derived from the Italian *commedia dell'arte*—the pedantic schoolmaster Holofernes, for example; the "braggart" Don Adriano de Armado, described as a "fantastical Spaniard"; the quick-witted fool Moth; and the slow-witted one, Costard. By Act Four the king is in love with the visiting princess, Dumain with Katherine, Longaville with Maria, and even Berowne, who ridicules the others for their hypocrisy, with Rosaline. Act Five indulges in a farce of mistaken identities, as the lords disguise themselves as Russians and the ladies don masks. This is followed by a masque of "The Nine Worthies": Pompey (Costard), Alexander (Nathaniel), Judas Maccabaeus (Holofernes), Hercules (Moth), and Hector (Armado). At the end the princess is recalled to France by the news that her father has died. Romantic consummation is therefore to be postponed for a year to test the lovers, secluded in a "forlorn and naked hermitage." Thus "Our wooing doth not end like an old play," Berowne advises the audience: "Jack hath not Jill."

The Film

By no means Shakespeare's most popular comedy, *Love's Labour's Lost* was not produced as a feature film until 1999, only to be released to tepid reviews in America in 2000. There were two television treatments, however: in 1965 BBC-2 captured a Bristol Old Vic performance directed by Roger Jenkins and the BBC "Shakespeare Plays" series production in 18th-century costume directed by Elijah Moshinsky in 1984, which was not a critical success. Perhaps a knowledge of these lackluster attempts prompted Kenneth Branagh's oddly flamboyant, oddly adapted, and greatly transformed approach. As *Variety* described it, Shakespeare's play was "hacked down into a faux, old-style Hollywood tuner and given the handle 'A Romantic Musical Comedy.'"

Because of the thinness of the contrived plot, director Kenneth Branagh decided to give the play a postmodern hydraulic life, setting it in the early 20th century (September 1939, to be exact) and striving mightily to turn it into a boulevardish comedy, into a Hollywood musical that would augment the language of Shakespeare with the music and lyrics of George and Ira Gershwin, Jerome Kern, Cole Porter, and Irving Berlin—anything that would make the play amusing for an audience less than attuned to the wordplay. Critics were dubious about whether the cast was up to the challenge of being Shakespearean actors, singers, and dancers. This is not so much an adaptation as a substitution. Stanley Kauffmann estimated that two-thirds of Shakespeare's language had been discarded, all the more surprising since in his previous Shakespeare outing, *Hamlet*, Branagh had produced a four-hour film that was absolutely faithful to every word of every speech in the published record of the play up to 1623. By appropriating the songs of other talents, Branagh had to jettison one of Shakespeare's most famous songs, because, he explained, "It just couldn't be reconciled with the great modern songs we decided to use."

Of course, *Love's Labour's Lost* is not *Hamlet* and not the product of Shakespeare's most mature art. Among the comedies, *Love's Labour's Lost* pales in comparison to *Twelfth Night* and *A Midsummer Night's Dream*, plays that had been done and redone before Branagh could have a go at them. Trevor Nunn beat him to the punch with *Twelfth Night* and Michael Hoffman with *A Midsummer Night's Dream*. So Branagh apparently opted for the overdone rather than the redone so as to avoid the redundant. As a consequence, Branagh decided to "face the music, and dance."

Branagh's concept seems to have sprung full-blown, not from the brow of Zeus, but from that of Woody Allen when Branagh was involved in another ill-advised project, Allen's *Celebrity*, after Allen had taken what Gary Arnold called "an eccentric swing at musical comedy in *Everyone Says I Love You*." However, Allen was not screwing around with Shakespeare in that film, and Woody Allen has a more finely honed sense of comedy than Kenneth Branagh, *Much Ado About Nothing* notwithstanding. Branagh had played the amorous king of Navarre in his Royal Shakespeare Company production, which, like Branagh's filmed *Hamlet*, had moved the play up in time to the 1870s. The film moved the time-frame forward by another 70 years so that Branagh could lard it with Schmaltz from the swing era and maybe a touch of *Casablanca*. This pop-culture extravaganza was not likely to impress the purists.

Stanley Kauffmann, a critic who understood theater as well as anyone reviewing films when *Love's Labour's Lost* was released, is not a purist, but he does respect the language of Shakespeare, which Branagh slighted. But Kauffmann was most displeased by the inadequacies of the cast. He found the casting of the two leads—Alessandro Nivola and Alicia Silverstone as the king and princess—"dull or dreadful." As the Spaniard Don Armado, Timothy Spaull—who had played the sleaziness of Eric Lyle brilliantly in Bernardo Bertolucci's *The Sheltering Sky* and who was a fine Guildenstern in Branagh's *Hamlet*—has trouble both dancing and delivering the Cole Porter song given to him to perform.

Of the eight principals, Kauffmann found only Branagh himself "impressive" and dismissed Alessandro Nivola and Alicia Silverstone as being "inadequate in every way," though the *Variety* reviewer claimed that Silverstone was able to "hold her own" in a "sporty" performance. Branagh gave himself the role of Berowne, the most verbal and eloquent of the attendant lords, who, with just under 600 lines, has the play's longest part. Natascha McElhone plays Rosaline to Branagh's Berowne, and Richard Briers, who played a sinister Polonius in Branagh's *Hamlet*, is cast as Nathaniel, a curate. Costard (Nathan Lane) is reimagined as a vaudeville clown, and Dull (Jimmy Yuill) as a police constable.

For Kauffmann the enterprise was "not completely lost," thanks to Geraldine McEwan, who plays the "schoolmistress Holofornia (Shakespeare's Holofernes transgendered) with her imperishable wit and charm," and Nathan Lane, who Kauffmann found impeccable as Costard, the clown who has the honor of singing the showstopper, "There's No Business Like Show Business." Because the 10 songs are so easy, familiar, and listenable, they make what's left of the text seem more difficult than usual. The film ends somewhat awkwardly on the eve of World War II, and the war enforces the postponement of marital bliss for the lovers, providing a grim little twist at the conclusion.

Predicting disgruntled and wicked reviews, *Variety* warned that Branagh would have difficulty selling the concept as an enjoyable, "slightly campy entertainment to the younger crowd" because there were "few recent precedents for such a picture," though one possible precedent may be the work of Dennis Potter, no doubt unknown to most younger viewers. Branagh assumed the mantle of Lord Olivier in 1989 with his spectacularly good treatment of *Henry V* and has gone on to become the world's foremost popularizer of Shakespeare. His previous attempts all hit the mark with varying degrees of accuracy, but *Love's Labour's Lost* surely misfired both with audiences and critics.

REFERENCES

Ansen, David, "Shakespeare Less Loved," *Newsweek* (June 12, 2000), 74; Arnold, Gary, "The Bard Keeps Branagh in Business," *The Washington Times*, June 16, 2000, C4; Elley, Derek, "Bold Tuner from Branagh," *Variety*, February 21–27, 2000, 50–51; Kauffmann, Stanley, "Well, Not Completely Lost," *The New Republic* (June 10 & 17, 2000), 32–33; Rothwell, Kenneth S. and Annabelle Henkin Melzer, *Shakespeare on Screen* (New York: Neal-Schuman, 1990).

—*J.M.W.*

MACBETH (1606)

Macbeth (1916), U.S.A., directed and adapted by John Emerson; Fine Arts/Reliance-Majestic.
Macbeth (1948), U.S.A., directed and adapted by Orson Welles; Republic Pictures.
Joe MacBeth (1955), U.K., directed by Ken Hughes, adapted by Philip Yordan; Film Locations/Frankovich/Columbia Pictures.
Throne of Blood/The Castle of the Spider's Web [*Kumonosu-Djo*] (1957), Japan, directed and adapted by Akira Kurosawa; Toho Films.
Macbeth (1971), U.K., directed by Roman Polanski, adapted by Kenneth Tynan and Roman Polanski, Playboy Productions/Columbia-Warner.
Macbeth (1979), U.K., directed by Trevor Nunn and Philip Casson, adapted by Thames Television.
Men of Respect (1990), U.S.A., directed and adapted by William Reilly; Central City/Ephraim Goldblatt.

The Play

Next to *Hamlet*, *Macbeth* is Shakespeare's best-known tragedy, a study of ambition's destruction of a man of conscience. First performed in 1606 and based on sources in Raphael Holinshed's *Chronicles*, the play recounts the fall of Macbeth, a military hero first introduced to us as a brave defender of King Duncan, whose reign has been threatened by foreign and native rebels. Returning to his castle and devoted wife following his army's victory, Macbeth and his fellow general Banquo are accosted by three witches who prophesy that the hero will become king, while his companion's children will one day wear the Crown. Banquo is skeptical, but Macbeth secretly embraces the prediction because it conforms to his desire for sovereignty. When Duncan and his train arrive at Macbeth's castle to celebrate, the king takes the occasion to announce that he has delegated his son Malcolm to succeed him. The news perplexes Macbeth, but Lady Macbeth urges him to remain firm and behave "like a man." She spawns a plan to stab Duncan in his sleep and blame the murder on his attendants. Macbeth's conscience troubles him, provoking in his mind's eye the vision of an imaginary dagger.

After their father's murder, Malcolm and his brother Donalbain flee to England, giving Macbeth the opportunity to hint at their guilt and assume Scotland's throne. To solidify his grip, the newly crowned king arranges the assassination of his rival Banquo on the eve of a royal banquet. Fleance, Banquo's son, manages to escape, however, keeping alive the possibility that he or his heirs might one day come to power. During the feast, Banquo's ghost takes Macbeth's place at the table, prompting the distracted host to hurl threats at the specter and declare his manhood to a stunned audience unable to see what he sees. Lady Macbeth proves incapable of restoring peace and urges the guests to depart in disorder and haste. The disruption of the banquet marks Macbeth's decline into despotism and Lady Macbeth's loss of control over her husband. He becomes more robotic, she more withdrawn and conscience-stricken.

Frantic to know "the future in an instant," Macbeth forces the witches to make clear his fate. They reassure him that "no man of woman born" will defeat him and that he will rule until "Birnam Wood come to Dunsinane [Macbeth's castle]." These pronouncements still his fears but give him unwarranted confidence in his invincibility. That confidence is shaken when Lady Macbeth suddenly dies, following a sleepwalking episode in which she reveals her guilt for Duncan's murder. Her death occurs at just the wrong moment for the besieged Macbeth: Malcolm, backed by loyal Macduff and English forces, leads his army toward Dunsinane under camouflage provided by branches from Birnam's trees. Desperate but undaunted, Macbeth battles the invaders, scorning those he kills as obviously born of women. Yet, when he confronts Macduff, whom he is reluctant to fight because he has already killed the thane's wife and children, Macbeth discovers to his dismay that his opponent was "untimely ripped" from his mother's womb. The play ends with Macduff beheading Macbeth and proudly championing Malcolm's rightful assumption of Scotland's throne. The resumed succession would have been particularly pleasing to James I, who ruled Scotland before becoming England's king and traced his lineage back to Banquo.

The Films

Several films of *Macbeth* appeared in the silent era, foremost of which was Sir Herbert Beerbohm Tree's 1916 production for the Fine Arts company (a component of the three-pronged Triangle Films studio), directed and adapted by John Emerson. (Publicity at the time claimed that the production was supervised by D.W. Griffith but was doubtless greatly exaggerated.) It was a time when stage stars by the dozens were being lured to Hollywood, and Tree's appearance promised to confer legitimacy on the production (indeed, his salary of between $3,000 and $4,000 a week was one of the highest salaries paid to an actor up to that time).

Costarring as Lady Macbeth was another stage star, Constance Collier. Because this *Macbeth* is a "lost" film, we have only historians' and contemporary critics' commentary to go on. In his history of the Triangle studio, Kalton Lahue notes that Tree "had no concept of motion pictures and continually moved out of range or frame, turning his back to the camera and grandly overexaggerating his pantomime." So bad was Tree, Lahue contends, that actor Monte Blue was called in to double many of his scenes. As for the contemporary reviews of the three-hour film, they were varied, to say the least. Writing in *The Moving Picture World* in June 1916, Lynde Denig praised the production as one that "not only visualizes the dramatic incidents completely and convincingly, but makes clear the mental processes of Macbeth and Lady Macbeth." When speech was necessary, Denig continued, "lines from the play are invariably used, and the arrangement of the scenario necessitates few explanatory leaders. It is a treat, indeed, to read so much of Shakespeare on the screen, even if some familiar quotations are slightly altered." Sir Herbert, moreover, was a "virile, compelling Macbeth, possessed of the rare art that makes possible the communication of emotional states." However, critic Julian Johnson demurred in the pages of *Photoplay* a few weeks later. He singled out Tree's performance as stiff and static: "After the first few episodes, this acting consisted, on the part of Sir Herbert, of staring and wobbling, and the staring eye when translated into black and white, becomes extremely monotonous." What is beyond dispute is that *Macbeth* was a failure at the box office. A few months later, Beerbohm Tree's movie career was likewise a footnote in history.

The first major sound production was Orson Welles's 1948 version for the B-movie studio, Republic Pictures. With the box-office failures and budget overruns of *The Lady from Shanghai* (1947) and *The Stranger* (1947) behind him, he determined to bring a film in on time and on a modest budget. Certainly Welles knew his way around Shakespeare's play, having already produced an experimental all-black "voodoo" version on Broadway for the Federal Theatre Project in the mid-1930s. The new film project, based on his production for the Utah Shakespeare Festival, and shot in just 23 days, was a daring effort, but a box-office disaster. The brilliant director of such films as *Citizen Kane* (1941) and *The Magnificent Ambersons* (1942) seemed not to care about the fate of the picture as it went into post-production. "The fact was," as biographer Barbara Leaming has written, "that as far as Orson was concerned, *Macbeth* was in a sense finished—not as a film of course, but as an experiment. In *Macbeth* Orson had never intended to make a great film; just to prove a point, to show what could be shot quickly and cheaply." As for the finished product, it transformed Shakespeare's tragedy into a morality tale about Christian good and pagan evil. This interpretation is evident in the opening sequence, during which the witches shape a mud doll representative of Macbeth that can be controlled by a kind of voodoo-like magic. Welles also created a character named Holy Father (Alan Napier) to oppose the witches; he conducts a general mass aimed at exorcising Satan after Duncan's party arrives at Macbeth's castle. During the action, he carries a cross-topped staff while the witches brandish sticks that look for all the world like television antennas. Macbeth seals his fate when he kills Holy Father with a spear during the siege of Dunsinane.

Working with a meager budget, Welles had to rely on Fred Ritter's cardboard-like sets, which looked more like leaky caves than monumental castles. He also asked his actors, many of whom had worked on his *Mercury Theatre of the Air* radio show, to speak in a Scottish burr, a decision that resulted in a garbled sound track to go along with the generally murky chiaroscuro of the cinematography. A weak performance by Jeanette Nolan as Lady Macbeth and drastic cuts and transpositions further hampered the film. Most telling was, as one critic complained, the director's decision to represent the hero as a "static, two-dimensional creature" capable of villainy from the tragedy's very beginning, which strips the role and the play of their compelling psychological dimension.

An even more problematic translation is Ken Hughes's 1955 *Joe Macbeth*. Hughes and screenwriter Philip Yordan displace the tragedy into the tale of a gangster who kills his way to the top of the mob. Set in Chicago, this genre piece begins with the gunning down of boss Big Duca's (Gregoire Aslan) rival in Tommy's Café. The man behind the hit is Joe (Paul Douglas), who celebrates his newfound status with his wife Lily (Ruth Roman) in another nightclub. During the celebration, a fortune-teller named Rosie (Minerva Pious) announces that Joe will soon become "Lord of Lakeview Drive," then "King of the City." Lily urges her husband to fulfill the prophecy when Big Duca comes to the mansion for a weekend party, accompanied by Bandy (Sid Jones) and Lennie (Bonar Coleano). These two lieutenants correspond to Banquo and his son, Fleance; Joe and Lily will try to pin Big Duca's murder on them. Instead of staying in his bed, however, the boss of bosses takes a late-night swim, forcing Joe to stab and drown him. Lily has to dive into the lake to retrieve the murder weapon when her frightened husband forgets it. Joe tries to consolidate his power by killing Bandy and Lennie's wife and children. During the banquet to confirm his ascension, however, he encounters Banky's ghost and delivers the classic mobster line, "Which one-a you guys done this?"

His paranoia increasing, the hero becomes a prisoner in his own home, where he barricades himself and, in a fit of blind terror, mistakenly guns down Lily when she tries to free him from his office. Lennie finally gains his revenge by shooting Joe, then running out into a hail of bullets from the police. The film ends as another morality tale about the bitter fruits of ambition told in the context of gangster culture. Marred by amateurish acting—Ruth Roman's performance is the sole exception—unintentionally funny dialogue, and pretentious noirish sequences, *Joe Macbeth* richly deserves its place at the bottom of the remaindered videos bin.

A more compelling offshoot is Akira Kurosawa's *Throne of Blood* (1957). Bearing the characteristics of a samurai fable and an American western, *Throne* (also translated as *The Castle of the Spider's Web*) traces the career of Washizu (Toshiro Mifune), a medieval Japanese warrior who with his comrade Miki (Minoru Chiaki) defeats the rebels challenging Kuniharu's (Takamaru Sasaki) reign. On the way back from the decisive battle, the two captains lose their way in a fog-shrouded forest and encounter a ghostly figure turning a spinning wheel and singing of Washizu's rise to the position of lord of the Forest Castle. From this point, the film generally follows the *Macbeth* plot, but with some interesting variations: Asaji/Lady Macbeth (Isuzu Yamada) performs a Noh-like ritual dance after Kuniharu's murder; she tells Washizu that she is pregnant to prevent him from tapping Miki's son as his successor; Miki's murder is signaled by the return of his riderless white horse to his castle; Asaji wears a strange-looking mask while sleepwalking; and Washizu, instead of being beheaded in the finale, is pierced by hundreds of arrows that rain down on him from the bows of his own vengeful troops. This ritualized ending, one of the most horrific scenes of violence in the history of film, underscores Kurosawa's morality message that the general's own men are the only proper judges and executioners of one whose ambition transgressed their samurai code.

Roman Polanski's 1971 treatment, financed by Playboy Productions and adapted by Kenneth Tynan, seemed to many reviewers to inscribe onto the story a highly personalized code, one dealing with the life of

Jon Finch portrayed Macbeth in Roman Polanski's screen adaptation. (COURTESY COLUMBIA PICTURES)

Francesca Annis portrayed Lady Macbeth in Roman Polanski's Macbeth. (COURTESY COLUMBIA PICTURES)

Polanski himself. His wife, Sharon Tate, and the baby she was carrying had recently been brutally murdered by members of the Manson family. Polanski's obsession with graphically bloody scenes, especially Duncan's murder, appeared to have been prompted by visions of the ritual killing of his wife. The director's obsession with sexuality was thought to be mirrored in Lady Macbeth's (Francesca Annis) nude sleepwalking scene, a gratuitous sequence perhaps bespeaking the *Playboy* underwriting.

The tragedy is marked by numerous references to blood and sex, notwithstanding Polanski's own private obsessions. There's the bloody captain, gore-smeared daggers, the sexually charged relationship between Macbeth (Jon Finch) and his lady—all of which underscore the links between eroticism and power. Polanski also stressed the play's social context by introducing dogs, bears, chickens, and other objects that tend to ground the action in its historical setting. We witness the witches burying a hangman's noose, dagger, and severed hand on the beach, the rebel Cawdor mouthing "long live the king" as he is hanged in chains; a bear-baiting sequence observed closely by a fascinated Lady Macbeth. The film's mise-en-scène has been described as "claustrophobic," creating a mood in which Macbeth and others struggle, like chained bears, to escape a certain, terrible fate. Indeed, Macbeth's severed head is mocked and treated like that of an animal when he is finally brought down. Instead of a morality fable, Polanski sees *Macbeth* as a Marxist tale about the unceasing hunger for power: The final shot is of Donalbain, who, following Malcolm's coronation, seeks shelter from a driving rain and finds himself drawn to the siren-like song of the witches in their hut. The wheel of fortune, Polanski suggests, continues to turn.

Trevor Nunn's 1976 Royal Shakespeare Company stage production of Macbeth emphasized the ritual elements of the play and was distinctive for its bare set, minimal props, and the fact that all the actors were seated in a circle on stage throughout the show, effects that Philip Casson preserved in the 1979 televised version. Although the camera work never calls attention to itself, it pulls the audience into the action with probing close-ups and forces them to view the play with the intimacy and immediacy of a participant. The camera moves very close, for example, when Ian McKellen, as Macbeth in slicked-back hair and with a black leather coat thrown over his shoulders, and Judi Dench, as Lady Macbeth in a straight black dress and a black cloth tight around her head, punctuate their discussion of the prophecy with a series of kisses. Barely distinguishable from the blackened background, they convey the eroticism of power in a close-up that focuses on their bare hands and faces as they caress. In this striking and somber film, only the porter scene, played by Ian McDiarmid in broad music-hall style and with a comic Scots accent, seems to interrupt the downward spiral of its two principal characters.

The ritual quality first appears in the opening shot of a lighted circle surrounded by chairs and darkness, where the shadows of the approaching players intersect like spokes in a wheel. The remarkable banquet scene has Macbeth holding a large silver chalice as each person drinks from it. After Lady Macbeth drinks, Macbeth looks for a place at the table and finds none, then realizes that he sees Banquo's ghost (John Woodvine). No one, including the film audience, sees the ghost, but Macbeth thrusts his face into the camera, in effect making it the ghost. Momentarily recovering, Macbeth finishes off the chalice as the assembled group claps rhythmically, as if for a drinking game, but when the fit worsens he begins to sweat profusely, foam and drool running down his chin. At this point Lady Macbeth begins to lose control; she pulls back, weeps, and seems to faint, until Macbeth pulls her up, saying "We are yet but young in deed." The second prophesy scene emphasizes a different sort of violated ritual when the three witches gather around a pair of lighted candlesticks with a chalice and pot nearby, suggesting the elements of a black mass, and seem to initiate Macbeth, taking off his coat, painting crosses on his bare chest and back, and giving him a drink that puts him into a trance. Michael Mullin comments that "the apparitions, perhaps aided by something psychotropic, arise from the coincidence of Macbeth's fears and the Witches' riddling replies." The apparitions are here represented by totem figures that Macbeth carries and displays at various points in the rest of the film, holding one, for example, when he fights Macduff (Bob Peck). The last shot in the film freeze-frames the crown and two bloody daggers, describing the past, suggesting the future.

Unlike Polanski's sociopolitical reading of *Macbeth*, William Reilly's *Men of Respect* (1990) recalls *Joe Macbeth* in its attempt to recontextualize the play in the gangster-movie idiom. John Turturro plays the hero Mike Battaglia as a young, neurotic climber who displays no signs of Macbeth's conscience when, in the opening, slow-motion sequence, he guns down several mafiosi in a New York restaurant. This sequence is preceded by a voice-over chorus declaring, "There is nothing but what has a violent end or violent beginnings." Relying on the success of *The Godfather* trilogy and Martin Scorsese's *GoodFellas*, Reilly transforms Mike into a schemer for whom "respect" means more than conscience or loyalty.

Like *Joe MacBeth* the film uses a fortune-teller (Lilia Skala) instead of witches for prophecies and substitutes New York (as opposed to Chicago) street idioms for Shakespeare's verse. This descent into banality shows up most strikingly when, for example, Mike learns that his boss Charlie D'Amato (Rod Steiger) has promoted him to *capo regime*. The good news is greeted with "Whatever happens, happens." As in *Joe MacBeth*, the best performance is given by the actress—Katherine Borowitz—playing Lady Macbeth, here named Ruth. She displays genuine emotion and psychological depth as she tries to steel Mike's resolve to kill Charlie. To underline her determination, for instance, she reminds the hero that she had an abortion to further his career! Unfortunately, Borowitz's performance is the only bright spot in a disappointing offshoot that ends with a fatally injured Mike observing, "Shit happens."

REFERENCES

Andrews, Nigel, "*Macbeth*," *Sight and Sound*, 41 (Spring 1972), 108; Berlin, Normand, "*Macbeth*, Polanski, and Shakespeare," *Literature/Film Quarterly*, 1:4 (1973), 291–298; Denig, Lynde, "Macbeth," *The Moving Picture World*, 28:13 (June 24, 1916), 2258; Eckert, Charles W., ed., *Focus on Shakespearean Films* (Englewood Cliffs, N.J.: Prentice-Hall, 1972); Johnson, Julian, "Macbeth," *Photoplay*, 10:3 (August 1916), 141; Lahue, Kalton, *Dreams for Sale: The Rise and Fall of the Triangle Film Corporation* (Cranbury, N.J.: A.S. Barnes, 1971); Leaming, Barbara, *Orson Welles: A Biography* (New York: Viking Press, 1985); Mullin, Michael, "Stage and Screen: The Trevor Nunn *Macbeth*, in *Shakespeare on Television*, eds. J.C. Bulman and H.R. Coursen (Hanover, N.H.: University Press of New England, 1988), 107–115; Perret, Marion D. "Double, Double: Trevor Nunn's *Macbeth* for Television," *Shakespeare Bulletin* 10:3 (1992), 38–39; Rosenthal, Daniel, *Shakespeare on Screen* (London: Hamlyn, 2000), 192; Willson, Robert F., Jr., *Shakespeare in Hollywood, 1929–1956* (Madison, N.J.: Fairleigh Dickinson University Press, 2000).

—R.F.W. AND R.V.

MEN OF RESPECT

See MACBETH

THE MERCHANT OF VENICE (1596–97)

Il mercante de Venezia (1910), Italy, directed by Gerolamo Lo Savio, Film d'Arte Italiana

Shylock, ou le More de Venise (1913), France, directed by Henri Desfontaines, adapted by Louis Mercanton, Eclipse/George Klein.

The Merchant of Venice (1969), U.K., directed by Jonathan Miller and John Sichel, adapted by John Sichel, Precision Video.

The Merchant of Venice (1980), U.K., directed by Jack Gold, adapted by David Snodin, British Broadcasting Company/Time-Life Television.

The Merchant of Venice (2001), U.K., directed by Trevor Nunn and Chris Hunt, adapted by Trevor Nunn. ExxonMobil Masterpiece Theatre, Public Broadcasting System.

The Play

The Merchant of Venice gave the world two of Shakespeare's best-known speeches, spoken by two of his most remarkable characters. Portia's "The quality of mercy is not strained . . ." (4.1.190–210) and Shylock's "Hath not a Jew eyes?" (3.1.57–71) have both enjoyed an existence almost separate from the play, the latter speech, for example, finding a remarkable application in Ernest Lubitsch's farcical satire of Nazis in *To Be or Not to Be* (1942). Shakespeare's play begins with the melancholy Antonio deciding to borrow money so that his friend, Bassanio, can sail to Belmont to win Portia, a woman whose father, now dead, concocted a test to ensure that his daughter marries the right man. Several chains of dependency pervade the play, and each action seems connected in remote ways to nearly every other one. Antonio borrows the money from a Jewish moneylender, Shylock, who feels mistreated by the Christians in Venice and resents their intrusions in his affairs and their judgment of his methods. Shylock agrees to loan Antonio the money with the stipulation that forfeiting the loan will cost Antonio "a pound of flesh." When Shylock's daughter, Jessica, runs off with Lorenzo, a Christian, and appears to reject and abuse both her heritage and specific things that her father held dear, Shylock becomes more hostile toward the Christians. The news that Antonio's ships have been lost at sea, making him unable to repay the loan, gives Shylock a means to vent his anger against the Venetian Christian society that he believes has victimized him.

Against this somewhat tragic line of development, Shakespeare juxtaposes an unusual romance story. Portia's father has left a will stating that his daughter can marry only the man who successfully passes the test of the three caskets. In separate scenes Shakespeare shows how the prince of Morocco selects the golden casket, the prince of Aragon picks the silver one, and Bassanio, whom Portia favors, chooses the lead casket, for which he is rewarded since he chose "not by the view" (3.2.131). No sooner has Bassanio won his lady, however, than he receives the message that Shylock is preparing to take his pound of flesh from Antonio. When Portia offers to pay the amount owed several times over, Bassanio returns to Venice to repay the debt. Meanwhile Portia decides to disguise herself as a young lawyer and follow him to Venice, where she will defend her husband's friend.

The last two acts of the play focus on the theme of commitment to a bond, presenting it first from a legal perspective and then from a romantic-comedy perspective. In the famous trial scene, Shylock presses for the letter of the law and asks that the bond should be paid as stated by taking a pound of flesh from Antonio, who by this time has become symbolic of the antagonistic Christian society. When a learned doctor, a young lawyer named Lorenzo, arrives, Shylock is encouraged by the new lawyer's strict interpretation of the law. Soon, however, the lawyer, actually Portia in disguise, turns the arguments against Shylock, who was apparently unaware of the further implications of a law that protects citizens of Venice from resident aliens. Her argument ultimately costs Shylock the case, his wealth, and even his religion, reducing him to an outcast who must renounce his faith and lose all he owns in addition to suffering the disgrace of his daughter's elopement and conversion. In a comic echo of the legalistic arguments, Shakespeare has Bassanio and his man Gratiano give up their wedding rings to pay Antonio's lawyer and assistant, the men's disguised wives. By having Antonio request the rings to pay the lawyer who has saved him from Shylock, Shakespeare, in effect, reverses the earlier chain of obligations.

Leaving the world of the court and Shylock's complaint about his fate, the last act returns the play to Belmont and opens with Jessica and Lorenzo recalling previous lovers and their fate. Portia and Nerissa enter in time to change back to women's clothing, greet their husbands, and chide them for not having the rings. Rather than hold the men to the strict letter of the law, after threatening to do so the wives reveal their former identity and forgive their husbands. Just at that moment, news comes that Antonio's ships have landed, and he is now financially restored by fate as he was earlier saved from death by his friend's wife when she was disguised as a young lawyer.

The Films

Several of the silent film companies that devoted some of their production to filming Shakespeare's plays made versions of *The Merchant of Venice*. Méliès apparently used at least the title for a short film which has not survived. In America, versions included one by Vitagraph in 1908, by Thanhouser Films in 1912, and by Carl Laemmle in 1914. An Italian version appeared in 1910, a French one in 1913, a British one in 1916, and a German one in 1923, with the Italian and British versions giving some emphasis to the stories of Jessica and Shylock. The Italian *Il mercante de Venezia*, for example, exists as a nine-minute condensation of the play, hand colored, and with several scenes apparently shot in Venice. Its opening title card shifts the usual emphasis of the play from Bassanio to "Lorenzo who is in love with Jessica, daughter of Shylock the Jew." What follows, however, is the scene in which "Bassanio who is in love with Portia, begs his friend Antonio for a loan to enable him to ask for her in marriage." Robert H. Ball speculates that among the missing portions of the film might be the casket choice, but, if the title card is accurate, the caskets might have been omitted. Indeed, whether from design or omission, the romance in this version belongs primarily to Lorenzo and Jessica, leading Kenneth Rothwell to say that "the movie should rightly be re-titled, 'Daughter of Shylock.'" However, after leaving with Lorenzo, Jessica appears again in this version only when she stands and smiles approvingly at Portia's decision to disguise herself and save Antonio from Shylock's revenge, a process which is simplified along the lines suggested by the title card's summary, "Portia disguised as a lawyer, saves Antonio by reminding Shylock of the law of Venice making confiscation of lands and good the penalty for the shedding of a drop of Christian blood." Shylock (Ermete Novelli), who is turbaned and sitting on the floor sharpening his knife as the scene opens, is soon reduced to making repeated pleas for the money, but then the film ends abruptly with no return to Jessica or to the play's final action in Belmont.

The French film *Shylock, ou le More de Venise*, with French stage actor Harry Baur in the title role, brought to America in 1913 by George Kleine, was not called Shylock because of its sympathy with that character. Although Shylock had been treated as a dignified character on the Victorian stage by Henry Irving, who wrote that he saw "Shylock as the type of a persecuted race; almost the only gentleman in the play and the most ill-used," this filmed Shylock owes nothing to that interpretation. Ball cites a contemporary reviewer who wrote that "M. Baur would seem to have gone back to earlier traditions for his impersonation of Shylock, reviving memories of the time when the Jew was regarded more or less as an object of ridicule and mirth rather than sympathy." The opening titles identify Shylock as "The crafty Money Lender who for centuries has stood forth a living symbol of cunning and greed." In part one of the film, just before Antonio (Romuald Joubé) and Bassanio (Jean Hervé) visit him to ask for the loan, Shylock is shown seated on the floor throwing gold coins over his head and running his hands through the money. When he finally agrees to the loan, Shylock has difficulty letting the money actually leave his hands. The second part of the film focuses on Bassanio's choice of the right casket. When Bassanio wins Portia (Pepa Bonafé), and she kisses him, a messenger comes to tell him of Antonio's predicament. The third and last part of the film opens with the court scene. Shylock enters wearing a turban, sits on the floor, and strops his knife on his shoe. When he finally loses the case, Shylock is carried off, and the action shifts to Bassanio's giving up his ring to the lawyer, then later facing Portia to confess that he no longer has her gift. Antonio stoutly defends his friend's honor, and Portia kisses both of them. Suddenly Shylock appears again, asking whether he can at least have the principal on the loan, and the Venetians tell him he can only have punishment. When Shylock leans against a door and weeps, they laugh at him. This abbreviated version, essentially reducing the play to the interaction of these four characters, echoes the elemental drama of the mummers' play, in which, typically, an English hero faces a foreign foe in ritualized combat, a doctor resuscitates the fallen hero, and the hero then rises to kill or drive off the foreigner.

A general shift in sensibility, together with the horrific events of World War II, changed forever the context of this play, but, as John Gross points out, "It was a long time before actors and directors felt obliged to take the new situation into account." Ernest Lubitsch in *To Be or Not to Be* (1942) and Elia Kazan in *Gentleman's Agreement* (1946) use Shylock's "Hath not a Jew eyes" speech in their films to plead for a common humanity, but no significant available film version of *The Merchant of Venice* appeared until 1969, when Jonathan Miller filmed his National Theatre production of the play with

Laurence Olivier as Shylock, setting it in a 19th-century mercantile society. Gross says that "Olivier's Shylock longed for social acceptance, but when it came to it, he found that the old prejudices were still bubbling away. And the bigotry of the well-bred Christian characters was meant to be all of a piece with their other vices. They were portrayed as corrupt, cold-hearted frauds." Olivier himself claims to have modeled his characterization on George Arliss's portrayal of Benjamin Disraeli and on his own Uncle Sydney, the first Lord Olivier and governor of Jamaica, whom, Olivier says, "had a beard and looked quite Jewish."

The characters in this film do, in fact, occupy a world in which money and privilege seem the primary values. Marion D. Perret makes the point that this version shows Shylock as "a successful financier," for whom "the 'bank' is his home," even as he "puts a top hat over his skullcap in a fruitless effort to seem one with the frock-coated gentlemen who speak frostily to him." Next to Olivier's Shylock, the other characters seem to live in a superficial dandified world like that inhabited by Oscar Wilde's characters, an impression reinforced perhaps by Miller's comment that he modeled Bassanio and Antonio on "the relationship between Oscar Wilde and Boise." In Belmont, Joan Plowright's Portia certainly seems as indolent and well-cared for as the women in a Wilde play, and the handling of the Belmont scenes suggests a continuing criticism of the values of this society. Portia's suitors, here a grandiose prince of Morocco and an aged prince of Aragon, are reduced to ethnic stereotypes. Later, when two sopranos, dressed alike, deliver the "Where is fancy bred" lines in an animated, operetta-like fashion, they leave Bassanio (Jeremy Brett) with no doubt as to which casket to choose and create the impression that Portia has disingenuously trivialized the choice. In this context, Portia's accounting of herself in metaphors of trade as she congratulates Bassanio seems, as June Schlueter comments, "testimony to the endurance of Venetian values over Belmont's."

Against this world stands Shylock, with many of his hate-filled lines excised and an emphasis instead on his sense of personal and familial loss. By turn, he is shaken when he discovers that Jessica has left, jubilant when he discovers Antonio's ships have foundered, and filled with grief when he finds his daughter has traded his ring for a monkey. Miller has the camera linger in a moment of silence on the broken Shylock pulling his shawl around himself. Other touches that reinforce this characterization include the surprising offstage wail of grief heard just after Shylock leaves the court and the mournful sound of the Kaddish, the Jewish requiem, played as a saddened Jessica separates herself from the cheerful Christians in Belmont to read the letter telling her father's fate. Gross believes that "Even Olivier's magnetism could not lend credibility to a Shylock who did not grow out of either Jewish history or Shakespeare's text, but who had been specially manufactured for the occasion," and he finds the "'authentic' Jewish touches . . . particularly false in context."

Jonathan Miller also produced the 1980 version of *The Merchant of Venice* that Jack Gold directed for the BBC series *The Shakespeare Plays*. The earlier National Theatre version emphasized Shylock's attempt to look like his 19th-century counterparts, and Olivier played the role with restrained emotions that burst out only at moments when he is isolated and therefore unconcerned with saving face. The BBC version puts Shylock back in the Renaissance world where the obvious dissimilarities in attire underscore the other differences between Shylock and the world around him. Olivier's clipped speech gives way to Warren Mitchell's heavy accent. In Mitchell's Shylock the pain seeps through the humor that he wraps around his sharpest lines. He is short, animated, gesturing and joking in his delivery; a kind of salesman trying to work a hostile audience, an earthy man who pumps his arm as he tries to explain "the work of generation." More of a conniver than Olivier's desperately dignified Shylock, Mitchell's Shylock, instead of having his less acceptable views omitted, delivers them in cautious asides, momentarily taking the audience into his confidence as he continually struggles between what he feels and what he can safely say.

In general, this BBC version presents a more openly hostile world than the National Theatre version, but it is a hostility that cuts both ways. Miller, in an interview, makes the point that, while "the play's central theme is the conflict between the world of the Old Testament and the world of the New Testament," Shakespeare also "shows us that those who are the exponents of mercy act unmercifully when given the opportunity to use the law against the Jew." If Shylock is violent in both his asides and his intentions, the Christians in this version are very physical in their contemptuous treatment of Shylock. When Salarino and Solanio taunt Shylock that his daughter Jessica has left him, this version has the hefty Venetians manhandle and then laugh at Shylock as he delivers the "Hath not a Jew eyes" speech. Later in the trial scene, when Shylock realizes he is defeated, Gratiano knocks him to the floor and pulls his beard, while the other Christians form a threatening circle around him. Ironically, after the

Duke points out that the Christians are more merciful, Gratiano knocks the yarmulke from Shylock's head, and Salarino takes an elaborate and large cross from around his own neck, and, placing it on Shylock, forces him to kiss it. Through all this, Shylock writhes in pain. Perret comments that "the anguish and horror on Shylock's face as Salerio drops his cross over the Jew's head proclaim that Shylock regards its chain as the noose Gratiano wished upon him." When Shylock asks that the papers be sent to his home because he is not well and will sign them there later, it is not difficult to believe that this Shylock will soon die. The effect is to make it seem that it is not just mercantile Venice that is villainous but Christian Venice.

Following the modern interpretation that Renaissance notions of friendship amount to sexual ambivalence, Antonio, as played by John Franklyn-Robbins, is visibly perturbed by Bassanio's request for money to pursue Portia (Gemma Jones), and, in the last scene at Belmont, when Bassanio (John Nettles) and Portia kiss, Antonio lowers his head. In the film's last shot, after the happy lovers have left the stage, Antonio walks slowly away as mournful music plays and sits alone for a final silhouette as the shot fades to a still frame. This version also emphasizes the sacrificial quality of Antonio's role, where, in the trial scene, Bassanio and the others hold Antonio's arms out while Antonio, pale and bare chested, braces himself for Shylock's knife, a visual image of the crucifixion. Yet, with the ensuing treatment of the defeated Shylock, the film suggests that the characters only change roles in repeated enactments of cruelty and revenge.

On balance, the other relationships in the BBC version also seem muted and murky. Jessica (Leslee Udwin), a particularly rebellious daughter to Shylock, seems less in love with Lorenzo than eager to escape her father. Given her sneering, mocking attitude, her stealing Shylock's money, squandering it, and selling his ring to purchase a monkey, suggest contempt and even a malice not too far removed from what his Christian tormentors deliver. In this version Portia seems cool and competent rather than romantic. When her lines call for her to judge the suitors, she imitates their speech, including Aragon's lisp. When the prince of Morocco leaves after making the wrong choice, the camera moves to a close-up for her to say "let all of his complexion choose me so." In the courtroom, the pale and delicate lady, when dressed as the young lawyer, seems somewhat reserved and unimpassioned, making her speech on mercy seem more like an attempt to define the term rather than an plea for compassion.

Trevor Nunn says that his Royal National Theatre production of *The Merchant of Venice*, restaged and filmed for ExxonMobil Masterpiece Theatre, broadcast on PBS, developed out of his attempt to reconcile the apparent racism in the play with his own sense "that Shakespeare is the greatest humanist who has ever lived." Nunn set his production in the late 1920s, he says, "Because it was that very period when anti-Semitic thought and anti-Semitic behavior was becoming current and even . . . voguish and the subject of wit and amusement." The effect of this shift in time looms over everything in the play, since all the emotions and incidents must somehow foreshadow the Holocaust. The slightly decadent world of this production opens in a smoky after-hours nightclub where the melancholy Antonio (David Bamber) punctuates his lines with a bit of piano playing. When Gratiano (Richard Henders) and Bassanio (Alexander Hanson) enter, dressed like the rest in tuxedos, Gratiano steps up to an open microphone to say some of his lines in a drunken voice. When Bassanio asks for the money, Antonio goes over to his table and tousles his hair before he agrees to stand for the loan. Meanwhile, back in Belmont, Portia (Derbhle Crotty) strikes languid poises while Nerissa (Alex Kelly) runs black-and-white movies of Portia's suitors as the two women evaluate their qualities. Henry Goodman's Shylock is somewhere between Olivier's and Mitchell's, a businessman in black suit and overcoat, revealing a yarmulke under his fedora, but accented, full of gestures and mannerisms, conspiratorially engaging the audience by speaking into the camera, but clearly a complex person in a complicated world.

The contrast between the café world of the Christians and the ghetto world of the Jews becomes an important part of this version. Shylock is patriarchal and imposing in his home and speaks Yiddish when he orders Jessica (Gabrielle Jourdan) about. She is an unhappy, frustrated young woman in a plain dress and a thin sweater, finding solace in the kindness of Launcelot (Andrew French) and seeking escape through her love for Lorenzo (Jack James). Later, when Shylock is getting ready to have supper with the Christians, he and Jessica have a tender moment in which they sing together in Hebrew, yet when he tells Jessica to shut his house against the Christian revelers, he slaps her in the face, seems to regret doing so, and then, just before he leaves, stares briefly at a photograph of his apparently dead wife.

This production gives a full range of responses to Shylock. In their bargaining about the loan, Antonio angrily and impatiently interrupts Shylock and seems to force him into their peculiar bond. Later, Launcelot's complaints about Shylock become a stand-up routine that he delivers to the café crowd, interrupted, however, when Shylock comes through on his way to his dinner with the Christians. Solanio and Salarino seem jarred by the intensity of Shylock's "Hath not a Jew eyes" speech. At the opening of the court scene, the young, suited Venetians react to Tubal as though he were an intruder in their club, their hostility civil and smiling, though no less insidious, even as they try to block Shylock's entrance to the courtroom. When Shylock says "The pound of flesh which I demand of him/Is dearly bought," he momentarily breaks down and has to pause. His behavior contrasts strongly with the bullying Gratiano who must be physically restrained. Then, as Portia sits and engages him with the "quality of mercy" speech, Shylock seems conflicted but then struggles through to his passion. When Shylock is about to take the pound of flesh, Tubal stands, comes close to Shylock, looks at him, then averts his eyes and leaves. Hearing Bassanio and Gratiano say they would sacrifice their wives to save Antonio, Shylock again becomes impassioned, regretting that his own daughter is married to one of these "Christian husbands." He holds the knife to Antonio's bare chest, hesitates quiveringly, falls back, and holds his hand to his forehead. Defeated at the end, Shylock drops his yarmulke on the scales before he leaves the courtroom, shaken but still working to preserve his dignity.

Finally, in Belmont, Jessica, whose material fortunes have clearly risen since she left her home and joined Lorenzo, remains under her father's influence. As Trevor Nunn explains, "She realizes that people continue to see her as alien and even joke about her alien nature, and she feels very much an outsider." At the end of the play, when Jessica breaks into song after reading the letter describing her father's fate, according to Nunn, "She sings that song again in Hebrew because that is her identity, and she is not going to masquerade in a different identity again." The Christian couples stare at her, then Portia notes that the sun rises, and the film ends.

REFERENCES:

Ball, Robert Hamilton, *Shakespeare on Silent Film* (London: George Allen and Unwin Ltd., 1968); Gross, John, *Shylock: A Legend and Its Legacy* (New York: Simon and Schuster, 1992); Hallinan, Tim, "Miller on the Shakespeare Plays," (*Shakespeare Quarterly* (1981): 134–145; Lelyveld, Toby, Shylock on the Stage (London: Routledge & Kegan Paul Ltd., 1961); Miller, Jonathan, *Subsequent Performances* (New York: Viking, 1986); Nunn, Trevor, "An Interview with Trevor Nunn," (*The Merchant of Venice,* ExxonMobil Masterpiece Theatre, www.pbs.org/wgbh/masterpiece/merchant/ei_nunn.html); Olivier, Laurence, *On Acting* (New York: Touchstone, 1986); Perret, Marion D., "Shakespeare and Anti-Semitism: Two Television Versions of *The Merchant of Venice,*" *Shakespeare on Television* ed. J. C. Bulmann and H. R. Courson (Hanover, N.H.: University Press of New England, 1988); Taylor, Neil, "National and Racial Stereotypes in Shakespeare Films," *The Cambridge Companion to Shakespeare on Film,* ed. Russell Jackson (Cambridge, England: Cambridge University Press, 2000): 261–273; Schlueter, June, "Trivial Pursuit: The Casket Plot in the Miller/Olivier 'Merchant'" (*Shakespeare on Television,* ed. J. C. Bulman and H. R. Courson, Hanover, N.H.: University Press of New England, 1988): 169–174; Willis, Susan, *The BBC Shakespeare Plays: Making the Televised Canon* (Chapel Hill: University of North Carolina Press, 1991).

—R.V.

A MIDSUMMER NIGHT'S DREAM (1595)

A Midsummer Night's Dream (1935), U.S.A., directed by Max Reinhardt and William Dieterle, adapted by Charles Kenyon and Mary C. McCall; Warner Bros.

A Midsummer Night's Dream (1964), U.K., directed by Joan Kemp-Welch, adapted by George Rylands; Rediffusion.

A Midsummer Night's Dream (1969), directed and adapted by Peter Hall; RSC Ent. Warner Bros.

A Midsummer Night's Dream (1982), U.S.A., directed by James Lapine and Emile Ardolino; ABC Video.

A Midsummer Night's Dream (1982), U.K., directed by Elijah Moshinsky, adapted by David Snodin; British Broadcasting Company/Time-Life Television.

A Midsummer Night's Dream (1996), U.K., directed and adapted by Adrian Noble; Channel Four Films.

William Shakespeare's A Midsummer Night's Dream (1999), directed and adapted by Michael Hoffman; Fox Searchlight Pictures.

The Play

The play begins in anticipation of the marriage of Theseus and Hippolyta and ends with their wedding celebration, and a comic masque, "A tedious brief scene of young Pyramus and his love Thisbe," involving "very tragical mirth," performed by a troupe of Athenian tradesmen led by Peter Quince and Bottom, the Weaver. But "the course of true love never did run smooth," and that is certainly the case for four young lovers who are unfortunately mismatched. Hermia loves Lysander, but is also loved by Demetrius, who is the choice of her father, Egeus, to marry her. Helena loves Demetrius, who has eyes only for Hermia. When Theseus rules that Hermia must marry Demetrius, Hermia and Lysander decide to elope into the forest and escape the obligations of Athenian law. They are pursued into the forest by Demetrius and Helena and find themselves caught up in a net of enchantment and frustration.

Deep in the forest, they are noticed by Oberon, king of the Fairies, who takes pity on Helena and instructs Puck, his mischief-making henchman, to enchant Demetrius with a love potion so that he will fall in love with Helena. By mistake Puck enchants Lysander instead, who rejects Hermia for Helena. Helena finds herself courted by two randy young men after Demetrius is also put under the spell of the love potion, and confusion ensues, until, toward morning, Puck reverses the spell on Lysander. Puck also works his mischief on Bottom the Weaver as the artisans rehearse their absurd play in the forest, transforming him into a half-beast with the head of an ass. Oberon has demanded that Titania, his Fairy Queen, surrender to him a young Indian boy, a changeling who has been in her service. When she refuses, Oberon tells Puck to work a spell on her while she sleeps that will humiliate her and teach her a lesson of submission. When she awakens, she will fall in love with the first creature she sees, monstrous Bottom, whom she takes for a lover. Bottom takes this all in stride, but after Titania has been humiliated, Puck lifts the spell and Bottom is restored to his former self.

The play ends at court, with multiple marriages: Theseus and Hippolyta, Demetrius and Helena, and Lysander and Hermia, despite her father's objections. The wedding masque is performed, and the rude mechanicals perform their absurd play of Pyramus and Thisbe. Puck concludes the play with his "If we spirits have offended" Epilogue, and all live happily ever after.

The Films

The first film to treat the play in part was a 1909 Vitagraph production directed by the stage actor Charles Kent, shot in Brooklyn's Prospect Park and Flatbush. Italian and German versions were filmed in 1913, and a later German version that appeared in 1925 employed double exposures and a female Puck. But Shakespeare demands sound, and the Warner Bros.' adaptation of Shakespeare's comedy was the first talking adaptation of the play, and certainly one of the most entertaining in its extravagance and silliness. The Austrian impresario Max Reinhardt, who had staged the play frequently between 1905 and 1934, directed the film with William Dieterle.

The production overloads the text with non-Shakespearean material. The orchestral music of Felix Mendelssohn and the fairy dance performed by a Russian ballet troupe extend the action and, although decidedly atmospheric, tend to be distracting for those expecting the language of Shakespeare, which is abbreviated and sometimes mangled by the studio contract players, with the exceptions of Ian Hunter (Theseus) and Victor Jory, who plays an imposing and imperious Oberon. Warner Brothers threw all of its resources into the film, including such contract players as Jimmy Cagney as Bottom, Mickey Rooney as Puck, Olivia de Havilland as Hermia, Jean Muir as Helena, Dick Powell as Lysander, Ross Alexander as Demetrius, and an unforgettable Joe E. Brown as Francis Flute, who is given the role of Thisbe in the masque. The film was nominated for three Academy Awards for 1935, including best picture, best cinematography (Hal Mohr), and best film editing (Ralph Dawson) and won the latter two. The film was designed as an escapist Depression fantasy and is most successful in the farcical action in the "Pyramus and Thisbe" masque, as well as in the confusions of the hexed forest. Its spectacle of enchantment seems artificial and contrived in retrospect, and the farcical action tends to obliterate the poetry.

Joan Kemp-Welch, in her 1964 production of *A Midsummer Night's Dream*, seems to preserve some of the visual felicities of Reinhardt's film, along with the dancers and the Mendelssohn music, and, though her version is far less spectacular and has a few obviously stagey settings, it has many virtues. The mechanicals, in particular, are rural and funny without being either demeaned or romanticized. Benny Hill, as Nick Bottom, demonstrates a dogged determination to overlook obstacles and press ahead; he is not a fool but an incorrigible optimist continually trying to offer a solution for every problem he can spy. As Hill plays the role, it is easy to see why the other would-be actors like and respect him. When he is transformed, he wears a large ass's head that covers his head completely and sits on his shoulders with a leafy wreath at its bottom edge. Appropriately puzzled by the Queens's attentions, he skips through the forest with the preteen fairies, amiably giving commands and trying to amuse his attendants rather than exercise his newfound powers. Waking from his dream, he seems mostly embarrassed by his memory of the events that he proposes to make into "Bottom's Dream." Later, when he seems to step out of character to explain the action of *Pyramus and Thisbe* to

A group portrait from Warner Bros.'s 1935 production of A Midsummer Night's Dream (COURTESY NATIONAL FILM SOCIETY ARCHIVES)

Theseus, he seems entirely true to the character he has established throughout the rest of the comedy.

The roles in the production are generally played with a kind of generosity to the characters, and it is entirely without the dark side that most productions have included since Jan Kott's famous essay revealed the play's ambiguities and the dangers of the formerly green world of the forest. Puck (Tony Tanner), for example, is not an annoying child but a young man with magical powers, poor judgment, and a quick wit. When he talks with the first fairy, he seems to flirt with her, and she giggles in response, apparently charmed by his rapid patter. Both fall back laughing and kick their legs in the air. This air of amiability extends to the royal couples. Theseus (Patrick Allen) and Hippolyta (Eira Heath) are obviously passionate, and their apparent restraint seems intended to intensify their passion rather than resulting from some hesitation or hostility. In the final act, however, Hippolyta is robbed of her lines about "something of great constancy," so Theseus's descriptions of how "the lover, the madman, and the poet are of imagination all compact" becomes the last word on interpreting those events. Oberon (Peter Wyngarde) and Titania (Anna Massey) are also very gentle in their disagreement about the little Indian boy, here about 10 years old, and this Oberon is not vengefully out to embarrass his queen. He seems thoughtful and concerned and is more than happy to comfort Titania when she recoils from Bottom, still wearing his ass's head and sleeping beside her. The four Athenian lovers are young and energetic, so that their quarrels, though raucous, remain good-spirited. The only part of this production that has not held up is perhaps the costumes. Theseus, in particular, looks less like the ruler of Athens and more as though he is king of a place that *Star Trek* voyagers might have visited.

The Peter Hall film of 1969 was graced by outstanding talent from the Royal Shakespeare Company, most notably Diana Rigg as Hermia, Helen Mirren as Helena, and Judi Dench as a far sexier Titania than had yet been filmed. The outstanding performance of this production is Ian Holm's panting Puck, whose comings and goings are enhanced by trick photography. The lovers are not interchangeable, as in the 1935 film, thanks to Diana Rigg and Helen Mirren, who sort out the differences between Helena and Hermia. The interpretation had surely been influenced by Jan Kott's *Shakespeare, Our Contemporary* (1964), which had been translated into English in 1966 and which put a nasty spin on a comedy that had hitherto been regarded as "innocent," emphasizing the bestial relationship between Bottom (Paul Rogers) and Titania. Hall manages to dirty-up the action as the lovers muck about in the forest in anger and frustration before Puck finally reverses the love spells. The Hall production took a low-budget approach. The "Athenian" setting appears to be a rural English one (actually filmed by Peter Suschitzky outside of Stratford-upon-Avon), and no attempt was made to dress it up. The costumes were also minimal, Carnaby Street coats with lace collars for the men, mini-skirts for the women, near nudity for the fairies, with green-toned body makeup. Hippolyta (Barbara Jeffords) wears a kinky leather mini-skirt and boots but is not a very forceful Amazon queen. Peter Hall wanted to use "the advantages of the cinema not to make a film in the accepted sense, but to communicate the words." Certainly this production attempts to be faithful to the text; but to include as much of the text as possible, the actors fairly race through their lines, which makes the language difficult to follow, especially since the sound recording is not very good. All in all, this is a competent but generally joyless rendering of the play.

The tone of Elijah Moshinsky's 1982 BBC version becomes apparent from the opening shot, in which a gray-bearded Theseus remains on one side of the room while he addresses a much younger, more wildly dressed, and somewhat grim-faced Hippolyta who stands on the opposite side, a window behind each of them and a tangible distance between them. Following the visual style established for the BBC Shakespeare by Jonathan Miller, the opening scenes recall 17th-century paintings of northern European interiors and make this part of the play seem a bit claustrophobic. In the library where Theseus hears their case, Hermia (Pippa Guard) and Lysander (Robert Lindsay) seem barely able to look at each other, and Helena (Cherith Mellor), as Susan Willis says, "is almost a parody of stereotypical librarian unattractiveness," here played with granny glasses, high arched eyebrows, and frizzy red hair. This production, clearly influenced by Jan Kott, also seems somewhat uncomfortable about what to do with the mechanicals. They sit in a row, all facing the same direction, and remain so in their opening scene as Peter Quince (Sebastian Shaw) assigns parts for their play. Later, a remarkably subdued Bottom (Brian Glover), wearing the ass's head, frightens himself when he sees his reflection in the water, though he looks a bit more like a large rabbit than an ass. He quickly sees the advantages of accepting Titania's attention. Later he is convinced of his own importance and decides to have Quince write a ballad of his dream. The comedy in this version shifts from the mechanicals to the performances of the young Athenian lovers, who, once they enter the woods and lose the stiff veneer of their earlier selves, suddenly become wonderfully screwball comedians. Cherith Mellor, in particular, is excellent as the earnest and grinning Helena, frustrated by her unrequited love and frustrated even further when, through Puck's mistake, both Demetrius and Lysander fight for her love.

The transition to the woods presents a visual shock, as the action moves from the carefully constructed perspectives of the court scenes to the moonlit wilderness. Here a pool of water magnifies the light from the torches and from the crescent moon which sits perched between the dark silhouettes of trees. A luminescent Titania (Helen Mirren) and her lovely followers, most of them dressed as she is in pearls and diaphanous gowns, seem to glide through an animation of Arthur Rackham's illustrations for the play, and, when they gather at Titania's bower, they become all wings and glowing hair. At the same time, this woods also contains the dangers of the night. Puck (Phil Daniels) has greasy hair and fangs, and growls his lines in a cockney accent. Susan Willis writes that "Moshinsky did not want a sweet, impish Puck; he wanted a character from *A Clockwork Orange*." He succeeded. Oberon (Peter McEnery) appears on a black horse, wearing black leather pants, and his dark-suited followers mostly seem to be miniatures of the adults of Theseus's court. All of Oberon's conversation with Puck is painful, as he pulls Puck's hair, grabs him, and dunks him in the water; there is a vein of cruelty behind every line. By the final act, back at the court, the various lovers, including Theseus and Hippolyta, seem to have warmed up to each other and to the evening's entertainment. Many of their sarcastic comments about the mechanicals' play seem to be missing, and what is left seems to reflect an attempt to understand this oddly unfunny version of *Pyramus and Thisbe*, rather than to be amused by it. They reward Pyramus's suicide with somber applause.

    Emile Ardolino directed the filming of a 1982 live performance of *A Midsummer Night's Dream* at the Delacorte Theatre in New York's Central Park as part of Joseph Papp's Shakespeare in the Park series. James Lapine directed the show. The natural setting of the park adds to the realism of the woods scenes, but obliterates any distinction between court and woods, so that the burden seems to have fallen on costuming. The people at court, including the Athenian lovers, wear a sort of country casual; all the men are in shirtsleeves, with Theseus (James Hurdle) and Egeus (Ralph Drischell) looking a bit more futuristic; Hermia (Deborah Rush) and Helena (Christine Baranski) wear long dresses with puffy sleeves, and Hippolyta (Diane Venora), in Jo McMurtry's phrase, "wears black leather and looks as if she might have arrived on a motorcycle." All three couples appear dressed entirely in nuptial white for the final act. The mechanicals, who are presented as blue-collar workers, though not as hardhats, all wear some sort of cap, with Peter Quince (Steve Vinovich) wearing a crimson beret and Bottom (Jeffrey De Munn) wearing a red baseball cap to match his red shirt, with the cap's bill turned up to expose a green underside. The fairies and other forest people, on the other hand, might have escaped from one of Maurice Sendak's books, such as *Where the Wild Things Are*. Oberon (William Hurt), who tends to enter by pushing himself up through a hole in the ground, wears a fringed vest and leggings, and Titania (Michele Shay) is appropriately radiant in a spangled nude-colored bodysuit with sheer pastel material draped across it.

    Christine Baranski adds effective comic turns to her role as Helena, but Jeffrey De Munn as Bottom and Marcel Rosenblatt as Puck seem to vie to capture the play's energy through noisily frenetic performances. Puck is inclined to laugh at odd moments and, irritatingly, to fall back and kick his legs in the air and watch stretches of the action from this position. Bottom tends to insist on having his say, and, as often as possible, his way. He is oddly modest when he returns to his fellows after the transformation, and, rather than give details, interjects, "Not a word out of me." When he hurriedly tells his companions that the Duke has selected their entertainment to be performed, he actually seems to be trying to change the subject. Certainly he remains the most active character in the play, and in some respects becomes the center of the play. In the transformation scene, Titania's followers strip him almost naked, revealing a black ass's tail attached to his polka-dot boxer shorts, hoist him aloft, set him down between the legs of a recumbent Titania, and then pile on to hide the implied coupling of queen and beast. Puck, in the one restrained gesture in his performance, responds in a close-up with a look of amazement, but later laughs when reporting the incident to Oberon. The handling of this scene perhaps fits with Bottom earlier addressing Peascod, Shakespeare's Peaseblossom, by shouting at his crotch, as though confusing "peascod" and "codpiece" might automatically be funny. It also fits with Oberon's glancing "quizzically at Helena's kinky desire to have Demetrius treat her as a spaniel," about which Kenneth Rothwell and Annabelle H. Melzer say, "these modernized touches decode Shakespeare into an idiom for modern discourse."

    Adrian Noble's 1996 film of his 1995 Royal Shakespeare Company stage production attracted some critical attention even though it was not widely seen. Michael Hattaway notes allusions to Lewis Carroll's *Alice in Wonderland* and to Ingmar Bergman's film of Mozart's *The Magic Flute*, among other works. Mark Thornton Burnett finds even more allusions and comments on the "postmodern mixture of childhood reminiscences, self-conscious literary allusions, sexual awakenings and reminders of a turn-of-the-century environment." This film's unusual device is to render the entire action through the eyes of a young boy (Osheen Jones). It opens with the camera gliding through banks of clouds then entering an upstairs window to pan across a roomful of wonderful toys before settling on a blond-haired boy asleep with his arm thrown over a blue-covered copy of *A Midsummer Night's Dream* with Arthur Rackham's illustrations. The clock on the boy's dresser shows that it is midnight. In the tilted frame sequence that follows, the boy suddenly appears walking through a series of brightly painted corridors. Then, peering through a keyhole, he sees the opening of *A Midsummer Night's Dream* with Theseus (Alex Jennings) and Hippolyta (Lindsay Duncan) suddenly interrupted by Egeus (Alfred Burke), who drags Hermia

(Monica Dolan) with the rival lovers behind her. Immediately the boy is involved in the action, hiding under the table and dodging a toppled chair. He hears the Hermia and Lysander (Daniel Evans) plot to meet in the woods, and he is sitting next to Helena (Emily Raymond) as she plots to tell Demetrius (Kevin Doyle). Running out of the room, he immediately falls down a dark space and soon pops out of a wood stove in the cottage where the mechanicals are planning their production of *Pyramus and Thisbe*. These mechanicals are more affluent than most. Bottom (Desmond Barrit) wears a biker's helmet and leather jacket. Peter Quince (John Kane) and Robin Starveling (Robert Gillespie) wear suits and ties. At the end of this scene, the boy watches an umbrella float upward until, finally, Puck (Finbar Lynch) catches it. The boy gazes admiringly as Puck speaks to rows of bright costumed fairies perched on the handles of floating umbrellas. Soon the boy becomes Titania's changeling which Puck has just described.

All this is not to say, however, that this production is aimed at children. The normal sexual undercurrent of the play seems intensified by localizing the dream in the experience of the preadolescent boy, by the dreamlike quality of the production, and, most especially, by the handling of Bottom's transformation. The ass's ears, enlarged teeth, a tail, and facial hair are not the only additions. Titania caresses Bottom's groin with her feathered coif and then with her foot. He takes her flying through the sky and past the full moon on his motorcycle, with the boy waving gleefully from the sidecar. Titania is anxious to get Bottom to her bower, here an inverted and cushioned umbrella in which they sail across a still water to the moon. Then, as Oberon looks into the camera and says, "This falls out better than I could devise," Bottom is shown braying as he makes love to Titania who arches in corresponding ecstasy. When he awakens from the spell, Bottom interprets the line "me thought I had" by checking in his pants. Meanwhile, the Athenian lovers punctuate their confusion by moving in and out of somewhat surreal freestanding door frames. When Puck correctly joins the lovers, the boy spins in approving delight.

Noble has also used doubling throughout the play with the Theseus/Oberon, Hippolyta/Titania, and Philostrate/Puck pairs being perhaps the most significant examples. The effect seems to be that the problems implied in the opening of the play have been somehow resolved through the dreamlike action of the middle. With their snide remarks somewhat deemphasized, the audience for *Pyramus and Thisbe* adds another level of response when, for example, Hippolyta turns lovingly to Theseus and reassuringly kisses his hand when Pyramus laments that "my Thisbe's promise is forgot," or when the audience of newlyweds is clearly moved when Pyramus holds up Thisbe's bloody cloak, and even the boy, from the wings, becomes tearful. Finally, when Theseus stands over the fallen Pyramus and says "he might yet recover, and prove an ass," Hippolyta starts as if suddenly remembering her other self through Theseus's apparent allusion to those events. At the end, the clock strikes midnight, and everything returns to that moment at the beginning of the dream when the boy woke up and shouted for his mother. The playhouse empties, the fairies reappear, and Puck addresses his final speech to the boy and to the camera audience.

The Michael Hoffman production updates the play by setting it in Tuscany during the late 19th century, making the production "operatic," though the music (Verdi's *La Traviata* and Bellini's *Norma*, combined with Mendelssohn's incidental music) seems mismatched. The director also decided to put his actors on bicycles, which must have seemed to him a good idea. In his *Variety* review (May 10–16, 1999), Emanuel Levy, who found the production inventive, noted that it "suffers from a lack of coherent vision and an incongruous tone." The standout performance here was Kevin Kline as Bottom, played without an ass's head,

Oberon (Rupert Everett) and his queen, Titania (Michelle Pfeiffer), in a romantic moment in Michael Hoffman's A Midsummer Night's Dream (COURTESY FOX SEARCHLIGHT PICTURES)

but given long ears and a snout with facial hair, as Charles Laughton had done in a stage production directed by Peter Hall at Stratford-upon-Avon in 1958. Calista Flockhart plays an appealing Helena against Anna Friel's Hermia, Christian Bale's Demetrius, and Dominic West's Lysander. Friel pouts mightily as the much-abused Hermia, and Bale and West personalize the look-alike *beaux* Demetrius and Lysander. Stanley Tucci plays an adult Puck, following the instructions of Rupert Everett's Oberon; Michelle Pfeiffer is a beautiful Titania.

The cast is fine, but the concept suffers. David Strathairn's Duke Theseus lacks the authority the play demands because his lines have been abridged in keeping with the near-contemporary Italianate setting. He appears to be the maitre d' of a resort hotel rather than a ruler whose nuptials are most central to the plot. Sophie Marceau's Hippolyta is presented as a genteel, aristocratic lady, a highly unlikely Amazon queen. One effective touch in the film is the way in which the fairies seem to interact with the townspeople, as one catches glimpses of them in the town from time to time. Stanley Tucci, gives a carefully modulated and thoroughly professional rendering of Puck, but he seems a bit cumbersome. This *Midsummer Night's Dream* is generally short on comic energy and is something of a snooze, but it is generally entertaining.

REFERENCES

Buhler, Stephen M., *Shakespeare in the Cinema: Ocular Proof* (Albany: State University of New York Press, 2002); Burnett, Mark Thornton, "Impressions of Fantasy: Adrian Noble's *A Midsummer Night's Dream*, in *Shakespeare, Film, Fin de Siècle*, ed. Mark Thornton Burnett and Ramona Wray (London: Macmillan Press Ltd., 2000) 89–101; Hattaway, Michael, "The Comedies on Film," *The Cambridge Companion to Shakespeare on Film*, ed. Russell Jackson (Cambridge: Cambridge University Press, 2000) 85–98; Jones, Gordon P., "Nahum Tate Is Alive and Well: Elijah Moshinsky's BBC Shakespeare Productions," *Shakespeare on Television*, ed. J. C. Bulman and H. R. Coursen (Hanover and London: University Press of New England, 1988) 192–200; Jorgens, Jack J., *Shakespeare on Film* (Bloomington: Indiana University Press, 1977); Manvell, Roger, *Shakespeare and the Film* (New York: Praeger, 1971); McMurtry, Jo, *Shakespeare Films in the Classroom* (Hamden, Conn.: Archon Books, 1994); Rothwell, Kenneth, *A History of Shakespeare on Screen* (Cambridge University Press, 1999); Rothwell, Kenneth, and Annabelle Henkin Melzer, *Shakespeare on Screen* (London: Mansell Publishing Ltd., 1990); Willis, Susan, *The BBC Shakespeare: Making the Televised Canon* (Chapel Hill: University of North Carolina Press, 1991); Willson, Robert F., Jr., *Shakespeare in Hollywood, 1929–1956* (Madison, N.J.: Fairleigh Dickinson University Press, 2000).

—*J.M.W. AND R.V.*

MUCH ADO ABOUT NOTHING (1598–99)

Much Ado About Nothing (1973), U.S.A., directed by A.J. Antoon, adapted by A.J. Antoon and Joseph Papp; New York Shakespeare Festival/Columbia Broadcasting System.

Much Ado About Nothing (1984), U. K., directed by Stuart Burge; British Broadcasting Company/Time-Life Television.

Much Ado About Nothing (1993), U.S.A., directed and adapted by Kenneth Branagh; Samuel Goldyn Company.

The Play

With *As You Like It* and *Twelfth Night*, Shakespeare's *Much Ado About Nothing* belongs to a series of "joyous" comedies. There are two primary relationships here. One is a comedy of courtship and the other is a comedy of marriage. The quick courtship nearly results in disaster, and the slow, reluctant marriage is successful. The quarto of 1600, the first published text of the play, notes on the title page that it had been performed publicly "sundry times" by the Lord Chamberlain's Men. The plot source is Ludovico Ariosto's *Orlando Furioso* (1516).

After helping Don Pedro subdue his malcontent brother, Don John, returning soldiers Benedick and Claudio find themselves quickly entangled in amorous wars. Benedick renews his battle of wits with Beatrice (his "Lady Disdain"), the niece of Messina's governor, Leonato, while Claudio, who distinguished himself in battle, realizes that he has been subdued by the beauty of Leonato's daughter, Hero. A confirmed bachelor, Benedick expresses dismay that his young friend is in love, but Don Pedro offers to intercede with Hero and her father, since Claudio himself seems uneasy about declaring his sudden affection. At a masked dance, Don Pedro will woo Hero in Claudio's name. Meanwhile Don John (who describes himself as "a plain-dealing villain") has found out about the affair and decides to get revenge on Don Pedro and Claudio by ruining it. He convinces Claudio that Don Pedro won Hero for himself, but his victory is short-lived since the others convince Claudio that this is not so. With the issue settled, and Claudio and Hero planning marriage, they, Don Pedro, and Leonato decide to find a way to bring Benedick and Beatrice together. The men arrange for Benedick to overhear them talking about Beatrice's great secret love for him, while Hero and the other women will do the same for Beatrice, convincing her that Benedick is also hiding his affection. The plot works and, although formerly well known for their stance against love, both Benedick and Beatrice are soon sure they are deeply in love.

Don John has not, however, given up and instead escalates his villainy with a plan to make Don Pedro and Claudio believe they see Hero being unfaithful. When Hero appears the next day to be married, she and the others are shocked to hear Claudio, with the support of Don Pedro, reject his bride-to-be and say she is unchaste. Hero faints, Leonato is outraged, but the priest suggests gaining time to prove Hero innocent by saying she has died. Beatrice is so angry with Claudio that she takes advantage of Benedick's declaration of love to ask him to kill his friend. Undercutting the seriousness of the broken nuptial, Shakespeare introduces Constable Dogberry and his Watch, who patrol the streets of Messina and have very accidentally overheard Don John's henchmen, Borachio and Conrade, boasting of how they tricked Claudio and Don Pedro. Without really understanding what has happened, Dogberry and his men arrest the conspirators and take them to be interrogated.

Meanwhile Leonato and his brother Antonio accuse Don Pedro and Claudio of having killed Hero. Don Pedro expresses sorrow, but insists the charges against Hero are true. He and Claudio next see Benedick, who calls Claudio a villain and challenges him to a duel. Though they at first think he is jesting, they soon realize Benedick is serious. Just then, Dogberry brings in Borachio, who confesses the whole plot. Suddenly repentant, Claudio tells Leonato to take his own revenge. Leonato tells Claudio to marry, sight-unseen, a niece who is "Almost the copy of my child that's dead." Called back from hiding, Hero, Beatrice, and the other women appear, masked, for a new wedding ceremony. When Claudio humbly agrees to marry this woman whose face he has not even seen, Hero suddenly removes her mask. With all corrected, Benedick and Beatrice try briefly once more to deny their affections, but Claudio and Hero produce love poems written by the reluctant lovers. Benedick concludes that "man is a giddy thing," and tells Don Pedro to marry. As the guests begin to dance, word comes that Don John has been captured.

The Films

The only feature film treatment of *Much Ado About Nothing* is the very popular version by Kenneth Branagh, who transforms Shakespeare's Sicilian city of Messina into the Tuscany region of sunny central Italy, and structures the film around a light/dark division. He creates a world in which the land and the lovers almost visibly ache for satisfaction, and impediments seem sure to evaporate in the hot sun. Only the villainous Don John and, in this film, the slightly psychotic Dogberry embrace the darkness. The emotional center of this production, as in most, is the relationship between Benedick (Kenneth Branagh) and Beatrice (Emma Thompson), here boosted by their star power and by the fact they were at the time married to each other. Opening the film with Thompson reading the cautionary song, "Sigh no more, ladies, sigh no more, Men were deceivers ever," director Branagh throws the emphasis on Thompson's thoughtful portrayal of Beatrice as a woman whose sense of humor is only one of several weapons against painful vulnerability. From this point of view, the Claudio-Hero story almost becomes an example of what might happen in a love affair of less depth, the kind of affair that this Beatrice would avoid to escape further pain. Branagh does not push this point too far, and yet Thompson conveys this sense of a deeper offense in her charge to "Kill Claudio." Branagh's Benedick, on the other hand, is less the former rake (Leonato jokes that he is confident of being Hero's father because Benedick was then himself a child) than the screwball comedy hero who wonders at how the world is bit by bit taking shape before him. This is not a cynical Benedick but a surprised Benedick. He is innocent in a benign way, whereas his friend Claudio's innocence threatens cruelty. Perhaps only Don John, however, is really allowed to threaten much of anything in this film. As played by Keanu Reeves, Don John is a character composed mainly of scowls. This bastard brother is the negative image of the courtly and amiable Don Pedro (Denzel Washington), a point Branagh underscores by making Don John white and Don Pedro black.

Branagh cut and transposed a considerable portion of the original play, primarily, he says, "where the plot (such as it is) was not advanced" or where he needed "to create a movie pace (quite different from that of the theater)." One section in which the characters seem most obviously altered are the scenes having to do with Dogberry (Michael Keaton). Branagh introduces Dogberry and the Watch earlier than the play does, placing them, in effect, where they need to be to foil Don John's plot when it unfolds. In addition, Branagh wanted "to amend the ugliness inherent in the wedding scene and in Claudio's behavior afterwards." To do this, he and Michael Keaton reduced Dogberry's verbal malapropisms and made him a "physical malaprop." To do this, they seem to have borrowed from a variety of types of physical comedy. Dogberry's invisible horses, for example, are from the British Monty Python group's film *Monty Python and the Holy Grail* (1975), where the knights ride similar mounts. The physical violence, especially Dogberry's abuse of Verges, seems to come from the Three Stooges.

The effect seems to push the characterization away from sympathy and closer to slapstick. Several of Dogberry's more sympathetic lines have been cut, such as his plaintive "and a rich fellow enough, go to, and a fellow that hath had losses, and on that hath had two gowns, and everything handsome about him." A similarly motivated change in the physicality of the action occurs when Branagh shows Hero's supposed adultery. Shakespeare has Don John tell Claudio that he "shall see her chamber-window entered," and later Borachio says he has "wooed Margaret, the Lady Hero's gentlewoman, by the name of Hero." In Branagh's film, we see the bare back of a woman who is being made love to standing up, leaning back over a balcony. Here too, the effect is very different. Several writers have pointed out that this rendering of the incident makes the viewer more sympathetic toward Claudio and more in a position to understand his later rejection of Hero at the wedding, but it is clearly a violent change from Shakespeare's more oblique description.

Of the two notable filmed performances of *Much Ado About Nothing*, the A.J. Antoon and Joseph Papp version was enjoying a run at the New York Shakespeare Festival when it was prepared for television and broadcast on CBS in 1973. The television performance, apparently to everyone's surprise, effectively killed the Broadway show, which closed within four days. Papp himself said, "I've never seen anything fall so rapidly in my life." Antoon had directed the stage version, but had no television experience. Eventually, he worked primarily with the actors, and assistant Nick Havinga took over the shooting, though Antoon kept final artistic control of the production. Papp, who saw the project as "an attempt to reach a mass audience for plays of quality and content," had shifted the location of the play to turn-of-the-century America. In this version,

Kenneth Branagh's Much Ado About Nothing *cast himself as Benedick and Emma Thompson as Beatrice.* (COURTESY SAMUEL GOLDWYN COMPANY)

Don Pedro, Benedick, Claudio, and the others ride into the opening scene wearing post Spanish-American War uniforms and surrounded by brass bands, red-white-and-blue banners, men waving American flags, women wearing long flowing dresses with high collars, and a Keystone Kops-style police force. Critic H.R. Coursen deplored this approach and said that by shifting time periods Antoon "obliterates what Shakespeare may be saying to us with *his* play" and called the result "a cultural disaster." Papp himself had said that "Whenever you put Shakespeare in a more modern period, it is diminished," and he questioned several of Antoon's choices, including the Keystone Kops chase.

The Papp-Antoon production differs from other versions of the play at least in part because of the selection of the time period, but perhaps more importantly because of the emphasis on the conventions associated with that time period. The effect of making Dogberry (Bernard Hughes) a Keystone Kop, for example, is to provide a context that explains his behavior, but also to draw on the popular understanding of both the early 1900s and silent film conventions. Because its antecedents are more likely to be found in *Meet Me in St. Louis* (1944) and *Abbott and Costello Meet the Keystone Kops* (1955) than in the films of Mack Sennett, the production's use of ragtime music, tubas, and slow waltzes, along with the speeded up chase scenes, freeze frames, and other photographic tricks, are not the product of studying the silent film era, as Coursen correctly points out, but instead of manipulating the late-20th-century expectations of what those conventions were.

Benedick (Sam Waterston) is a cigar-smoking, deliberately old-fashioned man, bemused by the world, but aware of the precariousness of his position in it. Beatrice (Kathleen Widdoes) is a proto-feminist, who takes Benedick's beer and drinks it when she bests him in a verbal battle and later sits on a porch with the other women to sneak a cigarette. In this world, Don John (Jerry Mayo) is a comic villain, rather than the sullen or potentially dangerous force of other productions. The first view of Don John shows him trying to shoot the ducks in the pond, about as threatening as Elmer Fudd. When he finds out that Claudio and Hero will marry, Don John pounds his piano in frustration, and, when he sits in a barber's chair and spreads rumors about Hero, he plops a lollipop in his mouth with childish glee and tells the audience, rather than just Claudio, "O'plague right well prevented! So will you say when you have seen the sequel." In general, this is a world without malice. Borachio and Conrade are visibly saddened when they hear that Hero has died. It is a safe world of Victrolas, gazebos, straw hats, crinoline skirts, and parasols. The most serious moment comes when Don Pedro (Douglas Watson) gets down on one knee at the end of the dance in Act Two and asks Beatrice "Would you have me, lady?" Rather than tongue-in-cheek playfulness, the line suddenly makes Don Pedro into a disappointed but gallant lover, a characterization consistent with Benedick's line at the end of the play "Prince, thou art sad, get thee a wife."

The BBC version of the play, directed by Stuart Burge, makes the play a generally darker experience. Don John himself is dressed all in black and everything is in shadow, as though he were somehow sensitive to the light, although obviously the implication is that his condition is more metaphorical than medical. Later, when Dogberry's men seize the black-cloaked Borachio and Conrade, the visual metaphor seems to suggest two kinds of darkness meeting. While this does not seem to be an inappropriate image, this production gives the connection an emphasis that it seldom has had. Given this pattern of visual signals, however, holding the wedding scene in a darkened room seems to be a somewhat heavy-handed commentary on the state of things. Leonato (Lee Montague) and Beatrice (Cherie Lunghi), for example, the bride's father and cousin, are both dressed in dark clothing. Certainly in close shots their dark figures contrast effectively with Hero's white dress, and later Beatrice's black dress and Benedick's dark red outfit both seem appropriate in the darkened church when their discussion turns to killing Claudio. This dark palette continues until the final wedding scene when the women enter wearing the lighter colored dresses of the earliest scenes in the play.

Burge has said that "the subtleties and sophistications of this play require some kind of stylized setting" and that designer Jan Spoczynski "succeeded very well in merging a stylized background and a real foreground." Perhaps this light/dark patterning is part of the intended stylization, although Susan McCloskey believes that "this production would obscure" the contrast "between the sunlit comedy of Beatrice and Benedick's courtship and the potentially tragic darkening of Claudio's love for Hero." As she points out, Beatrice "is seldom merry" and Benedick (Robert Lindsay) seems to be "in a prickly funk" during the opening scenes of the play. Part of the problem, however, seems to be that the other actors do not respond to the lines, or seldom do. Dogberry (Michael Elphick) rarely gets a reaction from the characters onstage to his malaprop humor. The effect, of course, is to diminish his comic effect in the play. A notable exception, for example, might be Beatrice, who has been somewhat shrewish in her humor in the opening scenes, but suddenly winces, and is caught doing so by a close-up shot, when Benedick says "I cannot endure my Lady Tongue." It is a reading that gives more weight to her next lines, when Don Pedro says ". . . you have lost the heart of Signior Benedick," and she replies "Indeed, my lord, he lent it me awhile, and I gave him use for it, a double heart for his single one." Toward the end of the play, when Benedick asks Beatrice "for which of my good parts did you first suffer love for me?" they again achieve the kind of romantic connection that genuinely suggests that something has been overcome and that they really have reached the level of romance that the play suggests they should.

REFERENCES

Barton, Anne, "Shakespeare in the Sun," *The New York Review*, May 27, 1993, 11–13; Branagh, Kenneth, *Much Ado About Nothing by William Shakespeare: Screenplay, Introduction, and Notes on the Making of the Movie* (New York: W.W. Norton, 1993); Coursen, H.R., "Anachronism and Papp's *Much Ado*," in *Shakespeare on Television*, eds. J.C. Bulman and H.R. Coursen (Hanover, N.H.: University Press of New England, 1988), 151–155; Little, Stuart W., *Enter Joe Papp: In Search of a New American Theater* (New York: Coward, McCann and Geoghegan, 1974); McCloskey, Susan, "*Much Ado About Nothing*," *Shakespeare on Film Newsletter* (April 1985), 5; Shuttleworth, Ian, *Ken and Em: A Biography of Kenneth Branagh and Emma Thompson* (New York: St. Martin's Press, 1995); Weiss, Tanja, *Shakespeare on the Screen: Kenneth Branagh's Adaptations of Henry V, Much Ado About Nothing, and Hamlet* (Frankfurt: Peter Lang, 1999); Willis, Susan, *The BBC Shakespeare Plays* (Chapel Hill: University of North Carolina Press, 1991).

—R.V.

MY OWN PRIVATE IDAHO

See HENRY IV, PART I (1596–97); HENRY IV, PART II (1598)

OTHELLO (1603–04)

A Double Life (1947), U.S.A., directed by George Cukor, adapted by Ruth Gordon and Garson Kanin; Universal-International/Kanin Productions.

Othello (1952), Morocco/Italy, directed and adapted by Orson Welles; Mogador/Mercury Productions.

Othello (1955), USSR, directed by Sergei Yutkevich, adapted by Boris Pasternak; Mosfilm/Universal-International.

Othello (1965), U.K., directed by Stuart Burge, based on National Theatre production directed by John Dexter; BHE Production/Eagle Films Ltd.

Othello (1995), U.K., directed and adapted by Oliver Parker; Dakota Films/Imminent Films/Castle Rock Entertainment.

O (2001), U.S.A., directed by Tim Blake Nelson and adapted by Brad Kaaya; Lions Gate Films.

Othello (2002), U.S.A., directed by Geoffrey Sax, adapted by Andrew Davies for LTW and WGBH Boston, in association with the Canadian Broadcasting Corporation.

The Play

Dismissed for many years by classical critics as a "domestic tragedy," *Othello* has received greater attention from modern readers and viewers because of its complex racial and sexual themes. The hero is a Moor serving as leader of the Venetian army who marries the daughter of a senator opposed to the union on the grounds that Othello has used magic to seduce his innocent child. But Desdemona's love for her noble husband proves more than just a passing dalliance, and Othello greets her passion with some of the most powerful romantic poetry in all of Shakespeare.

Their union is destroyed by Othello's jealousy, prompted by his diabolic ensign Iago, and proves compellingly tragic, striking a chord with contemporary audiences attuned to domestic violence. While *Othello* is a sensational story with contrived plot turns—the hero's rage is provoked by Desdemona's supposed gift of a treasured handkerchief to her lover—the drama thoroughly explores the psyches of passionate characters with whom we strongly identify.

The action begins when Desdemona's father, Brabantio, is rudely awakened by her suitor Roderigo, urged on by a disgruntled Iago, who informs the senator that his daughter has eloped with the Moor. Iago uses Roderigo to avenge himself on Othello because the captain promoted Cassio to lieutenant instead of him. When Brabantio doesn't find Desdemona in her bed, he rushes to the duke and senate to demand Othello's arrest. Called upon to explain himself, the composed

Moor tells his accusers that he has indeed married Desdemona but that he wooed her with descriptions of his military adventures, not magic spells. The duke overrides Brabantio's complain and orders Othello to Cyprus to defend the island against invading Turks. A frustrated Brabantio directs this parting shot at Othello: "Look to her, Moor, if thou had eyes to see; She has deceived her father, and may thee." Thus the seeds of doubt are planted.

As the Venetian party arrives at Cyprus aboard different ships nearly sunk in a storm, Othello learns that the Turkish fleet has been destroyed in the same storm. No longer required to prepare for invasion, he becomes vulnerable to Iago's innuendoes about an affair between Michael Cassio and Desdemona. He also arranges for Cassio to drink too much wine while on watch, then calls on Roderigo to provoke a noisy street brawl. His sleep disrupted, Othello blames Cassio and demotes him after hearing "honest" Iago's account of the struggle. Appearing to be everyone's friend and confidant, Iago weaves a web out of bits and pieces of volunteered information that eventually ensnares Cassio, Desdemona, and Othello.

When Desdemona vigorously urges that her husband reinstate his friend Cassio, Iago has the opening he has been hoping for. He tells his captain that Cassio has revealed his sexual relationship with Desdemona while talking in his sleep. He also claims he saw Cassio wipe his beard with the special handkerchief given to Desdemona by Othello on their wedding day. For the hero, now in a frenzied state, the gift also signifies the giving away of her body to Cassio. Thus wedded to Iago's will, Othello orders Iago to kill Cassio and assigns him the title of lieutenant. He also vows to stifle Desdemona in her wedding bed. On the fatal night, we first witness Iago's attempt on Cassio's life with Roderigo's help; they manage only to wound him, however, and Iago kills Roderigo to cover up the scheme. When Othello accuses Desdemona, she declares her innocence but is unable to convince her enraged husband, who proceeds to stifle her. As she is about to expire, her attendant Emilia, Iago's wife, rushes into the bedroom, embraces her dying mistress, and accuses Othello of cruel murder. He tells her that her husband has proved Desdemona's unfaithfulness, using the handkerchief as evidence. Emilia then turns on her just-arrived husband, naming him as the cause of these tragic events; in payment for her honesty, she is stabbed to death by her conscienceless husband. Wounded and finally exposed, Iago refuses to give a reason for his plotting; Othello, heartbroken and desperate, commits suicide with a dagger he has hidden from his captors. As Cassio takes over the governorship of the island and Iago is led away, Othello's dying self-description—"one that loved not wisely but too well"—reverberates as a tragic, yet ironic, truth.

The Films

A few silent versions of the tragedy were made in Italy and Germany early in the century; these might be better described as "scenes from *Othello*." A 1936 British offshoot, *Men Are Not Gods*, concerns the efforts of a London newspaperman to save the reputation of an actor playing Othello. *A Double Life* (1947) also uses the Othello plot within a frame but in a more unusual, inventive way than *Men Are Not Gods* had done. Ronald Colman plays Broadway star Anthony John, who is urged by his agent to revive the *Othello* production that won him fame. John reluctantly agrees because he hopes to regain the affection of his estranged wife Brita (Signe Hasso), who will reprise her role as Desdemona. As rehearsals commence, the hero begins to confound his stage role with his real-life persona; like Othello, he grows increasingly jealous of his wife. When Tony meets and pursues a waitress (Shelley Winters) who resembles Brita as Desdemona, the siege on his sanity grows more intense. Convinced that the waitress is indeed Desdemona, he murders her in her bed during one of their late-night encounters. Police investigating the murder have no leads until a newspaper reporter talks to the coroner and discovers that the waitress was stifled "with a kiss." This is exactly the way Desdemona is murdered every night in Tony's production. Aided by the show's publicist Bill Friend (Edmond O'Brien), whom Tony suspects as Brita's wooer, police detectives gather behind the scenes of the play, planning to arrest Tony. But he has grown so remorseful that he decides to use a real knife for Othello's onstage suicide. Distinguished by *film noir* elements and superior direction by Hollywood veteran George Cukor, *A Double Life* is an artistic success and won Colman an Academy Award for best actor.

Orson Welles's 1952 version has some of the same *film noir* touches as *A Double Life*, but it is a more faithful, if shortened, treatment of the play. Welles's first Shakespeare film was *Macbeth* (1948), an artistic and box-office failure. Though he brutally cuts the text and overacts in the title role, Welles manages to catch more of the spirit of *Othello* than he did of *Macbeth*. Michael MacLiammoir's Iago first appears suspended in a cage looking down on a funeral procession carrying Othello

Stuart Burge's Othello *cast Laurence Olivier as Othello, Maggie Smith as Desdemona, and Anthony Nicholls as her father.* (COURTESY WARNER BROS.)

and Desdemona's bodies. The cage, iron bars, and stone vaults are objects that suggest Othello's imprisonment in a destructive world where he is manipulated by an impotent Iago. Shot in Morocco and Italy, the film is aptly characterized by Jack J. Jorgens as "a mannerist montage of broken continuities, wrenched perspectives, clashing images, and surreal sound." Welles's voice-over narration is extratextual and often distracting; it seems designed chiefly to instruct audiences unfamiliar with the play. Still, he manages to coax strong performances from his actors: Suzanne Cloutier's Desdemona and Michael Lawrence's Cassio prove almost as powerful as MacLiammoir's Iago. Now available in a restored video format, the film deserves reconsideration by audiences and critics alike.

The 1955 Russian *Othello* is, by contrast with Welles's production, a more colorful spectacle with operatic overtones that recall Verdi's *Otello*. Director Yutkevich believed film to be the right medium to represent the expansive lifelikeness of Shakespeare's plays. The crowd scenes, especially in Cyprus, achieve this effect, and the color photography presents a vivid portrait of the characters and action. Though originally made with Russian-speaking actors, a later version was made with dubbed-in voices of British players. Sergei Bondarchuk's Othello and Andrei Popov's Iago are both impressive, although their acting appears melodramatic by comparison with Anglo-American style.

That style is brilliantly demonstrated in Stuart Burge's 1965 *Othello*, featuring Sir Laurence Olivier, Maggie Smith as Desdemona, and Frank Finlay as Iago. A filmed re-creation of the London National Theatre production (directed by John Dexter), this version does seem hemmed in by comparison with the Welles and Yutkevich interpretations. Shot on a stage-like set, the film follows theatrical—rather than realistic—conventions in movement and speech. Olivier plays Othello in blackface and employs a Jamaican accent that seems at times, especially during the great soliloquies, distinctly out of place. But Olivier's speech rhythms contrast interestingly with those of Frank Finlay's Iago, who uses the accent of a Cockney. Maggie Smith's performance as Desdemona strikes just the right note of sincerity and innocence, although the camera tends to bring out a matronly quality in her appearance. Olivier's Othello carries the day, however, especially in Act Three, Scene Three, when Iago persuades him of his wife's infidelity. The riveting murder scene (V.ii) uncovers the hero's ferocity and tenderness in a convincing way. On the whole, Burge's attempt to engage the film audience as a stage director would a theater audience yields mixed results.

A much more realistic translation of the tragedy is Oliver Parker's 1995 version. Kenneth Branagh as Iago controls the camera and action throughout as he delivers his soliloquies in close-up. His ability to speak Shakespeare's lines with clarity and precision adds to the naturalistic tone of the film; it also means that he holds our attention in ensemble scenes. Laurence Fishburne's Othello is likewise a powerful presence (though perhaps eclipsed by Branagh's Iago), his youth and dynamism suggesting a hero still in his prime. His relationship with Desdemona (Irene Jacobs) is convincingly portrayed, stressing her modesty and straightforward innocence. Yet when Fishburne's Othello begins to doubt, Parker has him visualizing a seductress entwining a naked Cassio in her arms. Sequences like this one suggest a parallel with MTV music videos, hinting at Parker's attempt to attract a younger audience to his film. While Branagh's riveting Iago and Fishburne's menacing Othello offer the viewer much to enjoy, the film cuts many lines of Othello's poetry and tends to focus more on the trappings of his world than on the tortured psyche of the hero.

Tim Blake Nelson's *O* is a modern updating of the play that might be tagged "*Othello* Goes to Prep School." It follows the trend started by *10 Things I Hate about You* (1999), which also starred Julia Stiles, and might have been tagged "*The Taming of the Shrew* goes to High School." But *Othello* is more problematic: not only is it far more serious, but it is also far more difficult to update and dumb down. As the only black male in an all-white high school, screenwriter Brad Kaaya presumably might have experienced some of the anguish ascribed to his version of Shakespeare's tragic protagonist. Kaaya somehow thought it might be a good idea to turn *Othello* into a backcourt tragedy, without realizing that a basketball star lacks the authority and tragic dimension of the Moor, elevated to a position of military leadership. Shooting hoops instead of Turks is a less than subtle difference. And the notion of the Moor as a preppy youngster is potentially ridiculous.

Moreover, this flawed strategy fails to take into consideration the problem of Othello's distinctive rhetoric, even though, as Todd McCarthy pointed out in *Variety*, Kaaya "has been faithful to the play's emotion and plot mechanics," perhaps true to a degree. The trouble is, can the high passions and extreme violence of the Shakespearean original survive a text that has not one whit of the original language? Language was the scaffolding upon which Shakespeare erected his improbable set of characters with their equally improbable motivations and behaviors. But without that glorious linguistic superstructure, can this prefab movie long endure?

Odin James (Mekhi Phifer as Othello's counterpart) is the star player of the Palmetto Grove Academy basketball team in Charleston, South Carolina. He's also the only black man in the school. Like his namesake, he's a warrior in battle—only in this case the combat is played out on the basketball court, a weak substitute for the real thing. He's in love with Desi Brable (Julia Stiles

Laurence Fishburne starred as the proud Moor in Oliver Parker's adaptation of Shakespeare's Othello.
(COURTESY CASTLE ROCK ENTERTAINMENT)

plays this Desdemona), and makes little attempt to conceal it. When Desi's father, the school's dean (John Heard, the Brabantio figure), reproaches her, she defends the relationship.

Meanwhile, Odin's best friend and teammate, Hugo Goulding (Josh Hartnett as Iago) is nursing a deadly grudge: Odin has usurped his place on the team, which is coached by his father, Duke Goulding (Martin Sheen). Hugo feels displaced both as the team star and as the coach's son. In revenge, Hugo contrives a way to make Odin jealous of Desi. He starts rumors that Desi is seeing teammate Michael Casio (Andrew Keegan as Cassio). He fuels the rumors with allegations that Desi and Michael have cast racist slurs on Odin. He pilfers the scarf that Odin had given Desi and gets it into Michael Casio's hands. He even stage-manages a conversation with Michael intended to mislead Odin into thinking Michael is talking about an affair with Desi (instead of another girl). Even Hugo's girlfriend, Emily (Rain Phoenix), succumbs to Hugo's machinations, participating in the conspiracy.

Odin's jealousy takes its toll. He loses his concentration in practice. During a dunk contest, he angrily shatters the backboard glass. He turns to drugs. Finally, he falls in with Hugo's scheme to kill Desi. Desi awaits him one night alone in her room. While the basketball team is warming up for its big game, Odin steals into her room and strangles her.

Then, several things happen very quickly, all at once. Hugo and a confederate, Roger Rodrigues (Elden Henson), who will do anything to be popular, have taken Michael Casio out on a joyride with the secret intention of having the confederate kill him. The scheme backfires, and Hugo has to kill Michael and Roger himself. Back in Desi's room, Odin confronts Hugo and realizes at last that he has been betrayed by Hugo. Odin shoots himself, his last words declaiming that he really loved Desi. Hugo is hauled away by the cops.

The story is framed by images of cooing doves and a marauding hawk. Hugo's voice-over intones a litany about wanting to fly, about wanting to be a hawk, a predator. Odin is such a hawk, and soon Hugo will be one, too. This framing device is very contrived and awkward. It is worsened by the use of the hawk as the basketball team's name and mascot. The ill-advised treatment turns Shakespeare's tragic plot into an absurd melodrama that cannot stand alone without the support of Shakespeare's diction and rhetoric. The twisted plot cannot survive the attempted transformation and the whole thing seems a bit silly. Odin's mounting rage and violent actions likewise strain credibility. On the other hand, the notorious shootings at Columbine High School in Colorado two years before the film was made were enough to withhold this film from circulation. Apparently, a lot of people thought the film mirrored rather too closely the sort of repressions and unleashed violence that can happen among teenagers.

The cast members acquit themselves well enough on the basketball court, especially Mekhi Phifer, who is even more convincing on the basketball court than as a betrayed lover. He convincingly demonstrates that he might have had plenty of hardcourt experience and skill. *Variety* predicted that Phifer and Stiles "are two fine, intelligent young people destined for bright futures." Also, there's some plausible attention paid to the extremes that Palmetto's basketball coach, Coach Goulding (Martin Sheen) will go to recruit and develop Odin. The coach is like a Bobby Knight in miniature, a touch that rings true to the sport, if not to Shakespeare. Odin is not only the team's ticket to a state championship but to the coach's possible future in the ranks of college ball.

As a story about racism and basketball in the American South, the film makes some sense, but not as a version of *Othello* to be taken seriously. Odin's initials are "O.J.," which might have made a better title than simply "O." Like O.J. Simpson, Odin is a promising young athlete who has difficulty functioning in white America. In Shakespeare's play, the Moor is also an outsider in Renaissance Italy, but the circumstances are so culturally different that the comparison seems facile.

This is the second film directed by Tim Blake Nelson, memorable for his portrayal of the dimwit in the Coen brothers comedy *O Brother, Where Art Thou?* (1999). Owen Gleiberman of *Entertainment Weekly* praised Nelson's direction (and *O*, for that matter) but questioned "one extraordinary moment of primal anger" when Odin shatters the backboard in the dunking contest, the first demonstration of Odin's escalating rage that carries "uncomfortable—if unintentional—racist overtones." In the violent conclusion Odin becomes O.J. "Unlike Othello," Gleiberman concluded, Odin "withdraws in his very vengeance, from the audience, and the movie, for all of its feeling, recedes from tragedy." And that, besides the unfortunate decision to sacrifice the language that would not set well with prep-school athletes, weakens the emotional impact.

Andrew Davies, whose previous television credits included *Moll Flanders* and the impressive *House of Cards* series about a cynical politician ambitious of becoming prime minister, adapted Shakespeare's plot (but not his poetry) in this version, updating the action to contemporary London, where Scotland Yard's "John" Othello (Eamonn Walker) becomes the newly appointed commissioner of the Metropolitan Police after quelling a race riot. The adaptation was influenced by a real-life controversy over the 1993 killing of a black teenager and the botched police investigation that followed. The film begins with Othello at a formal reception, intercut with the police riot. Othello leaves the reception and goes out to calm the rioters: "We're not about to surrender the streets to mob rule," Othello tells the rioters, speaking to them of dignity and justice, "justice under the law."

Because of the controversy, former commissioner Sinclair Carver (Bill Paterson) is forced to retire. He favors Ben Jago (Christopher Eccleston, the Iago figure) to replace him, but the home secretary (Nicholas Gecks) and the prime minister (John Harding) have other plans. Michael Cass (Richard Coyle, the Cassio figure) is ordered to bring Othello to No. 10 Downing Street to the prime minister, who intends to promote Othello over his mentor, Ben Jago, to police commissioner. At that meeting Othello is advised to find someone in whom he can confide, and he chooses Jago. After the meeting Jago throws a private fit, venting his outrage: "It should have been me!" He then begins to plot against Othello. Hence this adaptation gives Iago a clear motive for his campaign to destroy Othello, as he begins to e-mail neo-Nazi hate groups.

Othello is married to Dessie Brabant (Keeley Hawes, the Desdemona figure), who has married Othello against the wishes of her father, James Brabant (Joss Ackland). Lulu (Rachael Stirling, the Emilia figure) is Dessie's friend and former classmate at boarding school, rather than her servant. Roderigo, Shakespeare's "gulled gentleman," becomes PC (Police Constable) Alan Roderick (Del Synnott), but he is less important than was the case in Shakespeare's play. Otherwise, the updated adaptation generally follows Shakespeare's tragic trajectory, except that Michael Cass, assigned to protect Dessie while Othello is at work, at one point makes a pass at her, though he finds her unreceptive.

Christopher Eccleston is impressive as Jago and dominates the production from beginning to end. His monologues both open and close the drama: "It was all about love. Don't talk to me about race. Don't talk to me about politics. It was love. Simple as that." After Othello stifles Dessie with a pillow at the end, he then gets on the bed and shoots himself. When he realizes that Jago has lied to him, he asks "Why?" Jago's answer is plain and simple: "Because you took what was mine!" The end of the television drama is far more cynical than Shakespeare's. After Othello's death, Jago simply walks away and is rewarded at the end of the picture by being made the next police commissioner.

The Davies *Othello* features strong performances but has difficulty emerging from the shadow of Shakespeare. Presenting the program for the PBS series *Masterpiece Theatre* (January 28, 2002), series host Russell Baker could hardly contain his contempt for an adaptation that discarded Shakespeare's poetry for the "modern English of TV cop shows." *Baltimore Sun* television critic David Zurawik found "poetry in the performances by Walker and Christopher Eccleston," however, also claiming that "the camera can have poetry, too." Perhaps, but this is not exactly equivalent to what Shakespeare wrote, and many who know the play will be in sympathy with Russell Baker's comment on Davies, "He throws the poetry out." However, the alleged "poetry" of the images does transform the play into a powerful racial spectacle of miscegenation and violence.

REFERENCES

Crowl, Samuel, "Othello," *Shakespeare Bulletin*, 41 (Winter 1996), 41–42; Donaldson, Peter S., *Shakespearean Films/Shakespearean Directors* (Boston: Unwin Hyman, 1990); Eckert, Charles W., ed., *Focus on Shakespearean Films* (Englewood Cliffs, N.J.: Prentice Hall, 1972); Gleiberman, Owen, "Class Warfare," *Entertainment Weekly* no. 612 (Sept. 7, 2001), 132–33; McCarthy, Todd, "O." *Variety* (June 11–17, 2001), 18, 23; Jorgens, Jack J., *Shakespeare on Film* (Bloomington: Indiana University Press, 1977); Manvell, Roger, *Shakespeare and the Film*, rev. ed. (Cranbury, N.J.: A.S. Barnes, 1979); Rothwell, Kenneth S., and Annabelle Henkin Melzer, *Shakespeare on Screen: An International Filmography and Videography* (New York: Neal Schuman, 1990).

—*J.C.T., J.M.W. AND R.F.W*

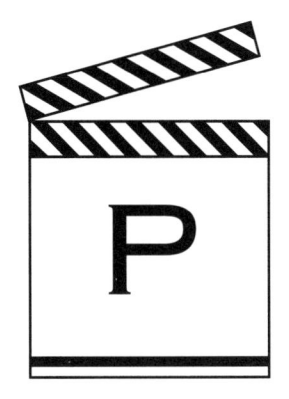

PROSPERO'S BOOKS

See THE TEMPEST

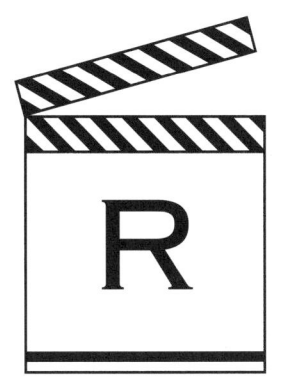

RAN

See KING LEAR

RICHARD III (1592)

Richard III (1912), U.S.A., directed by James Keane, adapted by Frederick Warde; M.B. Dudley Amusement Company.

Richard III (1955), U.K., directed by Laurence Olivier, adapted by Olivier and Alan Dent; London Films.

Richard III (1995), U.S.A., directed by Richard Loncraine, adapted by Loncraine and Ian McKellen; United Artists.

Looking for Richard (1996), U.S.A., directed by Al Pacino; Twentieth Century-Fox.

The Play

Although the play dates to 1592, the Quarto edition was not published until 1597. The Quarto's title page pretty well describes the action as follows: *The Tragedy of King Richard the Third, containing his treacherous plots against his brother Clarence; the pitiful murder of his innocent nephews; his tyrannical usurpation; with the whole course of his detested life, and most deserved death*. Though the title page lists this history play as a tragedy, it is only "tragic" in the medieval sense, in that it deals with the fall of a king. Shakespeare's source was Raphael Holinshed's *Chronicles* and Sir Thomas More's *History of King Richard the Third*, not a very flattering portrait, written circa 1514 but not published until 1557. Tudor historians tended to demonize Richard of Gloucester, and, following their lead, Shakespeare makes him deformed in body (the dowager queen Margaret, who has his number, calls Richard a "poisonous bunch-backed toad") and in mind. He is the equal of Othello's ensign Iago in his malice, though his villainy has a more apparent purpose.

Richard seeks the Crown and methodically goes about destroying those who stand in his way. This "elfish-marked, abortive, rooting hog" intends to usurp his dying brother, Edward IV, and cheerfully plots to dispose of George, duke of Clarence, his elder brother, who is framed by Richard, put in prison, and then drowned in a butt (cask) of malmsey wine, on Richard's orders. Informed of Clarence's death, King Edward IV dies of grief, but Richard has to overcome yet another obstacle. He thereupon orders the murder of the little princes, Edward, prince of Wales, and his brother Richard, duke of York, both of whom Gloucester, ironically their protector, has imprisoned in the Tower of London. He has already seen to the death of Edward, prince of Wales, the son and heir of King Henry VI and, outrageously, "woo'd and won" Edward's widow, the Lady Anne, who should despise him and yet succumbs to his poisonous charm.

Richard is constantly pleased with himself and his wicked plotting, and enjoys taking the audience into his confidence, but the spider king weaves a seductive verbal web as one evil scheme is eclipsed by the next, each increasingly more flamboyant, until Richard finally overreaches himself and alienates his henchman, the duke of Buckingham, whom he underestimates and stupidly slights. Buckingham then turns against Richard and joins his sworn enemy Henry, the earl of Richmond, who finally kills Gloucester at the battle of Bosworth Field.

The Films

This survey must begin in May of 1912, when a film of *Richard III*, directed by James Keare and starring the popular Shakespearean actor Frederick Warde, was released—and is most significant because it is now believed by archivists to be the oldest extant American feature film. (Film archivists define "feature" length as being at least four reels, or 40 minutes long; *Richard III* runs to 55 minutes.) The surviving print was donated to the American Film Institute in 1996 by William Buffum of Portland, Oregon, a retired flour mill manager who acquired the film in 1960 and carefully preserved the 35 mm print for 35 years but without understanding its historical importance. Archivist and historian Kevin Brownlow remarked to the *New York Times* that to find such a lost film that had been "expunged from the memory" but "complete in its original print is really astounding," because "over 70 percent of all feature films produced before the 1920s no longer exist."

According to Bernard Weinraub of the *New York Times*, the film was made in Westchester County and at City Island in the Bronx at a cost of $30,000 and is remarkable for its "lavish battle scenes," filmed with a cast of hundreds. Interviewed by *The Brooklyn Daily Eagle* in November of 1912, Frederick Warde expressed amazement at the "staging and methods of the moving-picture people," especially the way in which the director would tell "the other actors what to do, telling them when to look glad or sorry, when to shout and when to fight, without telling them why they did any of these things." The 1912 film was not the first film treatment, however. A one-reel Vitagraph abridgment was made in 1908 under the supervision of J. Stuart Blackton, and in 1911 a 27-minute abridgment was made in Britain, starring F.R. Benson.

The first major sound film to treat *Richard III* as a play—discounting the derivative *Tower of London* directed by Rowland V. Lee and scripted by Robert N. Lee in 1939—was Laurence Olivier's film made at Shepperton Studios, London, and shot in Technicolor and VistaVision. Again, Olivier set the standard, transforming himself into a bent and twisted stage villain, whose asides to the camera are used to hypnotize the viewers and lure them into his evil mentality. The credentials of the supporting cast are impeccable: John Gielgud (Clarence), Ralph Richardson (Buckingham), Cedric Hardwicke (Edward IV), Stanley Baker (Richmond), and Claire Bloom (Lady Anne).

Just as Olivier's *Henry V* had incorporated contextualizing material from *2 Henry IV*, Alan Dent's screenplay for *Richard III* incorporated portions of *3 Henry VI* as indicated by the film's full title: *Richard the Third, by William Shakespeare, with Some Interpolations by David Garrick, Colly Cibber, etc.* Such "interpolations" are in evidence from the play's opening "Now is the winter of our discontent" soliloquy that establishes Olivier's character unforgettably. The film offers none of the lavish spectacle of *Henry V,* but its inventive deployment of intimate stage settings suggestive of medieval woodcuts (designed

"My Kingdom for a horse!" shouts Laurence Olivier in the title role of Shakespeare's Richard III. (COURTESY NATIONAL FILM SOCIETY ARCHIVES)

Ian McKellen portrayed Richard III as a fascist dictator in the 1930s in Shakespeare's play. (COURTESY UNITED ARTISTS)

by Roger Furse and Carmen Dillon) as well as Olivier's stark facial makeup—producing a pasty white face crowned by coiling black curls—contrasts sharply with the film's muted pastel color palette and is distinctive in its stylization. The film's artful design allows Olivier's bravura acting performance to come to the fore.

Richard III, which Olivier first played on stage in 1944, was one of Olivier's defining roles, and for many years his interpretation was considered definitive. His achievement was so daunting that no one attempted another feature film treatment for 40 years, though there were two video interpretations. The first of these was produced in Georgia in the Soviet Union in 1980, directed by Robert Sturua, featuring Ramaz Chkhikvadze as Gloucester, and produced at the Rustaveli Theatre in Tbilisi. In 1983 Jane Howell directed a video interpretation for the BBC Shakespeare Series, adapted by David Snodin and starring Ron Cook as Gloucester.

In 1995 the play was given an astonishing postmodern fascist spin by director Richard Loncraine, who broke Olivier's spell by updating the action to the 20th century. Ian McKellen played the lead role of Richard, supported by Jim Broadbent (Buckingham), Maggie Smith (the duchess of York), Nigel Hawthorne (Clarence), Annette Bening (Queen Elizabeth), and Kristin Scott Thomas (Lady Anne). The film's design operates on the supposition that England had gone fascist during the 1930s and that Richard was a fascist dictator.

The Court scenes take place in elegant cafés, where a jazz baby sings a musical rendering of Christopher Marlowe's famous lyric, "The Passionate Shepherd's Reply." Chronology is fractured and the play is considerably streamlined and simplified, but the language is still Shakespeare's. At the stylized Victory Ball that begins the film, McKellen's Richard steps up to a microphone to begin his "Now is the winter of our discontent" monologue, then pisses away the rest of its more sinister implications in a urinal.

One derivative film that should not be ignored here is Al Pacino's *Looking for Richard* (1996), a sort of skewered documentary that might just as easily have been titled "Looking for Shakespeare." While trying to make sense of what may be Shakespeare's most frequently performed play, Pacino and his company also question the relevance of Shakespeare for today's audiences. (He might have saved some of this agonizing by looking carefully at Ian McKellen's political performance.) His man-on-the-street interview approach demonstrates only that the man on the street is not necessarily well informed about Shakespeare or history.

Establishing a proper focus seems to be a major challenge here, and it is not entirely clear what Pacino intends to document: the relevance of Shakespeare today? Behind-the-scenes preparations for a play performance? The shooting of a motion picture adaptation? Pacino himself seems not to be entirely certain. The film includes a pilgrimage to Shakespeare's Birthplace Museum in Stratford-upon-Avon, a visit to the site of the Globe Theatre reconstruction on the South Bank, and interviews with remarkable actors and directors, such as Sir John Gielgud, Vanessa Redgrave, Peter Brook, and Kenneth Branagh.

With his own cast (Alec Baldwin as Clarence, Winona Ryder as Lady Anne, Aidan Quinn as Richmond, Kevin Spacey as Buckingham) Pacino questions why American actors should be intimidated by the Bard, whether Richard and Buckingham should be treated as gangsters, the proper use of iambic pentameter, and the riddles of Shakespeare's densely packed rhetoric and the ambiguous motivation of his characters. He even brings in an educator, Frederick Kimball, for scholarly advice, whose advice he ends up rejecting.

Rehearsals, finished performances, and video replays of several scenes (Richard's seduction of the Lady Anne, for example, the arrest of Hastings, Gloucester's vexed nightmares and his death under Richmond's sword) are combined in a fascinating, seamless flow. Pacino will begin a line in his apartment, continue it on stage in costume, then review the finished product on a video monitor in the studio. Pacino creates a very interesting Richard, compounded of diffidence and deadly authority. What is the point? To show a serious actor attempting to find his character and attempting to perfect his craft. The questions raised about the play are well worth listening to.

REFERENCES

Colley, Scott, *Richard's Himself Again: A Stage History of Richard III* (Westport, Conn.: Greenwood Press, 1992); Manvell, Roger, *Shakespeare and the Film* (New York: Praeger, 1971); Mitchell, Deborah, "*Richard III*: Tonypandy in the Twentieth Century," *Literature/Film Quarterly*, 25:2 (1997), 133–145; Rothwell, Kenneth S., and Annabelle Henkin Melzer, *Shakespeare on Screen: An International Filmography and Videography* (New York: Neal Schuman, 1990); Weinraub, Bernard, "Movie History Emerges from a Basement," *The New York Times*, September 17, 1996, A1, B2.

—*J.M.W. AND J.C.T.*

ROMANOFF AND JULIET

See ROMEO AND JULIET

ROMEO AND JULIET (1595–96)

Romeo and Juliet (1936), U.S.A., directed by George Cukor, adapted by Talbot Jennings; Metro-Goldwyn-Mayer.

Romeo y Julieta (1943), Mexico, directed by Miguel M. Delgado, adapted by Jaime Salvadori, Posa Films.

Giuliete e Romeo/Romeo and Juliet (1954), Italy/U.K., directed and adapted by Renato Castellani; Verona Productions.

West Side Story (1961), U.S.A., directed by Robert Wise, adapted by Jerome Robbins, Arthur Laurents, and Ernest Lehman; United Artists.

Romanoff and Juliet (1961), U.S.A., directed and adapted by Peter Ustinov from his play; Universal-International.

Romeo and Juliet (1968), U.K./Italy, directed by Franco Zeffirelli, adapted by Franco Brusati and Maestro D'Amico; Paramount.

Romeo and Juliet (1978), U.K., directed by Alvin Rakoff, adapted by Alan Shallcross; British Broadcasting Company/Time-Life Television.

Romeo and Juliet (1982), U.S.A., directed and adapted by William Woodman; Bard Productions.

Valley Girl (1983), U.S.A., directed by Martha Coolidge, screenplay by Wayne Crawford and Andrew Lane, Valley 9000.

Fire with Fire (1986), U.S.A., directed by Duncan Gibbins, screenplay by Bill Phillips and Warren Skarren. Paramount Pictures.

China Girl (1987), U.S.A., directed by Abel Ferrara, written by Nicholas St.John; Vestron Pictures.

Romeo and Juliet (1988), U.K., directed and adapted by Joan Kemp-Welch; Thames Television.

Under the Boardwalk (1989), U.S.A., directed by Fritz Kiersch, screenplay by Robert King III, New World Entertainment.

Zebrahead (1992), U.S.A., directed and written by Anthony Drazan; Ixlan Corporation.

Romeo and Juliet (1993), Canada, directed and adapted by Norman Campbell; Canadian Broadcasting Company.

Romeo and Juliet (1994), U.K., directed by Alan Horrox, adapted by Grant Cathro; Thames Television.

Tromeo and Juliet (1996), U.S.A., directed by Lloyd Kaufman, screenplay by James Gunn II and Lloyd Kaufman. Troma Inc.

William Shakespeare's Romeo + Juliet (1996), U.S.A., directed by Baz Luhrmann, script by Craig Pearce and Baz Luhrmann; Twentieth Century-Fox.

Shakespeare in Love (1998), U.S.A., directed by John Madden, screenplay by Marc Norman and Tom Stoppard; Universal Pictures.

Romeo Must Die (2000), U.S.A., directed by Andrzej Bartkowiak, screenplay by Mitchell Kapner and Eric Bernt; Warner Bros.

The Play

Romeo and Juliet may be the best known of Shakespeare's works. Its balcony scene has become part of the cultural iconography, and even people who have never read the play know what it means to be called a "Romeo." Opening with a sonnet spoken by the figure of the Chorus who describes the action that will occupy "the two hours traffic of our stage," Shakespeare shows how a quarrel between the servants of opposing families quickly escalates into a fight that stops only when the prince of Verona intervenes. Distanced from the fighting, Romeo suffers from an unrequited love, while elsewhere Paris receives Capulet's permission to woo the 13-year-old Juliet. A party to be held at the Capulets' provides an intersection for these various lines of action. Benvolio believes the party will help his melancholy friend Romeo forget an infatuation with Rosaline, but Romeo is going because he learns Rosaline will be there. Capulet invites Paris, and Lady Capulet urges her daughter, Juliet, to judge the suitor's qualities. At the party, Capulet must calm Juliet's fiery cousin Tybalt, who recognizes Romeo and wants to fight him. Romeo and Juliet, of course, fall in love at first sight, compose a sonnet in their first lines to each other, and later pledge marriage when they meet alone outside Juliet's balcony.

The first half of the play contains many romantic and comic moments. The love between Romeo and Juliet allows Shakespeare the opportunity for some of his most memorable and frequently quoted lines. In addition, Juliet's nurse, who reminisces about Juliet's girlhood, and Romeo's friend, Mercutio, who invents the Queen Mab story, demonstrate a comic ability to spin a long-winded tale. The two later have a wonderful scene of bawdy bantering when the nurse comes to confirm Romeo's intentions. The nurse later pairs with Romeo's confessor, Friar Laurence, to bring the young lovers together, and, just before the middle of the play, the lovers are secretly married.

At this pivotal point, Mercutio and Benvolio encounter the angry Tybalt, who is looking for Romeo. When Romeo refuses to fight, Mercutio instead challenges Tybalt, and when Romeo tries to stop it, he succeeds only in causing Mercutio's death. Saying that his love has made him weak, Romeo goes after Tybalt, kills him, and then flees before the prince arrives to banish him. Meanwhile Juliet, waiting for news from her new husband, learns instead that he has killed her cousin. The lovers manage to spend one night together before Romeo escapes to Mantua. Distraught over the effect of Tybalt's death, Capulet decides to push forward with Juliet's marriage. When Juliet tells the friar she will kill herself rather than marry, he devises a risky plan to reunite the lovers. On the evening that her parents prepare for a second party, this one to celebrate Juliet's wedding, Juliet takes a sleeping potion that will make her appear dead. The next morning the nurse discovers the apparently dead Juliet, and the family must prepare for a funeral rather than a wedding.

In Mantua, Romeo has not received Friar Laurence's message that Juliet is alive, and instead Balthazar tells him that he has seen her buried. In despair, Romeo gets poison from an apothecary and travels to Verona to die next to Juliet. In a confrontation at the tomb, Romeo kills Paris, opens the tomb, weeps over Juliet, and then kills himself. When Friar Laurence arrives, he finds Romeo and Paris dead, and Juliet reviving from the drug-induced sleep. Hearing noises outside, the friar leaves, and Juliet stabs herself with Romeo's dagger. The prince arrives, finds out what has happened, and admonishes the families. Montague promises to raise a gold statue to Juliet, and Capulet promises to raise another of Romeo.

The Films

Next to *Hamlet*, *Romeo and Juliet* is Shakespeare's most often filmed play, and several major silent film companies tried their hand at it. Robert Hamilton Ball lists a *Burlesque on Romeo and Juliet* (1902) by Thomas Edison and speculates that it may be from an earlier George Méliès short. The largest of the early East Coast studios, Vitagraph, which often used "high-culture" material to gain respectability for the new industry, released a one-reel abridgment of *Romeo and Juliet* in 1908. The next year, Edwin Thanhouser, a theatrical producer before turning to films, made a two-reel *Romeo and Juliet*, of which about half survives. When Metro announced a *Romeo and Juliet*, staring Francis X. Bushman (the reigning matinee idol) and Beverly Bayne, to be released in October of 1916, William Fox hurried to produce a version starring Theda Bara (the original vamp) and Harry Hilliard, which managed to open at the same time.

The first sound version of the play followed the tradition of the prestige film treatment. The Irving Thalberg and George Cukor *Romeo and Juliet* boasted a large budget and a big-name cast. When Louis B. Mayer rejected Thalberg's original suggestion to film in Verona as being too expensive, designer Cedric Gibbons built a massive and elaborate set that eventually occupied more than five acres of the MGM lot. English actors took several key roles, including Leslie Howard as Romeo, Basil Rathbone as Tybalt, and Dame Edith Oliver as the nurse, but Thalberg's wife, Norma Shearer, played Juliet, John Barrymore played Mercutio, and comic actor Andy Devine gave his gravelly, rustic whine to the role of Peter. Agnes de Mille choreographed the Capulet ball, and scholars John Tucker Murray and William Strunk provided scholarly expertise, with Thalberg reportedly telling Strunk, "Your job is to protect Shakespeare from us."

Leslie Howard, who was not Thalberg's first choice among available English actors, was himself reluctant to take the part and wrote that Romeo "seems hardly to be a three dimensional figure since his principal function is little more than to be the object of Juliet's affection." In addition, Howard was 42 and Norma Shearer was 36—hardly budding adolescents. He agreed finally, at least in part, because he decided that the Romeo of the second half of the play, the Romeo banished to Mantua and stunned into suicide by the news of Juliet's death, was, as he put it, "a baby Hamlet," the role for which he wanted to prepare.

The film emphasizes the force of circumstance on individual action even more than the play. Although Shakespeare's play opens with a small incident—the thumb-biting gesture—that rapidly multiplies into a larger conflict, Cukor's film shows how the quarrel between servants grows out of the larger conflict between the families. As the film opens, the entire Capulet household seems to be in procession when they suddenly encounter the Montagues, coming from the opposite direction, in a similar procession. The thumb-biting incident develops as an overflow of the hatred generated by this accidental meeting of the two families. The film's charm, however, lies more in its gestures than in its passions. Examples are not hard to find. Andy Devine's role in the opening fight is immediately undercut by the fact that, in keeping with his slapstick characterization, he cannot get his sword out. Basil Rathbone's controlled performance as Tybalt makes him menacing and glowering, but projects cold-blooded malice rather than passionate fury. However appealing Norma Shearer's Juliet may be in her balcony, one cannot help noticing that she is enshrined in an intricate pulpit-like structure that seems to be about 30 feet above Romeo. Barrymore's wonderfully eccentric Mercutio bows and waves to the ladies of the square, delivers a fanciful and energetic reading of the Queen Mab speech, and is the only Mercutio that dies laughing, but in the central scene of the film his wounding happens so rapidly it is almost unexpected. The same is true of Romeo's fight with Tybalt, which lasts only 30 seconds, about half as long as the more dramatically staged fight with Paris where their shadows cross and loom against the walls as they fight in the labyrinthine crypt.

The film lost money and was not well received by critics, but seen from today's perspective, it possesses a kind of charm in its very artificiality. It is an example of that midnight-and-silver 1930s photography that makes black-and-white movies glisten, a contrast that is most apparent in the ball scene where Juliet's shimmering white dress and jewels contrast with Romeo's black outfit and white shirt. When he approaches her on the floor, the rest of the dancers fall into a shadow.

Renato Castellani in his *Giuliete e Romeo/Romeo and Juliet*, for which he won an award in the 1954 Venice Film Festival, makes an entirely different set of choices. His stars are less well known, and, in spite of the beautiful photography, Castellani gives the play perhaps the darkest, most enclosed feeling of any of these film versions. Shot in Italy, the film is notable both for its realistic settings and for its use of Renaissance art as pattern and backdrop for several of the costumes and scenes. Indeed, watching the movie can seem a bit like thumbing through a well-illustrated art book as one notices a dress from Botticelli, a fresco from Fra Angelico, the door from San Zeno Maggiore, and others.

More than just providing authenticity, however, Castellani's Renaissance world encloses and isolates his characters. After John Gielgud delivers the prologue, dressed in dark Elizabethan costume, the Italian neo-realist camera style leads the viewers into a walled city, through its gate, and up narrow streets whose high walls on either side make the streets seem almost like tunnels. Except for a shot of Romeo on a small finger of land near the water at the beginning of the film and the shots on the road to Mantua, neither the sky nor much else of undomesticated nature appears in this film. The fight scenes at the beginning and middle of the play seem to add to the oppressive atmosphere by cutting off the tops of the buildings. When Romeo (Laurence Harvey) and Juliet (Susan Shentall) meet for the balcony scene, they are framed by the pillars, windows, and walls of the building. Castellani deliberately puts architectural barriers between them at all times, and they are never together in a single unobstructed shot. This frustration extends to the wedding scene, not dramatized in the play itself, where they are married through an iron grille, exchanging a flower, the ring, and a chaste kiss. Romeo has to make his way through the labyrinth of Verona several times. Castellani eliminates Capulet's illiterate servant and the invitation episode, so Romeo and his friends seem accidentally to run into the partygoers. Romeo finds a passage, follows it to a door, and comes out in the middle of the party. Later, when he comes back from Mantua, he must get into the walled city, so he dismounts and sends his horse running up to the entrance. With the guards distracted, Romeo sneaks through the streets. Later, when he gets to the church and finds the doors closed, he again finds a way around and then must move a huge stone covering the entrance to the tomb before he can get to Juliet.

Capulet, as played by Sebastian Cabot, generates tremendous emotional energy both at the party when he restrains Tybalt and later when he threatens Juliet for not wanting to marry Paris, but for the most part Castellani focuses on the two main characters and diminishes the role of Mercutio, whose Queen Mab speech disappears altogether. In the central scene of the play, Romeo meets Tybalt alone and is joined soon after by Mercutio and Benvolio. Castellani also provides some unusual turns at the end of the play. For example, Romeo kills Paris with a huge candlestick rather than with a sword. Then, rather than take poison, Romeo must stab himself, since Castellani has eliminated the apothecary scene. He also adds some minor characters, such as Abraham, a young man killed in the opening fight, and Rosaline, who does not actually appear in Shakespeare's play but in this film attends the Capulet ball and warns Romeo to leave.

By contrast, Franco Zeffirelli's *Romeo and Juliet* seems to be a film about youth and spring, populated with long-haired, beautiful adolescents. Its charm and sexuality captured the youth movement of the late '60s and made this the most popular and lucrative adaptation of any Shakespeare play; it won Academy Awards for cinematography and for costuming. For the title roles, Zeffirelli picked Leonard Whiting and Olivia Hussey, unknown but attractive actors whose looks projected his vision of the play. He pared it down and gave the film a focus that eliminates moments such as Juliet's speech on consummating her marriage, her confusion later in this same scene over who has killed whom, her speech before she takes the potion, the nurse's discovery of Juliet's body, Romeo's visit to the apothecary, and the fight in which Romeo kills Paris. Among several cuts and rearrangements, these choices in particular indicate how Zeffirelli emphasizes the rapid development of the love story and eliminates aspects that might make the characters more reflective or otherwise complicate their image.

One of the accomplishments of the film is to present a solid and believable world of dimension and

Leonard Whiting and Olivia Hussey portrayed the star-crossed lovers in Franco Zeffirelli's Romeo and Juliet.
(COURTESY PARAMOUNT PICTURES)

substance. Zeffirelli uses some of the same locations that Castellani did, but while Castellani's version is dark and claustrophobic, Zeffirelli's version is light and open and spacious. If Castellani's characters seem oppressed by their environment, Zeffirelli's move through it with comfort. John McEnery's extraordinarily complex Mercutio, for example, not only fights in the square, he also bathes himself and washes his handkerchief in its fountain, climbs its stairs, and dies on one of its tiers. Perhaps following that same logic, this Romeo and Juliet are themselves very real and very attainable lovers. The balcony scene, for example, shows Zeffirelli attempting to balance Shakespeare's poetry against the physical images. While Cukor's lovers touch hands, and Castellani's do not touch at all, this Romeo sees his Juliet in a low-cut gown sitting on the edge of a long and spacious balcony that wraps part way around the building. Framed in the greenery of the Capulet garden, the lovers discover each other, then Romeo rather quickly climbs a tree and is on the balcony with her. Though many of the best-known lines of the play remain, they are punctuated by passionate kissing. Juliet at one point has to stop and catch her breath. When this Romeo asks "Oh wilt thou leave me so unsatisfied?" Juliet's startled face makes clear that she understands the term in its sexual context, and she seems relieved when he explains that the only satisfaction he wants is to exchange vows. She coyly presses her hand toward him, recalling the hand imagery of their first meeting.

Among Zeffirelli's embellishments is the suggestion that Capulet's statement about early marriage marring a woman might refer to Lady Capulet herself. When Capulet says the line to Paris, Lady Capulet appears in a window in the background, glares in his direction and then shuts it. Later she, rather than Capulet himself, calms Tybalt, who has caught sight of Romeo at the party. Finally, as Anthony Davies points out, she seems "devastated by the death of a lover rather than a nephew" when Tybalt dies. Another addition is the song, "What Is a Youth," whose mournful lines, "so dies the rose, so dies the youth," a young man sings as the Capulet guests encircle him, and as Romeo and Juliet are speaking their first words to each other. However irritating some critics found this and other sentimental additions, the song itself became a popular hit, perhaps underscoring Zeffirelli's accuracy in reaching his intended youthful audience.

William Shakespeare's Romeo + Juliet has been called the version for the Generation X, MTV, or postmodern sensibility, and more than one critic reviewing the film longed for the comparatively milder excesses of Zeffirelli's version. Certainly Baz Luhrmann refracts the Romeo and Juliet story through the conventions of contemporary pop media. A TV anchorwoman speaks the play's prologue and epilogue from the framed confines of a television screen. Characters are introduced through captioned freeze-frames from a news story. Almost immediately after the opening brawl between Montagues and Capulets, newspaper headlines announce it. When Leonardo DiCaprio's Romeo wanders back from his early morning reveries, he sees the video playback of the fight that opened the film. This is a nervous, frenetic film, visually and emotionally intense, characterized by rapid camera movement and fragmentation. Close-ups dissect their subjects, distorting faces and objects, while long shots tend to fill the screen with iconic images of, for example, a huge Christ statue positioned between the Montague and Capulet business towers, or a church interior glowing in the light of hundreds of candles, or the ruined proscenium arch that frames a junk-filled beach. In this world, Romeo and Juliet (Claire Danes) are constantly interrupted. When Juliet first meets Romeo gazing through an aquarium, the nurse immediately pulls her away. When they hold hands and kiss, they must seek refuge in an elevator. In the balcony scene, they evade security cameras by kissing underwater. In the aubade scene, the nurse and Lady Capulet are in the bedroom as Juliet kisses Romeo goodbye, and he once more falls into the pool. In the tomb scene, Romeo fights his way past the police who are searching for him with helicopters and spotlights. He is at the business of drinking the poison when Juliet awakens, and interrupts him too late. He dies in her arms.

Luhrmann, like Zeffirelli, selected young actors for the part, but neither Claire Danes nor Leonardo DiCaprio were unknowns. Both were familiar from television, and both had achieved recognition in coming-of-age films. The division of older and younger generation in this film, however, seems ultimately an illusion. The violence of the younger generation is clearly an extension of parental excesses, most notably Fulgencio Capulet's (Paul Sorvino) angry rebuke of Tybalt in the Fellini-esque party scene or his later fury when he tells Juliet she must marry Dave Paris, the governor's son whose face is on a magazine cover labeled "most eligible bachelor."

Perhaps it is not so much the changes in the actual lines as the unusualness of the accompanying visual images that makes this film so disconcerting. Attempting to reconcile Shakespeare's "swords" with the hip world of Verona Beach, Luhrmann uses a close-up of the

Baz Luhrmann's Romeo + Juliet *brought Shakespeare into the postmodern age.* (COURTESY TWENTIETH CENTURY FOX)

characters' guns to show that their brand name is "Sword" (instead of, one might suppose, "Colt"). Romeo and Juliet deliver most of the lines of the balcony scene in the Capulet swimming pool. Mercutio (Harold Perrineau), perhaps exploiting recent critical trends, comes to the party wearing a sequined minidress and makeup and then appears as the star of a Las Vegas-style production number. Romeo is unsure of his first vision of Juliet because he is recovering from the Queen Mab drug that Mercutio has given him. Friar Laurence (well played by Pete Postlethwaite) seems to be an advocate of alternative medicine, and other alternative solutions, rather than a well-intentioned confessor. He has a large crucifix tattooed on his back, clearly visible through his transparent guayabera, and has nearly mystical visions of how his intervention can end the violence. In addition, employing ethnic divisions that are often used in adaptations of this play, Luhrmann makes the Montagues Latin, with Paul Sorvino as Fulgencio Capulet, John Leguizamo as Tybalt, and dark-eyed Claire Danes as Juliet. The Montagues are Anglo, perhaps Irish, with Brian Dennehy as Ted Montague and Leonardo DiCaprio as Romeo. Interestingly, from this point of view, Mercutio is black, which gives a somewhat different weight to his dying lines, "a plague o' both your houses."

The several adaptations of the Romeo and Juliet story use various ways to divide their young lovers. Whereas *Romanoff and Juliet*, for example, makes the warring households the diplomatic outposts of the United States and Russia, *West Side Story*, *China Girl*, and *Zebrahead* rely on ethnic and racial differences. Shakespeare himself examined such differences as Christian and Jew in *The Merchant of Venice*, Moor and Venetian in *Othello*, and Egyptian and Roman in *Antony and Cleopatra*, but, in *Romeo and Juliet*, his Montagues and Capulets are feuding families of the same tribe, and seem to be more often paralleled than contrasted.

The Mexican comic actor Mario Moreno, known as Cantinflas, developed a parody of the *Romeo and Juliet* story as a vehicle for his customary comedic stance. His primary skill is his talent for verbal evasion, but the Cantinflas character, the *peladito*, shares with Chaplin's Little Tramp an identification with the oppressed poor, and his *Romeo y Julieta* in various ways pits rich against poor. The film, directed by Miguel M. Delgado, provides a frame tale in which Cantinflas pretends to be a Shakespearean actor and plays the role of Romeo in a production that in several scenes echoes George Cukor's 1936 version. Balancing formal diction with street slang and comic rhymes, Cantinflas deflates the pretensions of official high culture through verbal and visual twists on the play.

Cantinflas in this film is a *ruleterro*, a cabbie, whose cab is beyond antique and will not start when Cantinflas tries to take his girlfriend for a ride. Lifting the hood, he finds a box, a can, a cat, and, finally, her kitten. Just as the car backfires, covering the girlfriend in soot, another man in a shiny new car offers her a ride, and she leaves. Despondent, Cantinflas happens to pick up a fare, two men who become the Friar and the rejected lover of the story. They scheme to win over Juliet's father by appealing to his snobbish interest in theater, and particularly in Shakespeare. Offering him enough money to buy a new car, they convince Cantinflas to become "Abelardo del Monte," a Shakespearean actor just returned to Mexico after a distinguished career in Europe who will play the role of Romeo in a special production. In both this frame story and in the version of *Romeo and Juliet* that is played, Juliet's parents are pretentious and avaricious. In the role of Old Capulet, the father comments that Paris is stupid, but rich. Shortly after, Lady Capulet explains to Juliet that husbands are not meant to inspire passion but to pay bills. At the ball, Capulet becomes a ticket-taker, counting guests and collecting stubs.

Cantinflas, with some rearrangement of incidents, keeps to the general outline of the Cukor version. In the first confrontation between the Montagues and the Capulets, however, Cantinflas/Romeo bites his thumb at the Capulets, and the fight quickly disintegrates as the combatants empty out the trash, and vegetables go flying through the air. The dance scene, modeled on the famous dance in Cukor's film, features Cantinflas with his customary low-slung pants dancing comically with Juliet. In the balcony scene, Cantinflas knocks out the guard with a mandolin, sings a *ranchera* song to Juliet, and falls into a reflecting pool several times. In the central fight in the play, Cantinflas first distracts the combatants with a game of dice, then goes through the pockets of his dead friend Mercutio to collect a debt before challenging Tybalt. Later, in the apothecary scene, Cantinflas says he would rather have the poison in a little taco than in the large bottle the apothecary offers him. As the tomb scene concludes, Cantinflas's girlfriend from the frame tale storms onstage and starts a fight. Brought before a magistrate, Cantinflas tells the story that is the film's narrative line. In the film's conclusion, three Shakespeare critics, who have been watching the play, ask to see the actor. Cantinflas, believing they have come to praise his performance, goes into an adjacent room to reap his rewards. Instead the three men thrash him and march out of the room, holding their heads high, as Cantinflas's friends rush to comfort him.

In filming *West Side Story*, film director Robert Wise used actual street scenes for some of the musical numbers and perhaps drew on his background as an editor to create dynamic and interesting scenes from co-director Jerome Robbins' choreography. Wise managed to improve the genre of musicals just as he had earlier significantly contributed to the western (*Blood on the Moon*, 1948), the fight film (*The Set-Up*, 1949), and the science fiction film (*The Day the Earth Stood Still*, 1951). *West Side Story* won nine Academy Awards, including best director, best picture, best supporting actor (George Chakiris), best actress (Rita Moreno), and best scoring of a musical picture.

Based on the play by Arthur Laurents, with lyrics by Stephen Sondheim and music by Leonard Bernstein, *West Side Story* uses several elements from Shakespeare's play but casts them in a somewhat different context. In this telling of the story, the Capulets become the Puerto Rican gang, the Sharks, and Capulet and Lady Capulet are replaced by a big brother, Bernardo (George Chakiris), who watches out for this story's Juliet, Maria (Natalie Wood), who has recently arrived from Puerto Rico, but who also becomes the Tybalt of the film. Instead of a nurse, Maria has a best friend, Anita (Rita Moreno), and Paris becomes Bernado's fellow gang member, Chino (José De Vega). A rival gang, the Jets, show even fewer specific resemblances to the Montagues. Riff (Russ Tamblyn), who is actually the leader of the gang, seems most like Mercutio mainly in that Bernardo kills him. The Romeo character in the film, Tony (Richard Beymer), is retired from the gang and working in a drugstore for Doc, who resembles Friar Laurence to the extent that the friar is often pictured as being surrounded by alchemical instruments. At the end of the film, Tony, Bernardo, and Riff die, and only Maria remains to articulate the sense of anger and violation that Shakespeare's play gives to the prince.

In her reconstruction of the actual process of writing this play, Bernstein's biographer, Joan Peyser, says that various approaches to the main conflict included opposing Jews and Catholics, Anglos and Latinos in Los Angeles, and blacks and Puerto Ricans in New York, before they settled on the Sharks and the Jets, one gang composed of recently immigrated Puerto Ricans and the other composed largely of first-generation Americans, the children of European immigrants. The play is unusual also in its attention to the question of immigration and the idea of what it means to be an American. For Maria, Anita, Bernardo, and the other recently immigrated members of the Sharks, life in Puerto Rico is not so distant, and they frequently discuss the notion of going back there. Tony, on the other hand, is Polish, and the other members of the Jets are identified as Irish or Italian, members of the previous wave of immigrants. The New York accents of the Jets contrast strongly with the Spanish accents of the Sharks. Lieutenant Schrank, for example, very pointedly identifies himself and the Jets as "American," as opposed to the Sharks.

Peter Ustinov's original play, *Romanoff and Juliet*, focuses more on the quarrel between families than on the fate of the young lovers, and the film version, released the same year as *West Side Story*, reinforces the Shakespearean borrowing. From the beginning, Ustinov made Shakespeare's Montagues and Capulets into cold war–era Russians and Americans, but whereas the play opens with two soldiers who relieve the boredom of their watch by indulging in word games, the film plunges immediately into political comment with a shot of the United Nations building as Ustinov's voice-over explains that the film is dedicated to the UN, while the camera sweeps over rows of bored or sleeping delegates. For Ustinov, the love story of Romanoff and Juliet, the son of the Russian ambassador to Concordia and the daughter of the American ambassador to the same country, only underscores the political divisions. Ustinov himself appears as the leader of the tiny nation, which attracts the attention of the superpowers when he casts an abstention on a crucial UN vote. When both nations realize they must court the tiny country, Concordia finds itself offered aid, grain, and, among other things, performances by the Bolshoi Ballet. Seizing his opportunity, Ustinov's character becomes a more successful version of Shakespeare's friar and manages to get the lovers married, bringing peace and saving the day. Although the film has not received much attention and is not currently available, Ustinov was serious about his critique of governments and "huge supra-national corporations," and, in his autobiography, describes how he was pleased to receive a letter of praise from former president Harry Truman.

Abel Ferrara's *China Girl* retains several motifs from Shakespeare's play but also seems to draw on some of the visual imagery of *West Side Story*. The maze of chain-link fence, the graffiti-covered brick walls, the teen dance scene, the use of the fire escape for Juliet's balcony—all these elements establish the New York City atmosphere for both films. Where *West Side Story* depicted rival street gangs, *China Girl* presents, in effect, a second generation of gangs in which the disruptions caused by the younger gangs upset the carefully negotiated cooperation of the more established Chinese and Italian mobsters. The opening shots of the film make it clear that this is a neighborhood undergoing a significant transition. As a Chinese restaurant owner and his helpers transform an Italian restaurant into a Chinese one, Ferrara shows the angry and dismayed faces of the Italians in the neighborhood. Apparently later that same evening, the Romeo of this story, Tony Monte (Richard Panebianco), notices the film's Juliet, a beautiful Chinese girl named Tyan Hue, but called Tye (Sari Chang), dancing at a local dance club. When, without speaking, he begins to dance with her, their attraction is immediate and apparent, so much so that Tye's cousin and brother break up the dance and chase Tony through the streets. He crosses the Canal Street line between the territories, but the boys hesitate only briefly before following him down an alley to a chainlink fence, recalling one of the opening scenes of *West Side Story*. The Italian boys suddenly come out of the shadows on the other side of the fence and rescue Tony by attacking the Chinese. The fight stops only when the police arrive. Tye's brother, Yung Gan (Russell Wong), very much recalls Bernardo of *West Side Story*, and her cousin, Tsu Shin (Joey Chin), is clearly a Tybalt figure. Tony also has an older brother, Alby (James Russo), who parallels Tye's brother, and it is Alby's death that sets off the final violent action in the film. David Caruso plays a Mercutio, here called Mercury, who is more incendiary than mercurial, more a second Tybalt.

Director Ferrara's flair for urban violence gets ample display in this film as the multiple gangs come into conflict. In an odd travesty of cooperation, at one point a member of the older Chinese mob in a disciplinary raid stabs one of the rebellious young Chinese gang members, and when the young man gets up and moves toward the attacker, a member of the older Italian mob appears from the shadows and kills the young man by running a knife through his back. At the film's conclusion, in the middle of an Italian community celebration that features a procession of men carrying a statue of the Virgin Mary, violence erupts again, and both Tony and Tye are shot and die in the street, lying face up on the wet pavement, their hands touching.

Zebrahead, director Anthony Drazan's first film, and winner of the 1992 Sundance Film Festival's Filmmaker's Award, borrows the broader elements from the Romeo and Juliet story—a couple whose love is complicated if not prevented by family barriers, the death of an innocent friend who tries to break up a fight, a killer with a flammable temper, and a violent and fatalistic atmosphere. One of the recurring images in the film is of a character who drops matches on his lawn to show how pollution is seeping into his land and making everything flammable. This film, however, is less direct in its borrowing from either Shakespeare or other films, such as the influential *West Side Story*. The setting of this film is Detroit. Zach (Michael Rapaport), the Romeo of this film, is a redheaded, Jewish high school senior whose family owns a record store. The Juliet character, Nikki (N'Bushe Wright), is a young black girl who has just transferred from a Brooklyn high school and is the cousin of Zach's best friend Dominic, called Dee (DeShonn Castle). Shakespearean identities seem rather blurred in this film. While Dominic has some elements of Romeo's friend and confidant, Benvolio, he also has a protective role toward the film's Juliet. In this respect, he is like the older brothers in *West Side Story* and *China Girl*, except that he, like Shakespeare's Mercutio, dies in Romeo's place. The film's Tybalt character, named Nut (Ron Johnson), is volatile, but rather than being Juliet's cousin, he wants to date her and says he used to live in the house where she now lives.

While Zach apparently has an unrequited romance with a Rosaline-like character, his breaking up with her seems part of a broader effort to define love. In a scene at the record store, Zach's womanizing father (Ray Sharkey) says sex is a subspecies of rhythm and defines love by playing a Johnny Mathis album. Calling Zach's father a schmuck, Zach's grandfather says instead that love is responsibility. In another scene in the high school, a group of black girls point out different boys in the cafeteria and argue over which ones they would date and whether race would make a difference to them. Zack himself is accused by some of the black characters in the film of being a "wannabe," the word they spray-paint across his locker. He acts black, listens to black music, and is dating a young black woman. At the end of the film, although Dee has died, Zach and Nikki have survived, and Zach goes over to Nikki and embraces her, but over their shoulder, in the background, a bookish black militant and an Italian boy fight each other.

Shakespeare in Love, written by Tom Stoppard and Marc Norman, and directed by John Madden, is not so much a version of *Romeo and Juliet* as it is a cleverly imagined story of how the play might have been written, recalling somewhat the atmosphere of Anthony Burgess's 1964 novel *Nothing Like the Sun*. Norman has said that the idea for the film began when his son asked him to do a story about young Shakespeare. Stoppard, of course, has written speculatively about Shakespeare's work in *Rosencrantz and Guildenstern Are Dead* (1967) and has often toyed with the notion of the creative process and its relationship to reality in various plays from *The Real Inspector Hound* (1968) to *Arcadia* (1993). Following the logic of the story, and Stoppard's usual practice, the play contains several clever allusions and anachronisms that build a comedy around the construction of the tragic play. This Shakespeare (Joseph Fiennes) goes to see a doctor named Moth whose Freudian practice extends to what, in some future day, will become the traditional psychiatrist's couch. Dr. Moth gives him a serpent-shaped bracelet, obviously phallic, and, seeking amorous inspiration along with the other kind, Shakespeare gives the bracelet to Rosaline. Later, when he goes to Richard Burbage's house looking for Burbage (Martin Clunes), he instead finds his Rosaline in bed with Mr. Tilney (Simon Callow), the master of the revels. Later in the film, Christopher Marlowe (Rupert Everett) goes to the same house and finds Rosaline astride Burbage himself. It is Marlowe himself, in casual bar talk, who suggests the outline of Shakespeare's *Romeo and Juliet*; and Lady Viola De Lesseps (Gwyneth Paltrow), who, as she is leaving to go to America, outlines the plot of *Twelfth Night*.

Shakespeare in Love first constructs a huge log jam of obstacles, including an insolvent theater owner, Philip Henslowe (Geoffrey Rush), a creatively and sexually blocked Shakespeare, feuding theatrical companies, and an unpromising group of actors, including a Juliet whose voice changes just as the show is going on stage. Breaking through these barriers, however, is Lady Viola De Lesseps, representing the combined inspirations of love, beauty, and sex, who inspires Shakespeare to revise his proposed comedy, *Romeo and Ethyl, The Pirate's Daughter*, into the play we all know. (Stoppard's humor being what it is, it may be worthwhile noting that Ferdinand De Lesseps is the engineer who built the Suez Canal.) Assisting this process at a different level is Queen Elizabeth herself, who seems to represent intuition, good sense, and both practical and imaginative power. In the best tradition of movies about theatrical productions, everything that can go wrong does, but the play goes on and wins over even Viola's cuckolded husband Lord Wessex (Colin Firth), as well as a street preacher who was railing against plays when he was accidentally swept inside, and the hard-nosed money lender, Mr. Fennyman (Thomas Wilkinson), who goes from roasting Henslowe's feet in the opening scene of the film to reveling in the part of the apothecary, which Shakespeare adds for him (or at least says he does). The film won seven Academy Awards, including best picture, best actress for Gwyneth Paltrow, best supporting actress for Judi Dench, and best original screenplay for Norman and Stoppard.

Televised stage productions, although they tend to be more complete than versions prepared as theatrical films, generally suffer in comparison with theatrical films, sometimes regardless of either medium's individual merits or faults. That was perhaps the case with Alvin Rakoff's *Romeo and Juliet* for the BBC Shakespeare series, which Kenneth S. Rothwell says is "dismal . . . a shadowy replica of the dazzling Zeffirelli film," although Anthony Davies finds it "thematically more satisfying in its subtlety." Of historical note, Gielgud again plays the Chorus, though costumed very differently than his appearance 24 years earlier in Castellani's film. Also interesting is the fact that the black eye Rakoff gives to the Capulet servant Gregory is echoed in Luhrmann's film—same eye, same place.

Attempting to overcome the limitations of a filmed stage production, Rakoff uses a set that has several windows, stairways, and other openings. His camera almost never finds a blank wall. Besides the visual differences between Zeffirelli's version and this one, Rakoff attempts to give the complete play and to restore some dignity to Juliet's parents. Here they are more Juliet's concerned parents than Castellani's domestic tyrants or Zeffirelli's unhappily married couple. They often appear together and frequently touch Juliet, demonstrating both care and affection. Michael Hordern's Capulet is amiable and even a bit confused, recalling Hordern's wonderful portrayal of Baptista in Zeffirelli's *The Taming of the Shrew*, an impression oddly reinforced by the line "'Tis gone, 'tis gone, 'tis gone," which echoes the song in the earlier play. While Romeo (Patrick Ryecart) and Juliet (Rebecca Saire) are given back the inner life Shakespeare constructed for them, to look at this Juliet is to recall that 13-year-olds are today middle-school children. She seems brighter but also younger and less animated than some other Juliets. Finally, Rakoff sometimes strives too hard to illustrate lines, for example, on the way to the party when Mercutio throws out his hands and kicks up his heels when he tells Romeo to dance. Later Friar Laurence's proverbial "they stumble that run fast" becomes a response to Romeo's actually falling on his way out of the Friar's cell.

Bard Productions uses American actors and advertises on the video jacket that "Unfamiliar English accents, so prevalent in most Shakespearean productions, are absent from this series." In William Woodman's *Romeo and Juliet*, for example, Alex Hyde-White (son of actor Wilfrid Hyde-White) is Romeo, Blanche Baker (daughter of actress Carroll Baker) is Juliet, and black actress Esther Rolle is the nurse. All three had backgrounds in television and some movie experience at the time this play was filmed. Bard also claims the play is "staged as seen in the 16th Century." In fact, this is not Shakespeare's bare stage but a somewhat more ambitiously used two-level stage area, including several props, and some expertise in modern stage design and lighting.

Perhaps to illustrate the play's prologue, William Woodman opens with a close-up of the faces of the dead lovers, and, as a voice-over recites those opening lines, the camera pulls back to reveal a circle of people standing around the platform on which the two lovers lie. Juliet wears what looks very much like a white bridal gown, complete with veil. At the end of the play, Woodman returns to the same shot, almost suggesting the circularity of a tale told. In general, the costumes in this production tend to be bright and ornate, making Zeffirelli's seem comparatively restrained; in fact, the choice of cast and costumes suggests that sexual appeal was an important consideration in assembling this production. There are no unnoticed double entendres, and many of them are rewarded with clarifying gestures. Woodman's *Romeo and Juliet* is also a very physical play. In the opening scene, Gregory and Sampson are playing dice. Later, when Benvolio and Romeo talk, they punctuate their delivery by tossing oranges spilled in the previous fight. Lady Capulet is checking her makeup and adjusting her dress while she waits for Juliet's first appearance. Mercutio is prostrate at the end of both the Queen Mab speech and the conjuration speech. As one might expect, the fights are athletic and well choreographed. Mercutio tweaks Tybalt's nose, taunts him with a hat, and spits in his face. Unique to this production is the fact that Mercutio is stabbed in the back when Romeo spins him around to stop the fight. Occasionally the physicality is distracting, especially when Juliet gives a horsey motion to her reading of "Gallop apace, you fiery-footed steeds," or when Romeo, in the tomb, stands straddling Juliet's prone body just before taking the poison.

Relying frequently on mid-shots and close-ups, Joan Kemp-Welch's version of *Romeo and Juliet*, more than any other, sometimes has a "talking head" effect. Many of the soliloquies are spoken directly into the camera. When characters—such as the nurse, Mercutio, Friar Laurence, Juliet, and Romeo—have long speeches, the camera tends to come closer as they speak and then recede when they finish. On the other hand, scenes that seem to call for a more spacious treatment, such as the two fight scenes, seem a bit cramped, although the skillfully staged fights are lively and inventive, making up for the lack of space. Similarly there are only about a dozen dancers at the Capulet party, but Capulet and Tybalt position themselves immediately in front of the camera, and thus cut off some of the stage space. Verona itself seems to be a city of narrow alleys with sharp twists. In this town, distances seem to go back and forth in space but almost never left to right. Interiors generally seem more spacious, with Juliet's bedroom and the tomb, ironically, the most ample.

Like Zeffirelli and Rakoff, Kemp-Welch selected a very young Juliet, with a success that falls somewhere between the other two. Ann Hanson's Juliet is a pleasant young woman who smiles quite a bit of the time and does a reasonably good job with her lines, but she must be at least a foot shorter than Romeo, who seems uncomfortable as he bends over to give her their first kiss. The high-waisted dress she wears through most of the play unfortunately emphasizes this difference in stature. Positioning the camera below her, as in the balcony scene, seems to help, but too often she is viewed from over Romeo's shoulder. Patrick McNamee's Romeo somehow conveys the more poetic elements of Romeo's character. His features are somewhat delicate, he is inclined to stare off into space or into the camera, and, although he seems athletic enough in the fight scenes with Tybalt and later with Paris, the camera tends to focus more on his face. Mercutio is an introspective and droll man who seems acquainted with disappointment. When Romeo stops his Queen Mab speech, Mercutio rubs his temples and looks down reflectively as he says, "True, I talk of dreams . . . the children of an idle brain."

Norman Campbell's filming of the Stratford, Ontario, *Romeo and Juliet*, as staged by Richard Monette, is in many respects good precisely because it makes no attempt to disguise the fact that it records an excellent stage production, apparently before a live audience. Locations are suggested simply—arranging a few tables and chairs, for example, creates a restaurant; adding a piano and a candelabra makes it the Capulet party; and the grave is simply a pair of open doors in the floor of the stage. The second, smaller upper level, differently lit each time, becomes the platform from which the prince castigates the feuding families, the head of the stairs from which Juliet is presented before descending to the party, and later her balcony, and, finally, with gates around its supporting pillars, the graveyard. While transitions between scenes are conveyed by a fade, stagehands push props off and on. Backgrounds are kept dark, and locations seem to glide from one to the next, while characters are isolated simply by moving to a close-up. In the pauses between acts, the audience applauds, and the camera pulls back to show the full stage. At the end the cast comes out for a bow and the silhouetted figures of the audience stand in the foreground.

Set in Italy during Mussolini's time, this CBC production has the Capulet young men wear black and tan military uniforms, while the Montague men wear light-colored suits. The prince wears a white uniform, with gold epaulets, and a blue sash. Interestingly, when Romeo (Antoni Cimolino), Mercutio (Colm Feore), and Benvolio (Paul Miller) attend the Capulet party, they dress in Renaissance costume, so that the scene visually recalls the period of Shakespeare's play. The cast is almost uniformly excellent. Mercutio is a forceful character, clever, nimble, athletic, and funny. Juliet (Megan Porter Follows) makes a subtle transition from a child to a young woman apparently simply by changing her clothing and hair, although it is really her entire posture that changes. When we first see her, she is a child in a white nautical outfit and pinned up hair. Later, when she appears at the party standing on the upper level, wearing a golden dress, with her red hair combed out, her sparkle easily supports Romeo's comment about her shining like a jewel. The Capulets (Lewis Gordon and Kate Trotter) are also especially strong. Capulet himself is clearly in charge of things; bellowing, glad handing, and hugging, he is the ruler of his family. An interesting bit of characterization occurs when Capulet gets angry with Juliet after she resists the marriage to Paris; the nurse, Lady Capulet, and Juliet huddle together and hug as Capulet rants at all the women in his house.

Alan Horrox's *Romeo and Juliet* is abbreviated to about half the length of the BBC and CBC versions, and, although much is lost, he manages to develop a consistent look without straining the resources of the medium. The world of this production is neither sunny nor bright, and many scenes seem permeated by a smoky haze. The two fight scenes take place in an enclosed area with large pillars, which the duelists use to their advantage, and when Romeo fights Tybalt each holds a torch in one hand and the sword in the other. When the nurse brings Juliet's message to Romeo, she enters a room where Romeo, Benvolio, and Mercutio sit around a long table. The only exterior view in this production is through Juliet's window.

Romeo (Jonathan Firth) and Juliet (Geraldine Somerville) are not here children pitted against an adult world. Juliet, in particular, speaks with her mother (Jenny Agutter) and the nurse (Dearbhla Molloy) as an equal. When she pleads with Capulet not to force her into the marriage with Paris, she is a young woman hoping that she can manipulate her father by acting submissively, rather than a child cowering before him. Her reading of the line, "You kiss by the book," in response to Romeo's second kiss suggests that she has some basis of comparison. Yet her speech in Act Three wishing her marriage to be consummated and her speech before taking the potion are both cut. The cuts generally seem intended to focus the action and speed up the pace of the play. Horrox sacrifices the beginnings and endings of scenes and pretty much all of the extended comparisons. For example, the lines leading up to Mercutio's Queen Mab speech are cut, but Mercutio (Ben Daniels) is allowed to give a particularly animated delivery of the whole thing. When Mercutio dies, rather than have Benvolio lead him out and then return with the news that he has died, Mercutio dies seated with Romeo and Benvolio on either side of him. At the grave, Romeo enters by himself, Paris does not appear, and most of the friar's speech is cut, yet the production retains Montague and Capulet making their offers to build gold statues of the dead lovers.

A final group of *Romeo and Juliet* adaptations includes those films which make somewhat freer use of the play's elements. *Valley Girl* and *Under the Boardwalk*, for example, use parts of the story to develop light-hearted comic films with a happy ending. In *Valley Girl*, Julie (Deborah Foreman) is the title character, and Nicolas Cage, in his first movie appearance, is Randy, the punk from the city. The party scene motif remains intact, but for the balcony scene, Randy instead sneaks back into the household through the bathroom window and hides in the shower until Julie comes in to reapply her makeup. At the film's end, Randy shows up at the prom, takes Julie away from Tommy, the film's Paris character, and takes her in Tommy's limo to the room that Tommy had booked in the Valley Sheridan Hotel. In Fritz Kiersch's *Under the Boardwalk*, Nick Rainwood (Richard Joseph Paul) is one of the Vals, the surfers from the San Fernando Valley, and Allie Yorpin (Danielle von Zerneck) is one of the locals from Venice Beach, called Lowks. Advertised as a *Romeo and Juliet* story, this film uses only the basic idea of opposing families and young lovers. The beach party in *Under the Boardwalk*, for example, provides a parallel to Shakespeare's party scene but successfully evades opportunities to echo the famous meeting of Romeo and Juliet. At the end of the film, as the video jacket describes it, "All their hopes and fears come to a head in the final surf contest—a modern-day 'surf to the death' duel. At stake are both Nick's pride and his future with Allie. And only his board lies between Nick and his ultimate fate."

Other adaptations tend to emphasize the tragic qualities of the play. In Duncan Gibbins's *Fire with Fire*, Virginia Madsen is Lisa Howard, a wealthy girl at a Catholic boarding school who meets Joe Fisk, played by Craig Sheffer, a detainee at a nearby juvenile correctional facility. When the girls decide to invite the boys over for a dance as a good deed, the nuns and the prison officials provide the sense of opposing families who want to keep the youth apart. Staged in a gymnasium, the dance provides some visual parallels to the dance in *West Side Story*, except that here gender and social standing rather than gang membership divides the assembled groups. Lisa, the Juliet character, very consciously identifies herself with another Shakespeare character, Ophelia, who appears in paintings, photographs, and class discussion at various points in the film. At the end, the lovers seem to die when they jump off a cliff together, and the searchers in helicopters give them up for dead, but they surface downriver and escape into the woods.

Romeo Must Die in many respects is a martial arts film with rival Chinese and black gangs in Oakland fighting for control of the city. One of the notable features of the film is that when characters recoil from various martial arts blows, X-ray images of their bodies flash on the screen. The film's Romeo is Han Sing, a martial arts expert of the Bruce Lee and Jackie Chan variety, who escapes from a Hong Kong prison when he learns his brother has been killed. The Juliet, played by the late R&B artist Aaliyah, is Trish O'Day, daughter of the head of the black gang. The film does not really draw on the *Romeo and Juliet* iconography, although when Han Sing visits Trish for what would be the balcony scene, he has to fight his way down a stairwell that bears a passing resemblance to Juliet's balcony as depicted in *West Side Story* and *China Girl*. The film ends when all offenses are revenged, and Han Sing and Trish O'Day walk out of the frame.

Tromeo and Juliet offers a transgressive, often vile use of the play, allegedly to discuss a variety of social ills, including the treatment of women, patriarchal concepts of romantic love, and the practice of eating meat. In this film, Old Montague and Capulet have become Monty Que and Cappy Capulet, former partners in a pornographic film company. The action includes lesbian scenes between Juliet (Jane Jensen) and Ness (Debbie Rachon), a masturbating Tromeo (Will Keenan), and Cappy's sexual abuse of young Juliet. While Rothwell says the film belongs in a category he calls "Shakespeare movies of no kind," Margaret Jane Kidnie perhaps overstates the case when she says that *Tromeo and Juliet* "asks unsettling questions without offering tidy answers." Analyzing the world reflected in his film, director Lloyd Kaufman says that his generation of baby boomers "trumpeted peace and emotional freedom in the sixties. Now they've given way to a blind elitism which preaches coolness over feeling . . . these boomers have thus plasticized their own pasts, making the values they once trumpeted no more real than the Partridge Family, and therefore no longer dangerous to the status quo—that is, themselves." By contrast, according to Kaufman, "Contemporary Americans in their teens and twenties have turned inward, concocting their own universe of the cool, cold, and uncaring. To me, they can hardly be blamed. It's the same emotional response a man has after being repeatedly raped in prison." Commenting on his script, written by James Gunn, Kaufman says, "I felt more for the Juliet character; it was now the story of Juliet escaping from the bondage of her baby boomer father as a young person and as a woman." Following this logic, Kidnie argues that "Kaufman renders the familiar strange, a process of cultural disruption which enables his audience to question and re-evaluate modern value systems in a reflective manner." In this film's version of the balcony scene, Cappy has bound Juliet inside a Plexiglas case. To rescue Juliet, Tromeo bashes Cappy with a handy copy of the *Yale Shakespeare*, and Juliet helps out by smashing a television set over her father's head. Not yet defeated, Cappy holds a crossbow on the couple and is forcing them into another room when Juliet finishes him off by plugging the television cord into a wall, causing Cappy's head to explode. In response to Tromeo's parody of Shakespeare's lines from the balcony scene, Rothwell says that "Supposedly a redeeming element is that Shakespeare's dialogue is firmly separated from its grossest episodes, but even that hope is blasted with such inanities as, 'What light from yonder Plexiglas shines?'"

REFERENCES

Ball, Robert Hamilton, *Shakespeare on Silent Film* (London: George Allen and Unwin, 1968); Courson, H.R., *Shakespeare: The Two Traditions* (Cranbury, N.J.: Associated University Presses, 1999); Davies, Anthony, "The Film Versions of *Romeo and Juliet*," *Shakespeare Survey*, 49 (1996), 153–162; Flamini, Roland, *Thalberg: The Last Tycoon and the World of MGM* (New York: Crown, 1994); Goodale, Gloria, "How They Imagined *Shakespeare in Love*," *Christian Science Monitor*, March 5, 1999, 17; Howard, Leslie, *Trivial Fond Records* (London: William Kimber, 1982); Howard, Tony, "Shakespeare's Cinematic Offshoots," in *The Cambridge Companion to Shakespeare on Film*, ed. Russell Jackson (Cambridge, England: Cambridge University Press, 2000), 295–313; Kaufman, Lloyd, and James Gunn, *All I Needed to Know About Filmmaking I Learned from* The Toxic Avenger (New York: Berkley Boulevard Books, 1998); Kidnie, Margaret Jane, "'The Way the World is Now': Love in the Troma Zone," in *Shakespeare, Film, Fin de Siècle*, eds. Mark Thornton Burnett and Ramona Wray (London: Macmillan Press, 2000), 102–120; Levy, Emanuel, *George Cukor, Master of Elegance: Hollywood's Legendary Director and His Stars* (New York: William Morrow, 1994); Manvell, Roger, *Shakespeare and the Film* (New York: Praeger, 1971); Payser, Joan, *Bernstein: A Biography*, rev. (New York: Bill Board Books, 1998); Pilcher, Jeffery M., *Cantinflas and the Chaos of Mexican Modernity* (Wilmington, Del.: Scholarly Resources, 2001); Rothwell, Kenneth S., *A History of Shakespeare on Screen* (Cambridge, U.K.: Cambridge University Press, 1999); Thomas, Bob, *Thalberg: Life and Legend* (New York: Doubleday, 1969); Uricchio, William, and Roberta E. Pearson, *Reframing Culture: The Case of Vitagraph Quality Films* (Princeton, N.J.: Princeton University Press, 1993); Ustinov, Peter, *Dear Me* (Boston: Little, Brown, 1977); Willis, Susan, *The BBC Shakespeare Plays: Making the Televised Canon* (Chapel Hill: University of North Carolina Press, 1991); Willson, Robert F., Jr., *Shakespeare in Hollywood, 1929–1956* (London: Associated University Presses, 2000); Zeffirelli, Franco, *Zeffirelli: An Autobiography* (New York: Weidenfeld and Nicholson, 1986).

—R.V.

ROMEO MUST DIE

See ROMEO AND JULIET

ROMEO Y JULIETA

See ROMEO AND JULIET

S–T

SHYLOCK, OU LE MORE DE VENISE

See THE MERCHANT OF VENICE

THE TAMING OF THE SHREW (1593–94)

The Taming of the Shrew (1929), U.S.A., directed and adapted by Sam Taylor; United Artists.

Kiss Me Kate (1953), U.S.A., directed by George Sidney, adapted by Dorothy Kingsley; MGM.

The Taming of the Shrew (1966), U.S.A./Italy, directed by Franco Zeffirelli, adapted by Zeffirelli, Suso Cecci D'Amico, Paul Dehn; Royal Films International, F.A.I.

10 Things I Hate about You (1999), U.S.A., directed by Gil Junger, adapted by Karen McCullah Lutz; Touchstone Pictures.

The Play

The general reader may be surprised to know that *The Taming of the Shrew* does not immediately begin with the familiar story of Kate and Petruchio; rather, one of Shakespeare's earliest comedies begins with an extended "Induction" (prologue), involving a practical joke played upon a drunken tinker, Christopher Sly, who awakens to find himself treated like a lord, much to his amazement. Unaware of the joke being played on him, Sly assumes the lordly role and allows himself to be entertained by men employed by the true lord, who is the initiator of the joke. The performance for Sly becomes the core of Shakespeare's play, though, oddly, the Sly character disappears completely after the first act. The main plot of the play Sly is watching involves two sisters, Katharina and Bianca, the daughters of Baptista Minola. Baptista will not allow Bianca, the younger and more conventional, to marry until a husband has been found for her cantankerous older sister. The eligible bachelors of Padua prize the beautiful and docile Bianca, but none is interested in Katharina. Bianca's rivals, Hortensio, Lucentio, and Gremio, hire Petruchio, a gentleman from Verona, to woo Kate in order to clear the way for their courtship of Bianca. Upon hearing of Baptista's wealth, Petruchio seems mainly interested in Kate's dowry. Baptista readily accepts Petruchio's offer of marriage. Meanwhile, Lucentio and Hortensio disguise themselves as instructors to Bianca so as to woo her without her father's interference.

Petruchio arrives at his wedding outrageously garbed in beggar's clothing and insists Kate marry him as he is. This is merely his ploy to begin the process

Mary Pickford and Douglas Fairbanks, as Kate and Petruchio, brought Shakespeare to the talkies for the first time in The Taming of the Shrew *(1929).* (MARY PICKFORD FOUNDATION)

of Kate's "taming." Throughout the next several scenes, Petruchio denies Kate food, sleep, and a suitable wardrobe, as he attempts to establish himself as her "lord and master"; but although he humbles and humiliates her constantly until she blindly agrees to whatever he says, Petruchio never breaks her spirit. In contrast, Lucentio, disguised as Cambio, a tutor, woos and wins Bianca's love only after she is assured of his father's wealth; then they marry, secretly. Unaware that Cambio is really Lucentio, Hortensio, disgusted by Bianca's favoritism of a lowly tutor, withdraws his offer of marriage to Bianca and instead proposes to a wealthy widow. The final scene has Petruchio, Kate, Lucentio, Bianca, Hortensio, and his new wife all celebrating their nuptials. During the wedding feast, the men wager on the obedience of their wives, but, surprisingly, Petruchio wins the wager. Kate not only shows obedience to her husband but is also extremely critical of the other wives for their neglect. As Cordelia will later do in *King Lear*, Kate pledges her love according to her bond, on condition that Petruchio remain loving and honest. She proclaims Petruchio "her loving lord" and proves submissive to "his honest will." She even offers to place her hands beneath his feet, an offer that Petruchio does not accept. Instead, he kisses Kate, proclaiming her his equal, not his servant.

The Films

Among the first screen treatments of *The Taming of the Shrew* is the abbreviated version made by D.W. Griffith in 1908, which reduced the entire play to one reel of running time. Much later, the Sam Taylor adaptation was the first complete Shakespeare play to be filmed as a Hollywood talkie. It was a benchmark United Artists production that established the trend of a celebrity husband-and-wife team in the central roles that would be followed three decades later by Richard Burton and Elizabeth Taylor. The play was used as a vehicle to showcase the talents of Hollywood's most famous couple, Mary Pickford and Douglas Fairbanks, Sr. Mary, celebrated as "America's Sweetheart" for most of her career, essayed her second "mature" role (after having won the second best actress Oscar for *Coquette* in 1929) as Kate; and Douglas Fairbanks, the matinee idol who had built his reputation during the 1920s with several highly entertaining swashbuckling roles, starting with *The Mark of Zorro* (1920), drew upon his own Shakespearean experience (with the Frederick Warde Company) as Petruchio.

The sophistication of the talking picture technique is remarkable for its time. The broadly farcical action was influenced by conventions of silent comedy, and the "talk" was kept to a minimum (the wedding ceremony is nearly wordless, for example, as the scene is driven by Fairbanks's pantomimic comic talent). The action is certainly pared down, and there is no evidence of a screen credit alluding to "additional dialogue by Sam Taylor." The screenplay dispenses with the Sly Induction and most of the Bianca subplot so that the stars can shine immediately. Act One was considerably compressed in order to get Fairbanks on camera as quickly as possible (the camera tracking back before his broad stride down the streets of Verona is a nice touch), and the characters of Lucentio and Hortensio are conflated into a single suitor for Bianca. The movie really hits its stride with the wedding scene and its aftermath in Act Three. In the play Kate is deprived of food and sleep for days until she learns her lesson, but in the film this ordeal is compressed into a single night of comic abuse (perhaps reflecting something of the stormy relationship Fairbanks and Pickford were experiencing at the time of the production). The ending is simplified; the

100-crown wager is cut; the text is arguably corrupted, but the meaning is clear—reconciliation comes as the result of mutual respect and understanding. In 1954 the film, slightly abbreviated, was re-released with a new soundtrack. Long out of print, it is being replaced at this writing with a restored version of its original state.

Franco Zeffirelli's 1966 adaptation is far more traditional and complete (nearly twice as long as the 1929 version), incorporating lush sets and lavish costumes in an attempt to place the play in an appropriate Italianate setting. Even so, Zeffirelli does not incorporate the Induction scene, which introduces the motif of disguise and trickery. The film does clearly portray that Bianca (Natasha Pyne) only plays at being the dutiful daughter, hiding a shrewish nature that might rival her sister's. Richard Burton's Petruchio shows little artful finesse in his manipulation of Kate (Elizabeth Taylor); he is merely bigger and more bullying than the shrew he courts. Elizabeth Taylor's Kate, although humble and suitably submissive in her final speech, leaves the celebration feast at the end, leaving Petruchio to chase after her, perhaps implying that theirs is not the marriage of equal wit and passion suggested by Shakespeare, but merely a childish tug-of-war for power. Burton's Petruchio at first pretends not to notice Kate's hostility when he chases her with oblivious gusto over the rooftops of the Minola mansion, until they tumble into the woolstack, as Zeffirelli visualizes their initial sparring. This Petruchio first seems to be merely a vulgar, boorish, drunken lout; but these traits are countered by his verbal dexterity and diction, which suggest that this is not an utterly crude man.

The couple is not entirely mismatched since the two have a great deal in common and seem to arrive at a mutual understanding. Zeffirelli's Kate is more spirited, interesting, and appealing than her devious sister. From behind a stained-glass window, she watches Petruchio with longing and interest. Zeffirelli takes far

Real-life husband and wife Richard Burton and Elizabeth Taylor starred as Petruchio and Kate in Franco Zeffirelli's The Taming of the Shrew. (COURTESY ROYAL FILMS INTERNATIONAL)

more time to humanize the character of Petruchio than Sam Taylor had done and provides a better reason for Katharine's astonishing transformation. Her absolute loyalty to a domineering husband is mainly a matter of gamesmanship, as romantic comedy displaces the earlier farcical action. The film is made even more entertaining by the able supporting cast, including Michael Hordern's Baptista, Michael York's Lucentio, and Cyril Cusack's Gremio. The film was important in the way it reestablished the marketability and accessibility of Shakespeare for a mass audience.

The other titles listed above as adaptations represent more of a stretch. Cole Porter's masterful *Kiss Me Kate* premiered on Broadway in 1948 and is mainly a backstage musical rather than a true adaptation of Shakespeare's play. In the framing story a once happily married couple, now bitterly divorced, each still knowing the other's weak spots, exploit their past personal knowledge onstage and off as they rehearse a musical version of *The Taming of the Shrew*. Unlike Christopher Sly in Shakespeare's "Induction" scene, Lilli Vanessi (Kathryn Grayson) and Fred Graham (Howard Keel) do not merely watch the play-within-a-play but are its main participants. The imbedded play provides a rationale for role-changing as the actors compete for the limelight. Fred uses Lilli's vanity to manipulate her into accepting the part of Katharina before Lilli is at all sure that she really wants to play the role. Lilli flaunts gifts from her new fiancé, Tex, in order to make Fred jealous, but Lilli is herself jealous of Fred's offstage romance with Lois Lane (Ann Miller), the actress playing the part of Bianca. This offstage battle of the sexes parallels and compliments the onstage contest between Petruchio and Kate.

The actor playing Lucentio has accumulated a gambling debt under a false name and signed an I.O.U. using Fred Graham's name as his own. When gangsters come to the theater to collect on the debt, Fred gains an advantage by playing along with the gangsters and insisting that they use their brute charm to keep Lilli from running out mid-show. Being forced to stay with the production and perform only increases Lilli's hostility, which is carried over to her performance as Kate. When Lilli receives flowers from Fred, she thinks he has remembered the one-year anniversary of their divorce, but is later enraged to learn the flowers were intended for Miss Lane and delivered to Lilli by mistake. Lilli threatens to walk out of the theater and never return. The gangsters threaten her, but Fred allows her to leave with her fiancé and orders the understudy to complete the production for Lilli.

The final scene of the movie takes place onstage, the scene where Kate berates the other wives for their lack of service to their husbands. When Petruchio calls for Kate, Kate does not come onstage. When he calls again, whispering orders to the stage manager to find the understudy, Kate, played by Lilli Vanessi, returns to appear onstage. Both Kate and Lilli become willing captives of love, willing to assist their husbands, showing that the heart and not merely the taming method is truly the rationale behind their speech of obedience and devotion.

The last film, Gil Junger's *10 Things I Hate about You*, is even more of a stretch, reducing Shakespeare's play to a teenpic, set at Padua High School. Cameron Jones (Joseph Gordon-Levitt), an updated Lucentio, is a new transfer student who falls for the lovely Bianca Stratford (Larisa Oleynik), but in order to date her he has to pay off somebody foolish enough to date her formidable older sister, Kat (Julia Stiles). Here, the edict that Bianca cannot date until Kat does stems from Kat's basic unwillingness to date, not because her father fears that he will not otherwise be rid of his daughter. Enter Patrick Verona (Heath Ledger), the Petruchio figure, an Aussie with a reputation for being a Bad Boy. Patrick pockets the money and courts Kat. After a rocky start, including a party scene where Kat loosens up, gets drunk, and throws up on Patrick, the two find true romance at the senior prom. Cameron, meanwhile, finds bliss in Bianca's arms. At the prom Bianca defends Kat and the sisters actually reconcile their differences, a plot twist utterly alien

10 Things I Hate about You *translated* The Taming of the Shrew *into contemporary teen-speak.* (COURTESY TOUCHSTONE PICTURES)

to Shakespeare. At the end the wifely obedience speech is transformed into a reworked sonnet, assigned as a homework assignment, that Kat reads in front of the class, stating that her love for Patrick is greater than her humiliation at finding out that he was paid to date her. Her emotional honesty shows clearly what Shakespeare only hinted at, that love is greater than pride.

All the kids are freshly scrubbed, look great in their chic clothes, live in upscale homes, and go to a school that looks like a storybook castle. It is interesting to see a New Age spin on the traditional concept of a lusty, sexist beast of a Petruchio, and of a kittenish, bitchy Kate. He is now just a lovable hunk, and she is a feminist icon. In other words, the edges of both are dulled for the sake of political correctness. This is one twisted *Shrew* stripped of its language, elegance, and spirit. Purists may be justifiably horrified.

REFERENCES

Brownlow, Kevin, *Mary Pickford Rediscovered* (New York: Abrams, 1999); Manvell, Roger, *Shakespeare & the Film* (New York: Praeger, 1971); Tibbetts, John C., and James M. Welsh, *His Majesty the American: The Cinema of Douglas Fairbanks, Sr.* (Cranbury, N.J.: A.S. Barnes, 1977); Zeffirelli, Franco, *Zeffirelli: An Autobiography* (New York: Weidenfeld and Nicholson, 1986).

—J.C.T. AND J.M.W. AND H.O.

THE TEMPEST (1611)

The Tempest (1908), U.K., directed and adapted by Percy Stow; Clarendon Film Co.

Tempest (1939), U.K., directed and adapted by Dallas Bower; BBC-TV.

Forbidden Planet (1956), U.S.A., directed by Fred McLeod Wilcox, adapted by Cyril Hume from a story by Irving Black and Allen Adler; MGM.

The Tempest (1956), U.K., directed and adapted by Robert and Ian Atkins; BBC-TV.

The Tempest (1960), U.S.A., directed and adapted by George Schaefer; Hallmark Hall of Fame/NBC-TV.

The Tempest (1968), U.K., directed by Basil Coleman, adapted by Cedric Messina; BBC-TV.

The Tempest (1979), U.K., directed by John Gorrie, adapted by Alan Shallcross; "The Shakespeare Plays" Series/BBC-TV.

The Tempest: by William Shakespeare, as seen through the eyes of Derek Jarman (1980), U.K., directed and adapted by Derek Jarman; British Film Now.

Tempest (1982), U.S.A., directed by Paul Mazursky, adapted by Mazursky and Leon Capetanos; Columbia Pictures.

Prospero's Books (1991), U.K./France, directed and freely adapted by Peter Greenaway; Allarts-Cinea/ Camera One-Penta Co-Production/Miramax.

The Tempest (1999), U.S.A., directed by Jack Bender, adapted by James Henderson; NBC Studios/Trimark Pictures.

The Play

The play, believed to be Shakespeare's last before his retirement to Stratford-upon-Avon, was given special treatment in the First Folio of 1623, placed first among all the plays printed therein. It is possible that Shakespeare collaborated with John Fletcher on a later play entitled *The Two Noble Kinsmen* in 1613, but that play was not included in the Folio or in any other subsequent 17th-century editions. Strikingly original in its substance and execution, *The Tempest* later inspired artists outside the theater, such musical treatments as those by Hector Berlioz ("Dramatic Fantasy," 1830), Tchaikovsky ("Fantasy," 1873), the incidental music Sir Arthur Sullivan composed in 1872, as well as an opera, *Der Sturm* (1956), by the Swiss composer Frank Martin. Two of the filmmakers drawn to this play were trained artists as well: Derek Jarman was a painter and designer trained at the Slade School of Art in the late 1960s; Peter Greenaway was a trained draftsman, illustrator, and mural painter, an artist who happened to make films.

Prospero, the scholar-sorcerer and central character of *The Tempest*, was betrayed by his brother Antonio, who, aided by Alonso, the king of Naples, usurped Prospero to become duke of Milan 12 years before the plot begins, sending Prospero and his three-year-old daughter Miranda into exile. Adrift at sea in a leaky boat, Prospero eventually finds himself beached on a remote island. His only resources are his books on magic, given to him by his loyal friend Gonzalo. He puts these books to good use on the island. His knowledge gives him dominance over the native Caliban, the misshapen son of the dead witch Sycorax, who had claimed to rule the island. Prospero intends to educate Caliban, but after Caliban attempts to rape Miranda, Prospero makes Caliban his slave. He also uses his power to release the spirit Ariel, whom Sycorax had imprisoned in a cloven pine. Ariel becomes his faithful fairy servant.

Prospero conjures up a tempest that shipwrecks his former antagonists on the island—Antonio, Alonso, Alonso's son Ferdinand, and Alonzo's brother, Sebastian. Ariel takes Ferdinand, who landed apart from the others, to Prospero's lodgings, where Ferdinand meets and falls in love with Miranda. Prospero puts Ferdinand to work bearing logs to test the young man's mettle. Meanwhile, Ferdinand's father, Alonso, is grieving because be thinks his son has been drowned.

On its strange trajectory toward forgiveness and reconciliation, the play has sinister implications. Antonio and Sebastian conspire to murder Alonso, for example, but their plans are foiled by Ariel. This plot is paralleled by a comic subplot involving two lowlife characters, Alonso's butler Trinculo and his colleague Stephano, who introduce Caliban to alcohol, getting him drunk, then conspire with Caliban to kill Prospero so that Trinculo can rule the island with Miranda as his queen. These characters are stupid, however, and no match for Prospero's power, as Ariel distracts them and leads them away to a stagnant pond, where they sink chin-deep into the muck.

Ariel tells Alonso that the gods have taken his son in punishment for his previous crimes. Bewitched into contrition, Alonso, Antonio, and Sebastian become conscience-ridden, desperate men. Satisfied by the worthiness of Ferdinand, meanwhile, Prospero consents to his betrothal to Miranda and conjures up a masque in celebration in Act Four. In Act Five Ariel has imprisoned the castaways in a grove of lime trees and indicates that he feels sorry for them, which makes Prospero question his motives for revenge. Moved by compassion to forgive his enemies, Prospero reveals himself to them, dressed in the regalia of the duke of Milan and demands that his dukedom be restored. He shows Alonso his son, playing chess with Miranda, and explains to his guests how they were brought magically to the island.

Ariel appears with the ship's captain and boatswain and the news that the ship has been magically transformed, repaired, and made seaworthy. Ariel is instructed to release Caliban, Trinculo, and Stephano. Ariel is then given his freedom in reward for his service, and Prospero decides to break his staff, since he no longer needs his magic. He plans to return to Milan after stopping in Naples, where Ferdinand and Miranda will be married. Thus Prospero is restored and virtue is rewarded.

Critics have described the play as Shakespeare's fantasy meditation on the New World, with European seafarers discovering an exotic island populated by strange creatures who are transformed into servants and slaves by the superior colonist. Caliban's name has been recognized as an anagram of the word "cannibal." Coming at the end of Shakespeare's dramatic career, the play has also been discussed as an allegory in which Prospero is seen as a symbolic representation of Shakespeare himself. John Russell Brown writes that unlike a "straightforward valediction" (or leave-taking), the play "is packed with innovations." Although Shakespeare "may well have intended it to be his last play," Brown adds, "nothing is shirked." It was premiered in a command performance for King James I in the Banqueting House at Whitehall by Shakespeare's company, the King's Majesty's Servants, on Hallowmas (All Saints' Day), November 1, 1611.

The Films

The Tempest, a magical and enchanted play, has had a rich and imaginative history of media productions. Because *The Tempest* is one of the shortest plays in the Shakespeare canon, and one of the most interesting, it is more easily adaptable to the screen, though directors and adaptors have taken incredible liberties with Shakespeare's text, stripping away its poetry and transforming it into a science fiction space epic, as in *The Forbidden Planet* (1956), or into a modern fable, as in the Paul Mazursky transformation of 1982.

The first *Tempest* on film was made in 1908, directed by Percy Stow for the Clarendon Film Company in Britain. An unidentified cast sketches the action of Shakespeare's play in this one-reeler through vignettes such as Prospero's arrival at the island after his exile, Miranda in arms and books in hand, the release of the spirit Ariel from a tree, which is clearly not a "cloven pine," the discovery and taming of Caliban, the conjuring of the tempest. Although it is only 11 minutes long, the film attempts to follow Shakespeare's design. An American *Tempest*, no longer extant, was released by Thanhouser in 1911, and a French version was released by Eclair in 1912. The first extended sound adaptation would not come until 37 years later, surprisingly, through the medium of early television.

Arguably, the play has fared better on television than film, depending on one's reaction to the distinctive and peculiar treatments of Derek Jarman and Peter Greenaway. The first television treatment came as early as 1939, a low-budget BBC production directed by Dallas Bower with a high-profile cast, notably Peggy Ashcroft as Miranda, George Devine (later famous for his work at the Royal Court Theatre) as Caliban, and John Abbott as Prospero. The play was later produced for BBC in 1956 by the father-son team of Robert and Ian Atkins, with Robert Atkins playing Caliban as a monstrously deformed creature. A notably ethereal television adaptation was directed in America in 1960 by George Schaefer for the Hallmark Hall of Fame NBC television series, graced with a talented cast that included Maurice Evans (Prospero), Lee Remick (Miranda), Roddy McDowall (Ariel), and Richard Burton as "an unforgettable Caliban," in the words of Kenneth Rothwell. Shortened to a 90-minute performance, Schaefer's lighthearted treatment has been considered one of the most successful television adaptations.

According to Kenneth S. Rothwell and Annabelle Henkin Melzer, the Cedric Messina BBC television production of 1968 should be considered a benchmark in the "modern era" of BBC Shakespeare productions, since later, in 1976, Messina was named first producer of the ambitious BBC "Shakespeare Plays" series. Though prints are unavailable, the cast was impressive, featuring Michael Redgrave as Prospero, Ronald Pickup as Ariel, Tessa Wyatt as Miranda, Keith Michell as Caliban, and Douglas Rain as Stephano. Messina later produced the adaptation for "The Shakespeare Plays" series, directed by John Gorrie that featured Michael Hordern as Prospero, Warren Clarke as Caliban, Pippa Guard as Miranda, David Dixon as Ariel, and Nigel Hawthorne as Stephano. Kenneth Rothwell notes that the production follows the text faithfully: "there are no gross excesses." The play is enhanced by a spectacle of music and dance, performed by a "balletic fairy troupe."

There is simply no conventional film adaptation for this play, which seems a magnet for eccentric talents such as Derek Jarman, whose inventive and unconventional adaptation comes the nearest to the play itself, even if the betrothal masque is oddly imagined and the text restructured and abridged. Prospero's long expository monologues providing the backstory of his exile (I.ii) are broken up and patched in *passim* in order to avoid stagebound business that is inherently uncinematic.

Jarman first imagined "a mad Prospero, rightly imprisoned by his brother," and considered having Prospero speak all the lines, as Peter Greenaway was later to do; but this concept was later modified. Heathcote Williams plays a younger Prospero than is usual, preoccupied by "curious" knowledge. As a consequence, Miranda (Toyah Wilcox) is a neglected child, used to entertaining herself, adventuresome and curious about sex. Caliban (blind actor Jack Birkett) is merely a "voyeuristic nuisance," more "mooncalf" than "monster," and not a serious sexual threat to Miranda. "He is like a giant baby," as Diana Harris and MacDonald Jackson have written, "so that the bizarre flashback showing him sucking at the breast of his grotesque mother, the hookah-smoking Sycorax, seems strangely appropriate." On the other hand, Kenneth Rothwell, from an earlier generation of critics, found "the breast-feeding of a full-grown Caliban by his sow of a mother, Sycorax," surely "one of the most revolting spectacles ever filmed."

Karl Johnson's Ariel, according to Harris and Jackson, "fits Jan Kott's conception of the character" as resembling "a laboratory assistant working on an atomic reactor," hence, "the technician for Prospero's research." Wearing a pearl in his left earlobe, and "without the least suggestion of stereotypical homosexual mannerisms or the conventional androgyny," Harris and Jackson contend, "he comes across as knowingly and securely gay." They also discern an "ambiguous, homoerotically charged and sometimes tortuous" relationship between this Ariel and Prospero.

In this adaptation, Ferdinand (David Meyer) finds his way to Prospero's castle and sleeps naked in Caliban's lair, where he is discovered by Ariel, then humiliated by Prospero, who provides him with a white uniform and then manacles him to the wall, suggestive, perhaps, of bondage. An atmosphere of "carnivalesque gaity" is then established as Caliban "grinds out a merry tune on a hurdy-gurdy," as Harris and Jackson describe the scene. That atmosphere extends into the nuptial masque, done up as a high-camp extravaganza that combines elements of Gilbert and Sullivan's *H.M.S. Pinafore* and Busby Berkley's confections, as a troupe of Balkan sailor boys dance to the hornpipe, which Harris and Jackson describe as a "gay in-joke": "In his autobiography Jarman describes a party for Sir Francis Rose, where Jean Cocteau brought twenty-one sailor boys as a gift to Francis for his twenty-first birthday." Caliban then enters with Trinculo, garbed as a drag queen, and this spectacle is then topped by the entrance of blues singer Elisabeth Welch—"Iris, Ceres, and Juno rolled into one"—who does a knockout rendering of Harold Arlen's "Stormy Weather." The treatment is astonishing; some purists may object to its campy extravagance, but its originality cannot be denied.

Shakespeare's play has spawned a number of entertaining derivative features, the most famous of which is probably *Forbidden Planet* (1956). In this loosely adapted, futuristic science fiction rendering of the play set in the year 2257, Dr. Morbius (Walter Pidgeon), the Prospero figure, lives in exile with his daughter Altaira (Anne Francis) on a remote planet, Altair-4. They are assisted by Robby the Robot, a mechanical Ariel. They are visited by a United Planets Cruiser mission led by Commander Adams (Leslie Nielsen), who comes to take Dr. Morbius and his daughter back to Earth, but Morbius refuses and orders the crew to leave. Dr. Morbius's magic involves the "Krell" technology he discovered on the planet and mastered, but the technology gets out of control and Morbius is killed in the process. Altaira (Miranda) and Adams (Ferdinand) and his crew escape the planet, which is destroyed as they depart. The Shakespeare connection may seem a bit remote here, but the film is a popular science fiction "classic."

Another displaced derivative that was not so successful was Jack Bender's *The Tempest*, produced for NBC television in 1999. Set before and during the American Civil War, it tells the story of Gideon Prosper (Peter Fonda), who is more interested in the voodoo magic and sorcery known to his slaves than he is in the business of running his plantation. In a voice-over he explains that he was born into wealth and had no way of predicting the coming tempest, involving both the Civil War and a power struggle instigated by his brother. Gideon has given over the running of the plantation to his younger brother, Anthony (John Glover), who challenges Gideon's authority and accuses him of freeing a slave named Ariel (Harold Perrineau, Jr.), who earlier was seen being horsewhipped, while the white owners dance in the elegant plantation house. Anthony demands that Gideon be executed. Gideon escapes, however, with his young daughter (Katherine Heigl) to a Mississippi bayou, where Ariel helps him to start a new life. Twelve years later, while the Civil War rages around them, Gideon is forced to confront his murderous brother and give up his grown daughter and his ex-slave, releasing them to true freedom. This is a Civil War story of feuding brothers hung upon the framework of Shakespeare's play and stripped of Shakespeare's poetry. Without the language of Shakespeare, can it seriously be considered an adaptation?

Paul Mazursky's film updates and reconfigures the play as a contemporary comedy with a successful, 50-year-old American architect named Philip (John Cassavetes) as the Prospero figure, experiencing a mid-life crisis. Philip is fed up with his career, his life, and his wife Antonia (Gena Rowlands), an actress mainly interested in resurrecting her neglected career. Philip's employer, Alonzo (Vittorio Gassman), is a real estate tycoon. Although Shakespeare's Prospero was deposed of his dukedom and driven into exile, Philip leaves his profession by choice, forsaking Manhattan island for a Greek island in the Aegean Sea, where he takes his daughter Miranda (Molly Ringwald). Philip merely wants to escape a tempestuous marriage and to find himself. On his way to Greece, Philip meets a modernized version of Ariel, the twice-divorced Aretha (Susan Sarandon), who gives up her job singing in an Athens nightclub to accompany Philip to his island.

One problem is that there is hardly any magic in the modern world. Instead of a staff, Philip has a telescope, a poor substitution. Before he leaves New York, Philip observes a storm from his apartment window and says to himself "Show me the magic," but there is little to suggest that Philip is in control or has true magical powers until he arrives in Greece, where he is more in tune with Nature. There a storm has been forecast, so one has to take on faith the idea that Philip is able to conjure it up.

The Greek island is inhabited by a lusty goatherder named Kalibanos (Raul Julia) who has his lustful eye on Miranda but he is too foolish to pose much of a serious threat to her. His bestial nature is suggested only by his lust for Miranda, and this Caliban figure is humorously transformed into a banal materialist, obsessed with watching television. Philip lives at peace with himself until the tempest brings to the island the very people Philip had sought to escape from, when Alonzo's yacht is marooned there. With Alonzo is his son Freddie, played by Sam Robards (the son of Jason Robards, Jr., and Lauren Bacall).

This is a well-made and well-conceived film, but Shakespeare, it isn't. "I was originally going to try to do Shakespeare's play on film," Mazursky told the *New York Times*, but after 10 years, the project was languishing. "I found that it just wasn't right for me to do it," Mazursky explained. "The poetry of Shakespeare's language was so fabulous that somebody who was an expert on Shakespeare should do it—not me. But a couple of years ago, my friend Leon Capetanos and I came up with a way we felt we could modernize the story and use our language, rather than Shakespeare's language. The play is filled with a lot of mixtures of crazy things; at one point I was even going to do a sort of Marx Brothers version. Now it's probably a strange cross between some kind of lunacy and some kind of seriousness."

Director Paul Mazursky retold Shakespeare's The Tempest *in contemporary terms.* (COURTESY COLUMBIA PICTURES)

Mazursky was blocked for 10 years because he knew Shakespeare's language would not work for a contemporary story and mass audience. He finally realized that what appealed to him most was the plot: "A man and his daughter on an island. A man consumed with negative feelings about his past. A man who felt that terrible things had been done to him and who in the end would put down his magic and forgive." Capetanos explained that "Philip doesn't really have any power." No one does: "You only have the power to forgive people for their mistakes and become friends with them and see them as human beings and see yourself as a human being."

Consequently, the main focus was shifted to the father-daughter relationship. They decided the play was not about magic but about "a person who people believe has magic." Like Philip, Mazursky "loved the magic," however, and "loved the idea of forgiveness." Although the film is not exactly Shakespeare, it is awfully close in its way to Shakespeare's denouement of reconciliation, forgiveness, and sacrifice, as Philip gives up his hold on Miranda to Freddy, Aretha (Ariel) is "released," and Antonia and Alonzo are forgiven. The benign enchantment of this film is perhaps closer in spirit to Shakespeare's *A Midsummer Night's Dream* than to *The Tempest*. It is a derivative hybrid transformation, but the palimpsest of Shakespeare's play is still discernible.

The most astonishingly inventive adaptation of *The Tempest* is Peter Greenaway's *Prospero's Books*, starring John Gielgud as Prospero in a signature performance by one of England's most respected actors. Gielgud interpreted the role of Prospero three times on stage: at the Old Vic (1940), Stratford and Drury Lane (1957), and at the National Theatre (1974), and was Greenaway's natural choice to play Prospero, seen in his tub at the beginning of the film beginning to write a play called *The Tempest* and composing it as the action unfolds in a bizarre spectacle of nudity and revenge. The first word Gielgud utters—"Boatswain!"—is the first word of the play, and the text is both written and spoken throughout the film derivative.

Added to the recited text of Shakespeare are colorful and odd digressions concerning the books in Prospero's library, 24 of which are explained and defined, such as "The Book of Water" (volume one), "The Book of Mirrors" (volume two), "Architecture and Other Music" (volume three), and so on, each serving to illustrate the Renaissance worldview in microcosm. The whole film involves a process of illustration, in fact. The only actor to act and speak is the awesome John Gielgud as Prospero; the other "actors" are there only to illustrate the text. As Greenaway once wrote: "Film is far too rich and capable a medium to be merely left to the storytellers." *Prospero's Books* is not for the narratively challenged, and Greenaway expects his audience to know and understand the text as a prerequisite for viewing the film.

As surely as Prospero controls his island in the play, John Gielgud controls the film through his distinctive, mellifluous voice and his command of language in diction and inflection. At the age of 87 when the film was made, Sir John Gielgud was the last of a line of knighted and titled actors, including Sir Laurence Olivier and Sir Ralph Richardson and Dame Peggy Ashcroft, who had conquered the London stage. According to Peter Conrad, the casting of Prospero "was intended by the director as an homage to the actor and to his 'mastery of illusion.' Sir John's Prospero is Shakespeare, and having rehearsed the action inside his head, speaking the lines of all the other characters, he concludes the film by sitting down to write *The Tempest*." After quitting the stage Sir John considered *Prospero's Books* "a summary of his career" as well as a formal valediction.

Although the other players may be non-actors in this "illustrated" classic, they are not without impressive credentials. Erland Josephson, who plays Prospero's faithful friend Gonzalo and provides Prospero with his precious books, worked on many a film project with Ingmar Bergman. Mark Rylance came to the role of Ferdinand from the Royal Shakespeare Company. Kenneth Cranham (Sebastian) had acted for the Royal Shakespeare Company, the National Theatre, and the Royal Court Theatre in London. Michel Blanc (Alonso) had won the best actor prize at the 1986 Cannes Film Festival for his work in Bertrand Blier's *Menage*. Tom Bell (Antonio) had extensive experience in film and television. Isabelle Pasco (Miranda) began as a model but had acted in several French- and English-language films. Perhaps the only true non-actor in the film was Michael Clark (Caliban), a dancer and choreographer trained by the Royal Ballet School—but that should qualify for "theatrical" experience.

Of course, some reviewers were alienated or offended by Greenaway's "lavishly ornamental ordeal [that] smothers *The Tempest* with an illustrative gloss so prurient [that] it defeats the pleasures of the original material," as Gary Arnold protested: Greenaway "prefers manipulating actors as puppets or decor himself, so the idea of Prospero as the inventor and mouthpiece for the entire ensemble must have seemed irresistible. Sir John could be treated like royalty and the remainder of the cast like Mardi Gras flotsam." Against this tirade, is the more measured evaluation of Brian McFarlane, who thought the film gave "new meaning to the idea of film adaptation," taking "a great text in another medium" and altering, modifying, and reimagining "it in such a way that it becomes unthinkable as anything other than a film." *Prospero's Books* is "not just a matter of turning the original inside out or upside down, but rather, a dazzling tour de force in which the play has been shaken in the manner of a kaleidoscope. In the process, the eye is assailed with gorgeous imagery and the mind is kept panting with the effort to reconstruct the glittering pieces as they fall." Perhaps no critic has better defined the method behind Greenaway's alleged madness.

REFERENCES

Arnold, Gary, "Stormy Weather for Greenaway's Purient 'Prospero,'" *Washington Times*, November 27, 1991, E2; Bennetts, Leslie, "Paul Mazursky Brews a 'Tempest,'" *New York Times*, August 30, 1981, D19, D24; Brown, John Russell, *Shakespeare's The Tempest* (London: Edward Arnold, 1969); Cavecchi, Mariacristina, "Peter Greenaway's *Prospero's Books*: A Tempest between Word and Image," *Literature/Film Quarterly* 25:2 (1997), 83–89; Conrad, Peter, "From a Vigorous Prospero, A Farewell Without Tears," *The New York Times*, November 17, 1991, II:1, 18; Coppedge, Walter, "Derek Jarman's *The Tempest*," *Creative Screenwriting* (April 1998), 12–15; Harris, Diana, and MacDonald Jackson, "Stormy Weather: Derek Jarman's *The Tempest*," *Literature/Film Quarterly*, 25:2 (1997), 90–98; Jarman, Derek, *Dancing Ledge* (London: Quartet, 1984), 186–206; McFarlane, Brian, "*Prospero's Books*," *Cinema Papers*, 86 (1992), 57–58; Mazursky, Paul, and Leon Capetanos, *Tempest: A Screenplay* (New York: Performing Arts Journal Publications, 1982); Rothwell, Kenneth S., and Annabelle Henkin Melzer, *Shakespeare on Screen: An International Filmography and Videography* (New York: Neal Schuman, 1990); Stenmetz, Leon, and Peter Greenaway, *The World of Peter Greenaway* (Boston: Journey Editions, 1995); Sonnabend, Yolanda, "Designing *The Tempest* with Derek Jarman," in *Derek Jarman: A Portrait* (London: Thames and Hudson, 1996): 77–79; Taylor, Geoffrey, *Paul Mazursky's Tempest* (New York: New York Zoetrope, 1982); Vaughan, Virginia Mason, and Alden T. Vaughan, "Tampering with *The Tempest*," *Shakespeare Bulletin*, 10:1 (1992), 16–17; Woods, Alan, *Being Naked Playing Dead: The Art of Peter Greenaway* (Manchester, U.K.: Manchester University Press, 1996).

—*J.M.W.*

10 THINGS I HATE ABOUT YOU

See TAMING OF THE SHREW, THE

THRONE OF BLOOD/CASTLE OF THE SPIDER'S WEB

See MACBETH

TITUS ANDRONICUS (1594)

Titus (1999), directed and adapted by Julie Taymor; Fox Searchlight Pictures.

The Play

Shakespeare's early tragedy was staged on January 24, 1594, by the Earl of Sussex's men at the Rose Theatre. It was published later that year, then reprinted in 1600 and 1611. The 1611 quarto was reprinted in the First Folio of 1623. Dating its composition is problematic. Some scholars have questioned whether Shakespeare wrote all of it. As one of his earliest works, it has all the faults to be expected from an inexperienced, 30-year-old playwright. Its violence and butchery were clearly modeled after that exemplar of classical tragedy, Seneca, whose works include the story of Thyestes, in which the protagonist is served a banquet of his children's flesh. *Titus Andronicus* begins in Rome where the eponymous general has just returned from his victory over the Goths. Two of his captives are Aaron, a Moor, and Tamora, queen of the Goths. Titus orders that Tamora's eldest son is to be butchered in retribution for the deaths of two of his own sons. Seeking her own revenge, Tamora enlists the aid of Aaron and her two remaining sons to bring about the deaths of Titus's son-in-law (by stabbing) and two of his sons (by beheading). Moreover, Aaron tricks Titus into cutting off one of Titus's hands after his daughter Lavinia has been raped and mutilated and her tongue torn out. Unable to communicate to Titus the persons responsible for these outrages, Lavinia scratches out their names in the sand with a stick.

Now it is Titus's turn for vengeance. First he slays Tamora's sons, grinds up their bones into a pie, which he feeds to Tamora, and then he kills Tamora. For his actions, Titus is killed by the emperor (who in the meantime had married Tamora), and subsequently Titus's surviving son, Lucius, kills the emperor. As one of the only surviving nobles, Lucius assumes governorship of Rome, punishes Aaron, buries the growing pile of the dead, and instills peace at last over the city. Commentator Marchette Chute argues that rather than presume that Shakespeare was "carried away by his desire to please his audience" with "witless atrocities," Shakespeare was "trying to write a 'noble Roman history' and conform to the best standards of the classical drama as they were understood in his day." Chute seems to be writing as an apologist for what is generally considered an atrocious play.

The Film

Titus is too much of a bad thing, without question Shakespeare's cruelest and crudest play. As an unrelenting revenge tragedy repulsive in its grotesquerie, it is fair game for the sort of postmodern interpretation that Julie Taymor lends to it, giving an astonishingly high-tech, low-concept spin to the play's post-Senecan horrors. The film begins with a boy, identified as "Young Lucius," in a contemporary setting, playing cruel games with his toy soldiers. He is then transported back into a postmodern version of ancient Rome to witness the story of Titus as a bystander, incorporated into the action, witnessing it, and, presumably, learning from it. After the final spectacle of revenge and blood sacrifice, the image widens out to indicate that the performance has been enacted before a modern audience, clothed in black, in the Roman Coliseum, with microphones in place so that Lucius, the surviving son of Titus (not to be confused with the invented character of Young Lucius), may address the Coliseum audience at the play's conclusion.

The film is splendidly cast. Anthony Hopkins plays Titus, proud, dutiful, soon transformed through grief and madness into a fearsome avenger. Jessica Lange is an overly made-up, stone-hearted Tamora. But the standout performances belong to Alan Cumming, looking as though he had stepped out of *Cabaret* and into *Fellini Satyricon*, utterly decadent, self-absorbed, and evil, and, especially, to Harry Lennix as Aaron the Moor, the ultimate emblem of subconscious evil and one of Shakespeare's most powerful creations. The film production is marked by gross indulgence and hideous excess, but it is sometimes shockingly effective and even darkly humorous, as at the play's climax, when Titus scampers around dressed in a chef's uniform and hat at the Thyestian feast served to Saturninus, who finds it tasty, and Tamora, who clearly doesn't know what's cooking.

Taymor's stylization purposely jumbles together ancient and modern elements and motifs, lifting part of her concept from Fellini, not only from *Satyricon*, but also from *Fellini Roma*. "Modern Rome built on the ruins of ancient Rome, offered perfect stratification for the setting of the film," she wrote for a press release, without mentioning Fellini or Carlos Fuentes, both of whom

Anthony Hopkins played the title role in Julie Taymor's Titus, *an adaptation of Shakespeare's* Titus Andronicus.
(COURTESY FOX SEARCHLIGHT PICTURES)

have put the stratification of civilizations to metaphorical use. "I wanted to blend and collide time to create a singular period that juxtaposed elements of ancient barbaric ritual with Familiar, contemporary attitude and style." For her symbolic denouement, Taymor wanted the Roman Coliseum, "the archetypal theater of cruelty, where violence as entertainment reached its apex."

In the film's prologue, Young Lucius, involved in pretend "violence" with his toy soldiers, "falls through an 'Alice in Wonderland' time-warp, right into the Coliseum," as his toy soldiers are translated into Titus and his army, marching mechanically and in triumph into Rome. Young Lucius himself is transformed into Titus's grandson. The horrors of Shakespeare's play are framed through a coming-of-age metaphor as Young Lucius passes from innocence to experience, "to knowledge, wisdom, compassion, and choice." His final exit from the Coliseum toward the dawning of a new day with evil Aaron's baby in arms symbolically is a journey toward redemption.

REFERENCES

Chute, Marchette, *Shakespeare of London* (New York: E.P. Dutton, 1949); Welsh, J., and J. Tibbets, "'To Sup with Horrors': Julie Taymor's Senecan Feast," *Literature Film Quarterly*, 28:2 (2000), 155–156.

—J.M.W.

TROMEO AND JULET

See ROMEO AND JULIET

TWELFTH NIGHT, OR WHAT YOU WILL (1600–01)

Twelfth Night (1996), U.K., directed and adapted by Trevor Nunn; Fine Line Features.

The Play

Recognized as Shakespeare's most stageworthy comedy, *Twelfth Night* entertains with a complex plot and intriguing characters. Yet for all of its ribald fun, this farce also features notes of melancholy that call to mind the mood of the tragedies. Its central figure is Viola, who is shipwrecked on the coast of Illyria as the play begins. Believing that her twin brother Sebastian has been lost in the storm, she disguises herself (with the aid of a sea captain) as a page named Cesario and enters the service of Duke Orsino. She quickly falls in love with him, but he pines for the young countess Olivia, who is in extended mourning for a brother drowned at sea and has repeatedly refused the duke's many advances. Orsino, unfazed by these rebukes, sends Viola-Cesario to Olivia with more entreaties; Olivia finds herself immediately attracted not to the duke's words but to the charms of his young page. When Sebastian, who has also been swept ashore on Illyria, encounters Olivia while searching for his companion Antonio, she mistakes him for Viola-Cesario and persuades him to marry her. Orsino, believing himself betrayed by his page, threatens to kill Viola-Cesario, who stands utterly amazed by the turn of events. But when the twins finally meet and Viola discovers that her brother is alive, all is forgiven. The duke marries Viola and Sebastian, a beneficiary of fortune, wins the beautiful countess Olivia.

The play's subplot is equally diverting and filled with clever comic business. Malvolio, Olivia's steward, believes himself superior to the other members of the household and treats them with contempt. He harbors a desire for Olivia, yearning for the day when he can marry her and punish those who have challenged his rule. These characters include Olivia's drunken uncle Sir Toby Belch, her foppish suitor Sir Andrew Aguecheek, her clown Feste, and her clever gentlewoman Maria. To the delight of the others, Maria devises a plot whereby Malvolio finds a letter, apparently from Olivia, urging him to be bold, approach her smiling and in yellow cross-garters, and express his love for her. When he does so, Malvolio's mad behavior prompts Olivia to have him imprisoned. He is released only after Olivia discovers the plot and reprimands her wayward householders. Although Malvolio vows to seek revenge on all of them, his ambition and pomposity have forever been exposed. Sir Toby proves so enchanted by Maria's wit that he promises to marry her. Thus the madness-tinged story of twins reunited and a household restored to order ends with happy, transforming weddings, even though Feste reminds us in song of the rain that "raineth every day."

The Film

Trevor Nunn's 1996 treatment of *Twelfth Night* is framed by a melancholy Feste's (Ben Kingsley) song "With hey, ho, the wind and the rain." The song nicely catches the complex mood of this version, in which song, both joyous and somber, water, and windy emotions are artfully mixed. Feste's opening words fade as we see a 19th-century galley sailing on a stormy sea. Inside, Sebastian and Viola entertain the travelers in pantaloons and veils; when they remove the veils, both are wearing identical mustaches. This sequence strikes the keynote of gender confusion and its stormy consequences throughout the action. Indeed, Nunn seems to be inviting us to consider the dangerous assumptions underlying gender stereotypes in order to make the point that male and female differences can sometimes collapse into mirror-like similarities.

When the tempest blows up suddenly and wrecks the ship, Viola (Imogen Stubbs) can be seen underwater, struggling to reach the surface, then miraculously reborn on the shores of Illyria. She is a survivor and brings to the place a saving grace. Here she must quickly change her appearance because her country Messaline is at war with Illyria. This modification of Shakespeare's text provides a reason for her disguise but also oversimplifies the plot to no great advantage. It also undercuts the mystery of her rebirth.

Though saved from the sea, Viola-Cesario seems never far from drowning in the emotional tempest that follows. Tony Stephens's Orsino is attracted to her from the beginning of her service; his mansion, located near the seashore, is fittingly placed to suggest his strong association with love's watery siren-song. Helena Bonham Carter's Olivia sheds salt tears in mourning for her brother lost at sea, although she too finds in Viola-Cesario the means to save her from drowning. Both Stephens and Carter here reveal a kind of world-weariness and despair that often suggests not Shakespeare but Chekhov. Stubbs's Viola manages to keep her balance and the audience's attention throughout, but in the realistic medium of film her disguise proves an all-too-recognizable artifice.

As for the comic subplot, Nigel Hawthorne's Malvolio is depicted as an almost sympathetic character, instead of the hypocritical spoilsport of Shakespeare's text. Indeed, through some ingenious cross-cutting, Nunn suggests a parallel between Feste and Malvolio, characters whose melancholy humor sets them apart from the rest. This interpretation is reinforced by Mel Smith's Toby Belch, who behaves as a boorish fellow guilty of harassing Maria and embarrassing Olivia. The same can be said for Richard E. Grant's annoying Andrew Aguecheek. Nunn's treatment of the subplot might be called politically correct; the result is that these sequences lack the comic energy necessary to balance the more emotional main plot. But because of Nunn's fascination with cross-dressing and its gender-bending implications, the farcical scheme to expose Malvolio created by an ingenious Maria (Imelda Staunton) comes off as little more than a sick prank conducted by drunks and lechers. And while the lovers and siblings are finally joined in a festive wedding scene, Nunn cross-cuts shots of Malvolio, suitcase in hand, Toby and Maria, Aguecheek, Antonio, and Feste all departing Olivia's estate in various stages of disappointment. When, at the close, Kingsley's Feste reprises "With hey, ho, the wind and the rain" at sunset, the song reminds us that the spirit of inclusiveness marking Shakespeare's *Twelfth Night* is perhaps a watery dream not fully achieved at the turn of yet another century.

REFERENCES

Coursen, H.R., "Three Recent Shakespearean Films," *Shakespeare Bulletin*, 17 (Winter 1999), 38–41; Crowl, Samuel, "Twelfth Night," *Shakespeare Bulletin*, 15 (Winter 1997), 36–37; Lane, Anthony, "Tights, Camera, Action!," *The New Yorker*, November 25, 1996, 65–77; Rothwell, Kenneth S., *A History of Shakespeare on Screen: A Century of Film and Television* (Cambridge, U.K.: Cambridge University Press, 1999).

—*R.F.W*

U–W

UNDER THE BOARDWALK

See ROMEO AND JULIET

VALLEY GIRL

See ROMEO AND JULIET

WEST SIDE STORY

See ROMEO AND JULIET

WILLIAM SHAKESPEARE'S A MIDSUMMER NIGHT'S DREAM

See A MIDSUMMER NIGHT'S DREAM

WILLIAM SHAKESPEARE'S ROMEO + JULET

See ROMEO AND JULIET

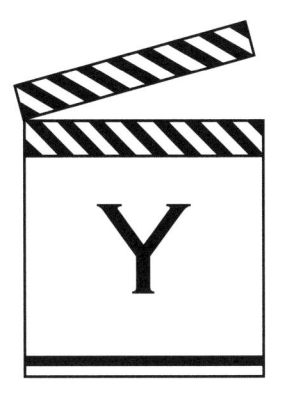

THE YIDDISH KING LEAR

See KING LEAR

ZEBRAHEAD

See ROMEO AND JULIET

Essays

The "Very Cunning of the Scene": Kenneth Branagh's *Hamlet*

On January 21, 1997, Kenneth Branagh's film version of *Hamlet* received its United Kingdom premiere at the newly opened Waterfront Hall in Belfast. It was an important event, as the audience was able to appreciate Branagh's four-hour realization of Shakespeare's play in a spectacular chrome and glass environment, a manifestation of the prosperity that has come to Belfast in the wake of the peace process. But the occasion also provided an opportunity to reflect upon the achievement of this extraordinary actor and director. If, in Britain, Branagh has been maligned for his "populist" readings of Shakespeare, film critics in the United States have praised him for his reworking of Renaissance theatrical traditions and acute cinematic intelligence.[1] In this essay, I will discuss the numerous virtues and isolated infelicities of Branagh's *Hamlet* in an attempt to discriminate between these judgments. While paying close attention to the film's textual sensitivity, I will also concentrate upon the "cunning" (or "art") of its "scene" (or representational devices).

I

Perhaps the most impressive element of the film is Branagh's performance as Hamlet, played in such a way as to bring out the multiple dimensions of a tortured psyche. Thus, from a grieving son lurking in the shadows at the start, Branagh moves to an explosive "man of action" in the later scenes, a knowing impersonator of madness and a theatrically dynamic presence. While Branagh clearly points up a personality-based and romantic reading of Shakespeare's play, the film is arguably more obviously dominated by its political resonances: This *Hamlet* constructs Denmark as a militaristic state. In the opening scenes, there are already glimpses of preparations for war. Hamlet strides through an arsenal on his way to encounter the ghost, and displays of fencing practice punctuate the narrative, foreshadowing the catastrophic conclusion. It is to Branagh's credit that he has restored to Hamlet its military subtexts, and the film does not hesitate to demonstrate the extent to which Denmark's power is dependent upon the cooperation of a gallery of soldierly underlings—Rosencrantz (Timothy Spall) and Guildenstern (Reece Dinsdale) wear regimental sashes; guards invade Ophelia's chamber; and the grave digger (Billy Crystal) arranges skulls side by side with all the precision of a campaigning general. Nor is this merely an extraneous interpretation. The play abounds in martial rhetoric, as when Claudius enjoins the "kettle to the trumpet speak,/The trumpet to the cannoneer without,/The cannons to the heavens" (V.ii.272–74). Branagh takes his cue from the specific orientation of Shakespeare's text in a persuasive reconsideration of the material bases upon which Elsinore's preeminence is founded.

It is part of the versatility of the film's representational scheme that Branagh also develops the Fortinbras subplot, which is so often omitted from modern productions. Frequent use is made of parallel montage whereby the scene cuts between unfolding wrangles at Elsinore and the relentless advances of Fortinbras's army. At one point, newspaper headlines are deployed to highlight the threat of the Norwegian commander, played with an icy implacability by Rufus Sewell. As the film progresses, it would seem as if there is every justification for the nervousness of the sentry who patrols the castle's gates.

The cunning of the film's representational devices can be apprehended no less forcibly in set design and staging procedures. Joel Fineman's work on fratricide and cuckoldry has established the importance of *Hamlet*'s "doubling" structures and assessment and mirrored arrangements. Branagh's *Hamlet* fits well with this assessment, since its interior scenes take place in a state hall lined with windows and mirrored doors. In such a setting, Hamlet is forced to confront reflections of himself, such as Claudius (Derek Jacobi), who, with his blond hair and clipped beard, bears an uncanny resemblance to Branagh's Dane. The points of contact between the characters are also incestuously underlined when Hamlet pushes Ophelia (Kate Winslet) against one of the hall's mirrors, not realizing that Claudius and Polonius are hidden behind it. Branagh himself has observed that the set was intended to suggest "a vain world . . . looking in on itself . . . that seems confident and open but conceals corruption" (quoted in LoMonico 6). It is a bold and critically current view, and one for which there is considerable textual support. Once again, Branagh is keen to place a visual slant upon the concerns of the text, and this imperative is ably demonstrated in the presentation of a court, which, as it contemplates its own self-image, faces only an inevitable decline.

To the broad brush strokes of the design can be added the nuanced local effects with which the film abounds. As the cunning of the film is displayed in its overall montage, so is it revealed in a spectrum of more specialized scenic details and connections. First, several fresh areas of meaning come into play in images of domestic intimacy. After an assignation with a prostitute, Polonius (Richard Briers) dresses himself to tutor Reynaldo (Gerard Depardieu) in the art of surveillance, which makes an intriguing link with the following scene in which Ophelia describes Hamlet's appearance before her "with all his doublet all unbrac'd" (II.i.78). As she recovers upon her father's bed, it is implied that Ophelia has been abused by Hamlet and will be prostituted by her brothel-frequenting father. Second, the density of scenic business reinforces the narrative continuum and creates unexpected poetic correspondences. Claudius and Laertes (Michael Maloney) quaff brandy together as they plot Hamlet's downfall. Their conspiratorial drinking is immediately overtaken by the description of Ophelia's drowning, and subsequently by the grave digger's observation that a tanner's hide "is so tanned with his trade that a will keep out water a great while, and your water is a sore decayer of your whoreson dead body" (V.i.164–66). Through such networks of liquid allusion, visual stimuli in the film enrich the play's textual fabric, exposing reductive, consuming systems in which a woman's innocence is at the mercy of paternalistic hypocrisy.

By concentrating key scenes of the play in particular locations, the film pushes to their furthest extent the areas of overlap between visual messages and verbal utterances. Notably the chapel, a dimly lit but ornate interior, serves as a suggestive site for the prompting of confessional revelations. Toward the beginning of the film, Polonius thrusts Ophelia into a confession box to quiz her about the "very ecstasy of" Hamlet's "love" (II.i.102). A more unsettling use of the box occurs when Claudius creeps into it to lament his "rank" (III.iii.36) offense. Lighting upon Claudius, Hamlet forces his knife through the grill, becoming an unpunctual but unconsoling father confessor. As well as enhancing the impression of a world suffering from the effects of withholding secrets, these locational moments complicate the implications of the play's rhetoric. When Hamlet urges Gertrude (Julie Christie) to "Confess [herself] to heaven" and "Repent what's past" (III.iv.151–52), for instance, one is reminded of a developing intrigue that finds its expression in parodic gestures toward absolution. As confessional textual details are taken up in the film's confessional sequences, a lively sense of escalating frustrations is elaborated.

The partnership between the verbal and the visual is demonstrated most eloquently in the scenes involving the ghost. Played by Brian Blessed and shot from a high-angle perspective, the ghost is discovered as a militant specter of colossal proportions. As the ghost confesses its secrets, bursts of flame break through the forest floor and smoke billows about the trees, apt metaphors for the opening of the sepulcher's "ponderous and marble jaws" (I.iv.50) and for the "blasts from hell" with which the supernatural visitation is associated. Similarly, when the ghost appears in Gertrude's chamber, an eerie music sounds, stressing again the possibility that Hamlet senior may be a demon in disguise. True to the infernal suggestions of Shakespeare's text, the film imagines the ghost as a force whose motives are questionable in the extreme.

Characteristic of both the general representational strategies and the local coloring is the productively restless camera work. Often, repeated camera movements illuminate psychological connections. In the opening scene, the camera zooms outward to show the disappearing ghost, a trajectory followed again for Hamlet's "How all occasions do inform against me" (IV.iv.32) speech: the comparable tracking shots hint at a revitalized paternal and filial alliance. More striking, it might be suggested, are the ways in which the camera prowls around groups of characters, often using 360-degree pans. When Claudius and Polonius agree to spy upon the prince, they are circled by the camera, as is Hamlet on confronting his mother in her "closet." In this scene, the voyeuristic impression is reinforced by the chamber's Tiepolo-like wall paintings of eavesdroppers leaning over balustrades to watch an event of clearly spellbinding significance. This innovative use of the camera has several effects. At once, it adds to the sense of a court dominated by dark secrets and political espionage. In the same moment, it sharpens an awareness of the ever-increasing danger of Fortinbras's army, a force that will eventually encircle the castle itself. The closer Fortinbras draws, the more exactly does he seem to represent the eye that subjects all of Elsinore to an uncompromising, comprehensive scrutiny.

II

Despite the obvious felicities of Branagh's interpretation, there are moments when the film suffers from a textually unwarrantable amount of scenic business. The enthusiasm to illustrate the action is such that the film occasionally provides the audience with a surplus of information. Admittedly, some of these additions are superficially attractive, as when Hamlet senior is presented sleeping in his orchard, only to be retrospectively upstaged by the Player King who appears in an identical colorful costume. At other points, however, ambiguities in the text are flattened by the assumption that the spectators are incapable of imagining for themselves. Jump cuts, flashbacks, and spliced narratives—such as images of Claudius's hand untying Gertrude's bodice, of Claudius keeping "wassail" (I.iv.9), and of Hamlet and Ophelia making love—take away from the plural meanings that the verse alone is able to generate. In this way, although the urge to fill in the text's open spaces makes for a clear story line, it also reduces the "heart" of the play's "mystery" (III.ii.357), substituting a one-dimensional reading for irresolution and elusive uncertainty.

Equally troubling is the recourse to sentimentality in scenes where a much harder or even ironic sensibility would seem to be at work. The score is generally excitedly august, but several musical themes seem inappropriate. As an example, one can cite the scene in which Laertes takes leave of Polonius, which provides the politician with an opportunity to bully his son into filial subservience. Yet in Branagh's *Hamlet*, romantic organ music (in conjunction with soft-focus camera work) is instrumental in subordinating the text's ironic potential to a bonding between father and son that can be dramatically supported only with difficulty. In the same mold are those moments when Hamlet views "man" (II.ii.303) as a "quintessence of dust" (II.ii.308), and when Ophelia laments the disruption to his "noble mind" (III.i.152): a romantic theme sounds precisely at the point where the text calls for a bitter or dissonant musical accompaniment. With such romantic musical evocations, the film runs the risk of muffling some of the more unpalatable dimensions of the text—including Hamlet's participation in the victimization of Ophelia—and comes close to putting a rose-tinted view of the Dane in the place of a more all-embracing political critique.

III

Notwithstanding individual shortcomings, Branagh's *Hamlet* most often captivates with its blend of sumptuous internal scenes and sweeping exterior visuals. If, moreover, the film caters to the postmodern viewer in piecing out textual gaps, it also manages to find new preoccupations in an all-too-familiar narrative. The film is perhaps freshest, and most absorbing, after the intermission, when the breakup of Elsinore is an urgent prospect. Clearly apparent in the film's latter stages is the shrunken character of the court: Only a handful of attendants are present at Ophelia's funeral, a stark contrast with the swelling numbers flocking to enjoy the play-within-the-play and an indicator of Claudius's waning control. Even before Fortinbras makes his spectacular final entrance, monarchical authority is wavering, as Gertrude's increasingly sour expressions indicate. When the climax arrives, Fortinbras's troops crash through the state hall's windows and mirrored doors, a timely lesson for a court that has been incapable of recognizing its own fragile illusions. Hamlet is given a soldier's funeral, a move that identifies him with Fortinbras, the commander whose superior military prowess allows him to declare himself the state's inheritor.

But Branagh's *Hamlet* goes beyond a simple dichotomy between military technology and political supremacy. In many respects, it probes deeper levels of meaning, which lie outside the merely filmic and textual relationship. Above all, this *Hamlet* is intertextual in that it repeatedly articulates its connections to a host of other texts and histories. Faithful to the 1623 First Folio version of the play, the film is suitably bookish, and a favorite retreat for Hamlet is his book-lined study: it is here, not accidentally, that he consults a treatise on demons before setting out to confront the ghost. Branagh, it seems, intends to authenticate himself as a leading Shakespearean by realizing the entire play, an undertaking unique in the theatrical record. In this endeavor, he is aided by many of the luminaries of the Shakespearean establishment. There is more than a passing intertextuality involved in casting Derek Jacobi as Claudius, for the actor played Hamlet in 1979 at the Old Vic, took the part in a BBC version of the play in 1980, and directed Branagh in the title role for the 1988

Renaissance Theatre Company production (Branagh vi–vii, 175). If Jacobi is Branagh's filmic father, then Branagh is Jacobi's theatrical son. A legitimating imperative would also appear to lie behind the casting of John Gielgud (Priam) and Judi Dench (Hecuba) in nonspeaking appearances, and an intertextual dimension is certainly detectable in Charlton Heston's cameo role as the Player King. By drawing upon the pooled resources of Stratford-upon-Avon dignitaries and Hollywood-epic veterans, Branagh, with typical audacity, sets himself up as another epic filmmaker, as a bardic interpreter with impeccable credentials.

Yet the film's intertextuality does not end with casting associations. Part of the grandeur of the film depends upon the numerous exterior views of Blenheim Palace (masquerading as the castle of Elsinore), which is shot in a wide-screen 70mm format. From this scene of architectural magnificence a number of intertextual resonances can be inferred. Following the defeat of the French at Blenheim in 1704, the palace was constructed for the duke of Marlborough as thanks for a landmark victory. Sir Winston Churchill was born at Blenheim in 1874, and members of the family still live at the palace. With these contexts in mind, it can be argued that Branagh's *Hamlet* operates as a metaphor for historical conflicts between England and France, between England and Germany, and even between the English royal family and a more powerful political entity. The film is too complex to be straitjacketed within a simple allegory, however, and equally provokes contrary readings that go against its more obvious contextual correspondences. At the close, the imposing statue of Hamlet senior is toppled to the ground, and any spectator attuned to the late-20th-century collapse of communist countries will not miss the parallel. Branagh's *Hamlet* is an eloquent disquisition on the perils of aristocratic and royal authority; it is also a "cunning" celebration of the plebeian forces that contest the ownership of power and privilege.

What, finally, of the premiere itself? By staging the premiere in Belfast, Branagh, poised between two cultures in that he was born in Belfast but brought up in England, is bringing Shakespeare back to an adopted Irish homeland. Something of this was hinted at in the promotional material about the charity that the screening supported: "First Run Belfast" sponsors local thespians to stage theatrical ventures or to study drama outside Northern Ireland. *Hamlet*, one might suggest, represents Branagh's attempt to negotiate, like Hamlet himself, a tricky trajectory (and a narrative of exile and return) between London, Hollywood, and Belfast, just as the Danish prince follows a similar journey from Wittenberg to England and finally to Denmark. When Julie Christie introduced the film at the premiere, she, too, made use of the homecoming motif, describing Branagh, strangely Gertrude-like, as "your boy." Branagh, however, was not present. Away in the United States filming *The Gingerbread Man*, he was available only as a simulacrum on a videotaped message, transformed into a ghostly echo of his cinematic counterpart.

—Mark Thornton Burnett
The Queen's University of Belfast

NOTES

1. See Christopher Goodwin, "Love Him, Loathe Him: Ken Divides Us All," *The Sunday Times* (January 19, 1997): 8–9; and Geoffrey O'Brien, "The Ghosts at the Feast," *The New York Review of Books* (February 6, 1997): 15–16.

WORKS CITED

Branagh, Kenneth. Hamlet *by William Shakespeare: Screenplay and Introduction*. London: Chatto and Windus, 1996.

Fineman, Joel. "Fratricide and Cuckoldry: Shakespeare's Doubles." *Representing Shakespeare: New Psychoanalytic Essays*. Ed. Murray M. Schwartz and Coppèlia Khan. Baltimore, Md.: Johns Hopkins University Press, 1980: 70–109.

LoMonico, Michael "Branagh's *Hamlet*—Power and Opulence." *Shakespeare* 1.1 (1996).

Shakespeare, William. *Hamlet*. Ed. Harold Jenkins. London and New York: Methuen, 1987.

Playing the Game: Branagh's *Henry V*

"We will in France, by God's grace, play a set,

Shall stike the father's crown into the hazard."

"The gentler gamester is the soonest winner."

"Play up, play up and play the game"

—*Sir Henry Newbolt,*
Vitai Lampada

When a television news crew asked some U.S. Air Force (USAF) pilots during the Gulf War what it was like waiting to fly over enemy territory, they replied that it was like waiting in the locker room before a really important game. The game metaphor for military activity is hardly new; it is there in Shakespeare's *Henry V* and in Branagh's film, though after reading some of the critical responses to the latter, you'd never think so. Branagh has shifted to different games—not the tennis of Shakespeare or the cricket of Newbolt but games more deeply bound up with contemporary English life, national image and self-image, and cultural attitudes. Royal Air Force (RAF) pilots echoed the sentiments of their American colleagues.

I sometimes feel that screen adaptations of Shakespeare send some academics into the visual equivalent of locomotor ataxia. The reactions to Branagh's *Henry V*, such as those of Bernard Richards in *The English Review* or of Ian Aitken in *Critical Survey*, demonstrate this syndrome, an aggravating symptom of which is the need to play the mysterious game of worshipping Olivier.

This English ritual has never appealed to me. I suppose I had better come out now and confess that I am not now, nor have I ever been, an admirer of Olivier's filmed Shakespeare. To borrow a cliché from our least attractive national sport, soccer, I never felt that the boy done good. Expressing this in phrases reminiscent of sexuality, politics, and sport is deliberate; the sexual and political dimensions of *Henry V* are clearly explored by Branagh, whose historical film returns us, via images of sport, to the cultural problems of the present. Olivier preferred to avoid such controversy, opting for a picturesque medievalism based on the *Book of Hours* that returns us to the never-never land of a mendaciously idealized past.

Given the visual acuity in Branagh, it is all the more surprising that the articles in front of me show no awareness of the metaphorical dimensions of images or any sign of a contemporary, popular visual literacy. This is the more ironic, since the popular images in Branagh are immediately themselves as well as elements in *Henry V*. Moreover, Aitken criticizes Branagh for lacking a popular political perspective, a perspective that is supplied precisely through, among other things, visual references to popular culture drawn from films and sport. The fault, dear Brutus, is in ourselves, not in our stars.

Let's consider one such reference: Henry's first appearance on the screen. The context for this is the cleverly condensed scene between Canterbury and Ely. These clerics trust no one, scarcely even each other. They have been in secret negotiation with the king, who himself does not seem party to the even more secret deal which has been struck between Canterbury and Exeter. This new court, like the imperial adventure it is about to make formal, is marked by hypocrisy, connivance, and duplicity, rather like the 1982 imperial adventure in the Falklands. So far, then, so English. Yet

Kenneth Branagh and Brian Blessed "playing the game" in Henry V (BRITISH FILM INSTITUTE)

rather than make Henry either the heroic dupe or the heroic master of his elders, Branagh chooses to intensify the atmosphere of imperial chicanery. Henry first appears as a black figure in the massive portal of the court. A literary critic might argue that he is as yet a blank, a cipher in the great account, a mysterious and unknown force waiting to fill out into a king or human being or both. Someone who's been to the movies, however, will take one look and see Darth Vader.

At which point any notion of Henry as heroic superstar or unknown quantity promptly vanishes. Henry is instantly and precisely known, as is his present position in the power structure. Moreover, the surprise registered by both Canterbury and Exeter as Henry refers to his "sleeping sword" of war is an indication of how far down the imperialist road Henry already is. Henry/Vader is the star of the story, yet he is the dark invader, the death star, a point supported as he moves into the court by the over-the-shoulder camera position that frames the back of his head and the faces of his courtiers in an obvious *Star Wars* trope. In a sense, this looks forward to that long tracking shot after Agincourt. This latter is quite clearly a swipe at Olivier, whose famous tracking shot is a naturalistic extension of his medieval pageant. Branagh doesn't even bother to show this mythologized moment. He saves his tracking shot for the exhausted and harrowing aftermath, in which the ground resembles not the green sward of Olivier but the landscape of the Somme. Henry carries a dead child through the corpses, in a more brutal working-out of the Vader story, for here the Vader figure vanquishes his own children and, by implication, the next generation, thus pitching us into the words of the final chorus, where the whole enterprise is revealed as, finally, pointless.

By the time we reach the tracking shot, though, things are no longer quite as simple as the Vader image at the start might suggest. Henry does indeed reveal all the ruthless ambition of that other invader, and the French tremble at his name as much as Vader's rivals do. The comparison suggests more, though—a terrified and sycophantic court and an essentially corrupt and dehumanized regime; these notions seem to fly in the face of the text's rhetoric about the king, much of which is cut, only to be restored visually later on. Branagh's visuals here subvert the text, posing the fundamental question of sincerity or cynicism about Henry, which is really the question of the presence or absence of radical ambiguity in the text. To reinforce it, Branagh is prepared to let the French represent civilized values, though whether this is quite as enlightened as it seems is something we'll come to later on. Confronting us with this image of Henry right at the start certainly shows an ambitious and potentially radical approach to the text. With Henry as Vader, the start of the French venture is a foregone conclusion; the discussion in court no more than a rationale for the record.

Not that we need to recognize the Vader image just to understand that. In the English court, the courtiers in their dreary uniforms occupy hard wooden pews facing each other in the manner of a private-school chapel or the benches in a locker room. Note the near bonfire that burns behind one of the rows of pews; its flickering light through the arches is a clear precursor of the fire glimpsed through the breach in the walls of Harfleur. We are, in a sense, already there, a neat visual counterpoint to Westmoreland's remark that Henry's subjects' hearts "have left their bodies here in England/And lie pavilioned in the fields of France."

Once in France, the implications of the Vader image are further extended. Exeter arrives on his embassy to the king of France provocatively dressed in full armor. Bernard Richards picks up this ball but doesn't run with it. He begins by complaining that this is unhistorical—a surely rather quaint notion given the text we are dealing with—going on to remark, in tones suggesting Branagh's failure, that Exeter looks like Robocop—which is precisely the point. Exeter, clearly the power behind the throne to begin with, is as dehumanized as his king: a killing machine praying for war. The only time Exeter looks happy is when he's bludgeoning Frenchmen. He is the dispenser of authoritarian terror. Presented as Robocop, he brings cyborg associations appropriate to Henry's Vader, with additional echoes from films like *The Terminator*. By touching on such popular movies in visually obvious ways, Branagh is more than just popularizing his film text. He is aligning it within the Western cultural and visual obsession with apocalypse, figuring Henry and Exeter in an unavoidable critique of the cult of the warrior—a literary tradition that stretches from Archilochus to Auden.

It is not a mistake, though how fully thought through it is may be another matter. In one way, it all seems simple enough. Just as *Mad Max 2* is a reworking of *The Iliad* told from the Trojans' point of view, presenting them as the guardians of civilized community values and the Greeks as invading barbarians, thus inviting us to reappraise the foundations of our culture, so, too, is Branagh careful to make the French models of civilization and Henry hungry for war. Within the larger critique of the cult of the warrior is a more specific exploration of Englishness.

The French court is well lit, comfortable, warmed with a domestic brazier while the furniture is set out as a conference room rather than a locker room. England, seen from here, is the uncultured invader of Europe, a situation familiar today to readers of the sporting press. Even in the crisis of World War II, the English establishment, through Olivier, couldn't resist presenting the French as effete over-reachers, just as Galtieri was caricatured as a "tin-pot general." As regards the French, these attitudes are still in place today, with a government that sees the European Community as a Franco-German plot to wrest sovereignty from Westminster and which rallies the electorate around the totemic image of the currency as a profound marker of national identity. Thatcher's response to the proposal for a single European currency was expressed in a mode familiar on the terraces of soccer grounds: "No, no, no!" In the terms in which we started, the French are the Federation, the English the Empire.

Yet this simple scheme won't hold. Branagh's film is as ambiguously unstable as the Shakespearean text. For all that Henry is a Vader figure, Branagh nevertheless leaves uncut and unsubverted his speech before Agincourt which culminates in the impassioned tears and penance for the death of Richard. Why humanize him to this extent now, when the cynically laid plans to steal France are about to come to fruition? One can understand why Shakespeare did it, but why should Branagh feel constrained? Looking back, one can see that this process of humanizing is visible much earlier, not just in the weeping for Bardolph, which from one point of view is a disgustingly cynical performance and from another a revelation of genuine regret, or even in the scene with Scroop, but with earlier images. In the scene before Harfleur, Henry sits astride his rearing horse like the Lone Ranger, or even Indiana Jones. Branagh, interviewed on this very set for BBC-1, remarked that he wanted Henry to come across as Batman.

Consider the French at Agincourt. As the constable dies, the French nobility are framed in a beautifully composed slow-motion tableau, lit by that lovely pale sunlight which shines only on them. They are the flower of chivalry; civilization and culture overcome by the raw energy of the barbarians in a frankly elegiac moment. Yet not much before this, we were listening to Henry's Crispin's Day speech. Whatever one makes of that as just one more piece of Henry's manipulative rhetoric, here it almost transcends that. I don't agree with Richards that the musical score is intrusive here: it is frankly operatic—a combination of the very moving and openly contrived, rather like the speech itself. These ambiguities aren't just a question of Branagh attempting a sort of liberal evenhandedness; they end up, it seems to me, making the film a radically different experience at the end than the one promised at the beginning. *Moving* and *contrived* are precisely the terms in which one might describe Henry's self-communings before Agincourt. This combination of features is typical of right-wing rhetoric, and Branagh's playing of the speech adds to the extemporary quality that in particular has come to characterize the kind of discourse deployed by Margaret Thatcher, who makes a point of departing from her texts much in the way nonconformist preachers will depart from theirs to utter spontaneous witness. The extemporary, in this kind of discourse, is a mark not just of sincerity but of connection with transcendent truth. The most valued speech is the least fixed, if only because it is individual. In one sense Shakespeare's text is constantly seeking to discover and establish Henry as an individual, led by the demands, not of any social role, but the purely personal, self-redemptive: "No King of England if not King of France."

This causes problems, for other key moments when Henry is obliged to deploy language spontaneously, such as before Harfleur, take on this aura of sincerity. Thus, despite its being carefully planned, the arrest of the traitors becomes a moment when Henry can speak intimately to Scroop, his lover, turning this sincere utterance to official use only in the final phrases. Do we see key moments like this from the perspective of the opening scenes, where all is cynicism and manipulation, or do we see them from the high emotion of the Crispin's Day speech?

At Harfleur things are still relatively straightforward. Here, Henry is playing in the sense of performing. "Once more unto the breach" is a textbook example. As historian Paul Fussel writes in *Wartime*: "What, then, keeps the soldier from giving way to fear? The answer is simply—his desire to retain the good opinions of his friends and associates . . . his pride smothers his fear. The whole trick for the officer is to seem what you would be, and the formula for dealing with fear is ultimately rhetorical and theatrical: regardless of your actual feelings, you must stimulate a carriage which will affect your audience as fearless."

That this is a performance becomes quite clear when the charge is repulsed and Henry comes away swearing to himself, immediately going on to give another linguistic performance to the governor of the town. As he does so, we see shots of his soldiers: lines of faces that are in one sense the team photo, anticipating the game discourse later on; in another the ironically gentled yeomen; in another, barbarians ready to commit murder and rape on command. At this point there is little doubt that the last of these is dominant. Apart from anything else, it fits exactly with the ruthlessness of the Vader image. The Empire strikes back.

This image is part, not just of Branagh's rhetoric, but of Henry's, too. Henry carefully contrives his first appearance in court to be as impressive as possible to his courtiers; he wishes to project himself as vast, mysterious, and dominant. Branagh's use of the Darth Vader image amply reveals the overweening nature of this ambition. In this sense, Branagh's rhetorical project runs parallel to Henry's, both revealing and subverting it. The Lone Ranger image is a good example.

By the time we reach the Crispin's Day speech, however, things have changed. Branagh's project is no longer parallel to Henry's but identical with it; the film's rhetoric has been seduced. Henry no longer plays in the sense of performing but in the sense of taking part in the great game. Vader becomes Skywalker. The situation is a precise echo of the absent Act I, Scene ii, where Henry is coshed with the mythology of kingship, forbears, and English tradition in advance of his spoken decision to invade France. At the very moment that Henry raises practical objections, such as invasions by the Scots, Canterbury steps in with the fully developed analogy of the beehive, Henry's response to which is to immediately make the decision to see the French ambassador, that is, to invade France. Henry's decision is made not in response to practicalities but mythicalities; he absorbs and redeploys the mythic rhetoric exactly as Branagh does.

Part of the problem seems to lie in the visual discourses through which Branagh attempts to return us to the present. The game discourse culminates in the closing shot of Agincourt, a close-up of Henry against an out-of-focus, misty background, as he surveys the field. It is cold and wet; he is spattered with mud and traces of blood. The image is accompanied by the fully orchestrated finale of the *Non nobis*. The rhetorical impact of this image is quite clear, particularly when Henry bows his head slightly. Here, he is, stooping to accept the Olympic gold medal in the traditional and familiar close-up of a successful challenger. The Olympics are a set of aggressively chauvinistic events, of course, in which the ritual allows the public display of male emotion, usually in association with the playing of the victor's national anthem, for which the *Non nobis* here stands. The emotive force of this, both here and in the wider cultural context gestured at, leaves this image looking like a piece of unpleasant imperial nostalgia unless we're prepared to see an ironic tension between the high emotion and the fundamentally ephemeral nature of the achievement; for all the slaughter, it remains, for Henry, a game. The image is seductive and repellent by turns.

There is more to this Olympian image, though, than a suggestion of an England that can once again beat the world (Shakespeare's text consciously recalls Crécy; Branagh's, as we shall see, World War I); the grayness, focus, framing, mud, and blood make this a typical press photo of a victorious player. Yet in what game?

Obviously, the national one. Or, rather, two. The first is soccer. Henry's haircut is a modern trim like that worn by the northern lager lout. It is also closely allied to Gascoigne's, the crown prince of soccer. Gascoigne, or "Gazza," played an interesting role in England's attempt at the World Cup. His performance in the semifinals involved what many saw as a piece of cynical professional fouling, for which he blamed his opponent. Some, in other words, thought he cheated. This is not a world away from Henry's constant shifting of blame onto others. Yet, when booked by the referee, Gazza wept openly because he had, as a result, lost his place in the squad (note the military metaphor) for the final. As national reaction showed, the coexistence of this "professional" attitude and the tears was not seen as cynical, or even particularly strained. Gazza, like Henry with Bardolph, was suddenly sentimentalized in the middle of his own brutalities. Gazza's tears, like Henry's, were not simply a cynical performance, though there was, I am sure, an element of that, as the presentation of a feeling genuinely there but amplified beyond its intrinsic value by the ritual context. The kind of thing, in other words, that Shakespeare is constantly doing in play after play. In situations like these, the tears are literally religious; they bind spectators and actors into the ritual which becomes one of trial and suffering rather than aggression and victory. The degree of ambivalence is hard to gauge. Soccer is a game replete with overemotional responses of varying degrees of authenticity. It is also a game where cheating and rule breaking are both expected and tolerated as part of the rite. What this means is that soccer players are professionals—players, not gentlemen.

That's not a bad assessment of Henry. Yet Harfleur and Agincourt are experiences that supposedly gentle the condition of all the participants. If Henry is a licensed hooligan called a player, he must also be a gentleman, which is why at Agincourt the game metaphor changes. The critique shifts, seeming to validate the text's positive view of Henry. The second game—rugby—is a game linked, in a way soccer is not, with the ruling class. It is a private-school game; it was invented, after all, at the Rugby School. Agincourt is thus an appropriate male ritual for a court presented at the outset as a private school. It is, among other things, a rugby match.

For those who played rugby in school the signs are clearly visible: the climate foggy, raw, and dull (a neat touch, this, the French being invaded by the English weather); the mud; the bloodstained teeth; the matted hair; the rolling, sliding piles of mud-soaked bodies; York rising out of the scrum like a frustrated forward in a maul; Henry's slow-motion dash down the wing. As I write this paragraph, the rugby World Cup final is live on television in the next room. The weather is grayly English, the ground soft, and Roebuck, the Australian fullback, has a face dramatically streaked with blood.

The English, then, are professionals, not gentle gamesters. At Agincourt, York dies barbarically in a scrum produced by his own energetic leading of the vaward. The Constable, by contrast, dies in that tableau of immaculately clad and beautifully lit knights. In this momentary recovery of their climate, the French look cultured, even in their dying. This tableau positions the English as barbarians, a word that is, incidentally, the name of a powerful English rugby team. This barbarian energy is, like York's death, terrifying and admirable. It accounts for the English going bareheaded to face fully-armored cavalry. Bernard Richards complains of a lack of realism here, yet the judgment "it would not have been like that" is surely a poor way to assess any historical fiction, whose discourse is much more heavily franked with the cultural conditions of its point of production than its point of reference. Branagh shows that the civilized and armored French are vulnerable to the internally-armed English who are represented by Henry as gentleman team captain and Exeter as, still, Robocop. The mixture of imperial critique and imperial nostalgia is difficult to disentangle here. Thank God Britain won the Falklands, against great odds, because now we can afford to be liberal about it.

The World Cup began a while back with the singing of national anthems to music by the band of the Royal Marines, an elite force. Agincourt begins with every Englishman kissing the sacred turf. The rugby discourse is further promoted by the conversation between Henry and Fluellen. What's been retained is a highly emotive conversation about Welshness, ending with tears and a male hug. This is, in part, the buddy-movie trope that ends so many violent sequences in films and successful tries in rugby, yet the insistent emphasis on Welshness reminds one forcibly of the fact that where rugby is concerned (a game played by the French, incidentally), the Welsh have a habit of winning. The ambivalence of all this is just beginning to show, as we have seen, in the shots of Henry's soldiers before Harfleur.

It is at Harfleur that another discursive line is introduced; that of World War I. Fluellen, Jamy, and MacMorris converse in a trench from which the English make their attacks. Like those World War I attacks, these, too, prove vain. This World War I reference crops up again at Agincourt in the rain, mud, and blood-filled puddles that litter the field like shell craters.

There are surely few now who would argue that the Great War was a glorious enterprise. Presumably, therefore, it is part of Branagh's critique of Englishness and warriorhood. It is closely connected with the setting up of the court in the first scene as a private school. Bernard Richards writes about the film in the language of a school report but ironically misses the connection. The power distribution within the scene supports the school metaphor. Henry as head boy is technically junior but in practice socially senior to the older, supposedly wiser, advisors around him. Canterbury in particular sounds like a housemaster reading a lecture, even having to slap the document against his hand at one point to wake the boys up. Henry's court is youthful; many of the faces and haircuts would not be out of place in a private-school drama. This affects the reading of the traitor scene, which is the equivalent of the head boy summoning some recalcitrant younger boy for a formal thrashing. Hence the small wooden room (equivalent to a gym, the traditional masculine place for such activity), the bolting of the door (to keep the lowly out), and the overt demonstration of that boys'-school vice, homosexuality. The film that underpins all this is, of course, Lindsay Anderson's *If . . .* .

The scene is played with great openness. Exeter describes Scroop as "the man who was [Henry's] bedfellow," a phrase that has no secondary meaning and which elicits no surprise from his auditors. Indeed, Exeter saves an extra slap for Scroop at the unmasking ritual, as if to punish love betrayed. At one point, as he lies on top of Scroop, Henry looks as if he will kiss him at any moment. Henry's hand and finger movements prior to this are those of the lover.

Rugby itself is, of course, a homosexual male ritual; few other games require men to thrust their heads between the thighs and buttocks of other men. The traditional communal bath and rather desperate singing of obscene songs (transformed here into the *Non nobis*) after the match point in the same direction—which leads us back to that long tracking shot after Agincourt, as Henry carries and finally kisses the dead boy, in a rearticulation of Shakespeare's description of York's death, to the strains of the *Non nobis*, which is now, of course, the school song. There is a deep ambivalence in this dual role: the music is both rousing and mendacious, like a traditional hymn.

Branagh doesn't shirk depicting Agincourt as a product of a private-school ethos. He makes it obvious from the maps, marked with famous towns like Abbeville, as well as from the trenches at Harfleur and the mud of Agincourt, that the fields that saw Crécy also saw the Great War; that conflict which, to the private-school mind, was "the greatest game of all." To that extent, Branagh's rhetorical project still subverts Henry's. The problem is that the game metaphor isn't a fully subversive visual rhetoric. The battle itself is depicted as nasty and squalid but also, like so many sports photographs, as an elegiac meditation on heroism, an attitude supported by the utterly unambiguous playing of these scenes. While the text speaks openly of mutilation, the film is discreet, preferring to figure even the unpleasant death of York within the rugby metaphor. This does reveal the actual consequences of this game mentality but it also sentimentalizes and distorts it in a manner similar to Shakespeare. At the same time, the psychopathic violence of the cyborg genre has been underplayed; Exeter hits Frenchmen but isn't seen dismembering any.

With all these contemporary cultural references, as well as the Chorus delivering his opening lines in a film studio, Branagh is clearly concerned not to return us to an idealized past but to a visibly constructed present. In this sense it is just wrong to suggest that the film lacks any political element. Presenting any event as the Great War is to construct it as negative and futile. Branagh goes one step further and visualizes Shakespeare's game metaphors to reveal the kind of thinking that was by no means unfamiliar in 1914—or in 1991.

Nor is it hard to see in the official English enthusiasm for war and the woefully inadequate task force a loose allegory of the Falklands conflict. Yet by moving that much closer in time and by developing the game metaphors, Branagh strays into potentially destabilizing territory. The weeping-for-Bardolph Henry; the bare-headed, I'm-one-of-the-lads Henry; the Olympic victor Henry; the damn-nearly-singing-St. Crispin's Henry all suggest a dangerously seductive figure and an equally dangerous and seductive nationalism. Yet which discourse, the critical or the nostalgic, is pulling which inside out? To put that another way, does the Vader image inform our view of Henry throughout, or is it rather a case of love on the rebound? By contrast with the Vader figure, the Henry of Agincourt looks positively human, his chicanery redeemed by his heroism. That, I suggest, is indeed the popular perspective of the film: Gazza-like and Thatcherite.

That Agincourt should be a matter of personal and familial redemption for Henry makes it the site of *his* struggle preeminently. Aggression and victory are turned into trial and suffering, though not for the victims. The tears, as with Gazza, belong to the aggressor. No one remembers who Gazza "fouled" or how he felt about it. Thatcher talks about *our*, meaning *her*, struggle. Again, the carrying and kissing of the dead boy is that strange mixture of sincerity and opportunism that characterizes so much right-wing discourse. The wooing of Katherine in Act V, despite the linguistic and visual shift into naturalism, is in much the same vein, though at a much lower level of emotion, since she's only a woman. If the marriage is to set the closure on Henry's redemption, then what we are watching is hardly subversive discourse.

Whether the film finally reveals or revels in that discourse isn't as clear as it might be. To construct war as a game can be radical or reactionary, depending on where, like those USAF and RAF pilots, you are coming from. Players can't be gentlemen any more than hooligans can be heroes, except, perhaps, in the schizoid world of the cyborg or *Henry V*. It is this problem that makes Branagh's film so very English: the attempted liberal critique in the end falls under the spell of established values, producing a text with all the compromised ambivalence of the Cenotaph, that monument to the Olympian greatest game.

—*Michael Pursell*
Gedling English Faculty
Nottingham, U.K.

WORKS CITED

Aitken, Ian. "Formalism and Realism in *Henry V*," *Critical Survey*, III:3 (1991).

Fussell, Paul. *Wartime*. New York: Oxford University Press, 1989.

Richards, Bernard. "Olivier's and Branagh's *Henry V*," *The English Review*, I:1 (1990).

"Every Project Has Its Season": Mel Gibson and Franco Zeffirelli on the Challenges of *Hamlet*

As the Italian director Franco Zeffirelli recalls in his autobiography, he was born a *bastardino*, or "little bastard," near Florence in 1923. Unable to take the name of his biological father, Corsi, he was a *nescio nomen*, or "no name." Later, he took the name "Zeffirelli," which was adapted from a reference in an aria in Mozart's *Così fan tutte* to the *Zefiretti*, or "little breezes." He studied architecture as a student and later fought in the Resistance in the hills around Florence during World War II. He claims that his ambitions to work in stage and cinema were confirmed by a screening of Olivier's *Henry V* and by a subsequent association in the 1940s and early 1950s with his screen mentor, Luchino Visconti. Zeffirelli became a successful opera director, guiding the careers of such luminaries as Maria Callas and Joan Sutherland. But his theatrical films, including Shakespearean adaptations such as *The Taming of the Shrew* (1967), *Romeo and Juliet* (1968), *Otello* (1986), and *Hamlet* (1990) have established his reputation for general audiences.

Zeffirelli has been frequently criticized for a style he describes as "lavish in scale and unashamedly theatrical." Yet, undeniably, his pictures (which also include *Brother Sun, Sister Moon* [1973], *Jesus of Nazareth* [1978], and *Endless Love* [1981]) have appealed to mass audiences because of their blend of flamboyant imagery and spectacle with scrupulous care and craftsmanship. Arguably, more viewers have encountered grand opera and Shakespeare through his films than through the work of any other contemporary artist. He is the complete filmmaker who oversees every aspect of the design, story, and production. As Laurence Olivier remarked during the filming of *Jesus of Nazareth*, "No matter what we do, in the end Franco has the scissors!"

Mel Gibson was born in Peekskill, New York, in 1956, and moved to Australia at the age of 12. After graduating high school, Gibson enrolled at the National Institute of Dramatic Arts in Sydney. After completing his studies there, he auditioned for a role in George Miller's low-budget action movie, *Mad Max* (1979), which made him an instant star. Even so, he joined the State Theatre Company of South Australia in Adelaide to strengthen his stage credentials. *Mad Max* sequels followed in 1982 and 1986, but more substantial was his work with Peter Weir in *The Year of Living Dangerously* (1983). Already a screen star, he appeared on stage in a revival of Arthur Miller's *Death of a Salesman*. Regarding *Hamlet*, Gibson remembered, "I auditioned for it once when I was about 28 and paid it some mind. But somebody else got [cast], and I hadn't thought that much about it again until Franco [Zeffirelli] offered me this part. He met me at a restaurant, and then I wanted to do it. You can't *not* do it! Franco presented it to me like a gauntlet, like a slap in the face. So, you do it."

The interviews that follow took place in New York City during January 1991.

—*John C. Tibbetts*
University of Kansas

JCT: Is Shakespeare a "hard sell" these days?

ZEFFIRELLI: Impossible! We tried to interest studios here, but they weren't interested at all. We had to go the independent route. I don't know why they were nervous; we had had great success with *The Taming of the Shrew* and *Romeo and Juliet*. I remember more than 10 years ago when the people at Paramount told me that Shakespeare never worked in the movies. Now, you are young and may not know that when I had done *Romeo and Juliet* a few years before, it had resurrected Paramount from the ashes! No matter, they just decided that Shakespeare doesn't work. You go to them with figures and a track record, but they don't listen. The way we did *Hamlet*, finally, was to go with three different companies, including Nelson, Carolco, and Sovereign Pictures. Barry Spikings, with Nelson, is English, and I've known him for years. He's been a great fan and friend of mine. When we got [Mel] Gibson and Glenn Close, he was the one who finally said, come on, let's do it.

JCT: How important was getting the Gibson name?

ZEFFIRELLI: It was vital in finding financial backers. But it was a two-edged thing. On the one hand, for anything with Gibson, you can find financing; on the other hand, you get people who doubt, who say, "Gibson? Gibson as Hamlet?" For Gibson, it was extremely risky. He was very brave. He put his career on the line. Imagine, if we did not succeed, he might be the joke of the industry. He has a new audience now. His fans go, too. But I'll tell you, it took great nerves from Mel.

JCT: Was it also a risk when you did *The Taming of the Shrew* with Burton and Taylor?

ZEFFIRELLI: They were at the peak of their careers. Richard Burton was the most famous Shakespearean actor of his time. Elizabeth Taylor was the greatest beauty of the day. It was extremely easy. It was supported by him, personally, and by Columbia. The big problem was later, with *Romeo*. Despite the success of *The Taming of the Shrew*, when I immediately suggested a little, lean *Romeo*, instead of a big, fat-budget thing—just a crust of bread—everybody said, "No way!" I wanted to prove that Shakespeare can work without big names.

JCT: How difficult was it to bring *Hamlet* in at just over two hours?

ZEFFIRELLI: The kind of story we wanted to do automatically meant some areas of the original play became unnecessary. They fell away by themselves, like dried branches. I never cut down so little from the first assembly to the final version than I did here. At first it was two hours and 40 minutes. We cut down only half an hour—unheard of! My first cut of *Romeo and Juliet* was five hours 20 [minutes]. I'd love to go back to my original!

JCT: Describe your first meeting with Mel Gibson.

ZEFFIRELLI: I come from the city of Machiavelli. I know one thing: In the heart of every actor, no matter how big or famous, there is this thorn, this stinging thing, that they wish to do Shakespeare. I talked with

Mel Gibson's animated Hamlet for Franco Zefferelli (WARNER BROS.)

Dustin Hoffman before and I told him I was going to do *Hamlet*. He asked me, "With whom?" I told him, "Mel Gibson." Dustin just almost fainted. He told me, "My dream has always been to play Hamlet!" Everybody wants to do Hamlet. So you can be sure that you hit a note there, you ring an alarm, a bell, in the ears of every actor. He will not say no. With Mel, we had a brunch, which turned into a lunch, and then into a tea and dinner. We separated, and he was convinced.

JCT: Did anything about Gibson come as a surprise to you?

ZEFFIRELLI: I was already informed that he had done some Shakespeare when he was young. I also was madly in love with his voice. It was something I liked, perhaps because of my operatic training, whatever. And his voice is magnificent, bronzed, rich voice. There was something in him that made me very, very excited about the possibility. It was mainly that he could be a 16th-century character. He looks like a young Michelangelo now, with his hair and beard. The classical structure. And the humor. He's capable of a very nasty humor! That's one of my main regrets in the adaptation—that we did not trust ourselves enough to put in more humor. Because Shakespeare knew perfectly well what he was doing. He injected a sudden humor. Perhaps people are uneasy about *Hamlet* now, though—they don't know if they should laugh or not.

JCT: Generally speaking, what are the challenges in bringing Shakespeare to a modern audience?

ZEFFIRELLI: I think it's making the language acceptable, so that you can understand it, that it's almost colloquial. You look at Shakespeare's earlier plays, like *Romeo and Juliet*, and [there is] a much more baroque language, a more flourishing language than, say, *Antony and Cleopatra* or *King Lear*. I think our actors have done this miracle. They have to speak a language that is beautiful, yes, but more "primitive" and spare, in a way. Look at the scenes with Paul Scofield. You're not aware of a "classical barrier" between you and him. He speaks in a way that you understand every single word. And Mel, for all his realism, he makes "To be or not to be" not a poetical aria, but a real suffering and a real problem that you understand. People who are not familiar at all with the speeches tell me that for the first time they understand it. In trying to make it clear to himself, Mel helps the others to understand it better. That was for me the main problem. The story is already so magnificent!

GIBSON: It's the language of Shakespeare that's the real difficulty for everybody. I mean, the words were a barrier to *me*. You learn it by first understanding it yourself. But that doesn't necessarily mean you can make anybody *else* understand it. It's all in the inflection, the emotion, the *sense* of what they are saying. Then you can put your own layers, or colors, on it. You take a line like, "Oh, most wicked speed, to post with such dexterity to incestuous sheets." Very abrasive words, "incestuous sheets." The iambic pentameter grinds itself into a rhythm in the brain after a while, so that even your ordinary conversation takes on that style.

JCT: So what insight does the language give you into Hamlet's character?

GIBSON: You can hear his wheels [turning]. . . . He's very smart, and he's always in motion—either thinking too much or acting too impulsively. Extremes, either way, but they come from the same energy. Take those lines when Hamlet is welcoming Rosencrantz and Guildenstern to Denmark in Act II, scene ii. Hamlet tells them "Denmark's a prison." And they reply that Denmark is not a prison, it's just his mind that makes it so. And Hamlet says [meaning "Are you crazy?"], "I could be bounded in a nutshell and count myself a king of infinite space." You can't pin him down. And don't forget, all this time he's enjoying messing with their heads. He's always doing that, you know.

JCT: Did you see any of the other classic *Hamlet* portrayals, like those of John Barrymore, Maurice Evans, or Laurence Olivier?

GIBSON: No, I don't think anyone can *give* you Hamlet. You're on your own. It's a very personal thing. No matter who you are, you can identify with some aspect of that character. Shakespeare has put the whole of the human condition into one person. And that's why it's such an intriguing thing—why it has had such longevity. And always will. Maybe I'll do it on a stage sometime. Another time. Right now, it's a blessed relief to get onto something else. It all seems so much easier after this.

JCT: Is reaching a mass audience your biggest priority?

ZEFFIRELLI: You know, I think culture—especially opera and Shakespeare—must be available to as many people as possible. It irritates me that some people want art to be as "difficult" as possible, an elitist kind of thing. I want to give these things back to the people. All my training has been a preparation for the one medium that can do that, the motion picture.

JCT: Let's get back to *Hamlet*. Have you ever staged it before?

ZEFFIRELLI: I did it on stage in Italy with a superb cast and brought it to the Festival des Nations in Paris. Later, we toured it to Russian and eastern Europe. That was 1964.

Always I wanted to bring it to the cinema. Either the actor wasn't ready, or I was not, or the money was not. . . . Every project has its own season.

JCT: In *Hamlet* you achieve a distinctive kind of "look" with cinematographer David Watkin. Could you tell us about your work with him?

ZEFFIRELLI: I like always to work with him. We did *Jesus of Nazareth* together. I had lost my cameraman, Armando Nannuzzi, who had become a director himself. David knows how to recreate the look of the "Old Masters." He can make a "still life" out of each set. I enjoy how we worked out a special kind of light for the dueling scene in *Hamlet*. We shot in that huge area with light coming in from openings in the walls. Then we took huge white sheets and placed them from one end of the hall to the other to bounce the light, to reflect it back into the scene. Even the white shirt of Hamlet became a kind of reflector, and you can see the light on Laertes' face brighten when he gets closer. An extraordinary effect. All of this is possible, too, with special lenses and the film stock. And we kept the colors to a more black-and-white look, yes?

JCT: Quite a difference from the charge that you usually work in highly saturated, vivid colors!

ZEFFIRELLI: Color is devastating here, but in this way: I keyed the whole movie to mostly grays and ash colors, a medieval "primitive" look, the look of a society that is brutal and made of stone. Whenever a few rich colors *do* come out, the effect is even more vivid. In that sense, this is one of the most colorful films I've ever done—but only because the few rich colors stand out so much from the grays. That way, you become inebriated by those colors.

JCT: Hamlet himself continues to fascinate us?

ZEFFIRELLI: Hamlet really was a window opened onto the future. He invented the "modern man." You'd like to meet him personally, if you could, today, because he'd be so exciting and interesting.

JCT: Some critics complain that Mel Gibson's character is too old, compared to the relative youth of Glenn Close's Gertrude.

ZEFFIRELLI: They absolutely don't know what they're talking about! Hamlet here is 33 or 34, which at that time was a mature adult. His mother is still young enough to be exuberant sexually, a wildcat who wants to have sex with her new husband at every minute, behind every pillar. She's so hungry for sex. She must be around 45, and that fits very well. She could have had Hamlet at a very young age, you see, even as early as 13—which was common to that time because women were married as soon as they were capable of having children. It works perfectly for us.

JCT: And what about Hamlet's relationship with Gertrude?

GIBSON: I don't think it's sexual, but they do know each other *very well*. And they're totally dependent on each other. They touch and hang on to each other a lot. But with her new husband she's found something she likes better for the moment. And Hamlet can't bear it. By the laws of that time, her marriage to his uncle really was incestuous. Hamlet is disgusted with her. And when he confronts her in the chapel, he wants to shock her. Freudian? That's a crock!

JCT: In *Zeffirelli: An Autobiography* [Weidenfeld & Nicolson, 1986] you claim that from childhood the world of theater has always represented something larger than life. Can you recall an example of that?

ZEFFIRELLI: We've been talking about the Middle Ages, yes? Well, I grew up in the Tuscan countryside, which has always had for me a taste of the real Italy of the Middle Ages. I spent summers watching the traveling troupes of performers who would come and perform. They kept lamps on the floor in front of them, which would throw diabolical shadows on the walls behind them—something I often do in my movies. They told stories and acted them out with shouts and blows and gestures. I have always felt these players were the true descendants of the world of Boccaccio, and I've always believed more in their fantasies than in anything else.

TO "SEE IT FEELINGLY": *KING LEAR* THROUGH RUSSIAN EYES

It would not be entirely accurate to say that 70 years of cinema history were to pass before any film director could meet the challenge of *King Lear*. Some attempts were made in the early years during that flurry of Shakespearean exploitation when the movies were still novelties seeking an appropriate substance to which style could be molded. But even then, in comparison to the numerous *Hamlet*s and *Othello*s, there were very few *Lear*s. A Vitagraph *Lear* in 1909, for example, apparently tried to pack the big dramatic moments of the play into a little film; but *Lear* is arguably too big for the stage, and, as Robert Hamilton Ball reasonably observed in *Shakespeare on Silent Film: A Strange Eventful History*: "Of all the plays *King Lear* seems least suited to radical condensation without audible language" (52). In short, it is doubtful that any of these early attempts really met the challenge.

And a formidable challenge it is! *King Lear*, it almost goes without saying, is Shakespeare's richest and most complex dramatic poem. Of all the plays, it certainly deserves to be filmed. Yet not until the 1970s did directors of the international cinema have the presumption or the courage to approach it. The two who finally took up that challenge both approached the filming of this tragedy through the theater. Peter Brook had directed *Lear* for the Royal Shakespeare Company in England, and he brought this dramatic version to the screen with Paul Scofield in the title role; Grigori Kozintsev also worked toward his visualization of *Lear* through a dramatic production, in his case at the Bolshoi Dramatic Theatre in Leningrad. Each cinematic adaptation was distinctly different in its approach. Peter Brook's was both unconventional and controversial, following the theoretical and political interpretation offered by the Polish poet and critic Jan Kott in his book, *Shakespeare, Our Contemporary* (1966), who entitled his chapter on the play "*King Lear* or *Endgame*," and who regarded the grotesque brutality of the play as absurdist rather than merely tragic. "In Shakespeare's play," Kott wrote, "there is [no] Christian Heaven." *Lear* "makes a tragic mockery of all eschatologies: of the heaven promised on earth, and the Heaven promised after death." In this play, "both the medieval and the Renaissance orders of established values disintegrate. All that remains at the end of this gigantic pantomime, is the earth—empty and bleeding." Kott concludes, "The theme of *King Lear* is the decay and fall of the world." That world is governed by an "absurd mechanism."

Kozintsev's approach to the play was far more conventional and, for many, far more agreeable. It was appropriately scholarly, pragmatic, exegetical, and effective. Appropriately, therefore, his film was released in North America to a demanding academic audience attending the World Shakespeare Congress in Vancouver, British Columbia, in August 1971. According to Maurice Yacowar, who reviewed the film for the Canadian journal *Take One*, the film was well received by this audience of Shakespeareans, who gave the director a five-minute standing ovation after the film had been screened.

In 1971 Grigori Kozintsev was 66 years old. Over the years he had grown and developed with the cinema in his native Russia. Few directors—if any—have come equipped for the task of filming Shakespeare with the cinema credentials of Grigori Kozintsev. His artistic genius was tempered in the postrevolutionary crucible of dramatic and cinematic experimentation in the Soviet Union. This was his training ground: Kozintsev was one of the founding directors of the "Factory of the Eccentric Actor" (FEX). Consequently, Kozintsev and his colleague Leonid Trauberg experimented with cinema as part of the FEX group effort at about the same time another experimenter, Sergei M. Eisenstein, from the Proletkult Theatre, was involved in making his first film, *Strike* (1924). But even though Kozintsev was present at the creation of the Soviet cinema, so to speak, he was at first eclipsed by other innovative talents—Eisenstein, Pudovkin, Dovzhenko. Well after the passing of these gifted compatriots, the achievement of Kozintsev's *Hamlet* (Lenfilm, 1964) brought him international acclaim and recognition. Sadly, however, his *King Lear*, representing a culmination of his artistic career, was destined to be his last adaptation of Shakespeare to the screen. Kozintsev died in Leningrad on May 11, 1973.

Kozintsev's *Lear* was therefore the director's last, and arguably his greatest, achievement, concluding a long and productive career. It undertakes a bicultural transformation of its Shakespearean original and translates Shakespeare's poetry into a coherent structure of unforgettable images. Its approach is "traditional" in that it does not undertake an interpretation of the play currently in fashion. Kozintsev does not attempt to Kotterize Lear, for example. Rather, he orchestrates a black-and-white symphony of gore and bloodletting only insofar as is necessary to demonstrate through his visualization the disintegration of the king and his kingdom into a state of chaos and anarchy. His Lear is placed in a cruel and questioning universe, but it is not necessarily an absurd one.

King Lear is, of course, many things, but it is, at least in part, a play that demonstrates the deleterious effects of division, fragmentation, dissolution, and disintegration. The opening of the play represents a willfully imperceptive violation of a moral principle of unity and authority as the king attempts to divide himself from his responsibilities. A once-admirable man capable of commanding the love and loyalty of such as Kent and Cordelia now speaks reasonably of unreasonable things and, when challenged or thwarted, speaks unreasonably of reasonable things. Division is central here: Lear divides his daughters by dividing his kingdom among them. This material division first has psychological, then metaphorical repercussions, until, finally, we find the tormented king, his mind divided between the rational and irrational forces that vie for control, commanding the very heavens to crack and divide. Kozintsev attempts to visualize the process of division and moral disintegration that governs the play.

Through the carefully structured details of his mise-en-scène Kozintsev creates an appropriate atmosphere and moral landscape for this tragedy, as he had earlier done for *Hamlet*. As the doting and self-indulgent benefactor is transformed into a rash and angry tyrant, Kozintsev ties together the idea of king and kingdom by his handling of a large, symbolic map. Through his casting of Lear, Kozintsev presents us with a clue to his understanding of the man and his tragedy. King Lear is played by a wizened old man (Yuri Jarvet), possessed of a quiet dignity in his moments of composure, but capable of conveying and sustaining the building rage that dominates him in his moments of "hideous rashness." But Jarvet's Lear is also frail and defenseless against loneliness and isolation, against the brutal forces in human nature that his abdication has unleashed against the elemental forces in Nature that batter him on the heath. This idea is captured in a shot from the shooting script that Sergei Yutkevich has described (No. 566, not included in the final released version): "The wind throws Lear off his feet. But he rises and goes forward, a tiny figure against the vast, raging sky" (196). But Shot No. 566 was overstated, and, Yutkevich believes, excised for that reason. Nonetheless, its perception of Lear is evident—a vulnerable man thrown off balance by forces larger than himself.

So strong is this Lear's desire "to shake all cares and business from our age" that he will not even speak his own proclamation at the beginning of the film. Rather, he sits at rest, warming himself by an open hearth while an underling reads part of it. So comfortable and secure is he that his understanding of Cordelia's defiance is slow in coming. Though slightly agitated, his initial response to her—"Nothing will come of nothing. Speak again" (I.i.90)—is relatively calm. But when Cordelia is then forced to quantify her love—to divide between her future husband and her father that which cannot be divided—his anger heats, and, as his choler grows, we hear the flames from that open hearth crackling behind his words on the soundtrack. Then we see

Paul Scofield as Peter Brook's King Lear, *with Irene Worth as Goneril*

the now furious king shaking and unfurling that oversized map of his kingdom, which ripples unsteadily like a flag across the entire and considerable width of the CinemaScope frame.

The process of division follows a widening course, as in the Gloucester subplot brother is divided against brother and son is divided against father. Later still in the affairs of Goneril and Regan, wife will be divided against husband, servant against master, and sister against sister, until, finally, the whole realm will be thrown into the division and chaos of civil war. This film's particular genius is its masterful visualization of the process. It is worth pausing a moment, therefore, to examine in some detail how this is achieved.

In Act IV we find Lear mad on the heath. Kozintsev presents him as a stationary, dwarfed figure (in long shot), standing still in the center of the wide frame, as the heath grass tosses in the wind on either side of him—a man strangely at odds with his environment. The camera then moves in close to show Lear crawling through the grass as he asserts, "I am the King himself!" (IV.vi.84), visually recalling the grotesque irony of his stated desire in his opening speech in Act I to "unburdened crawl toward death." After the recognition scene with Gloucester, Lear is discovered and borne on a stretcher to Cordelia. Here we finally see Lear momentarily at peace, serene, utterly oblivious to what is going on around him, as men are slaughtering each other on the field of battle. That "future strife" that Lear had hoped somehow to avoid by dividing his realm is here being enacted all around him as the process of political disintegration seems to have become universal.

When Lear and Cordelia are reunited (IV.vii), Kozintsev adds an intelligent and effective touch by including the Fool, now fettered in chains, in the scene, but off to one side (once again, carefully utilizing the width of the CinemaScope frame). When the by now "mightily abused" Lear says to Cordelia, "Pray, do not mock me," Kozintsev immediately cuts to a close-up of the Fool, who, upon hearing these words, lowers his head to the ground in shame. The final confrontation with Cordelia, where the king is forced to acknowledge the reality of her death but fights against the recognition, is handled brilliantly. Kozintsev has set all the remaining characters in the drama momentarily adrift. People come and go and fight and die for no clear reason. Friend is indistinguishable from foe as swords are drawn and fires set and catapults released. Against this shifting and destructive chaotic background, Goneril and Regan wander in search of Edmund, until they meet and one poisons the other. Crosscut with this action is the image of Edgar, walking across the heath with a purpose—to seek out and avenge himself and his father on his bastard brother. In this way moral and dramatic tension is created through the effective use of parallel montage.

Meanwhile, in the midst of all this chaos and uncertainty, Lear and Cordelia have been taken prisoner. Yet Lear is utterly serene and happy: "Come, let's away to prison./We two alone will sing like birds i' th' cage" (V.ii.8–9). When next we see Lear, however, this serenity will have shattered. And even as these lines are uttered, father and daughter are divided by the faceless, helmeted soldiers who surround them. As Cordelia kisses her father's hand—her final parting gesture—Kozintsev cuts to Edmund as he states "To be tender-minded does not become a sword"—portentous words that ironically anticipate his final confrontation with Edgar, his nemesis.

The final tragic scene is introduced with the camera staring into an empty courtyard as we hear an incredible, anguished howling on the soundtrack—like a wounded animal in terrible pain. Even the camera seems puzzled, but curious and determined to seek out the source of this disturbing scream. It starts to track, seemingly uncertain of precisely where to go. It then moves up a flight of stairs, where it discovers, standing on the castle walls, the bent figure of King Lear, frozen before the hanging body of Cordelia in an archway. And we know that we are at Act V, Scene iii, where Lear enters (line 258), bearing the body of Cordelia in his arms. As Lear utters his final chorus of negation ("Never, never, never, never, never"), the camera returns in a visual trope to that archway on the castle wall where he had discovered Cordelia's body, the severed rope used to hang her still dangling there, the turbulent sea churning far below in the vista beyond the portal. Just before this, the father has lifted up his daughter so that her motionless face touches his own as he remarks: "What is't thou say'st? Her voice was ever soft." Immediately afterwards, Lear dies, and father and daughter are again united as they are borne off together on the same stretcher, serene and motionless, and finally at rest. As the camera tracks back in order to follow this action, soldiers bearing the bier kick the fettered Fool out of the way in order to pass. His grief becomes our grief. The film ends with the Fool, hunkered on the ground, playing his lament on his flute—his anguish translated beyond words into music.

The details of Kozintsev's handling of the Gloucester "echoplot" are equally affecting. Edgar's explanation of his disguise (II.iii) is not verbalized in the film, nor does it need to be. Instead, Kozintsev shows us the process by which Edgar develops his plan. He sees a band of itinerant "Bedlam beggars" passing by; he hears their "roaring voices" (one of which repeats the phrase "Poor Tom's a-cold"); and on this cue Edgar tears his clothes and begrimes himself with filth, then joins them. Later, the whole group joins Lear and the Fool on the heath, forming a lunatic chorus and mad jury for the mock trial that the king stages (at III.vi).

The blinding of Gloucester is also distinctive in Kozintsev's adaptation; it is filmed in such a way that the anguished questioning of the victim is emphasized, rather than the spectacle of this repulsive violence. As Cornwell says "Upon these eyes of thine I'll set my foot" (III.vii.68), the camera moves in to a close-up of his spurred boot poised over the face of Gloucester, who has been pinned to the floor. Shakespeare does not include Edmund in this scene, but Kozintsev does. As the blinded Gloucester screams Edmund's name, Kozintsev's camera takes us to a chamber above, where we see Edmund, obviously unmoved by Gloucester's grief and pain, calmly going about his business as his father's screams reverberate throughout the room.

In contrast to this unfeeling bastard, we later see Edgar's reaction to his blinded father when he discovers him on the heath. While the camera zooms in to a tight close-up to mark the point of recognition, Edgar as Poor Tom groans in agony to see his suffering father. Later still, Kozintsev chooses not to represent the play's suicide ruse, wherein Gloucester is led to believe his guide (Edgar disguised as Poor Tom) has taken him to the cliffs of Dover. Instead, he interprets the final reconciliation between father and son in remarkably visual terms, Gloucester's recognition of Edgar (and his own misjudgment) just before "his flawed heart . . . 'twixt two extremes of passion, joy, and grief/ Burst smilingly" (as Edgar's report describes it in the play). The scene begins in longshot, the figures of father and son isolated on a rocky plane. The camera moves ever closer, as the father's hands grope toward the face of his son. The final recognition, then, is subtly suggested and conveyed through understated gesture—a *perfect* visualization of Gloucester's answer to mad Lear's question on the heath when he asks blind Gloucester if he sees "how this world goes"—"I see it *feelingly*."

If one consults Kozintsev's theoretical writings about Shakespeare, one can see his ideas behind both *Hamlet* and *King Lear* in gestation. One learns, for example, that the director considered the reestablished affection between Lear and Cordelia as "an illustration of wisdom." Kozintsev's own writings clearly anticipated his filmed treatment of the reconciliation of father and daughter in Act V: "An instant of harmony is so beautiful that the rest of life is like utter darkness beside it. The optimism of *King Lear* does not only lie in the idea that evil men either are punished or kill one another; it lies mainly in the feeling of victory of the worthy over the unworthy, even though their moral victory be a factual defeat at the same time. This is evinced in the last scene between Lear and Cordelia," as Kozintsev wrote in his book *Shakespeare: Time and Conscience*. "It seems that their enemies have won a sweeping victory. Nevertheless these vulnerable two are the victors. They prevail because they know happiness" (102).

Kozintsev contends that "Lear finds true wealth" in that instant of harmony: "No matter how much more time he has to live, Lear spends these few moments as a wise man. He has come to know what is counterfeit and what is real." The thrust of this film is to amplify those qualities that the loving Cordelia comes to represent. "I tried to strengthen the voice of Good," Kozintsev explained for the World Shakespeare Congress at Vancouver in 1971, "even in those instances when it has no words to speak." Silence and the expressiveness of gesture cinematically adorned is the key to his method—Edgar recoiling in horror at the sight of his blinded father, for example, or the Fool in chains lowering his head in shame at the end, or Gloucester's recognition of Edgar by his ability to "see feelingly." One is not likely to encounter a more haunting or moving portrayal of Shakespeare's *King Lear*. For me, this is the definitive film adaptation.

—*James M. Welsh*
Salisbury University

Note: The ideas that shaped this essay were influenced in part by my colleague Bill Zak, who taught *King Lear* brilliantly in 1975 at Salisbury University while working out the thesis of his own book on the play, *Sovereign Shame*, published in 1984.

WORKS CONSULTED

Ball, Robert Hamilton. *Shakespeare on Silent Film: A Strange Eventful History*. New York: Theater Arts, 1968.

Kott, Jan. *Shakespeare Our Contemporary*. Trans. Boleslaw Taborski. Garden City, N.Y.: Doubleday/Anchor, 1966.

Kozintsev, Grigori. "*Hamlet* and *King Lear*: Stage and Film," *Shakespeare 1971*. Ed. C. Leech and J.M.R. Margeson. Toronto: University of Toronto Press, 1972.

———. *Shakespeare: Time and Conscience*. New York: Hill & Wang, 1966.

Leaming, Barbara. *Grigori Kozintsev*. Boston: Twayne, 1980.

Yacowar, Maurice. "*Lear* in Vancouver," *Take One* III:3 (January/February 1971): 28+.

Yutkevich, Sergei. "The Conscience of the King," *Sight and Sound* 40 (Autumn 1971): 196+.

Zak, William F. *Sovereign Shame: A Study of* King Lear. Lewisburg, Pa.: Bucknell University Press, 1984.

Macbeth: Polanski and Shakespeare

It is not possible to present a great dramatist's work in another form, like film, and still be altogether faithful to that work. Since the dramatist's greatness depends on the fact that his drama *is* the form, changing the form will distort the work. This must be granted. But this does not mean that the new work cannot have its own value or that this new work cannot tell us much about the original drama. This is precisely the case I wish to argue, using Roman Polanski's screen version of Shakespeare's *Macbeth*. We may wish to regret that tragedy has become melodrama, that the camera has replaced the word, and that Shakespeare's play has been reduced both morally and metaphysically. But these regrets should not blind us to the virtues of the film, not only its energy and visual excitement, but its value as an interpretation of Shakespeare. How Polanski sees (or reads) *Macbeth* indicates the rich suggestiveness of Shakespeare's art; it also indicates Polanski's personal vision of the modern world.

My concern here is what Polanski does with (or to?) Shakespeare, how he *uses* what Shakespeare presents or suggests, and to what purpose. I should add that my concern here was my concern when I viewed the film, for if this movie were treated by itself, without thought of the original, it would be little more than a romp, visually exciting but essentially thin. However, with Shakespeare's play as the underpinning, the point of reference throughout, the film becomes interesting and original as an *interpretation* of Shakespeare and as a view of life in our time.

Both Shakespeare and Polanski begin with the witches, and, for both, the witches set the emotional climate. Thunder and lightning punctuate their entrance in Shakespeare, and one witch asks, "When shall we three meet again/In thunder, lightning, or in rain?" The witches are described two scenes later as "withered" and as having "beards." They are usually played as old hags, with raspy voices, mannish ("they should be women," says Banquo, but their beards make him unsure) and sexually repulsive. From their skinny lips comes the phrase that serves as the keynote to Shakespeare's play, "Fair is foul, and foul is fair," a phrase which underscores the play's most important theme—confusion of values, life as ambiguity, puzzlement, equivocation. The witches disappear, usually together in a cloud of smoke, as they prepare to "hover through the fog and filthy air." Fog and filth set up the physical conditions for Shakespeare, with most of the play taking place in the haziness of fog or the darkness of night. Because Shakespeare's scene is firmly planted in the viewer's mind, Polanski's opening sequence shocks by its difference. No thunder or lightning, no thick fog, but a day that is hazy, and three women in the middle of what seems to be a wet, sandy beach, with no trace of sea. As they utter Shakespeare's words, they are busy burying a severed hand in the sand. Two of the witches are old hags of the Shakespeare variety; one is a young girl. Surprisingly, after the initial shock to one's expectations, it seems right that one of the witches is young. Her youth (17 or 18 years old) and good looks indicate "fair," whereas her company and her action indicate "foul." Her age makes one realize that witches possess an ongoing quality in time; a particular witch grows, matures, and dies, but witches remain forever, and the young learn from the old. When Polanski's witches leave, instead of disappearing together, they separate—the young witch, pushing a wheelbarrow containing who knows what kind of grotesque items, travels with one old witch, the third witch walks alone—and the stationary camera watches as they walk in two directions in a V pattern, isolated figures in a bare landscape, stretching from a buried hand to encompass a wide space. Polanski's point, it seems clear, is that the witches cover a lot of space; in fact, they cover the world. Shakespeare's words indicate that they are separating to meet again, but only in Polanski—if my memory of previous stage and movie versions serves me—do they literally separate. This is no small point, for their widening movement, coupled with the youth of one of the witches, strongly suggests the all-encompassing (space and time) quality of the witches and what they represent.

War pervades the next scene in both play and film, a bloody sergeant telling Duncan how the battle was

Jon Finch as Macbeth in Roman Polanski's adaptation
(COLUMBIA PICTURES)

"lost and won" (to use the witches' equivocal phrase) and reporting how brave Macbeth, with great flourishes of his bloody sword, won the day for Scotland. When we first see Polanski's Macbeth, leaving the battle and soon to see the witches, we are surprised by his youthful appearance. He possesses, at first glance, an aura of innocence, or at least an aura of clarity and cleanliness, that seems not to fit so bloody and seasoned an executioner. As Macbeth and Banquo ride from the battle, it is Banquo to whom the grimy and bloody qualities of war cling. In fact, on first viewing I was unsure which was Banquo, which Macbeth. (Was Polanski playing with puzzlements here also?) The witches, "imperfect speakers" though they are, set us right as to Macbeth's identity when they address him directly. They are now near a dark cave over which the camera hovers, clearly establishing this geographical spot for later use in the film. The witches hail Macbeth as Glamis, Cawdor, and King-to-be, words which cause Macbeth to stare in a kind of trance—and here the camera catches a quality in the eyes of Macbeth (played by Jon Finch) that belies the clarity and innocence of our first impression. A touch of Satanism seems to have possessed Macbeth, a mystic bond with the witches, captured beautifully by Polanski as the camera reinforces Shakespeare's words. A few moments later, when Ross and Angus arrive to hail the new Thane of Cawdor, Macbeth's fate seems sealed. His face betrays the fire enkindled within, and the large iron pendant that Ross hangs around his neck, symbolizing his new status as Cawdor, presses against a heart no longer free.

The youth and attractiveness of Polanski's Macbeth, when we first see him, is matched by his wife's. Lady Macbeth (played by Francesca Annis) was disarmingly pleasant to look at and listen to, possessing none of that hardness and bitterness usually associated with Shakespeare's lady. Polanski does not take seriously the words that Shakespeare gives to Lady Macbeth—"unsex me here"—and presents a young woman physically attractive to audience and husband. When we see Macbeth and Lady Macbeth together for the first time, theirs seems an ideal marriage of bodies and minds; they are one in youth and beauty, and an air of domesticity hangs over their scene together. For only this time, however, because the murder of Duncan, soon to follow, changes Macbeth from young loving husband to callous king, and his bloody acts eventually lead his wife to madness. Precisely because Shakespeare's play is behind us, we realize that the young Lady Macbeth, like the young witch, fair on the outside, is foul within. Although Polanski simplifies Shakespeare's more complex view of the pair, he does, by means of his direction and his actors' intelligent rendering of Shakespeare's lines, set up a close physical and emotional relationship that will serve as a clear foil to what happens afterward to the beautiful Macbeths.

Beginning with Duncan's murder, the film seems to revel in gore, a criticism leveled against it by reviewers and spectators. Polanski does accentuate the blood and brutality. Because his wife, Sharon Tate, was murdered so brutally and senselessly by Charles Manson's "family," it seems easy to see in the movie's emphasis on bloodshed a working out of Polanski's personal obsession. Whatever truth such a view may have, it should not stop us from investigating Polanski's use of the horror. (Do not many directors and writers transform their private obsessions into art?) If the violence and gore are there for their own sake, merely to arouse, to titillate, to appeal to our basest emotions, then Polanski's art is decadent. If, however, they serve a larger purpose, as I think they do, then their presentation deserves the kind of respect we are willing to give to the blinding of Oedipus or Gloucester or to the horrors found in Webster's

Duchess of Malfi. There is no denying that Polanski has an imagination that is essentially gothic. Mystery and horror abound in his work: witness *Repulsion* and *Rosemary's Baby* and *The Fearless Vampire Killers*. But his gothic sensibility serves artistic purposes. Violence is part of the reality of the world as Polanski sees the world, and in his *Macbeth*, Polanski uses Shakespeare's setting to present his personal vision of bloodshed, mutilation, violence, and horror—a vision not altogether unfounded in the light of Auschwitz and, we should add, the Manson family murders.

Macbeth's savage slaughter of Duncan sets the tone for the rest of the film. Whereas Shakespeare brilliantly evokes the murder without showing it on stage, presenting the haunting and nervous reactions of Macbeth and Lady Macbeth, Polanski takes full advantage of his medium to *show* us the murder. The sleeping Duncan awakens to see Macbeth hovering over him. Duncan's look of fright meets Macbeth's look of death. Macbeth plunges his dagger again and again into Duncan's body; the effort is great, and Polanski forces us to hear knife hitting bone. Blood gushes from the many wounds. One must borrow Lady Macbeth's later question: "Who would have thought the old man to have had so much blood in him?" During the stabbing, Duncan's crown falls from a table near his bed to the floor, the camera remaining with it for a couple of seconds. It is for this crown that Macbeth will suffer his "deep damnation." Polanski's focus on the crown so vividly associates the crown with blood and death that this will be its association later when Macbeth is crowned in a formal ceremony—outside, under a hazy sky, in that bleak, wet desert landscape—and at the end of the film when the crown is placed on Malcolm's head. The most important prop in the movie, the symbol of the imperial theme, the circle of iron for which Macbeth kills, this crown gathers to itself a complex of associations: ambition and kingship *and* blood and slaughter. In Shakespeare the crown, symbol of kingship, carries with it trouble and responsibility and sleepless nights, but not necessarily blood and havoc, so that when Malcolm acquires the crown at the end of Shakespeare's play, it represents a return to order and harmony. In Polanski the association of crown with violence is so accentuated, set up in this sequence showing Duncan's murder, that the crown itself is tainted, and we are forced to realize that Malcolm's crowning at the end of the film is a continuation of violence and blood.

Once this brutal act of violence is behind him, there is no turning back for Macbeth. He travels a narrowing path to his own destruction, acting as butcher along the way. Shakespeare allows us to see the inside of Macbeth, and we come to sympathize with this man caught up in an ambiguous world, isolated, sensitive to what he has lost, unable to free himself from the fate he created. Polanski gives us the outside only, making the film more melodramatic than tragic. But we must not forget that Shakespeare wrote life, and his play is large enough to contain Polanski's view. Murder and violence beget murder and violence. There is no end to the process in Polanski. It is not necessary to pinpoint the brutality that dots the rest of the film. Mutilated bodies, hacked limbs, throats cut, heads lopped off, bloody faces—a parade of horrors. The film is bathed in gore, as life is bathed in gore, according to Polanski's vision of reality. It is a reality hard to face, and both Shakespeare and Polanski demonstrate that Lady Macbeth cannot face it. Many commentators on Shakespeare's play believe that Lady Macbeth feigns fainting in Act II, Scene iii to get her husband out of a difficult situation. But Polanski has clearly captured Shakespeare's intention, I believe, by having Lady Macbeth faint *at the sight of* Duncan's murdered grooms. Her fainting is a genuine reaction to a bloody scene. It indicates her essential weakness—a weakness which will lead her to delirium—and it accentuates the separation of Macbeth and his wife at a crucial dramatic moment. Lady Macbeth does not altogether know her husband; she is shocked by his brutality. He will now travel his bloody path alone. Polanski, in this sequence, offers an intelligent interpretation of a Shakespearean crux.

The murder of Banquo is a high-action sequence in the film. In Shakespeare the scene takes place at night, with Fleance holding a torch for his father. We hear from the murderers that Banquo and Fleance must leave their horses behind and walk to the palace (because horses could not appear on Shakespeare's platform stage). Polanski, unhampered by Elizabethan stage conditions, presents his sequence in the hazy daylight with Banquo and Fleance on their horses. An exciting fight ensues, the three murderers (one of them is Ross) against father and son. Fleance escapes, but Banquo, after his horse is felled, receives an ax in his back and plops into a muddy, shallow lake. In the banquet scene, his gory figure returns as a ghost, so excessively gruesome that we fully understand Macbeth's horror when he gazes at it. The horrible imaginings that Macbeth knew would result from murder haunt him with a vengeance. Polanski does not relent in his visual presentation of the horror.

Shaken by Banquo's apparition, Macbeth rides across the bleak landscape to the witches' cave, this time going inside the cave. Again, Polanski stuns us with his interpretation of Shakespeare, for the cave is filled with nude witches, some young, but most old. Conventional wisdom holds that nudity in a young woman (whether witch or Lady Macbeth) is pleasing to the eye; nudity in old hags, with breasts hanging and shapes distorted, is offensive, grotesque, disgusting. That young and old are together forces us to realize that the young will become the old, fair turning to foul; that the cave is crowded makes us realize that the world contains *many* witches—both ideas reinforcing the all-encompassing quality of witches that is suggested in Polanski's first sequence. The grotesqueness of their bodies is matched by the wildness of their looks. Joyfully they place items—a hand, a baby, and the like—into a steaming cauldron. The items, listed by Shakespeare, are disgustingly visible in the film. Polanski goes beyond Shakespeare by having Macbeth drink the hellish brew. When the camera moves from a view of the many nude witches to the cauldron where "things" are thrown, to a large goblet, going from witch's hand to Macbeth's hand and from his hand to his lips as he drinks, we have a progression that stunningly reveals how far Macbeth has entered the world of the witches. The shot of Macbeth gulping the liquid, greedily and sloppily, punctuates his desperation and wildness and his complete oneness with the witches. Their brew is now within him; he now possesses them; he has literally "supped full with horrors." Here is a director's addition to Shakespeare which remains true to the play, visually heightening both meaning and feeling. We are inside the cave, the horrible deepening quality of Macbeth's commitment to horror, to all that is foul and unnatural.

The witches' prophecies give Macbeth that false sense of security which pushes him further along the bloody path to his own death. Along the way, he orders that Lady Macduff and her children be murdered, providing Polanski with another sequence of slaughter and nudity this time part of a domestic scene. Macduff's young son is bathing nude in a tub of water (in the previous scene, the witches' cauldron contained a nude bloody child) when the murderers enter. His cries and his mother's shrieks sound the havoc in a world created by Macbeth, and images of gore and violence once more invade the viewer's consciousness. Along the way, too, we witness the quieter scene of Lady Macbeth's delirium. Macbeth hath murdered her sleep as well as his own, and she reenacts, in her sleepwalking, the murder of Duncan. Her face is harder now, and older. She seems completely isolated from her husband as she walks alone in darkness. The candle that Lady Macbeth holds is Shakespeare's and Polanski's image of an essentially frail nature which once burned brightly and passionately in pursuit of a crown, but which now flickers precariously before it finally goes out.

The climactic battle between Macbeth and Macduff is an editorial stage direction in the Shakespeare text: "They fight"; "*Exeunt* fighting." We can be sure that the Elizabethans enjoyed the battle on their platform stage, and we can be equally sure that whatever happened on that stage could not have matched the shocking violence of Polanski's sequence. In Shakespeare the decapitation of Macbeth takes place offstage; in Polanski we see it. The two savage warriors engage in an even match—armor clashing, bodies receiving mighty and bone-breaking blows. Their swords are heavy, and become heavier as the battle progresses. Then, as Macbeth climbs stairs to get to Macduff, Macduff's large and furious stroke severs Macbeth's head from his body. Polanski's camera follows the head as it leaves the body and rolls on the floor (reminding us of Duncan's crown), and then the camera cuts to the body, sans head, which balances for a second on the steps before it sways backward, crashing down the steps. It is a horrible, sordid, realistic sequence. Shakespeare has Macduff return to the stage with Macbeth's head on a pole; Polanski shows us how it got there. Both Shakespeare and Polanski, true to their respective forms, present a fitting and awesome climax to Macbeth's bloody career.

Shakespeare's play ends with Macbeth's head on a pole and with Malcolm asserting his kingship in a speech that allows the audience to believe that the time is now free, that thanks will be given to loyal followers, and that Scotland will be healthy again. In short, in Shakespeare "fair" is reestablished, and Malcolm will be going to Scone to be crowned king. Polanski refuses to give us so positive a picture. We see Malcolm crowned—his expression duplicating Macbeth's when he was crowned, the crown itself the focus of Polanski's attention. Polanski does not want us to forget that it was *this* crown that fell in Duncan's bedroom when he was savagely slaughtered, that it was *this* crown that the slaughterer wore in the days of his terrible reign. Emphasis on the symbol of ambition and destructive violence at the end of this film penetrates to the heart of Polanski's belief that no relief seems possible in so horrible a world. Because Polanski wishes to make this point without equivocation, he gives us a brief concluding sequence not found in Shakespeare. Malcolm's brother, Donalbain (who walks with a limp, thereby calling attention to himself even in the early part of the movie), is seen riding swiftly across the wet, sandy landscape and stopping at the cave of the witches, a brilliant touch. He, too, is ambitious; he, too, will seek supernatural ties; he, too, will confront lies that seem like truth; he, too, will be caught in a puzzling "fair-foul" world. And the violence will go on. This sequence is pure Polanski, going beyond Shakespeare's text, but it is strongly suggested by the potent equivocal atmosphere of Shakespeare's play, by the ongoing quality of fair-foul, foul-fair; and it seems absolutely right as an ending to this modern adaptation of *Macbeth*.

By way of conclusion, I would like to examine a specific poetic image in Shakespeare which becomes a visual sequence in Polanski. Hearing that Birnam Wood is coming to Dunsinane, ready to face his doom, Shakespeare's Macbeth utters these words: "They have tied me to a stake, I cannot fly./But bearlike I must fight the course." The reference here is to the sport of bearbaiting, much enjoyed by the Elizabethans, in which a bear, tied to a post by a long rope or chain, tries to retaliate against four or five large dogs who attack the bear. Shakespeare often used the image in his plays, and in *Macbeth* it perfectly suits a rugged, bearlike Macbeth who realizes he is tied (the inevitability of tragedy) and soon to be attacked, but bravely faces his end. The poetic quality of Shakespeare's image is lost in Polanski's film, but its cinematic potentiality is fully exploited. In the banquet scene, when we see Macbeth as king and where we expect to find good cheer and merriment, as part of the entertainment a bear is brought in, chained to a stake (with Polanski giving us a single shot of the iron ring that holds the chain, forcing us to recall the ring that is a crown) and attacked by yelping mastiffs. We witness the bearbaiting for a few seconds before the camera moves to Macbeth talking to the murderers and then to the confrontation of Macbeth with the gory apparition of Banquo. After the banquet, which ends in disorder, the dead and bloodied bear and two of the dogs are seen dragged along the halls of the castle, a cinematic epiphany of violence in a Macbethian world. Shakespeare's poetic image at the end of his play becomes a visual image in the film's middle, allowing us to witness the condition of the world and foreshadowing the end of Macbeth, another bear tied to his own stake because of his murders, his ambition, his wife, and his mystical ties with those juggling fiends, the witches. Here is a perfect example, I think, of the rich suggestiveness of Shakespeare's art providing an intelligent director with a perfect cinematic image and idea.

Roman Polanski's *Macbeth*, although its form distorts Shakespeare and exploits Shakespeare's melodramatic side, is a valid modern interpretation of Shakespeare's play. Bloody, violent, unremitting in its horror, the film presents a vision of a world filled with confusions and madness, a world in which both brave Macbeth and limping Donalbain will always seek Satanic ties, a world containing only bears and dogs, a world where tomorrows are as brutal as todays. His filmic interpretation of Shakespeare's *Macbeth* allows Polanski to present a comment on our time. What seems to be his personal obsession with violence (we cannot forget the Manson family) has been objectified in an energetic piece of cinematic art.

—*Normand Berlin*
University of Massachusetts,
Amherst

Scotland Saved from History: Welles's *Macbeth* and the Ahistoricism of Medieval Film

I want to consider Welles's *Macbeth* in a different frame from the usual ones, viewing it less as a Shakespearean or Wellesian film than as a medieval one. From its opening words, the film stakes a claim to historicity—claiming to depict the period of Christianity's first penetration of a barbarian world—that is belied by virtually everything that follows: the visual invocations of westerns and film noir, the anachronistic grotesqueries of costuming, the fabular simplification of character to the demands of a parable about the resistible rise of gothic tyranny, what Michael Anderegg (84) has called the "postnuclear" devastation of its landscape. In creating this notional and abstract version of the Middle Ages as a theater in which to play out an estranged version of the political concerns of the late 1940s, Welles works against Shakespeare to suppress the Renaissance context of the original play, substituting in particular a myth of the eternal return of tyranny—"Peace, the charm's wound up"—for the linear and progressive development of Scotland and England invoked in Shakespeare's text. In Welles's version, as in Polanski's later and better one, Macbeth doesn't lead to King James; he leads to another Macbeth.

In so doing, Welles both conforms to and helps to shape the conventions that have controlled the depiction of the Middle Ages since at least the 1950s. Arguably, this film has had a greater impact, for better or (mostly) for worse, on medieval films than on Shakespeare or Shakespearean film. Part of that impact has been to reinforce the prevailing confusion of "dark ages" with Middle Ages; this Macbeth is, after all, an extreme example of that equation of the medieval with mud, murk, monks, and mayhem common to people who know little about the period and care less. Welles's own attitude toward the period is concisely expressed in the version of the coming of the Renaissance given in his introduction to *The Mercury Shakespeare*:

> Down in Italy . . . men had taken the hoods of the dusty, dusky old Middle Ages off their heads and begun to look around. . . . Books were being written instead of copied; people had stopped taking Aristotle's word for it and were nosing around the world, taking it apart to see what made it run. (Quoted in Kodar 210)

Cruel as it is to cite a man's popularizations against him, this constitutes fair warning. If you start from this view

Orson Welles as Macbeth

of the Middle Ages, you are unlikely to use them as anything except a pretext for talking about something else. In that, unfortunately, Welles is the precursor of an entire genre of medieval films. I want to put his *Macbeth* in the context of that genre.

For five years at the National University of Singapore, I taught an honors-year seminar in film and history, originally designed to compare and contrast the ways in which films of the Middle Ages and those dealing with recent history reconstruct the past. I quickly figured out that almost all the "history" was in the latter, modern half of the course. Soon after, I realized that virtually none of my medieval films—Welles's included—was reconstructing the past at all, at least not in the detailed, furniture-fixated way of, say, Scorsese's *The Age of Innocence* (1993). Also unlike Scorsese but more importantly, the medieval films did not work from the assumption that the past was of inherent interest or historically connected to the present. While the recent past is customarily presented as causatively connected to the present, the medieval past is virtually always presented as an analog—usually for our basest behavior—a distant, alienating mirror, as Welles's Scotland is an estranged version of Germany or that more abstract place, "Fascism-land."

To see what I mean, let's look at one of the most familiar opening sequences in nominally historical film: the one from Bergman's *The Seventh Seal* (Sweden, 1957), a work which shares to a remarkable extent the stylistic vocabulary of *Macbeth*. Let me remind you of the elements of that famous sequence: the hawk hanging in the stormy sky accompanied by a notably shrill version of the *Kyrie Eleison*; a rocky shore under dark cliffs between an empty sea and an empty sky; two isolated figures, one with a dagger at hand, waking on the rocks; a Wellesian voice-over reading of Revelations 8; the chess set with the sea behind it; Block's failed attempt to pray; the appearance of the monastically robed Death; the two figures sitting down to play.

Is this the Middle Ages? While notionally in 1349, we are actually in Beckett time (that is, Any or No time), the major difference being that in this case Godot has come and turned out to be just what we thought he would be, though disguised as Mephistopheles. The place, nominally if namelessly Swedish, is a beach midway between T.S. Eliot's and Neville Shute's. The actors we meet later are on their way to Elsinore, presumably to entertain Fortinbras. We are looking, in short, at the painfully familiar Never-Never-but-Always land of mid-20th-century European high modernism, the same territory inhabited by Jeanette Nolan's furred and Freudianized Lady Macbeth in Welles's film. If we are in any historical period, it is less the 1340s of the plot premise than the subatomic early 1950s, with universal death looming out of the northern sky. As Peter Cowie has written, the film "reflect[s] the trepidation of the Cold War era." A child of the fifties myself, I react to that hawk by wanting to crawl under my school desk.

The music is medieval—if you assume that the *Kyrie* is automatically "medieval"—but filtered through modernist, electronic distortion. Even Block's chess set has clearly been borrowed from another, more highly polished age. And, of course, Antonius and Jons have landed on this beach conspicuously without ship or other means of transport, called, like Death himself, by the needs of allegory, and landed in a notional 1340s derived more from mystery plays and woodcuts—and an earlier Bergman play—than from any but the flimsiest of historical records. Even the meals they later eat will be symbolic: from beatific (and intertextual) strawberries and milk to bitter bread. Not to belabor an obvious point, we are looking—as we are in Welles's *Macbeth*—at a version of the Middle Ages that has been carefully lifted out of historical sequence in order to serve as an alienating device for viewing the midcentury present and/or the timeless present of parable. This is not a fault, merely a fact. What is perhaps more striking is how many films, even those ostensibly committed to reproducing the medieval past—Vincent Ward's *The Navigator* (New Zealand, 1988), even Mel Gibson's *Braveheart* (1995)—put it to similarly ahistoric purposes. In so doing, they reflect a way of seeing that is enshrined in *Macbeth* and perfected in *The Seventh Seal*. I once thought the ahistoricism of Bergman's film an exception; in fact, it's the rule. *The Age of Innocence* manages to be both a meticulous reconstruction of its recent period and a meditation on the evolution of modern sexual mores and visual codes. There is no inherent reason why medieval films could not do likewise—those, at least, with the money Welles lacked to afford meticulous reconstruction—but, in my experience, they don't.

Not, of course, that one can imagine Welles wanting to do that sort of film. Virtually every significant stylistic element in *Macbeth* serves the common purpose of dehistoricizing its world: the elaborately and insistently expressionist setting (a castle of dripping, subterranean rock whose layout persistently refuses to make literal sense); the self-reflexivity that regularly calls our attention to the soundstage and the diorama against which Banquo's murderers are posed; the use of simultaneous and/or abstract staging which allows

Macbeth, for example, to change scenes by crossing directly from one part of the set to another, and which constantly invokes the stage versions from which the film evolved; the anachronistic and cross-cultural voodoo doll picked up in Welles's passage through Harlem; the extensive cross-referencing to other genres about other times—galloping horseback riders out of Republic westerns or Jeanette Nolan's embarrassing attempts at film noir seductiveness; the erasure of historical references, especially the sequence of kings from Macbeth's last encounter with the witches; the parabolic simplification of Macbeth to a transhistorical type, even as immersion in his point of view encourages us to view the film as psychodrama, concerned with the psychology of evil, not its history.

The cumulative effect of all these devices has registered on even the film's most sympathetic critics, such as Jean Cocteau:

> "Clad in animal skins like motorists at the turn of the century, horns and cardboard crowns on their heads, his actors haunt the corridors of some dreamlike subway, an abandoned coal mine, and ruined cellars oozing with water. . . . Sometimes we wonder in what period this nightmare is unfolding" (Bazin 29).

Andrè Bazin located it in "a prehistoric universe," even while noting that it could be seen as a transposition of the drama of *Citizen Kane* (101). More recently, Michael Anderegg has suggested both that "insofar as it resembles anything other than a studio set, the world [of the film] suggests postnuclear devastation," and that "Welles's Scotland is not so much prehistoric as outside history; his specific time and place exists as a blur; indeed we are *beyond* history" (84). Scotland, in my formulation, is rescued from mere history—a presumptively dead past—and lifted onto the plane of eternal, or at least contemporary, relevance: the allegorical landscape of *Godot* and *The Seventh Seal*.

If that is so, why—aside from a fidelity to the text nowhere else shown in this film—should Welles bother to place Macbeth in the Middle Ages at all? Basically, because that is where old archetypes go to die and be reborn. Once they have done so, you can—untrammeled by the demands for plausibility, surface realism, and characterization made by more recent, better-known periods—stage the sort of conflicts Welles was always drawn to: superstition versus religion, barbarism versus civilization (at least civilization in a barbaric medieval form), id versus superego, witches versus Holy Father. (The merely individual Macbeth, remember, is equivalent to that voodoo doll: a grubby little object in the hands of the capitalized Forces of the universe.) This is, of course, the strategy of a film like John Boorman's *Excalibur*, where Malory is restaged as a Jungian psychodrama whose archetypal figures play out rites of passage in a once and future world. It is the strategy of *Ladyhawke*, with its courtship of boy/wolf and girl/falcon. The prevalence of this mode may explain why archetypes of essential sexual identity persist in medieval film when correctness has expunged them from virtually every other mode. It certainly explains why films about Robin Hood outnumber even those about St. Joan, virtually the only historical figure from the Middle Ages to have a body of films devoted to her, by so vast a margin.

I am, of course, aware that Shakespeare's *Macbeth* is not (quite) a historical figure, though he is located in the linear sequence Shakespeare took from Holingshed. One problem with the film is that Welles wants to historicize that legendary figure—by placing him at the notional point of victory by the Christian force he has invented the Holy Father to embody—and to dehistoricize him at the same time. That Bergman faces no such conflict of impulses may suggest that the rules of the medieval film were more rigid in 1957 than they were for Welles 10 years earlier.

I am also well aware that the "reconstructions" of the past are inherently constructions, shaped, as Hayden White has taught us all, by the genres of literature.[1] And, while the value of film creations of the past is far better understood than it was, say, in the early 1990s when Robert Rosenstone had to struggle to get the *American Historical Review* to accept a panel of essays on historical film, it is less well understood that there are fundamentally different ways of creating these pasts. Those ways, it seems to me, are differentiated chiefly by whether we are trying to imagine only ourselves and our concerns or our ancestors—that is, other people—and theirs. In both cases, the bottom line of interest may be present relevance—historical film is always about the present—but in one case you imagine something different—Newland Archer and his society, say—becoming like you; in the other, you admire (or cringe from) your own image in a distant mirror. There is, I suspect, an ethical difference (as well as a psychological one) between the two modes.

In a sense, we are dealing with a simple difference between two discursive constructs of history, one linear and the other nonlinear. However, the type of construct exemplified in Welles's *Macbeth* incorporates a denial of historical process and connection, and that is the one usually applied to the filming of the Middle Ages. The dominant mode of medieval film—regardless of country of origin or degree of commercial calculation—is fabular, whatever claims, usually unfounded, a given film (*Macbeth* or its more sophisticated descendant, *Braveheart*) may make to factuality.

In practice, we automatically privilege the current signified over the medieval signifier, referring the boat people who are attacked and driven off by the villagers in *The Navigator*, for example, to their 1980s equivalents. The historical accuracy of that scene is clearly not the point. When we ask casually what the film of *The Name of the Rose* (Italy/Germany/France, 1986) is "about," we usually mean "what's the relevance?" (Nazis? Red Brigades? Liberal impotence in times of terrorism? These parallels are reenforced by the color-coding which equates Benedictines with Blackshirts and by the casting of Sean Connery in the role of tainted liberal). When *Film Comment* interviewed F. Murray Abraham about his role as the Inquisitor, Abraham talked exclusively and automatically about Nazis (Bachmann 16–20).

If we ask what *The Navigator* is about, the most obvious answers are AIDS, environmental and spiritual devastation, and the ills of modern technology. While *Braveheart* gets an occasional fact right—some of the tactics at Stirling Bridge, for example, or the carnival elements of medieval executions—historical chronicle is not the mode in which it operates; its occasional ventures into accuracy serve only to license critical abuse. Its subject, clearly signaled, is not Scotland in the 1290s but Ireland and the rest of the Celtic fringe in the 1990s, prominently including Scotland, that "nation colonized by wankers" memorialized in *Trainspotting* (U.K. 1996), *Braveheart*'s antiheroic bookend. Why else has Wallace been given a fictive Irish colleague devoted to talking—in conspicuously modern dialect—about the liberation of his island? Why else does Wallace paint his face with the colors of a Scottish football supporter and lead an army that resembles nothing so much as a soccer crowd on the terraces at Ibrox Park? This war is the continuation of football by other means. Of course, Wallace's appeals to "freedom" are anachronistic; surely in the context of so many proleptic references—even down to the substitution of Irish pipes for Scottish on the soundtrack—they are meant to be? The opening line of the film's voice-over warns us that this is not so much a true story (though "some say" it is) as a contending fiction. It is a fiction, however, that acts by almost allegorical substitution: 13th-century struggles do not lead to 20th-century ones, but mirror them. The real connection is through an ahistorical essentialism:

the English always torment the Scots because it is in their eternal, sexually inadequate nature to do so; Celts resist so erratically because it is in their lovable, virile but shambolic nature to do so, ever and always. Superficial changes of technology or dress serve only as distancing devices, allowing a Scottish audience in particular to see with renewed clarity what might be hidden behind a common currency. The past is the present and so, by an obvious extrapolation, is the future. Or, in the Welles version, "the charm's wound up"; the plot, ever and always, loops back to its beginning.

The difference between the modes of modern and medieval historical films can be summarized in a brief example. When Daniel Vigne shot *The Return of Martin Guerre* in its original 16th-century context, he treated it as a timeless parable of acting and identity. Natalie Zemon Davis, who collaborated on but later rejected the film, says that she wrote her later study, "to dig deeper into the case, to make historical sense of it" (Davis 8).[2] When that story is remade as *Sommersby* (1993) and is reset in the post–Civil War American south, its hero becomes an early proponent of racial integration and agricultural cooperatives who is persecuted mainly for his progressive views. He is historicized as an agent of social evolution; he is located in linear history as part of that fable of progress so common to films of recent history—think, for example, of *Glory*, *Little Women*, *The Age of Innocence*, or virtually any Merchant-Ivory film—and so strikingly absent from medieval films. When you think of the distant past as an estranged equivalent to the present (as Welles does) or as superior to it by virtue of faith (as Ward does), you are unlikely to think of history in terms of progress or indeed of any kind of linear development whatsoever. Having positioned his film at a point of historical change—the triumph of Christianity over the chthonic forces represented by the witches—Welles is compelled by the conservatism of his vision not only to make the Holy Father nearly as barbarous as what he opposes but to kill off the supposed winner so that the witches can have the last word, which is, of course, that nothing has changed.

Such a version of history inevitably entails some losses; in the case of Welles's *Macbeth*, those losses include Shakespeare, that awkward Renaissance intervention in the otherwise seamless connection of ancient barbarism with modern. As is widely recognized, Welles largely excludes references to the play's Elizabethan cosmology and historiography. He not only marginalizes the saintly King Edward even more than the original play does, but, as we have seen, substitutes a closed loop of evil begetting further evil for the providential pattern by which the natural order expels Macbeth in order to return to its proper condition, and by which Macbeth's crimes beget the line of Banquo, stable kingship, and the eventual union of Scotland and England. Shakespearean providentialism, however severely qualified it is in the play, fits awkwardly with the film's simplified and ahistorical primitivism. As a result, Shakespeare is present in the film mostly as a transmitter of messages from the unconscious translated into the Viennese of Welles's psychologizing and as a dignifying pretext for the substitution of Welles's cruder cosmology. Scotland as a notional and subjective place is thus rescued from Elizabethan as well as medieval history and relocated in the same timeless landscape as the *Godot*-influenced opening scenes of *The Seventh Seal*, with its two chivalric tramps bereft on the barren shore of 1950s high modernism. And, yes, that does seem to me a form of solipsism (as well as a rejection of the work of memory) that is common to the genre of medieval film, at least in part because of the influence of Welles filtered through Bergman.[3]

—Arthur Lindley
National University of Singapore

NOTES

1. See especially Hayden V. White, *The Content of the Form: Narrative Discourse and Historical Representation* (Baltimore: Johns Hopkins University Press, 1987) and, of course, White's *Metahistory: The Historical Imagination in Nineteenth-Century Europe* (Johns Hopkins, 1973).

2. Davis's full account both locates the original story in the specific context of the peasant culture of Foix in the 1550s and treats it as a chapter in the evolution of gender identities and what she regards as Protestant attitudes toward clerical authority.

3. An earlier version of this paper was read at Shakespeare on Screen: The Centenary Conference, Malaga, Spain, September 21–24, 1999. Four paragraphs of this article appeared in slightly different form in my article "The Ahistoricism of Medieval Film," in the electronic journal *Screening the Past* 3 (May 1998), URL: http://www.latrobe.edu.au/www/screeningthepast.

WORKS CITED

Anderegg, Michael. *Orson Welles, Shakespeare and Popular Culture*. New York: Columbia University Press, 1999.

Bachmann, Gideon. "C.I.A.: F. Murray Abraham Interviewed by Gideon Bachmann." *Film Comment* 22:5 (Sept.-Oct. 1986): 16–20.

Bazin, André. *Orson Welles: A Critical View*. London: Elm Tree Books, 1978.

Cowie, Peter. "*The Seventh Seal*." Voyager, April 1998. http://voyager.com/criterion/indepth.cgi?seventhseal.

Davis, Natalie Zemon. *The Return of Martin Guerre*. Cambridge, Mass.: Harvard University Press, 1983.

Kodar, Oja, Jonathan Rosenbaum, and Peter Bogdanovich, eds. *This Is Orson Welles*. New York: HarperCollins, 1992.

Lindley, Arthur. "The Ahistoricism of Medieval Film." *Screening the Past* 3 (May 1998). URL: http://www.latrobe.edu.au/www/screeningthepast.

Richard III on Film: The Subversion of the Viewer

> Why, I can smile, and murder whiles I smile,
>
> And cry 'Content!' to that which grieves my heart,
>
> And wet my cheeks with artificial tears,
>
> And frame my face to all occasions.
>
> —*Richard, Duke of Gloucester, later King*

I

For almost 400 years the Chorus has made his appeal to audiences of Shakespeare's *Henry V* to imagine scores of horses and fields of men in battle. With the emergence of film we surely find the means to cast off such a device, perhaps with a desire to present a minimally altered script (after all, we can hardly imagine *Henry V* without the Chorus). Kenneth Branagh employs veteran Derek Jacobi as Chorus in his 1989 production. Jacobi, dressed in modern attire, calls for "a muse of fire" (I.i.1) and reflects on the limitations "within this wooden O" (13) on a soundstage littered with props and filmmaking equipment. Despite this inherent appeal of this "behind the scenes" introduction to the film, it could be done without. As we fully expect when sitting to watch a film, we will see the horses and the men and the battles; the "two mighty monarchies" of France and England will appear in full on the screen (I.i.20). Yet this opening scene, in the Branagh film at least, does more than prime the viewer's imagination. It establishes a relationship with the viewer which continues through the close of the film. Direct relationships between actor and viewer are rather unconventional in the film genre, but not altogether absent. Indeed, filmed productions of *Richard III* consistently insist upon such a relationship. It is upon this relationship between actor and viewer that the following focuses.

"In linguistic communication," explains Roland Barthes, "I and you are absolutely presupposed by one another" (260). Of course this is true, almost banal as Barthes himself admits; however, this presents a rather overlooked issue in the case of *Richard III*. For all of Richard's Proteus-like[1] acting and assuming, there exist two distinct audiences: the duped characters at his side and the viewers watching him upon the screen. Much has been said to elucidate the relationship that Richard shares with his audience, but such commentary applies to productions of the play in general. For example, we of course begin as sympathizers, progress to accomplices and confidantes, and ultimately come to our senses alongside the "circumspect" Buckingham (IV.ii.32). My interests lie in the manner in which specific actors approach this relationship and particularly the realization of this feat on film. By looking at the filmed performances of Laurence Olivier (1955), Ron Cook (1983), and Ian McKellen (1995) as Richard, we shall see exactly what role we, as viewers, play and how each actor forces us into it.

Why film? First a clarification: H.R. Coursen, in *Watching Shakespeare on Television*, distinguishes between film and television with a discussion of the loss of spectacle as films are reduced to the "nineteen diagonal inches in the domestic and domesticated space of our playroom" (22).[2] McKellen's romantic performance, in fact, draws its success from keen use of this "domesticated space," but Coursen's point remains: Television pales in comparison to the "big screen" atmosphere with its deafening digitized sound and full audience. For our purposes, however, we will be thinking about the films as they appear in video format, for that is how they are most likely to be screened (be it in classroom or living room). So again, why film (video)? First, filmed productions are widely available and can be viewed repeatedly. Theater productions, on the other hand, contain some degree of improvisation and, as with any other performance-oriented art, exist only once in time in the same way. This is not to dismiss theatrical performances, however. *Richard III* remains a widely performed play, and looking to some specific production reviews will help to establish the traditional conventions against which the film versions react. Second, film and theater, while related, are quite different modes of production. Susan Sontag offers the following generic distinction:

> Theatre is confined to a logical or continuous use of space. Cinema (through editing, that is, through the change of shot—which is the basic unit of film construction) has access to an alogical or discontinuous use of space. In the theater, actors are either in the stage space or "off." When "on," they are always visual or visualizable in contiguity with each other. In the cinema, no such relation is necessarily visible or even visualizable. (108, original emphases)

To unpack this difference is to first acknowledge the selective exclusion/inclusion of the camera, described by André Bazin as "a mask which allows only a part of the action to be seen" (105). However, Sontag walks a fine line here. With the technical capabilities of the modern stage, namely, set design and lighting, along with a strong imagination, the distinction between uses of space can be overcome. A stronger distinction yet exists between the film and theater experience: film as *visual* and theater as *physical*. Traditionally, say with Hitchcock or any of the slew of recent "action" films, this is a distinction that holds up. Our role in *The Birds* or *Psycho* is that of terrified onlooker peering through "the invulnerable voyeuristic eye" of the camera (Sontag 363). The likes of *The Terminator* and *Independence Day* add excitement and thrills with intense and expensive special effects, but again we remain removed from the world on the screen. With Shakespeare, in particular *Richard III*, even this distinction becomes blurred: film Richards, taking their cue from Olivier's 1944 groundbreaking production of *Henry V*, look directly through the lens of the camera and invite, even insist, that we do matter, that we do play a role in the drama of the screen.

This convention, while new to film, traces back in form to Greek theater, in which actors spoke in monologue.[3] The technique of directly addressing the audience, known as soliloquy, became commonplace in Seneca's tragedies, most notably *Thyestes*, *Hercules Furens*, and *Troades*, which were available to Shakespeare in a 1581 translation. It is with *Richard III* that this technique firmly reasserts itself upon the Elizabethan stage:

> [S]oliloquy, with its note of dramatic irony giving histrionic point to the crude plottings of the villain, subsequently becomes conventionalized, and gains its ultimate expression in the superb declarations of Gloster at the opening of Shakespeare's *Richard III*. (Arnold 8)

A brief look at Seneca reveals the precursor to both the Chorus in *Henry V* and Richard's opening "confession":

> I syster of the Thunderer, (for now that name
>   alone
> Remaynes to me) Jove evermore as though
>   devorst and gone,
> And temples of the highest ayre as wydowe
>   shunned have,
> And beaten out of skyes above the place to
>   Harlots gave.
> I must dwell beneath on ground, for Whoores
>   do hold the sky,
>   * * *
> Let hateful hurt now come in anger wood,
> And fierce impyety imbrew himselfe with his
>   owne bloud,
> And errour eke, and fury arm'd agaynst itself
>   to fight.
> This meane, this meane, let wrath of myne
>   now use to shewe
> my might. (*Hercules Furens* 1–5; 97–100)

As this prologue continues, Juno reveals her impending revenge against her brother and husband Jupiter which includes a plot to have his "base Sonne Hercules" kill his own wife and child. This entire prologue closely parallels Richard's soliloquies of the first act in which he complains of his disadvantage and then reveals his "plots" and "inductions." In Richard's hands the soliloquy becomes a sharpened sword with multiple edges: it introduces and sets the scene much like the Chorus does in the later *Henry V* (I.i.13); it serves to introduce Richard (I.i.13–27) and his plans (I.i.27–40, III.v.101–104, IV.ii.62–67); it announces the entrance of characters (I.i.41, I.iii.337); it allows him to gloat over his successes (I.iii.215–50, I.iii.322–36, III.i.82–83,

IV.iv.362). Perhaps most importantly, and unquestionably so for the purposes of this study, the soliloquy provides the vehicle through which Richard relates to the audience. This is also the aspect of the soliloquy with which individual actors most freely experiment.

On stage we find a plethora of Richards: a pathetic Richard so "'rudely stamped' that not only can he not 'strut before a wanton ambling nymph' but he cannot strut at all—at least not without the help of crutches" (Shaw 20); the condescending Richard of McKellen's 1992 Royal Shakespeare Company stage production (the precursor to his film) who stands "stiffly downstage center and [addresses] the audience in a distinctly upper class accent"[4] (Oberlander 10); an intimidating Richard who seems to both threaten and eyeball the audience "as if totting up the box-office take" (Smallwood 327); a friendly Richard who delivers the opening soliloquy as he prowls among the audience before mounting the stage to meet Clarence (Shaltz 43); a rallying Richard who treats the audience throughout as troops being prepared for the upcoming battle (Shurgot 28); a "hyperactive, peevish, spastic" Richard "with a trace of Tourette's Syndrome and attention deficit disorder" (Timpane 19) who offends and repels the audience. Actors playing Richard on film are no more consistent than their theatrical counterparts: Olivier chooses to awe and oppress; Cook plays to our sympathies; McKellen romances us. Despite their differing approaches, each succeeds to the desired and expected denouement in which we ally ourselves with Richard's (and our) victims and freely invite the vengeance exacted upon our former "friend." We shall now closely examine each actor's technique and approach in winning the favor of his audience.

II. OLIVIER (1955)

"In Olivier's hands," writes Constance Brown in her groundbreaking "re-evaluation" of the film, "one of Shakespeare's better plays . . . is transformed into an intricate, subtle, coolly ironic plunge into one of those recesses of human nature that are generally avoided through the same fastidious impulses that make the manufacture of sewer covers a profitable business" (23). Indeed, if frequency of performance is a measure, one would certainly agree with Brown's claim that this is one of the "better plays." Throughout the performance history of *Richard III* actors have eagerly risen to the challenge offered by its title role. In fact, scholars believe that *Richard III* is privileged as the first production of Shakespeare in America,[5] and it has since been performed with surprising frequency. What, then, is the appeal of Richard? Perhaps the following, spoken to the reader by Kurt Vonnegut's villain-hero Howard W. Campbell, Jr., from his novel *Mother Night*, offers some insight: "I doubt if there has ever been a society that has been without strong and young people eager to experiment with homicide, provided no very awful penalties are attached to it" (120). Both Brown, in identifying a "recess of human nature," and Vonnegut help to make our point: Human nature draws us to Richard. More specifically, our predatory instincts seize upon this opportunity to take advantage of unsuspecting, and in most cases, deserving victims. Moreover, the play is constructed so as to allow us opportunity to withdraw from the relationship which feeds upon our inherent bloodlust, return to the side of the moral and the just, and leave Richard alone in his despair.

Despite this universal appeal of the play, which translates into the appeal of a perfect crime, the actor must still develop a technique to convince us of our desires. Not until we have been convinced to go along with Richard do we find we enjoy it. Laurence Olivier chooses to overpower us to the point in which we feel compelled to go along with him. By including an excerpt of Richard's extended soliloquy from *Henry VI, Part 3* in his opening address, Olivier begins to paint his Richard as omnipotent. The following lines in particular suggest the almost superhuman nature of Olivier's Richard:

> I'll play the orator as well as Nestor,
> Deceive more slyly than Ulysses could,
> And, like a Sinon, take another Troy.
> I can add colours to the chameleon,
> Change shapes with Proteus for advantages,
> And set the murderous Machiavel to school.
> Can I do this, and cannot get a crown?
> Tut, were it further off, I'll pluck it down.
> (III.ii.188–95)

Not only does Richard compare himself to the best orators and deceivers known to history, he believes without a doubt that he will outperform them. The fact that Richard controls the majority of the action of the play as histrionic dissembler can only strengthen his control over us, for after all we too play a role, however passive, in this drama directed by Richard. Richard sees himself as actor in a play larger than life, a play in which he not only takes the lead, but takes the lead better than anyone else. This role places him in a specific position of power from which he "pulls the strings" of his victims, including Clarence, Anne, and the young Princes.

Laurence Olivier with Claire Bloom in Richard III

Moreover, in the *Henry VI, Part 3* passage he hints at a supernatural disposition in comparing himself to Proteus and the chameleon, and professes confidence in redefining the methods of Machiavelli's Prince. Machiavelli explains that while a man may rise to power by "murder[ing] his fellow citizens, betray[ing] his friends . . . be[ing] devoid of truth, pity, or religion" (25), he will not thus gain glory; while such a man may become a powerful ruler, "his fearful cruelty and inhumanity, along with his innumerable crimes, prevent us from placing him among the really excellent men" (25). Olivier's Richard fully intends to prove this wrong, as we shall see when he mounts the throne and expects our unconditional praise and submission. We shall also see how it is this desire which turns us from his side and saves us from sharing his punishment and despair.

By fully cutting Margaret from the film, Olivier channels all of the supernatural and psychic powers through Richard.[6] He becomes the sole manipulator in the play and the source of our awe and wonder. Margaret's curses (IV.iv), which in the original text seem informed by some greater power as they come to fruition in turn, are replaced by Richard's own prophecies:

> I'll make my heaven to dream upon the crown,
> And whiles I live, t'account this world but hell,
> Until my misshaped trunk that bears this head
> Be round impalèd with a glorious crown.
> (*Henry VI, Part 3* III.ii.169–71)

> This day should Clarence closely be mewed up
> About a prophecy which says that 'G'
> Of Edward's heirs the murderer shall be.
> (I.i.38–40)

In fact, each plan that Richard shares with us, such as his plans to marry Anne (I.i.53ff), becomes a revelation of his own foresight. With the realization of each prediction, our fear and admiration of Olivier's Richard grows.

But such editing and script rearranging, along with Olivier's sinister appearance,[7] can be fully realized on stage. We must focus primarily on Olivier's filmic techniques and the way he specifically demands our complacency by controlling and directing us. The central conventions to the omnipotence and omniscience of Olivier's Richard and his manipulation of the viewer include spatial dynamic, set design, and use of shadows. As outlined by Lorne Buchman in the first chapter of *Still in Movement*, Olivier uses the spatial field accessible in film by alternating the depth of the shot to create a tension between two distinct Richards: the "distant schemer" of the long shot and the "conspiring friend" of the close shot (18). With the close shot we are drawn into Richard's confidence: "'We'll do it together, you and I,' he seems to suggest, making sleepy eyes at the camera, looking up and down as some men contemplate a prospective lover" (Brown 30). But with the long shot of Richard dressed in black standing menacingly against a wall decorated with his "bruiséd arms" we are reminded that we are not his equals.

His ability (as director and actor) to control our point of view demonstrates his authority over us. Conversely, our role as viewers taking in the images offered us displays our submission to his will. Along with Olivier's camera techniques, his set design plays a significant role in shaping what we see and establishing Richard as omnipresent. The set facilitates Richard's view of scenes in which he does not directly play a role. For example, Richard peers down into the courtroom as King Edward condemns Clarence and then watches later as his brother details his dream to Brackenbury. In both cases Richard controls us by controlling our vision. In the first he opens window shutters to reveal the courtroom below and invites us to peer in with him. The latter scene begins and ends with a shot of the barred window of Clarence's cell and we realize as it comes to an end that "we have unknowingly witnessed [Clarence's confession] through [Richard's] eyes . . . like the characters he manipulates, we the audience find ourselves controlled and directed by him" (Singer 191).

While Anthony Davies suggests that this "reinforces the suggestion of our having been drawn into voyeuristic complicity with Richard" (68), the fact that we are forced to view what we do remains. Unlike our experience in the theater where we can freely shift our focus from character to character, film actively and consciously chooses and directs our attention. Susan Sontag draws this distinction in defining film as "mediated art" and theater as "relatively unmediated art":

> We can see what happens on stage with our own eyes. We see on the screen what the camera sees. In the cinema, narration proceeds by ellipsis (the "cut" or change of shot); the camera eye is a unified point of view that continually displaces itself. But the change of shot can provoke questions, the simplest of which is: from *whose* point of view is the shot seen? (110, original emphasis)

The techniques of film allow for such creative and shocking situations as our viewing of the commotion caused by the beheading of Macbeth *through* the eyes of the head as it is swung around on the end of a halberd in Roman Polanski's film.[8]

Shadows also play an important role in the construction of Olivier's Richard, and much has been already noted in this area. Constance Brown sees the shadow as the punctuation to each goal Richard realizes and as metaphorical subtext. For example, his shadow overtakes the train of Anne's white dress after the successful wooing scene to signify his victory and domination over her just as it engulfs the screen to represent Richard's tyrannous conquering of England (25). But this is not all there is to it. Through this manipulation of his shadow, Olivier finds yet another way to bridge the world of the play with the world of the viewer and, moreover, another means of oppression and intimidation. The shadows which accompany virtually every movement in the first act repeatedly expand to drown the entire screen in darkness; what begins as a trace movement caught in the corner of the camera's (and the viewer's) eye builds to a threatening force which reaches out to pull us under its constrictive hold. We become entrapped by Olivier the director by these carefully placed and precisely driven shadows of Olivier the actor. Not only do these shadows stand for the metaphorical engulfing of the state of England, but they stand for Richard's tyrannous hold over us. Again we fall victim to manipulation in the hands of a peremptory Richard.

Jack Jorgens, in his excellent *Shakespeare on Film*, admits he is "not really frightened by Olivier's entertaining

Richard, who is a handsome devil" (142). Such a misconception speaks for Olivier's overall success in orchestrating the role of Richard. While we are indeed drawn under an oppressive rule by precise machinations, we do not come to realize this until Richard agrees to accept the crown. And this is of course part of Olivier's game. We are meant to feel at ease and comforted by this "handsome devil," but we are also kept under constant management. The perpetual affirmations of our alliance with Richard keep us ignorant of his increasing hold over us; that is, until he gains the throne and finds it only seats one (something he knows all along, but something our ignorance keeps us from seeing). Olivier descends from his position between the "two props of virtue" (III.vii.96) on the rope of a bell causing it to spin wildly out of control. As he lands amid the clamoring of the crowd of citizens and the clanging of the bell, he vehemently juts his gloved hand forward for Buckingham to kiss:

> He thrusts it forcibly toward the camera, and holds it extended in the air like a huge, black claw. The hand is extended toward the audience as much as toward Buckingham. For the first time, the audience is advised that what it has approved by laughter and condoned in the earlier part of the film is its own destruction. (Brown 31)

While Brown may underscore the earlier domination of an "amused" audience, she is right in identifying this as the point in which Richard ends *any* relationship that may have existed between him and his viewers. If our innocent ignorance of this "handsome devil" has otherwise kept us from realizing the true nature of our situation, this scene, with its overt symbolic and physical demand for submission, surely sets us straight.

III. RON COOK (BBC 1983)

With the screening of Olivier's film on American television in 1955, more people were introduced to the play than the sum total of those who had ever seen it performed onstage; understandably, Olivier's Richard left an impact. While actors have since struggled to escape Olivier's shadow in their own portrayals of the role, perhaps none do so as well as Ron Cook. Cook, in Jane Howell's BBC production of the play, takes an approach precisely the opposite of Olivier's in his characterization and presentation of Richard. Rather than appropriate the image of a powerful and commanding duke plotting to gain the throne by force as introduced in the extended soliloquy from *Henry VI, Part 3*, Cook emphasizes Richard's physical deformities:

> But I, that am not shaped for sportive tricks
> Nor made to court an amorous looking-glass,
> I that am rudely stamped and want love's majesty
> To strut before a wanton ambling nymph,
> I that am curtailed of this fair proportion,
> Cheated of feature by dissembling nature,
> Deformed, unfinished, sent before my time
> Into this breathing world scarce half made up—
> And that so lamely and unfashionable
> That dogs bark at me as I halt by them-
> (I.i.14–23)

Such are the lines that receive specific attention in Cook's emotional delivery. The Proteus-like, commanding, and treacherous Richard of Olivier is replaced with a sniveling, disheveled, and pathetic Richard. Though the relationship suggested by an introductory scene in which Cook first makes contact with us and laboriously writes "Richard III" on a blackboard is one of teacher-student, the actual relationship that develops boasts no such degree of respect. While the title, written at a downward slant, symbolizes the decline of England in Richard's hands, as well as for Richard's own downfall, it more importantly serves as the pattern for the relationship between Cook's Richard and his audience.

Unlike Olivier's intimidating opening soliloquy delivered strongly and convincingly, Cook's opening utterance reeks of pity and sorrow. Cook enters through a door on one end of the stage (for indeed the set is a stage) to the sounds of laughter and music coming from the "lady's chamber" where we assume Edward IV "capers." He immediately and deliberately moves across the stage to shut out the celebratory music that he cannot appreciate. Cook, short in stature, plays a severely crippled Richard, hunched over and complete with highly visible leg brace. Even without comparing him to Olivier, we notice a lack of concern for self-appearance: his clothing careless, his hair ungroomed and greasy, his demeanor humble and withdrawn. His every action, from shutting the music out to limping around the room, emphasizes his exclusion. He systematically plays the plainspoken injured man of Act I, Scene iii, who breaks in upon the king's kindred to complain of their "dissentious rumours" against him (42–53), and we, at least at first, systematically fall victim to his performance.

Again we see an actor's manipulation of his audience; however, while Olivier chooses to physically dominate, Cook preys upon the emotions. As R. Chris Hassel notes, "Cook's speech is stage-Cockney on occasion, as though the blood royal were no different from the newly minted bloods from Elizabeth's line" (10). Coupled with his lowly physical appearance, Cook's voice becomes one we can relate to, one we can in fact pity; he almost reminds us of a nagging little brother down on his luck. Hassel continues to say that for all Cook "lacks [in] magnetism and stature" (11) his Richard "rises to our esteem" (12) in the first wooing scene. This may indeed prove true on an initial viewing; however, a closely tracing of the relationship between the audience and Richard reveals how this scene offers our first hint that Cook is indeed playing a role and that he is manipulating us right along with Anne. When Anne spits in his face, we catch a brief glimpse of the true man hiding behind this meek facade. Cook becomes enraged and forgets his role for a moment, yet sure enough he switches right back into character and delivers with injured eyes, "Why dost thou spit at me?" (I.ii.144) as the pathetic wretch to whom we have become attached. While his brief flash of rage adequately scares Anne, it does not serve as warning enough to frighten us from his side.

Director Jane Howell plays an important role in establishing the relationship between the audience and Cook's Richard. Michael Manheim believes "her *Richard III* is not so effective in 'descanting' on a tyrant's evil" and that "other directors are more engaged with the inventions of the arch-villain than she" (138). Exactly, but this should not concede to any degree of failure on her part or of the production as a whole. Howell concerns herself with presenting a *likable* Richard wrought with pathos, a Richard very well suited to Ron Cook as well as the series in general. Susan Willis, who chronicled the taping of the BBC collection, notes that Cook shows signs of visible fatigue in the production. Indeed, one might expect the actors to be quite tired by the time they got to filming *Richard III*, the last play of the tetralogy which was filmed in its entirety in 28 days.[9] Howell makes Cook's lethargy work for the production by placing extra emphasis upon it. Instead of a worn-out actor failing to measure up to Olivier's Richard, she presents a worn-out Richard both physically and mentally taxed from the civil war which has just ended. While this tactic perhaps becomes more evident when screening *Richard III* as the conclusion to the first tetralogy, a screening of *Richard III* on its own does indeed suggest Howell's approach. The final tableau of the film works to suggest a rather unsettling possibility, but one that supports Cook's weary Richard: the Richard of the BBC may in fact be the biggest victim of the play. Before we can fully appreciate such a claim, however, we must first look at Margaret and her role in this production.

As mentioned previously, Olivier chooses to eliminate Margaret, and in doing so sets Richard up as the only supernatural presence and surely the most powerful character in the play. Howell's production, remaining true to the BBC's mission to capture the unadulterated Shakespeare canon on film, reinstates Margaret to her rightful role as supernatural and omniscient force. Margaret's commanding presence, in which she looks more like one of the weird three from *Macbeth* with her drab clothing and chin wrap, helps to further set our sympathies on Richard. While Richard still betters her by deflecting her curse, we see that he is uncomfortable with her presence. In the face of a Margaret even more disheveled than Cook's Richard, we happily defer our attention and sympathies back to him. We may wonder, however, what connection should be made between former queen and future king: both are untidy in appearance; both reek with pathos; both hobble about, suffering from physical setbacks (for Margaret limps about only with the help of a cane). While the final tableau of the play may only hint at some answers to this question, it most assuredly reminds us that our initial relationship with Richard is one based on our humanitarian response to Cook's presentation. The camera pans back and forth over a pile of corpses to rest upon Margaret cackling, her hair in wild array, cradling the lifeless Richard as if he were a baby.[10] Critics remain uncertain as to the precise meaning of this scene and tend to dislike it for its departure from Shakespeare's text.[11] Perhaps this final image pushes the concept of Richard as scourge of a supernatural force for whom he serves as instrument and performs vile deeds to ensure the purification of England.[12] Such interpretation aside, however, this image strongly reinforces the Richard offered from the beginning of the play by both Howell and Cook. The final image shocks us and forces us to think that, despite all of the trickery and careful acting, Richard might have been deserving of our compassion and pity after all. If the woman who curses Richard as "slave of nature and the son of hell" (I.iii.227) can in fact comfort him in death, then perhaps we were right to extend our trust to this pathetic and wronged soul.

Though Cook appropriates Olivier's technique of direct address to the camera, he is not the only one to do so in the BBC production. In Act I, Scene iv, Brackenbury peers into our eyes after Clarence recounts the terrors of his nightmare. The fact that another character has access to the audience is not an insignificant one. If another character in Olivier's film had turned to address us directly, much of Olivier's commanding and fixating hold over us would have dissipated. The reverse holds true in the BBC production. Brackenbury's lines spoken to us reveal the pathetic nature of Clarence:

> Sorrow breaks seasons and reposing hours,
> Makes the night morning and the noontide
>   night. (I.iv.72–3)

Here Brackenbury channels Clarence's sorrow to us. The concern that Brackenbury shows for Clarence when he asks "Why looks your grace so heavily today?" (I.iv.1) is reflected in his eyes as he stares directly into ours. We cannot but help feel sorry to know that the repentant Clarence is about to meet his death. This happens again as Buckingham speaks to us before fleeing in Act IV, Scene ii. Such scenes invite our sympathies to play a role in the film. In such cases Howell further establishes the convention that allows for the sense of compassion transmitted between Richard and his viewers.

Cook as Richard gladly takes the part of the bullied over the bully. He wears a sword but convinces us that he is too meek to wield it. Cook plays this pathetic Richard so congenially that we are loath to turn on him. While we do eventually distance ourselves from him in the latter half of the play, Cook continues to give us glimpses of his pathetic Richard. He rouses our sympathies in Act IV, Scene ii, when Buckingham does not immediately agree to slaughter the princes. He looks hurt and truly betrayed when Buckingham asks for "some little breath, some pause" (25); Olivier shrugs it off as mere inconvenience. When Olivier mounts the throne and openly projects his dominance, we see him for what he truly is. When Cook mounts his throne, he appears as a young child lost in a sizable chair. Our pity turns to concern: will he be able to fill the throne? Even when Cook takes the lives of the young princes we can almost identify with his fear for preserving his rule. On the battlefield on eve of his death he is visibly frightened, a fear that invites us back into our relationship with him. Even the gratuitous slaughter of Richard appeals to our emotions. He fights death off valiantly, and when he does eventually yield it is with multiple spears jutting from his body like lifeless tentacles. Is it a coincidence that the initial blow comes from behind? That when he finally dies it is upon his knees in a position of prayer? The combination of these factors and the comments made above about the image of the final tableau seem to suggest that, despite his treachery and villainy, Cook's Richard may deserve our sympathies after all. Richard's evil acts can be rationalized:

> Why, love forswore me in my mother's
>   womb,
> And, for I should not deal in her soft laws,
> She did corrupt frail nature with some bribe
> To shrink mine arm up like a withered shrub,
> To make an envious mountain on my back—
> Where sits deformity to mock my body—
> To shape my legs of an unequal size,
> To disproportion me in every part,
> Like to a chaos, or an unlicked bear whelp
> That carries no impressions like the dam.
>   (*Henry VI, Part 3* III.ii.152–62)

While he is decidedly not the Richard whom Olivier constructs from the extended soliloquy in *Henry VI, Part 3*, he is in fact some variation of this "rudely stamped" (I.i.16) man.

IV. MCKELLEN (1995)

Ian McKellen, under the direction of Richard Loncraine, presents yet a third characterization of Richard in the 1995 film adaptation of Richard Eyre's 1992 stage production. Many have suggested a connection between Olivier's Richard and Hitler,[13] and indeed the theme of domination and oppression facilitates such a parallel. While the political message of Olivier's film remains implicit, McKellen's film, set in the 1930s, insists upon a Richard who undeniably mirrors the Nazi leader. With such an agenda, then, we might expect an overtly suppressive Richard; however, we find much to our surprise a romantic and soft Richard. Rather than conquer us by force and intimidation, McKellen's Richard persuades us with charm.

The film opens in the headquarters of King Henry. Prince Edward sits down to his dinner with a picture of his beloved Anne; a tickertape warns that "Richard Gloucester is at hand"; the king prays in his bedroom. Violence soon shatters this quiet scene, however, and the ground begins to shake. We are given a quick shot of Anne's picture as it symbolically topples over, and then a tank rips through the fireplace. Soldiers in gas masks enter with machine guns, and assassination follows. Edward is shot in the outer room, and the camera cuts to Henry kneeling in prayer. A solitary man enters the room, and we hear the report of his pistol as he shoots the king. He pulls off his mask, and we catch our first glimpse of McKellen; his grin turns to full smile as if the murder was performed for our sake. Thus begins the courtship.

The next scene is set in an extravagant ballroom. The king and queen dance the first dance of the evening which begins the celebration of peace. All of the characters are present, even Richmond, who dances with his future bride to the satisfaction of the king and queen. Richard roams through the crowd and mingles with various guests; he shares a quick laugh with Buckingham. He not only stands out for his full military dress uniform, complete with a battery of medals and ribbons, but for the fact that when the camera zooms out we find him standing alone amidst the dancing couples. Though he speaks the first few lines (1–8) of the opening soliloquy into a microphone on a platform in front of the crowd, our relationship with him does not become fully established until he slinks off to the restroom: a rather unromantic place, but a private one. McKellen waits to make any further contact with us until we are quietly removed from the public affairs of the lavish ballroom. His Richard prefers solitude to Olivier's omnipresence. He continues the soliloquy as he enters the lavatory and begins to urinate. He apparently spots our reflection in the mirror in front of him, but does not directly address us until the last few lines of his speech. Rather than show annoyance at our eavesdropping, McKellen immediately warms in our presence and beckons us seductively with a wag of his finger to follow as he goes to meet his brother Clarence.

"In Shakespeare's play," explains Phyllis Rackin, "Richard's monopoly of both male and female sexual energy is vividly portrayed in his seduction of Anne" (109). As we watch McKellen remove his ring, the key implement in this seduction, with his mouth we experience this sexual energy in full force. Tight camera work pervades this wooing scene and makes up for the extensively cut material.[14] As McKellen kneels before Anne (Kristin Scott Thomas) to invite her revenge with his own blade (a blade perfectly suited to this "soft" Richard: it more resembles a steak knife than the hefty swords of Olivier and Cook), alternating close-ups of Richard and Anne direct our attention to their facial expressions and eye movements and replace the stichomythic dialogue of the original text. The result is a more relaxed and passionate wooing, not one marked by raised voices and resentment. McKellen's sleepy, bespectacled eyes and relaxed face sap all of Anne's anger. Such a face just could not be that of a killer, the camera

Ian McKellen's Richard with Annette Bening's Queen Elizabeth in Richard III (UNITED ARTISTS)

insists. Working solely with his good arm, he transfers the ring to Anne's finger; she almost faints from the power of this gesture and can barely voice her rebuttal: "To take is not to give" (I.ii.190). Like his first soliloquy, this scene takes place in a most unromantic setting: a morgue filled to capacity with bodies. Once again McKellen transforms a most unexpected place into a lover's chamber.

If it appears that McKellen gives himself to Anne, his following actions convince us otherwise. He speaks to us as if to say "Not to worry, I'll be rid of her soon enough" with his "Was ever woman in this humour wooed?/Was ever woman in this humour won?" soliloquy (I.ii.215ff). He invites us again with a smile and a wink, as music comes up, to dance with him back to the ballroom. He wants us to see that he is in fact capable of dancing and celebrating given the right partner. As he skips and hops up the stairs we begin to realize that we are his chosen partners.

Certain other factors also contribute to our seduction by McKellen. The first half of the film is accompanied by colorful music arranged by Trevor Jones. "Come live with me and be my love," invites the singer over close-ups of our seducer.[15] The music proves almost subliminal with its message of love; we find our feet tapping along to the beat even as Richard mounts the stairs from the morgue in victory. We truly dance with McKellen in this scene. The music becomes the cue for McKellen's romantic endeavors. Whenever it begins to play expect an accompanying shot of his smiling face. The cigarettes that constantly dangle from McKellen's lips invite our attention; his squinting eyes draw us in behind tight glasses, and the swirling smoke that always seems to cloud his face mesmerizes us. The smoke which leaks from his mouth carries his words to us directly from the screen, and at the same time keeps his true nature hidden from us. We are dazzled by his eloquence and the dexterity of his good arm. This is a Richard who truly likes us and whom we want to like back.

While McKellen's relationship with his viewers begins as mere flirtation, it soon gains a sexual edge. When he sees proof of his victims' deaths he becomes visibly excited. McKellen receives some degree of stimulation when he holds Clarence's spectacles and later when he flips through photographs of Hastings's lifeless body. As he enjoys the proof of his brother's death, he spies Anne standing on a stair across the room in a sheer nightgown. As he smiles and gets up to walk to her we assume they will mount the stairs together. Yet, as if to display his faith to us, he reaches for a lightswitch next to his wife, flips it, and then leaves her to mount the stairs alone in darkness, embarrassment, and rejection. Moreover, when he examines the photos of Hastings, he puts on a recording of the same song from the end of the wooing scene and lies upon a couch dropping the photos on his body. Again he invites us to dance as he taps his foot, hums, and nods along to the music. Let there be no mistake, he assures us, we are the sole target of his affections.

If this relationship builds to suggest a love affair, it culminates in rape. For all of his romantic overtones and suggestive winks, McKellen's Richard finally demands our submission to his rule. We may have in fact been wooed, but we are not his equal. Just before his coronation he holds a rally from which he emerges as fascist ruler and we as victims of our own ignorance. Row upon row of soldiers hail him as their leader, and we are smacked in the face with reality.[16] What we assume as an innocent and seductive romance turns to utter horror as the camera pans up to reveal McKellen, dressed in black, smiling his biggest smile yet. We see, in those red banners and uniforms that remind us of Nazis, that Richard's love affair has been with power from the very beginning. We discover that we have been used by this monster now standing before us. Rather than demand our submission to his rule, he systematically ignores us except for a brief glance after he demands the deaths of the young princes, yet even then he seems only to say "What did you expect?" From this point on, McKellen refuses to make eye contact with us, only reinforcing our feelings of isolation and betrayal.

Amazingly, it is the Richard who invites us as close companions into his lavatory and to celebrate his successes in dance—the Richard to whom we are most attracted—who becomes the most despised. Even to the end of the film, when he is caught unarmed by a crazed Richmond and shot in cold blood, we cheer for his justice. While Olivier and Cook may disgust us, neither one becomes as much an object of our hatred as does McKellen. We feel violated, betrayed, and ignorant in his subversive manipulation of our emotions and feelings, and the final image of the play, unlike that of the BBC production, does nothing to resurrect him: he topples off a high scaffold into the flames of hell below. Interestingly, however, this is not the end of the film. Perhaps with a nod to Polanski's *Macbeth*, in which Donalbain seeks out the witches after Macbeth's death, the music comes up one last time and Richmond looks into our eyes and grins seductively. Will we find solace in the hands of this new king?

V. CONCLUSIONS

A young Orson Welles made the claim that "every single way of playing and staging Shakespeare—as long as the way is effective—is right" (27). Jay Halio shows a little more concern: "How can we know whether we are seeing Shakespeare performed or something that passes under the name of Shakespeare but is really something else, not Shakespeare at all?" (3). Olivier, Cook, and McKellen each play *effective* Richards, as put forth above, but is any one interpretation more authentic than another? Do any of the three play the role according to Shakespeare's original script? With little more than personal accounts of members from Elizabethan audiences we will never be able to tell who plays the "purest" Richard. One account seems to suggest a romantic Richard:

> 13 March 1601/2 . . . Upon a tyme when Burbidge played Rich. 3. there was a citizen grue so farr in liking with him, that before shee went from the play shee appointed him to come that night unto hir by the name of Ri: the 3. (Chambers 212)

Such evidence may perhaps speak for McKellen's seductive Richard, yet such anecdotal references remain quite ambiguous. The patron may have just as easily been charmed by a powerful Richard much like Olivier's, or she may have been struck with pity for a Richard like Cook's. The appeal of this text to actors is the simple fact that Richard may indeed be played in any of these ways. The appeal to the audience is that we may be taken in by Richard in any number of ways; each time we watch the play, whether onstage or onscreen, we do not know exactly what to suspect. Even as we watch cautiously for a forceful Richard, we may be caught offguard by performances such Cook's and McKellen's.

In the cinematic space, *Richard III* becomes a performance in the purest sense: It becomes the chronicle of a private relationship between Richard and his viewer. On film the soliloquy, when spoken in direct address to the camera, becomes most intimate and most successful. While stage actors play to the general space of a collective audience, film casts play to the solitary eye of the camera, an eye that both reveals and conceals. It is no wonder that a play in which a villain-hero not only acts, but directs, manipulates, and deceives, works so well on film, a medium itself given to manipulation and deception.

—*Christopher Andrews*
University of Connecticut

NOTES

1. Coincidentally, *Proteus* is the name emblazoned on Richard's airplane in which the Duchess of York (Maggie Smith) escapes to France in McKellen's film.
2. See also Coursen's "The Bard and the Tube." *Shakespeare on Television*. Ed. J.C. Bulman and H.R. Coursen.
3. It is held that Thespis began this tradition on the Greek stage in 535 B.C.E. (Arnold 2).
4. A decidedly different technique than that employed in the film version (as we will see below).
5. Scott Colley (*Richard's Himself Again: A Stage History of Richard III*), among others, suggests that a 1750 New York production of *Richard III* was in fact the premier of Shakespeare in America, though he also directs us to Charles Shattuck (*Shakespeare on the American Stage*, vol. 1) "for other possible 'firsts'" (1).
6. The elimination of Margaret is one of a number of changes to the original text made by Colley Cibber (1700) that Olivier chooses to keep; another is the substitution of Prince Edward's body for that of Henry VI.
7. Olivier's costuming and physical appearance (black tights, black cloak, straight black hair, and darkened, sunken eyes) became the paradigm for future actors playing the role. Roger Manvell describes Olivier's Richard as having "crowlike feet, shod in black shoes with long, pointed toes" (48).
8. *Macbeth*. Dir. Roman Polanski. Playboy Productions/Caliban Films, 1971.
9. The taping dates were October 13–19, 1981 (*Henry VI, Part 1*); December 17–23, 1981 (*Henry VI, Part 2*); February 10–17, 1982 (*Henry VI, Part 3*); March 31–April 6, 1982 (*Richard III*) (Willis 329–30).
10. Hassel extracts certain "unmistakable" (28) Christ imagery in this final tableau, but the effect is the same: Margaret holds a powerless Richard.
11. See Hassel (28), who also directs us to Warren (340) for support of his criticism, and Manheim (138).
12. For extended discussion of Richard as scourge, see Hunter, Quinn, Rossiter, and Stampfer.
13. See Brown (132–33) and Kenneth Tynan's 1966 interview with Olivier (*New York Times*, August 21, 1966, Sec. 2, p. 6).
14. Of the three productions, McKellen's cuts the most material. A conservative estimate suggests that only a third of the 3,600 lines are retained. The 250 lines of Act I, Scene ii are cut to 89.
15. This number is an adaptation of Christopher Marlowe's "The Passionate Shepherd to His Love": "Come live with me and be my love,/And we will all the pleasures prove."
16. The concept of a fascist rally appears quite often in film; see, for example, *Pink Floyd: The Wall* (1982) in which this same image is used to define the inverted peak of a character's descent into madness.

WORKS CITED

Filmography/Primary Sources

Greenblatt, Stephen, et al., eds. *The Norton Shakespeare*. New York: W.W. Norton and Company, 1997.

Machiavelli, Niccoló. *The Prince*. 2nd ed. Trans. Robert M. Adams. New York: W.W. Norton and Company, 1992.

Pink Floyd: The Wall. Dir. Alan Parker. Metro-Goldwyn-Mayer, 1982.

Seneca, Lucius Annaeus. *Seneca: His Tenne Tragedies*. 2 vols. Ed. Thomas Newton. 1581. Reprint, New York: Knopf, 1927.

Vonnegut, Kurt. *Mother Night*. New York: Dell, 1961.

Secondary Sources

Arnold, Morris LeRoy. *The Soliloquies of Shakespeare*. Columbia University Press, 1911. Reprint, New York: AMS Press, 1965.

Barthes, Roland. "Introduction to the Structural Analysis of Narratives." In *Image-Music-Text*. Trans. Stephen Heath. New York: Hill and Wang, 1977.

Bazin, André. *What Is Cinema*? Trans. Hugh Gray. Berkeley: University of California Press, 1967.

Brown, Constance. "Olivier's Richard III–A Re-evaluation." *Film Quarterly* 20.4 (1967): 23–32.

Buchman, Lorne M. *Still in Movement: Shakespeare on Screen*. New York: Oxford University Press, 1991.

Bulman, J.C., and H.R. Coursen, eds. *Shakespeare on Television: An Anthology of Essays and Reviews*. Hanover, N.H.: University Press of New England, 1988.

Chambers, E.K. *William Shakespeare: A Study of Facts and Problems*. Vol. 2. New York: Oxford University Press, 1930.

Colley, John Scott. *Richard's Himself Again: A Stage History of Richard III*. New York: Greenwood Press, 1992.

Coursen, H.R. *Watching Shakespeare on Television*. Rutherford, N.J.: Fairleigh Dickinson University Press, 1993.

Davies, Anthony. *Filming Shakespeare's Plays*. Cambridge, England: Cambridge University Press, 1988.

Davies, Anthony, and Stanley Wells, eds. *Shakespeare and the Moving Image: The Plays on Film and Television*. Cambridge, England: Cambridge University Press, 1994.

Eagleton, Terry. *William Shakespeare*. Rereading Literature series. Oxford: Basil Blackwell, 1986.

Halio, Jay L. *Understanding Shakespeare's Plays in Performance*. Manchester, England: Manchester University Press, 1988.

Hassel, R. Chris. *Songs of Death: Performance, Interpretation, and the Text of Richard III*. Lincoln: University of Nebraska Press, 1987.

Hunter, Robert G. *Shakespeare and the Mystery of God's Judgments*. Athens: University of Georgia Press, 1976.

Jorgens, Jack. *Shakespeare on Film*. Bloomington: Indiana University Press, 1977.

Manheim, Michael. "The English History Plays on Screen." In *Shakespeare and the Moving Image: The Plays on on Film and Television*. Ed. Anthony Davies and Stanley Wells. Cambridge, England: Cambridge University Press, 1994: 121–45.

Manvell, Roger. *Shakespeare and the Film*. London: J.M. Dent and Sons, 1971.

Oberlander, Marjorie J. "Review of *Richard III*. Royal National Theatre of Great Britain, New York." *Shakespeare Bulletin* (Winter 1993): 10.

Quinn, Michael. "Providence in Shakespeare's Yorkist Play." *PMLA* 10 (1959): 45–52.

Rackin, Phyllis, and Jean E. Howard. *Engendering a Nation: A Feminist Account of Shakespeare's English Histories*. New York: Routledge, 1997.

Rossiter, A.P. *Angel with Horns*. New York: Theater Arts Books, 1961.

Shaltz, Justin. "Review of *Richard III*. The Stratford Festival, Ontario." *Shakespeare Bulletin* 16.1 (Winter 1998): 43–4.

Shattuck, Charles. *Shakespeare on the American Stage*. Washington: Folger Shakespeare Library, 1976.

Shaw, William P. "Review of *Richard III*. RSC, London." *Shakespeare Bulletin* (November 1984/December 1985): 19–20.

Shurgot, Michael W. "Review of *Richard III*. Tygres Heart Shakespeare Company, Portland, Oregon." *Shakespeare Bulletin* 15.2 (Spring 1997): 28–29.

Singer, Sandra Sugarman. "Laurence Olivier Directs Shakespeare: A Study in Film Authorship." Dissertation, Northwestern University, 1978.

Smallwood, Robert. "Review of *Richard III*. RSC, Stratford." *Shakespeare Bulletin* 4 (1996): 326–29.

Sontag, Susan. *Styles of Radical Will*. New York: Farrar, Straus and Giroux, 1969.

Stampfer, Judah Leon. "Ideas of Order in Shakespeare's Histories and Tragedies." Dissertation, Harvard University, 1959.

Timpane, John. "Review *Richard III*. New Jersey Shakespeare Festival, Madison." *Shakespeare Bulletin*. 15.2 (Spring 1997): 19–20.

Welles, Orson. *Everybody's Shakespeare*. Woodstock, Ill.: Todd Press, 1934.

Willis, Susan. *The BBC Shakespeare Plays: Making the Televised Canon*. Chapel Hill: University of North Carolina Press, 1991.

Baz versus the Bardolaters, Or Why *William Shakespeare's Romeo + Juliet* Deserves Another Look

Baz Luhrmann's version of Shakespeare's *Romeo and Juliet* provoked in 1997 almost as much passion and violence of expression as the action of the play itself. Conservative opinion spluttered in outrage at Luhrmann's film. While audiences responded to the latest film with considerable enthusiasm, and cinematic criticism provided enlightening insights,[1] those who have allied themselves with Shakespeare-as-bulwark-of-tradition tended to dismiss *William Shakespeare's Romeo + Juliet* as a "monumental disaster" (LaSalle) or a "violent swank-trash music video that may make you feel like reaching for the remote control" (Gleiberman 1). Earnest critics decried: "there are 'bad films,' there are 'worst films of all time,' and then there's Baz Luhrmann's *Romeo & Juliet*."[2] Such a reaction of abhorrence is almost as interesting as the reluctance of academic publications to treat the film as a work worthy of scholarly attention.[3]

Before beginning a study of Shakespearean interpretations, it is important to note that the sense of definitive scripts, against which adaptations must be measured, is a product of 20th-century textual scholarship. Biblical study notions of textual purity (or Manichean notions of "good" and "bad" quartos) and authenticity are firmly attached to our understanding of the plays we read and perform, yet these artifacts are modernized for us, and any scholarly edition will elucidate the decisions made in the collating of a series of recollections by actors and audience (Holderness). Theoretical developments take us further: Reception theory points out that any text is partly created by the reader/viewer and we generally accept that no interpretation is definitive. In the light of these considerations, it is intriguing to observe critics' ambivalence. A recent text on this subject appears open to the "multiple possibilities" available in interpretations in its introduction (Boose 3); again the chapter by the editors admits that a "single, unified Shakespeare whose works could be covered" has always been an illusion (18), yet mourns, on the following page, "the disappearance of an older sense of the actor as someone who actually knew Shakespeare, who communed with him, understood his mind, and perhaps at times even thought that he himself was Shakespeare."[4] It seems that the author is dead, but that the author-function of Shakespeare makes for an intimidating ghost.

The action of adapting Shakespearean plays into film has mostly been dangerous for those game enough to make the attempt. The plays remain in the realm of prestige entertainment, whereas it has taken many years for film to be accepted as art. The dominance of the visual in film can struggle with the preeminence of the word in Elizabethan drama. Given that it had been accepted for critics to despise theatrical productions of Shakespeare's plays, allowing that true appreciation was only possible on the page, film was always destined to face opposition. The Shakespeareans' reluctance or inability to read the visual adaptation of linguistic elements of the plays leaves their comprehension of the cinematic version impoverished, and the works, therefore, often despised. Translation of the play to film requires a number of stylistic decisions to be made to assist in conveying stories told often in blank verse, in archaic language, in the presence of an overwhelming tradition of an overwhelming tradition. Olivier opted for a deliberate staginess—Branagh for a stronger cinematic intertextuality in worlds distanced by time and space. Zeffirelli and Luhrmann have taken a work that is strongly familiar to one section of the audience and frighteningly off-putting to the Shakespeare-shy and made it over.

Zeffirelli's *Romeo and Juliet*, revolutionary in its time, was more apparently traditional in its use of the original, and so the criticism he received, for his cutting of text and casting youthful actors who spoke the lines "sagging with puppyfat" and bereft of poetry, was more muted in nature (Simon 208). The glorious scenery of this "Renaissance Verona," superb in the attempt to evoke the history and the atmosphere of familiar paintings, belongs firmly in the lineage of the Victorian interpretation and production of the plays of Shakespeare (Collick). Here Shakespeare's work is directed toward a youthful audience, sexy and violent, filled with the heat and passion conveyed by the text, incorporating a critique of the adult world with its fatal thread of masculine violence. Yet it does so without betraying its "high art" trappings and threatens less the code of respectable Shakespeare: Some of the film's actors have Shakespearean experience, the period setting balances the "flower child" allusions, and the associations, mise-en-scène and musical, are with classical cultural traditions. While it is subversive of its own culture,[5] this production seems more respectful toward the "rules" of dealing with the Bard.

Luhrmann, on the other hand, summons a hallucinogenic range of youth and popular-culture details, attempting to translate the power of Shakespeare's story to a visually attuned generation. Of these, only a lucky few avoid having this text murdered by classroom desiccation, while others might never encounter it at all. That Luhrmann's subversive version should be produced has aroused reactions almost physical, calling to mind Kristeva's description of the reaction to abjection. Within the Shakespearean monotheistic economy, this film operates as "transgression of the Law" or "sin," that which is excluded and taboo (Kristeva 17). Luhrmann presumably sees his enterprise as displaying grandeur in its amorality (4) or as a "crime . . . that flaunts its disrespect for the law—rebellious, liberating, and suicidal" and thus not abject. It seems, however, that the critics view him as an Iago/abject: "immoral, sinister, scheming, and shady: a terror that dissembles, a hatred that smiles, a passion that uses the body for barter instead of inflaming it, a debtor who sells you up, a friend who stabs you" (4). Like any crime, his film "draws attention to the fragility of the

Claire Danes in the crypt scene of Baz Luhrmann's Romeo + Juliet (TWENTIETH CENTURY FOX)

law" (4). His film appears to be among those elements which cause abjection, that which "disturbs identity, system, order. What does not respect borders, positions, rules." The abject "lies outside, beyond the set, and does not seem to agree to the [superego's] rules of the game. And yet, from its place of banishment, the abject does not cease challenging its master" (2). The abject is "perverse because it neither gives up nor assumes a prohibition, a rule, or a law; but turns them aside, misleads, corrupts; uses them, takes advantage of them, the better to deny them" (16). The establishment critics' "unshakable adherence to Prohibition and Law" aims to hem in and thrust aside this perverse interspace, enforcing "Religion, Morality, Law," themselves always arbitrary (17). It is as though the traditionalists experience the intensely physical reaction that Kristeva describes.[6] Why this should be so deserves some consideration.[7]

Links with the biblical tradition mentioned above point the way. As the preeminent figure and guardian of the British literary tradition, Shakespeare has taken on an almost godlike status, and scholarly attention to his work figures as a tradition, with nearly as many defenders and attackers as the Christian churches can boast in their own history. (Or, in Bourdieu's terms, he is "canonized.") The same sense of sin applying to those who transgress the rules of religion is cast against those treating the Swan of Avon without the appropriate reverence; the Bardolaters will take no blasphemy from heretics. The abject nature of sin is discovered in the sacrilegious interpretations of radicals. In theater, the interpretation is ephemeral and raciness perhaps expected with the differing demographic involved in production and viewing. Film is trapped for the duration of its existence or reputation, reaching a wider, less-cognizant audience, and perhaps its very permanence draws out fears of irreparable devastation and rapine.

Despite the impression a reader might gather from any dismissive "MTV-generation trash" review assuming that the project is committed to no more than its own "eye-candy," the film repays closer study (Gleiberman 46). Luhrmann has given considerable attention to taking Shakespeare's play and making it work within the contemporary setting.[8] Respecting Zeffirelli's achievement as a "gorgeous piece for its time," he did not wish to cover the same territory. He desired from the first scenes to "disarm our audience, many of whom thought they knew what to expect" and make them see the play afresh (Evans 58). Romeo and Juliet could not enthrall a new generation as scions of the 20th-century cultural elite; the tale must be told in a setting where its internal logic remains. This is a world that is modern and yet unfamiliar: a world where the youth might conceivably always go armed; a world where love can still be so thwarted and endangered; where the innocence and passion of the protagonists can be so out of step with the current mood. His approach is frenetic and modern, rendering the play almost immediately accessible to 1990s youth and the conflict more recognizable. His Capulets and Montagues are as violently and passionately enmeshed as the play suggests, but the trappings that here carry them into the late 20th century have alienated that audience which finds even Branagh's apparently safe adaptations too iconoclastic and accessible to suit its desire to keep Shakespeare the familiar property of the educated elite.

Shakespearean drama is often used to reinforce the status quo, yet the ideologies conveyed through the drama are far more diverse and conflicting than conservative critics will allow, hence the fiery debate regarding the nature of views espoused in the plays. Often the undercurrents are more transgressive than reinforcing, and this movement is captured in Luhrmann's film. Elements of Bakhtin's Carnivalesque, where established powers are called into question and the people's culture celebrated, for example, abound in Shakespeare's play in the feasting, insults, and ribald wordplay. These are echoed in the scenes at the Capulets' party most strongly. Luhrmann wanted the feast to be somewhat sinister; he wanted "Romeo and Juliet and the audience to walk into a grotesque, Bacchanalian example of what their parents' world is" (Press Kit 12). Just as in the Bakhtinian understanding, the excesses occur in a wild and exaggerated way, filled with grotesque imagery skewed by Romeo's "acid"-addled gaze. Mercutio's cross-dressing and the camera angles focusing up from Capulet's groin and belly are strongly Carnival elements. Zeffirelli's feast, by comparison, is much more an "official feast," asserting and reinforcing a stability rejected by the family's offspring (Morris 199). These elements, part of the undermining of the prestige possession of the plays, discomfort those who are used to an unchallenging familiarity with their Shakespeare.

For Luhrmann this familiarity is stultifying; the choice of name for his film gives an indication of his mission in approaching the complications of adaptation. He has tried to reclaim the play from its association as rarefied and stagy. Recognizing the rambunctious, sexy, and violent elements in Shakespeare's storytelling, as well as the boisterous comedy and passion, was significant for him in returning to the play's roots. Shakespeare knew that he was providing entertainment, a fact seemingly often forgotten. Luhrmann sees the driving force behind the film as "addressing the original Shakespeare," reclaiming the play from the snobbery of the Victorian inheritance in theater and redeeming the power of the Shakespearean tale for a less hidebound audience; the original audience did not watch it as a British classic. The chosen approach to delivery of the language, analogous to the Branagh dictum, hoped to do "the words justice" while making the impression "conversational." Elizabethan language is a demanding medium for any contemporary audience; delivered in traditional versified manner, it would be an unthinkable obstacle for the youth market at which the film is pitched. The aim was to be "obvious, precise, and clear" and every detail in the mise-en-scène is intended to elucidate (Press Kit 2, 3).

A "created world" results: "a collage of modern and classic images, drawn from religion, theater, folklore, technology and pop-culture"; varied 20th-century icons, which are intended to be overtly comprehensible. The setting, Verona Beach, equates for us Elizabethan perceptions of Verona: a hot, sexy, violent, and Catholic (signifying exotic and dangerous) location (Press Kit 7). While this world is recognizably modern, it is neither the future nor the past, partly aided by being so much composed of the "world of the movies."[9] The intention was that this eclectic mix would be familiar on some level, making it easier for the audience to accept, and comprehend, the stylized language. The sets themselves were designed to convey information about the characters who move within them in the clearest possible way, so that "people will know instantly where they are and will be able to concentrate on the language the actors are speaking"(Press Kit 10). The girlish yet privileged innocence of Juliet's room, the garish showiness of the ball, contrasted with the simplicity of the lovers, all work as visual shorthand.

The costumes and related clues both work to make the characters swifter to comprehend, and to detract as little as possible from the attention necessary to understanding the dialogue. Drawing on characters recognizable from the film tradition was part of this. Gloria Capulet (Diane Venora) is a Southern belle, and the elements of 1950s design in her clothing comment on the nature of her role in her marriage. Romeo's and Juliet's costuming favors blues, silvers, and whites, remarkable for simplicity. In a way they are like "specters, the ones whose hold on life is the most tenuous," and this is augmented by the degree to which the camera dwells on the gawky and often wounded vulnerability of Romeo. Other examples of succinct use of mise-en-scène in characterization are evident in the ball scenes. Tybalt, for example, with all his Marian tokens, has more than a little of the devil to him, not only in the styling of his hair and mustache, but also in his choice of Mephisthophelean masque costume. His gunplay is as exotically skilled as Mercutio suggests the original's swordplay to have been; links to the western film are playfully suggested by musical accompaniment as well as posturing, not to mention the extreme focus on the grinding out of his cigarette. Old Capulet is a Mafia boss and is robed as a Caesar in his riot of excess. The Count Paris is characterized by his appearance as that all-American, clean-cut hero of the modern age—the astronaut. Everything is about "revealing the language, making it less distant and more potent" for its intended audience (Press Kit 15).

Another element to the mise-en-scène working to overcome the dangers of disjunction lies in the careful attention to justifying anachronistic allusions, as evidenced by touches such as the guns labeled "Rapier 9mm." The sycamore grove, for example, not actually visited in the play, provides the setting for much of the jostling for power and prestige among the gangs of young men in this version. It has become "Sycamore Grove," a dilapidated, almost post-holocaust wreck of an amusement park. The wording figures over the remnants of a proscenium arch, the tincture of a dilapidated staginess which informs both Romeo's pining and Mercutio's death (itself further dramatized by the fortuitous arrival of a hurricane).

Disrespectful elements to disturb the establishment include a number of visual Shakespearean jokes, including one played at the expense of the revered Globe Theatre, now a seedy pool hall. Also pilloried is religion, which plays a constant and clashing role in this mise-en-scène. The cathedral dominates the landscape and the montages establishing this city, itself dominated by the giant statues of Mary and Jesus. This society, permeated by violence, drugs, adultery, and revenge, is undoubtedly Catholic and matches Shakespeare's Verona (not to mention Protestant England) for hypocrisy in the duty paid to this faith. All have lost the "pious underpinnings" to this overt religious display (Press Kit 15). But the surreal element continues. This is a Catholicism virtually unrecognizable to the contemporary adherent: neon-lit crosses; choral versions of "Prince" songs accompanying the mass; a priest with tattoos, Hawaiian shirts, and sinister relationships with his young charges.[10]

Nor is *William Shakespeare's Romeo + Juliet* filmed in the traditional "continuity" style of editing, which seeks to efface the existence of camera as mediator of the narrative experience. The camera work and editing again undermine any pretense toward realism that the unwary viewer might be tempted to read. The screenplay is full of the camera "slamming" in and out, and Luhrmann has his editor fast-forwarding (anxious, like Zeffirelli, to maintain pace [Hapgood 82]) through bridging sequences, with dizzying editing of montages building the overview of the city as well as establishing the edgy and vertiginous atmosphere of this town where the work of seconds can radically alter one's fate. In contrast to this frenetic pace, Romeo and Juliet are surrounded by moments of stillness, and some of the longest unmoving takes of the film are in the extreme close-ups of their faces, creating a "sweet counterpoint to the chaos" (Gilbey 7). The recurrent water imagery usually reflects this sense of peace. The cinematographer, Donald McAlpine, aimed to remove every vestige of "stage," every hint of highbrow "classic" by trying "to develop as much movement and change of perspective as possible, every cinematic trick we [could] think of to make it look as much like a movie as we [could]."[11] The camera work furthers the sense of transgression: Stability and perpetuation are reinforced by the classic Hollywood continuity editing that "serves to suture up the gaps, potential fissures in the unity of the diegesis" (Nichols 83). By failing to mask these to ensure the film process remains hidden, the work challenges our desire to suspend disbelief and succumb to the inevitable rightness of the status quo.

The first and last moments of this production indicate starkly that this is not a realist text. The chorus's words are spoken on the television that moves in on the black screen from the distance (filling or replacing the cinema screen?[12]) and then finally diminishes out of it. The awareness of itself as construct urged regularly by editing, and mise-en-scène (not to mention by its overtly made-for-album musical soundtrack) is signaled from the first moment. This becomes even more apparent when the film is viewed as video, with a television screen growing to full size within another television screen. This is not merely included as a distancing device, however; for Luhrmann, "television is the chorus of our lives" (Adamek).

Both Zeffirelli and Luhrmann transgressed in the direction of their balcony scenes. Traditionally, this was the moment for the poetry to dominate, and the lovers never touched. A decade before Zeffirelli's film, the Castellani version, with Susan Shentall and Laurence Harvey, presented the ever-parodied placement of plum-mouthed wooer below and winsome virgin above,

never touching, ever yearning; this traditional theatrical enunciation and formalized gesture was the norm. The 1968 and 1996 versions' degrees of transgression highlight the break made and also the differences between the two films. Both have excised some of the poetry, but it was in the "stage-business" that they shocked. Zeffirelli allows his Romeo and Juliet to touch and kiss, adding a pungent eroticism to the wordy, sonnet-shaped wooing, perhaps, too, adding to the plausibility that they should choose to wed by the end of the scene.

Luhrmann, in his attempt to make this excessively familiar scene completely new, has much of it conducted within the Capulets' swimming pool, his Romeo and Juliet entwined. The scene is framed by humor; the tradition is parodied as Romeo stares longingly at the balcony at the light breaking through yonder window, but the Nurse (Miriam Margolyes) appears, provoking shocked laughter and renewed attention. The conclusion offers the Nurse's silhouette waggling in frustration behind that same window. Tension, however, is not sacrificed. It mounts as images of the lovers are intercut with the surveillance by guards and Nurse: both remind us of the perilousness of the meeting. Romeo enters a darkened, traditional setting to have it flooded with the gaudy glow of Christmas lights. A classical statue of a youth resembling Romeo points to the prestige associations of the play, DiCaprio's coltish clumsiness contrasting with its static grace. Juliet (Danes) then appears at ground level from a surprising elevator; a scream and the splash of the pair tumbling into the pool end the worst disruptions to the spectators' desire to immerse themselves in the lovers' exchange.

The aqueous embraces serve a similar purpose to Zeffirelli's, creating the bond between the lovers. The stillness of the camera, the prolonged and close focus on their faces, enshrining their individual passion and intense eye contact, convey their swift-growing intimacy. The images further illustrate the couple's abstraction from their society. The shimmering of this unearthly light as it reflects upon their faces suggests incorporeality, a ghostly fragility; their movement is a dance of such slowness and delicacy that it melts the memory of the earlier ball. Finally, Juliet mounts the stairs to the balcony scenes, re-creating her as the traditional Juliet and forming a visual echo of Zeffirelli's version. This is not a travesty, but renewal.

The possessiveness expressed in the appalled reactions of devastated Anglophiles toward this film is intriguing. The idea that Zeffirelli's adaptation, which spoke so powerfully to its own contemporaries, signaling its significance for the peaceniks and free-love generation, ought to be the last word on the matter is extraordinary.[13] As most recognize, no interpretation is definitive. Luhrmann has merely taken up the challenge which Shakespeare's work continues to pose of reworking and revising to keep it fresh. It is worth recalling that "Shakespeare's work was popular culture when it was produced."[14] These directors adopt very different cinematographic techniques to smooth the contrast between the visual and the language. Branagh has commented: "We see something in the latest *Romeo and Juliet* that is utterly different and radical and quite dazzling in its way, and yet the more traditional version [by] Zeffirelli is also a very fine film. They're polar opposites, but the writing, the work and the feeling in the play is still there" (quoted in Sinden). Both interpretations are valid and stimulating; they should be able to live alongside the passionate actor with nothing but bare boards to support his incarnation of the poetry (Eyres). The cinematic and theatrical arts can both explore the play in the ways best suited to their own strengths. This never needed to be a war.

—Lucy Hamilton
Monash University
Clayton, Victoria, Australia

NOTES

1. One of the best is José Arroyo's "Kiss Kiss Bang Bang," in *Sight and Sound*, March 1997. It should not be forgotten, however, that the film is transgressive of Hollywood cinema tradition as well: "AFI Conversations on Film: Jill Bilcock and Roger Savage on the Making of Baz Luhrmann's *Romeo + Juliet*," Metro 1998: 113–14.
2. Luhrmann quoted in Adamek. Among others: "manipulative fluff" from Matthew Gold in *Book-lover's Guide to Cinema* www.panix.com/~mgold/romeo.htm. Or, Luhrmann puts "Shakespeare's greatest Romance in a choke-hold and takes it slam-dancing" from Desson Howe, *Washington Post*, www.washingtonpost.com/wp-srv/style/longterm/movies/videos/romeoandjuliet.htm. One presumes these critics have not seen the extraordinary *Tromeo and Juliet* (1997) which makes Luhrmann's film appear positively staid. (She: "Parting is such sweet sorrow." He: "Totally sucks!")
3. The most recent Shakespeare edition of *Literature/Film Quarterly* gives an intelligent but brief review: see Jim Welsh 25:2 (1997): 152-53. *Shakespeare Bulletin* is the only journal to have devoted extended serious attention to the film; Robert Kole's thorough piece is, however, descriptive rather than analytical, and Peter Newman's reflects the understanding that Luhrmann's film is mainly interesting for the way it speaks to "youth" (Summer 1997). The two issues of *Post Script* devoted to Shakespeare on film, one published in 1997(17:1), and another to be released soon, give no space to this film.
4. See p. 19. Yet *Sight and Sound* dismisses this text: it "will do nicely as a prime exhibit of pop leveling run amok" (February 1998): 31–32.
5. Lord Brabourne comments that the rebelliousness expressed in the film assisted in making it one of the most successful films ever made, earning an "unheard-of" $17 million. From Brian McFarlane, *An Autobiography of British Cinema by the Authors and Filmmakers Who Made It*, London: Methuen, 1997, 94.
6. "I experience a gagging sensation and, still farther down, spasms in the stomach, the belly; and all the organs shrivel up the body, provoke the tears and bile, increase heartbeat, cause forehead and hands to perspire" ibid. 3.
7. Chedgzoy perceives it slightly differently. On Shakespeare and abjection, she begins, "It is tempting to relate this evocative phrase to the massive investments of yearning and desire which cultural history has cathected on to the semi-mythical aesthetic bounty represented by the figure of Shakespeare. It precisely evokes the insatiable longing for aesthetic self-presence and plenitude which Shakespeare's plays seem somehow more able than other texts to offer the possibility of recuperating, but nevertheless always elude" (50).
8. Luhrmann begins with soundtrack elements that link him to classical tradition. After the screen image of the television, dramatic orchestration from Mozart's Symphony No. 25 overlays the setting of the scene. Postlethwaite's more-or-less English accent clearly enunciates "star-crossed lovers." But, as the title wipes the screen, so rap music wipes the classical associations of the play's past.
9. Familiar elements include *Rebel Without a Cause*, *Dirty Harry* and the Busby Berkeley musicals. Press Kit 9.
10. This last element may sadly be more recognizable.
11. McAlpine adds that the interplay of a "down, hard style" and "lyrical language" augment the contrast between the lovers and their world, in a "broad anamorphic format" which creates the cinematic feel. Anamorphic: gives "space on the screen to encompass two people talking to each other, while providing room for background detail" (Press Kit 16/17).
12. Thanks to Brian McFarlane for this idea.
13. Roger Ebert's damning review, for example, harks repeatedly back to Zeffirelli: "I think back to the tender passion of the 1968 version, and I want to shout: 'Romeo! Quick! Poison yourself!'" from "*Romeo and Juliet*," www.suntimes.com/ebert/ebert_reviews/1996/11/110104.html.

14. Marjorie Garber interviewed in Hannah Feldman, "Some Like It Haute," *World Art* no. 1 (1995): 30.

WORKS CITED

Adamek, Pauline. "*Romeo and Juliet*." *Cinema Papers*, February 1997:14.

Boose, Lynda, and Richard Burt. *Shakespeare the Movie: Popularizing the Plays on Film, TV, and Video*. London and New York: Routledge, 1997.

Bourdieu, Pierre. *The Field of Cultural Production*. Cambridge, England: Polity Press, 1993.

Branagh, Kenneth. *Hamlet Screenplay and Introduction*. London: Chatto and Windus, 1996.

Bristol, Michael. *Carnival and Theatre*. London: Methuen, 1985.

Chedgzoy, Kate. *Shakespeare's Queer Children: Sexual Politics and Contemporary Culture*. Manchester, England and New York: Manchester University Press, 1995.

Collick, John. *Shakespeare, Cinema and Society*. Manchester, England: Manchester University Press, 1989.

Evans, Dean. "Guns 'n' Roses." *Total Film* 3 April 1997.

Eyres, Harry. "Shakespeare: Do We Need Him?" *The Spectator* 24 May 1997.

Feldman, Hannah. "Some Like It Haute." *World Art* 1 (1995): 30–33.

Gilbey, Ryan. "*William Shakespeare's Romeo + Juliet*." *Premiere* April 1997.

Gleiberman, Owen. "Where for Art?" *Entertainment Weekly*, no. 352 (Nov. 8, 1996): 46–47.

Gray, Marianne. "*Romeo and Juliet*." *Film Review*, April 1997.

Hapgood, Robert. "Popularizing Shakespeare: The Artistry of Franco Zeffirelli." *Shakespeare the Movie: Popularizing the Plays on Film, TV, and Video*. London and New York: Routledge, 1997.

Holderness, Graham, and Andrew Murphey. "Shakespeare's England: Britain's Shakespeare." *Shakespeare and National Culture*. Manchester, England, and New York: Manchester University Press, 1997.

Kristeva, Julia. *Powers of Horror: An Essay on Abjection*. New York: Columbia University Press, 1982.

LaSalle, Mick. "This 'Romeo' Is a True Tragedy: DiCaprio, Danes Weak in Shakespeare Update." *San Francisco Chronicle* (Nov. 1, 1996)

McFarlane, Brian. *An Autobiography of the British Cinema by the Authors and Filmmakers Who Made It*. London: Methuen, 1997.

Morris, Pam. *The Bakhtin Reader*. London and New York: Edward Arnold, 1994.

Nichols, Bill. *Ideology and the Image*. Bloomington: Indiana University Press, 1981.

Simon, John. "Romeo and Juliet," in *Film 68/69*. Ed. Hollis Alpert and Andrew Sarris. New York: Simon and Schuster, 1969: 208–09.

Sinden, Peter. "Do the Bard, Man!" *Film Review* March 1997: 52–55.

Welsh, Jim. "Postmodern Shakespeare: Strictly Romeo," *Literature/Film Quarterly* 25:2 (1997): 152–53.

William Shakespeare's Romeo + Juliet. 20th Century-Fox press kit, 1996.

Peter Greenaway's *Prospero's Books*: A Tempest between Word and Image

This study analyzes the way Peter Greenaway in his film *Prospero's Books* reinterprets Shakespeare's *The Tempest* by underlining the way he organizes the material from the Shakespearean play to bring about a specific imaginative response. My analysis will be limited to the exploration of the spatial field (Buchman 12–32) created by Greenaway in the first sequences of the shipwreck, particularly interesting and characteristic of the film, since, according to Greenaway himself, "the start of a film is like a gateway, a formal entrance-point" (*Watching Water* 14).

In his film, Greenaway develops and focuses on the aesthetic and mannerist aspects of the Shakespearean text, while he does not seem to care too much about the other very important Shakespearean themes, such as power or history.[1] As far as it is possible to generalize about the relation between *Prospero's Books* and *The Tempest*, I am suggesting that the filmmaker reinterprets the Shakespearean text as a mannerist text and creates a new, artificial, and mannerist world by making use of devices and techniques that constitute a cinematic equivalent to Shakespeare's theatrical illusionism. He exasperates and amplifies those aspects, which were already there in Shakespeare, where the crisis makes itself felt most fully and explicitly (Hoy 49–67),[2] namely the metadramatic reflection upon the concept of art and the work of art-artist-spectator relationship and the mannerist tendency to disrupt the spatial unity and to combine things from different spheres of reality (Hauser).

In spite of his cinematic translation and exasperation of certain Shakespearean "tricks," the filmmaker imposes his meaning on the original text and, by reducing it to a formal mechanism and a huge stock of images and languages, he creates his own cerebral world which, in turn, offers him the opportunity for a discourse upon the cinema. The film is directed by a filmmaker who is also a painter, who tries to redefine the properties of the filmic frame. Greenaway's magic, like Prospero's, is a strange mixture of science and art. If Shakespeare, like Prospero, is a playwright who exploits all his "*charms*" (*Tempest* 1)[3] —namely, the technical tricks of his days, to stage "the direful spectacle of the wrack" (I.ii.26)— Greenaway uses both conventional film techniques and the resources of high-definition television to layer image upon image, superimposing a second or third frame within his frame. As a matter of fact, his use of the digital Graphic Paintbox, which he defines as the "newest Gutenberg technology" (Greenaway, *Prospero's Books* 28),[4] offers a relatively new way of producing cinematic space; and the frame, no longer two-dimensional, reveals multiple layers of spatial dimension. One of those layers refers to the plot traced by Shakespeare's plays; the others are not chronologically or spatially continuous with previous frames. Since Greenaway's premise is that Gonzalo stowed away 24 magic books on the leaky boat he provided for Prospero and Miranda's escape from Italy, his film opens each book, offering the spectator the possibility of reading Prospero's developing play in relation to the books he has already read. Each book is placed over the frame of the play's action, only partially covering the image, so that it gives virtually every frame at least two space-time orientations.

The film shows the enactment of the plot of *The Tempest* as Prospero writes and delivers it. We see and hear Prospero building up the scene before us while we simultaneously witness him taking pleasure in this creation. The magical force of his words conjures up his characters before our eyes in elaborate dumb shows.

Within the space of a completely artificial world Greenaway offers his audience spatial dynamics that counterbalance Shakespeare's dramaturgical design. Throughout his film Greenaway/Prospero creates two different space fields: the space of word and the space of image. The word/image juxtaposition parallels not only the relationship of a playwright to a scene—of Prospero/dramatist to Prospero/actor—but also that of a filmmaker to his spatial field. Prospero's activities can thus be interpreted as a metaphor for director Greenaway's filmmaking strategies and for Gielgud's

John Gielgud in Peter Greenaway's Prospero's Books (MIRAMAX)

long career as a Shakespearean actor. What prevails is this deeply complex identification, Prospero-Gielgud-Greenaway-Shakespeare, which is crucial in a film characterized by the continuous interplay of parallel creations, reflections, overlaps, and duplications.

THE SPACE OF THE WORD

Greenaway experiments with the possible relationships between the word pronounced, written, and materialized; and in the film there is an extraordinary amount of writing: words etched in air, on water, in stone, on parchment, in the image itself create a dimension of writing unusual for the cinema. In addition, Prospero's books are placed prominently, and written pages and sheets of paper are scattered throughout the film. The film is also highly literary and self-referential in its constant reminders that *The Tempest* is a text: Greenaway conceives the play as Prospero's own creation, and we see the magician-playwright speaking each verse until the final act, as well as his pen as it moves across the parchment. The recurring image of the inkwell is like a "magician's hat" (Rodgers 15), where anything can appear, as an acknowledgment of Shakespeare's creation of the original text. According to Greenaway himself, the film "deliberately emphasizes and celebrates the text as text, as the master material on which all the magic, illusion and deception of the play is based" (9). As a matter of fact, from the very beginning Greenaway emphasizes the importance of books, and the film opens with Gielgud uttering in voice-over the words from *The Tempest* as he writes them in close-up: "Knowing I lov'd my books, he furnis'd me/From mine own library with volumes that/I prize above my dukedom" (I.ii.166—68).

Greenaway presents shots of Prospero standing white and naked, like a De la Tour St. Jerome or a Bellini St. Anthony (*Prospero's Books* 39–40),[5] in a bathhouse, which he deftly contrasts with his close-ups of words being written on a blank sheet of crisp, off-white paper. Prospero begins to conjure up the idea of a scenario for a storm by using the single word "boatswain."[6] He plays with this word by experimenting with different recitative styles and by repeating it ruminatively, curiously, and interrogatively, while close-ups of the word, handwritten on a sheet of paper, repeatedly fill the screen. The evocation of the word "boatswain" in conjunction with the first book of the film, which is the *Book of Water*, supposedly compiled by Leonardo da Vinci,[7] opens the film; and this link between the ink and the tempest in a game of interference between the graphic sign and the image referent is significant.

THE SPACE OF THE IMAGE

Thanks to the classical/mannerist columns of the bathing room, the architectural capriccios scaled prophetically to Piranesi's romanticism, the books superimposed, and the connotation of characters and situations with reference to precise figures and *tableaux vivants* in the history of painting, there is an artificiality about that world, deeply reminiscent of the theater itself. But the spectacle of the shipwreck is enhanced by a plurality and density of images, achievable only through cinema.

Thus the tempest is created through an accumulation of metaphors: a series of associations with watery elements, linked together by the recurring image (and the loud and abrupt noise) of drops of water splashing—in slow motion—into a black pool, probably also an echo of Gonzago's words "every drop of water swears against it" (I.i.56), and authorial self-reference to the first sequence of Greenaway's film *Making a Splash* (1984). Pages from the *Book of Water* are the first to be framed with their drawings of seas and climate and with the small design of an ink-drawn galleon floating on the choppy water. This same three-masted galleon (or a similar one) is soon seen in the hands of Prospero, who sets it on the bath water where it trembles and bucks in the rough water caused by the urinating (but the word used by Greenaway in his film script is "peeing") Ariel—a Spirit of Air inspired by the dancing child in Bronzino's mannerist masterpiece *Allegory of Venus, Cupid, Folly, and Time*.[8] As Prospero, in the bathhouse, is confronted by a mirror-image from the *Book of Mirrors* of the drenched ship's company, the storm he has conjured up becomes a reality (but one might ask which level of reality) and on the line "Out of our way, I say!" the soundtrack grows suddenly more complex with the "massive burst of aggressively 'musical' sound" by Michael Nyman (Greenaway 43). When the peak of magic is attained, we see a pattern of alternative images of smiling Ariel, hovering above the edge of the bath and still urinating into the pool; of a full-screen flame (appearing eight times throughout the sequence), probably an echo of the strong perception of fire in Ariel's vision of the shipwreck in *The Tempest* (I.ii.196—206); and of Prospero dressing himself with linen under-robe and a black cloak, magically changing its color, to look like the Venetian Doge Leonardo Loredan in Bellini's portrait.

At the very beginning of the film the audience realizes that Greenaway attempts to create a very particular kind of illusionism. In the decision to create an outdoor effect indoors, the filmmaker follows Shakespeare's mounting a storm, complete with a shipwreck, on an indoor stage.[9]

Indeed, in Shakespeare it is a bravura staging device and the effect dictates the ruling conceit for the whole play. *The Tempest* in fact depends on the initial illusion of the shipwreck scene, which is the verification of Prospero's magic and the declaration that it is all the work of illusion, a harmless "spectacle" (I.ii.26). Against the scenery of the Banqueting House at Whitehall,[10] the shipwreck is set off by Prospero's magic, consisting in scenic and mechanical skills, the same magic Inigo Jones deployed in his masques. At the beginning of the play, the spectators watch the "direful spectacle of the wrack," which they recognize as having the conventions of Elizabethan courtly drama. There is nothing in the text to suggest any doubt about what they are seeing, and the brief scene is marvelously evocative as well as terminologically exact. But this first perception of the shipwreck is then replaced by the compelling pictures of Miranda's (I.ii.1–13) and Ariel's (I.ii.195–206) perspectives, alluding to the other spectacle of the theatrical devices employed to mount the storm.[11] The pattern of shifting perception (Pierce 167–73) characterizes *The Tempest* as a play which consistently arouses, challenges, and disappoints the spectators' expectations. The audience is being kept in suspense and, like the courtiers in the shipwreck, is never shown which layer of illusionism is presented on the stage.

In *Prospero's Books*, the image of the model galleon, which is also a hint at the special effects of the cinema (since many storm scenes have been shot using model ships), is followed by an accumulation of images and figures taken from literature and painting and therefore existing at a different level of reality (or illusion). Spirits impersonating classical and Old Testament myths associated with water—such as Moses, Leda, Neptune, a drowning Icarus, Jason, Hero, Leander, and Noah—indicate the growth and wrath of the storm.[12] The storm is also visualized through reference to painting and in particular, according to Greenaway himself, to Botticelli's *Birth of Venus*: the storm of papers swirling around the library, constructed to look like a facsimile copy of Michelangelo's Laurentiana Library in Florence, is in fact stirred up by naked mythological figures standing on tables, grouped in pairs, their cheeks puffed out, like Botticelli's winds. But, as a matter of fact, this intertextual reference to the winds also has a different source, since Robert Fludd used the image of the blowing winds in the frontispiece of his *Meteorologia Cosmica* (Yates 60), which is a source of inspiration for Greenaway's *Book of Universal Cosmography*.

In the film, far from any attempt at realism, Prospero's island has become a place of illusion and deception, full of superimposed images, shifting mirrors, and mirror images where pictures conjured by texts, such as the one of the galleon, can be "as tantalizingly substantial as objects; and facts and events [are] constantly framed and re-framed" (12). Thus, the film's multilayered narrative, with Prospero writing the story in which he is also a character, is matched by a kaleidoscope of images inset in other images so that Shakespeare's island "full of noises" (III.ii.133) and voices, since Prospero's is just one of the possible versions of the story—Caliban's, for example, is a different one—has become an island overflowing with superimposed images derived from the original text by association and contiguity.

In the film I have identified three main kinds of relationships between the images which contribute to visual density: frames-within-frames, mirrored images, and iterated images.

Framing

In *Prospero's Books* framing and reframing becomes "like a text itself—a motif—reminding the viewer that it is all an illusion which is constantly fitted into a rectangle, into a picture frame—a film frame" (12). The recurring geometrical figure of the film—that of a rectangle, alluding to the frame, to the proscenium arch stage, and also to the cinema screen—reveals Greenaway's deep concern with the medium he is using, so that the references to theater, literature, and painting contribute to his self-conscious reflection upon the cinema, its nature, and its possibilities. Thus, there is an interesting coincidence between the number of the books and the 24 frames per second in cinema, and often in the film the camera frames Prospero's image reflected in a TV screen; in particular, at the end of the film, on the last lines of the Epilogue, the camera retreats on Prospero's close-up to show, disruptively, that it is a close-up on a huge screen.

Greenaway uses the frame-within-frame as the cinematic equivalent of Shakespeare's play-within-play: it offers him the possibility to analyze the work of the art/artist/spectator relationship; and, besides, however imperfectly, each frame-within-frame undermines the credibility of the surrounding action. He not only revives this Shakespearean device but he also exasperates and exploits it to the utmost so that almost every frame contains a frame within or refers to one outside the screen by means of intertextual quotations to literature, architecture, art, and so on.

Frames-within-frames and mirrors contribute to that representation of different kinds and levels of reality, which is a feature Shakespeare himself shared with 16th-century mannerist painting (Hoy 49–67).

In *The Tempest* Shakespeare deals centrally with ideas and concepts of art, and in Prospero's magic he gives full expression to a theme close to the core of his artistic self-consciousness. Despite its realistic dialogue and details, the shipwreck is a show, and in the Epilogue (1–20) Shakespeare deliberately eliminates any barrier between the play world and the real. The audience is invited to enter the play world and assume a role, since their hands must release Prospero and their "gentle breath" (Epilogue 11) supply the "auspicious gales" (V.i.314), which he has promised Alonso. The Epilogue thus serves as a bridge between play and audience: a transitional link between art and reality (Egan 171–82).

The artful world of *Prospero's Books* is built upon different levels of illusion as well: the world of animated books melts into the world of the written words on the off-white pages and into the images of the bathing room with its many columns. The model ship itself enjoys different levels of illusion since it is at the same time an animated picture in a book, a model galleon on the desk of Prospero/dramatist, a toy in his hands as actor, and it is actually the ship transporting the members of the court. In addition, the film animates textual images: the *Vesalius Anatomy of Birth* disgorges bloody organs, while from the *Book of Architecture* three-dimensional buildings spring out like models in a pop-up book and Prospero is shown descending "textual" stairs. Furthermore, each character enjoys intertextual links with literature and painting, and the island is referenced with the architecture, paintings, and classical literature Prospero has imported. Greenaway delights in baffling the audience as to where reality (if there is one) actually turns into illusion.

Mirrors, or a Labyrinth of Optical Illusions

Mirrors are also recurrent in the film, adding a further layer of illusion and therefore a further element of confusion between reality and illusion. But these mirrors, held by minions and spirits of a Roman/Greek/Renaissance mythology, are very particular "distorting mirrors" (Eco 25–28) since they reflect Prospero's imaginings—good and bad—as though he always needs a mirror to make them manifest. In the first sequences of the film we first see Prospero reflected in the carried mirror, and soon after, with a flash, the mirror shows what Prospero sees: the victims of the storm.

The recurring rectangular mirrors enrich the "framing game" and, because of their nature, disrupt the link mirror image/image referent,[13] therefore reflecting optical illusions.

Repetition, or an Aesthetic of Redundancy

As a matter of fact, repetition is a fundamental recurring stylistic device in *The Tempest*. Lexical repetition is largely responsible for the incantatory appeal of *The Tempest* (Bower 131–50, McDonald 15–28).

In the same way, the film derives much of its metaphoric power from the interplay of repeated images during a sequence, such as the images of the galleon or the inkwell, or the visual allusions to fire and water. In addition, the Shakespearean text undergoes a further process of duplication; to quote an example from the first scenes, Shakespearean lines such as "Bestir, bestir" (I.i.4) or "Here, master: what cheer?" (I.i.2), are repeated as if they were an echo effect and are also reiterated by Prospero's writing them in full onscreen many times. In the film the characters are multiplied, too: Gielgud interprets two Prosperos and Ariel is played by four actors.

Verbal patterns are congruent with and supported by larger networks of reiteration, most of them narrative and structural; the symmetries and parodic constructions are obvious in *The Tempest*, and many critics have pointed to the density and congruity of its mirrored actions, which are emphasized even more in Greenaway as the mechanism of doubling is further amplified by multiple intertextual references. *The Tempest* is also flagrantly intertextual, and this audacious kind of authorial self-cannibalism contributes another layer of complexity, on which Greenaway feeds (Liberti 24).

The prominence of the figure of repetition in both the verbal style and dramatic structure of *The Tempest* encourages the audience to analyze the linguistic and structural patterns for meaning, but the text never fulfills the expectations of clarity that the discovery of such patterns engenders (McDonald 15–17). Since order and comprehension are continually promised but never thoroughly realized, the audience participates directly in the atmosphere of evanescence and instability of the play.

Iteration of images, characters' multiple layers of illusion, mirrors, and frames-within-frames in *Prospero's Books* work in the same way and carry out the same function: to entice the audience by promising and withholding illumination, demonstrating the impossibility of "significational certainty and creating an atmosphere of hermeneutic instability" (McDonald 16). As a matter of fact, Greenaway's film is informed with a precise pattern made up of the 24 magic books,[14] but this pattern is built up by an intricate network of allusions and intertextual references so that, in the end, the filmmaker provides the elements of spectacle but leaves the task of ordering them to the viewer, who becomes, therefore, the final interpreter of the film's shape.[15] The audience is thus established as the subject of the film, occupying a polysemic site where a multiplicity of possible meanings and intertextual relations intersect. To the Shakespearean text, Greenaway adds a visual and conceptual density that seems to defy any possibility of finding a stable pattern or meaning. What Derrida terms "the seminal adventure of the trace" (*Structure Sign and Play* 265) is nowhere better exemplified than in Greenaway's film. We move around among the sights, sounds, and accidentals which constitute the film, assembling and disassembling meanings as they fleetingly present themselves.

Prospero's Books is a cultural caprice: The flow of textuality overflows the traditional barriers of what we once called a "text" into what Derrida calls a "differential network, a fabric of traces, referring endlessly to something other than itself" (quoted in Atkins and Bergeron 40). The visual and symbolic hyperstratification and the endless process of quotations lead to a disruption of the filmic unity so that the film absorbs *The Tempest*'s imagery and text and turns into an encyclopedic container of images drawn from literature, painting, architecture, music, and so forth. By presenting too much to take in at a glance, Greenaway pushes to the limit his ideal of a "painterly cinema" (Masson 36–37), and to complete the effect, text, image, and sound constantly blur into each other in an infinite overlapping of languages and images: "Words making text, and text making pages, and pages making books from which knowledge is fabricated in pictorial form" (Greenaway, *Prospero's Books* 9).

Like the written word, the spoken word also changes into a visual image. The linguistic richness and nuances of Shakespeare's characters turn into the powerful and authoritative, but monotone, voice of Gielgud-Prospero, who speaks the Shakespearean lines aloud, shaping the characters so powerfully through his words that they are conjured before us. In Greenaway's mannerist (or postmodern) interpretation, the Shakespearean word becomes flesh, or metal, or any of the other metamorphoses the books exhibit. A mannerist hieroglyphic. A postmodern hieroglyphic. Celluloid. Cinema.

—*Mariacristina Cavecchi*
University of Milan

NOTES

1. "Since the film is deliberately built and shaped around the writing of the text of *The Tempest*, the script follows the play, act by act and scene by scene, with few transpositions and none of any substance to alter the chronology of the original. There have been some shortenings, the greatest being the comedy scenes with Stephano and Trinculo" (Greenaway, *Prospero's Books* 12).
2. See also Georg Weise, *Il Manierismo* (Florence: Olschki, 1976).
3. The Arden edition of *The Tempest* has been consulted throughout this study.
4. See also John Wrathall, "Mosaic Mindscapes," *Screen International* 824 (September 13, 1991): 16–18; and Michael Ciment, "Une conflagration de l'art," *Positif* 368 (October 1991): 43.
5. See also Liberti 22–24.
6. In an interview with Adam Barker, Greenaway notes that the first word of the play is "Bosun . . . which is a very interesting word because it is one that is never written down. It was used by seamen who were basically illiterate, so that when they came to write the word down it was 'boatswain.' It's a nice opening point about the topsy-turvy use of oral and written language" (28).
7. According to Greenaway, da Vinci "was an indefatigable enthusiast for the quality, motion and substance of water and an ideal authority to consult in the creation of a tempest" (*Prospero's Books* 38). It is also interesting to note the fascinating analogy between Leonardo's calligraphy in his drawings and Greenaway/Prospero's handwriting. See also J. Kott, "Prospero's Staff," *Shakespeare Our Contemporary* (London: Methuen, 1964): 197–202.
8. It is Greenaway himself who gives the indication in *Prospero's Books* 42.
9. *The Tempest* was the first play Shakespeare unquestionably wrote for the Blackfriars rather than for the Globe. It was moreover presented by Shakespeare's company at court on Hallowmas Eve in 1611 and again during the winter of 1612–13, as part of the astonishing round of entertainment provided during the period of the Elector's visit, particularly between the betrothal and the marriage. See Frank Kermode's introduction to *The Tempest*, Arden edition, xxi–xxii.
10. A sustained attempt to visualize a court performance of the play is Sir Ernest Law's "Shakespeare's *Tempest* as originally produced at Court," *Shakespeare Association Pamphlet* (1919).
11. For a visualization of the performance see also Anna Anzi Cavallone, *Varie e strane forme. Shakespeare: il masque e il gusto manieristico* (Milan: Edizioni Unicopli, 1984): 55–61.
12. In one of the sections of Greenaway's exhibition *Watching Water* (Venice, Palazzo Fortuny, June–September 1993), the video *A Walk through Prospero's Library* (1991) presents one by one all the characters that in *Prospero's Books* are somehow connected with water.
13. The expression "image referent" is my translation of Eco's *referente dell'immagine* (20; see also 9–37).
14. "I have not infrequently made use of mathematical structures, numbers and counting as an adjunct and companion to the narrative of a film. As author in control of the plot I can choose and dictate the fall-out of events from any number of infinite possibilities—which is a very volatile state of affairs, suggesting the ephemerality of fictional narrative" (Greenaway, *Watching Water* 28).
15. "I am interested in an audience that moves, that is not necessarily subject to a fixed frame, that does not have to remain in a fixed seat. Audiences that move are not unknown, but they are rare. Should we attempt to achieve audience movement as a prerequisite of cinema?" (Greenaway, *Watching Water* 49).

WORKS CITED

Atkins, G. Douglas, and D.M. Bergeron. *Shakespeare and Deconstruction*. New York: Peter Lang, 1988.

Barker, Adam. "A Tale of Two Magicians." *Sight and Sound* (May 1991): 26.

Brower, Reuben A. "The Mirror of Analogy." *Shakespeare: The Tempest: Casebook Series*. London: Macmillan, 1991.

Buchman, Lorne M. "Spatial Multiplicity: Pattern of Viewing in Cinematic Space." *Still in Movement. Shakespeare on Screen*. New York: Oxford University Press, 1991.

Derrida, Jacques. "Structure Sign and Play." *The Structuralist Controversy*. Ed. Richard Macksey and Eugenio Donato. Baltimore, Md.: Johns Hopkins University Press, 1970.

Eco, Umberto. "Freaks: gli specchi deformanti." *Sugli specchi e altri saggi*. Milan: Bompiani, 1985.

Egan, Robert. "This Rough Magic: Perspectives of Art and Morality in *The Tempest*." *Shakespeare Quarterly* 23, no. 2 (Spring 1972).

Greenaway, Peter. *Prospero's Books. A Film of Shakespeare's* The Tempest. London: Chatto & Windus, 1991.

———. *Watching Water*. Milan: Electa, 1993.

Hauser, Arnold. *Der Manierismus. Die Krise der Renaissance und der modernen Kunst*. Munich: C.H. Beck'sche Verlagsbuchhandlung, Oscar Beck, 1964.

Hoy, Cyrus. "Jacobean Tragedy and the Mannerist Style." *Shakespeare Survey* 26 (1973).

Liberti, Fabrizio. "Autoreferenzialità di *Prospero's Books*." *Cineforum* 311 (Jan.-Feb. 1992).

Liberti, Fabrizio. " Prospero e San Girolamo." *Cineforum* 311 (Jan.–Feb. 1992).

Masson, Alain. "This insubstantial pageant. *Prospero's Books*." *Positif* 368 (Oct. 1991).

McDonald, Russ. "Reading *The Tempest*." *Shakespeare Survey: An Annual Survey of Shakespeare Studies and Production* 43 (1991).

Pierce, Robert B. "'Very like a Whale': Scepticism and Seeing in *The Tempest*." *Shakespeare Survey* 38 (1965).

Rodgers, Marlene. "*Prospero's Books*-Word and Spectacle. An Interview with Peter Greenaway." *Film Quarterly* 45.2 (Winter 1991–92).

Shakespeare, William. *The Tempest*. Arden edition. London: Methuen, 1989.

Yates, Frances. *Theatre of the World*. London: Routledge & Kegan Paul, 1969.

Stormy Weather: Derek Jarman's *The Tempest*

British filmmaker Derek Jarman died in February 1994. Any comprehensive account of his achievements must include a reevaluation of his 1979 screen adaptation of Shakespeare's *The Tempest*, which anticipated many of the distinctive strategies of Peter Greenaway's *Prospero's Books* (1991). Greenaway's film is high-tech, with lavish crowd scenes and a kaleidoscopic profusion of images created with the aid of the "digital, electronic Graphic Paintbox."[1] Jarman's film was low budget, employing an orthodox mix of "masters, mid-shots and close-ups" (Jarman 194).[2] Yet, in their vastly different idioms, both movies dwell on the original script's obsession with the interaction between life, art, dream, and play, subtly shifting through different planes of reality and representation. In filling the frame, each director draws on a rich European artistic heritage. Greenaway recalls Piranesi, Bronzino, Da Messina, Michelangelo, Leonardo da Vinci, Botticelli, Veronese, Rembrandt, Bellini, and others. Jarman playfully alludes to Velázquez's "Las Meninas" and composes candlelit shots with the balance and beauty of paintings by Caravaggio or De la Tour.

Where Greenaway adds a postmodern self-consciousness about the relations between signifiers and the signified, and the ways in which text, as it is inscribed, conjures a world into being, Jarman's contemporaneity is more "social," the product of an exotic sensibility rather than of a modish intellect.[3] Jarman's films have been widely perceived as "statements of the late-1970s and early 1980s British counterculture, intended for punk and gay audiences" (Vaughan and Vaughan 209), and his version of *The Tempest* certainly reimagines the play, foregrounding the same-sex relationship between Prospero and Ariel, desentimentalizing the romance of the young lovers, Ferdinand and Miranda, with comedy, burlesque, and fun, and emphasizing dream as a Jungian search for selfhood.

Jarman jettisons the bulk of Shakespeare's dialogue and reorders most of what he keeps. The remains of the play's speeches may be scattered over several film sequences. Gonzalo's amiable garrulousness, for example, is enhanced by being protracted in this way. After Alonso's group arrives on shore in a dinghy, they trek through sandhills toward Prospero's mansion, and Gonzalo's Pollyanna-like chatter as he attempts to cheer the king or expounds his vision of Utopia percolates through three of the sequences showing this journey. We gain the impression that Alonso has an idée fixe, about which he cannot stop talking.

Shakespeare's long expository monologues, in which Prospero, in scene ii, tells Miranda of historic grievances, risk an audience's boredom and are thoroughly uncinematic. Jarman avoids tedium by dispersing them over several episodes, extending well into the middle of the film. Like Zeffirelli in his 1990 *Hamlet*, Jarman repeatedly breaks Shakespeare's scenes into smaller units, which he interweaves. The effect is to compress the time-scheme of a play that is already one of only two in which Shakespeare preserves the Aristotelian unities,[4] and to suggest that several related events are happening at the same time. The film's closing wedding-masque sequence assembles the whole cast and draws all the threads of the plot together.

The opening tempest is itself a challenge to a director. Shakespeare creates it through his dialogue, with the aid of a few primitive sound effects. On the modern stage, designer pyrotechnics and the electronic speaker system are apt to obliterate the words. In the cinema we expect to see a frothing ocean and a masted ship foundering, but may regret the loss of Shakespeare's evocative language and the metaphorical link between the storm and Prospero's inner turmoil. Jarman's solution to the practical problem becomes a key to the main significances of his film. In *Prospero's Books*, Greenaway has Gielgud as Prospero speak all the dialogue. Jarman had toyed with this idea: in his "first cut-up of the text . . . a mad Prospero, rightly imprisoned by his brother, played all the parts" (183). But in the final version it is only during the opening sequence that Prospero (in voice-over) utters other characters' speeches.

Throughout his film, Jarman uses blue filters for outdoor scenes. This establishes a nighttime, illusory quality, and the opening shot of sea, sky, and clouds is quickly assimilated into the imagination of Prospero, as he dreams in a shadow-haunted gothic castle on the Northumbrian coast.[5] The ship-master's "Bestir" is an urgent, echoing whisper in sleep; the wind of the tempest merges with the exhaling of breath as Prospero tosses and turns on his bed, his face netted under a gauze scarf. The shouts of the storm-tossed sailors become the anxious disembodied utterances of nightmare. "We split, we split!" (I.i.61) is as much a comment on disintegration of the personality as a reference to the breaking up of the vessel. Through Jarman's montage, the dark-blue shots of the lurching ship, crew scrambling along the rigging, and turbulent seas are linked with the mind of the troubled dreamer. The sleeper is conjuring up not only the shipwreck of his enemies but memories of his own maltreatment by them, when, ousted from his dukedom, he was hurried aboard a rotten bark, which was providentially washed ashore upon the island where he now reigns supreme. "The very rats/Instinctively have quit it" (I.ii.147–48), recalls Prospero, when later narrating his ordeals to Miranda; and in Jarman's film a white rat, heralded by a squeak on the soundtrack, scuttles across Prospero's bed. A little later a rat's eye glints momentarily through the gloom. More rodent screeches signal the ship's destruction. As the word "aground" reverberates, Prospero gasps himself awake, sits upright, and stares ahead in horror, to amplified sounds of a wave crashing. Miranda in her bed also stirs, as though implicated in her father's nightmare, but sticks her fingers back into her mouth, and curls up again under the covers.

Jarman's transitions from the sleeping Prospero to the stricken ship are very subtle. The bedroom is mostly shot in full color, but as he cuts back and forth between indoors and outdoors, or dreamer and dream, Jarman sometimes for a split second shows Prospero and his bed in virtual monochrome, which thus mediates between the two orders of reality. At the end of the sequence, Jarman cuts to a shot of Prospero striding toward his study, where he will evoke Ariel. Jarman thus constructs the first half of a frame that encloses Prospero's, Shakespeare's, and the director's fantasy. Thereafter, deep breathing is heard intermittently over the soundtrack to maintain the theme, and lines such as Miranda's "'Tis far off;/And rather like a dream" (I.ii.44–45) and Ferdinand's "My spirits, as in a dream, are all bound up" (I.ii.487) are given prominence.

Heathcote Williams is an unusually youthful Prospero, a 40-something "cross between Heathcliff in grunge and Dr Who" (Harris) with a hands-off approach to parenting. His hair recalls Beethoven. But his study is cluttered with the pseudoscientific equipment of a Renaissance magician like the German Cornelius Agrippa, the Italian Giordano Bruno, or the Elizabethan adept Dr. John Dee. There are mathematical and cabbalistic formulae, astrological diagrams, alchemical symbols, Egyptian hieroglyphs, the runic inscriptions of Agrippa's *Occult Philosophy*, a model of the zodiac, arrays of candles, perspective glasses, and crystal balls. Prospero's wand derives from Dee's *Monas Hieroglyphica*, "which symbolized the unity of spirit and matter" (Jarman 188). The indoor scenes were shot in Stoneleigh Abbey in Warwickshire, and this crumbling Kafkaesque pile with its gloomy stairwells becomes the natural habitat of a scholar, recluse, mad inventor, master of the occult. It is also well stocked with paraphernalia for play, like a Theatre Costume and Properties Hire shop. An alabaster bust resembling Prospero raises our awareness of questions of identity and mimesis.

Like many Shakespeare plays, *The Tempest* looks very different to most modern critics than it looked a few decades ago.[6] Instead of Prospero the benign mage, wise ruler over his island kingdom, stand-in for a Shakespeare who was delivering his farewell to the London stage after having emerged from the anguish of his tragic phase into a mood of reconciliation and faith in natural renewal, commentators find a deeply disturbed protagonist, whose tyrannical and repressive urge to control reflects his own inner insecurities, and who represents the vein of British empire-building that robs indigenous peoples of their native inheritance in the name of civilization. Nineteenth-century critics accepted Prospero's attitude toward Caliban. Recent critics are apt to sympathize with Caliban's impulse to overthrow the oppressor. The patriarch, imposing his will on others, must take a measure of blame even for his subject's attempted rape of Miranda. The play's keynote was once thought to be "forgiveness"; lately it has more often been seen as preoccupied with "power."

Certainly *The Tempest* bears some relation to the Renaissance revenge play. Prospero is like the wronged avenger-hero, who now has his enemies at his mercy. An emotional and psychological struggle within him between passion and reason, vengeance and forgiveness, can introduce "a sense of dramatic conflict necessarily lacking in an action moving at the will of an omnipotent being."[7] Modern critics have explored the conflict within Prospero—and behind him Shakespeare—between his need to see himself as humane, benevolent, and forgiving and his innate aggression, resentment, vindictiveness, and rage.[8] The plot itself moves toward Prospero's recognition that "the rarer action is/In virtue than in vengeance" (V.i.27–28), but his anger surfaces in the verbal details: the threats with which he controls the recalcitrant Ariel and Caliban, his mouth-filling descriptions of the cramps and convulsions to be visited on Stephano and Trinculo, the relish with which he pretends enmity toward Ferdinand. Against his brother Antonio he wields his forgiveness like a shillelagh: "For you, most wicked sir, whom to call brother/Would even infect my mouth, I do forgive/Thy rankest fault—all of them" (V.i.130–32). Jarman brings out Prospero's unacknowledged rancor through some striking images. As he addresses the spellbound Antonio, he holds a rapier point just below his treacherous brother's eye. Approaching the sleeping Ferdinand, he raises an ax, as though about to behead him, but smashes it down into the chopping block that Ferdinand is thus implicitly commanded to use. "The concept of forgiveness in *The Tempest* attracted me," wrote Jarman (202), who exposes the strain with which Prospero subdues his animosity and achieves that compassion which Ariel says he would feel were he human: "if you now beheld them, your affections/Would become tender" (V.i.18–19). Jarman's tricksy spirit utters this key speech as a wistful face peering out of a bundle of straw; his expression registers pleasure as Prospero resolves to forgive.

Toyah Wilcox's Miranda, a neglected child turned adolescent, is obviously used to creating her own entertainment. She invents herself with the help of a fertile imagination and a chest of clothing. Her hairdo, dreadlocks adorned with wisps of thread, is even more outlandish than her father's. She tries on hooped petticoat and bridal veil, blows a handful of feathers from a balcony, and arranges larger ones in her hair. She has the air of a self-absorbed but engaging urchin, with an infectious sense of fun. But she is also a curious, adventurous, sexually awakened young woman. Ariel sets her on the path to marriage with Ferdinand by intoning the wedding-masque verses forecasting fertile union, "Honor, riches, marriage-blessing" (IV.i.106), as he rocks astride her old rocking-horse, his motion lightly hinting at the consummation to come, while the toy itself serves as reminder of the child now poised on the verge of womanhood. In response, she mimes being a princess with airs and graces as she descends a flight of stairs to a xylophone accompaniment, but slips over on her backside and has to start again! Recapitulating Ariel's benediction, she herself recites scraps from the masque during her playacting. She appears to treat Ariel as a familiar playmate, but he has cast himself in the role of nurse or surrogate mother, supervising her maturation. But she remains a lively teenager with a gleeful chuckle, playing battledore and shuttlecock with Ferdinand before their game of chess.

Miranda has very little fear of Caliban, as portrayed by the blind harlequin Jack Birkett, "The Incredible Orlando." This Caliban is more "mooncalf" than "monster" (Vaughan and Vaughan 210). He is slack-jawed, camp, very physical but hardly a sexual threat to Miranda, who regards him as a voyeuristic nuisance. After her first encounter with him, he flaunts his open flies as she hurries away. Later he bends over and makes farting noises. This merely amuses her. Bald, shambling, baring his ugly teeth in vacant grimaces, he cackles and leers, a drooling natural. He is like a giant baby, so that the bizarre flashback showing him sucking at the breast of his grotesque mother, the hookah-smoking witch Sycorax, seems strangely appropriate. On his first appearance his hands are rummaging in a still-life platter of bruised fruit and stale vegetables in search of a raw egg. Finding one, he breaks it with his teeth and sucks the contents with slavering relish. He lisps and whines and croons. Prospero treats him with sadistic contempt, trampling on his fingers, as though corporal punishment is the only language he really understands.

Toyah Wilcox as Miranda in Derek Jarman's The Tempest

Caliban often seems like the embodiment of some despised element of Prospero's own psyche, an incarnation of the Freudian id; he lurks, motionless, in the background, like some dark shadow-self, while Prospero informs Miranda of past happenings. He is indeed a "thing of darkness" that Prospero must acknowledge as his (V.i.275–76). But he is clothed, as he sweeps the stairs, like an old-time Deep South butler. Drake, Purchas, or Raleigh might have called him a "mulatto." Racially unclassifiable, this Caliban might be the modern commentators' colonized native of disputed origin. His broad North Country-inflected "This island's mine by Sycorax my muvver" (I.ii.331) brings specifically English considerations of class and regionalism into his characterization, and he is vehement in his accusations that Prospero has robbed and enslaved him.

The inset of Sycorax is one of a sharply contrasting pair. With her mountain of naked flesh, lurid lipstick, and short peroxided hair in Medusa ringlets, Caliban's dam looks as though she belongs in the seamiest kind of 1930s Berlin nightclub, where Ariel suffers, rather than enjoys, bondage: Sycorax hauls him toward her by a long chain attached to his metal collar, while Caliban watches and sniggers. These images accompany Prospero's reminder to Ariel of the torment from which the mage had freed him. Jarman similarly illustrates Prospero's assurance to Miranda that during their sufferings at sea she was "a cherubim . . . that did preserve me" (I.ii.152–53): through an enchanter's scrying-glass Prospero shows his daughter a curly-headed blonde cherub, smiling as though lifted from some pastel-tinted Shirley Temple postcard; the adoring father, a spruce young aristocrat, beams with pride as she shyly parades in her Sunday best to music-box tinklings. Both flashbacks—to decadence and to innocence—have an air of camp excess that includes a hint of parody, but they are effectively antithetical nonetheless: cherubim as opposed to sorceress, preserver to torturer, virgin to whore.

Ariel (Karl Johnson) is a fascinating counter to Prospero. Dressed in a white boiler-suit and gloves, he is the technician for Prospero's research. This Ariel fits Jan Kott's conception of the character as like "a laboratory assistant working at an atomic reactor" (206). Yet he manages to convey a curiously disengaged quality that makes him more authentically a "spirit" than many conventional Ariels. He is like Prospero's Jungian anima figure—the mysterious "other" who complements him. He seems already to have gone through the angst that plagues Prospero, is more worldly wise, more cryptic, older even, and unsurprisable. He wears a pearl in his left earlobe, and, without the least suggestion of stereotypical homosexual mannerisms or the conventional androgyny, he comes across as knowingly and securely gay. His pallor is otherworldly. Spotlighting emphasizes it, especially when Prospero sits in contrasting shadow. The relationship between Prospero and Ariel is ambiguous, homoerotically charged, and sometimes tortuous. The dynamics of power are held in balance, often slipping or oscillating between them. We are aware that master can become slave and slave can become master. Prospero's dominance is most evident when he pins Ariel behind a glass screen; both Prospero's vision of Ariel and Ariel's of Prospero are shown as consequently blurred. Williams's lines are spoken softly and sensitively, "not bawled across the footlights" (Jarman 194), and Ariel's delivery is flat and impassive, and sometimes droll. He crouches in the long marram grass of the dunes, as he sings (in *Sprechgesang* style) "Full fathom five" to Ferdinand or "Awake, awake!" to Alonso and Gonzalo; the effect is to indicate his affinity with sea, sand, and sky, rather than to hint that he is potentially visible to the courtiers.

Ariel's nervousness about reminding Prospero that he has promised him his freedom is brought out by the way he rehearses his brief rebuke, accompanying his words with hand gestures mimicking the playground power-game "Scissors-Paper-Stone," where the aim is to anticipate the opponent's countermove. He is curious about Prospero's knickknacks. Corpselike himself, he toys with a miniature skull, clicking its jaws as he clicks his own, as though puzzling over what makes him different from mere mortals. When he recounts his escapades with Ferdinand, he appears, greatly diminished in size, as a floating projection on the wall above the mantelpiece in Miranda's bedroom, and at another point he goes to open a door, finds it stuck, glances at Prospero, shrugs deprecatingly, and with a snap of his fingers disappears. This looks almost like a parody of the antics of screen fairy folk, including the BBC Ariel, with his trick exits.[9] In general, this Ariel's nonhuman nature is established in more subtle ways. His first arrival is genuinely spooky: as Prospero repeats his commands, "Come away, servant, come; I am ready now" (I.ii.187), a doorknob turns, chandeliers sway and tinkle, a spider scuttles across a prayer book open at the communion service, a beaker of red wine (adjacent to "The Thirty-Nine Articles") falls on its side, and Ariel's voice is heard, as at a séance, before he materializes in person in a lightning flash and a clap of thunder. Madame Blavatsky could not have managed a more effective spirit entry. Jarman's cuts back and forth between close-ups and medium or long shots are perfectly calculated to produce the required frisson.

Sometimes you might half wonder whether there is anyone corporeal inside Ariel's overalls. In several other characters there is a contrasting emphasis on the body. The shipwrecked Ferdinand, for instance, wades to shore in blue-filtered light, a male Venus emerging from the waves, and staggers to Prospero's castle, to sleep naked in the straw of Caliban's lair before a blazing fire. There he is discovered by Ariel, who is joined by Prospero, Miranda, and Caliban in turn. After Prospero's feigned threats and accusations, Ferdinand, standing face to a wall, is manacled and made to wear a white uniform, while Caliban grinds out a merry tune on a hurdy-gurdy. The disjunction between the carnivalesque gaiety of the music and the pathos of Ferdinand's humiliation is unsettling. Miranda feels only pity: the next shot shows her weeping as she gently handles a dead butterfly. This aligns her with Shakespeare's other compassionate maidens, such as Marina, who in *Pericles* "never kill'd a mouse, nor hurt a fly" and wept when she "trod upon a worm" (IV.i.77–78).

Judging that "if one deals with unconventional subject-matter, experimental camera work can push a film over into incoherence" (194), Jarman restricted himself throughout to an orthodox repertoire of shots, but his masterly editing creates a remarkable visual poetry, with rhythms that enhance a sense of mystery. The skull-clicking episode, for example, begins with a close-up of a hand swinging a small glass pendulum, cuts to an extreme close-up of a wan-faced Ariel intently staring diagonally downward as he clicks his teeth, tilts slowly down his boiler-suited torso to settle on the object of his gaze, the miniature skull whose jaws he opens and shuts, and only then moves to the long-shot overview that reveals Ariel in the foreground with Prospero in the background sitting at a table, each engrossed in his business; the holder of the pendulum turns out to have been Prospero. Ariel drops the skull on the table as Prospero addresses him. Through the ordering of the shots, which reverses the normal progression from master to close-up, we have been made to share Ariel's puzzlement, sense his strangeness, meditate on mortality, and deepen our understanding of the relationship between spirit-servant and sage.

The soundtrack is no less inventive. The whirring of wings may signal Ariel's arrival, departure, or unseen presence. Frogs croak as Alonso's benighted group heads for the castle. The sound of marching feet serves as a backing to Prospero's tale about the usurpation of his dukedom. Seagulls cry as Ferdinand wades ashore or Caliban plods along the strand. An owl hoots as Prospero performs his nighttime rituals. Drumbeats or a synthesized rolling hum, blending with the sough of wind, intensify foreboding, mystery, or menace.

The comedy surrounding Trinculo and Stephano, escapees from a Butlins Holiday Camp, is reduced to a few giggled phrases, supplemented by visual gags—funny walks and drunken dancing—though the conspiracy against Prospero, like that of Sebastian and Antonio against Alonso, is retained, together with some effective sorcery as punishment, with Ariel in close-up snarling and howling like a bayhound, dwarves screeching and clawing at the offenders like angry cats, and the contents of Prospero's costume room, with its skull-masked dummies, taking on a life of their own. The rocking-horse whinnies and snorts as it pitches back and forth to the soundtrack's excited hunting scene. Later Ariel pants with his tongue hanging out, an exhausted hound, but also resembling an epileptic whose fits confer a psychokinetic power. There are also suggestions of postcoital lassitude. Over the whole episode there hangs a vague air of erotic exhilaration. Sex, domination, magic: Jarman's Prospero is no Aleister Crowley, but there is more than a smack of eros in his "so potent art."

The plan to murder Prospero is always patently doomed to failure. Events are so arranged that Jarman's Prospero is never distracted into forgetting about it, and he has the clairvoyance to keep track of all his enemies.

The pièce de résistance is Jarman's stunning wedding-masque finale, the "vanity of his art," to use Prospero's phrase for his show of spirits (IV.i.41). Alonso and his entourage have finally reached the castle. Warily treading its dark passageways, they hear unexpected sounds: "What harmony is this?" asks Alonso; "Marvellous sweet music!" exclaims Gonzalo (III.iii.18–19). We catch, muffled behind closed doors, the strains of a dance band and the shouts and laughter of convivial partygoers. Turning an engine that resembles some primitive forerunner to the orrery, Ariel weaves cobwebs to symbolically envelop the courtiers and transports them spellbound to the ballroom, which is garlanded in coronation splendor. Before the loving couple arrive—Miranda gorgeously attired as a cross between Scarlett O'Hara and the improved Eliza Doolittle—Prospero instructs Ariel to go to the king's ship and rescue "the mariners asleep/Under the hatches," waken them and "enforce them to this place" (V.i.98–100). "Presently," urges Prospero, meaning "immediately," and the room is forthwith invaded by the whole ship's company of sailors, miraculously dressed in modern naval uniform as if on leave from *H.M.S. Pinafore* and dancing a speeded-up hornpipe in a hilarious send-up of chorus-line revues and spectaculars from Gilbert and Sullivan on: Hollywood blockbusters, Esther Williams/Busby Berkley productions, and perhaps the Reinhardt-Dieterle film of *A Midsummer Night's Dream*.[10] It is a joyous celebration of male bonding. (In fact, it is also a gay in-joke. In his autobiography *Dancing Ledge* Jarman describes a party for Sir Francis Rose, where Jean Cocteau brought 21 sailor boys as a gift to Francis for his 21st birthday.) After the dark-blue outdoor and chiaroscuro indoor scenes, the blaze of light that fills the room is itself invigorating, and the music is witty and cheerful to the point of frenzy. Ariel, master of ceremonies in white jacket and bow tie, remains an onlooker but seems close to contentment amidst this bevy of sweating men. Shakespeare's nautical concerns are brilliantly fused with Jarman's homoerotic theme. If this *Tempest* is Prospero's dream, the dance routine is the symbolic fulfillment of repressed desire. It is liberating and parodic at the same time. But it is also an apt entertainment for a Miranda who has been isolated from humankind and now bubbles over with delight. "How many goodly creatures are there here!" indeed (V.i.182).

Next to appear are Caliban and his fellow conspirators, with Trinculo, dressed as a drag queen, eliciting wolf whistles from the sailor lads. In Shakespeare's play Stephano and Trinculo do in fact don the "trumpery" by which Prospero has diverted them from their murderous scheme, but Jarman gives their frivolity a characteristic twist. Then Ariel's wizardry plucks down a shower of rose petals, which becomes a deluge when supplemented by the contents of the sailors' upturned hats. We view the beaming bride and groom through this confetti, until down the florally carpeted corridor formed by the naval guard of honor walk Iris, Ceres,

Elizabeth Welch sings "Stormy Weather" in Derek Jarman's The Tempest. (BRITISH FILM INSTITUTE)

and Juno rolled into one—Elisabeth Welch, Sycorax's antitype, a black woman in the sophisticated garb of 1920s chanteuse, golden as a sunflower. With feathery imitation cornstalks in her hair, she conveys the promise of the harvest goddess and the reminder of pain from the "brave new world": the pain of racial difference in a world of slavery, the pain of sexual relationships in a world of inconstancy. The text of Harold Arlen's "Stormy Weather," in Welch's marvelously soulful rendition, harmonizing music and tempest, resonates with echoes from the rest of the film and from Shakespeare's play:

> Don't know why, there's no sun up in the sky,
> Stormy weather, since my man and I ain't
>   together,
> Keeps raining all the time.
>
> Life is bare, gloom and misery everywhere,
> Stormy weather, just can't get my poor self
>   together,
> I'm weary all the time.
>
> When he went away, the blues walked in and
>   met me,
> If he stays away, old rocking chair will get me,
> All I do is pray the Lord above will let me
> Walk in the sun once more.
>
> I can't go on, everything I had is gone,
> Stormy weather, since my man and I ain't
>   together,
> Keeps rainin' all the time,
> Keeps rainin' all the time.

There is something in "Stormy Weather" for each character to recognize. Caliban hears the sound of slavery and resistance in the classic 12-bar blues, the sound he unwittingly echoed in his own stumbling slave song, "'Ban, 'Ban, Ca-Caliban" (II.ii.184). Miranda and Ferdinand hear the complexities of lovers' relationships exposed. Ariel acknowledges the pain of losing Prospero: "Since my man and I ain't together/Keeps rainin' all the time." A touching close-up shows a sad and pensive Ariel, forefinger brushing his lips, as those lines are sung. Ferdinand and Miranda reassure each other with a tender kiss.

"Can't get my poor self together": the theme of psychic integration is touched on even here. "I can't go on"—"unless I be reliev'd by prayer" (Epi. 16): Prospero will renounce his magic and retire to Milan "where/Every third thought shall be my grave" (V.i.311–12). "Everything I had is gone"—"The cloud-capp'd towers, the gorgeous palaces,/The solemn temples, the great globe itself" (IV.i.152–53).

A blues number is the ideal 20th-century song form to encompass love and hate, vengeance and forgiveness, estrangement and reconciliation; to acknowledge how hard it is to limit desire, proscribe sexuality, exact penitence, or contain suffering. And what song could be more apt to the tempest conjured up by Prospero's so potent art than "Stormy Weather," with its refrain echoing Feste's wistful coda to the reunions and marriages that end *Twelfth Night*: "the rain it raineth every day."

"When he went away, the blues walked in and met me," sings Welch, and the blues have indeed walked in and complicated the jollity. At the end of the song, after Welch's yellow headdress has momentarily drenched the screen in sunshine, this world is plunged back into blue-black night. Ariel picks his way through the deserted ballroom, which looks, now that the lights are out, oddly like an autumnal woodland dell, littered as it is with confetti, streamers, and faded flowers. He clambers onto the vacant "throne," looks toward Prospero, slumped asleep in a chair, gives a rueful smile, glances sadly about the room, falteringly sings "Merrily, merrily, shall I live now" (V.i.93) in a doleful voice, tiptoes past his master, pausing for one last lingering look, runs up a flight of stairs, and vanishes to the sound of beating wings. It is a poignant moment. The camera focuses on a close-up of Prospero, whose breathing serves as background to his sleeptalking voice-over:

> Our revels now are ended. These our actors
> (As I foretold you) were all spirits, and
> Are melted into air, into thin air . . .
> We are such stuff
> As dreams are made on; and our little life
> Is rounded with a sleep. (IV.i.148–58)

Although Jarman maintains an interest in power relations, and the shipwrecked nobles sport the regalia of evangelical imperialism (admiral's cap, scarlet ecclesiastical robes, war medals, military uniform, pendant crucifix), there is, finally, more of "Shakespeare's farewell to his stage" in this film than of "an allegory of colonization." Prospero's release of Ariel and abjuration of his art throb with our knowledge that Shakespeare's genius would soon cease to manifest itself in the creation of new scripts for the London theaters and that his life itself was nearing its end. While the relationship between Prospero and Ariel is at the emotional center of Jarman's *Tempest*, Miranda's guileless teenage response to Ferdinand's courtship and her unaffected joie de vivre may also touch the heart. Greenaway's *Prospero's Books* bombards the ear and eye with stimuli and teases the intellect, but it remains emotionally sterile. Jarman's movie, though often bizarre, engages the feelings; it is genuinely moving, and the emotions it arouses are essentially those aroused by Shakespeare's play. It captures many key aspects of the original, being particularly deft at hinting at the element of psychodrama involving the central trinity of Prospero, Ariel, and Caliban. It raises questions about body and mind, restraint and liberty, freedom and control, desire and fulfillment; it balances joy and sadness, innocence and experience, hope and despair; above all, it powerfully conveys a sense of the shifting boundaries between illusion and reality, waking and dreaming, the playful and the serious, life and art. Jarman's antiestablishment style challenges or mocks "the designs of empire," gender stereotyping, and other forms of ideological policing. But, as every actor of Prospero knows, the speeches that, through their poetic richness, most move an audience are those conveying the playwright-magician's sense of mortality and the impermanence of all earthly things. A memorial to Jarman's mother, as the final frame announces, his *Tempest* stands both as a memento mori and as a monument to a filmmaker of idiosyncratic flair.[11]

—*Diana Harris and MacDonald Jackson*
University of Auckland

NOTES

1. Greenaway's term in his book of the film, *Prospero's Books*.
2. Jarman notes that most American reviews of his *Tempest* "saw it as deliberately wilful, and the *New York Times* mounted an attack which destroyed it in the cinemas there" (206). Frank Kermode slated the film in his review in the *Times Literary Supplement*, May 16, 1980, 553, but granted that "it sustains a mood" and "has a dreamlike, underwater quality, cold, dimly magical."
3. The sensibility exhibited in Jarman's *Tempest* bears a close relation to that defined by Susan Sontag in her "Notes on Camp" in *Against Interpretation and Other Essays* (London: Eyre and Spottiswoode, 1967): 275–89. "Camp" is not "homosexual," but there is considerable overlap. Recent theorizing of gay literature and film, as by Eve Kosofsky Sedgwick in *Between Men*, *Epistemology of the Closet*, and *Tendencies*, has potential application to Jarman's films, but our interest in his *Tempest* is as an example of "Shakespeare on screen."
4. The other is, of course, *The Comedy of Errors*.
5. Jarman shot exteriors on the Northumberland coast near Banburgh Castle, where the viewer assumes the interiors to be, though they were actually shot in Stoneleigh Abbey in Warwickshire. See Samuel Crowl, *Shakespeare Observed: Studies in Performance on Stage and Screen* (Athens: Ohio University Press, 1992): 77. Crowl gives a brief, mainly positive, account of Jarman's film.
6. Two major, Frank Kermode's Arden edition 1954) and Stephen Orgel's Oxford edition (1987), mark the shift in critical thinking.
7. Review in *The Times* (London) of Peter Brook's 1957 production, as quoted by Hayman 178.
8. Especially Bernard J. Paris, "*The Tempest*: Shakespeare's Ideal Solution," in Norman N. Holland, Sidney Homan, and Bernard J. Paris, eds., *Shakespeare's Personality* (Berkeley: University of California Press, 1989): 206–25.
9. However, the BBC/Time Life version of *The Tempest* was released in 1980, after Jarman's film had been made.
10. The connection with Reinhardt and Dieterle is made by John Collick, *Shakespeare, Cinema, and Society* (Manchester, England: Manchester University Press, 1989): 98–103. Collick discusses Jarman's film in rather different terms from ours. David L. Hirst offers some brief observations in his "Text and Performance" booklet on *The Tempest* (London: Macmillan, 1984): 41–60 passim.
11. We are grateful to Maggie Taylor for allowing us to see her notes taken from the Jarman archives in the British Film Institute, London.

WORKS CITED

Greenaway, Peter. *Prospero's Books*. London: Chatto and Windus, 1991.
Harris, Diana. "Stormy Weather: Three Screen Adaptations of *The Tempest*." ANZSA Conference. Perth, Feb. 1994.
Hayman, Ronald. *John Gielgud*. London: Heinemann, 1971.
Jarman, Derek. *Dancing Ledge*. London: Quartet Books, 1984.
Kott, Jan. *Shakespeare Our Contemporary*. London: Methuen, 1964.
Shakespeare, William. *The Tempest*. The Riverside Shakespeare. Ed. G. Blakemare Evans. Boston: Houghton Mifflin, 1974.
Vaughan, Alden T., and Virginia Mason Vaughan. *Shakespeare's Caliban: A Cultural History*. Cambridge, England: Cambridge University Press, 1991.

Returning to Naples: Seeing the End in Shakespeare Film Adaptation

The singular difference between the ending of a Shakespeare play and that of a film adaptation of it is that in the text and on stage the ending is spoken by the characters, whereas on film it is visualized by the camera. Instead of events coming to an end through the characters' words, the endings of recent screen adaptations take place in extensive reframings of the scene, camera movements, and shifts away from the characters and the scene of their end. These interventions of cinematic editing change the image and scene to supplant and supplement the characters' ends in death, marriage, reunion, and farewell with the spaces or places, rather than the moment, of ending. This foregrounding of sight over speech in the narration of the ending alters the event from a temporal to a more spatial one. In so doing, it draws attention to another seeing of the play, in a difference unique to the medium and its means of presenting it, and to a cinematic culture of reproduction and consumption that demands its own, additional ending in a visual equivalent of the last word. In this sense, the displacements produced by the closing images clearly show the excess and the slippage of holding the play in place. Comparable to Prospero's verbal crossing back from the island to Naples in his epilogue, the pressure of concluding and returning from the story to the real world in which it belongs is felt in a supplementarity of spaces, self-conscious and surprising, interjected at the end and after it. The closing visual sequences thus represent the extra narration, or question, of where we should place the reproduction of the text. Negotiating the point of exit from the story, then, involves seeing rather than speaking one's way out of it. This essay examines the differences that cinematic reproduction makes to the endings of Shakespeare in several recent film versions of the plays, in terms of the more—or less—that we see, of the other, alternative ending, and of the medium of cinematic space and visuality as a medium of revising through re-visioning.

An ending can be thought of as constituting the finitude of the plot, and it can fulfill, resist, and transform what Frank Kermode has described as the "need for ends consonant with the past" (88). All modern production of Shakespeare, however, is properly speaking reproduction, and therefore has to conclude double pasts: that of the events represented in the play, and that of the particular production's interaction with the audience's prior knowledge and expectations of the "original" play, or even of other productions of it. According to how intertextual exchange has directed or disposed the form of the production, what Patrice Pavis terms "the context of utterance" (90) has, by the time we reach the end, refigured the events of the play in specific intertextual and intercultural terms. Consequently, the sense of an ending works toward multiple and disparate ends: of plot, the cultural framing of Shakespeare, the competition with Shakespeare for authorship or with other productions for uniqueness, to name only the most obvious of the ends of reperformance. Pavis proposes that the mise-en-scène of the staging orders the confrontation between the dramatic text and its performance: "the fictional universe of the performance encompasses and permeates the fictional universe of the text uttered on stage, furnishing it with a specific context of utterance; and the fictional universe of the performance is liable to be at any moment contradicted and broken up from within by the text uttered in performance" (94). In cinematic reproduction, not only is the mise-en-scène much more dense than on stage and more equal in status to the actors as part of the total image, but mobile framing and editing between simultaneous spaces combine to retell and resell Shakespeare in terms of the performance of the *image*. The tensions of reproducing Shakespeare through the visual alterity of the cinematic medium can be seen in the strikingly divisive endings of recent film adaptations that reframe the ending and produce multiple spaces in which it takes place. In the recent box-office hit adaptation of *Romeo and Juliet*, *Shakespeare in Love*, the filmically realistic world of Elizabethan London is set dialectically against, yet often merges with, the theatrical space where the play is rehearsed and performed, thereby providing for a parallel storyline and a reopening of the question, after the first successful performance of *Romeo and Juliet* is over and the title characters are dead, "How is this to end?" (Norman and Stoppard 149).

A play's ending is crucial and defining to how it is remembered (and the reproduction of that ending to how a production or adaptation will be remembered). To audiences participating in the reenactment of the play, it is the anticipated point of arrival, but while current film adaptations often reproduce the known ending as a highly ritualized event, the ritual is threatened with disruption or displaced by the counteraction of alternative, surprise endings. Prolonged, intense stillness surrounds the famous and familiar last moments of Gielgud speaking Prospero's epilogue in Peter Greenaway's *Prospero's Books*, Hamlet's dying speech in Kenneth Branagh's version of the play, and Romeo and Juliet's separate approaches to death in Baz Luhrmann's *Romeo + Juliet*. This stillness solemnizes not only the deaths and farewells of the characters, but the closure of the ritual of rewatching these plays. Marking the space, or more precisely the setting, of the ending, the long runways that frame the spectator's view of the characters in all three films function as a symbol for the ritual progression to the end. Above all, there is the repeated use of an unusually long take, with a very slow track-and-crane out from the scene to a long shot. This kind of shot deliberately protracts the moment of the spectator's final gaze, creating and indulging in a scene of visual farewell, for instance in Luhrmann's crane shot of the dead lovers. The extravagant flooding of the image with candle flames in this scene, the clapping of the actors in *Prospero's Books*, and the soundtracks of all these films self-consciously produce, and invoke the spectator's conscious consumption of, the ending as a ritual of memory, nostalgia, and farewell.[1]

Stephen Heath points out that the long shot is a "master shot" derived directly from Quattrocento codes of perspective, which center the spectator as the subject of an ideal vision: "The long shot . . . in classical narrative cinema . . . subsequently develops as the constant figure of this embracing and authoritative vision, providing the conventional close to a film, the final word of its reality" (384). While Luhrmann's shot does produce an idealized image of the lovers' death, this idealization is placed at an unrealistically high angle above the lovers (as it is throughout this scene), creating a sensational effect that increases as the camera rises. The shot destabilizes the authoritative, unified vision of *Romeo and Juliet* by drawing attention to the spectator's access to, and indeed constituting the excess of, spectacle from that particular viewing position in the scene. Heath cites Edward Branigan on the disturbance created by this kind of camera position: "To the extent that the camera is located in an 'impossible' place, the narration questions its own origin, that is, suggests a shift in narration" (quoted in Heath 401). In this instance, "the impossible place" represents the pleasure of reenvisioning the scene: the only movements to continue the event are the camera's ever-so-slow withdrawal and the flickering of the recapitulatory images, and these together change that event of the lovers' death to the scene of our desire for and in it.

Explicit ritualization in these adaptations, however, neither seals the ending as inviolable, nor performs our attachment to it as such, but has the reverse effect of confronting the audience with what it expects and desires from watching Shakespeare. These strategies promote a self-consciousness about the desire for ritual reenacting and rewatching, such that desire becomes the field of play to which the tension and excitement of a challenge, a possible rupture to the ritual, is equally vital. In this sense, the scene of ritual closure and the scene of the alternative ending(s) stage a conflict that is not actually a conflict but a meta-drama of completing, of our own knowingness. Hence the storyline of John Madden's *Shakespeare in Love* depends quite openly upon the complicities of both our interest that *Romeo and Juliet* be written and successfully staged, and our pleasure in the obstacles to its success. In Branagh's *Hamlet*, the repeated cross-cutting from Elsinore to brief, silent images of Fortinbras and his army generates a mounting anxiety, at first undefined, but later crystallizing in a real threat to the ending as a vast battalion runs down the avenue toward Elsinore and assaults it, while so much remains yet uncompleted in the last scene taking place inside it. The continuous disruption of and return to the scene of the play's ending here constitute the rhythm of a confrontation between not only the text and its performance, but the mediums of theater and cinema. What is interesting in Branagh's reproduction of another ending to *Hamlet* is his expansion of another space, outside Elsinore, one that ostensibly provides the plot with an historical "context of utterance" closer to home, but which makes itself felt as the cinematic and cultural space of the scale and spectacle of Hollywood historical epics. The cut from Horatio's farewell to Hamlet to the second-story gallery as Fortinbras's soldiers crash through the windows in mass synchrony, stormtrooper style, clearly presents a spatially divided scene, and the invasion of

Hollywood spectacle into the play's ending. Thus the climax as it is reproduced is that of the competition between these two scenes of very different fulfillment, Hamlet's and Fortinbras's, and the split-second timing of their explosions in a single place. Hamlet's killing of Claudius and his last speech are made partner to, altered by, and ultimately subsumed in the context of Fortinbras's military coup, and this accounts for the strange sense of meta- or intertextual defeat as Fortinbras is crowned and takes over Denmark, a defeat objectified in the smashing of King Hamlet's statue.

To stress that another ending is produced as another space, and an alternative sight line, is to stress the editing of narrative space by which the story is redefined for cinematic cultures of watching. In both Branagh's *Hamlet* and Luhrmann's *Romeo + Juliet*, cross-cutting produces the double vision of "how it might otherwise end," by editing an "unseen" into the original endings. Luhrmann creates the contestational space of a possible alternative ending that would avert the expected tragedy, not by doubling locations as Branagh does, but by breaking up a unified scene into parts in conflict. The editing generates a cliffhanger by alternating between extreme close-ups that split the lovers spatially: when the close-up shows us Juliet's face stirring, Romeo is out of the frame, putting the ring on her hand, and when it shows her fingers moving, Romeo is again off-screen, at her face.[2] Thus the mechanism of dramatic irony that turns on Romeo's misapprehension is superseded by one that turns on his missed sight. This supplanting of what he does not know for what he does not see in the kind of tragic mistake made performs cinema's ingenious extension or appropriation of the verbal in the terms of the visual. But it also abandons the space of time between the two events of Romeo's death and Juliet's awakening (and the significance of that timing, however close) for the virtuoso effect of splitting the embrace of the lovers' bodies, dislocating a single event spatially. Although stage productions have also merged the two moments,[3] Luhrmann's reproduction of the mistake in terms of the simultaneously artificial and hyper-real close-up parodies the irony of fate with a trick of sight *played by the camera*; it is the build-up of conflict in the stimulus to the spectator's sight, not knowledge, that creates the suspense and delivers the shock of the climax.

The climax to this sequence of alternating close-ups is in fact preemptive, arriving before time at the instant Juliet's eyes snap open to look straight at us, intensely and abnormally close. The physical shock of her sudden awakening at such close range, the possibility that she may be just in time to change the ending, and the unexpected citation of Zeffirelli's version, which used the same extreme close-up of Juliet's eyes to capture her reaction when Romeo catches her hand, combine to rupture the membrane of the screen separating seer and spectacle by "returning the gaze," and so exposing the spectator's watching.[4] In the conflated look of different Juliets (Shakespeare's, Luhrmann's, Zeffirelli's, our own), the spectator's part of remembering the play, while desiring a difference, is confronted and thus performed into the scene of reproduction. This direct, close-up meeting of the character's eyes with the spectator's occurs at crucial points in almost all the endings of recent adaptations, as an inevitable fold in the visual re-narration at which the spectator becomes object, included in the field of the spectacle.

One of the chief difficulties of discussing the looking structures in (and of applying theories of the gaze to) situations of cinematic watching is that the camera's eye cannot be taken as the spectator's: its point of view is always as if it were our own, and is not seamlessly joinable or fully identifiable with the spectator's own sense of seeing. The camera's eye has the double function of both presenting to our eyes and pretending to be our eyes, and this break or hinge in the jointure between the camera's point of view and the spectator's seeing is particularly felt when we are made to see against the grain. In the cinematic reproduction of Shakespeare, the camera is almost obliged to discomfort the spectator's sight as part of the difference of reperformance that it asserts. But the specific difference that the eye of the camera stands to make to the always intertextualized watching of Shakespeare is that it positions, and indeed creates, subject-object relations of viewing for the spectator: just as reproduction looks back at us through Juliet's eyes in Luhrmann's film, it can enforce an alienated subjectivity through point-of-view shots. The closing moments of Branagh's film circulate the exchange of looks through Fortinbras's point of view, where the spectator alternately adopts Rufus Sewell's cold gaze around Elsinore, and is in turn stared straight back at (and quite menacingly, too). The looking structures perform against the grain of the viewer's subjective identification with Hamlet in the space of the ending, and produce the outsider and contender—for the throne and the ending—as the focal point, the subject matter.[5] Fortinbras's gaze is another sight line, which acts to change the place where events have ended by looking at them differently, but that direct, confrontational difference in point of view is threateningly opaque in that it is narratively inaccessible, unsecured by, and more than, the plot entails—in fact, it takes its place.

Branagh's film returns to and ends at the cinematic space outside Elsinore: following a dissolve that subtly transforms the image of Hamlet's body into one dressed for his state burial, the camera slowly tracks back and up to reveal the unexpected, enormous spectacle of amassed mourners in black arrayed outside Elsinore, at the same time gradually losing sight of Hamlet. This movement away from the scene of the play's end is also pronounced and self-conscious in the films of Luhrmann, Greenaway, and Madden. Whereas Shakespeare usually leaves the characters' return undramatized, as the expected closure deferred until after the play has ended, the movement of images forms a visual crossing back, a passage of exit out from the place of the story. Its changes of the scene or place of the ending appear to proffer a new framework for capturing the play, that is, to use space as context, and to effect that crossing as a connecting with scenes of habitual contemporary viewing. So Branagh re-places *Hamlet* in the Hollywood epic depicting the fall of regimes, and Luhrmann relocates *Romeo and Juliet* in a news broadcast on TV. However, the successive and conspicuous reframing or revisualizing of the space where the film ends does not so much resituate the scene as displace it, because the cinematic stylishness with which images of a changing narrative space are crossed and joined, especially through mobile framing and dissolves, puts the performance of transition itself on display. When the process of editing becomes the primary action in this way, the scenes become illusionistic, screen spaces rather than representations of a real context, defined by their dissolving into and disruption of each other, and by the visual pleasure and surprise of their combination.

As one might expect, it is the figure (not the idea) of the author that provides Shakespearean film adaptations with both a subject and site for transforming the ending, in the correlative of his creative imagination. Greenaway's *Prospero's Books* maps its close onto the author's, while Madden's *Shakespeare in Love* closes with Shakespeare's affirmation of his art; these two films offer a neat contrast between how the image of Shakespeare takes its place in the narration that ends at the ending, and at the beginning, of the author. In Greenaway's final long take, the camera tracks slowly out from a close-up on Gielgud-as-Prospero-as-Shakespeare's face speaking the epilogue in what appears to be the ending, but as the camera moves out, his face is surprisingly disclosed and reframed as a two-dimensional image on a screen. This movement recontains the actor-dramatist's art within the filmmaker's, and *makes space* in front of that screen-within-a-screen for the "live" eruption of three-dimensional images that break up and obscure the long farewell shot on it. Greenaway thus returns the plenitude of seeing to the spectator, after it had apparently been shed in the stripped-bare image of Gielgud's face, and invokes our pleasure in the renewal of "magical" sight when Ariel dives into sudden water. As counteraction to the relinquishment of art, Greenaway's visual magic here takes over from Prospero's and Shakespeare's. This sequence is a virtuoso display of cinematic showmanship that is unsecured by narrative motivation, unlike Prospero's or Shakespeare's arts; it is a meta-performative rejection of the return at the end of *The Tempest*, through a reassertion of the action of the magic eye of what cannot any longer be called the camera, because it does not mediate objects as images, but generates them. So even as the running of the child Ariel into our gaze to leap out of the frame prompts our uncomplicated identification with his joy, the increasingly slowed motion defines that pleasure of anticipation in terms of the artifice by which it is prolonged, expanded, and arrested. The story is superseded by the art—or the technology.

In *Shakespeare in Love*, the tragic ending of the play is a success in the real life of the film, and the tragic ending in real life is deflected into the start of a comedy. This circle of tragedy and comedy, which turns life back into art and endings into beginnings, is accomplished by revolving between three scenes that dissolve continuously into each other: the writer Will Shakespeare at his desk, his words being written on the page, and the underwater vision of his imagination. The effect of these dissolves is not merely to merge different scenes, but to treat the cinematic screen as literally a screen that absorbs and merges other mediums of representation and action: the picture-perfect Shakespeare, writing on the page, water. More precisely, the screen converts the different physical natures of these mediums into the common currency of the cinematic image by drawing attention to their framing and filming—only the camera can show action underwater. In the visual match of the parchment and blank beach, they become merging images of a ground, onto which the tiny figure of Viola materializes in front of the huge colon being written after her name. While the sequence seems directed toward a narrative epilogue, the merging mediums in fact persuade the spectator out of the need to conclude, and into an imaginary circle starting afresh: the voice-over of the author narrating the prelude to *Twelfth Night* as a "new beginning," for Viola uses Miranda's words at the opening of *The Tempest* to integrate the scenes of Shakespeare's last play with his first as a professional. Thus the rhythms of the music and editing track a passage out of this adaptation's story that is actually a recursive starting again. Indeed, *Shakespeare in Love* returns to Naples in a celebratory fashion, by beginning all over again where Prospero and Shakespeare ended, at the new place that is also the old one of Illyria, Prospero's island, America.[6]

In these film adaptations of Shakespeare, the action of visual metamorphosis replaces plot conclusion and resolution as the end of cinematic reproduction. This transformative drive seems both inescapable and confounding: it satisfies the compound imperatives to metamorphosis exerted by the cinematic medium, the differences of culture, the reauthorizing and reengagement of the story. In short, it represents the desire to say—or rather to show and see—something more as the end of the story. At the same time, the dissolves, reframings, and visual matches resist or avoid conclusion by reflexively deferring the placing of the story onto the medium of representation: the virtual space of the cinematic, televisual, or electronic image.

In the meta-narrative of our relation to Shakespeare, what might otherwise be perceived as a fictional space in which the story concludes, transforms into a virtual one in which such conclusions change form or format, rather than shift ground. In an alternative ending to the film, packaged with the Collector's Series release of *Shakespeare in Love*, Viola is met on the beach by two men, one white, one black, to whom she speaks her first line in *Twelfth Night*, "What country is this, friends?" and they answer "This is America"; her reply is "Well then, good." Yet another ending was scripted but not filmed, in which she moves past the line of trees blocking our vision at the shore to discover behind them the gleaming towers of Manhattan.[7] These alternatives, like a shadow behind the ending released, manifest what we already know in retrospect, that the film arrives at America—the Academy Awards, to be precise. More significantly, the proliferation of endings and the choice to leave "another shore" unnamed indicates the reluctance to form and fix a framing image of our space for Shakespeare's play, or the reproduction of it. The transformative movements, then, take the place of any concrete representation of our context for remaking Shakespeare. Yet they also represent the effort to break the limits of a defining position. Walter Benjamin noted that "[w]ith the close-up, space expands; with slow motion, movement is extended . . . Evidently a different nature opens itself to the camera than opens to the naked eye—if only because an unconsciously penetrated space is substituted for a space consciously explored by man" (229–30). In an ambivalent relation to this "different nature" of virtual space, each of these four films rejects dimensionality in favor of a flat two-dimensional image for the closing shot: Branagh's blocks, Luhrmann's television screen, Madden's beach, Greenaway's map, all present the endpoint of adaptation as a surface which seals off the spectator's interaction in any space at the level of the gaze.

—*Yong Li Lan*
National University of Singapore

NOTES

1. The violins of Patrick Doyle's soundtrack are particularly noticeable in Branagh's *Hamlet* during all the key speeches of the play, marking out their value and evoking a nostalgic response to them.
2. This tactic of alternating close-ups is repeated in the second cliffhanger scripted into the ending in the screenplay, which was not part of the film as released, where Father Lawrence nearly succeeded in getting the gun from Juliet and forestalling her suicide (Pearce and Luhrmann 159–60).
3. In the Royal Shakespeare Theatre's production in 1976, with Ian McKellen and Francesca Annis in the title roles, Juliet began to move her hand over Romeo's back, unnoticed by him, as he held her in his arms during his dying kiss.
4. The notion of the "returned gaze" has been extensively theorized, especially by Merleau-Ponty, Lacan, and Sartre, in terms of the otherness it produces in the subjective act of seeing, and some discussions of the relations between spectacle and spectator have adapted theories of the gaze to the situations of performance. Elizabeth Klaver, for instance, discusses how "the exchange of an object for a subject in the spectacle that looks back . . . unmasters the privilege of viewing the world (or visual art) as a representation, but also catches up the relations between viewer and viewed in a performative modality" (312).
5. Russell Jackson's "Film Diary" records Rufus Sewell's performative appearance in this scene: he "looks as though he really wants it, but knows it's easily won. Intense eyes, darkly handsome, calmly self-assertive," and Branagh's remark: "no glam spared on this film" (197).
6. The last long shot, held throughout the titles, is scripted as "DISSOLVE slowly to VIOLA walking away up the beach towards her brave new world" (Norman and Stoppard 155).
7. I am indebted to Russell Jackson, the production's textual advisor, for this information.

WORKS CITED

Benjamin, Walter. "The Work of Art in the Age of Mechanical Reproduction." *Illuminations*. Ed. Hannah Arendt. Trans. Harry Zohn. London: Fontana, 1992. 211–44.

Heath, Stephen. "Narrative Space." *Narrative, Apparatus, Ideology*. Ed. Philip Rosen. New York: Columbia University Press, 1986. 379–420.

Jackson, Russell. "Film Diary." *Kenneth Branagh*, Hamlet *by William Shakespeare: Screenplay and Introduction*. London: Chatto & Windus, 1996. 179–213.

Kermode, Frank. *The Sense of an Ending*. New York: Oxford University Press, 1967.

Klaver, Elizabeth. "Spectatorial Theory in the Age of Media Culture." *NTQ* 11:44 (1995): 309–21.

Pavis, Patrice. "From Text to Performance." *Performing Texts*. Eds. Michael Issacharoff and Robin F. Jones. Philadelphia: University of Pennsylvania Press, 1988. 86–100.

Pearce, Craig, and Baz Luhrmann. *William Shakespeare's* Romeo & Juliet: *The Contemporary Film, The Classic Play*. New York: Bantam Doubleday Dell, 1996.

Black and White as Technique in Orson Welles's *Othello*

In his film adaptation of *Othello* (1952) Orson Welles does much to strip Shakespeare's play of its racial thematics, or at least to reduce racial difference to the fundamentally cinematic grid of black-and-white photography. The play of light and shadow achieves clarity, focus, and distinction without resorting to effects of high contrast. The editing is fast, at times dizzying, as one would expect from the director of *Citizen Kane*. But the quick cutting and splicing of the film, like the way it is lighted, serves to keep black and white separate. A firm geometry of vertical and horizontal axes reinforces the grid of black and white, though there is no fixed mapping of one color onto one axis of spatial orientation. These elements of distinction, separation, and refusal to blur are best epitomized in the frequent use of barred gates, iron cages, trellised pergolas, the slatted floor of a bathhouse, the latticed rigging of a ship, and the like, to cast a grid of shadows across the faces of actors and the walled spaces that enclose them. These foregrounded patterns unsubtly but powerfully foreshadow the fatality that is in process of imposing itself, even as early as Welles's decision to open the film at its fatal terminus, with a death march, unfolding on the horizontal axis, of the bodies of Othello (Welles in blackface) and Bianca (the always pale, unpowdered, and ethereally white Suzanne Cloutier), suddenly intercut by Iago dragged on an unceremonious diagonal across the funeral scene, stuffed in a cage, and hoisted vertically up the city walls.[1] The contrast of the black and white faces of the lovers in death sets the stage for Welles's consistent portrayal of them in the life scenes to follow, and the framing of Iago's face by the black-and-white grid of the barred cage points to a relentless image pattern in the film: the coordinates of black and white determine a smothering grid, an inescapable prison, a fatal claustrophobia.[2] There is no space for soft-focus, blurring-of-boundaries sentimentality in Welles's cinema.[3]

Insofar as the film stresses them, Othello's racial self-doubts are the effect of the director's technique and the camera's point of view, not the passions of the man. For Welles the demise of Othello is a function of seeing himself in the eyes of his detractors, of hearing himself belittled by tendentious gossip as unworthy of Desdemona's love and therefore fit to be cuckolded. Welles cuts the references in the text to the possibility of Othello's impotence and thus avoids Shakespeare's suggestion that racism and sexual malfunction are mutually implicated. It is not the case in this film that Othello's racial self-doubts either give rise to or are caused by sexual self-doubts. This Othello is vigorous, forceful, of deep and resonant voice, and his self-doubts in soliloquy are reduced in the screenplay, or else spoken with such stiff and oracular orotundity that they scarcely qualify as self-doubt. Othello questions his racial fitness only when preyed upon directly by Iago in dialogue. In the temptation scene, Othello lets Iago insinuate himself by echoing him, thereby hollowing him out and making a "monster" (3.3.107) of him. In the latter part of this scene, a convex mirror sits on a dressing table at close range to the actor's face. It creates a fish-eye effect, a blurring and an elongation, a stretching of the face beyond the point of familiarity. At intervals we see Othello from above his rear shoulder reflected in the mirror as he intermittently catches uneasy sight of himself. The effect is of an anamorphic Othello bloating and about to break with jealousy. When Iago, standing behind the mirror, puzzles Othello with the question of why Desdemona failed to affect one "of her own clime, complexion, and degree" (3.3.230), Othello averts his gaze from the mirror image precisely when he hears the word "complexion." His reflected image is distorted, his spirits a little dashed, and whatever sense of racial integrity he had is deferred. Welles's formal technique as director, not the emotion of Welles the actor, is what expresses the chink in Othello's psychic armor. Race is reduced to a mirror trick, an image that does not reflect the ego's ideal image of itself since the camera lens looks awry.[4]

Welles employs a dizzying range of optical and audio distortions to indicate Othello's lapse into madness: fracturing the hero's sight lines, enclosing him in small spaces, using fast editing and audio reverberation to perform the echoing of Iago's consciousness in his head. The fevering of jealousy in 4.1 results when Othello gets the proof that he so desperately craves. Iago stations him behind the slit of a wall where he is made the captive audience of a masquerade. He becomes framed as the cuckold whose eye seeks voyeuristically to frame others in adultery; he gets the very "fate" (3.3.168) he desires. Even as he thinks he is framing Cassio in the act of gesturing and talking about sex, Othello's vigilance traps him in the narrow aperture of a camera obscura. Exterior light enters through the slit that circumscribes and is fully occupied by Othello's eyes—the eye-slit of the dark, enclosed stairwell where he stands unobserved. Othello achieves his privileged position as voyeur only at a price: he becomes diminished to a mere mechanical part, the oculus in a machine for imaging the ocular proof, a precursor of the moving picture camera behind which actor/director Welles frames the shot.[5] As Othello gazes through the narrow oculus, from a much wider range the camera returns the perspective and, unbeknownst to Othello, frames him as a partial pair of eyes detached from the body. These eyes bulge in excitation.[6] The voyeur is all eyes, only eyes. The reduction to eyes is important in indicating the centrality of the ocular for constituting Othello as the subject of jealous desire. He receives aural and visual images in inverted form, mistaking the referent of Cassio's flirtations to be Desdemona rather than Bianca. In the narrow and distorting perspective that crowds Othello's perception, the handkerchief that he sees is divorced from its proper context of purloined love token and is taken instead as the ocular proof positive of Desdemona's willful betrayal.

Jealousy-induced vertigo results as much from a disequilibrium of the ear as from a narrowing of perspective of the eye. The encounter between Cassio and Bianca which Iago stages for Othello's eyes depends for its effect as much on what is not heard as on the dumb show that is partially seen. The soundtrack manifests variations in volume, echo, and reverberation that depend on whether the sound is recorded from Othello's position within the receiving chamber or from that of Cassio, Iago, and Bianca without. The former is distorted, the latter clear. Othello's perch places him as much in the position of a muffled ear as in that of a camera obscura. Iago plays the flirt as he laughs and slaps Cassio in the face and teases him about Bianca's doting. His remark that "I never knew a woman love man so" (4.1.110) excites much laughter in Cassio. Othello hears this out of context, for he conflates automatically and unthinkingly Cassio's "customer" (4.1.119) Bianca with his wife, whom he will label "public commoner" (4.2.73) and "cunning whore of Venice" (4.2.89) in the brothel scene.

Welles grants to Iago a field of operations much wider than Othello's enclosure. After Cassio departs, Iago crosses over the threshold between Cassio and Othello, moving freely back and forth between perspectives—in front of and behind the chink—whereas Othello remains fixed in his station. As at other moments of psychic intensity in the film (for instance, immediately after Othello stabs himself), Othello's head swims in vertigo, in this case due to the echoes that hollow out what he has always assumed to be true: that Desdemona is honest. He is an easy subject for Iago's powers of suggestion, the tempting rationalizations that insinuate themselves under the confounding reverberations and vertiginous images. As in the temptation scene, the boundaries between Othello and Iago blur, unlike the never-merging blackness of Othello and whiteness of Desdemona. In what follows I want to turn again to how Welles keeps Othello and Desdemona separate from each other, even in the scenes that they share, and how the grid that separates them from each other also distinguishes their relation from the echoic fusion of Othello and Iago.[7]

The scene of Desdemona's death achieves its remarkable climax by once again deracializing race, by reducing the murderous conflict of black and white to a geometric-cinematographic grid. Or so I view the film, as a vehicle for bravura technical achievement at the expense of the anatomizing of the politics of representation that we value today in dramatic production and its criticism. As it approaches Desdemona's bedroom and overlooks her bedtime toilet, Othello's frame casts large and menacing shadows on the wall, making of the intruder a virtual caricature of the faceless villain in black. Welles cuts to Othello's eyes regarding the tumbling down of Desdemona's hair through a jealousy frame that atypically casts no shadows across her face. She remains bright white, inviolate, uncontaminated by the gaze of Othello behind the jealousy bars, yet her white face recalls nothing so much as a corpse. Even after Othello puts out the light, Desdemona, laid out upon the wedding bed, continues to beam forth marmoreal whiteness, abruptly crossed by Othello's face which rises like a hungry predator on the vertical axis from beneath the bed.

On the soundtrack the gasps of the chorus rise and throb as Othello mounts Desdemona in an act of murder and sex at once, her mouth sealed shut under his lips, her face smothered under the upturned wedding sheets. To the psychoanalytic eye the sheets appear to be recast as an undulant white undergarment, under whose folds the lips strive vainly to enunciate their innocent purity. Welles's climactic dream sequence performs a wish: that the sex-murder and sealing with a kiss realize in fantasy the (impossible) restoring of the hymen by reclosing the orifice of the devirginated bride. The lost hymen, whose symbolic analogue is the stained and lost handkerchief, is recovered by the white fabric that stops Desdemona's mouth. Cloth re-covers the broken hymen and makes it whole again.[8] In the arresting image of Othello pulling the sheet taut over Desdemona's face, traces of her eyes and lips bulge through the whiteness in a desperate effort to communicate, but only silence issues from the veil turned death mask. As the searing whiteness of the garment presses indelibly against Desdemona's face, it manifests all the panicked marks of a rape victim struggling beneath a gauze stocking. The attempt to restore the woman to virginity (via the wedding sheet) is paradoxically an act of rape (via the suffocating gauze stocking). Othello's internal confusion of love and death is made visible on film in the conflation of the lovers' sheet with the instrument for snuffing out the beloved.[9]

The way that Othello towers vertically over the recumbent Desdemona in her death scene echoes other scenes in which the camera's performance of the vertical sublime designates the threat of death: Iago hoisted in his cage up the city walls; Iago plunging his sword into Roderigo cringing beneath the slats in the bathhouse floor; Othello threatening to throw Iago over the ramparts if he is lying to him about Desdemona's treachery while the camera plummets to waves crashing on the rocks below. At the end of the film the vertical precipitance into blackout down the city wall terminates in the gentle light upon calm waters of the credit sequence.[10] This is a welcome reprieve from the association of plunging verticality with violence elsewhere in the film. The camera returns to a mode seen only once before in the film, in Venice: the gentle flickering and mingling of white light and black shadow on the waters, so different from the tempestuous, breaking seas of Cyprus. Rippling water raising light and shadow by turns unfixes the rigid axes of black-white and vertical-horizontal—the deathly grid, the menacing cage—and provides a brief glimpse of the beautiful in a film otherwise dominated by the melodramatic sublime. The score swerves from the portentous and hectoring bass harpsichords of the death scenes to the sweet détente of the lute, redolent of calm and release. Only in the credit sequence and in the impressionistic Venetian scenes does Welles allow black and white to mingle, and then only in the register of an aesthetic effect of light, outside the context of race. Its cosmopolite waters and dissolving frame reflect Venice's unmenacing urbanity. But Cyprus more accurately represents Welles's vision of a disciplinary and repressive culture, one in which the camera captures its subjects framed in a cage, distorted in a mirror, or barred in shadow. The cinematic frame displaces the textual and characterological thematics of race.

—*James W. Stone*
The American University in Cairo

NOTES

1. The cage or its shadow alone will hang at various points in the film against the city walls. Empty, it beckons towards the fate that is it is foredestined to accomplish. It is a lure whose emptiness mocks as well as a symbol of the ultimate public display of Iago's villainy. Anthony Davies examines the grid of bars and cages, the "trap motif," in *Shakespeare and the Moving Image*, eds. Anthony Davies and Stanley Wells (Cambridge, England: Cambridge University Press, 1994), pp. 196–210.

2. Jack J. Jorgens distinguishes between an Othello style in Venice and an Iago style in Cyprus. The former is monumental, open, and stately; the latter is claustrophobic, vertiginous, and fragmentary, and its cinematography revels in distorted angles and grotesque shadows. *Shakespeare on Film* (Lanham, Md.: University Press of America, 1991), pp. 175–180.

3. A relevant contrast to Welles's cinematography is that of Franco Zeffirelli, whose *Otello* is a tedious blur of emotion bathed in melting soft focus. Oliver Parker's 1995 *Othello*, photographed in sumptuous color, dwells fetishistically on rich costumes and furnishings at the expense of psychological probing. I have been unable to carry out my initial project of comparing the Welles to the Parker film since I was unable, in my far-flung locale, to obtain a video of the latter by mail.

4. In the next scene, after Othello gets upset when Desdemona tries to bind his pained forehead with her napkin, he approaches another convex mirror, this one mounted on the wall, in which he sees himself from close range and Desdemona reflected at some distance behind him. Then the camera pulls away for a medium shot of Othello in the

mirror with Desdemona's image seeming to stand above him, haunting him like a ghost. The locus of Othello's self-doubt lies not in his psychology but in the play of images.

5. In *Techniques of the Observer: On Vision and Modernity in the Nineteenth Century* (Cambridge, Mass.: MIT Press, 1990), Jonathan Crary offers an unwonted genealogy of the camera obscura that sets it distinctly apart from still and motion picture photography, but he does see it as a model for the interiority of the mind.

6. The bug-eyed Welles is a favorite target of critics eager to point to the actor's penchant for exorbitant overacting and canned melodrama. See Walter Kerr, "Wonder Boy Welles," *Theatre Arts* 35 (September 1951), pp. 50–51. One also sees in Welles's reduction of Othello to a caged animal's bulging eyes a capitulation to racial stereotyping of the type employed by Othello's persecutors, especially Iago, whose purpose in directing this scene is to degrade Othello to a victim who rages unwittingly on cue. Iago makes the caged bull jump at the drop of a handkerchief.

7. Critics are struck by Welles's much greater emphasis on the Iago-Othello bond than on Othello and Desdemona's marriage. The gay thematic upstages both the heterosexual and racial motives. See David Thomson, *Rosebud: The Story of Orson Welles* (New York: Knopf, 1996), p. 299.

8. Othello's fantasy of "revirginating" the woman whom he tragically initiated into sexuality is most cogently analyzed by Janet Adelman, *Suffocating Mothers: Fantasies of Maternal Origin in Shakespeare's Plays*, Hamlet *to* The Tempest (New York: Routledge, 1992), pp. 63–75.

9. After repeated viewings of this scene, I find myself unable to determine whether the instrument for suffocating Desdemona is the wedding sheet or her white wedding dress. The hem appears to suggest the latter, but most critics opt for the former. Jorgens provocatively assumes that the choke-cloth is the handkerchief! This interpretation begs the psychoanalytic reading in spades: the virgin love token, transformed into a sign of promiscuity, in turn becomes the agent of murder/revirgination. Jorgens points out that "the Moor makes a symbol of love a hideous death mask" (182).

10. Anthony Davies sees the blackouts after the funeral procession at the start of the film and again before the final credits as Welles's way of marking original departures from Shakespeare's text. *Filming Shakespeare's Plays* (Cambridge, England: Cambridge University Press, 1988), pp. 100–118. See also Gregg Andrew Hurwitz, "Transforming text: Iago's infection in Welles's *Othello*," *Word & Image* 13.4 (1997), pp. 333–339.

Nostalgia for Navarre: The Melancholic Metacinema of Kenneth Branagh's *Love's Labour's Lost*

With *Love's Labour's Lost* (2000), Branagh's narrative image found its animating logic in a generic transformation.[1] In what was by far the most radical interpretive gesture of his career, *Love's Labour's Lost* was mooted as reinventing one of Shakespeare's lesser-known plays as a Hollywood musical from the 1930s.[2] Prerelease machinery reiterated the singularity of the metamorphosis time and time again, contributing to the forcefully generic coherence of the film's intertextual relay. In the newly diverse context of Shakespearean cinematic appropriation, the potential merging of the drama and a musical in one of the least known plays appeared viable. When Harvey Weinstein of Miramax Films came on board for the American rights, predictions of box-office smashes, Academy Awards, and widespread acclaim ensued. Indeed, such was mogul confidence that *Love's Labour's Lost* was signaled as the first of a new Branagh/Shakespeare movie trilogy.

On release, however, *Love's Labour's Lost* proved not to be the success that had been predicted. Critical comment was divided between a minority that regarded it as a curiosity and a majority that branded it "Branagh's nadir as a director" (Grant 27), "a thing of shreds and patches . . . a failure" (Porter 9). The film, which had cost $8 million, took in less than £350,000 in the United Kingdom and $635,000 in the United States. (Dantrey 42), making it, according to the *Daily Express* reviewer, "one of the biggest box office flops of 2000" ("Ken's Labour's" 39). As a result, the futures of both *Macbeth* and *As You Like It*, the second and third elements of the trilogy, were placed briefly in doubt.

At an early stage in the publicity process, Branagh himself had professed an anxiety about exactly how his generic focus would be received: "What we've done with *Love's Labour's Lost*," he stated, "might provoke hostile debate" (Gristwood 9). Certainly, by any standards, his generic transformation was risky: in the latter half of the 20th century, commercially successful film musicals have been the exception rather than the rule. Moreover, as many critics have failed to appreciate, Branagh's musical is a conscious attempt to recreate a particular period in the history of the musical (the 1930s), rather than an endeavor to offer, as in *Grease* (1978), *Dirty Dancing* (1987), or, *Moulin Rouge* (2001), a contemporary reworking or appropriation of the musical form.[3] Purposefully sited in a reconstruction of a past chronology, *Love's Labour's Lost* further dares the box office by consciously invoking vocabularies at some distance from the modern viewer.

Conventions of the Hollywood musical are everywhere apparent in *Love's Labour's Lost*.[4] Almost three-quarters of the Shakespearean text disappears, ensuring that music registers as the dominant pull on audience attention. As in a traditional musical, the sets are few in number and familiar (library, quadrangle, riverside, and garden). Conventional iconic features include period dress, a combination of gaudy and sepia tones, and a series of impossibly extravagant physical elevations. Choreography is mainly inspired by Hermes Pan's routines in RKO Astaire-Rogers musicals, and most dance numbers are captured in long takes, with full body shots. At most points, the music functions as it would have done in its earlier Hollywood incarnation; that is, it helps to pinpoint romantic connections (couples are formed through the choreographed visuals of Jerome Kern's "I Won't Dance, Don't Ask Me"), to interrupt the narrative with vignettes and interludes (such as in the aquatic rendition of Irving Berlin's "No Strings [I'm Fancy Free]" à la Busby Berkeley); and, most importantly, to propel the plot. In the main, songs are woven into the film fabric, musical lyrics working as a correlative to the play's 16th-century rhetorical expression. Thus Berowne's condemnation of academic monasticism is converted into the George Gershwin and Desmond Carter number "I'd Rather Charleston."

And, when Berowne, contemplating love's elemental power, concludes "And when Love speaks, the voice of all the gods/Make heaven drowsy with the harmony" (Iv.iii.320–21), the film slips smoothly into a joint performance of Irving Berlin's "Cheek to Cheek," with its celestial refrain, "Heaven, I'm in heaven."

Love's Labour's Lost's facsimile of a pivotal period in the history of the musical sets it apart from, to take a Shakespearean instance, Robert Wise and Jerome Robbins's *West Side Story* (1961), a musical that invents as contemporary and conterminous the content of the story and the conventions of the genre. Instead, *Love's Labour's Lost* exemplifies a type rarely seen outside of parody, a style of film designated by Rick Altman as a "genre film" as opposed to a "film genre"—that is, a cinematic work "self-consciously produced and consumed according to . . . a specific generic model" (Altman 1999: 144). Perhaps Branagh's first mistake was overestimating his audience's familiarity with his generic model. As the multiplicity of media reactions makes clear, his target audience proved largely incapable of appreciating the film's signifiers of generic familiarity. Many commentators were uncertain about how to read the film: the alien associations of the adjective "surreal" are frequently utilized to describe a cinematic mode divorced from popular conceptions.[5] Examining the film without an appropriate interpretive lens, critics tended to judge *Love's Labour's Lost* literally, and noted the visuals only in order to label them "self-indulgent" (Hunter n.p.) and "fatuous" (Walker n.p.). Moreover, there is evidence to suggest that acting and gestures modeled on the style of the 1930s, and the tendency to slip into song and dance, are viewed today with sentiments akin to shame. "Embarrassing" recurred as a salient epithet in reviews, pointing to a particularly awkward filmic encounter (Andrews n.p.; Quinn n.p.). Few reviews, even those that were more kindly disposed, could resist poking fun at the performers, which implies that a critical suspension of disbelief—a dissolving into the film's imaginative landscape—had only imperfectly taken place. In particular, Branagh's age and physical appearance were singled out for unflattering remarks, in such a way as to indicate a skewed target of comic involvement. *Love's Labour's Lost* may have been designed as "a homage to the classical Hollywood musicals" ("*Love's Labour's Lost*": *Production Information* 27), but the critical reception makes visible the fact that, in the context of a late capitalist, postmodern movement, the musical is experienced largely through the perspective of a posthumous movement and ironic cynicism.

To pay filmic homage, it might be suggested, is also inevitably to participate in nostalgia. Susan Bennett has noted the way in which "nostalgia performs as the representation" (Bennett 5) of the utopian face of the past, and Branagh's perspective on the 1930s reveals just such a romantically filtered selectivity. The conventionally postmodern nostalgia evoked in *Love's Labour's Lost* where a potent impression of the decade is manufactured, as Fredric Jameson would have it, "through stylistic connotation" (Jameson 19), typically simplifies into symbolic objects (such as radiograms, cocktails, cigarette holders, and suitcases) the material realities of the time. Important to Branagh's romantic construction of the decade is his move away from the musical's defining identity as an original score and his decision to utilize, instead, melodies that, in the filmmaker's words, "give Shakespeare a run for his money." Assuming for themselves a canonical position in the popular consciousness, classic songs by Berlin, Kern, and Gershwin have sentimental networks of association outside of any incorporating narrative. They evoke an illusion of "period," conjuring a sense of certainty, clarity, and *communitas*, without specifically identifying a particular moment in history. The emotive charge with which the songs are invested accords with Branagh's conception of the 1930s as a "last idyll in the twentieth century . . . a stolen, magical, idyllic time which nevertheless had a clock ticking" (Wray and Burnett 174). This is reinforced in musical numbers that prefigure a troubled future, conjure up a glorious immediacy (Jerome Kern's "The Way You Look Tonight," while focusing on the present, has as its central theme the anticipation of "some day" when the "world is cold"), and help to construct the decade as a moment tragically eclipsed. For Branagh, it seems, the protected innocence of the 1930s is inextricably entangled in the fantastic musical forms that the decade produced. Indeed, in *Love's Labour's Lost*, the 1930s are realized as the musical, an elegant example of what Jameson describes as the "history of aesthetic styles" displacing "real history" (Jameson 20).

A deployment of the Hollywood musical as "history" has national implications which come into play during the faux newsreel sequences. A mélange of studio-created and historically authentic Pathé newsreels appear throughout the film.[6] As a material reminder of the war to come, this distinctively British instrument of reportage, which was pioneered in the 1930s, is key to the film's establishment of the decade as a privileged yet circumscribed moment. The opening newsreel, for example, informs the viewer about the European situation as well as the dramatic story, bringing two headlines—"New ideas in Navarre" and "War imminent"—into a precisely dated chronological juxtaposition. In a visual continuation of the headline disparity, medium shots of the male protagonists sharing a joke are interspersed with images of bombers, while a comparative voice-over announces:

> September 1939. Ominous clouds of war may be hovering over Europe But here in Navarre, the young King, seen here returning from military Manoeuvres, has announced an audacious plan. . . . He and his companions Are to cast off their military uniforms, while world events still allow, and Devote themselves to a rigorous three years of study. That's right, three years. (Branagh 2)

Paralleling the action of retirement with a gathering European crisis, the commentary constructs the musical sequences ahead as simultaneously hermetically sealed and about to be ruptured. The procedure is bolstered by the visual contrast between the heightened color of the action sequences and the scratchy black and white of the newsreels, which, like early experiments with Technicolor, works to increase, in the words of Jane Feuer, "the voluptuousness of those parts of a film which . . . represent fantasy" (Feuer 67), effectively fostering a dual reality effect (a type of "play-within-a-play").[7]

To these kinds of filmic alternation difficulties are attached. The immediate problem with a movement between external and internal events is that it has the effect of making the protagonists' flight into romance seem self-indulgent and irresponsible. As a result of *Love's Labour's Lost*'s uncertain fit between global conflict and romantic retrenchment, such a withdrawal is at least partially politicized. The point is underlined via images that emphasize the class-bound, familial, and locational obligations of the leading personalities. Much as he did in *Hamlet* (1997), Branagh consistently reminds his viewer that, as members of royal and aristocratic families, the drama's players have the potential to act in an internationally important fashion. The death of the king of France, for example, is realized both as a personal tragedy (a close-up shot of the princess's tears) and as a national disaster with ramifications beyond the immediate familial context (newspaper headlines suggest that France will fall without its figurehead).

Throughout these sequences, the camera continues to keep characters at a distance. When the princess learns of the retreat from a newspaper, the point-of-view shot scans the columns to remind us that the wider interpretive community is more preoccupied with the progress of England's most famous son, Winston Churchill. The move is awkward, leaving one uncertain of a gaze which relegates Allied foreign policy to a filmic grammar inspired by Hollywood. Once paralleled, moments of political withdrawal intersect, in turn, with the play's metatheatrical allusions. Comments such as Berowne's "The scene begins to cloud" (V.ii.717) and "That's too long for a play" (V.ii.867) inevitably reflect upon the escalating situation peripheral to the main plot, while pointing up issues of political neglect.[8] Maintaining the two-world narrative and retaining audience identification with the protagonists becomes a delicate balancing act, one that is destabilized by the very nostalgic sensibility necessary for its inception and survival.

Most unpredictably, perhaps, the common denominator of nostalgia underlining *Love's Labour's Lost* is further compromised by its oddly "British" inflections. If the songs, sets, international accents, and cross-racial casting evince a retrospective experience open to all, these parts of the film simultaneously mark nostalgia off as a strictly English prerogative. Nowhere is this more evident than in the scenes that discover, rather in the manner of Laurence Olivier's *Henry V* (1944), World War II as a nationally cohesive and exclusive enterprise. In Branagh's filmic comedy, an accelerated montage flits between six wartime scenarios: the princess and her waiting gentlewomen are led away to internment; Armado languishes in a prisoner-of-war camp; the king executes heroics at the front; his comrades have resumed their roles as fighter pilots; Berowne attends to the wounded; and Nathaniel and Holofernes are seen "digging for victory." Common to the sequences as a whole is a registration of the film's personalities as glamorously resilient and courageously corporate. But the wider field of activity is figured in highly local terms. With the exception of the quick glimpse of Boyet, who has been recuperated as a member of the French Resistance, all of the shots privilege a "British" context and figure Shakespeare's Gallic protagonists as little more than the English on holiday; the film both collapses and re-sorts the war's messy global trajectory. V.E. Day is constructed as an accomplishment in which all types of people play a part, yet the roles elaborated are manifestly unequal. The fate of the French is to be passive victims; the achievement of the British is to win glory in domestic and international spheres.

At once, of course, this is a species of nostalgia that removes to the periphery the Continental and American consumer.[9] At a deeper level, the essentially British orientation of the newsreel comes into tension with the musical's all-American modality. Crucially, the shift from one landscape to another (from the play script to the war script) does not only constitute a surface component of the literal narrative. It inevitably becomes, in the context of the film, a generic choice. The move into the musical environment is necessarily symbolically freighted—at best, foolhardy evasion, at worst, political cowardice. Rather than imagining the musical (and the decade that is elaborated through its signifiers) as politically neutral, the ill-matching nature of *Love's Labour's Lost*'s dual modes of representation mounts a challenge to the film's nostalgically sedimented dependencies. Constructing the musical as a distractive indulgence, generic discontinuity suggests an oppositional analysis of the 1930s in terms of a self-serving political myopia and a policy of appeasement. Certainly, the fact that the immersion in music has a costly consequence is made clear in the newsreel's closing montage, which includes glimpses of fascist regalia. Here, more than at any other point, are stressed not only the human ramifications of a politics of distraction, but also the concomitant competition between British and American styles of self-representation.

While the newsreel appears critically at odds with its generic enclosure, however, it also enthusiastically contributes to the musical's escapism, suggesting that unmediated authenticity is not freely available. "Royals Camping," a typical headline, is shown to take precedence over a vital update on French border disputes, which illustrates the kind of skewed priorities that the newsreel itself attacks elsewhere. In fact, by prioritizing glimpses into the protagonists' private lives, the newsreel becomes a microcosm of the displacing fantasies animating the film as a whole.[10] Further, the formal cast of the Cinétone voice means that its invitations to participate take on discernible political resonances, betraying its shaping role as a linguistic instrument of ideological coercion. The fact that newscaster's voice is Branagh's own works to implicate *Love's Labour's Lost* in just such a process. The director is identified as controlling agent, the paradoxical effect of which is to ensnare him in unresolved reflections upon censorship and creativity. The unsettling effect increases as the film progresses, because it is Branagh as authoritative voice that impresses throughout. Berowne, whom Branagh plays, is the only character able to move among the film's generic and ideological polarities. Thus, when the montage shows a visibly anxious Berowne listening to news of encroaching enemy troops, the revealing next cut is to the king and his colleagues, laughing about the "ladies." Presiding over the film world in the guise of newscaster, and flitting in and out of its layered environments, Branagh is kept continually at the screen's imaginative forefront, in such a way as to suggest a Shakespeare who must be mediated and an interpreter who must be privileged. At times, Branagh's role even extends to a simultaneously retrospective and prescient rehearsal of his career thus far. His performance as Berowne harks back to his rendition of a similar Shakespearean type, Benedick, in *Much Ado About Nothing* (1993), while the ensemble numbers and general camaraderie evoke the spirit of *In the Bleak Midwinter* (1995, also known as *A Midwinter's Tale*), with its "show must go on" philosophy. Even in this connection, however, the film reveals more than it might intend. A number like Irving Berlin's "There's No Business Like Show Business," for instance, can be seen to mediate Branagh's own pivotal role in the Shakespeare industry.[11] But it also comments on his increasingly marginal role within the cinematic revival of the dramatist for which he has, in large part, been responsible: viewed in the spotlight of the film's commercial failure, lines such as "Even with a turkey that you know will fold/You may be stranded out in the cold" (Branagh 53) reflect unflatteringly on the uncertain purchase of Branagh's recent Shakespearean outings.

The self-consciousness that clusters around Branagh as controller extends into the self-consciousness of the film's singing and dancing technique. Branagh's decision to cast untrained performers for roles that demanded classical performance skills rides roughshod over a basic musical convention: even if a plot constructs a character as an amateur, he or she is expected to demonstrate superlative qualities of movement and voice.[12] Confusion over this casting decision was rehearsed in many pejorative reviews.[13] In interview, Branagh stated that he was "happy to encourage . . . a certain rawness in the singing and dancing," since this illuminated the situation of "ordinary people . . . striving to express romantic urges and finer feelings in unaccustomed ways" ("*Love's Labour's Lost*": *Production Information* 20). However, Branagh's belief in the authenticity of music as a channel for vernacular feeling notwithstanding, *Love's Labour's Lost* in practice has a contrary effect: the film disindividuates its participants, the sheer appropriative weight robbing them of a felt articulacy. Obviously, the war is an external script that has an impact upon the lovers' life choices, but, through its particular amalgamation of different generic forms, *Love's Labour's Lost* reveals other scripts (such as its songs, and, of course, the Shakespearean text itself) as equally powerful prompts for self-representation. It is precisely this idea that is visually and aurally encapsulated when the four male protagonists not only write comparable love letters, but also express their situations through a single song, George and Ira Gershwin's "I've Got a Crush on You." By making of the song a simultaneously choral and communal set piece, the direction ensures that, rather than the stress falling on individuation, a similarity of experience is underlined. A related emphasis finds meaning in one of Branagh's favorite pieces of camera work, in which sequences of flash-frame close-ups show either the "girls" or the "boys" registering identical emotional expressions.

At an intertextual level, a cultivated amateurishness of technique becomes one of the instruments whereby the film reaches out to connect itself with cinematic history. An implicit ambition in *Love's Labour's Lost* is to dissolve the myth of the 1930s into a 20th-century paradigm, but this is prevented by the histories that have intervened between the two poles. In particular, the gradual disappearance of performative versatility, and its replacement by the more powerful virtues of celebrity, are unwittingly engaged in *Love's Labour's Lost*'s casting arrangements. Alicia Silverstone (the princess of France) may be the established U.S. star required to satisfy the box office; in terms of her musical abilities, however, she is clearly the weakest link. Silverstone functions as a constant reminder of the obliteration of singing and dancing as essential qualifications in modern Hollywood. As part of its replacement of "reality" with the trappings of genre, *Love's Labour's Lost* also conjures a narrower filmic trajectory, which leads from the buoyant vitality of the musical to the bleaker and more dispassionate reflectivity of the wartime romance (in which lovers often part and passion does not always prevail).[14] Bolstering the idea that the 1930s constituted a privileged space, the shift from musical to romance constructs World War II in terms of its aesthetic ramifications. The film's iconography gradually incorporates familiar motifs from films from the 1940s, mapping a cinematic route from innocence to cynicism, and from security to uncertainty. The movement culminates in a company performance of George and Ira Gershwin's "They Can't Take That Away from Me." One genre yields to another as the song, with its "we'll-always-have-Paris" sentiments, complements a leave-taking scene purposefully presented as a reworking of *Casablanca*'s (1942) celebrated ending.[15] On the one hand, the generic dissolution comments upon the multivalent dynamic of cinematic memory; on the other hand, it reinforces the notion, that, in Bennett's words, "Nostalgia might best be considered as the inflicted territory where claims for authenticity are staged" (Bennett 7). By filtering its romantic conceits through a mesh of accreted influences, *Love's Labour's Lost* inefficaciously searches for celluloid sincerity that will simultaneously revitalize and respect the integrity of the Shakespearean original.

Having inaugurated a development which should allow contemporary audiences to understand the play's ending (arguably, the least palatable part), Branagh chooses not to pursue it, preferring instead to reinstate the happy conclusion denied by both the drama and his wartime cinema narrative models. The tactic makes sense, however, within the context of the faux newsreel narrative, which demands that the immersion in romantic fantasy, like the cinematic dominance of the musical, is always only a phase. In a not wholly successful endeavor to restore an authentic masculinity, the play's 12-month separation period is extended to World War II's six-year hiatus.[16] The final narrative resolution attempts a reconciliation of the film's polarized values—material realities now blend with the world of imagination, with notions of spontaneity, impulse, and pleasure. This is signaled at the level of the film's appearance: gradually, a wash of color seeps in, a visual and ideological replacement for the similarly symbolically-loaded sequences of black and white. Once again, America is omitted in a montage of harmonizing visuals that underscores the cultural preeminence of London and Paris. If the reintegrated cinematography represses the spirit of "Old Sam," it simultaneously returns the film to its generic roots. The ending constitutes Branagh's reworking of the classical conclusion of the musical, although here filmic opposites are merged in the experiences of couples joined through a shared bond of global conflict.

In the absence of a Shakespearean script, a final set of clichés stands in for a concluding narrative. Visions of the reunited couples are filtered through the staged reunion photographs of V.E. Day in a revealing illustration of Susan Stewart's thesis that "the narration of the photograph itself becomes an object of nostalgia" (Stewart 138). But the unpredictable operations of nostalgia continue to assert themselves when one of the concluding shots shows a newspaper bearing the wrong date: 11 November was when World War I, not World War II, ended. The temporal breakdown stands as an overdetermined moment, robbing the decade of the distinctive identity *Love's Labour's Lost* works so hard to establish elsewhere. By breaking down the boundaries between the wars, this parting chronological rupture introduces a notion of historical indeterminacy, which works against the rest of the film's multiple constructions of the 1930s in general—and the musical genre in particular—as specially demarcated arenas. Executing a repressive function, it highlights the characteristically postmodern ways in which nostalgia is driven, not from a knowledge of or even a desire for the past, but from a fear or dislike of the present. Since throughout this discussion, I have argued that, in *Love's Labour's Lost*, such a sense of loss is made manifest at multiple levels—material, historical, and metacinematic—it is additionally appropriate that the newspaper in which the dating mistake appears is entitled *The Globe*. The title harks back to a bardolatrous construction of Shakespearean production, to an idealized moment when the dramatist's legacy was indisputably English, and when the right of interpretation was owned only by the man dubbed Olivier's heir. In so doing, it alerts us to the embattled locations of Branagh himself in the increasingly precarious universe of the Shakespearean present. As Jean Baudrillard states, "When the real is no longer what is used to be, nostalgia assumes its full meaning" (Baudrillard 12).

—Ramona Wray
Queen's University, Belfast

NOTES

1. My thanks to Pascale Aebishcher, Mark Burnett, Ewan Fernie, Aaron Kelly, Clare McManus, and Sharon O'Dair for their generous help with earlier drafts of this essay.
2. Criticism has yet to engage with *Love's Labour's Lost*. The only items published thus far are Crowl 237–38; Lanier 164–65; and Osborne 10–11.
3. For discussion of the evolution of the traditional musical into the "rock musical," see Feuer 130–38.
4. For a discussion of prototypical features, see Altman 1987: 28–58.
5. See the radio and TV clips reproduced on *"Love's Labour's Lost": U.K. Broadcast Coverage*. This video compilation forms part of the Kenneth Branagh Archive, donated by the filmmaker to Queen's University, Belfast.
6. For an overview of the evolution of this peculiarly British form, see Low 9–59.
7. On MGM's reliance on an internal narrative audience, see Feuer 31–34. Of course, the Cinétone announcer occupies a position analogous to the chorus in Shakespearean drama, a device Branagh had previously appropriatred to excellent effect in his film version of *Henry V* (1989).
8. See Branagh 54, 58.
9. Films such as Roberto Benigni's *Life Is Beautiful* (1997) demonstrate that trading upon received ideas about American intervention and liberation is a necessary ingredient in the achievement of commercial success.
10. As Branagh was planning *Love's Labour's Lost*, he was rehearsing a starring role in Woody Allen's *Celebrity* (1998), a film that addresses the late-20th-century fascination with the famous.
11. In moments such as these, Branagh is close to that other major Hollywood genre of the 1930s, the biopic.
12. The exception to the generally only average singing and dancing is Adrian Lester's superlative performance. Since Lester is black, this lends an interesting edge to Courtney Lehmann's article on Branagh's populism coming unstuck on multinational grounds. See Lehmann 1–22.
13. Critics such as Christopher Tookey, for example, "left wondering why real singer-dancers were not called in to do the job properly," were presumably reacting to the way in which an amateurishness of technique calls attention to the fictionality of the screen action and the implausibility of the film's personalities. See Tookey 52.
14. A similar trajectory is traced in Shindler *passim*.
15. The idea of a final bow for the musical is captured in the rendition of the penultimate song (Irving Berlin's "There's No Business Like Show Business"), which involves the entire company and is presented as a generic finale.
16. In this connection, there are stylish linguistic correspondences—Rosaline's requirement that Berowne should "Visit the speechless sick" (V.ii.840) to "jest a twelvemonth in an hospital" (V.ii.860) is translated into a sequence that shows Berowne working in a military hospital under the potent symbol of the Red Cross.

WORKS CITED

Altman, Rick. *The American Film Musical*. Bloomington: Indiana University Press, 1987.

———. *Film/Genre*. London: British Film Institute, 1999.

Andrews, Nigel. "Ken and Patricia's Labours Wasted." *The Financial Times*, March 30, 2000, n.p. Kenneth Branagh Archive, Queen's University, Belfast.

Baudrillard, Jean. *Simulations*. New York: Semiotext(e), 1983.

Bennett, Susan. *Performing Nostalgia: Shifting Shakespeare and the Contemporary Past*. London and New York: Routledge, 1996.

Branagh, Kenneth. "*Love's Labour's Lost*": *A Musical Adapted from the Play by William Shakespeare: Screenplay* [2000]. Kenneth Branagh Archive, Queens University, Belfast.

Crowl, Samuel. "Flamboyant Realist: Kenneth Branagh." *The Cambridge Companion To Shakespeare on Film*. Ed. Russell Jackson. Cambridge: Cambridge University Press, 2000, 222–38.

Dantrey, Adam. "Distributor Report Cards." *Variety*, December 11–17, 2000: 42.

Feuer, Jane. *The Hollywood Musical*. Basingstoke, England: Macmillan, 1993.

Grant, Steve. "Video," *The Sunday Times*, Culture section, August 27, 2000: 27.

Gristwood, Sarah. "What Is This Thing Called *Love's Labour's Lost*?" *The Guardian*, March 27, 2000: 9.

Hunter, Alan. "Film," *The Express*, March 31, 2000: n.p. Kenneth Branagh Archive, Queen's University, Belfast.

Jameson, Fredric. *Postmodernism, or, The Cultural Logic of Late Capitalism*. London: and New York: Verso, 1991.

"Ken's Labour's Lost on the Bard." *The Daily Express*, January 30, 2001: 39.

Lanier, Douglas. "'Art Thou Base, Common and Popular?': The Cultural Politics of Kenneth Branagh's *Hamlet*." *Spectacular Shakespeare: Critical Theory and Popular Cinema*. Ed. Courtney Lehmann and Lisa S. Starks. Teaneck: Fairleigh Dickinson University Press, 2002. 149–72.

Lehmann, Courtney. "Much Ado About Nothing? Shakespeare, Branagh, and the 'National-Popular' in the Age of Multinational Capital," *Textual Practice* 12 (1998): 1–22.

"*Love's Labour's Lost*": *Production Information*. London: Intermedia, 2000.

"*Love Labour's Lost*": *U.K. Broadcast Coverage*. Video compilation in the Kenneth Branagh Archive, Queen's University, Belfast.

Low, Rachael. *The History of British Film 1929–1939: Films of Comment and Persuasion of the 1930s*. London and New York: Routledge, 1997.

Osborne, Laurie E. "Introduction." *The Colby Quarterly* 37 (2001): 5–14.

Porter, Edward. "Musical Dares." *The Sunday Times*, Culture section, April 2, 2000: 9.

Quinn, Anthony. "Film," *The Independent*, March 31, 2000: n.p. Kenneth Branagh Archive, Queen's University, Belfast.

Shindler, Christopher. *Hollywood in Crisis: Cinema and American Society 1929-1939*. London and New York: Routledge, 1996.

Stewart, Susan. *On Longing: Narratives of the Miniature, the Gigantic, the Souvenir, the Collection*. Durham: Duke University Press, 1993.

Tookey, Christopher. "Bard Is Beyond Our Ken," *The Daily Mail*, March 31, 2000: 52.

Walker, Alexander. "Let's Face the Music and Prance." *The London Evening Standard*, March 30, 2000: n.p. Kenneth Branagh Archive, Queen's University, Belfast.

Wray, Ramona, and Mark Thornton Burnett. "From the Horse's Mouth: Branagh on the Bard." *Shakespeare, Film, Fin de Siècle*. Basingstoke, England: Macmillan, 2000. 165–78.

Shakespearean Authorship in Popular British Cinema

In the 1998 film *Shakespeare in Love*, Shakespeare's writer's block is cured by his passionate affair with a stage-struck aristocrat called Viola de Lesseps. But if love reinvents Shakespeare as an author, his authorship is also what arouses Viola's desire. At one point she asks the bashful poet, "Are you the author of the plays of William Shakespeare? Then kiss me again."

"Shakespeare on film" usually means the adaptation of Shakespeare's plays, rather than any representation of the poet himself. But such adaptations, by their very displacement of Shakespeare as author figure, inspire films which strive to make the dramatist present to the audience and which celebrate his authorship. This essay is concerned with three such films: *The Immortal Gentleman* (1935), *Time Flies* (1944), and *Shakespeare in Love* (1998). Where the 1998 film has achieved international renown and much critical attention, the earlier British films have been largely ignored by film critics and Shakespeareans alike. I will argue that *Shakespeare in Love* must be understood in terms of these earlier works, for all three films respond to an authorial absence created by adaptation.[1] Moreover, *The Immortal Gentleman*, *Time Flies*, and *Shakespeare in Love* use the same strategy to defend Shakespearean authorship, enacting a comic ritual in which the death of the author is threatened but finally averted. These films play with the possibility that Shakespeare could not write. They ask whether the man from Stratford really was the author of "Shakespeare's works." Finally, they question the poet's originality by identifying his work as collaborative. But in each instance, Shakespeare emerges with his status as an original genius both authenticated and exalted.

In *The Genius of Shakespeare*, Jonathan Bate reminds us that

> the Romantic idea of authorship locates the essence of genius in the scene of writing. With Romanticism, the quintessential image of the poet becomes that of Samuel Taylor Coleridge alone in a farmhouse, transcribing his opium-induced dream of 'Kubla Kahn' onto a blank piece of paper . . . (82)[2]

These films about Shakespeare immediately evoke a Romantic conception of authorship by privileging such scenes of writing.

The Immortal Gentleman is set in a tavern at Southwark in 1606 where Shakespeare, Jonson, and Drayton meet for a drink. Here, Shakespeare is wont to reflect on his literary and theatrical triumphs, and in the course of the film, these memories are interspersed with filmed reproductions of the most famous scenes.[3] Although its nostalgic view of the Shakespearean canon precludes the possibility of showing Shakespeare at work, the poet's reminiscences include scenes of writing. He draws attention to the wistful expression of a young woman in the tavern and declares "When I wrote my *Romeo and Juliet*, it was so I saw my Juliet."

In *Time Flies*, a time machine transports a group of Americans to Elizabethan England. Backstage at the Globe, one of the travelers, a vaudeville star called Susie, notices a poster advertising a performance of *Love's Labour's Lost*. Moments later, we see Shakespeare for the first time, seated at a desk on the Globe stage, with a quill in one hand and a piece of parchment in the other. He is reading aloud a passage he has apparently just written from *Romeo and Juliet*. This image of "our bending author" recalls the Gheerart Janssen monument in Holy Trinity Church, Stratford-upon-Avon, which also holds a quill in its right hand and a piece of paper in its left. Thus, *Time Flies* eschews other famous images of Shakespeare such as the Droeshout engraving or the Chandos portrait, images with a greater claim to authenticity, in favor of a monument which not only represents the author writing but which was remodeled thus by a later generation's desire to see Shakespeare at work.[4]

Shakespeare in Love responds to the same cultural pressure. Again, our first glimpse of the playwright is of him seated at a desk with a quill in his hand, apparently at work on *Romeo and Juliet*. The desiring eye of the camera encourages us to venerate the act of writing, and that particular cursive which is Shakespeare's own. Unlike biopics in which other hands replace the actor's when he has to play the piano, paint, and so on, *Shakespeare in Love* insists that Joseph Fiennes' ink-stained hands do the writing.[5] Moreover, this scene comments upon the fetishism inspired by Shakespeare's lost manuscripts. We approach tremulously the text that Shakespeare is composing, and are further tormented by a background shot of a chest spilling over with Shakespearean manuscripts. But the film also mocks our solemnity, for when we are allowed to view the product of Shakespeare's labors, it is merely a list of signatures. This disappointment contains a sophisticated academic joke,[6] but it also signals the first major threat to Shakespearean authorship, namely the possibility that Shakespeare suffered from writer's block.

In *Time Flies*, Shakespeare has problems with a specific line. In *Shakespeare in Love*, the dramatist is unable to begin his play and laughs at his title, *Romeo, and Ethel the Pirate's Daughter*. As far as both films are concerned, to give Shakespeare a case of writer's block is to make him more familiar and sympathetic to a 20th-century audience.[7] In a review of *Shakespeare in Love*, Richard Combs referred to the "naive delight" the film inspired in audiences by its representation of Shakespeare "not as an ivory-tower poet but a journeyman scribbler with money problems" (33). There is similarly something "populist" in this representation of the Romantic genius as fallible, easily distracted, unimaginative. That this perception of Shakespeare might undermine his iconic status seems to have occurred to Harold Bloom. In at least two reviews, Bloom is cited refuting the idea that Shakespeare could ever have suffered from writer's block (Forrest 5; Bloom interview 13).[8] And yet, the writer's block theme can easily be read as a confirmation of Shakespeare's genius. The poet's frustration anticipates scenes of inspiration. The depiction of sterility throws into relief the rare and wonderful power of invention. In *Time Flies*, when Susie realizes that she has been involved in the composition of *Romeo and Juliet*, she is awestruck. In *Shakespeare in Love*, the dramatist's passion for Viola cures his writer's block and leads to a number of passionate writing scenes in which the lovers pronounce the words of the play during sex. But the scenes in which Shakespeare writes alone, feverish with imagination, are hardly less eroticized.

The second major threat to Shakespeare's authorship is much older in provenance than this prospect of his faltering genius, namely the possibility that behind Shakespeare was someone else's genius. Like the theme of writer's block, this controversy reveals a fascination with the process of literary composition and assumes that a writer's brain is the primary source of his invention.[9]

In *The Immortal Gentleman*, Shakespeare has just appeared in the doorway of the tavern when he is recognized by one of its customers. The latter begins to sing a song from *As You Like It*, "It was a lover and his lass." He pauses to address the poet: "A pretty song, Master Shakespeare, but they say you did not write it." Shakespeare is not even slightly discomposed and agrees that he did not write it: "My pen wrote it, I only thought of it." We might be surprised that a film with such an apparently conservative agenda behind it, namely the desire to celebrate "our national poet," should deal with the authorship controversy at all. But the ease with which Shakespeare asserts his originality, wrong-footing the man with a riddle, more than justifies its inclusion. The authorship controversy works here to legitimize Shakespeare's identity as author of the works.

In *Time Flies*, the matter is taken more seriously. The poet is having trouble with Romeo's speech before the balcony scene. When Susie calls out the "correct" line to him ("He jests at scars that never felt a wound"), Shakespeare is about to write it down when he reflects that this was not the inspiration of his muse but a voice from outside. He asks who is there and Susie responds, "What's in a name? That which we call a rose by any other name would smell as sweet." "Another perfect line," Shakespeare cries, and is about to write this one down when he pauses. In tones of anxiety and some weariness he asks, "It's not one of Francis Bacon's, is it?" "Oh, no, no, no, no, no," Susie reassures him in a moment of Shakespearean epizeuxis. The significance of the authorship controversy here does not seem to reside in any contemporary academic debate on authorship: the Baconian theory was at least 60 years old by this point. It rather reflects the appropriation of Shakespeare by British filmmakers during World War II, and, in particular, their use of the authorship question as a metonym for the German threat to British national identity.[10]

Shakespeare in Love goes further in its representation of the authorship controversy than its predecessors but it also offers a more complete resolution of the issue. In this film, the contender for Shakespeare's laurels is Christopher Marlowe, a figure more familiar to the 1990s audience than Francis Bacon. The Marlovian theory rests on the assumption that Marlowe did not die but continued to write abroad, publishing his plays under the name of a common player, William Shakespeare.[11] *Shakespeare in Love* differentiates between Shakespeare and Marlowe immediately by presenting them as rival playwrights. The film also insists that Marlowe's plays end with his death. Shakespeare confides to Viola: "I would exchange all my plays to come, for all of his that will never come." Although what happened at Deptford remains a mystery, with Shakespeare himself not believing that it was simply a tavern brawl, there is no question that Marlowe is dead.

But if the film casually shakes off the aspersion that Marlowe was Shakespeare, it redefines the authorship controversy as something less sensational though still radical in terms of Shakespeare's cultural status. The question "Who wrote Shakespeare?" arises, not because of the confusion of Marlowe and Shakespeare, but because of Shakespeare's tremendous debt to his predecessor. It is a debt he explicitly acknowledges: "Marlowe's touch was in my *Titus Andronicus*. My *Henry VI* was a house built on his foundation."

Moreover, Marlowe's death is represented as Shakespeare's subconscious wish and the precondition of his greatness. It is here that the film seems to draw upon Harold Bloom's theory of misreading. In *The Anxiety of Influence* (1973), Bloom describes how the descendant of a great poet tries to cast off his sense of inferiority towards his precursor by misreading the other's work. Thus, he wrests it to his own purposes and becomes an influence himself. Bloom does not recognize the relationship between Marlowe and Shakespeare as such an agon since Marlowe was "very much smaller than his inheritor" (11). But recent critical studies have challenged this opinion. Indeed, in *The Genius of Shakespeare*, Bate redefines the relationship between Marlowe and Shakespeare in Bloomian terms: "Metaphorically, not literally, Shakespeare was the rival who killed Marlowe" (105). The representation of Shakespeare wishing for and subconsciously bringing about the death of his rival, is one of the most interesting of the film's interventions in Shakespeare lore. And yet, the film posits something more fundamental. It insists that Shakespeare's plays were created from polyphony.

If we look back at our earlier films, the question of literary debt hardly features. *The Immortal Gentleman* presents a Shakespeare who draws his inspiration from the people he sees around him and from his experience of life in general. But there is no suggestion that he gains anything from Jonson or Drayton despite the fact that they are his constant drinking companions. Moreover, Shakespeare's denial that any other hand was involved in the composition of "There was a lover and his lass" could be taken as a denial of any literary debt.

Shakespeare declares that he "only," that is, he alone, wrote it. *Time Flies* is a more complicated case. This Shakespeare takes lines from the American time traveler, Susie, anxious that they might belong to Bacon but not otherwise chary of exploiting someone else's wit. But although Shakespeare thinks that he is indebted to Susie, the words that she gives him are his own. This Shakespeare remains the solitary and self-sufficient genius of the Romantic period.

Shakespeare in Love, however, makes a point of attributing Shakespeare's text to a variety of sources. Through our privileged access to the creation of *Romeo and Juliet*, we see that the play is a "tissue of quotations." It interweaves the voices of an antitheatricalist preacher ("A plague on both your houses"); of Viola, Ned Alleyn, and Marlowe who suggest the play's plot and title, and the name of Mercutio; and the idiom of Shakespeare himself ("O, I am Fortune's fool!"). More importantly, by suggesting that what has been already spoken and written finds its way unconsciously into Shakespeare's text, the film alludes to theories of intertextuality that might challenge its whole conception of the author.

Roland Barthes' 1968 essay "The Death of the Author" begins with some examination of the way in which writing displaces meaning. Rather than preserving authorial intention, "writing is the destruction of every voice, of every point of origin. Writing is that neutral, composite, oblique space where our subject slips away, the negative where all identity is lost, starting with the very identity of the body writing" (168). The fact that in *Shakespeare in Love*, the poet is seen writing his name over and over again is a joke that Barthes might have appreciated. Moreover, Barthes' authorial absence is predicated upon the theory of intertextuality. The text is "a multi-dimensional space in which a variety of writings, none of them original, blend and clash" (170).

Shakespeare in Love has already deployed intertextual theory through its Bloomian representation of Marlowe and Shakespeare. Indeed, it could be said to go beyond Bloom who refuses to accept the relevance of any nonliterary context. But how far does *Shakespeare in Love* go in its challenge to authorial intention?[12] Like *The Immortal Gentleman* and *Time Flies*, the film is adept at averting threats to authorship, namely the danger that Shakespeare could not write, or that someone else wrote him. Although its treatment of collaboration is remarkable in the history of such films, there are places *Shakespeare in Love* will not go, conclusions it disdains.

The most obvious omission from its representation of an intertextual Shakespeare is any suggestion that Shakespeare culled his plots from other literature or that he read anything at all. While a book is present on the desk as he writes *Romeo and Juliet*, Shakespeare does not refer to it, nor is the book identified. Like the volume on the desk in *Time Flies*, it merely sets the scene. But given the resonance of the other props at this point in *Shakespeare in Love* (the skull, the Stratford mug)[13], this coyness about the book seems deliberate. What the film consciously ignores here is the fact that *Romeo and Juliet* was based on Arthur Brooke's poem *The Tragical History of Romeus and Juliet* (1562). In its insistence on Shakespeare's individual genius, the film also "forgets" that the story of *Romeo and Juliet* was already well-known and popular when Shakespeare began the play.[14] One might argue that this disregard for the book is dictated by the visual demands of cinema, or perhaps by the power struggle between text and image that goes on in Shakespeare films. However, we need only compare this film with *Prospero's Books*, in which *The Tempest* is seen to be the product of 24 volumes which come alive before the audience's eyes, to see how relatively illiterate this Shakespeare is.[15]

Perhaps more important, Shakespeare's collaboration with other authors and with the theater itself is limited. His manuscripts are represented as immaculate literary artifacts, written in his own hand, relatively unaffected by the process of staging. Previous Shakespeare films make small reference to the fact that Shakespeare was a dramatist. In *The Immortal Gentleman*, the playwright reflects upon *Hamlet*'s success in the theater. *Time Flies* makes a concession to Shakespeare as dramatist by simply placing his writing desk on the Globe stage. In contrast, *Shakespeare in Love* is deeply committed to presenting Shakespeare as part of the theater of the day. We see the dramatist negotiating with the theater owners, auditioning the players, attending rehearsals, and acting the part of Romeo. In the course of rehearsals, Shakespeare does make some alterations to his tragedy. When the lead actor of the Admiral's Men, Ned Alleyn, suggests that the play should be renamed *Romeo and Juliet*, he concurs. When Ned suggests there is a scene missing, Shakespeare writes one. But at no point in the rehearsal period is a line changed, either deliberately or by accident. Nor in the final performance is there any element of improvisation or error. Shakespeare and Viola play it by the book.

But perhaps the most obvious indication that the film successfully defends Shakespearean authorship is apparent in its reception. Reviewers praised the fact that this Shakespeare was not a Romantic stereotype, scribbling alone in a garret (see Peachman, Kemp, and "Where there's a Will"). But those same reviewers revealed a fascination with authorship clearly inspired by the film. Questions of authorship recur again and again: Who wrote *Shakespeare in Love*? Does credit for the film go to the theatrical heavyweight and Shakespearean Tom Stoppard, or to the writer of Hollywood swashbucklers Marc Norman? Is the screenplay plagiarized from the novel *No Bed for Bacon* by Caryl Brahms and S. J. Simon (1941)?[16] Is the film a true reflection of Shakespeare's creative process? More revealingly, Gilbert Adair responded to the prestige afforded to the author in *Shakespeare in Love* by wishing that the film had an auteur. Comparing film with opera, Adair wrote: "Opera, like cinema, may arguably be a 'collective' form, but one individual's artistry remains supreme—and so it does, or ought to do, with film" (5). Although Shakespeare in Love deploys contemporary scholarship which threatens to undermine its conception of the author, the author emerges triumphant, more formidable after his encounter with the giant-killers of poststructuralism.

Critics in the 1990s have bewailed the disappearance of Shakespeare in film adaptations of his plays. Shakespeare is displaced by the film's director, marginalized by references to popular cinema, and even deliberately deconstructed.[17] Moreover, Richard Burt suggests that in popular culture as a whole Shakespeare's visibility is becoming a kind of invisibility. Burt attests to the increasing distance between mass culture representations of Shakespeare and "the Shakespearean," defined as whatever is characteristic of the poet in his writing. As the distinction between the hermeneutic and post-hermeneutic breaks down, Burt argues that "it may soon be time to speak of the Shakespeare apocalypse" (Burt 227). And yet, Shakespeare's eminence has long been founded upon absences, the loss of his manuscripts, the lack of biographical information, the ambiguities within the plays. These gaps have not only fueled debates about Shakespeare but have inspired reinventions of his work. That Shakespeare should again be threatened by absence in the cinema and other forms of popular culture is then no great cause for concern since our culture continues to respond to this absence by reimagining Shakespeare.

When asked why the public should see *Shakespeare in Love*, the film's director, John Madden, replied: "Go and see it because this is a portrait of Will Shakespeare as you have never thought about him before" (21).[18] But though it presents Shakespeare as a sexier, more romantic, more insecure figure than hitherto, *Shakespeare in Love*, like *The Immortal Gentleman* and *Time Flies*, endorses the ways in which we have thought about Shakespeare for centuries. These films represent a cinematic form that is inherently conservative, a by-product of the increasingly radical process of adapting Shakespeare's plays for the screen.

—*Jane E. Kingsley-Smith*
University of Hull

NOTES

1. With each wave of popular film adaptation of Shakespeare's work comes a film in which Shakespeare is made present as an author. *The Immortal Gentleman* responds to the 1935-36 resurgence of Shakespeare on film, represented by Max Reinhardt's *A Midsummer Night's Dream*, George Cukor's *Romeo and Juliet*, and Paul Czinner's *As You Like It*. *Time Flies* was released in the same year as Olivier's groundbreaking *Henry V*. *Shakespeare in Love* responds to the popularity of Baz Luhrmann's *William Shakespeare's 'Romeo + Juliet'* (1996) and to the resurgence of what Ian Christie has called the "Elizabethan Romance," represented by Sally Potter's *Orlando* (1992) and Shekhar Kapur's *Elizabeth* (1998) (77).

2. See also Bate's *Shakespeare and the English Romantic Imagination*.

3. The reviewer for *Kine Weekly* called it a "serviceable, if not too subtle, formula for screen presentation of more popular Shakespearean excerpts." The film clearly acts as a prologue to later full-length adaptations on film. But it also has specific authorial intentions. It was based on a story entitled "An Evening with our National Poet, William Shakespeare," and not only the appearance of Shakespeare as a character but these filmed extracts are intended to make the poet familiar to the public.

4. In Dugdale's 1653 illustration of Janssen's work, published in *Antiquities of Warwickshire* (1656), there is no quill or parchment, suggesting that these were later additions by a Bardolatous age. Even with these additions, the bust has received considerable criticism for being insufficiently literary. John Dover Wilson declared it the likeness of a "self-satisfied pork butcher," presumably referring to the legend that Shakespeare's father was indeed a butcher. As recently as 1996, John Michell expressed his own disappointment: "A less appropriate image of any poet, let alone the great Shakespeare, could hardly be imagined" (90).

5. In an interview, Fiennes declared that he had written all the manuscripts in the film, including, presumably, the titles which appear in calligraphic form across the screen as Shakespeare writes ("Where There's a Will" 15). The fact that all this text should be Fiennes/Shakespeare's own is clearly related to the film's negotiations with the authorship controversy and with contemporary bibliographical scholarship, both areas to be examined shortly.

6. Shakespeare's doodling is seen to be responsible for the fact that there are 83 different spellings of Shakespeare's name and a confusing variety in his style of signature (Chambers 2: 371–372). More generally, this disappointment may remind the scholar that although he or she has tacitly accepted the theory that there is no original, holographic manuscript, in line with new bibliographical and performance studies, he or she still secretly longs for a glimpse of the "real thing."

7. In an interview with Maggie O'Farrell, Fiennes explained that "If you want to make idols accessible—which I think Shakespeare should be—then you have to bring a human touch, make it self-effacing and warm" (2).

8. In both articles, Bloom is identified as the author of *Shakespeare: The Invention of the Human*, a book which was being reviewed in the British press at about the same time as *Shakespeare in Love*. The film's reinvention of Shakespeare does not sit well with Bloom's assertion in this book that it is Shakespeare who invented us.

9. As Howard Felperin remarks, both the Bardolater and the anti-Stratfordian share "an overriding, even obsessive, concern with the 'author'" (135).

10. *Time Flies* may be located within a cycle of "heritage films" of the 1940s which aimed to boost patriotism by inspiring pride in Britain's cultural achievements. The references to Shakespeare in this cycle were varied—the film might be based on a Shakespeare play (Olivier's *Henry V*), it might quote passages from the works (*Words for Battle* [1941]), or simply take its title from a play (*This England* [1941]). See Barr (12). The authorship controversy plays a small but crucial role in a World War II espionage drama called *The Yellow Canary* (1943). The film begins with two air-raid wardens discussing whether Shakespeare or Bacon wrote the plays, a debate that clearly reflects the film's preoccupation with the identity and slander of its protagonist, Sally Maitland. Sally is accused of being a German spy but is eventually revealed to be a true patriot, working for British intelligence. At the end of the film, Sally's family triumphantly declares that "the myth of Sally Maitland is exploded," just as the air-raid warden refused to countenance the Baconian myth.

11. On the Marlowe/Shakespeare conspiracy see Calvin Hoffman's novel, *The Murder of the Man Who Was Shakespeare* (1955) and A.D. Wraight's *The Story That the Sonnets Tell* (1995).

12. The novelist Howard Jacobson was provoked by the film into a bitter tirade against post-structuralism. He condemned the practice of prioritizing the historical and social context of a work of literature over other considerations: "Any interest in the writer's intelligence or imagination, the largeness of his mind, his power to infuse particular experience with general thought, is considered uneducated, unacademic, fanciful and unreliable" (1).
13. The skull obviously anticipates *Hamlet*, while the mug, inscribed with the words "A present from Stratford-upon-Avon," alludes to Shakespeare's future commodification and the tourist industry he will inspire in his hometown.
14. Marlowe suggests the plot of the play as if he were imagining it on the spot rather than repeating a tale already familiar in prose and drama. Similarly, the Admiral's Men react with astonishment when the play which they believed about to end happily becomes tragic, though Brooke's poem advertised its nature as tragedy in the title.
15. On *Prospero's Books* and the bibliocentrism of other Shakespeare films, see Murphy and Lanier.
16. See French and Williams. That Shakespeare was himself a kind of plagiarist is suggested by Kemp.
17. Boose and Burt suggest that "in some ways, the present historical moment only clarifies the way Shakespeare has always already disappeared when transferred onto film" (11). On the search for the "true" Shakespeare in film adaptations, see Collick (1–10).
18. One reviewer for whom Madden's comments would clearly strike a chord is Owen Gleiberman: "Many of us carry around a mythical dream image of Shakespeare in our heads—a portrait of the artist as walking soul. *Shakespeare in Love* brings that image to life with a fervid theatricality and wit, a boisterous wholeheartedness, that is nothing short of enchanting."

WORKS CITED

Adair, Gilbert. "Shakey? It's pretty thin," *Independent on Sunday*, January 31, 1999: 5.

Barr, Charles. "Introduction: Amnesia and Schizophrenia." *All Our Yesterdays: 90 Years of British Cinema*. Ed. by Charles Barr. London: BFI, 1986. 1–30.

Barthes, Roland. "The Death of the Author." *Image-Music-Text*. Trans. Stephen Heath. London: Fontana, 1977: 142–148.

Bate, Jonathan. *The Genius of Shakespeare*. London: Picador, 1997.

———. *Shakespeare and the English Romantic Imagination*. Oxford, England: Clarendon Press, 1986.

Bloom, Harold. *The Anxiety of Influence: A Theory of Poetry*. New York: Oxford University Press, 1973.

———. Interview. *The Times*. January 16, 1999: 13.

Boose, Lynda E., and Richard Burt. "Totally Clueless? Shakespeare Goes Hollywood." In *Shakespeare, the Movie*. London and New York: Routledge, 1997: 8–22.

Burt, Richard. " 'Shakespeare in Love' and the End of the Shakespearean: Academic and Mass Culture Constructions of Literary Authorship." *Shakespeare, Film, Fin de Siècle*. Ed. Peter Thornton Burnett and Ramona Wray. London: Macmillan, 2000: 203–31.

Case, Brian. "Where There's a Will," *Time Out*, January 27-February 3, 1999: 14–15.

Chambers, E. K. *William Shakespeare: A Study of Facts and Problems*. 2 vols. Oxford: Clarendon Press, 1930.

Christie, Ian. "'As Others See Us: British Film-making and Europe in the 90s." *British Cinema of the 90s*. Ed. Robert Murphy. London: BFI, 2000: 68–79.

Clark, Peter. "The Divine Gwyneth and the Lovestruck Bard," *Evening Standard*, January 20, 1999, 20–21.

Collick, John. *Shakespeare, Cinema and Society*. Manchester, England: Manchester University Press, 1989.

Combs, Richard. "Shakespeare's 'Words, words, words,' " *Film Comment*, May/June 1999: 32–35.

Felperin, Howard. "Bardolatry Then and Now." *The Appropriation of Shakespeare: Post-Renaissance Reconstructions of the Works and the Myth*. Ed. by Jean I. Marsden. London and New York: Harvester Wheatsheaf, 1991: 129–44.

Forrest, Emma. "To Be a Hit or Not to Be a Hit," *Observer*, January 24, 1999: 4–5.

French, Philip. "William the Conqueror." *Observer*, January 31, 1999: 6.

Gleiberman, Owen. "*Shakespeare in Love*," *Entertainment Weekly*, December 4, 1998.

Jacobson, Howard. "Tis True Tis Pity and Pity Tis Tis True, Tis Total Tosh," *Independent*, January 23, 1999: 1.

Kemp, Philip. "*Shakespeare in Love*," *Sight and Sound*, February 1999: 53.

Lanier, Douglas. "Drowning the Book: 'Prospero's Books' and the Textual Shakespeare." *Shakespeare, Theory and Performance*. Ed. James C. Bulman. London: Routledge, 1996: 187–209.

Michell, John. *Who Wrote Shakespeare?* London: Thames and Hudson, 1996.

O'Farrell, Maggie. "Joseph Fiennes," *Independent on Sunday*, January 17, 1999: 2.

Peachman, Chris. "A Ruff Guide to the Amorous Bard, " *Mail on Sunday*, January 31, 1999: 34.

"Time Flies." Review. *Kine Weekly*, March 28, 1935: 31.

Williams, Rhys. "'Shakespeare' film script in copycat dispute," *Independent*, February 4, 1999: 6.

Appendix

BACKSTAGE WITH THE BARD:
OR, BUILDING A BETTER MOUSETRAP

Hamlet, Prince of Denmark, pauses a moment, sword at the ready, and takes the measure of his opponent, Laertes. Suddenly, with a deft stroke, he slices off Laertes' arm. Blood spurts 10 feet in the air as the severed limb falls to the stage. "A hit," declares Osric. "A palpable hit!" Laertes, in turn, ripostes with a lunge and cuts off Hamlet's arm. Another jet of blood arches across the stage. With a second thrust Laertes stabs Hamlet through the throat. Blood is now gushing everywhere, splashing onto the stage and spilling out into the audience seats. Stunned and horrified, the viewers are transfixed with horror.

Hamlet and Laertes, sans a few limbs and spouting fountains of blood, come down to the stage apron and cheerfully take their bow.

The interpreters of this extraordinary *guignol* version of Shakespeare's play are none other than those wayward children of the notorious Addams Family, Wednesday and Pugsley. They have just brought down the curtain on their school's kiddie talent pageant. More importantly, for our purposes, they have deconstructed every sugar-sweet children's show that parents and kids have ever had to endure.

Surely the Bard would have been pleased.

This moment, this brief play-within-a film, typifies just one of the many ways in which a Shakespearean "moment" may be cited within a motion picture to comment on its surrounding contexts. In the case of *The Addams Family*, it, like Hamlet's "mousetrap" play, creates seismic responses in the play's onlookers, each according to his or her particular disposition. While it outrages the hidebound stuffed shirts in the audience, it delights Wednesday and Pugsley's proud parents, Morticia and Gomez Addams, who rise to their feet, wildly cheering and applauding.

As Hamlet knew, it is all in how you look at it.

STAGING THE MOUSETRAP

Not all theatrical films directly adapt stage plays to the screen. Another category is a form of meta-cinema, that, taking the play-within-a-play in Shakespeare's *Hamlet* as its precedent, employs theatrical allusions as "mousetraps" that "capture the conscience," as it were, of the action and the characters. All too often, unfortunately, films of this kind are neglected in standard studies of theatrical films. But where would we be without masterpieces like George Cukor's *A Double Life* (1947), Jean Renoir's *The Golden Coach* (1952), Merchant-Ivory's *Shakespeare Wallah!* (1975), Kenneth Branagh's *A Midwinter's Tale* (1996), and that greatest of all theatrical films, Marcel Carné's *Children of Paradise* (1944)? These films do not adapt plays so much as they assimilate them into their primary texts. "The theater as a metaphor for life's madness is hardly new," says Kenneth Branagh, "and movies that use the stories of particular productions to provide a microcosmic view of human nature abound."

Actually, the idea of a play-within-a-play goes back further than *Hamlet*, to Thomas Kyd's *The Spanish Tragedy* (ca. 1583–87), in which the hero Hieronimo stages a play to trap his enemy. His revenge is complete when he substitutes a real dagger for the fake one in the final scene. The situation, it will be remembered, is similar in *Hamlet*. A troupe of traveling players has come to Elsinore. Hamlet asks them to present a play called *The Murder of Gonzago* before his uncle, King Claudius, to which Hamlet will add a few lines. The play, which is about a murder by poison, is designed to be a kind of "mousetrap" (indeed, that is the title Hamlet later gives the play): "The play's the thing wherein I'll catch the conscience of the king," he muses to himself. In this action, which transpires in Act Three, Scene Two, Claudius attends the show only to humor Hamlet. The performance begins with a dumb show, wherein a conspirator pours poison into the ears of the sleeping player-king. He subsequently woos the player-queen, who seems disposed to accept his favors. A dialogue ensues that identifies the dramatis personae as Gonzago, the victim and Lucianus, Gonzago's nephew as the murder/aspirant to the throne. King Claudius watches this performance with growing agitation. Hamlet assures him, "We that have free souls, it touches us not. Let the galled jade wince; our withers are unwrung." Nonetheless, Claudius abruptly rises, calls for lights, and stops the play. Hamlet's suspicions are confirmed.

Hamlet's little mousetrap dissolves the barriers between the fictive and the real. On the stage is a play in which an actor is playing a king. He is observed by Claudius, who is also seated on the stage (as was the custom). Attentively observing both of them is Hamlet. And all around them are Gertrude, Rosencrantz, Guildenstern, and Polonius. Lastly, we in the theater or in the movie house look on at these several tiers of audiences, knowing them all to be players.

Selected Classics— Backstage with the Bard

1. *TO BE OR NOT TO BE* (1942), U.S.A., directed by Ernst Lubitsch

Ernst Lubitsch's *To Be or Not to Be* employs its own "mousetrap" to foil Nazi tyranny in Poland. It belongs to a select company of backstage theatrical films set in World War II that also include Istvan Szabo's *Mephisto* (1981) and François Truffaut's *The Last Metro* (1980). Whereas *Mephisto*, adapted from Klaus Mann's long-suppressed novel, is a devastating indictment of artistic compromise in the service of the Nazi Party—the character of Hendrik was based on the opportunistic actor Gustaf Gründgens, who sold his soul, as it were (hence the title *Mephisto*), to curry the favor of Hermann Goering—the Lubitsch and Truffaut films are glorious tributes to the role that theater plays in the battle for personal and political freedom. (The Truffaut film will be examined presently in these pages.) *To Be or Not to Be* tells the story of the Josef Tura Troupe's involvement in the dangerous politics of World War II. Taking its cue from the title, a production of *Hamlet* is exploited for a variety of seriocomic possibilities. The setting is Poland in 1939. Jack Benny portrays Josef Tura, "that great, *great* Polish actor," as he describes himself on several occasions. A running gag in the film is his intonation of the lines of Hamlet's famous soliloquy—which are always interrupted by the departure from the audience of a handsome, young Polish flyer (principally, Robert Stack as Lieutenant Sobinski). Tura misunderstands the action: He thinks it is a critique of his acting, when in reality, unbeknownst to him, those particular lines are a signal arranged by his wife, Maria (Carole Lombard), for an assignation. It is doubtful if the Bard's words had ever before functioned as a coded message for extramarital dalliance. Those words may also be construed as the burning question that will decide Poland's fate.

But I get ahead of myself. Ernst Lubitsch's classic seriocomedy, written by Edwin Justus Mayer, depicts the adventures of a troupe of actors in war-torn Poland who find themselves utilizing their talents to outwit the Gestapo and support the Resistance. The movie opens with Adolph Hitler striding through the streets of Warsaw. But it is not Hitler. It is Bronski, an actor in Josef Tura's troupe, rehearsing a play called *Gestapo* that satirizes the Nazis. Sent out into the streets to test the effectiveness of his impersonation, he "fails" when a little girl comes up to him and asks him by his stage name for an autograph. Unlike the child, we movie viewers have been fooled at the outset (later in the film, this same impersonation will succeed with the Nazi Gestapo officers). Illusion and reality jostle for our attention. As Robert Willson has pointed out, this opening anecdote establishes at once not only the theme of the film but also the essential parallel between the movie and Shakespeare's *Hamlet*, i.e., "the feared German tyrant" proves to be "nothing more than a bad actor trying to convince us he is more powerful than he is." Hitler, like Claudius, "is little more than a player-king, incapable of ruling himself, let alone the kingdom."

When it is learned that a presumed Polish patriot, Professor Siletsky (Stanley Ridges), is in reality a Nazi agent bent on turning over the names of loyal Poles to the Nazis, the Tura troupe springs into action to intercept him and, at the same time, to effect the escape of the Polish aviator Sobinski. Josef Tura impersonates the Gestapo officer Erhardt (Sig Rumann), and interviews Siletsky. Smelling a rat, Siletsky almost escapes before he is killed by Sobinski. (This moment is one of the highlights of the film: Siletsky flees to Tura's theater, where he is shot dead on center-stage, a spotlight full upon him.) Tura now turns to his next challenge, impersonating Siletsky ("I'm going to have to do the impossible; I'm going to have to surpass myself"). As Siletsky, he goes to the real Erhardt in order to procure a plane for the fleeing Sobinski. But Erhardt, too, sees through the disguise, although he is unsuccessful in preventing Tura-Siletsky from escaping. The problem remains—Sobinski still has to be spirited out of the country. Now the stage is set, as it were, for the last and most ambitious of the Tura impersonations.

Learning that the real Hitler is coming to Tura's theater to witness a celebration performed in his honor, Tura contrives to use the occasion to effect Sobinski's escape. He may be motivated by more than just patriotism—after all, his troupe's Nazi satire, *Gestapo*, had been cancelled by the censors, and here is a chance at last to bring the play to the public. Using the uniforms from *Gestapo*, he and his actors invade the lobby *before* the arrival of the real Hitler. One of Tura's actors, Greenberg (Felix Bressart), has in the meantime been planted in the restroom in advance. He rushes out to confront "Hitler" (Bronski again) and commences Shylock's Rialto speech ("Hath not a Jew eyes?") from *The Merchant of Venice* (3.1.55–69). It is Greenberg's finest hour, and he recites the lines with poignant simplicity. While the fake Hitler orders the man's arrest, Tura (also in disguise as an SS officer) uses the ruckus as a diversion to spirit away Sobinski along with the rest of the fake soldiers. It is a subtle irony that while Bronski had not fooled the Poles with his Hitler impersonation, he is able to fool the Germans.

That the machinations of an acting troupe are central to the plot resolution and the deception of the villains underscores yet another link between the film and the "mousetrap" of Shakespeare's play. Significantly, as Danny Peary points out, it takes ham-handed actors to "have the tremendous egos that can compete with those of the Nazis"; and it takes their skills in theatrical deception to compete with the spy Siletsky.

The "To Be or Not to Be" words are declaimed one last time at the end of the film. Tura and his troupe have come to England to perform *Hamlet*. To the astonishment of Tura—and of Sobinski seated in the audience—at the utterance of the famous lines, *another* serviceman rises from his seat and heads for the exits! It is the last stroke in a world full of illusion and deception. Or, as Willson suggests, perhaps this last exit is indeed a critical reaction to Tura's performance (his rendition of Hamlet had earlier been criticized as comparable to what the Nazis were doing to Poland). Thus, by extension, "Lubitsch also seems to be suggesting that such poor players or player-kings as Hitler and Mussolini will likewise be exposed and hooted off the world stage."

It is worth noting that in Mel Brooks's remake in 1983 the play being performed by the Polish troupe is not *Hamlet*, but a series of excerpts from a collage play

Shakespeare's Hamlet *came to the backstage seriocomedy* To Be or Not to Be, *which starred Jack Benny and Carole Lombard as members of a Polish theater troupe.* (COURTESY NATIONAL FILM SOCIETY ARCHIVES)

entitled *Highlights from Hamlet*. That in itself is perhaps a commentary upon our modern-day penchant for bowdlerizing Shakespeare and abbreviating him for modern consumption.

2. *A DOUBLE LIFE* (1947), U.S.A., directed by George Cukor

A Double Life is one of many films that utilize theatrical events to illuminate psychological truths about the particular characters involved. To digress a moment, in *The Dresser* (1983), based on Ronald Harwood's 1980 play, a performance of *King Lear* salvages the wreckage of the unstable mental and emotional life of the actor known only as "Sir" (Albert Finney). With the support and urging of his loyal dresser, Norman (Tom Courtenay), Sir, who had earlier confused his lines, is able to pull himself together to deliver the last and definitive performance of his life. Perhaps appropriately, at the curtain's fall, Sir dies. Clearly, the character of Lear is an extension, or reflection, of Sir himself. Thus, the film emerges as a commentary on the excessive degree to which an actor identifies with a role.

More germane to *A Double Life* are the several films that have selected another Shakespeare play, *Othello*, to explore the darker implications of role identification. From the silent era comes *Carnival* (1921), which stars the great Italian Shakespearean actor Silvio Steno who, during a performance of *Othello*, goes crazy with jealousy and nearly strangles his wife to death while she is playing Desdemona. Two films from Britain have similar plot lines. *Men Are Not Gods* (1936) features an actor playing Othello, Edmund Davey (Sebastian Shaw), and his Desdemona, his wife (Gertrude Lawrence), who find themselves in a real-life triangle that nearly results in her murder onstage.

The most famous entry in this list—and one of mainstream Hollywood's finest treatments of Shakespeare—is undoubtedly *A Double Life* (1947), directed by George Cukor and scripted by Garson Kanin and Ruth Gordon. Shakespeare is dragged, all too willingly, one might suspect, into the world of late-1940s *film noir*. Ronald Colman (who won an Oscar for his performance) is Anthony John, an aging Broadway stage star who is currently costarring with his newly divorced wife, Brita (Signe Hasso), in a drawing-room comedy called *A Gentleman's Gentleman*. As a publicity stunt and a career boost, Tony considers mounting on Broadway a production of *Othello*, which will feature Brita as Desdemona. A gimmick will be that he will not smother Desdemona to death, but stifle her with a kiss. Ex-wife Brita is dubious about his taking on the role of Othello, since she knows all too well that Anthony has a tendency to identify too much with his roles. Sure enough, Tony immediately takes to the streets to ponder the new project, reciting lines from the play as he walks. Stopping at a café, he continues to recite lines to himself while chatting with a waitress named Pat Kroll (Shelley Winters). Throughout their exchange, Tony's interior voice declaims lines like "We do call these delicate creatures ours. . . ." from *Othello*. More lines whirl through his brain as he goes to her apartment and discovers that her bed is partitioned from the rest of the room, just as Desdemona's is in the play. "Have you prayed tonight, Desdemona?" The next morning Tony leaves Pat to begin rehearsals. Tony's interior monologue continues throughout, as he says to himself, "Look within yourself to find the key—jealousy!"

A remarkable montage takes us through the months spanning pre-production preparations to the successful opening night. We catch swift glimpses of the preliminary blocking, the first run-through, adjustments of the script, the costume tryouts, the glitches during technical rehearsals, and the night of the premiere. "The part begins to seep into your life and the battle begins," muses Tony. "Imagination against reality. Keep each in its place. That's the job, if you can do it." Although the production is a success, Tony is increasingly plagued by these interior voices and by the jangling sounds of bells.

The play is now in its second successful year. But as Tony's attempts to reconcile with Brita fail, his acting becomes more agitated, and his murder scenes with Desdemona become increasingly realistic. Things come to a head when Brita refuses Tony's marriage proposal, and he follows her to her rooms. "Yet she must die lest she betray more men," intones his interior voice. "Heaven truly knows that thou art false as hell. Oh, now, forever, farewell the tranquil mind." In a deranged state, he leaves her and staggers out into the night to Pat's room. After asking her repeatedly if she

George Cukor

has had other lovers, he murders her. "Put out the light, and then put out the light," he intones. The newspapers are full of the scandal, reporting that the victim was dispatched by a "kiss of death." It's a press agent's dream, aided by Tony's publicist and rival for Brita's affections, Bill Friend (Edmund O'Brien). But when Tony spots the story, he furiously rushes to Bill's flat and unsuccessfully tries to strangle him, shouting lines from the play all the while. Suspicious of Tony's complicity in the murder, Bill determines to set a trap for Tony, a "mousetrap" device. (Bill himself may be acting out of a combination of an altruistic search for justice and jealousy over Tony's relations with Brita.) Bill "auditions" several prospective actresses to impersonate the dead Pat Kroll. After selecting one, he has her made up and dressed like Pat, down to wearing her earrings. He then positions her in a bar where he will contrive to have Tony run into her. Tony's guilty reactions convince Bill he is indeed guilty of Pat's murder. Meanwhile, Tony prepares for the evening's performance of *Othello*. He confesses to Brita that nightmares and distractions are plaguing him. He summons up his strength, however, and goes on. After the murder scene with Desdemona, he speaks the lines, "Speak of me as one who loved not wisely but too well. . . ." Before the police waiting in the wings can capture him, he produces Othello's knife, for which he has substituted a real blade, and fatally stabs himself. While the audience reacts in shock, Tony is dragged backstage where he confesses his crime to Brita, Bill, and the police. At the moment of his death a shadow falls across his face, and at the same time the curtain closes and the spotlight is extinguished.

Veteran stage actor-manager Walter Hampden supervised the generous helping of *Othello* sequences. Cinematographer Milton Krasner photographed many of the exterior scenes in the New York streets and the interior, theatrical sequences in a heavily cloaked chiaroscuro lighting. Miklos Rozsa's music "doubles" as diegetic music for the play and as nondiegetic music to accompany and enhance the offstage action.

There are many levels of reality and illusion, each "doubling" for the other. Indeed, the "double" motif permeates all aspects of the film and the play-within-the-film (while Bill's little "mousetrap" device constitutes yet another level, *another* play-within-the-film). Just as Shakespeare demonstrated that Othello was himself a divided soul, as capable of noble-hearted generosity as he was of lethal jealousy, Tony John is immediately depicted as a man possessed also of a double personality. When we first see him, he is standing in the foyer of the Empire Theatre before a large painting of himself. Tony turns toward the camera; and before his face blocks out the painting we see two Tonys, the enormous painting towering above and behind him. Moments later he pauses and silently regards his bust, the two faces in a "two-shot," as it were. Later in the street he encounters two actresses. "What a darling," one says. "What a stinker," retorts the other.

Clearly, there are *two* Tony Johns to consider. When he first seriously considers performing in *Othello* he shuffles through some drawings while the image of the bearded, dark-skinned Othello superimposes over his face. "Oh, beware, my lord, of jealousy. It is the green-eyed monster," says a voice in his head. It is our first encounter with another "double"—we realize that Tony has *two* voices. The interior one functions throughout as the equivalent of the Shakespearean soliloquy, i.e., it both enhances and comments upon the action. When Tony first follows Pat to her apartment, he has difficulty telling her his name, his *real* name. Instead, he catalogues the names of many roles he has played. Immediately thereafter as he turns to a mirror and tries on one of her earrings, declaiming Othello's lines, "the bawdy wind that kisses all it meets . . .," the camera pans from his face to the mirror image, positioning the two together within the shot.

Desdemona's deathbed scene is also doubled, finding its real-life counterpart in Pat's bedroom. The scene is depicted four times. The first time we are on the Empire stage for opening night, and the scene is played virtually intact. "Yet I would not shed her blood, yet she must die," declaims Tony. At that same moment his interior voice comments: "You're two men now, grappling for control. You and Othello." He strangles Desdemona, then kisses her intently until her spasms cease. He then stabs himself, saying, "No way but this, killing myself to die upon a kiss." All is played strictly according to the book; but a disturbing moment, a discordant grace note, as it were, polishes off the scene. Tony remains in place, taking his curtain calls, even though the curtain has fallen and the audience departed. Having established the basic outline of the scene, Desdemona's murder is played a second time in more truncated form. A series of views from the wings and backstage, along with several powerful close-ups, give it a more intimate quality. Tony is now somewhat deranged and his strangling of Desdemona is frighteningly real—so real that she has to call for a doctor afterward.

The third replay of the scene occurs in Pat's apartment. Her bed, the curtain partition, even details of the décor echo the stage set. Her blonde hair has tumbled loose, and she is wearing a white nightgown, very much like Desdemona. As she brings him a cup of coffee, he interrogates her about other men in her life. Tony grows more agitated as she asks him to "put out the light." It's a fatal mistake. Her remark reminds him of Desdemona's line, and he responds, now wholly caught up in the play, "If I quench thee, thou flaming minister . . ." He strangles, then kisses her. Her clutching hand grips the partition and draws it across the scene like a closing curtain. For the fourth and final enactment of the scene we are back on the Empire stage. Distraught and anxious, Tony nervously awaits the scene. He is at the end of his rope, and the police are closing in. This time the action begins after the murder, when Othello is about to be taken away by his councillors. Instead of stabbing himself with the prop knife, he procures a real blade (another "double" motif). "Then must you speak of one who loved," he intones brokenly, "not wisely but too well; of one not easily jealous but being wrought perplexed in the extreme." As the interior noises rise in a crescendo in his head, he collapses.

Commentator Robert F. Willson argues persuasively that the role of Othello functioned as an Iago-like device that precipitated Tony's homicidal tendencies and his own death. "*A Double Life* represents Iago as a psychological demon that in the modern world has become internalized; relying on the device, the writers and director explore depths of character that the Freudian age has come to regard as determinate and psychopathic rather than 'tragic.'" Putting it another way, the play—indeed, the acting profession generally—functions as a kind of potion that can stimulate alternate personalities in an actor, just as the elixir of the noble Dr. Jekyll frees Mr. Hyde.

3. *THEATER OF BLOOD* (1973), U.K., directed by Douglas Hickox

Theater of Blood trumps *A Double Life* several times over. An actor chooses not just one, but 10 methods of Shakespearean-inspired homicide. In a brilliant stroke, Vincent Price is cast as the vengeful Edward Lionheart, a most theatrically flamboyant, if ham-handed, serial killer.

Setting the scene is a prologue containing clips of death scenes from several black-and-white Shakespearean silent films. The eerily mute succession of suffocations and stabbings takes on the elegantly Grand Guignol character of drawings by Edward Gorey. The story proper begins on March 15 (appropriately enough, as it turns out) with the savage stabbing death of theater critic George Maxwell (Michael Hordern). After being lured to an abandoned building, Maxwell finds himself confronting a knife-wielding mob in a scene straight out of *Julius Caesar*. He is brutally attacked and hacked to pieces. Looking on is the costumed character of Mark Antony. "Pardon me, thou bleeding piece of earth," Antony mocks, "that I am meek and gentle with these butchers." Discarding the broken corpse, Antony turns to his bedraggled accomplices and intones his eulogy of the dead Caesar, "Friends, Romans, countrymen, lend me your ears!"

Edward Lionheart, once presumed dead, is very much alive. Assisted by his deranged daughter, Edwina (Diana Rigg), and a motley crew of accomplices, he has begun his vendetta against the critics who savaged his performances. Each murder will be patterned after one of the Shakespearean plays that marked Lionheart's last season on the boards. Like Caesar himself, back from the dead, he is ready to "Cry 'Havoc!' and let slip the dogs of war. . . ."

In *Troilus and Cressida* Achilles slays Hector and lashes his corpse to the tail of a wild horse. Lionheart's second victim, critic Hector Snipe (Dennis Price), suffers the same fate. "Look, Hector, how the sun begins to set, how ugly night comes breathing at his heels," declaims Lionheart, dressed in the armor of Achilles, as he thrusts his spear into Snipe's body. "Even with the violent darkening of the sun to close the day up, Hector's life is done." Lionheart orders his accomplices, "Come tie his body to my tail, along the field I will the Trojan trail . . ."

Just as in *Cymbeline*, Imogen wakes up and finds the headless body of Cloten in the bed with her, so now does Lionheart arrange a like fate for his third victim, critic Horace Sprout (Arthur Lowe). Lionheart and his accomplice (Diana Rigg disguised as a man) invade Sprout's bedchamber, drug him and his wife with a hypodermic, lay out their surgical tools, and proceed to saw off Sprout's head. Jets of blood spurt upward while dreamy music is heard on the soundtrack. Beside her decapitated husband, Mrs. Sprout sleeps on. She is due for a rude awakening.

In *The Merchant of Venice* the vengeful Shylock wants to claim his pound of flesh from Antonio, but his daughter, Portia, dissuades him. Lionheart has worked out his own version of the play for his fourth victim, critic Trevor Dickman (Harry Andrews). Dickman protests that Antonio is spared in the play. "We have revised this script," retorts Lionheart, dressed in the robes of the Jew, as he cuts out Dickman's heart. "You spurned me such a day," recites Lionheart. "Another time you called me dog. . . . But if I am a dog, beware my fangs." He weighs the bleeding tissue on the scales. Two ounces too heavy. He snips off a tiny piece. *Now* he has his pound of flesh. Later, viewing the dead man's remains, another critic quips, "Only Lionheart would have the temerity to rewrite Shakespeare."

In *Richard III* the scheming Richard has his henchmen murder George, the duke of Clarence, by drowning him in a cask of wine. Lionheart duly lures his fifth victim, critic Oliver Larding (Robert Coote) to a fake wine tasting, where he is thrust upside down into a wine cask. "Now is the winter of our discontent," snarls Lionheart, wearing the wig and mincing the walk of Richard, "made glorious summer by this son of York. . . . As I am subtle, false, and treacherous, this day should Clarence be closely mewed up."

The sixth murder attempt is a curiously unfinished affair. Critic Peregrine Devlin (Ian Hendry) goes to his fencing school, where instead of his teacher, he confronts Lionheart, rapier in hand. Like Tybalt and Romeo in *Romeo and Juliet*, they go at it, hurdling barriers and bouncing on trampolines. But then, curiously, Lionheart lets him go, delaying the kill for another day.

Inspired by Othello's deadly jealousy, Lionheart contrives to stage-manage a scene where his sixth victim, critic Solomon Psaltery (Jack Hawkins), finds his wife in bed with a lover (Lionheart disguised as a masseur). Psaltery seizes a pillow and suffocates his wife. Lionheart may not have killed Psaltery, observes a police detective, but he has managed to consign the poor man to prison for the rest of his life.

Henry VI, Part I has a grisly scene where Joan of Arc is burned at the stake. Lionheart's seventh victim, critic Chloe Moon (Carol Browne), faces a similar fate when she goes to an appointment at a hair salon. Lionheart, affecting a limp-wristed persona, waits on her. He hooks her hair curlers to the electricity and turns on the juice. "Bring forth that sorceress condemned to burn," he intones. "Break thou in pieces and consume to ashes, thou foul, accursed minister of Hell." Chloe is left in the chair, burnt to a cinder.

Titus Andronicus contains Shakespeare's most notorious piece of Grand Guignol revenge as Titus feeds his arch enemy, Queen Tamara, a meat pie consisting of her two sons. This is the fate reserved for Lionheart's eighth victim, critic Meredith Merridew (Robert Morley). Merridew dotes on his two poodle dogs with the same enthusiasm as he relishes a gourmet meal. Lionheart contrives to combine both pleasures. He fakes a live performance of a popular cooking television show,

This Is Your Dish, where the delighted Merridew is treated to a succulent dish. But the meat pie that Merridew consumes with such pleasure turns out to made from his two dogs. "I will grind your bones to dust and make two pasties of your shameful head," quotes Lionheart as Titus, as he stuffs food down Merridew's throat with a funnel. Moments later, Lionheart smirks, "Pity, he didn't have the stomach for it."

Lionheart reserves critic Peregrine Devlin for the fate of Gloucester in *King Lear*. Devlin is tied to a bench while two red-hot daggers slowly descend toward his eyes. Lionheart offers mercy if Devlin will admit that he is a great actor. Refusing, Devlin gazes at Edwina, who is all too willingly assisting her father. "What have you done to your daughter?" Devlin protests. Edwina, standing in for Lear's loyal daughter, Cordelia, turns toward her father: "Good my lord you have begot me, bred me, loved me," she says, assuming her own role. "I return those duties back as are right fit. Obey you, love you, most honor you." Before Devlin's eyes can be put out, the police burst in. Edwina is injured and Lionheart, clasping her body to his breast, staggers off and sets the theater on fire. "Come, fire," he moans, "consume this petty world; and in its ashes let my memory lie." He and Edwina exchange their last words. "How does my royal lord," she whispers. "How fares your majesty?" He responds, "You did me wrong to take me out of the grave. Thou art a soul in bliss, but I am bound upon a wheel of fire. Mine own tears do scald like molten lead." She breathes her last, "We are not the first, who best meaning, have incurred the worst."

Both perish in the fire. It remains for Devlin, the only surviving critic, to have the last word: "Yes, it was a fascinating performance, but of course he was madly overacting, as usual. But you must admit, he did know how to make an exit."

If Lionheart identifies with his Shakespearean characters, so surely does Vincent Price empathize with his character of Lionheart. Both, near the end of their careers, suffered critical jibes for their broad-brush theatrics. And in this film both have the chance to wreak revenge most foul. *Theater of Blood* is the most erudite piece of Grand Guignol in film history; and Lionheart/Price is the most articulate of serial killers.

4. *SHAKESPEARE WALLAH* (1965), U.K., directed by James Ivory

The term "wallah" in Hindustani means a small-time operator. Here it refers to a small troupe of touring English players. The film is loosely based on the diaries of actor-manager Geoffrey Kendal while touring India with his "Shakesperiana" troupe in 1947, the year India achieved independence from Britain. When filmmaker James Ivory read the diary, he showed it to novelist Ruth Prawer Jhabvala, who collaborated with him on a screenplay. Kendal and his wife, Laura Liddel, portrayed their fictional counterparts, the Buckinghams. Their daughter Felicity was cast in the key role of Lizzie Buckingham. Popular actor Shashi Kapoor portrayed Sanju, Lizzie's romantic lead. And Madhur Jaffrey played Manjula, a popular Bollywood actress. The film was made on a shoestring budget of $80,000 and shot on locations in the hill station of Kasauli, in the Punjab; in the vice-regal summer capital of Simla; in Alwar, in Rajasthan; in Lucknow; and in Bombay.

The story spins out against the background of the passing of British culture in post-independence India. It is a world too impatient for Shakespearean drama and too preoccupied with the novelties of musical films. The disasters that befall the Buckingham Players exemplify the schisms opening up between worlds old and new, between classical and popular entertainment. The Buckinghams are slow to adapt to these changes. "One is always conscious of them as being constrained by their theatrical calling," notes Patrice Sorace, "which has lost popularity to Indian films that represent the new, indigenous Indian culture."

Indeed, the Buckinghams' tour is marked by disasters of all kinds. At the film's beginning, when they are performing Sheridan's *The Critic* in front of a chateau near Lucknow, a runaway cow stampedes the actors and audience. Their next performance, of Shakespeare's *Antony and Cleopatra*, transpires in the renovated palace of the maharaja of Betawar, who complains that current conditions have forced him to rent out half his palace as office space. Later, at a private school the troupe learns that they will have to cut back on the usual number of performances. Mr. Buckingham protests: "But surely Shakespeare is still in your curriculum. I mean, our shows are very popular with schools and colleges. We do a kind of package—Hamlet, some comedy, some tragedy, a bit of *Twelfth Night*. . . ." But the department head only shakes him off, citing the importance of allowing time for a game of cricket: "I don't want to put undue stress on our sports activities, but they do take a lot of time. . . ." To Buckingham's dismay, the troupe is dismissed after just one performance. "It all changed, slowly, over these past years," he says bitterly. "I keep thinking about it. I can't help it. We should have gone home in '47 when the others went. But we were too sure of ourselves."

Tensions of a different sort arise when young Lizzie Buckingham meets and falls in love with Sanju, a wealthy young Indian playboy. Sanju conveys his admiration of the troupe's performance of *Hamlet* to his friend, the celebrated Indian actress Manjula. In particular, he extols Lizzie's artistry: "She is a very fine artist. For such people one can have some respect." Manjula, who has no inkling of what classical drama is all about, retorts that she, too, has played "many great dramatic roles in my time." To which Sanju admits, "People don't care for the theater so much these days. Only for films."

Ignoring Manjula's jealousy, Sanju follows Lizzie when the troupe takes to the road toward Simla. He watches her performance as Maria in *Twelfth Night* and as Desdemona in *Othello*. During the latter performance, Manjula unexpectedly bursts in, and her ostentatious entrance literally stops the show. Mr. Buckingham advances to the footlights and requests silence. Unabashed, Manjula maintains her grand manner and signs autographs during the murder scene. In mock horror at the violence of Desdemona's death, Manjula departs with considerable commotion. "How can you like something like that?" she asks Sanju. "All that moaning and groaning, so bloodthirsty." Later, when Sanju tries to apologize to Buckingham, he shrugs, saying, "Let's just call it the victory of the moving pictures over the theater." The final humiliation comes during the Buckinghams' performance of *Romeo and Juliet*. Lizzie's entrance onstage as Juliet is greeted with rude whistles and comments from the audience. As she declaims the lines, "But my true love is grown to such excess/I cannot sum up half my wealth," a fight breaks out between Sanju and the offending toughs. A near riot ensues and the performance is halted. Minutes later, Sanju objects to Lizzie's choice of a lifestyle that constantly exposes her to the public. "It's a wonderful life," she replies defensively; "I wouldn't want to be anything else. Acting's my whole life." Yet, it is obvious she is prepared to give it up if Sanju would ask her to marry him. But it is just as obvious that Sanju will never understand her devotion to the theater, and that he is not prepared to take that final step. The lovers part. In the concluding scene, at the behest of her parents, a saddened Lizzie boards a ship bound for England.

Although the original source material of the film, the Kendal diaries, had depicted the adventures of the troupe as a positive experience, it was decidedly the intention of Ivory and Jhabvala to negate that. The Buckinghams' failure was designed to be emblematic of the larger failure of classical drama in the face of the culture of a New India—a culture at once rooted both in Eastern traditions and in the pop culture of Bollywood. Similarly, Lizzie's devotion to her craft was also out of place in the face of Sanju's traditionalist—some would say "sexist"—attitudes toward a woman's place in society. "The Kendals felt uncomfortable," recalled James Ivory, "were hard put sometimes even to bring out their dialogue, which seemed to give utterance to thoughts which were at variance with everything they believed. It did not help that the stuff of their lives was being used in order to create a drama symbolic of a moment in history."

5. *A MIDWINTER'S TALE* (1995), U.K., directed by Kenneth Branagh (released in the U.K. as in THE BLEAK MIDWINTER)

In *A Midwinter's Tale* (1995) the redoubtable Shakespearean Kenneth Branagh chronicles the glitches, twitches, and occasional glories of a theatrical troupe desperately trying to ready a performance of *Hamlet* for a Christmas Eve opening in an abandoned English country church. Fiction merges with reality in that the actors are drawn from Branagh's own troupe, the Renaissance Theatre Company. Thus, you can believe what you're seeing on screen is the real thing, drawn from their shared experiences. "It was the cumulative experience of this group that informed and changed the script," recalled Branagh. "All the mad audition sequences come from life, as do many of the characters. The film itself was made in the spirit of the story.... The spirit of generous collaboration (not without the odd fit of temper) made for a shoot... which, as Hamlet would, held 'the mirror up to nature.'" Moreover, Branagh serves it up with quick wit, swift pacing, peppery dialogue, and a no-nonsense camera style. "The more 'serious' the play the more likely rehearsals are to create amusement," says Branagh, "although the hijinks may not always be intentional and may not always be enjoyed by the people involved.... In Shakespeare particularly, the great tragedies tread such a fine line between laughter and tears, that any group working on them can find themselves in the grip of hysteria.... It's

Backstage with the Bard: A theater troupe prepares its production of Hamlet in Kenneth Branagh's A Midwinter's Tale.
(COURTESY CASTLE ROCK ENTERTAINMENT)

the very stuff of drama, inside the drama." Critics of the film agreed. "[It] starts off as an amusing free-for-all spoof of the acting profession," wrote Stephen Holden, "and eventually turns into a comic valentine to diehard thespian dedication."

Much of the film is frankly autobiographical, both of the adventures Branagh has experienced on the road, and of his childhood delight in watching Hollywood backstage musicals. In particular, Branagh wanted to emulate the cycle of backstage movies that teamed up director Busby Berkeley with Judy Garland and Mickey Rooney—*Babes in Arms* (1939), *Strike up the Band* (1940), *Babes on Broadway* (1942), and *Girl Crazy* (1943)—wherein the determination of a bunch of squabbling, disparate kids to "put on a show" transforms them into a solidly organized and creatively productive theatrical unit.

A Midwinter's Tale begins as Joe (Michael Maloney) holds auditions for an upcoming production of *Hamlet*: A dancer tap-dances the "To Be or Not to Be" soliloquy. A ventriloquist and his dummy proclaim the "Alas poor Yorick" lines. A madwoman enacts with hand puppets the characters of Mrs. and Mrs. Macbeth. A balding man belts out "Mule Train" while hitting himself on the head with an aluminum tray.

What a mismatched assortment of players is finally brought together! As Kenneth Rothwell says, they are "losers, not glamorous stars, making pathetic efforts to interest the world in their Shakespearean tragedy." There's Michael Maloney as Joe, the intense producer rolling the dice on this production; Julia Sawalha as Nina, his Ophelia, a nearsighted klutz who can't even find a creek to drown in; Nicholas Farrell as Tom Newman, who plays Laertes, slipping in and out of unlikely accents ("from another solar system") and motivations like a shopper trying on suits; John Sessions as Terry Du Bois, a campy gay man who takes on Gertrude (and who will supply his own frocks and breasts for the role); Richard Briers as Henry Wakefield, the company's Claudius (who staunchly declares, "The English theater is dominated by the class system and a bunch of Oxbridge homos"); and Celia Imrie as Fadge, the production designer with singularly inventive ideas, including populating the empty auditorium seats with cardboard cutouts of spectators "just to keep the actors company," she confides to Joe (the sight of these bizarre, stiff forms mixed in with the living patrons accounts for the funniest scenes in the movie). "If we don't get a natural audience, I want to create a World for you. You should at least have people watching you. Even if they are cardboard."

The company arrives in Joe's car at the village of Hope. They tumble out and admire the picturesque little church situated at the top of a hill. But no, this is the wrong site. The *real* church is down by the village, an "ugly red church" that is damp and cavernous. At the first read-through, Joe admits, "I see it as a very long play." "I see it as a *very* long play, darling," retorts one of the players. "Sally Scissors is going to appear, we hope?" Everybody bickers about what lines are to be cut, details of costuming, who will play multiple roles, what period to set the play in, how to advertise. They worry about attracting the locals to see the play. "Hello kids," mocks Molly. "Do stop watching Mighty Morphin Power Rangers and come and watch a four-hundred-year-old play about a depressed aristocrat. I mean it's something you can really relate to."

The first rehearsals. One actor defends his preposterous "grande dame" accent in Gertrude's opening lines ("They don't talk like they do in the real world—they put on the old cigarette gravel—the tragic thrill—the emotional break in the middle of the line—the operatic cadenzas"). So caught up is she in Ophelia's madness, poor nearsighted Nina shouts "Oh, my lord, I have been so affrighted"—and races right off the edge of the stage. One actor finds himself having to play Rosencrantz and Guildenstern *at the same time.* There are worries about paying the landlord overdue electric bills. And there is not enough time for sufficient rehearsal. "We have set ourselves a challenge there is no doubt," declares Joe. "But at Shakespeare's own theater, a six-week season would have produced 35 performances of 17 different plays including at times four world premieres. So, as Polonius says, 'Sometimes Brevity can be the soul of wit.' But I don't think we should lose our nerve." The closet scene between Hamlet and Gertrude is interrupted by the revelation that the actor playing Gertrude had abandoned a child years before.

As things keep going wrong and the prospect of additional needed funding looks bleak, Joe at last loses his temper: "What is the point? . . . You're a perfectly decent bunch of people. A group of actors with all the normal insecurities and vanities. But basically I know you want to be here, we all want to do what's best for the show. But look at us. We argue. We're depressed. We've set ourselves too great a target. It is too personal for us all. It's a big play and we keep running up against it and hurting ourselves, and I for one can no longer remember what I'm doing or why I'm doing it." But the next day things look better. The scenes snap into focus. The cast comes up with the extra money.

Now comes the technical rehearsal. Too much smoke. Nobody can see anything. The opening words, "Who's there?" take on extra meaning. Meanwhile, no one (least of all the movie viewers) has a clue as to what is the time period for the play. Relations among the cast are likewise indeterminate, as they keep falling in and out of love with each other.

In a last-minute crisis, Joe's agent, Margaretta (Joan Collins), gets him a lucrative movie job acting in a science fiction trilogy. She arrives on Christmas Eve to announce that the show will have to close and that Joe has to leave that night. The actors, by now united into a family group, protest that the show must go on: "That's what actors do . . . they hang on, they stick it out." Joe's Ophelia reminds him, "You put your whole life into this, Joe. Right from the start. You needed this job. You needed it then and you need it now. It's not about fame or money or so-called wealth and security, it's about nourishing your soul, nourishing your heart." Molly prepares to go on at the last minute as Hamlet. She receives a canny piece of advice: "If I ever forget my lines in Shakespeare, I always say, 'Crouch we here awhile and lurk.' Always seems to do the trick."

At last the performance begins as smoke envelops the stage (and the audience). At the words, "Who's there?" Horatio, clad in a trench coat, fires a machine gun over the heads of the startled audience. From the back of the church comes Hamlet's first words: "A little more than kin and less than kind." It is Joe, to the rescue, clad in his winter coat, returned unexpectedly at the last minute for opening night. Quick onstage scenes intercut with Fadge backstage clinking glasses with Molly. The Nunnery Scene. Nina's Ophelia is clad in a silver turban and glittery dress, making her look for all the world like Theda Bara. Clearly upset with Joe's last-minute grandstanding, Nina concludes her lines—"Rich gifts wax poor when givers prove unkind"—with a hard slap to his face. Quick glimpse of the Mousetrap Scene (with Claudius clad in military tunic and epaulettes). Cut to the Closet Scene, where Hamlet says, "What is a man if his chief good and market of his time be but to sleep and feed, a beast no more." The sword fight features Hamlet and Laertes, bare-chested, in trousers and suspenders, exchanging lines and blades as they whirl about the room. Hamlet declaims his last lines, "The rest is silence." Fortinbras says: "Go, bid the soldiers shoot." Darkness. Drum. Gong. Wild applause. The whole performance has taken up a mere four minutes of screen time. Tom Stoppard could not have abbreviated the whole thing in a more trenchant and succinct manner. It is the Bard played at top speed.

The theatrical improbabilities spill out into the post-performance sequence with several tearful reunions and last-minute revelations. One of the audience members turns out to be a Hollywood celebrity. After dubbing Joe and Nina "Mickey" and "Judy" ("The whole thing was like a Judy Garland movie"), she offers Tom Newman a leading role and Fadge a job as designer in her new science fiction movie. Another audience member turns out to be Terry's long-lost son; and they reconcile with a tearful embrace as Terry says, "I think you're a wonderful queen, in every way." In the meantime, it is revealed that Joe really has turned down the movie part for the sake of being with the play and with Nina. A mollified Nina falls into his arms and they dance, their future romance assured. Against an exterior night shot of the church, the words of the company are heard: "Merry Christmas!"

The triumph of this performance is nothing less than a Christmas apotheosis for the lowly cast members. "The enchantment of assuming the identities of fabled persons like Hamlet, Gertrude, and Ophelia casts its spell," writes Kenneth Rothwell, "and their play turns into a Christmas miracle in which wretchedness is transfigured into sublimity."

A Midwinter's Tale serves as a comic curtain-raiser for the real treat to come—Branagh's full-scale production of *Hamlet* (1996), which presented the complete play, intact, for the first time on screen. (There's a private joke in *A Midwinter's Tale*, incidentally, when the director reassures his troupe that they'll perform the play with cuts.) For some of us, however, Branagh's *Midwinter* deserves its own privileged place alongside his *Hamlet*.

6. *LOOKING FOR RICHARD* (1996), U.S.A., directed by Al Pacino

Al Pacino's *Looking for Richard* (1996) might be subtitled *Looking for Shakespeare*. While trying to make sense of what is probably Shakespeare's most frequently performed play, Pacino and his company also cast about for the relevance of Shakespeare for today's audiences. To make *that* long story short, dozens of brief interviews with "the man in the street" persuade us that he doesn't mean a heck of a lot. As Anthony Lane wrote in *The New Yorker*, "This reaching out to an ideal public is bound to be a disappointment, because the majority of the population doesn't care a whit for Shakespeare and never will."

To be sure, just what Pacino intends this project to be is never made clear. Just what is it documenting: the

Al Pacino and Winona Ryder embark on a search for Shakespearean relevance in Looking for Richard.
(COURTESY FOX SEARCHLIGHT PICTURES)

relevance of Shakespeare today; the behind-the-scenes preparations for a play performance; or the shooting of a motion picture adaptation? Pacino himself is not quite sure, and he drifts through the proceedings like a Shakespearean version of Marcello Mastroianni trying to make sense of his creative vision in Fellini's *8 1/2*. There are discussions of the proper use of iambic pentameter, a trip to Shakespeare's birthplace in Stratford-upon-Avon (where Pacino inadvertently trips the fire alarm), a brief visit to the site of the Globe Theatre (which at the time was beginning its reconstruction), and interviews with stalwart Shakespeareans like Kenneth Branagh, Sir John Gielgud, Vanessa Redgrave, and Peter Brook. Pacino gathers his cast—Alec Baldwin as Clarence, Winona Ryder as Lady Anne, Aidan Quinn as Richmond, Kevin Spacey as Buckingham, and Pacino himself as Richard—and they tussle mightily over issues of why American actors are intimidated by performing the Bard, how to make sense of some of the more densely textured rhetoric, how Richard and Buckingham can be related to today's gangsters (but "high-class gangsters"), and the riddles of character motivation (just why does Richard feel he has to marry Lady Anne?). Pacino has also brought along an educator, Frederic Kimball, for his scholarly savvy.

Predictably, rarely does anyone agree on anything. "Nobody knows *Richard III*," mutters Pacino in exasperation. "It's very confusing. I don't know why we're doing this [movie] at all." Later, as he begins to settle into his character, Pacino doesn't hesitate to reject the advice of Kimball. Kimball erupts in very real anger. "You hired me as a scholar to explain things," he shouts, "yet you *actors* seem to think your ideas are better than mine." Pacino only smiles and grabs a sword to confer a mock knighthood on the poor man, dubbing him "Sir Ph.D."

Meanwhile, Pacino, who does not exactly enjoy an extensive experience in matters Shakespearean, struggles with the convoluted plot. He is bemused but not abashed at its complexities. "There is something sly and rather Richard-like in the throwaway glee with which [Pacino] approaches matters of grave intent," notes Anthony Lane. He also credits Pacino's experience in the three "Godfather" movies with his understanding of the "diplomatic savagery" that Richard employs to place himself on the English throne. There is the backstory of the War of the Roses and the recent defeat of the house of Lancaster to unravel; the complicated relationships among King Edward's presumptives to the throne; Richard's campaign to eliminate his rivals (in order, Clarence, the two princes, and Hastings); and the circumstances of the battle of Bosworth.

Rehearsals, finished performance, and video replay all combine in a seamless flux and flow. In a series of quick edits, Pacino begins a line in his apartment, continues it on stage in full costume, and then reviews the finished product on the video monitor in the studio. Punctuating the proceedings are a number of brief scenes when Pacino's Richard, clad in black tunic, hair wisping from beneath his black cap, addresses the camera with smarmy familiarity. His pale face emerges from out of the enveloping darkness, and his dissipated eyes flicker warily while his lips curdle in an ever so slight smirk. This is a most interesting Richard, a compound of diffidence and deadly authority. In the second half of the film are several protracted sequences that give us our Shakespeare "straight," as it were. These include, in order, Richard's seduction of Lady Anne ("'Twas thy beauty that provoked me," he suggests softly), his charge to two assassins to murder Clarence, the council meeting and the arrest of Hastings, and his exhortation to Buckingham to kill the two princes, and his nightmarish sleep when he is visited by the specters of his past crimes.

Unimpressed by all this are two filmmakers who protest Pacino's extravagance with the whole thing. Finally, after the battle of Bosworth and Richard's death under Richmond's sword, one of them stands back from the set and asks in deadpan, "Is Richard dead? Is that *it*?"

The other retorts sarcastically, "If I had told [Pacino] about that other ten rolls of film, he'd want to use it!"

7. *SHAKESPEARE IN LOVE* (1998), U.K., directed by John Madden

Shakespeare in Love (1998) would have us believe that an ill-starred love affair between young Shakespeare and a beauteous woman named Viola De Lesseps (Joseph Fiennes and Gwyneth Paltrow) directly inspired—and was in turn inspired by—the romantic tragedy, *Romeo and Juliet*. What is backstage comes to the forestage—and returns full circle. This play-within-a-play-within-a-movie is cunningly written by Shakespeare veteran Tom Stoppard (*The Fifteen-Minute Hamlet* and *Rosencrantz and Guildenstern Are Dead*) and Marc Norman; and directed by John Madden (who displayed a deft touch with actress Judi Dench in another historical film, about Queen Victoria, *Mrs. Brown*).

London, 1593. Two theaters are contending for popular (and royal) favor—the Curtain Theatre, which claims the talents of the Chamberlain's company and playwright Kit Marlowe; and the Rose Theatre, with the Admiral's company and young Will Shakespeare. The latter house is deep in debt, and its manager, Philip Henslowe (Geoffrey Rush), must get Shakespeare to write a sensational melodrama to fill the coffers. But poor, scruffy, ink-stained Will is suffering from writer's block and sexual impotence ("I dreamed I was trying to pick a lock with a limp herring," he innocently tells his astrologer/councillor in an early scene). The play that's resisting his pen is a melodrama called *Romeo and Ethel, the Pirate's Daughter*.

But inspiration springs up afresh, so to speak, when Will espies a young man at the play auditions named Thomas Kent, who speaks his lines with extraordinary eloquence. Amazed, Will pursues him and tracks him down to a wealthy estate across the Thames. He does not find Thomas Kent, but he does encounter a dazzling, golden-tressed damsel named Viola. Will is instantly smitten with her and impetuously crashes a dance party to see her. But because Will is from the wrong side of the tracks—from the far shore of the Thames, as it were—he's tossed out by her angry suitor, Lord Wessex (Colin Firth). Back at the Rose Theatre, rehearsals begin for *Romeo and Ethel, the Pirate's Daughter*. The mysterious Thomas Kent reappears and joins the theater cast as the character of "Romeo." It's only a little later that Will realizes at last that he has been hoodwinked—that this boy is in actuality his beloved Viola in disguise ("I am theater mad," she says, "and dream myself into a company of players"). It's a delicious moment, as Will waxes eloquently to the "boy" about Viola's charms, and "he" in response suddenly kisses Will.

Keeping their secret, Will and Viola rehearse by day onstage at the Rose and make love by night in her chambers (her parents are conveniently out of town); and, newly inspired, Will transmutes their tender moments into scenes for the new play. In this way life, love, and the theater blissfully intertwine—until Viola's ruse is discovered by the angry Lord Wessex, who first attacks Will in a sword fight and then has the Master of the Revels close down the Rose Theatre on the grounds of the illegality of having a woman appear on the stage. But Burbage's, the Chamberlain's company, comes to the rescue and offers its Curtain Theatre to put on the play (by now retitled, at the casual suggestion of one of Will's actors, *Romeo and Juliet*). The play commences, but Will is brokenhearted because Viola is now married to Lord Wessex. Little does he know that not only has Viola run away from Wessex to attend the opening day of the play, but that she has also taken the place of the boy portraying Juliet. When she comes on to the stage—a real woman playing Will's real love—she and the character of Juliet have melded into one (just as Will is now a real-life Romeo). After the play ends to tumultuous applause, the Master of the Revels shows up determined to close down the theater. But who should rebuke him but Queen Elizabeth herself, who emerges from the gallery to closely examine Viola and slyly declare that her "illusion" as a "woman" is very convincing. The queen sends Viola off with Wessex. Will, after a tearful departing scene with Viola, settles down to write *Twelfth Night*, with a heroine named Viola. "Write me well," Viola says, "with a new life beginning on a stranger shore."

Joseph Fiennes' Shakespeare is a portrait of a man on the run. He's an artistic chameleon, alive to the vivid colorations of life on the street. He cadges plot tips from Kit Marlowe and lines of dialogue from street conversations—like "a plague on both your houses," overheard from a local minister fulminating against the wicked stage. And he writes like he makes love—at top speed, the quill pen splattering ink across the snow-white foolscap. Gwyneth Paltrow is certainly an intriguing sight sporting a mustache and dressed in men's clothes, quite at home, ironically, amidst a crowd of men dressed like women! Other memorable touches include the boy who periodically shows up, torturing cats and mice, who says his name is John Webster and that he likes blood and murder (who, of course, will grow up to become the Jacobean author of such blood-and-thunder revenge dramas as *The Duchess of Malfi*). There's some business with Kit Marlowe (Rupert Everett in a subdued mood), whose death from a tavern brawl Shakespeare mistakenly supposes to have been caused by his inference to Wessex that it is Kit, not he, who has been visiting Viola at night. Meanwhile, the show's benefactor, the "money man," as he declares himself, ends up a stagestruck idiot playing the character of the apothecary. Philip Henslowe, the manager of the Rose, has a continuing bit of business wherein he declares that some "mysterious" power always comes to the rescue of even the most disaster-ridden theatrical enterprise (and sure enough, at the last moment the tongue-tied character portraying Chorus miraculously declaims his opening speech perfectly). It is also Henslowe who has the best line: After hearing Will describe the action of the play, Henslowe rolls his eyes and responds sarcastically, "*That'll* have 'em rolling in the aisles." And maybe best of all is Judi Dench, who appears in only a few extended scenes (attending a farce with Will Kemp on stage, conferring her blessing on the marriage between Viola and Wessex, and settling matters after the premiere of *Romeo and Juliet*), who with a flash of an eye or a grimace of the mouth can convey more of Elizabeth's hauteur and sly wit than all the arm-waving histrionics of another actress could have.

The play, *Romeo and Juliet*, indeed permeates the entire film, both on- and off-stage. Many set pieces illustrate the point. First is the long montage sequence wherein scenes of Will and Viola's nocturnal lovemaking are cross-cut with the actions of the daily stage rehearsals. In a seamless interchange, desperate embraces and impassioned speeches begin in the bedchamber,

Joseph Fiennes as Shakespeare in John Madden's Shakespeare in Love (MIRAMAX)

continue onstage, and conclude back in the bed. Similarly, in the extended scene of the play's premiere, Will/Romeo and Viola/Juliet come together to enact their and the play's anguish of frustrated love. As in the play, Will's first declaration of love to Viola is a veritable balcony scene. Again, as in the play, her nurse becomes the accomplice through which they conspire to meet. Throughout, the impossibility of his love against her life of privilege and her arranged marriage parallels the play's "star-crossed" fatalism. Events come to blows between Will and his rival, Wessex, just as they do between Romeo and Tybalt. And there's also the rivalry between his company of players and Burbage's men, echoing that between the houses of Capulet and Montague.

Love and artifice, private life and public performance are indistinguishable. These lovers are actors in their own lives and participants in their own drama. It's a grand game, one in which they, and the viewers, become willing conspirators. The play-within-the-film functions not just to imitate the offstage action but also to inflect it, to reveal that the true theatrical clichés and artifices reside in the real world, not just on stage. Truly, art has only imitated life.

Revisiting a Classic

No theatrical film can rival Marcel Carné's classic *The Children of Paradise* (1944) in its variety of theatrical evocations, complex layerings of reality and illusion, and in its enduring charm. "*Les Enfants du Paradis* is a tribute to the theater," said director Carné in 1944, shortly after completing the film. It generously alludes to many forms of theatrical event, including pantomime, farce, and melodrama; and its central theme, the frustrations and jealousies of love, derives particularly from Shakespeare's *Othello*.

In the words of commentator Edward Baron Turk, Jacques Prévert's screenplay "glorifies the capacity of theatrical fictions to confer coherence upon real-life experience." That applies as much to the film's directly contemporaneous context (it was made during the German Occupation) as it does to the fictions depicted on screen. The setting is Paris, beginning in the year 1827, during Carnival time. The action is framed by the rise and fall of a theater curtain and begins on the "Boulevard of Crime" (the Boulevard du Temple), Paris' theater district, which teems with acrobats, clowns, barkers, peepshows, and animal acts. Many of the patrons who come here are from society's lower ranks. They occupy *le paradis*, "the gods," slang for the highest and least expensive gallery seats, where they vent their frustrations and shout their enthusiasms to the actors (the "children of the gods"), disporting themselves on the stage. It is clear that these crowds are a metaphor not just for the oppressed compatriots of the French Occupation (during which time the film was made) but for today's audiences who come to movie theaters seeking relief from worldly burdens. "They're poor people, but I am like them," declares an actor. "I love them, I know them well. Their lives are small, but they have big dreams. And I don't only want to make them laugh, I want to move them, to frighten them, to make them cry."

Two of the principal characters of the story are based on real-life figures—the elegant mime Jean-Gaspard Deburau (played by Jean-Louis Barrault under the altered name of Baptiste Deburau) and the flamboyant Shakespearean performer Frederick Lemaître (Pierre Brasseur). Each has his own theater—Baptiste at Les Funambules and Lemaître at the Grand Theatre. The comedy and farce of the commedia dell'arte (Pierrot, Columbine, Harlequin, and Pantalone) and the tragedy and melodrama of *Othello* (Othello, Desdemona, Iago, and Brabantio), respectively, reflect and govern the actions of these men. What unites them—and links them with the more peripheral characters of the story, the villainous Lacenaire (Marcel Herrand) and the slimy aristocrat Edouard de Montray (Louis Salou)—is their fascination and involvement with the enigmatic beauty, Garance (Arletty). "Jealousy belongs to everyone," says Lemaître. "Even if women belong to no one!"

Baptiste and Lemaître must turn to their art to survive. For both the theater offers not only solace but also a kind of creative whetstone. As Lemaître observes, "When I act, I am desperately in love, desperately, do you understand? But when the curtain falls, the audience goes away, and takes 'my love' with it. You see, I make the audience a present of my love. The audience is very happy, and so am I. And I become wise and free and calm and sensible, again, like Baptiste!"

Thus, Lemaître transmutes his murderous jealousy into the role of Othello. Upon learning that Garance is in love with Baptiste, Lemaître tells her that she is like a "Desdemona." He declares, "Thanks to you . . . I shall be able to play Othello! I have been trying to find the character, but I didn't feel him. He was a stranger. There it is, now he's a friend, he's a brother. I know him . . . I have him in my grasp." Later, while performing *Othello* at the Grand Theatre, we witness a portion of the scene wherein Othello plots with Iago against Desdemona: "Get me some poison, Iago—this night. I'll not expostulate with her, lest her body and beauty unprovide my mind again. . . ." Iago advises him to strangle her instead. Lemaître/Othello's eyes stray toward one of the boxes, where Garance/Desdemona is seated with her lover, the Count Edouard de Montray. Cut to the count, who is beginning to suspect that Garance has had an affair with Lemaître. He audibly complains at this point of the play's "debased violence." Onstage, meanwhile, Lemaître/Othello continues: ". . . for she shall not live. No, my heart is turned to stone: I strike it, and it hurts my hand." Minutes later, while watching the bedroom scene as Lemaître/Othello prepares to strangle Desdemona, de Montray, by now beside himself, threatens to murder Lemaître. Cut to the stage, where Lemaître/Othello is clearly addressing his lines not to his Desdemona on stage, but to his Desdemona in the box beside the count:

> Therefore confess thee freely of thy sin;
> For to deny each article with oath
> Cannot remove nor choke the strong
>   conception
> That I do groan withal.
> Thou art to die.

The theatrics don't end with the curtain, however. Minutes after the performance, the drama continues backstage in the Green Room, when the count angrily confronts Lemaître. He insults Lemaître, and in the process tries to insult the whole institution of Shakespearean theater:

COUNT: Monsieur, you played the part of this simpleminded and bloodthirsty brute as if you found it perfectly natural.

FREDERICK: You are too kind, Monsieur, but I hope that above all I played it as Shakespeare wrote it—as if it was the most natural thing in the world!

COUNT: A very peculiar character, this "Monsieur Shakespeare!"

I have been given to understand that he served his literary apprenticeship . . . chopping meat on a butcher's slab.

FREDERICK: And why not?

COUNT: Which would explain the bestial and savage character of his plays, and why, when he was alive, he was a great favorite among such people as dockers, carters . . .

FREDERICK: And kings!

Before this protracted disquisition can be revealed for what it really is, a deadly exchange between these two rivals for the affections of Garance, it is interrupted by the arrival of Lacenaire, who clearly has something up his sleeve, as it were. In a nifty piece of theatrics of his own, he approaches his enemy, the count, and then wounds him more sorely than if he thrust a sword into his back. "I'm not a character out of a bedroom farce," he tells de Montray, at which point he draws aside a curtain, revealing Garance and Baptiste in a passionate embrace. What the astonished onlookers see is a perfect stage picture, nicely framed by the curtain, calculated to humiliate the count and drive him into a duel with his rival, Lemaître. Lacenaire has wrought as beautiful a piece of tragically dangerous theatrics as if he had just staged *Othello* himself. Putting it another way, he has played Iago to de Montray's Othello. Whereas Lemaître was able to purge himself of his deadly jealousies by enacting them on stage, de Montray will inevitably fall victim to them. Before he can duel with Lemaître, he will be slain by Lacenaire's knife thrust the next morning.

As for the neurotic, lovelorn Baptiste, he, like Lemaître, also finds in his art both a reflection and an expression of his own frustrations. As his pantomimes become darker and more violent, he observes that there is not really such a great difference between pantomime and tragedy. After all, he says, *Othello* would "make a nice pantomime." Bitterly, he continues: "A man who kills his love, and dies of it. Poor man. A sad and ridiculous story, like so many others. . . ." His great performance, not unlike Lemaître's aforementioned role as Othello, is a pantomime called "The Rag and Bone Man." It opens with Baptiste, clad in his silken white costume, face masked with makeup, arriving at a sumptuous evening party. His attempts to enter are rejected. Alone, under a street lamp, he encounters a rag merchant. Realizing he must attire himself in suitable evening dress, he tries to purchase the merchant's clothes. When he is unable to come up with the money, Baptiste draws a sword and runs the man through. The audience, startled but delighted at the unexpectedly morbid tone of the performance, applauds wildly.

In the course of these events we realize that the other characters, the non-actors like Garance, Lacenaire, and the count, have likewise donned masks of their own. As Garance has dallied with Lemaître, Baptiste, and the count, she has donned the twin masks of comedy and tragedy, assuming the "roles" of Columbine and Desdemona. The count has found himself the object of a very deadly piece of theatrics (he ultimately dies at Lacenaire's hands), and Lacenaire himself has assumed the role of *metteur en scène*, or master stage director.

The film is not free of moments of delicious theatrical parody. One of the set pieces is when Lemaître chafes at having to act in a blood-and-thunder melodrama, *L'Auberge des Adrets*. ("The Brigand's End"). During the rehearsal, which is attended by the play's authors, Lemaître, as the hero, Robert Macaire, ridicules the absurdities of the play. Example: When the play's heroine, Marie, asks Macaire if it is possible that he has committed many crimes, Lemaître, as Macaire, replies: "What do you expect, Marie; everyone has their little weaknesses!" The outraged authors protest that the line was not in the text. Lemaître replies: "Since there's absolutely nothing in your play, it's got to be padded out a little." In retaliation, the authors remind Lemaître that this is the sort of thing one would expect from "someone who started his career at the Funambules . . . walking on his hands." Lemaître smiles and retorts, "And why not on my hands? You've certainly managed to write a play with your feet!" Later, on opening night, Lemaître completes the devastation of the play he had begun in rehearsal. In perhaps the most hilarious moment in the film, Lemaître quits the stage and mounts to a stage box. Now, as an audience member, he vigorously applauds the play and shouts his "Bravos." Now declaring himself to be not Robert Macaire but "Frederic Lemaître," he continues to improvise to the consternation of his fellow cast members and the delight of the audience. At last, feigning death, he adlibs that his were not the real crimes of the story; indeed, "the real criminals, the ones who plotted everything . . . are the AUTHORS!" And he rises magnificently to point to the playwrights seated below him. Preposterous as all this is, moments later a rather similar melodrama transpires in Lemaître's dressing room when the villainous Lacenaire arrives and demands blackmail money from Lemaître. "Well, I'll be," smiles the actor; "It's exactly like the *Brigand's Inn*."

In the largest sense, *Children of Paradise* is about the enduring legacy of 19th-century French theater. The casting of Jean-Louis Barrault and Pierre Brasseur as, respectively, Baptiste and Lemaître, constituted a tribute to those two great traditions of the French theater, the pantomime and the romantic drama, and their two greatest 19th-century exponents, Deburau and Lemaître. At the time of the film's release, Barrault, newly elected *societaire* of the Comédie Française, had already initiated a general resurgence of interest in pantomime—for what Antonin Artaud called "the irresistible significance of gesture." His identification with Deburau was unquestioned. Pierre Brasseur was likewise a highly respected actor-playwright. In his excessive energies and self-indulgences, he was ideally suited to convey the raw power and fierce individuality of the actor-rebel Lemaître—who had once been dubbed by Hugo as "the French Kean." In evoking these traditions, says Turk, Barrault and Brasseur contributed to the film's theme that theater is the proper arena in which to claim one's authentic being. Indeed, it has been demonstrated that theatrical activity, not political action, was France's chief bulwark against the Nazi oppression that gripped Paris during the German Occupation. In the words of Turk, France's theaters were "the 'safe houses' of those collective dreams that take the form of plays and movies [and which] provided a public site for relief from political oppression."

Inevitably, perhaps, Shakespeare has entered the Age of Dogme 95 with Kristian Levring's *The King Is Alive* (2001). Levring, along with cofounders of the Dogme movement, Lars Von Trier, Thomas Vinterberg, and Soren Kragh Jacobsen, established Dogme in Copenhagen in March 1995 with the expressed goal of countering "certain tendencies" in the commercial cinema. Their manifesto was a "Vow of Chastity" that challenged filmmakers to shoot only on location, reject nondiegetic sound and music, use only hand-held cameras, rely only on natural lighting, and avoid all optical effects. *The King Is Alive* is the fourth film in the official series, preceded by Von Trier's *The Idiots*, Vinterberg's *Celebration*, and Jacobsen's *Mifune*.

This "vow" has now been applied to Shakespeare's *King Lear*, stripping it down to a handful of lines and situations and grafting it on to a dramatic study of human survival against natural and psychological challenges. Set in the Namibian desert in southwest Africa, the story begins when a tour bus strays from the highway and runs out of gas, leaving 10 tourists and a bus driver to fend for themselves. One hardy soul, Jack (Miles Anderson), offers to trek across the desert for help. "If I am not back in five days," he instructs them, "take the tires off the bus and burn them as a signal for help." A Shakespearean actor, Henry (David Bradley), decides that they should all keep busy in the interim by rehearsing a makeshift performance of *King Lear*. He writes out the parts and assigns them. As the weary, sunbaked travelers spend their days slogging through the play, each descends into his or her own primal hell: Liz (Janet McTeer) attempts to seduce the black bus driver (Peter Kuheka) in an attempt to make her husband Ray (Bruce Davison) jealous. The hapless driver is also the recipient of the racist hate of the bully of the group, Charles (David Calder). When Gina (Jennifer Jason Leigh), resists an older man's sexual advances, he dresses up in coat and tie and hangs himself. Finally, at the end—with the play still unfinished—rescuers arrive, attracted by the fires that have been set.

Director/writer Kristian Levring inserts the *King Lear* mousetrap device into the story to trigger a series of confrontations among the group that, by turns, both unify and disrupt them. They behave as if under the influence of Shakespeare's lines, "This cold night has transformed us all into fools and madmen." When Ray asks his wife what *King Lear* is all about, she replies, "You don't have to worry, you know. Nobody has to fall in love and everybody gets to die in the end." Well, love proves to be fickle and not everyone dies; and, excepting the obvious correlations between Henry and Shakespeare and Gina and Cordelia, not everyone easily corresponds to their assigned characters in the play. Nonetheless, *Lear*'s theme of the disruption of family unity handily mirrors the strained relationships among these stranded travelers during a time of crisis.

Finally, no survey of these mousetrap films, however brief, is complete without reference to Tom Stoppard's stage play, *Rosencrantz and Guildenstern Are Dead*, which he himself adapted and brought to the screen in 1990. Appropriately, it brings this discussion back to where it started, with Shakespeare's *Hamlet*. Stoppard's play had been an immediate success upon its premiere in London in 1966, and launched Stoppard's career. It is still the work most associated with his name.

Both play and film are truly a byzantine exercise in mousetraps, a veritable *Citizen Kane* of mousetraps, a construction of mousetraps within mousetraps, if you will. What results is a cross between the meta-theater of Pirandello's *Six Characters in Search of an Author* and the absurdist drama of Beckett's *Waiting for Godot*. It would take a cross-section of many commentators and many exhaustive analyses of this work to do it justice—volumes by Felicia Hardison Londre (1981), Anthony Jenkins (1987), and Susan Rusinko (1986) come to mind—but space permits only a brief examination here.

The narrative begins in medias res as two English courtiers find themselves on the road to Elsinore, only dimly aware that they have been directed to appear at the court of Prince Hamlet. On the road they encounter a troupe of strolling players also headed for Elsinore. The troupe's leader, known simply as Player, tries to interest them in witnessing a performance. But before they can begin, there is a sudden change of the light, and the characters of Hamlet and Ophelia appear. Queen Gertrude and King Claudius follow, and they engage Rosencrantz and Guildenstern in dialogue directly from Shakespeare's *Hamlet*. Similar interruptions, or breaches between the world of Rosencrantz and Guildenstern and that of the Shakespearean play, occur at irregular intervals on the road, in the palace at Elsinore, and on the boat bound for England. "Never at a moment's peace!" declares Rosencrantz at these mysterious appearances and disappearances, "in and out, on and off, they're coming at us from all sides" (73). Meanwhile, Player and his troupe find themselves fleeing an outraged Claudius after an aborted performance of *The Murder of Gonzago*. They, Hamlet, and Rosencrantz and Guildenstern all wind up on a boat bound for England. It is at this time that Rosencrantz and Guildenstern learn that they are the bearers of an order for Hamlet's execution. But Hamlet escapes during a pirate attack, leaving his two friends confounded to know that now *they* are to be executed. Despite their protests at their fate, in mid-speech they disappear. According to the stage directions, the lights now go full up, revealing the tableau of court and corpses constituting the last scene of *Hamlet*. The two ambassadors from England report to Horatio the famous words, direct from Shakespeare, that "Rosencrantz and Guildenstern are dead."

If Shakespeare uses the mousetrap play in *Hamlet* to throw light upon events external to the play, Stoppard reverses the process and uses peripheral events and the characters of Rosencrantz and Guildenstern—mere walk-ons in Shakespeare's original—as well as the Player, as a mousetrap device to examine the meaning of the play known as *Hamlet*. (To a degree, and in a more direct and accessible way, he did much the same thing in his screenplay for *Shakespeare in Love*.) To paraphrase Player's lines, they enact on stage the things that are barely alluded in Shakespeare's text, while standing apart from the ongoing performance of the play *Hamlet* ("We do on stage the things that are supposed to happen off, which is a kind of integrity, if you look on every exit being an entrance somewhere else," 28).

However, that barrier separating the onstage *Hamlet* from the offstage *Hamlet*; art from life; the story from the play; the play from the play-within-the-play—call them alternative realities, if you wish—is porous. Sporadically, unpredictably, these worlds interpenetrate. For example, there is the aforementioned Act I encounter between Rosencrantz and Guildenstern and Gertrude and Claudius. Then, the first 50 lines of *Hamlet*'s Act II, scene ii are enacted, uncut, as Rosencrantz and Guildenstern witness Gertrude and Claudius' discussion about Hamlet's "affliction." At the beginning of Stoppard's Act II Rosencrantz and Guildenstern again find themselves impressed into Shakespeare's *Hamlet*, this time in Act II, scene ii, where they exchange their colloquial diction for the proper Elizabethan speech as they discourse with Hamlet and Polonius. Other scenes from *Hamlet* that Stoppard interpolates into the action include 30 lines of dialogue from Act III, scene i, in which Claudius and Gertrude learn about the advent of the traveling players; Claudius' request to Rosencrantz and Guildenstern in Act IV, scene i that they find out from Hamlet where Polonius' body is hidden; Hamlet's conversation with a soldier in Act IV, scene iv; while other scenes, like Hamlet's "to be or not to be" soliloquy, are alluded to only in a comically oblique fashion.

These encounters trigger many discussions, nonsensical and ironic by turns, among Rosencrantz, Guildenstern, and Player that serve as a hilarious postmodernist critique of the meanings, or the lack of them, in Shakespeare's text. Stoppard himself has said that he chose to employ Rosencrantz and Guildenstern as leading characters precisely because "these two guys in Shakespeare's context don't really know what they're doing. The little they are told is mainly lies, and there's no reason to suppose that they ever find out why they are killed" (quoted in Rusinko, 28). Thus, they completely miss the point of many of the scenes they witness from *Hamlet* (or, to put it another way, their obtuseness suggests the possibility that there was no point in the first place). With a lethal, deadpan flatness, Rosencrantz summarizes some of Hamlet's more peculiar (offstage) remarks in a way that drains them of any significance, much less poetry: "Denmark's a prison and he'd rather live in a nutshell; some shadow-play about the nature of ambition, which never got down to cases, and finally one direct question which might have led somewhere and led in fact to his illuminating claim to tell a hack from a handsaw" (57). Another discussion of Hamlet's mental state resolves into palaver worthy of Lewis Carroll's Mad Tea Party:

GUIL.: He's melancholy

PLAYER: Melancholy?

ROS: Mad.

PLAYER: How is he mad?

ROS: Ah. How is he mad?

GUIL: More morose than mad, perhaps.

PLAYER: Melancholy.

GUIL.: Moody. . . . I think I have it. A man talking sense to himself is no madder than a man talking nonsense not to himself.

ROS: Or just as mad.

GUIL: Or just as mad.

ROS: And he does both.

GUIL.: So there you are.

ROS: Stark raving sane (67–68).

According to commentator Felicia Londre, this sort of thing "sums up centuries of scholarly debate over the question of whether Hamlet is really mad" (26).

In another striking scene, Player relates to Rosencrantz and Guildenstern the action of the play his troupe will perform before the king. This narration, in Londre's words, "goes much further than the play-within-the-play that one sees in *Hamlet*" (28), including the closet scene with Hamlet and his mother, his stabbing of Polonius, and his being sent to England with Rosencrantz and Guildenstern, who bear a letter that seals their deaths.

Yet, Rosencrantz and Guildenstern, in the end, make little sense of all this. The true "author" of the events that entangle them remains unknown. "It is written," is the only truth vouchsafed them. "What a fine persecution," laments Guildenstern, "—to be kept intrigued without ever quite being enlightened . . . " (41). Moreover, their efforts to alter their fate are useless. "Wheels have been set in motion," says Guildenstern in stoic exasperation at one point, "and they have their own pace, to which we are . . . condemned. Each move is dictated by the previous one—that is the meaning of order . . . (122). Later, he declares, "We can move, of course, change direction, rattle about, but our movement is contained within a larger one that carries us along as inexorably as the wind and current" (60). These remarks in turn echo Hamlet's own: "There's a divinity that shapes our ends,/Rough-hew them how we will." Stoppard's mousetrap device not only stimulates our meditation on the frustrating ambiguities of *Hamlet*, but also serves as a commentary on the essential artifices of theatricality and on the absurdity of our attempts to make sense of our lives and to define reality itself.

At the Curtain's Fall

As commentator Francis Fergusson has noted, the subtlety of Hamlet's "mousetrap" play suggests that it is designed not only to "catch" the conscience of Claudius but also to provoke reaction from any other auditors—and that includes all of us in the audience. Part of that reaction, as critic Anthony Lane has suggested, is that movies like these "perplex a settled theatrical tradition" in altering the contexts in which theatrical events are perceived and measured. They "break a long line of grand performing masters in favor of something not just more sneaky but also, in an odd way, more democratic." And that, in its own way, is a method and consequence of the grandest kind of theatrical endeavor.

—*John C. Tibbetts*

WORKS CITED

Branagh, Kenneth, *A Midwinter's Tale: The Shooting Script*, with an introduction. New York: Newmarket Press, 1995.

Brooke, Dinah, tr., *Children of Paradise: A Film by Marcel Carne*. New York: Simon and Schuster, 1968.

Denby, David, "Under the Lights," *The New Yorker*, January 3, 2000, 130–132.

Fergusson, Francis, *Shakespeare: The Pattern in His Carpet*. New York: Delacorte Press, 1970.

Holden, Stephen, "A Midwinter's Tale," *New York Times*, February 9, 1996, C5:1.

Houseman, John, *Run-Through: A Memoir*. New York: Simon and Schuster, 1972.

Ivory, James, "Introduction" to *Shakespeare Wallah*. New York: Grove Press, 1973)

Jenkins, Anthony, *The Theatre of Tom Stoppard*. Cambridge and New ork: Cambridge University Press, 1987.

Kael, Pauline, *For Keeps: 30 Years at the Movies*. New York: Dutton, 1994.

Kauffmann, Stanley, "Listening Again," *The New Republic* (January 10, 2000): 26–27.

Lane, Anthony, "Stagestruck," *The New Yorker*, December 13, 1999, 111–113.

———, "Tights! Camera! Action!" *The New Yorker*, November 25, 1996.

Londre, Felicia Hardison, *Tom Stoppard*. New York: F. Ungar Publishing Company, 1981.

O'Brien, Geoffrey, "Stompin' at the Savoy," *The New York Review of Books*, February 24, 2000, 16, 18–19.

Pearson, Hesketh, *Gilbert: His Life and Strife*. New York: Harper, 1957.

Peary, Danny, *Cult Movies*. New York: Delta Books, 1981.

———, *Cult Movies 2*. New York: Dell, 1983.

Robbins, Tim, *Cradle Will Rock: The Movie and the Moment*. New York: Newmarket Press, 2000.

Rothwell, Kenneth S., *A History of Shakespeare on Screen*. Cambridge, Eng.: Cambridge University Press, 1999.

Rusinko, Susan. *Tom Stoppard*. New York: Twayne Publishers, 1986.

Silver, Allan, "Maedchen in Uniform," in Arthur Lennig, *Classics of the Film*. Madison: Wisconsin Society Press, 1965: 126–131.

Storace, Patricia, "The Poet of Karma," *The New York Review*, October 17, 1999, 26.

Turk, Edward Baron, *Child of Paradise: Marcel Carné and the Golden Age of French Cinema*. Cambridge: Harvard University Press, 1989.

Willson, Robert F., Jr., *Shakespeare in Hollywood, 1929–1956*. Madison N.J.: Fairleigh Dickinson University Press, 1999.

Wilmington, Michael, "Cradle Will Rock," *Film Comment*, 35:6. November–December 1999), 79.

Contributors

Christopher Andrews teaches at the University of Connecticut. His comparative essay on film adaptations of Shakespeare's *Richard III* was published in *Literature/Film Quarterly*, Vol. 28, No. 2 (2000).

Normand Berlin, a Renaissance scholar educated at New York University (B.A.), Columbia University (M.A.), and the University of California, Berkeley (Ph.D.), was a professor of English at the University of Massachusetts, Amherst, when he wrote the essay on Polanski's *Macbeth* for *Literature/Film Quarterly*. He is the author of *Thomas Sackville* (1974), *The Base String: The Underworld in Elizabethan Drama* (1968), and *The Secret Cause: A Discussion of Tragedy* (1981).

Mark Thornton Burnett is Reader in English a the Queen's University of Belfast. he is the author of *Masters and Servants in English Renaissance Drama and Culture: Authority and Obedience* (1997), the editor of *The Complete Plays of Christopher Marlowe* (1999), the coeditor of *New Essays on "Hamlet"* (1994) and *Shakespeare, Film, Fin de Siècle* (2000).

Mariacristina Cavecchi teaches at the University of Milan in Italy and has published on Peter Greenaway in *Literature/Film Quarterly*, Vol. 25, No. 2 (1997).

Hugh H. Davis, educated at the University of Tennessee, teaches English at Chowan College in North Carolina. He published an article on Gus Van Sant's *My Own Private Idaho* in *Literature/Film Quarterly*, Vol. 29, No. 2 (2001).

Lucy P. Hamilton studied with Brian McFarlane at Monash University in Clayton, Victoria, Australia, near Melbourne. Her essay on the Australian director Baz Luhrmann was published in *Literature/Film Quarterly*, Vol. 28, No. 2 (2000).

Diana Harris teaches in New Zealand at the University of Auckland. Her interest in *The Tempest* began with a paper entitled "Stormy Weather: Three Screen Adaptations of *The Tempest*," presented at the ANZSA Conference held in Perth, Australia, in February 1994.

MacDonald Jackson teaches with Diana Harris in New Zealand at the University of Auckland. His essay, coauthored with Diana Harris, on Jarman's *The Tempest* was published in *Literature/Film Quarterly*, Vol. 29, No. 2 (2001).

Jane E. Kingsley-Smith teaches at the University of Hull in England and is a contributor to *Literature/Film Quarterly*.

Yong Li Lan teaches at the National University of Singapore and has published on Shakespeare in *Literature/Film Quarterly*, Vol. 29, No. 2 (2001).

Arthur D. Lindley is a senior lecturer of English at the National University of Singapore and has published on the Welles *Macbeth* in *Literature/Film Quarterly*, Vol. 29, No. 2 (2001).

Heather Owings was educated at Kent State University in Ohio and recently completed her M.A. at Salisbury University in Maryland.

Michael Pursell, a British scholar trained at Nottingham University, teaches English in Nottingham at the Gedling School. He has published frequently in *Literature/Film Quarterly* on Franco Zeffirelli's *The Taming of the Shrew* (Vol. 8, No. 4, 1980), Zeffirelli's *Romeo and Juliet* (Vol. 14, No. 4, 1986), and Branagh's *Henry V* (Vol. 20, No. 4, 1992). He also has served on the editorial board of *Literature/Film Quarterly*.

Kenneth S. Rothwell, Professor of English Emeritus at the University of Vermont, was the founding editor of *Shakespeare on Film Newsletter* with Bernice Kliman. He cochaired the Shakespeare on Film seminar at the 1991 Tokyo World Shakespeare Congress and produced the Shakespeare on Film festival at the 1996 Los Angeles World Shakespeare Congress. He edited *Shakespeare on Film IV: Papers from the World Shakespeare Congress* (1981), compiled with Annabelle Henkin Melzer *Shakespeare on Screen: An International Filmography and Videography* (1990), and is the author of *A History of Shakespeare on Screen: A Century of Film and Television*, published by Cambridge University Press in 1999.

Neil Sinyard is Head of the Department of English at the University of Hull and a contributing editor for *Literature/Film Quarterly*. He is the author of numerous film studies, including *Filming Literature: The Art of Screen Adaptation* (1986) and *Children in the Movies* (1992). Currently he is writing *Graham Greene: A Literary Life* and *Make It New: Modernism in the Arts, 1910–1914*.

James W. Stone is Assistant Professor of English and Comparative Literature at the American University in Cairo and a contributor to *Literature/Film Quarterly*.

John C. Tibbetts, associate professor of theater and film at the University of Kansas, Lawrence, has served as the president of the Literature/Film Association. His books include *The American Theatrical Film* (1985), *Dvor·k in America* (1993), and several coauthored and coedited with James M. Welsh, including *The Encyclopedia of Novels into Film* (1998), *The Cinema of Tony Richardson: Essays and Interviews* (1999), and *The Encyclopedia of Stage Plays into Film* (2001).

Richard Vela, a professor of English at the University of North Carolina, Pembroke, was a major contributor to *The Encyclopedia of Stage Plays into Film* (2001) and to the forthcoming *Encyclopedia of Orson Welles*, to be published by Facts On File.

James M. Welsh, professor of English at Salisbury University in Maryland, is the editor of *Literature/Film Quarterly* and the coauthor and coeditor (with John C. Tibbetts) of several books, including *The Encyclopedia of Novels into Film* (1998), *The Cinema of Tony Richardson: Essays and Interviews* (1999), *The Encyclopedia of Stage Plays into Film* (2001). He was educated at Indiana University, Bloomington (B.A.) and the University of Kansas (M.A. and Ph.D.) His earlier books include *Abel Gance* (with Steven Philip Kramer, 1978) and *Peter Watkins: A Guide to References and Resources* (1986).

Robert F. Willson, Jr., former chair of the Department of English at the University of Missouri, Kansas City (1975–90), was educated at Wayne State University (B.A.) and the University of Wisconsin, Madison (M.A. and Ph.D.) In 2000, his book *Shakespeare in Hollywood, 1929-1956*, was published by Fairleigh-Dickinson University Press.

Ramona Wray is Lecturer at the Queen's University of Belfast. She is the coeditor of *Shakespeare and Ireland: History, Politics, Culture* (1997). She is currently completing two books, *Women Writers of the Seventeenth Century* and *Women, Writing, Revolution: An Anthology of Writing by Women*.

James N. Yates is associate professor of English at Northwestern Oklahoma State University. He has published in the *Journal of Popular Culture* and in the forthcoming *Columbia Companion to Film and History*, edited by Peter C. Rollins.

Bibliography

Anderegg, Michael. *Orson Welles, Shakespeare, and Popular Culture*. New York: Columbia University Press, 1999.

Ball, Robert Hamilton. *Shakespeare on Silent Film: A Strange Eventful History*. London: Allen and Unwin, 1968.

Boose, Lynda E., and Richard Bart, eds. *Shakespeare, The Movie: Popularizing the Plays on Film, TV, and Video*. London: Routledge, 1997.

Branagh, Kenneth. *Hamlet, by William Shakespeare: Screenplay and Introduction*. New York: W.W. Norton, 1996.

———. *Henry V, by William Shakespeare: A Screen Adaptation*. London: Chatto and Windus, 1989.

———. *Much Ado About Nothing, by William Shakespeare: Screenplay, Introduction, and Notes on the Making of the Movie*. New York: W.W. Norton, 1993.

Brode, Douglas. *Shakespeare in the Movies: From the Silent Era to Shakespeare in Love*. New York: Oxford University Press, 2000.

Buchman, Lorne M. *Still in Movement: Shakespeare on Screen*. New York: Oxford University Press, 1991.

Buhler, Stephen. *Shakespeare in the Cinema: Ocular Proof*. Albany, N.Y.: SUNY Press, 2002.

Bulman, J.C., and H.R. Coursen, eds. *Shakespeare on Television*. Hanover, N.H.: University Press of New England, 1988.

Burt, Richard. *Shakespeare After Mass Media*. New York: Palgrave, 2002.

———. *Unspeakable Shaxxxspeare: Queer Theory and American Kiddie Culture*. New York: St. Martin's Press, 1998.

Cartmell, Deborah. *Interpreting Shakespeare on Screen*. New York: St. Martin's Press, 2000.

Coursen, H.R. *Macbeth: A Guide to the Play*. Westport, Conn.: Greenwood Press, 1997.

———. *Shakespeare in Production: Whose History?* Athens: Ohio University Press, 1996.

———. *Shakespeare in Space*. New York: Peter Lang, 2000.

———. *Shakespearean Performance As Interpretation*. Newark: University of Delaware Press, 1992.

Crowl, Samuel. *Shakespeare Observed: Studies in Performance on Stage and Screen*. Athens: Ohio University Press, 1992.

Davies, Anthony. *Filming Shakespeare's Plays: The Adaptations of Laurence Olivier, Orson Welles, Peter Brook, and Akira Kurosawa*. Cambridge, U.K.: Cambridge University Press, 1988.

Davies, Anthony, and Stanley Wells, eds. *Shakespeare and the Moving Image: The Plays on Film and Television*. Cambridge, U.K.: Cambridge University Press, 1994.

Donaldson, Peter S. *Shakespearean Films/Shakespearean Directors* Boston: Unwin Hyman, 1990.

Eckert, Charles W., ed. *Focus on Shakespearean Films*. Englewood Cliffs, N.J.: Prentice-Hall, 1972.

Ehrens, Patricia. *Akira Kurosawa: A Guide to References and Resources*. Boston: G.K. Hall, 1979.

Forman, Milos, and Jan Novak. *Turnaround: A Memoir*. New York: Villard Books, 1994.

Geduld, Harry M. *Filmguide to Henry V*. Bloomington: Indiana University Press, 1973.

Gielgud, John, and John Miller. *Shakespeare: Hit or Miss?* London: Sidgwick and Jackson, 1991.

Goodwin, James, ed. *Perspectives on Akira Kurosawa*. New York: G.K. Hall, 1994.

Hall, Joan Lord. *Henry V: A Guide to the Play*. Westport, Conn.: Greenwood Press, 1997.

Homan, Sidney, ed. *Shakespeare's More Than Words Can Witness: Essays on Visual and Nonverbal Enactment in the Plays*. Lewisburg, Pa.: Bucknell University Press, 1980.

Howlett, Kathy M. *Framing Shakespeare on Film*. Athens: Ohio University Press, 2000.

Jackson, Russell, ed.. *The Cambridge Companion to Shakespeare on Film*. Cambridge, Eng.: Cambridge University Press, 2000.

Jorgens, Jack J. *Shakespeare on Film*. Bloomington: Indiana University Press, 1977.

Kliman, Bernice W. *Hamlet: Film, Television, and Audio Performance*. Rutherford, N.J.: Fairleigh Dickinson University Press, 1988.

———. *Macbeth: Shakespeare in Performance*. Manchester, U.K.: Manchester University Press, 1992.

Kozintsev, Grigori. "*Hamlet* and *King Lear*: Stage and Film," in *Shakespeare 1971: Proceedings of the World Shakespeare*

Congress, Vancouver, August 1971, ed. Clifford Leech and J.M.R. Margeson. Toronto: University of Toronto Press, 1972.

———. *King Lear: The Space of Tragedy. The Diary of a Film Director*, tr. Mary Mackintosh. Berkeley: University of California Press, 1977.

———. *Shakespeare: Time and Conscience*, tr. Joyce Vining. New York: Hill and Wang, 1966.

Lehman, Courtney, and Lisa Starks, eds. *Spectacular Shakespeare: Critical Theory and Popular Culture*. Rutherford, N.J.: Fairleigh-Dickinson University Press, 2002.

Lippmann, Max, ed. *Shakespeare in Film*. Wiesbaden: Saaten Verlag, 1964.

Lusardi, James P., and June Schlueter. *Reading Shakespeare in Performance: King Lear*. Rutherford, N.J.: Fairleigh Dickinson University Press, 1991.

———, eds. *Shakespeare Bulletin* (incorporating *Shakespeare on Film Newsletter* since 1972), English Department, Lafayette College, Easton, Pennsylvania.

Lyons, Bridget, ed. *Chimes at Midnight, Orson Welles, Director*. New Brunswick, N.J.: Rutgers University Press, 1988.

Maher, Mary Z. *Modern Hamlets & Their Soliloquies*. Iowa City: University of Iowa Press, 1992.

Manvell, Roger. *Shakespeare and the Film*. London: J.M. Dent, 1971.

Mazursky, Paul, and Leon Capetanos. *Tempest: A Screenplay*. New York: Performing Arts Journal Publications, 1982.

Morris, Peter. *Shakespeare on Film*. Ottawa: Canadian Film Institute, 1972.

Parker, Barry M. *The Folger Shakespeare Filmography A Directory of Feature Films Based on the Works of William Shakespeare*. Washington, D.C.: Folger Shakespeare Library, 1979.

Pilkington, Ace G. *Screening Shakespeare from Richard II to Henry V*. Newark: University of Delaware Press, 1991.

Richie, Donald. *The Films of Akira Kurosawa*, rev. Berkeley: University of California Press, 1984.

Rothwell, Kenneth S. *A History of Shakespeare on Screen: A Century of Film and Television*. Cambridge, U.K.: Cambridge University Press, 1999.

Rothwell, Kenneth S., and Bernice W. Kliman, eds. *Shakespeare on Film Newsletter*. Published 1976 to 1992.

Rothwell, Kenneth S., and Annabelle Henkin Melzer. *Shakespeare on Screen: An International Filmography and Videography*. New York: Neal-Schuman, 1990.

Shaughnessy, Robert, ed. *Shakespeare on Film*, New Casebooks Series. New York: St. Martin's Press, 1998.

Silviria, Dale. *Laurence Olivier and the Art of Film Making*. Rutherford, N.J.: Fairleigh Dickinson University Press, 1985.

Skovmand, Michael, ed. *Screen Shakespeare*. Aarhus, Denmark: Aarhus University Press, 1994.

Stalpaert, Christel, ed. *Peter Greenaway's Prospero's Books: Critical Essays*. Ghent: Academia Press, 2000.

Taylor, Geoffrey. *Paul Mazursky's Tempest*. New York: New York Zoetrope, 1982.

Tibbetts, John C., and James M. Welsh. *His Majesty the American: The Films of Douglas Fairbanks, Sr.* South Brunswick, N.J.: A.S. Barnes, 1977.

Welsh, James M., and John C. Tibbetts, eds. *The Cinema of Tony Richardson: Essays and Interviews*. Albany, N.Y.: SUNY Press, 1999.

Welsh, James M., and Thomas L. Erskine, eds. *Literature/Film Quarterly*. Shakespeare Issues: 1:4 (1973), 4:2 (1976), 5:4 (1977), 11:3 (1983), 14:4 (1986), 20:4 (1992), 22:2 (1994), 25:2 (1997), 28:2 (2000), 29:2 (2001).

Willis, Susan. *The BBC Shakespeare Plays*. Chapel Hill: University of North Carolina Press, 1992.

Willson, Robert F., ed. *Shakespeare: Entering the Maze*. New York: Peter Lang, 1995.

Willson, Robert F., Jr. *Shakespeare in Hollywood, 1929–1956*. Madison, N.J.: Fairleigh Dickinson University Press, 2000.

Wollen, Roger. *Derek Jarman: A Portrait; Artist, Film-maker, Designer*. London: Thames and Hudson, 1996.

Woods, Alan. *Being Naked Playing Dead: The Art of Peter Greenaway*. Manchester, U.K.: Manchester University Press, 1996.

Index

Italicized page numbers refer to illustrations.
Boldface page numbers refer to the main discussion of a topic.

A

Aaliyah, in *Romeo Must Die* (2000) 89
Abbott, John, in *The Tempest* (1939) 97
Abraham, F. Murray, in *The Name of the Rose* (1986) 144
Ackland, Joss, in *Othello* (2002) 72
Adair, Gilbert, on *Shakespeare in Love* (1998) 204
adaptations, criteria for xxx
The Addams Family 207
Addy, Wesley, in *Hamlet* (1953) 20
aesthetic criticism xiii–xiv
Agate, James, on *The Taming of the Shrew* (1929) xi
Agee, James, on *Hamlet* (1948) 19
The Age of Innocence (1993) 142
Agutter, Jenny, in *Romeo and Juliet* (1994) 89
Aitken, Ian, on *Henry V* (1989) 117
Alberg, Mildred Freed, *Hamlet* (1953) 17
Alexander, Peter xvi
Alexander, Ross, in *A Midsummer Night's Dream* (1935) 57
Alexander Nevsky (1938) 29
Algero, Augusto 2
All About Eve (1950) 34
Allen, Patrick, in *A Midsummer Night's Dream* (1964) 58
Allen, Woody
  Celebrity (1998) 44
  Everyone Says I Love You (1996) 44
  in *King Lear* (1987) 41
All I Need to Know about Filmmaking I Learned from The Toxic Avenger (Kaufman) xviii
Almereyda, Michael, *Hamlet* (2000) xxviii–xxix, 25
Altman, Rick 194
Anderegg, Michael A. xiii, xvii
  on *Macbeth* (1948) 141, 143
Anderson, Miles, in *The King Is Alive* (2001) 223
Andrew, Dudley xv
Andrews, Christopher, on *Richard III* 147–157
Andrews, Harry, in *Theater of Blood* (1973) 212
Andrews, Nigel, on *Karol Lir* (1970) 39
animation xxx
Annis, Francesca, in *Macbeth* (1971) 50, *50*, 136
Antony and Cleopatra **1–3**
  Heston (1972) 2–3
  plot of 1–2
  Scoffield and Nunn (1974) 3
Antoon, A. J., *Much Ado About Nothing* (1973) 64–65
The Anxiety of Influence (Bloom) 203
Arai, Yoshio xiii
Arcadia (Sydney) 38
Ardolino, Emile, *A Midsummer Night's Dream* (1982) 60
Ariosto, Ludovico 62
Aris, Ben, in *Hamlet* (1969) 22
Arlen, Harold 181
Arliss, George, in *The Merchant of Venice* (1969) 54
Arnold, Gary
  on *Everyone Says I Love You* (1996) 44
  on *Prospero's Books* (1991) 100
"Art and Artifice in Franco Zeffirelli's *Romeo and Juliet*" (Pursell) xiv
Artaud, Antonin 223
Ashcroft, Peggy, in *The Tempest* (1939) 96
Aslan, Gregoire, in *Joe MacBeth* (1955) 49
As You Like It **3–8**
  Coleman (1978) 7
  Czinner (1936) xxvii–xxviii, 5–6
  Edzard (1992) 6–7
  Kent (1912) 4–5
  plot of 4
  Roland (1985) 7–8
Atkins, Ian, *The Tempest* (1956) 97
Atkins, Robert, *The Tempest* (1956) 97
Auberjonois, Rene, in *King Lear* (1977) 40–41
authorship, Shakespearean 201–205
Aylmer, Felix
  in *Hamlet* (1948) 19
  in *Henry V* (1944) 30

B

Bacon, Francis 202
Baker, Blanche, in *Romeo and Juliet* (1982) 87
Baker, Russell, on *Othello* (2002) 72

Baker, Stanley, in *Richard III* (1955) 76
Baldwin, Alec, in *Looking for Richard* (1996) 78, 218
Bale, Christian
    in *Henry V* (1989) 31
    in *A Midsummer Night's Dream* (1999) 62
Ball, Robert Hamilton x, xii, xxvii
    on *Burlesque on Romeo and Juliet* (1902) 79–80
    on Coghlan (Rose) 5
    on *King Lear* 129
    on *Il mercante de Venezia* (1910) 53
    on *Shylock* (1913) 53
ballets xxx
Bamber, David, in *The Merchant of Venice* (2001) 55
Banks, Leslie, in *Henry V* (1944) xiv, 30
Bara, Theda, in *Romeo and Juliet* (1916) 80
Baranski, Christine, in *A Midsummer Night's Dream* (1982) 60
Barber, C. L. xv
Barrault, Jean-Louis, in *The Children of Paradise* (1944) 221, 223
Barrie, J. M., *As You Like It* (1936) 3
Barrit, Desmond, in *A Midsummer Night's Dream* (1996) 61
Barrymore, John, in *Romeo and Juliet* (1936) 80
Barthes, Roland 147, 203
Bartkowiak, Andrzej, *Romeo Must Die* (2000) 79
Barton, John, *Hamlet* (1970) 17
Bate, Jonathan 201, 203
Bates, Alan, in *Hamlet* (1990) 23, *23*, 24
Baudrillard, Jean 198
Baudry, Jean-Louis xvii
Baur, Harry, in *Shylock* (1913) 53
Bayne, Beverly, in *Romeo and Juliet* (1916) 80
Bazin, André
    on limitations of camera 148
    on *Macbeth* (1948) 143
The BBC Shakespeare Plays (Willis) xv

BBC/Time-Life television series xiii
Béchervaise, Neil E. xvi
Beck, Reginald, *Henry V* (1944) 28
Beddington, Jack 29
Bell, Tom, in *Prospero's Books* (1991) 100
Bellini, Vincenzo 61
Bender, Jack, *The Tempest* (1999) 98
Ben-Hur (1959) 2, 34
Bening, Annette, in *Richard III* (1995) 77, *155*
Benjamin, Walter ix, 187
Bennett, Alan, in *Hamlet* (1970) 22
Bennett, Jill, in *Julius Caesar* (1969) 34
Bennett, Rodney, *Hamlet* (1980) 22–23
Bennett, Susan 194
Benny, Jack, in *To Be or Not to Be* (1942) xxx, 208, *209*
Benson, F. R., in *Richard III* (1911) 76
Bergman, Ingmar, *The Seventh Seal* (1957) 142, 143, 145
Bergner, Elisabeth, in *As You Like It* (1936) xxvii–xxviii, 5–6
Berlin, Irving 44, 193, 194, 196
Berlin, Normand
    on *King Lear* (1971) xiii–xiv
    on *Macbeth* (1971) 135–139
Berlioz, Hector 95
Bernhardt, Sarah x, 19
Bernstein, Leonard 84
Bernt, Eric, *Romeo Must Die* (2000) 79
Beymer, Richard, in *West Side Story* (1961) 84
Bioscope (journal) x
Birch, Margaret, *As You Like It* (1912) 5
Birkett, Jack, in *The Tempest* (1980) 97, 177
Birkett, Michael xii
Blackton, J. Stuart x
    King Lear (1909) 39
    A Midsummer Night's Dream (1909) xxvii
    Richard III (1908) 76

Blakely, Colin, in *King Lear* (1983) 41
Blanc, Michel, in *Prospero's Books* (1991) 100
Blessed, Brian
    in *Hamlet* (1996) xxvi, 25, 114
    in *Henry V* (1989) 31, *118*
Bloom, Claire
    in *Cymbeline* (1982) 11
    in *Hamlet* (1980) 23
    in *Richard III* (1955) 76, *150*
Bloom, Harold 202, 203
Blue, Monte, in *Macbeth* (1916) 48
The Blue Angel (1930) xviii
Bonafé, Pepa, in *Shylock* (1913) 53
Bondarchuk, Sergei, in *Othello* (1955) 69
Bonham-Carter, Helena
    in *Hamlet* (1990) 23
    in *Twelfth Night* (1996) 103
Boorman, John, *Excalibur* (1981) 143
Boose, Lynda xvi
Borghi, Vanni xiii
Borowitz, Katherine, in *Men of Respect* (1990) 51
Bower, Dallas
    Henry V (1944) 28
    The Tempest (1939) 96–97
Bradley, David, in *The King Is Alive* (2001) 223
Brahms, Caryl 204
Branagh, Kenneth
    Hamlet (1996) xvi, xxvi, *24*, 24–25, 113–116, 184–186
    Henry V (1989) xxiv, xxv, 30–31, *31*, 117–123, *118*, 147
    in *Looking for Richard* (1996) 78, 218
    Love's Labour's Lost (2000) 44–45, 193–198
    A Midwinter's Tale (1995) 196, *215*, 215–217
    Much Ado About Nothing (1993) 63–64, *64*
    vs. Olivier 117, 118
    in *Othello* (1995) 70
    on plays within plays 207
    on *Romeo and Juliet* 164

INDEX

Brando, Marlon, in *Julius Caesar* (1953) 34
Branigan, Edward 184
Brasseur, Pierre, in *The Children of Paradise* (1944) 221, 223
Braveheart (1995) 142, 144
Bressart, Felix, in *To Be or Not to Be* (1942) 209
Brett, Jeremy, in *The Merchant of Venice* (1969) 54
Briers, Richard
    in *Hamlet* (1996) 25, 114
    in *Henry V* (1989) 31
    in *Love's Labour's Lost* (2000) 44
    in *A Midwinter's Tale* (1995) 216
Broadbent, Jim, in *Richard III* (1995) 77
Brode, Douglas xvii
Broken Lance (1954) xxx
Brook, Peter
    King Lear (1953) 39
    King Lear (1971) xiv, 39–40, 40, 129
    in *Looking for Richard* (1996) 78, 218
Brooke, Arthur 204
Brooks, Mel, *To Be or Not to Be* (1983) 209
Brown, Constance xii
    on *Richard III* (1955) 149, 151, 152
Brown, Joe E., in *A Midsummer Night's Dream* (1935) 57
Brown, John Russell, on *The Tempest* 96
Browne, Carol, in *Theater of Blood* (1973) 213
Browning, Kirk, *Hamlet* (1990) 17
Brownlow, Kevin, on *Richard III* (1912) 76
Brusati, Franco, *Romeo and Juliet* (1968) 78
Buchanan, Judith xvi
Buchman, Lorne xvii
    on *Richard III* (1955) 151
Buffum, William 76
Bulman, J. C., on *As You Like It* (1978) 7
Bulman, James xiii, xv–xvi

Burge, Stuart
    Julius Caesar (1969) 34–35
    Much Ado About Nothing (1984) 65–66
    Othello (1965) 69, 69–70
Burgess, Anthony 86
Burke, Alfred, in *A Midsummer Night's Dream* (1996) 60–61
Burkeley, Busby 216
Burlesque on Romeo and Juliet (1902) 79–80
Burnett, Mark Thornton xvi
    on *Hamlet* (1996) 113–116
    on *A Midsummer Night's Dream* (1996) 60
Burt, Richard xvi, xviii, 204
Burton, Richard
    in *Hamlet* (1964) 21
    in *The Taming of the Shrew* (1966) 93, *93*, 126
    in *The Tempest* (1960) 97
Bush, W. Stephen ix, x
Bushman, Francis X., in *Romeo and Juliet* (1916) 80

C

Cabot, Sebastian, in *Giuliete e Romeo* (1954) 81
Cage, Nicolas, in *Valley Girl* (1983) 89
Cagney, James, in *A Midsummer Night's Dream* (1935) xi, 57
Calder, David, in *The King Is Alive* (2001) 224
Calhern, Louis, in *Julius Caesar* (1953) 34
Callas, Maria 125
Callow, Simon, in *Shakespeare in Love* (1998) 86
Cambridge Companion to Shakespeare on Film (Jackson) xvi
Campbell, Norman, *Romeo and Juliet* (1993) 88
Canby, Vincent xvii
Cantinflas, in *Romeo y Julieto* (1943) 84
Capetanos, Leon, *The Tempest* (1982) 98
Carné, Marcel, *The Children of Paradise* (1944) 221–223

Carney, Art 41
Carnival (1921) 210
Carter, Desmond 193
Caruso, David, in *China Girl* (1987) 85
Caselli, Chiara, in *My Own Private Idaho* (1991) 28
Cassavetes, John, in *The Tempest* (1982) 98
Casson, Philip, *Macbeth* (1979) 50–51
Castellani, Renato, *Giuliete e Romeo* (1954) 80–81, 82, 163
Castle, DeShonn, in *Zebrahead* (1992) 86
Castle, John 2
Cathro, Grant, *Romeo and Juliet* (1994) 79
Cavecchi, Mariacristina, on *Prospero's Books* (1991) 167–172
Celebrity (1998) 44
Century (magazine) x
Chakiris, George, in *West Side Story* (1961) 84
Chamberlain, Richard
    in *Hamlet* (1970) 22
    in *Julius Caesar* (1969) 34
Chang, Sari, in *China Girl* (1987) 85
Charnes, Linda xviii
Charney, Maurice 7
Chatterton, Ruth 20
Chiaki, Minoru, in *Throne of Blood* (1957) 49
The Children of Paradise (1944) 221–223
Chimes at Midnight (1967) xv, xvi, xvii, 26–28
Chin, Joey, in *China Girl* (1987) 85
China Girl (1987) 85–86
Chkhikvadze, Ramaz 77
Christie, Julie, in *Hamlet* (1996) 25, 114, 116
Chronicles (Holinshed) 38, 47, 75
Churchill, Sarah 20
Churchill, Winston 116
Cimolino, Antoni, in *Romeo and Juliet* (1993) 88
Cirillo, Albert R. xvii
Clark, Michael, in *Prospero's Books* (1991) 100

Clarke, Warren, in *The Tempest* (1979) 97
Close, Glenn, in *Hamlet* (1990) 23, *23*, 126, 128
Cloutier, Suzanne, in *Othello* (1952) 69, 189
Clunes, Martin, in *Shakespeare in Love* (1998) 86
Cocteau, Jean 143, 180
Coghlan, Rose 4–5
Coleano, Bonar, in *Joe MacBeth* (1955) 49
Coleman, Basil
  As You Like It (1978) 7
Colleran, Bill, *Hamlet* (1964) 17
Collick, John xv
Collier, Constance, in *Macbeth* (1916) 48
Collins, Joan, in *A Midwinter's Tale* (1995) 217
Colman, Ronald, in *A Double Life* (1947) 68, 210
Combs, Richard, on *Shakespeare in Love* (1998) 202
Condee, Ralph xiii
Condell, Henry 18
Connery, Sean, in *The Name of the Rose* (1986) 144
Conrad, Peter 100
Cook, Ann xiii
Cook, Ron, in *Richard III* (1983) 77, 152–154
Coolidge, Martha, *Valley Girl* (1983) 78
Cooper, Frederick, in *Henry V* (1944) 30
Coote, Robert, in *Theater of Blood* (1973) 213
Coppedge, Walter R. xiv
costume sketches xv
Coursen, H. R. xv–xvi, xvii
  on film vs. television 147
  on *Hamlet* (1980) 23
  on *Much Ado About Nothing* (1973) 65
Courtenay, Tom, in *The Dresser* (1983) 209
Cowie, Peter, on *The Seventh Seal* (1957) 142
Coyle, Richard, in *Othello* (2002) 72

Cranham, Kenneth, in *Prospero's Books* (1991) 100
Crawford, Wayne, *Valley Girl* (1983) 78
criticism, literature and film
  categories of xiii–xiv
  history of ix–xviii
  stages of ix
Croft, Emma 6
Cronyn, Hume, in *Hamlet* (1964) 21
Crotty, Derbhle, in *The Merchant of Venice* (2001) 55
Crowden, Graham 11
Crowl, Samuel xvii
  on *Julius Caesar* (1969) 34
Cruze, James 10–11
Crystal, Billy, in *Hamlet* (1996) 25, 113
Cukor, George *210*
  A Double Life (1947) xxx, 68, 209–212
  Romeo and Juliet (1936) xi–xii, xv, 80
Culen, R. J., *As You Like It* (1936) 3
Cumming, Alan, in *Titus* (1999) 101
Curtice, Sally, in *My Own Private Idaho* (1991) 28
Curtiz, Michael xxviii
Cusack, Cyril, in *The Taming of the Shrew* (1966) 94
Cymbeline **9–12**
  Moshinsky (1982) 11–12
  plot of 9–10
  Sullivan (1913) 10–11
Czinner, Paul, *As You Like It* (1936) xxvii–xxviii, 5–6

D

D'Amico, Maestro, *Romeo and Juliet* (1968) 78
D'Amico, Suso Cecci, *The Taming of the Shrew* (1966) 91
Dancing Ledge (Jarman) 180
Danes, Claire, in *Romeo + Juliet* (1996) 82, 83, *83*, *160*, 163
Daniels, Ben, in *Romeo and Juliet* (1994) 89

Daniels, Phil, in *A Midsummer Night's Dream* (1982) 59–60
Darth Vader, Henry V as 118–119, 120
Dash, Irene xiii
Daves, Delmer, *Jubal* xxx
David and Bathsheba (1951) 2
Davies, Andrew, *Othello* (2002) 71–72
Davies, Anthony xvi
  on *Chimes at Midnight* (1967) xv
  on *Richard III* (1955) 151
  on *Romeo and Juliet* (1968) 82
  on *Romeo and Juliet* (1978) 87
Davis, Natalie Zemon, on *The Return of Martin Guerre* (1982) 144
Davis, Pamela, *Antony and Cleopatra* 1
Davison, Bruce, in *The King Is Alive* (2001) 223
Dawson, Ralph 57
Day, Clarence xxviii
"The Death of the Author" (Barthes) 203
de Havilland, Olivia, in *A Midsummer Night's Dream* (1935) 57
Dehn, Paul, *The Taming of the Shrew* (1966) 91
Delgado, Miguel M., *Romeo y Julieta* (1943) 78
Delgado, Roger 2
de Mille, Agnes 80
De Munn, Jeffrey, in *A Midsummer Night's Dream* (1982) 60
Denby, David xxix
Dench, Judi
  in *Hamlet* (1996) 24, 116
  in *Macbeth* (1979) 51
  in *A Midsummer Night's Dream* (1969) 59
  in *Shakespeare in Love* (1998) xxvi, 87, 220
Dennehy, Brian, in *Romeo + Juliet* (1996) 83
Denig, Lynde, on *Macbeth* (1916) 48
Dent, Alan
  in *Chimes at Midnight* (1967) 27
  Hamlet (1948) 17
  Henry V (1944) 28
  Richard III (1955) 76

INDEX

Depardieu, Gerard, in *Hamlet* (1996) 25, 114
derivatives, Shakespeare xxix–xxx
Derrida, Jacques 171
Desfontaines, Henri, *Shylock* (1913) 52
design sketches xv
De Vega, José, in *West Side Story* (1961) 84
Devine, Andy, in *Romeo and Juliet* (1936) 80
Devine, George, in *The Tempest* (1939) 96–97
Devlin, William, in *King Lear* (1948) 39
DeVore, Christopher, *Hamlet* (1990) 23
Dexter, John, *Othello* (1965) 69
Díaz-Fernández, José Ramon xiii
DiCaprio, Leonardo, in *Romeo + Juliet* (1996) 82, 83, *83*, 163
Dickson, W. K. L. xii, xxvii
Dieterle, William, *A Midsummer Night's Dream* (1935) xi, 57, *58*
Dignam, Mark, in *Hamlet* (1969) 22
Dillane, Stephan, in *Hamlet* (1990) 24
Dillon, Carmen 77
Dinsdale, Reece, in *Hamlet* (1996) 113
Dixon, David, in *The Tempest* (1979) 97
Dmytryk, Edward
  Broken Lance (1954) xxx
  Hamlet (1960) 20
documentaries xxx
Dogme movement 223
Dolan, Monica, in *A Midsummer Night's Dream* (1996) 61
Donaldson, Peter xiv, xvii
A Double Life (1947) xxx, 68, 209–212
doubling 211–212
Douglas, Paul, in *Joe MacBeth* (1955) 49
Doyle, Kevin, in *A Midsummer Night's Dream* (1996) 61
Doyle, Patrick 31
Drake, Alfred, in *Hamlet* (1964) 21

Drazan, Anthony, *Zebrahead* (1992) 86
The Dresser (1983) 209
Drexler, Peter xvi
Drischell, Ralph, in *A Midsummer Night's Dream* (1982) 60
Duncan, Lindsay, in *A Midsummer Night's Dream* (1996) 60
Duncan-Jones, Katherine, on *Cymbeline* (1982) 12
Dunsmore, Rosemary 7

E

Early Modern Literary Studies xvi
Eccleston, Christopher, in *Othello* (2002) 72
Eckert, Charles xvi
Edison, Thomas 79
educational films xxx
Edzard, Christine, *As You Like It* (1992) 6–7
Eisenstein, Sergei
  Alexander Nevsky (1938) 29
  Strike (1924) 129
Elliott, Michael, *King Lear* (1983) 41
Elphick, Michael, in *Much Ado About Nothing* (1984) 65
Emerson, John, *Macbeth* (1916) x, 48
Emmerton, Roy, in *Henry V* (1944) 30
endings, of plays *vs.* films 183–187
Les Enfants du Paradis (1944) 221–225
Engel, Susan, in *King Lear* (1971) 40
The Entertainer (1960) 22
Evans, Daniel, in *A Midsummer Night's Dream* (1996) 61
Evans, Maurice
  in *Hamlet* (1953) 20
  in *The Tempest* (1960) 97
Everett, Rupert
  in *A Midsummer Night's Dream* (1999) 61, *62*
  in *Shakespeare in Love* (1998) 86, 220

Everyone Says I Love You (1996) 44
Excalibur (1981) 143
Eyre, Richard
  King Lear (1997) 41
  Richard III (1992) 154

F

Factory of the Eccentric Actor (FEX) 129
The Faerie Queen (Spenser) 38
Fairbanks, Douglas, in *The Taming of the Shrew* (1929) x, *xii*, xxvii, 92, *92*
Faithfull, Marianne 22
Farrell, Nicholas
  in *Hamlet* (1996) 25
  in *A Midwinter's Tale* (1995) 216
Fellini, Federico 101–102
Fenwick, Henry xvi
Feore, Colm, in *Romeo and Juliet* (1993) 88
Fergusson, Francis 226
Ferrara, Abel, *China Girl* (1987) 85–86
Feuer, Jane 195
FEX. *See* Factory of the Eccentric Actor
Fiennes, Joseph, in *Shakespeare in Love* (1998) xxvi, 86, 219, *220*
film(s)
  endings of 183–187
  vs. television 147
  vs. theater xxiii–xxviii, 148, 151, 183
Film d'Art x
Filming Shakespeare's Plays (Davies) xv
Film Quarterly (journal) xii
Films and Filming (journal) xii
Films in Review (journal) xii
Finch, Jon, in *Macbeth* (1971) 50, *50*, 136, *136*
Fineman, Joel 113
Finlay, Frank, in *Othello* (1965) 69
Finney, Albert, in *The Dresser* (1983) 209
Fire with Fire (1986) 89
The First Part of the Mirror for Magistrates (Higgin) 38

Firth, Colin, in *Shakespeare in Love* (1998) 87, 219
Firth, Jonathan, in *Romeo and Juliet* (1994) 89
Fishburne, Laurence, in *Othello* (1995) 70, *70*
Flea, in *My Own Private Idaho* (1991) 28
Fletcher, John 95
Flockhart, Calista, in *A Midsummer Night's Dream* (1999) 62
Fludd, Robert 170
The Folger Shakespeare Filmography (Parker) xiii
Follows, Megan Porter, in *Romeo and Juliet* (1993) 88
Fonda, Peter, in *The Tempest* (1999) 98
Forbes-Robertson, Johnston 19
Forbidden Planet (1956) xxx, 97–98
Ford, John, *My Darling Clementine* (1946) xxx
Foreman, Deborah, in *Valley Girl* (1983) 89
Fox, James 6
Fox, William 80
framing 170
Framing Shakespeare on Film (Howlett) xvii, xviii
Francis, Anne, in *Forbidden Planet* (1956) 98
Franklyn-Robbins, John, in *The Merchant of Venice* (1980) 54
French, Andrew, in *The Merchant of Venice* (2001) 55
Friel, Anna, in *A Midsummer Night's Dream* (1999) 62
Fuentes, Carlos 101–102
Furnival, Robert, *Julius Caesar* (1969) 33
Furse, Roger 77
Fussel, Paul 120

G

Gabold, Annelise, in *King Lear* (1971) 40
Gale, Peter, in *Hamlet* (1969) 24
Garland, Judy 216

Garrick, David 38
Gascoigne, Paul 121, 123
Gassman, Vittorio, in *The Tempest* (1982) 98
gaze 185
Gecks, Nicholas, in *Othello* (2002) 72
The Genius of Shakespeare (Bate) 201, 203
Gentleman's Agreement (1946) 53
Geoffrey of Monmouth 38
Gerdes, Peter xxiv
Gershwin, George 44, 193, 197
Gershwin, Ira 44, 197
Gibbins, Duncan, *Fire with Fire* (1986) 78
Gibbons, Cedric 80
Gibson, Mel 125
  Braveheart (1995) 142, 144
  in *Hamlet* (1990) 23, 125–128, *126*
  interview with 125–128
Gielgud, John
  in *Chimes at Midnight* (1967) 27
  in *Giuliete e Romeo* (1954) 81
  Hamlet (1964) 21
  in *Hamlet* (1970) 22
  in *Hamlet* (1996) 24, 116
  in *Julius Caesar* (1953) 34
  in *Julius Caesar* (1969) 34
  in *Looking for Richard* (1996) 78, 218
  in *Prospero's Books* (1991) xxx, 99–100, 167–168, *168*, 175, 186
  in *Richard III* (1955) 76
  in *Romeo and Juliet* (1978) 87
Gilbert, John xxvii
Gillespie, Robert, in *A Midsummer Night's Dream* (1996) 61
Gillies, Andrew 7
Giuliete e Romeo (1954) 80–81, 82, 163
Gleiberman, Owen, on *O* (2001) 71
Glover, Brian, in *A Midsummer Night's Dream* (1982) 59
Glover, John, in *The Tempest* (1999) 98
Godard, Jean-Luc, *King Lear* (1987) 41
Goering, Hermann 208

Gold, Jack, *The Merchant of Venice* (1980) 54–55
Goodman, Henry, in *The Merchant of Venice* (2001) 55
Gordon, Lewis
  in *As You Like It* (1985) 7
  in *Romeo and Juliet* (1993) 88
Gordon, Ruth, *A Double Life* (1947) 67, 210
Gordon-Levitt, Joseph, in *10 Things I Hate about You* (1999) 94
Gorey, Edward 212
Gorrie, John, *The Tempest* (1979) 97
Gough, Michael, in *Cymbeline* (1982) 12
Graham, Clive, in *Hamlet* (1969) 22
Grant, Kathy xiii
Grant, Richard E., in *Twelfth Night* (1996) 104
Grayson, Kathryn, in *Kiss Me Kate* (1953) 94
Greenaway, Peter 95
  Prospero's Books (1991) xv, xxx, 99–100, 167–172, 175, 184, 186
Griffin, Alice xii
  on *Hamlet* (1953) 20
Griffith, D. W.
  Macbeth (1916) 48
  The Taming of the Shrew (1908) 92
Gross, John
  on *The Merchant of Venice* (1969) 54
  on World War II 53
Gründgens, Gustaf 208
Guard, Pippa
  in *A Midsummer Night's Dream* (1982) 59
  in *The Tempest* (1979) 97
Gunn, James, *Tromeo and Juliet* (1996) 90
Guntner, Lawrence xvi

H

Halio, Jay xvi
  on *Hamlet* (1964) 21

INDEX

on *Hamlet* (1970) 22
on performance of Shakespeare 156
Hall, Mordaunt, on *The Taming of the Shrew* (1929) xi
Hall, Peter
  A Midsummer Night's Dream (1958) 62
  A Midsummer Night's Dream (1969) 59
Hamilton, Lucy, on *Romeo + Juliet* (1996) 159–164
Hamilton, Victoria, in *King Lear* (1997) 41
Hamlet **17–25**
  Almereyda (2000) xxviii–xxix, 25
  Bennett (1980) 22–23
  Branagh (1996) xvi, xxvi, *24*, 24–25, 113–116, 184–186
  editions of 17–18
  essays on xiv
  Gade (1920) x
  Gielgud (1964) 21
  Kline (1990) 24
  Kozintsev (1964) 20–21, 130
  Lyth (1984) xv, xvi
  Olivier (1948) 19–20
  play-within-a-play in 207–208
  plot of 18–19
  Richardson (1969) xxvi, 21–22, 24
  Schaefer and McCleery (1953) 20
  Wirth (1960) 20, *20*
  Wood (1970) 22
  Zeffirelli (1990) *23*, 23–24, 125–128
Hamlet: Film Television and Audio Performance (Kliman) xv
Hampden, Walter 211
Hampton, Benjamin xii
Haney, Mary 7
Hanson, Alexander, in *The Merchant of Venice* (2001) 55
Hanson, Ann, in *Romeo and Juliet* (1988) 88
Hapgood, Robert xvi
Harding, John, in *Othello* (2002) 72
Hardison, O. B. xiii, xv

Hardwicke, Cedric, in *Richard III* (1955) 76
Harris, Diana, on *The Tempest* (1980) 97, 175–182
Harry and Tonto (1974) 41
Hartnett, Josh, in *O* (2001) 71
Harvey, Laurence, in *Giuliete e Romeo* (1954) 81, 163
Harvey, Rodney, in *My Own Private Idaho* (1991) 28
Harwood, Ronald 209
Hassel, R. Chris, on *Richard III* (1983) 153
Hasso, Signe, in *A Double Life* (1947) 68, 210
Hattaway, Michael, on *A Midsummer Night's Dream* (1996) 60
Havinga, Nick 64
Hawes, Keeley, in *Othello* (2002) 72
Hawke, Ethan, in *Hamlet* (2000) 25
Hawkins, Jack, in *Theater of Blood* (1973) 213
Hawthorne, Nigel
  in *Richard III* (1995) 77
  in *The Tempest* (1979) 97
  in *Twelfth Night* (1996) 103
Heard, John, in *O* (2001) 71
Heath, Eira, in *A Midsummer Night's Dream* (1964) 58
Heath, Stephen 184
Hedges, Inez xviii
Heigl, Katherine, in *The Tempest* (1999) 98
Helpmann, Robert, in *Henry V* (1944) 30
Heminges, John 18
Henders, Richard, in *The Merchant of Venice* (2001) 55
Henderson, James, *The Tempest* (1999) 95
Hendry, Ian, in *Theater of Blood* (1973) 213
Henry IV, Parts I and II **26–28**
  plot of 26
  Van Sant (1991) (*My Own Private Idaho*) 28
  Welles (1967) (*Chimes at Midnight*) xv, xvi, xvii, 26–28

Henry V **28–31**
  Branagh (1989) xxiv, xxv, 30–31, *31*, 117–123, *118*, 147
  essays on xv
  Olivier (1944) xiv, xv, *xv*, xxiv–xxv, 29–30, 117, 118
  plot of 28–29
Henson, Elden, in *O* (2001) 71
Hepworth, Cecil 19
Herlie, Eileen
  in *Hamlet* (1948) 19
  in *Hamlet* (1964) 21
Herrand, Marcel, in *The Children of Paradise* (1944) 221
Hervé, Jean, in *Shylock* (1913) 53
Heston, Charlton
  Antony and Cleopatra (1972) 2–3
  in *Hamlet* (1996) 24, 116
  in *Julius Caesar* (1969) 34, 35
heuristic criticism xiii–xiv
Hickox, Douglas, *Theater of Blood* (1973) 212–213
Higgin, John 38
Hill, Benny, in *A Midsummer Night's Dream* (1964) 57–58
Hilliard, Harry, in *Romeo and Juliet* (1916) 80
Hinman, Charlton, on *Hamlet* (1948) 19
Hirsch, John, *As You Like It* (1985) 4, 7
Historia Regum Britanniae (Geoffrey of Monmouth) 38
A History of Kinetograph (Dickson) xii
History of King Richard the Third (More) 75
A History of the Movies (Hampton) xii
History of Shakespeare on Screen (Rothwell) xxvii, xxx
Hitchcock, Alfred 148
Hitler, Adolf 154
Hodgdon, Barbara xiii, xiv
Hoffman, Dustin 126
Hoffman, Michael, *A Midsummer Night's Dream* (1999) xv, *61*, 61–62
Hogg, Ian, in *King Lear* (1971) 40

Holden, Anthony 5
Holden, Stephen, on *A Midwinter's Tale* (1995) 216
Holderness, Graham xiii, xvi
Holinshed, Raphael 38, 47, 75
Holland, Peter xviii
Holm, Ian
 in *Hamlet* (1990) 23–24
 in *Henry V* (1989) 31
 in *King Lear* (1997) 41
 in *A Midsummer Night's Dream* (1969) 59
Hooker, Brian x
Hopkins, Anthony
 in *Hamlet* (1969) xxvi, 21, 22
 in *Titus* (1999) 101, *102*
Hordern, Michael
 in *Cymbeline* (1982) 12
 in *King Lear* (1975) 40
 in *Romeo and Juliet* (1978) 87
 in *The Taming of the Shrew* (1966) 94
 in *The Tempest* (1979) 97
 in *Theater of Blood* (1973) 212
Horrox, Alan, *Romeo and Juliet* (1994) 88–89
House of Cards 71
Houseman, John, *Julius Caesar* (1953) 33–34
Howard, Leslie, in *Romeo and Juliet* (1936) xii, 80
Howell, Jane, *Richard III* (1983) 77, 152–154
Howlett, Kathy xvii, xviii
Hughes, Bernard, in *Much Ado About Nothing* (1973) 65
Hughes, Ken, *Joe MacBeth* (1955) xxx, 49
Hunter, Ian, in *A Midsummer Night's Dream* (1935) 57
Hurdle, James, in *A Midsummer Night's Dream* (1982) 60
Hurt, John, in *King Lear* (1983) 41
Hurt, William, in *A Midsummer Night's Dream* (1982) 60
Hussey, Olivia, in *Romeo and Juliet* (1968) 81, *81*
Hyde-White, Alex, in *Romeo and Juliet* (1982) 87

I

The Immortal Gentleman (1935) 201–205
Imrie, Celia, in *A Midwinter's Tale* (1995) 216
In the Bleak Midwinter. See A Midwinter's Tale
Ingber, Nachman xiii
International Film Index xiii
International Movie Database xiii
Irving, Henry 53
Ivory, James, *Shakespeare Wallah* (1965) 213–215

J

Jackson, Freda, in *Henry V* (1944) 30
Jackson, Gordon, in *Hamlet* (1969) 22
Jackson, MacDonald, on *The Tempest* (1980) 97, 175–182
Jackson, Russell xvi
Jacobi, Derek
 in *Hamlet* (1980) 22–23
 in *Hamlet* (1996) 25, 113, 115–116
 in *Henry V* (1989) 30, 147
Jacobs, Irene, in *Othello* (1995) 70
Jacobsen, Soren Kragh 223
Jaffrey, Madhur, in *Shakespeare Wallah* (1965) 214
James, Jack, in *The Merchant of Venice* (2001) 55
Jameson, Fredric, on *Love's Labour's Lost* (2000) 194
Jarman, Derek, *The Tempest* (1980) 95, 97, 175–182
Jarvet, Yuri, in *Karol Lir* (1970) 39, 130
Jarvis, John 7
Jeffords, Barbara, in *A Midsummer Night's Dream* (1969) 59
Jenkins, Roger, *Love's Labour's Lost* (1965) 44
Jennings, Alex, in *A Midsummer Night's Dream* (1996) 60
Jennings, Talbot, *Romeo and Juliet* (1936) 78
Jensen, Jane, in *Tromeo and Juliet* (1996) 90

Jesson, Paul 11
Jhabvala, Ruth Prawer 214
Joe MacBeth (1955) xxx, 49
Johnson, Ian xii
Johnson, Julian, on *Macbeth* (1916) 48
Johnson, Karl, in *The Tempest* (1980) 97, 178
Johnson, Richard
 in *Antony and Cleopatra* (1974) 3
 in *Cymbeline* (1982) 11
 in *Hamlet* (1970) 22
 in *Julius Caesar* (1969) 34
Johnson, Ron, in *Zebrahead* (1992) 86
Johnson, Samuel 10
Jolson, Al xvi
Jones, Barry 20
Jones, Gemma, in *The Merchant of Venice* (1980) 54
Jones, Inigo xxv, 169
Jones, James Earl, in *King Lear* (1977) 40
Jones, Osheen, in *A Midsummer Night's Dream* (1996) 60
Jones, Sid, in *Joe MacBeth* (1955) 49
Jones, Trevor 155
Jonson, Ben xxv, xxvi–xxvii
Jorgens, Jack J. xiii, xv
 on *As You Like It* (1978) 7
 on *Hamlet* (1964) 21
 on *Othello* (1952) 69
 on *Richard III* (1955) 151–152
Jory, Victor, in *A Midsummer Night's Dream* (1935) 57
Josephson, Erland, in *Prospero's Books* (1991) 100
Joubé, Romuald, in *Shylock* (1913) 53
Jourdan, Gabrielle, in *The Merchant of Venice* (2001) 55
Jubal (1956) xxx
Julia, Raul
 in *King Lear* (1977) 40
 in *The Tempest* (1982) 98
Julius Caesar **33–35**
 Burge (1969) 34–35
 Cines (1914) x

INDEX

Mankiewicz (1953) 33–34
  plot of 33
"*Julius Caesar* in the Cold" (Miller) xiv
Junger, Gil, *10 Things I Hate About You* (1999) 70, 94–95

K

Kaaya, Brad, *O* (2001) 70
Kael, Pauline
  on *Chimes at Midnight* (1967) 27
  on *King Lear* (1971) xvii
Kane, John, in *A Midsummer Night's Dream* (1996) 61
Kanin, Garson, *A Double Life* (1947) 67, 210
Kapner, Mitchell, *Romeo Must Die* (2000) 79
Kapoor, Shashi, in *Shakespeare Wallah* (1965) 214
Karol Lir (1970) 39, 129–132
Kauffmann, Stanley
  on *Hamlet* (2000) 25
  on *Love's Labour's Lost* (2000) 44
Kaufman, Lloyd, *Tromeo and Juliet* (1996) xviii, 90
Kazan, Elia, *Gentleman's Agreement* (1946) 53
Kean, Edmund 38
Keane, James, *Richard III* (1912) xxvii, 76
Keaton, Michael, in *Much Ado About Nothing* (1993) 63–64
Keegan, Andrew, in *O* (2001) 71
Keel, Howard, in *Kiss Me Kate* (1953) 94
Keenan, Will, in *Tromeo and Juliet* (1996) 90
Kelly, Alex, in *The Merchant of Venice* (2001) 55
Kemp-Welch, Joan
  A Midsummer Night's Dream (1964) 57–59
  Romeo and Juliet (1988) 88
Kendal, Geoffrey, in *Shakespeare Wallah* (1965) 214

Kent, Charles
  A Midsummer Night's Dream (1909) xxvii, 57
  As You Like It (1912) 4–5
Kenyon, Charles, *A Midsummer Night's Dream* (1935) 56
Kermode, Frank 183
Kern, Jerome 44, 193, 194
Kidnie, Margaret Jane, on *Tromeo and Juliet* (1996) 90
Kiersch, Fritz, *Under the Boardwalk* (1989) 78
Kimball, Frederick, in *Looking for Richard* (1996) 78, 218
King, Robert, III, *Under the Boardwalk* (1989) 78
The King Is Alive (2001) 223–224
King John xi, xxvii
King Lear 37–41
  Blackton and Ranous (1909) 39
  Brook (1971) xiv, 39–40, *40*, 129
  commentary on xiv, xxvii
  Elliott (1983) 41
  Eyre (1997) 41
  Godard (1987) 41
  Kozintsev (1970) (*Karol Lir*) 39, 129–132
  Kurosawa (1985) (*Ran*) xv, xxix, 41
  McCullough and Brook (1953) 39
  Miller (1975) 40
  Miller (1982) 40
  Morley (1948) 39
  plot of 37–39
  Sherin (1977) 40–41
  Thomashefsky (1934) (*The Yiddish King Lear*) 39
  Warde (1916) x, 39
Kingsley, Ben
  in *Antony and Cleopatra* (1974) 3
  in *Twelfth Night* (1996) 103
Kingsley, Dorothy, *Kiss Me Kate* (1953) 91
Kingsley-Smith, Jane E., on authorship 201–205
Kleine, George 53
Kliman, Bernice W. xiii, xv, xvi
Kline, Kevin
  Hamlet (1990) 24

  in *A Midsummer Night's Dream* (1999) 61–62
Knight, Esmond, in *Henry V* (1944) 30
Kott, Jan
  and *Hamlet* xxix, 20
  on *King Lear* 129
  on *A Midsummer Night's Dream* 58, 59
  on *The Tempest* 178
Kozintsev, Grigori
  Hamlet (1964) 20–21, 130
  Karol Lir (1970) 39, 129–132
Krasner, Milton 211
Kuheka, Peter, in *The King Is Alive* (2001) 223
Kurosawa, Akira xxix
  Ran (1985) xv, xxix, 41
  Throne of Blood (1957) xxix, 49
Kustow, Michael
  on *Hamlet* (1948) 19
  on *Hamlet* (1964) 20
Kyd, Thomas 207

L

LaBadie, Florence 10–11
Ladyhawke (1985) 143
Laemmle, Carl, *The Merchant of Venice* (1914) 53
Lahue, Kalton, on *Macbeth* (1916) 48
Lan, Yong Li, on endings 183–187
Lane, Andrew, *Valley Girl* (1983) 78
Lane, Anthony
  on *Looking for Richard* (1996) 217, 218
  on mousetrap plays 226
Lane, Nathan, in *Love's Labour's Lost* (2000) 44–45
Lange, Jessica, in *Titus* (1999) 101
language, evolution of xxviii
Lapine, James, *A Midsummer Night's Dream* (1982) 60
Lapotaire, Jane 2
Last Action Hero (1993) xxx
The Last Metro (1980) 208
Laughton, Charles, in *A Midsummer Night's Dream* (1958) 62

Laurents, Arthur 84
Lawrence, Gertrude, in *Men Are Not Gods* (1936) 210
Lawrence, Michael, in *Othello* (1952) 69
Leaming, Barbara 48–49
Ledger, Heath, in *10 Things I Hate about You* (1999) 94
Lee, Robert N. 76
Lee, Rowland V. 76
Leguizamo, John, in *Romeo + Juliet* (1996) 83
Lehman, Ernest, *West Side Story* (1961) 78
Leigh, Jennifer Jason, in *The King Is Alive* (2001) 224
Leighton, Margaret, in *Hamlet* (1970) 22
Lemmon, Jack, in *Hamlet* (1996) xxvi, 24
Lennix, Harry, in *Titus* (1999) 101
A Letter to Three Wives (1949) 34
Levring, Kristian, *The King Is Alive* (2001) 223–224
Levy, Emanuel, on *A Midsummer Night's Dream* (1999) 61
LFQ. See *Literature/Film Quarterly*
Liddel, Laura, in *Shakespeare Wallah* (1965) 214
Life with Father (1947) xxviii
Lindley, Arthur, on *Macbeth* (1948) 141–145
Lindsay, Robert
 in *Cymbeline* (1982) 12
 in *A Midsummer Night's Dream* (1982) 59
 in *Much Ado About Nothing* (1984) 65
Ling, Nicholas 17
Lipkov, Alexander xiii
Lippman, Max xiii
Literature/Film Quarterly (LFQ) xiii, xxxi
Lloyd, Robert, in *King Lear* (1971) 40
Lombard, Carole, in *To Be or Not to Be* (1942) 208, *209*
Loncraine, Richard, *Richard III* (1995) xxix, 77–78, 147, 154–156

Londre, Felicia, on *Rosencrantz and Guildenstern Are Dead* 225
long shots 184
Look Back in Anger (1959) 22
Looking for Richard (1996) 77–78, 217–219, *218*
looking structures 185
Lo Savio, Gerolamo, *The Merchant of Venice* (1910) 53
Love's Labour's Lost **43–45**
 Branagh (2000) 44–45, 193–198
 plot of 43
Lowe, Arthur, in *Theater of Blood* (1973) 212
Lubitsch, Ernest, *To Be or Not to Be* (1942) xxx, 52, 53, 208–209
Luhrmann, Baz, *Romeo + Juliet* (1996) xxv, xxviii, 82–83, *83*, 159–164, 184, 185
Lunghi, Cherie, in *Much Ado About Nothing* (1984) 65
Lutz, Karen McCullah, *10 Things I Hate About You* (1999) 91
Lynch, Finbar, in *A Midsummer Night's Dream* (1996) 61
Lyons, Bridget xv
Lyth, Ragnar, *Hamlet* (1984) xv, xvi

M
Macbeth **47–51**
 Emerson (1916) x, 48
 essays on xiv
 Hughes (1955) (*Joe MacBeth*) xxx, 49
 Kurosawa (1957) (*Throne of Blood*) xxix, 49
 Nunn and Casson (1979) 50–51
 plot of 47–48
 Polanski (1971) xiv, xxv, 49–50, *50*, 135–139
 Reilly (1990) (*Men of Respect*) 51
 Welles (1948) xxv, 48–49, *141*, 141–145
MacGowan, Jack, in *King Lear* (1971) 40, *40*
MacLachlan, Kyle, in *Hamlet* (2000) 25

MacLiammoir, Michael, in *Othello* (1952) 68
Madden, Ciaran, in *Hamlet* (1970) 22
Madden, John, *Shakespeare in Love* (1998) xxvi, 86–87, 183–184, 186–187, 201–205, 219–221
Mad Max (1979) 125
Mad Max 2 (1982) 119
Madsen, Virginia, in *Fire with Fire* (1986) 89
Maher, Mary 24
Mailer, Norman, in *King Lear* (1987) 41
Maloney, Michael
 in *Hamlet* (1996) 25, 114
 in *A Midwinter's Tale* (1995) 216
Mamet, David xxviii
Manheim, Michael xiii
 on *Richard III* (1983) 153
Mankiewicz, Joseph L., *Julius Caesar* (1953) 33–34
Mann, Klaus 208
Manson, Charles 136, 137, 139
Manvell, Roger xii–xiii
 on *Chimes at Midnight* (1967) 27
 on *Julius Caesar* (1969) 34–35
Marceau, Sophie, in *A Midsummer Night's Dream* (1999) 62
Margolyes, Miriam, in *Romeo + Juliet* (1996) 163
Marlowe, Christopher 77, 202–203
Marsh, Linda, in *Hamlet* (1964) 21
Martin, Frank 95
Mason, James, in *Julius Caesar* (1953) 34
Massey, Anna, in *A Midsummer Night's Dream* (1964) 58
Maxwell, Roberta 7
Mayer, Edwin Justus 208
Mayer, Louis B. 80
Mayo, Jerry, in *Much Ado About Nothing* (1973) 65
Mazursky, Paul
 Harry and Tonto (1974) 41
 The Tempest (1982) xiv, xxx, 98–99, *99*
McAlpine, Donald 163

INDEX

McCall, Mary C., *A Midsummer Night's Dream* (1935) 56
McCarthy, Todd, on *O* (2001) 70
McCleery, Albert, *Hamlet* (1953) 20
McCloskey, Susan, on *Much Ado About Nothing* (1984) 65
McCullough, Andrew, *King Lear* (1953) 39
McCullough, Christopher xiii
McDiarmid, Ian, in *Macbeth* (1979) 51
McDowall, Roddy, in *The Tempest* (1960) 97
McElhone, Natascha, in *Love's Labour's Lost* (2000) 44
McEnery, John
    in *Hamlet* (1990) 24
    in *Romeo and Juliet* (1968) 82
McEnery, Peter, in *A Midsummer Night's Dream* (1982) 59–60
McEwan, Geraldine, in *Love's Labour's Lost* (2000) 45
McFarlane, Brian, on *Prospero's Books* (1991) 100
McKellen, Ian
    in *Macbeth* (1979) 50–51
    in *Richard III* (1995) 77, 147, 154–156, *155*
McKern, Leo, in *King Lear* (1983) 41
McKernan, Luke xiii
McLean, Andrew xiii
McMurtry, Jo xiii
    on *A Midsummer Night's Dream* (1982) 60
McNamee, Patrick, in *Romeo and Juliet* (1988) 88
McTeer, Janet, in *The King Is Alive* (2001) 223
medieval films 141–145
Meerson, Lazare 6
Méliès, George, *Romeo and Juliet* (1902) 80
Mellor, Cherith, in *A Midsummer Night's Dream* (1982) 59
Melzer, Annabelle xiii, xxx
    on *As You Like It* (1912) 5
    on *A Midsummer Night's Dream* (1982) 60
    on Thanhouser 10

Men Are Not Gods (1936) 68, 210
Mendelssohn, Felix 57, 61
Men of Respect (1990) 51
Menzies, William Cameron xi
Mephisto (1981) 208
Il mercante de Venezia (1910) 53
Mercanton, Louis, *Shylock* (1913) 52
The Merchant of Venice **52–56**
    Desfontaines (1913) (*Shylock*) 53
    Gold (1980) 54–55
    Lo Savio (1910) 53
    Miller and Sichel (1969) 53–54
    Nunn (2001) 55–56
    plot of 52–53
Meredith, Burgess, in *King Lear* (1987) 41
Messina, Cedric, *The Tempest* (1968) 97
Meteorologia Cosmica (Fludd) 170
Meyer, David, in *The Tempest* (1980) 97
Michell, Keith, in *The Tempest* (1968) 97
A Midsummer Night's Dream **56–62**
    Ardolino and Lapine (1982) 60
    Blackton and Kent (1909) xxvii, 57
    essays on xv
    Hall (1969) 59
    Hoffman (1999) xv, *61*, 61–62
    Kemp-Welch (1964) 57–59
    Moshinsky (1982) 59–60
    Noble (1996) 60–61
    plot of 56–57
    Reinhardt and Dieterle (1935) xi, 57, *58*
A Midwinter's Tale (1995) 196, 215, 215–217
Mifune, Toshiro, in *Throne of Blood* (1957) 49
Miller, Ann, in *Kiss Me Kate* (1953) 94
Miller, Anthony xiv
Miller, Jonathan
    King Lear (1975) 40
    King Lear (1982) 40

The Merchant of Venice (1969) 53–54
    and *A Midsummer Night's Dream* (1982) 59
Miller, Paul, in *Romeo and Juliet* (1993) 88
Milli, Robert, in *Hamlet* (1964) 21
Mirren, Helen
    in *As You Like It* (1978) 7
    in *Cymbeline* (1982) 12
    in *A Midsummer Night's Dream* (1969) 59
    in *A Midsummer Night's Dream* (1982) 59
mirror(s) 170, 171
mirror movies xxx
Mitchell, Elvis, on *Hamlet* (2000) 25
Mitchell, Warren, in *The Merchant of Venice* (1980) 54
Mohr, Hal 57
Molloy, Dearbhla, in *Romeo and Juliet* (1994) 89
Monette, Richard, *Romeo and Juliet* (1993) 88
Montague, Lee, in *Much Ado About Nothing* (1984) 65
Monty Python and the Holy Grail (1975) 64
More, Thomas 75
Moreno, Mario, in *Romeo y Julieto* (1943) 84
Moreno, Rita, in *West Side Story* (1961) 84–85
Morley, Robert, in *Theater of Blood* (1973) 213
Morley, Royston, *King Lear* (1948) 39
Morris, Peter xiii
Moshinsky, Elijah
    Cymbeline (1982) 11–12
    Love's Labour's Lost (1984) 44
    A Midsummer Night's Dream (1982) 59–60
Mother Night (Vonnegut) 149
Motonari Mori 41
Mounet-Sully, Jean x
mousetrap plays 207–226
The Moving Picture World and View Photographer (journal) ix

Much Ado About Nothing **62–66**
    Antoon (1973) 64–65
    Branagh (1993) 63–64, *64*
    Burge (1984) 65–66
    plot of 62–63
Muir, Jean, in *A Midsummer Night's Dream* (1935) 57
Murphy, Andrew xvi
Murray, Bill, in *Hamlet* (2000) 25
Murray, John Tucker 80
musicals xxx
    Love's Labour's Lost (2000) 44–45, 193–198
    West Side Story (1961) 84–85
My Darling Clementine (1946) xxx
My Own Private Idaho (1991) 28
The Mystery of Hamlet (Vining) 19

N

The Name of the Rose (1986) 144
Nannuzzi, Armando 128
Napier, Alan, in *Macbeth* (1948) 49
The Navigator (1988) 142, 144
Neil, Hildegard 2
Nelson, Tim Blake, *O* (2001) 70–71
Nettles, John, in *The Merchant of Venice* (1980) 54
Newton, Robert, in *Henry V* (1944) 30
New York Times (newspaper) x
Nicholls, Anthony, in *Othello* (1965) 69
Nielsen, Asta 19
Nielsen, Leslie, in *Forbidden Planet* (1956) 98
Nieto, Jose, in *Chimes at Midnight* (1967) 27
Nivola, Alessandro, in *Love's Labour's Lost* (2000) 44
No Bed for Bacon (Brahms and Simon) 204
Noble, Adrian, *A Midsummer Night's Dream* (1996) 60–61
Nobre, F. Silva xiii
Nolan, Jeanette, in *Macbeth* (1948) 49, 143
Norman, Marc, *Shakespeare in Love* (1998) xxvi, 86, 87, 204, 219

normative criticism xiii–xiv
Nosworthy, J. M., on *Cymbeline* (1982) 12
Nothing Like the Sun (Burgess) 86
Novelli, Ermete, in *Il mercante de Venezia* (1910) 53
Nunn, Trevor
    Antony and Cleopatra (1974) 3
    Macbeth (1979) 50–51
    The Merchant of Venice (2001) 55–56
    Twelfth Night (1996) 103–104
Nyman, Michael 169

O

O (2001) 70–71
O'Brien, Edmond
    in *A Double Life* (1947) 68, 211
    in *Julius Caesar* (1953) 34
O Brother, Where Art Thou? (1999) 71
Oleynik, Larisa, in *10 Things I Hate About You* (1999) 94
Oliver, Edith, in *Romeo and Juliet* (1936) 80
Oliver, May xii
Olivier, Laurence *xxiv*, xxiv–xxv
    in *As You Like It* (1936) 5–6
    vs. Branagh 117, 118
    Hamlet (1948) 19–20
    Henry V (1944) xiv, xv, *xv*, xxiv–xxv, 29–30, 117, 118
    in *King Lear* (1983) 41
    in *The Merchant of Venice* (1969) 54
    On Acting 5
    in *Othello* (1965) *69*, 69–70
    Richard III (1955) 76, 76–77, 149–152, *150*
    on Zeffirelli 125
On Acting (Olivier) 5
operas xxx
Orlando Furioso (Ariosto) 62
Orson Welles: Shakespeare and Popular Culture (Anderegg) xvii
Osborne, John 22
Othello **67–72**
    Burge (1965) *69*, 69–70
    Cukor (1947) (*A Double Life*) xxx, 68, 209–212

    Davies (2002) 71–72
    essays on xiv
    Nelson (2001) (*O*) 70–71
    Parker (1995) 70, *70*
    plot of 67–68
    Welles (1952) 68–69, 189–191
    Yutkevich (1955) 69

P

Pacino, Al, *Looking for Richard* (1996) 77–78, 217–219, *218*
Paltrow, Gwyneth, in *Shakespeare in Love* (1998) xxvi, 86, 87, 219
Panebianco, Richard, in *China Girl* (1987) 85
Papp, Joseph
    King Lear (1977) 40–41
    Much Ado About Nothing (1973) 64–65
Parfitt, Judy, in *Hamlet* (1969) 22
Parker, Barry M. xiii
Parker, Oliver, *Othello* (1995) 70, *70*
Pasco, Isabelle, in *Prospero's Books* (1991) 100
Pasco, Richard 7
Pasternak, Boris
    Hamlet (1964) 17
    Karol Lir (1970) 39
    Othello (1955) 67
Paterson, Bill, in *Othello* (2002) 72
Paul, Richard Joseph, in *Under the Boardwalk* (1989) 89
Pavis, Patrice 183
Pearson, Roberta E. xii
Peary, Danny, on *To Be or Not to Be* (1942) 209
Peck, Bob, in *Macbeth* (1979) 51
pedagogical criticism xiii
Pendleton, Tom xvii
Pennell, Nicholas 7
Pennington, Michael
    in *Cymbeline* (1982) 12
    in *Hamlet* (1969) 22
Perret, Marion D., on *The Merchant of Venice* (1969) 54
Perrineau, Harold
    in *Romeo + Juliet* (1996) 83
    in *The Tempest* (1999) 98
Peyser, Joan 85

INDEX

Pfeiffer, Michelle, in *A Midsummer Night's Dream* (1999) 61, 62
Phifer, Mekhi, in *O* (2001) 70, 71
Phillips, Bill, *Fire with Fire* (1986) 78
Phoenix, Rain, in *O* (2001) 71
Phoenix, River, in *My Own Private Idaho* (1991) 28
Pickford, Mary, in *The Taming of the Shrew* (1929) x, xi, *xii*, xxvii, 92, *92*
Pickup, Ronald, in *The Tempest* (1968) 97
Pidgeon, Walter, in *Forbidden Planet* (1956) xxx, 98
Pilkington, Ace G. xiv, xvii
Pinter, Harold xxviii
Pious, Minerva, in *Joe MacBeth* (1955) 49
Pirandello, Luigi xxvii
play(s)
    within plays 207–226
    vs. screenplay xxiv
Plowright, Joan, in *The Merchant of Venice* (1969) 54
Polanski, Roman, *Macbeth* (1971) xiv, xxv, 49–50, *50*, 135–139
"Pop Goes the Shakespeare" (Walker) xiv
Popov, Andrei, in *Othello* (1955) 69
Porter, Cole 44, 94
Porter, Eric
    in *Antony and Cleopatra* (1972) 2
    in *Hamlet* (1980) 23
positivist criticism xiii–xiv
Postlethwaite, Pete, in *Romeo + Juliet* (1996) 83
postmodernism xviii, xxix
Potter, Dennis 45
Potter, Lois xiii
Powell, Dick, in *A Midsummer Night's Dream* (1935) 57
Preece, Patricia, *King Lear* (1982) 37
Prévert, Jacques 221
Price, Dennis, in *Theater of Blood* (1973) 212
Price, Vincent, in *Theater of Blood* (1973) 212, 213

Prospero's Books (1991) xv, xxx, 99–100, 167–172, 175, 184, 186
Pursell, Michael
    on *Henry V* (1989) 30–31, 117–123
    on *Romeo + Juliet* (1996) xiv
Pyne, Natasha, in *The Taming of the Shrew* (1966) 93

Q

Quinn, Aidan, in *Looking for Richard* (1996) 78, 218
Quinn, Edward xv
Quiz Show (1994) xviii
Quo Vadis? (1951) 2, 33, 34

R

Rackham, Arthur 59, 60
Rackin, Phyllis, on *Richard III* 155
radio xxviii
Rain, Douglas, in *The Tempest* (1968) 97
Rakoff, Alvin, *Romeo and Juliet* (1978) 87
Ran (1985) xv, xxix, 41
Ranous, William V., *King Lear* (1909) 39
Rapaport, Michael, in *Zebrahead* (1992) 86
Rathbone, Basil, in *Romeo and Juliet* (1936) xii, 80
Raymond, Emily, in *A Midsummer Night's Dream* (1996) 61
recontextualizations xxx
Redgrave, Corin, in *Antony and Cleopatra* (1974) 3
Redgrave, Michael
    in *Hamlet* (1970) 22
    in *The Tempest* (1968) 97
Redgrave, Vanessa, in *Looking for Richard* (1996) 78, 218
Rees, Angharad 7
Reeves, Keanu
    in *Much Ado About Nothing* (1993) 63
    in *My Own Private Idaho* (1991) 28
Reframing Culture (Uricchio and Pearson) xii

Reilly, William, *Men of Respect* (1990) 51
Reinhardt, Max, *A Midsummer Night's Dream* (1935) xi, 57, *58*
Remick, Lee, in *The Tempest* (1960) 97
The Return of Martin Guerre (1982) 144
revues xxx
Rey, Fernando, in *Chimes at Midnight* (1967) 27
Richard III 75–78
    commentary on 147–157
    Howell (1983) 77, 152–154
    Keane (1912) xxvii, 76
    Loncraine (1995) xxix, 77–78, 147, 154–156
    Olivier (1955) 76, 76–77, 149–152, *150*
    Pacino (1996) (*Looking for Richard*) 77–78, 217–219
    plot of 75–76
Richards, Bernard, on *Henry V* (1989) 117, 119, 120, 121, 122
Richardson, Ralph
    in *Chimes at Midnight* (1967) 27
    in *Richard III* (1955) 76
Richardson, Tony, *Hamlet* (1969) xxvi, 21–22, 24
Richert, William, in *My Own Private Idaho* (1991) 28
Ridges, Stanley, in *To Be or Not to Be* (1942) 208
Rigg, Diana
    in *Julius Caesar* (1969) 34
    in *King Lear* (1983) 41
    in *A Midsummer Night's Dream* (1969) 59
    in *Theater of Blood* (1973) 212
Ringwald, Molly
    in *King Lear* (1987) 41
    in *The Tempest* (1982) 98
Ritter, Fred 49
Ritzav, Tue xiii
Robards, Jason, in *Julius Caesar* (1969) 34, 35
Robards, Sam, in *The Tempest* (1982) 98
Robbins, Jerome 84
The Robe (1953) 2

Robey, George, in *Henry V* (1944) 30
Rodway, Norman, in *Chimes at Midnight* (1967) 27
Rogers, Paul, in *A Midsummer Night's Dream* (1969) 59
Roland, Herb, *As You Like It* (1985) 7–8
Rolle, Esther, in *Romeo and Juliet* (1982) 87
Roman, Ruth, in *Joe MacBeth* (1955) 49
Romanoff and Juliet (1961) 85
Romeo and Juliet **78–90**
   Bartkowiak (2000) (*Romeo Must Die*) 89–90
   Campbell (1993) 88
   Castellani (1954) 80–81, 82, 163
   Coolidge (1983) (*Valley Girl*) 89
   Cukor (1936) xi–xii, xv, 80
   Delgado (1943) 84
   Drazan (1992) (*Zebrahead*) 86
   essays on xiv
   Ferrara (1987) (*China Girl*) 85–86
   Gibbins (1986) (*Fire with Fire*) 89
   Horrox (1994) 88–89
   Kaufman (1996) (*Tromeo and Juliet*) xviii, 90
   Kemp-Welch (1988) 88
   Kiersch (1989) (*Under the Boardwalk*) 89
   Luhrmann (1996) xxv, xxviii, 82–83, *83*, 159–164, 184, 185
   Madden (1998) (*Shakespeare in Love*) xxvi–xxvii, 86–87, 183–184, 186–187, 201–205, 219–221
   plot of 79–80
   Rakoff (1978) 87
   Ustinov (1961) (*Romanoff and Juliet*) 85
   Wise (1961) (*West Side Story*) 84–85
   Woodman (1982) 87–88
   Zeffirelli (1968) xiv, *81*, 81–82, 87, 126, 159–160, 163–164
Romeo Must Die (2000) 89–90

Rooney, Mickey
   in *A Midsummer Night's Dream* (1935) 57
   and *A Midwinter's Tale* (1995) 216
Rose, Francis 180
Rosenbaum, Jonathan xvii
Rosenblatt, Marcel, in *A Midsummer Night's Dream* (1982) 60
Rosencrantz and Guildenstern Are Dead (Stoppard) 86, 224–225
Rosenstone, Robert 143
Rothwell, Kenneth S. xiii, xxvii, xxx
   on *As You Like It* (1912) 5
   on *As You Like It* (1936) 6
   on *As You Like It* (1992) 6
   criticism survey by ix–xviii
   on *Hamlet* (1980) 22, 23
   on *Julius Caesar* (1969) 34
   on *Il mercante de Venezia* (1910) 53
   on *A Midsummer Night's Dream* (1982) 60
   on *A Midwinter's Tale* (1995) 216, 217
   on *Romeo and Juliet* (1978) 87
   on *The Tempest* (1960) 97
   on *The Tempest* (1979) 97
   on *The Tempest* (1980) 97
   on Thanhouser 10
   on *Tromeo and Juliet* (1996) 90
Rowlands, Gena, in *The Tempest* (1982) 98
Rozsa, Miklos 211
rugby, *Henry V* and 121–122
Rumann, Sig, in *To Be or Not to Be* (1942) 208
Rush, Deborah, in *A Midsummer Night's Dream* (1982) 60
Rush, Geoffrey, in *Shakespeare in Love* (1998) 86, 219
Russo, James, in *China Girl* (1987) 85–86
Rutherford, Margaret, in *Chimes at Midnight* (1967) 27
Rutherford, Mary, in *Antony and Cleopatra* (1974) 3
Ryder, Winona, in *Looking for Richard* (1996) 78, 218, *218*
Ryecart, Patrick, in *Romeo and Juliet* (1978) 87

Rylance, Mark, in *Prospero's Books* (1991) 100
Rylands, George, *A Midsummer Night's Dream* (1964) 56

S

St. John, Nicolas, *China Girl* (1987) 78
Saire, Rebecca, in *Romeo and Juliet* (1978) 87
Salou, Louis, in *The Children of Paradise* (1944) 221
Salvador, Jaime, *Romeo y Julieta* (1943) 78
Sammons, Eddie xiii
Sand, Tom, *Hamlet* (1953) 17
Sarandon, Susan, in *The Tempest* (1982) 98
Sasaki, Takamaru, in *Throne of Blood* (1957) 49
Sawalha, Julia, in *A Midwinter's Tale* (1995) 216
Sax, Geoffrey, *Othello* (2002) 67
Schaefer, George
   Hamlet (1953) 20
   The Tempest (1960) 97
Schell, Maximilian, *Hamlet* (1960) 20
Schildkraut, Joseph 20
Schlueter, June, on *The Merchant of Venice* (1969) 54
Schreiber, Liev, in *Hamlet* (2000) 25
Schwarzenegger, Arnold xxx
Scofield, Jon, *Antony and Cleopatra* (1974) 3
Scofield, Paul
   in *Hamlet* (1990) 24, 127
   in *Henry V* (1989) 31
   in *King Lear* (1971) 40, *40*, 129, *130*
Scorsese, Martin, *The Age of Innocence* (1993) 142
Scott, John 2
Screening Shakespeare (Pilkington) xvii
screenplay, *vs.* play xxiv
scripts, film xv, xxiv
Sellers, Peter, in *King Lear* (1987) 41

INDEX

Seneca 148
Sessions, John, in *A Midwinter's Tale* (1995) 216
The Seventh Seal (1957) 142, 143, 145
Sewell, Rufus, in *Hamlet* (1996) 113
SFNL. See *Shakespeare on Film Newsletter*
Shakespeare: A Hundred Years on Film (Sammons) xiii
Shakespeare and the Films (Manvell) xii
Shakespeare and the Moving Image (Davies) xvi
Shakespearean Films/Shakespearean Directors (Donaldson) xvii
Shakespeare Bulletin xiii
Shakespeare, Cinema and Society (Collick) xv
Shakespeare, Film, Fin de Siècle (Burnett and Wray) xvi
The Shakespeare Hour: A Companion to the PBS-TV Series xv
Shakespeare in Hollywood, 1929–1956 (Willson) xvii–xviii, xxx
Shakespeare in Love (1998) xxvi–xxvii, 86–87, 183–184, 186–187, 201–205, 219–221
Shakespeare in Production. Whose History? (Coursen) xvii
Shakespeare in the Movies (Brode) xvii
Shakespeare Observed (Crowl) xvii
Shakespeare on Film (Jorgens) xiii, 151–152
Shakespeare on Film Newsletter (SFNL) xiii, xv
Shakespeare on Screen (Rothwell and Melzer) xiii, xxx
Shakespeare on Silent Film (Ball) xii, xxvii, 129
Shakespeare on Television (Coursen and Bulman) xv–xvi
Shakespeare, Our Contemporary (Kott) xxix, 59, 129
"Shakespeare Plays" series 97
Shakespeare Quarterly xii
Shakespeare Survey (Wells) xvi

Shakespeare: Time and Conscience (Kozintsev) 132
Shakespeare Wallah (1965) 213–215
Shallcross, Alan xvi
  As You Like It (1978) 4
  Hamlet (1980) 17
  Romeo and Juliet (1978) 78
  The Tempest (1979) 95
Sharkey, Ray, in *Zebrahead* (1992) 86
Shaughnessy, Robert xvi
Shaw, Martin, in *Hamlet* (1970) 22
Shaw, Sebastian
  in *Men Are Not Gods* (1936) 210
  in *A Midsummer Night's Dream* (1982) 59
Shaw, William P. xiv
Shay, Michele, in *A Midsummer Night's Dream* (1982) 60
Shearer, Norma, in *Romeo and Juliet* (1936) xii, xviii, 80
Sheen, Martin, in *O* (2001) 71
Sheffer, Craig, in *Fire with Fire* (1986) 89
Shentall, Susan, in *Giuliete e Romeo* (1954) 81, 163
Shepard, Sam, in *Hamlet* (2000) 25
Sherin, Edwin, *King Lear* (1977) 40–41
Shodin, David, *King Lear* (1982) 37
Shostakovich, Dmitri 21, 39
Shylock, ou le More de Venise (1913) 53
Sichel, John, *The Merchant of Venice* (1969) 52
Sidney, George, *Kiss Me Kate* (1953) 91
Sight and Sound (journal) xii
silent films x, xxvii
Silent Shakespeare (compilation video) xxvii
Silverstone, Alicia, in *Love's Labour's Lost* (2000) 44, 197
Simmons, Jean, in *Hamlet* (1948) 19
Simon, S. J. 204

Skaaren, Warren, *Fire with Fire* (1986) 78
Skala, Lilia, in *Men of Respect* (1990) 51
Skarsgård, Stellan xv
Skovmand, Michael xvi
Smiley, Jane xxx
Smith, C. Aubrey xii
Smith, Maggie
  in *Othello* (1965) 69, 69–70
  in *Richard III* (1995) 77
Smith, Mel, in *Twelfth Night* (1996) 104
Smoktunovski, Innokenti 21
Snell, Peter, *Julius Caesar* (1969) 34
Snodin, David xvi
  Cymbeline (1982) 9
  The Merchant of Venice (1980) 52
  A Midsummer Night's Dream (1982) 56
  Richard III (1983) 77
soccer, *Henry V* and 121
soliloquy 148–149
Somerville, Geraldine, in *Romeo and Juliet* (1994) 89
Sommersby (1993) 144
Sondheim, Stephen 84
Sontag, Susan, on film *vs.* theater 148, 151
The Sopranos (television show) xxviii
Sorace, Patrice, on *Shakespeare Wallah* (1965) 214
Sorvino, Paul
  in *King Lear* (1977) 40
  in *Romeo + Juliet* (1996) 83
Spacey, Kevin, in *Looking for Richard* (1996) 78, 218
Spall, Timothy, in *Hamlet* (1996) 113
The Spanish Tragedy (Kyd) 207
Spaull, Timothy, in *Love's Labour's Lost* (2000) 44
Spenser, Edmund 38
Spikings, Barry 126
Spoczynski, Jan 65
sports, *Henry V* and 121–122
St. John, Nicholas, *China Girl* (1987) 78

Stack, Robert, in *To Be or Not to Be* (1942) 208
Starks, Lisa xvi
Star Wars, *Henry V* and 118–119, 120
Staunton, Imelda, in *Twelfth Night* (1996) 104
Steiger, Rod, in *Men of Respect* (1990) 51
Steno, Silvio, in *Carnival* (1921) 210
Stephens, Tony, in *Twelfth Night* (1996) 103
Stewart, Patrick
   in *Antony and Cleopatra* (1974) 3
   in *Hamlet* (1980) 23
Stewart, Susan 197
Stiles, Julia
   in *Hamlet* (2000) 25
   in *O* (2001) 70, 71
   in *10 Things I Hate About You* (1999) 94
Still in Movement (Buchman) xvii, 151
Stirling, Rachael, in *Othello* (2002) 72
Stirner, Brian 7
Stone, James W., on *Othello* (1952) 189–191
Stoppard, Tom
   Rosencrantz and Guildenstern Are Dead 86, 224–225
   Shakespeare in Love (1998) xxvi, 86, 87, 204, 219
"Stormy Weather" (song) 181
Stow, Percy, *The Tempest* (1908) xxvii, 96
Strathairn, David, in *A Midsummer Night's Dream* (1999) 62
Strike (1924) 129
Strunk, William B. xii, 80
Stubbs, Imogen, in *Twelfth Night* (1996) 103
Sturua, Robert 77
Sullivan, Arthur 95
Sullivan, Frederick, *Cymbeline* (1913) 10–11
Suschitzky, Peter 59
Sutherland, Joan 125

Suzman, Janet, in *Antony and Cleopatra* (1974) 3
Sydney, Basil, in *Hamlet* (1948) 19
Sydney, Philip 38
Synnott, Del, in *Othello* (2002) 72
Szabó, István, *Mephisto* (1981) 208

T

Tamblyn, Russ, in *West Side Story* (1961) 84
The Taming of the Shrew **91–95**
   Junger (1999) (*10 Things I Hate About You*) 70, *94*, 94–95
   plot of 91–92
   Sidney (1953) (*Kiss Me Kate*) 94
   Taylor (1929) x–xi, *xii*, xxvii, 92–93
   Zeffirelli (1966) *93*, 93–94, 126
Tanner, Tony, in *A Midsummer Night's Dream* (1964) 58
Tate, Nahum 38
Tate, Sharon 50, 136
Taylor, Elizabeth, in *The Taming of the Shrew* (1966) 93, *93*, 126
Taylor, Neil, on *Hamlet* (1980) 23
Taylor, Sam, *The Taming of the Shrew* (1929) x–xi, *xii*, xxvii, 92–93
Taymor, Julie, *Titus* (1999) xxvi, xxix, 101–102, *102*
Tchaikovsky, Peter Ilich 95
television productions xiii, xv–xvi, 147
The Tempest **95–100**
   Atkins and Atkins (1956) 97
   Bender (1999) 98
   Bower (1939) 96–97
   Coleman (1968) 97
   Gorrie (1979) 97
   Greenaway (1991) (*Prospero's Books*) xv, xxx, 99–100, 167–172, 175, 184, 186
   Jarman (1980) 97, 175–182
   Mazursky (1982) xiv, xxx, 98–99, *99*
   plot of 95–96
   Schaefer (1960) 97
   Stow (1908) xxvii, 96
   Wilcox (1956) (*Forbidden Planet*) xxx, 97–98

10 Things I Hate about You (1999) 70, *94*, 94–95
Terris, Olwen xiii
Thalberg, Irving xi–xii, xviii, 80
Thanhouser, Edwin
   Cymbeline (1913) 10–11
   King Lear (1916) x
   Romeo and Juliet (1909) 80
   The Tempest (1911) 96
Thanhouser, Gertrude 10
Thanhouser Film Corporation 10
Thatcher, Margaret 119, 120, 123
theater
   endings in 183–187
   vs. film xxiii–xxviii, 148, 151
Theater of Blood (1973) 212–213
Theater and Film (Manvell) xii–xiii
Thomas, Hugh 11
Thomas, Kristin Scott, in *Richard III* (1995) 77, 155
Thomashefsky, Harry, *The Yiddish King Lear* (1934) 39
Thompson, Emma, in *Much Ado About Nothing* (1993) 63, *64*
A Thousand Acres (1997) xxx
Throne of Blood (1957) xxix, 49
"Through the Camera's Eye" (Griffin) xii
Tibbetts, John C.
   on *Hamlet* (1990) 125–128
   on plays within plays 207–226
Tiernan, Andrew 6
Timber, or Discoveries (Jonson) xxvi
Time Flies (1944) 201–205
Titus Andronicus **101–102**
   plot of 101
   Taymor (1999) xxvi, xxix, 101–102, *102*
To Be or Not to Be (1942) xxx, 52, 53, 208–209, *209*
To Be or Not to Be (1983) 209
Tower of London (1939) 76
The Tragedy of Romeo and Juliet. See *Romeo and Juliet*
The Tragical History of Romeus and Juliet (Brooke) 204
Trainspotting (1996) 144
Trauberg, Leonid 129
Tree, Herbert Beerbohm
   in *King John* (1899) xi, xxvii
   in *Macbeth* (1916) x, 48

INDEX

Trier, Lars Von 223
Tromeo and Juliet (1996) xviii, 90
Trotter, Kate, in *Romeo and Juliet* (1993) 88
Troughton, Patrick, in *King Lear* (1948) 39
Troupe, Tom, in *My Own Private Idaho* (1991) 28
The True Chronicle History of King Leir (play) 38
Truffaut, François, *The Last Metro* (1980) 208
Truman, Harry 85
Trundell, John 17
Tucci, Stanley, in *A Midsummer Night's Dream* (1999) 62
Turk, Edward Baron, on *The Children of Paradise* (1944) 221, 223
Turturro, John, in *Men of Respect* (1990) 51
Tutin, Dorothy, in *King Lear* (1983) 41
Twelfth Night, or What You Will **102–104**
    Nunn (1996) 103–104
    plot of 103
"Two King Lears" (Hodgdon) xiv
Tynan, Kenneth, *Macbeth* (1971) 49

U

Udwin, Leslee, in *The Merchant of Venice* (1980) 54
Under the Boardwalk (1989) 89
Unspeakable ShaXXXspeares (Burt) xviii
Uricchio, William ix, xii
Ustinov, Peter, *Romanoff and Juliet* (1961) 85

V

Valley Girl (1983) 89
Van Sant, Gus, *My Own Private Idaho* (1991) 28
Vaughn, Robert, in *Julius Caesar* (1969) 34
Venora, Diane
    Hamlet (1990) 24
    in *Hamlet* (2000) 25

in *A Midsummer Night's Dream* (1982) 60
in *Romeo + Juliet* (1996) 162
Verdi, Giuseppe 61
Vigne, Daniel, *The Return of Martin Guerre* (1982) 144
Vining, Edward P. 19
Vinovich, Steve, in *A Midsummer Night's Dream* (1982) 60
Vinterberg, Thomas 223
Visconti, Luchino 125
Vitagraph Company of America x, 4
Vonnegut, Kurt 149
Von Trier, Lars 223
von Zerneck, Danielle, in *Under the Boardwalk* (1989) 89

W

Walker, Eamonn, in *Othello* (2002) 72
Walker, Elsie xiv
Ward, Vincent, *The Navigator* (1988) 142, 144
Warde, Ernest C., *King Lear* (1916) x, 39
Warde, Frederick
    in *King Lear* (1916) x
    in *Richard III* (1912) xxvii, 76
Warren, Roger, on *Cymbeline* (1982) 12
Wartime (Fussel) 120
Washington, Denzel, in *Much Ado About Nothing* (1993) 63
Watching Shakespeare on Television (Coursen) 147
Waterston, Sam, in *Much Ado About Nothing* (1973) 65
Watkin, David, *Hamlet* (1990) 23, 127–128
Watson, Douglas, in *Much Ado About Nothing* (1973) 65
Webb, Alan, in *King Lear* (1971) 40
Weimann, Robert xvii
Weinraub, Bernard, on *Richard III* (1912) 76
Weinstein, Harvey 193
Weir, Peter 125
Welch, Elizabeth, in *The Tempest* (1980) *180*, 181

Welles, Orson xxv
    Chimes at Midnight (1967) xv, xvi, xvii, 26–28
    commentary on xvii
    essays by xii
    in *King Lear* (1953) 39
    Macbeth (1948) xxv, 48–49, *141*, 141–145
    Othello (1952) 68–69, 189–191
    on performance of Shakespeare 156
Wells, Stanley xvi
Welsh, James M. xiv, xvii, xxiii–xxxi
    on *Karol Lir* (1970) 129–132
    on *The Taming of the Shrew* (1929) x
West, Dominic, in *A Midsummer Night's Dream* (1999) 62
West Side Story (1961) 84–85
What Happens in Hamlet? (Wilson) 24
White, E. B. xii
White, Hayden 143
Whiting, Leonard, in *Romeo and Juliet* (1968) 81, *81*
Widdoes, Kathleen, in *Much Ado About Nothing* (1973) 65
Wilcox, Fred McLeod, *Forbidden Planet* (1956) xxx, 97–98
Wilcox, Toyah, in *The Tempest* (1980) 97, 177, *177*
Wilde, Oscar 54
Wilders, John xvi
Wilds, Lillian, on *Hamlet* (1960) 20
Wilkinson, Thomas, in *Shakespeare in Love* (1998) 87
Williams, Harcourt, in *Henry V* (1944) 30
Williams, Heathcote, in *The Tempest* (1980) 97, 176
Williams, Robin, in *Hamlet* (1996) 25
William Shakespeare's A Midsummer Night's Dream (1999) xv, *61*, 61–62
William Shakespeare's Romeo + Juliet (1996) xxv, xxviii, 82–83, *83*, 159–164, 184, 185

Williamson, Nicol, in *Hamlet* (1969) xxvi, 21–22
Willis, Susan xv
  on *Cymbeline* (1982) 12
  on *A Midsummer Night's Dream* (1982) 59
  on *Richard III* (1983) 153
Willson, Robert F., Jr. xvii–xviii, xxix–xxx
  on *A Double Life* (1947) xviii, 212
  on *To Be or Not to Be* (1942) xviii, 208, 209
Wilson, John Dover 24
Wilson, P. W. xi
Winslet, Kate, in *Hamlet* (1996) 25, 114
Winters, Shelley, in *A Double Life* (1947) 68, 210
Wirth, Franz Peter, *Hamlet* (1960) 20, *20*
Wise, Robert, *West Side Story* (1961) 84–85
Wong, Russell, in *China Girl* (1987) 85
Wood, Natalie, in *West Side Story* (1961) 84
Wood, Peter, *Hamlet* (1970) 22
Woodbridge, Linda xviii
Woodfall Productions 22
Woodman, William, *Romeo and Juliet* (1982) 87–88
Woodvine, John, in *Macbeth* (1979) 51
World Shakespeare Bibliography xvi
World War I, *Henry V* and 122
Worth, Irene, in *King Lear* (1971) 40, *130*
Wray, Romana xvi
  on *Love's Labour's Lost* (2000) 193–198
Wright, N'Bushe, in *Zebrahead* (1992) 86
Wyatt, Tessa, in *The Tempest* (1968) 97
Wyngarde, Peter, in *A Midsummer Night's Dream* (1964) 58

Y

Yacowar, Maurice, on *King Lear* (1970) 129
Yamada, Isuzu, in *Throne of Blood* (1957) 49
The Year of Living Dangerously (1983) 125
The Yiddish King Lear (1934) 39
Yordan, Philip, *Joe MacBeth* (1955) 49
York, Michael, in *The Taming of the Shrew* (1966) 94
Yuill, Jimmy, in *Love's Labour's Lost* (2000) 45
Yutkevich, Sergei xiii
  on *Karol Lir* (1970) 130
  Othello (1955) 69

Z

Zebrahead (1992) 86
Zeffirelli, Franco 125
  Hamlet (1990) 23, 23–24, 125–128
  interview with 125–128
  Romeo and Juliet (1968) xiv, *81*, 81–82, 87, 126, 159–160, 163–164
  The Taming of the Shrew (1966) *93*, 93–94, 126
Zukor, Adolph x
Zurawik, David, on *Othello* (2002) 72